*It's not the book you buy that you regret.
It's the book you didn't buy.*

Anonymous

*Nobody who can read is ever successful
at cleaning out an attic.*

F. Jones

The Used Book Lover's Guide To The Midwest

Ohio, Indiana, Illinois, Michigan,
Wisconsin, Minnesota, Iowa,
Missouri, Kentucky and West Virginia

By

David S. and Susan Siegel

Book Hunter Press
P.O. Box 193
Yorktown Heights, NY 10598

The Used Book Lover's Guide To The Midwest: Ohio, Indiana, Illinois, Michigan, Wisconsin, Minnesota, Iowa, Missouri, Kentucky and West Virginia by David S. and Susan Siegel.   © Copyright 1999. Book Hunter Press.

Printed and bound in the United States of America

Library of Congress Catalog Card Number 98-092978

ISBN 0-9634112-9-2

Dedication

This book is dedicated to our 1993 Mazda which has served us faithfully for over 90,000 miles as we've traveled across the United States visiting book stores for six of the nine *Used Book Lover's Guides* we've published since beginning the Series in 1992.

Acknowledgments

We would like to thank the over 1,300 book dealers listed in this Guide who patiently answered our questionnaire, responded to our phone calls, and chatted with us during our visits. Without their cooperation, this book would not have been possible.

We would also like to thank the Mid-Michigan Antiquarian Book Dealers Association, the Midwest Bookhunters and the Northern Ohio Bibliophilic Society for their membership directories and the dealers who compile the Indiana, Illinois, Minnesota, Madison, Wisconsin and Kansas City/Independence, Missouri state and local guides.

Thanks also our many readers who have provided us with leads on new listings for this book.

And a special thanks to David G. Nussmann for his continuing feedback.

Also Available From Book Hunter Press

The Used Book Lover's Guide to New England, a guide to over 750 used book dealers in Maine, New Hampshire, Vermont, Massachusetts, Connecticut and Rhode Island.

The Used Book Lover's Guide to the Mid-Atlantic States, a guide to over 1,000 used book dealers in New York, New Jersey, Pennsylvania and Delaware.

The Used Book Lover's Guide to the South Atlantic States, a guide to over 950 used book dealers in Maryland, Washington, DC, Virginia, North Carolina, South Carolina, Georgia and Florida.

The Used Book Lover's Guide to the Pacific Coast States, a guide to over 1,350 used book dealers in California, Oregon, Washington, Alaska and Hawaii.

The Used Book Lover's Guide to the Central States, a guide to over 1,200 used book dealers in the Rocky Mountain, Plains, Southwest and Southcentral States.

If you've found this book useful in your book hunting endeavors and would like to order copies of any of the other guides, you will find a convenient Order From at the back of this book. Or, you can call or write to us at:

Book Hunter Press
PO Box 193
Yorktown Heights, NY 10598
(914) 245-6608
Fax: (914) 245-2630
bookhuntpr@aol.com
http://members.aol.com/bookhuntpr/

Table of Contents

List of Maps	3
No Matter How Hard We Try	5
On the Road Again	6
How To Get The Most From This Guide	7
Illinois	11
Indiana	95
Iowa	133
Kentucky	153
Michigan	181
Minnesota	263
Missouri	307
Ohio	349
West Virginia	426
Wisconsin	435
Specialty Index	481
Keeping Current	510

List of Maps

	Map Number	Page
Illinois		
State Map	1	24
Champaign	2	26
Chicago	3	31
Chicago/downtown	3A	34
Chicago Suburbs	4	66
Evanston	5	49
Indiana		
State Map	6	100
Indianapolis	7	110
Iowa		
State Map	8	136
Des Moines	9	142
Kentucky		
State map	10	159
Lexington	11	167
Louisville	12	171
Michigan		
State Map	13	184
Upper Peninsula	14	192
Ann Arbor	15	197
Detroit Suburbs	16	192
Minnesota		
State Map	17	268
Minneapolis/St. Paul Suburbs	18	290
Minneapolis/St. Paul	19	282
Missouri		
State Map	20	312
Kansas City/Independece	21	326
St. Louis	22	336
Springfield	23	342
Ohio		
State Map	24	352
Akron	25	360
Cincinnati	26	368

4

Ohio (continued)
Cleveland and Suburbs	27	375
Columbus	28	385

West Virginia | 29 | 426

Wisconsin
State Map	30	440
Madison	31	454
Milwaukee	32	460

No Matter How Hard We Try

No matter how hard we try—and we do try for perfection—perfection just "ain't" possible.

Despite the countless hours we spend gathering the information for our Guides, both prior to and during our road trips, and in additional follow up phone calls and e-mail messages once we begin to transfer the raw data into a usable book format, last minute changes do happen. New area codes are announced. Dealers change their hours. A shop unexpectedly closes—or moves. A new shop opens.

What to do? If the book hasn't gone to press yet, we grit our teeth and make the changes, even if it means redoing page layouts and changing maps.

What about changes that occur once the book has gone to press? These changes are saved in our "Update" files and are incorporated into the annual Supplements we publish for each Guide in which we let our readers know about shop closings and relocations, new shop openings and area code changes. (See Keeping Current in the back of this book.)

With all of the above in mind, each time we learn that a change has been made that could result in frustration to one of our readers who planned on visiting a particular establishment, we wince slightly and ask ourselves if that reader will look to us and say, "Was this book worth it?"

We're pleased to report that to date, at least, the vast majority of our readers, even those who have been occasionally frustrated when they've encountered some unrecorded changes, continue to rely on our books and understand that, like a certain president, "we feel their pain."

David S. & Susan Siegel
September, 1998

6

(Reprinted from first edition)

On The Road Again

We say in the introduction to our first Used Book Lover's Guide that our inspiration was *Drif's Guide To The Secondhand & Antiquarian Bookshops In Britain*. We discovered the guide when we were planning a trip to Great Britain which was to combine sight seeing with book hunting.

Three guides and several reprintings later, and before setting out for the Midwest to research this, our fourth guide, we decided we owed ourselves that long postponed trip.

For advanced bibliomanics like David, we'd like to share some of our relfections on book hunting in Great Britain.

Alas, we were disappointed in Charing Cross Road which was more of a bustling commercial thoroughfare than the quiet book-lined street we had pictured in our minds. (Cecil Court, just off Charing Cross does retain some of the former flavor, however.) And of course, we enjoyed our visit to Hay on Wye, the used book capital of Great Britain.

For the most part, what we found were smaller collections than most American open shops, older collections and a large number of specialty dealers.

While the quality and desireability of what we saw varied greatly, our conclusion is that unless you're looking for truly rare British firsts or early editions of volumes of a most scholarly nature, you're likely to find better buys and a better selection in the USA. (We hope this conclusion doesn't make us too unpopular with the very friendly and knowledgable dealers we were privileged to meet in our travels.)

When you do travel to Great Britain, perhaps the greatest thrill you can promise yourself as a true bibliophile is a lengthly visit to the rare book rooms at the British Museum.

And now that we've returned to our true love, book hunting in America, we wish you happy book hunting in America's heartland.

David S. and Susan Siegel
November, 1994

How To Get The Most From This Guide

This guide is designed to help you find the books you're looking for, whether you visit used book shops in person or "browse" by mail or phone from the comfort of your home. It's also designed to help you access the collections of the three categories of used book dealers: open shop, by appointment and mail order.

Open shop dealers maintain regular store hours. Their collections can vary in size from less than a 1,000 to more than 100,000 books and can either be a general stock covering most subject categories or a specialized collection limited to one or more specialty areas.

By appointment or chance dealers generally, but not always, have smaller collections, frequently quite specialized. Many of these dealers maintain their collections in their home. By phoning these dealers in advance, avid book hunters can easily combine a trip to open shops as well as to by appointment dealers in the same region.

Mail order only dealers issue catalogs and/or sell to people on their mailing list or in response to written, phone or e-mail inquiries.

Antique malls. A growing number of dealers in all three of the above categories also rent space in multi dealer antique malls and some malls have more than one dealer. The size and quality of these collections vary widely from a few hundred fairly common titles to interesting and unusual collections, sometimes as large as what we have seen in individual book shops. While we include antique malls where we knew there were used book dealers, we have not, on a systematic basis, researched the multitude of antique malls in the Midwest.

How this book is organized.

Because we believe that the majority of our readers will be people who enjoy taking book hunting trips, we have organized this guide geographically by state, and for open shop and by appointment dealers, within each state by location. Mail order dealers are listed alphabetically at the end of each state chapter.

To help the reader locate specific dealers or locations, at the beginning of each state chapter we have included both an alphabetical listing of all the dealers in that state as well as a geographical listing by location.

Within each listing, we have tried to include the kinds of information about book sellers that we have found useful in our own travels.

• *A description of the stock:* Are you likely to find the kinds of books you're searching for in this shop? Are the books reading copies or of collectible quality? Are they fairly common volumes or more difficult-to-find unusual ones? Are they recent publications or do they date back to earlier decades? What condition are the books in? How many volumes does the dealer have? What percentage of the store's stock is paperback? (When collections are a mix of new and used books, and/or hardcover and paperback, we have indicated the estimated percentage of the stock in each category, listing the largest category first.)

• *Detailed travel directions:* How you can get to the shop, usually from the closest major highway exit.

• *Special services:* Does the dealer issue a catalog? Accept want lists? Have a search service? Offer other services? Note that if the dealer issues a catalog, we generally have not listed "mail order" as a separate service.

• *Payment:* Will the dealer accept credit cards?

• *Comments:* Perhaps the most unique feature of this guide is the *Comments* section that includes our personal observations about a shop. Based on our actual visits to the shops, the comments are designed not to endorse or criticize any of the establishments we visited but rather to place ourselves in the position of our readers and provide useful insights.

• *Specialty Index:* If you're interested in locating books in specific categories, take a close look at the Specialty Index in the back of the book.

• *Owner's name:* Note that the owner's name is included in each listing only when it is different from the name of the business.

Maps

The guide includes a series of 33 state, regional and city maps designed to assist readers plan book hunting safaris to open shops and by appointment dealers.

Locations with open shops are shown in regular type while locations that only have by appointment dealers are in italics. Note that the maps are not drawn to scale and are designed to be used in conjunction with actual road maps.

Comments

We're often asked, "Do you actually visit every dealer who appears in your books?" The answer, we must confess, is "No." To do so, would require far more time than one could possibly imagine and would make this book far too expensive.

We try instead to visit the kinds of shops the majority of our readers are most interested in: open shops with a predominately hardcover general collection. We do not normally visit specialty open shops or by appointment and mail order dealers. There are, of course, exceptions, such as when a shop is either closed on the day that we're in the area or is too far off the route we have laid out for ourselves in order to make the most economical use of our travel time. For this reason, we always welcome input from readers who may have personal knowledge of such shops so that we can share the information with other book lovers in future editions.

A few caveats and suggestions before you begin your book hunting safari.

Call ahead. Even when an open shop lists hours and days open, we advise a phone call ahead to be certain that the hours have not changed and that the establishment will indeed be open when you arrive.

Is there a difference between an "antiquarian" and a "used" book store? Yes and no. Many stores we visited call themselves antiquarian but their shelves contain a large stock of books published within the past ten or fifteen years. Likewise, we also found many pre-20th century books in "used" book stores. For that reason, we have used the term "antiquarian" with great caution and only when it was clear to us that the book seller dealt primarily in truly antiquarian books.

Used and Out-of-Print. Some used book purists also make a distinction between "used" books and "out-of-print" books, a distinction which, for the most part, we have avoided.

Paperbacks. The reader should also note that while we do not list shops that are exclusively paperback, we do include "mostly paperback" shops, although these stores are generally not described in great detail. While philosophically we agree with the seasoned book dealer we met in our travels who said, "Books are books and there's a place for people who love to read all kinds of books," because we believe that a majority of our readers are interested in hardcover volumes, we have tried to identify "mostly paperback" shops as a caveat to those who might prefer to shop elsewhere. In those instances where we did visit a "mostly paperback" shop, it was because, based on the initial information we had, we thought the percentage of hardcover volumes was greater than it turned out to be.

Size of the collection. In almost all instances, the information regarding the size of the collection comes directly from the owner. While we did not stop to do an actual count of each collection during our visits, in the few instances where we observed a significant difference between the owner's estimate and the size of the collection we saw displayed, we recorded our observation in the *Comments* section. Readers should note, however, that the number of volumes listed may include books in storage that are not readily accessible.

Readers should also note that with a few exceptions, only dealers who responded to our questionnaire or who we were able to contact by phone are included in the guide. If the dealer did not respond to our multiple inquiries, and if we could not personally verify that the dealer was still in business, the dealer was not listed.

And now to begin your search. Good luck and happy hunting.

A fishing and hunting corner for wild game? Or rare books?

Ex Libris
Frederick Eugene Hartnell

ILLINOIS

Alphabetical Listing By Dealer

Aah! Rare Chicago	85	Black Bird Books	74
About Books	22	Blake's Book Nook	68
Abraham Lincoln Book Shop	29	Book Court	75
Norma Adler	46	Book Keeper Paperback Exchange	77
After-Words	29	Book Market Paperback Sales	59
The Aleph Bookshop	48	The Book Nook	64
Alkahest Bookshop	48	The Book Rack	79
Allison's Signed Books & Autographs	85	The Book Shelf	74
Amaranth Books	49	Book Stall Of Rockford	78
The American Botanist, Bookseller	45	The Book Stop	56
Americas Antiquarium	86	The Book Stop	77
Ancient Society Books	86	Book World	23
The Antiquarian, Ltd.	30	Bookends and Fine Collectables	51
The Armadillo's Pillow	30	The Bookies Paperbacks & More	32
Armchair Books	70	Booklady	50
Articles of War	79	Booklegger's Used Books	32
Autumn Leaves Books	58	Bookman Extraordinaire	46
Babbitt's Books	26, 62, 69	Bookman's Alley	50
Back Door Antiques	74	Bookman's Corner	33
Bank Lane Books	86	Booknook Parnassus	94
Richard S. Barnes & Co.	86	Books & Beyond	87
Beadsman Books	86	Books & Bytes	68
Bearly Used Books	21	Books & Things	46
Beasley Books	30	Books 'N' Bits	67
Beck's Used Books	49	Books From The Past	75
Beverly Books	32	Books on the Square	81
Frank G. Bezak - Bookseller	63	Booksellers Row	33
Bibliodisia Books	32	The Booksmith	71
Bits & Pieces of History	70	The Booksmith	23

The Bookstore	77	Heartland Books	84
Bookstores of America	63	Heritage Trail Mall	83
Bookworks	33	Historical Newspapers	80
Bookzeller	68	History Hardbacks	74
Robert S. Brooks, Bookseller	87	Hooked On History	67
Thomas W. Burrows, Bookseller	87	Horizon Bookstore	27
Richard Cady-Antiquarian Bookseller	34	ICS Used Book Store	82
Casterbridge Books	87	The Illuminated Eye	89
Chicago Book Mart	87	Insight Metaphysical Bookstore	27
Chicago Historical Bookworks	51	Jack's Used Books	67
Chicago Rare Book Center	94	Jane Addams Book Shop	27
Choice Books	26	Jane Austen Books	89
Gerald J. Cielec-Books	88	Thomas J. Joyce and Company	36
Clinton Antique Mall	45	Kankakee Antique Mall	59
Stephen Daiter Gallery	34	Kay's Treasured Kookbooks	60
Dr. J's Books	53	Dorothy V. Keck Out-of-Print Books	90
Drummer and Thumbs Bookstore	20	Ashley Kennedy	90
Ann Dumler Children's Books	59	Charles H. Kerr Co.	36
D & E Books & More	72	Joyce Klein (Little Treasures)	71
Les Enluminures Ltd.	35	Gail Klemm-Books	90
Epperson Books, Etc.	80	Klimas Books	90
Marilynn Ervin Books	21	Barry A. Klaung	90
Especially Maine Antique	64	Larry Laws	90
Estate Books	88	Leekley Books	84
Ex Libris Theological Books	35	Left Bank Bookstall	91
N. Fagin Books	35	Legibus	60
First Impressions	88	Anne W. Leonard Books	37
The Fisherman's Bookshelf	88	Little Shop on the Prairie	65
Flying Moose Books	52	Maddie's Book Nook	61
D. J. Flynn-Books	88	Madigan's Books	91
Four Seasons Books	55	Magazine Memories	67
Galaxy Of Books	85	Magic, Inc.	37
The Gallery Bookstore	35	Main Street Fine Books & Manuscripts	54
Gemini Fine Books & Arts	58	Anthony Maita	91
General Store Antiques	55	March, Inc.	37
Gerhart's Rare & OP Auto Books	89	John Wm. Martin-Bookseller	60
Gift Music Book & Collectibles	45	Martinton Book Co.	91
Ginkgo Leaf Press	89	Mary's Antique Mall	69
Joe Girardi	60	McNeilly Books	92
Globe International Antiquarian Books	36	Metro-Golden Memories Shop	37
Good Books	89	Dorothy Meyer	38
Graton & Graton	57	David Meyer Magic Books	92
Green Hat Bookstore	69	Monastery Hill Bindery	38
Roger Griffith Bookseller	23	Montagnana Books	92
Half Price Used Book Store	54	More O'Books	29
Hamill & Barker Antiq. Booksellers	51	More O'Books	27

Myopic Books	38	Bob Rund-Books	54
The Mystery Nook	75	John Rybski, Bookseller	42
National Law Resource	92	Dale St. Peter Books	82
Kenneth Nebenzahl, Inc.	56	M. Sand Books	93
Neuman's Oak Point Books	62	Joe Sarno's Comic Kingdom	42
The Neverending Story	56	Edwin Schaeffer	47
Ralph Newman Bibliopole Ltd.	38	Scotland Yard Books	84
Novel Ideas	45	Barry Scott	42
Occult Bookstore	39	Second Chance Books	76
Officer Bob's Paperbacks	39	Second Reading Book Shop	19
O'Gara & Wilson Booksellers	39	Selected Works	42
Old Book Barn	52	Shake, Rattle & Read	43
The Old Bookseller	71	The Stars Our Destination	43
Old House Bookstore	69	State Street Antique Malls	78
Old Main Book Shoppe	28	Harry L. Stern, Ltd.	43
ORT Alley Bookstore	57	Stan Stites Books	93
Pages	19	Stonehill's Books	28
Palos Books	73	Storey Book Antiques & Books	81
Paperback Encore	79	Helena Szepe, Books	44
Paperbacks Plus	22	Phyllis Tholin, Books	51
Paragon Book Gallery	39	3R's HoneyBee Bookshoppe	55
Pastime Book Exchange	22	Thrifty Scholar	47
Peace of the Past	54	Titles, Inc.	58
The Peddler's Books & Things	62	Toad Hall Books & Records	78
Persistence Of Memory	72	Tomorrow is Yesterday	64
Pine Stock Books and Antiques	61	Top Shelf Books	73
Plain Tales Books	92	Turtle Island Books	44
Frank S. Pollack	57	Twice Read Books	61
Powell's Bookstore, South	40	Uncle Buck's Mysteries	93
Powell's Bookstore, Burnham Park	40	The Used Book Store	28
Powell's Bookstore, North	40	Victoria's Books	20
Prairie Archives, Booksellers	80	Village Books	76
Prairie Avenue Bookshop	41	The Village Reader	76
Priceless Books	81	Waukegan Bridge Center	82
Puffabelly Station	65	Mary Wehler, Books	20
Rain Dog Books	41	Weidler Book Source	94
Reader's Haven Paperback Books	47	Wheaton Antique Mall	83
Rhythm & Views	93	Bernard Wheel	72
Gerald Rilling	64	White Chapel Productions	53
Ed Ripp: Bookseller	41	The White Elephant Shop	44
George Ritzlin Maps & Books	57	Wilder Books	48
River Gallery	59	Rbt Williams Bound To Please Books	94
Riverboat Molly's Book Company	19	World Exonumia Press	94
Riverside Antiques	79	Ye Olde Book Worm	21
Richard Owen Roberts, Booksellers	83	Yesterday	44
Paul Rohe Books	93	Yesteryear Books	62
Bernie Rost-Books	42		

Alphabetical Listing By Location

Location	Dealer	Page
Albion	Pages	19
Alton	Riverboat Molly's Book Company	19
	Second Reading Book Shop	19
Arlington Heights	Drummer and Thumbs Bookstore	20
	Gail Klemm-Books	90
	Plain Tales Books	92
	Victoria's Books	20
Aurora	Mary Wehler, Books	20
Batavia	Chicago Book Mart	87
Belleville	Bearly Used Books	21
	Uncle Buck's Mysteries	93
Bensenville	Ye Olde Book Worm	21
Berkeley	Estate Books	88
Berwyn	Marilynn Ervin Books	21
Bloomington	About Books	22
	Paperbacks Plus	22
	Pastime Book Exchange	22
Bourbonnais	Roger Griffith Bookseller	23
Bradford	The Booksmith	23
Carbondale	Book World	23
	Choice Books	26
Champaign	Babbitt's Books	26
	Horizon Bookstore	27
	Insight Metaphysical Bookstore	27
	Jane Addams Book Shop	27
	More O'Books	27
	Old Main Book Shoppe	28
	Stonehill's Books	28
	The Used Book Store	28
Charleston	Madigan's Books	91
	More O'Books	29
Chicago	Abraham Lincoln Book Shop	29
	After-Words	29
	Americas Antiquarium	86
	The Antiquarian, Ltd.	30
	The Armadillo's Pillow	30
	Beasley Books	30
	Beverly Books	32
	Bibliodisia Books	32
	The Bookies Paperbacks & More	32
	Booklegger's Used Books	32
	Bookman's Corner	33
	Books & Beyond	87
	Booksellers Row	33
	Bookworks	33
	Richard Cady-Antiquarian Bookseller	34
	Casterbridge Books	87

Chicago	Chicago Rare Book Center	94
	Gerald J. Cielec-Books	88
	Stephen Daiter Gallery	34
	Les Enluminures Ltd.	35
	Ex Libris Theological Books	35
	N. Fagin Books	35
	The Gallery Bookstore	35
	Ginkgo Leaf Press	89
	Globe International Antiquarian Books	36
	Jane Austen Books	89
	Thomas J. Joyce and Company	36
	Charles H. Kerr Co.	36
	Larry Laws	90
	Anne W. Leonard Books	37
	Magic, Inc.	37
	March, Inc. (Movimiento Artistico Chicano)	37
	Metro-Golden Memories Shop	37
	Dorothy Meyer	38
	Monastery Hill Bindery	38
	Myopic Books	38
	National Law Resource	92
	Ralph Newman Bibliopole Ltd.	38
	Occult Bookstore	39
	Officer Bob's Paperbacks	39
	O'Gara & Wilson Booksellers	39
	Paragon Book Gallery	39
	Powell's Bookstore, South	40
	Powell's Bookstore, Burnham Park	40
	Powell's Bookstore, North	40
	Prairie Avenue Bookshop	41
	Rain Dog Books	41
	Rhythm & Views	93
	Ed Ripp: Bookseller	41
	Bernie Rost-Books	42
	John Rybski, Bookseller	42
	Joe Sarno's Comic Kingdom	42
	Barry Scott	42
	Selected Works	42
	Shake, Rattle & Read	43
	The Stars Our Destination	43
	Harry L. Stern, Ltd.	43
	Helena Szepe, Books	44
	Turtle Island Books	44
	The White Elephant Shop	44
	Yesterday	44
Chicago Heights	Gift Music Book & Collectibles	45
Chillicothe	The American Botanist, Bookseller	45
Clinton	Clinton Antique Mall	45
	Stan Stites Books	93

Decatur	Dorothy V. Keck Out-of-Print Books	90
	Novel Ideas	45
Deerfield	Norma Adler	46
	Bookman Extraordinaire	46
Downers Grove	Thomas W. Burrows, Bookseller	87
	M. Sand Books	93
Eldorado	Books & Things	46
Elgin	Reader's Haven Paperback Books	47
Elk Grove Village	Edwin Schaeffer	47
Elmhurst	Thrifty Scholar	47
	Wilder Books	48
Evanston	The Aleph Bookshop	48
	Alkahest Bookshop	48
	Amaranth Books	49
	Bank Lane Books	86
	Richard S. Barnes & Co.	86
	Beck's Used Books	49
	Booklady	50
	Bookman's Alley	50
	Booknook Parnassus	94
	Robert S. Brooks, Bookseller	87
	Chicago Historical Bookworks	51
	Hamill & Barker Antiquarian Booksellers	51
	Ashley Kennedy	90
	Montagnana Books	92
	Paul Rohe Books	93
	Phyllis Tholin, Books	51
Forest Park	Bookends and Fine Collectables	51
	Flying Moose Books	52
Forsyth	Old Book Barn	52
	White Chapel Productions	53
Freeport	Dr. J's Books	53
	Half Price Used Book Store	54
	Bob Rund-Books	54
Galena	Main Street Fine Books & Manuscripts	54
	Peace of the Past	54
Galesburg	General Store Antiques	55
	3R's HoneyBee Bookshoppe	55
Glen Ellyn	Four Seasons Books	55
Glencoe	Kenneth Nebenzahl, Inc.	56
Glenview	Aah! Rare Chicago	85
	Anthony Maita	91
Glenwood	David Meyer Magic Books	92
Grayslake	The Book Stop	56
Havana	The Neverending Story	56
Highland Park	Graton & Graton	57
	ORT Alley Bookstore	57
	Frank S. Pollack	57
	George Ritzlin Maps & Books	57
	Titles, Inc.	58

Hinsdale	Gemini Fine Books & Arts	58
Homewood	Autumn Leaves Books	58
Joliet	Book Market Paperback Sales	59
	River Gallery	59
Kankakee	Kankakee Antique Mall	59
Kenilworth	Ann Dumler Children's Books	59
	Joe Girardi	60
	Kay's Treasured Kookbooks	60
Kewanee	Weidler Book Source	94
La Grange	Legibus	60
	John Wm. Martin-Bookseller	60
	Twice Read Books	61
La Moille	Pine Stock Books and Antiques	61
Lake Forest	D. J. Flynn-Books	88
Le Roy	Maddie's Book Nook	61
Lebanon	The Peddler's Books & Things	62
Lewistown	Neuman's Oak Point Books	62
Lincoln	Babbitt's Books	62
	Yesteryear Books	62
Lisle	Bookstores of America	63
Lockport	Frank G. Bezak - Bookseller	63
Long Grove	Especially Maine Antique	64
Loves Park	Tomorrow is Yesterday	64
Machesaey Park	Gerald Rilling	64
Macomb	Ancient Society Books	86
Martinton	Martinton Book Co.	91
Mattoon	The Book Nook	64
McLean	Puffabelly Station	65
Mendota	Little Shop on the Prairie	65
Morris	Books 'N' Bits	67
Morton Grove	Magazine Memories	67
Mount Prospect	Hooked On History	67
	Jack's Used Books	67
Mundelein	Blake's Book Nook	68
Naperville	Allison's Signed Books & Autographs	85
	Books & Bytes	68
	Bookzeller	68
	Mary's Antique Mall	69
Nauvoo	Old House Bookstore	69
Niota	Green Hat Bookstore	69
Normal	Babbitt's Books	69
Oak Lawn	Bits & Pieces of History	70
Oak Park	Armchair Books	70
	The Booksmith	71
	Gerhart's Rare & Out-of-Print Automobile Books	89
	Joyce Klein (Little Treasures)	71
	Left Bank Bookstall	91
	McNeilly Books	92
	The Old Bookseller	71
	Persistence Of Memory	72

Oak Park	Bernard Wheel	72
Olney	D & E Books & More	72
Orland Park	First Impressions	88
Palatine	Top Shelf Books	73
Palos Hills	Palos Books	73
Paris	The Book Shelf	74
	History Hardbacks	74
Park Ridge	Beadsman Books	86
Peoria	Back Door Antiques	74
	Black Bird Books	74
	Book Court	75
	Books From The Past	75
	The Mystery Nook	75
	Second Chance Books	76
Petersburg	The Village Reader	76
Preemption	Robert Williams Bound To Please Books	94
Princeton	Village Books	76
Quincy	The Book Stop	77
River Forest	The Fisherman's Bookshelf	88
Rock Falls	The Bookstore	77
Rock Island	Book Keeper Paperback Exchange	77
Rockford	Book Stall Of Rockford	78
	Barry A. Klaung	90
	State Street Antique Malls	78
	Toad Hall Books & Records	78
	World Exonumia Press	94
Saint Charles	The Book Rack	79
	Riverside Antiques	79
Sandwich	Paperback Encore	79
Skokie	Articles of War	79
	Historical Newspapers	80
Springfield	Epperson Books, Etc.	80
	Good Books	89
	The Illuminated Eye	89
	Prairie Archives, Booksellers	80
Sycamore	Storey Book Antiques & Books	81
Urbana	Priceless Books	81
Virden	Books on the Square	81
Warrenville	Klimas Books	90
Watseka	Dale St. Peter Books	82
Waukegan	ICS Used Book Store	82
	Waukegan Bridge Center	82
Wheaton	Richard Owen Roberts, Booksellers	83
	Wheaton Antique Mall	83
Wilmette	Heritage Trail Mall	83
Winnetka	Scotland Yard Books	84
Winthrop Harbor	Leekley Books	84
Woodstock	Heartland Books	84
Zion	Galaxy Of Books	85

Albion
(Map 1, page 24)

Pages
41 South 5th Street 62806

Collection:	General stock of paperback and hardcover.
# of Vols:	20,000
Hours:	Tue-Fri 10-6. Sat 10-5.
Travel:	One block south of Rte 15 at the square.
Credit Cards:	No
Owner:	Barbara Wallace
Year Estab:	1996
Comments:	Stock is approximately 65% paperback.

Alton
(Map 1, page 24)

Riverboat Molly's Book Company
515 East 3rd Street 62002

Open Shop
(618) 465-1084
Fax: (618) 465-1085
E-mail: ttaylor@prairieghosts.com

Collection:	General stock of used and new hardcover and paperback.
Hours:	Mon-Sat 10-6. Sun 12-5.
Travel:	From St. Louis: proceed north on Rte 67, then right on Broadway and left on 3rd. From I-55: Rte 140 exit. Proceed west on Rte 140 which becomes College Ave, then left on Alby and left on 3rd St.
Credit Cards:	Yes
Owner:	Troy Taylor
Year Estab:	1998
Comments:	Not yet open when we were traveling through Illinois, the owner anticipates that once all the boxes are unpacked, the stock here will be similar to the collection at his shop in Forsyth (see the Old Book Barn below).

Second Reading Book Shop
301 East Broadway 62002

Open Shop
(618) 462-2830

Collection:	General stock of hardcover and paperback.
# of Vols:	60,000-70,000
Hours:	Tue-Sun 12-5.
Services:	Appraisals, search service, accepts want lists.
Travel:	From St. Louis, proceed north on Rte 67, then left after bridge on East Broadway. Shop is two blocks ahead on left in Mineral Springs Mall.
Credit Cards:	No
Owner:	John & Susan Dunphy
Year Estab:	1979
Comments:	At the time of our visit, the shop consisted of three rooms (one of which was almost exclusively paperback) of used books shelved in a completely unorganized fashion. Most of the books were older volumes and

showed their age. When we selected a book by an obscure writer, we were advised that the price clearly marked on the inside could not be correct. The dealer then indicated that he would have to check the price guide (we doubt he would ever find a price for a 5th edition of the book). Somehow, when a $1 book becomes a rare item, we begin to look for the cheese we know is lurking in Denmark.

Arlington Heights
(Map 4, page 66)

Drummer and Thumbs Bookstore   **Open Shop**
1 East Campbell Street 60005   (847) 398-8968
                                                          E-mail: drandth@aol.com

Collection:	General stock of mostly used paperback.
# of Vols:	30,000 (combined)
Hours:	Mon-Fri 9-6, except Thu till 8. Sat 9-5. Sun 12-5.
Services:	Search service, accepts want lists, mail order.
Travel:	Arlington Heights Rd exit off I-90. Proceed north on Arlington, then left on Campbell. Shop is two blocks ahead.
Credit Cards:	Yes
Owner:	Rob Baker
Year Estab:	1987
Comments:	Stock is approximately 75% used, 80% of which is paperback.

Victoria's Books   **Open Shop**
13 West Campbell Street 60005   (847) 788-1313
                                                          Fax: (847) 788-9645

Collection:	General stock of hardcover and paperback.
# of Vols:	15,000
Specialties:	First editions; signed; children's series.
Hours:	Mon-Fri 10:30-6:30, except Thu till 8. Sat 9-5. Sun by appointment.
Services:	Search service, accepts want lists, mail order.
Travel:	Rte 53 (Arlington Hts Rd) exit off I-90. Proceed north on Rte 53, then Euclid exit off Rte 53. Proceed east on Euclid, then south on Wilke Rd and east on Campbell.
Credit Cards:	Yes
Owner:	John C. Meinhardt
Year Estab:	1997
Comments:	A very nice little shop with interesting titles and a good mix of most subjects. The books were in reasonably good condition.

Aurora
(Map 1, page 24)

Mary Wehler, Books   **By Appointment**
244 South Elmwood Drive 60506   (630) 896-0169

Collection:	General stock.
# of Vols:	5,000-6,000

Specialties: Children's illustrated; Civil War; Abraham Lincoln.
Services: Appraisals, mail order.
Credit Cards: No
Year Estab: 1979

Belleville
(Map 1, page 24)

Bearly Used Books   **Open Shop**
18 East Main Street 62220   (618) 235-0099
    Fax: (618) 235-7326

Collection: General stock of paperback and hardcover, gifts and music.
# of Vols: 20,000
Hours: Mon-Sat 10-6.
Travel: In downtown, one block east of town square.
Year Estab: 1993
Comments: Stock is approximately 75% paperback.

Bensenville
(Map 4, page 66)

Ye Olde Book Worm   **Open Shop**
115 West Main Street 60106   (630) 616-1590

Collection: General stock of mostly used hardcover and paperback.
# of Vols: 100,000 (See Comments)
Hours: Mon-Fri 11-6:30. Sat 10-4.
Services: Appraisals, search service, accepts want lists, mail order.
Travel: Lake St exit off I-290 or I-294. Proceed east on Lake, left on York Rd and left on Main. Shop is 1½ blocks ahead across from train station.
Credit Cards: Yes
Owner: Dale & Ann Brownewell
Year Estab: 1973
Comments: The books are tightly packed in the rear of a shop that in olden days would have been referred to as a "candy store" selling candy, soda, lottery tickets and similar items. The stock was divided almost evenly between hardcover and paperback books. The hardcover volumes were generally older but not necessarily collectible. Some children's items. An alert scout conceivably might find an item or two of importance; we failed in that endeavor. At the time of our visit, only about half of the stock cited above was on display.

Berwyn
(Map 4, page 66)

Marilynn Ervin Books   **By Appointment**
3517 Wisconsin Avenue 60402   (708) 795-4928

Collection: General stock.
# of Vols: 10,000

Services: Accepts want lists, mail order.
Credit Cards: No
Year Estab: 1972

Bloomington
(Map 1, page 24)

About Books   **Open Shop**
221 East Front Street 61701   Tel & Fax: (309) 829-3999
                                                  E-mail: sstruck@aol.com

Collection: General stock of mostly hardcover.
# of Vols: 80,000
Hours: Tue-Fri 10:30-5:30. Sat 10:30-4.
Services: Appraisals, search service, accepts want lists.
Travel: Exit 160 (Market St) off I-74. Proceed east on Market, right on Madison (Bus Rte 51) and left on Front.
Credit Cards: Yes
Owner: Steve & Carol Struck
Year Estab: 1992
Comments: In 1994, after our first visit to this bi-level shop, we made the following observation:
                   When we visited this shop, it had been in operation for less than two weeks. The size of the store and the enthusiasm of its owners lead us to believe that the collection will be growing and that the quality of the items offered will be above average. The stock we did see was eclectic in vintage and generally in good condition Prices were fair.
                   In 1998, when we returned to the shop, we found that it had more than fulfilled its promise. The shop offers a fine selection of books in almost every subject. The books are generally well cared for and prices are reasonable. In addition to some new items, the shop has a good share of collectibles.

Paperbacks Plus   **Open Shop**
1201 East Oakland 61701   (309) 829-5475

Collection: General stock of mostly paperback.
# of Vols: 4,000-5,000
Hours: Mon-Fri 10-5. Sat 9:30-1:30. Sun 1-3.

Pastime Book Exchange   **Open Shop**
618 North Main Street 61701   (309) 829-6394

Collection: General stock of paperback and hardcover.
# of Vols: 7,000
Hours: Mon-Fri 10-4. Sat 10-1.
Travel: Market St exit off I-74. Continue on Market then left on Main. Shop is at corner of Main and Locust.

Bourbonnais
(Map 1, page 24)

Antique Mall

300 Larry Power Road   Mall: (815) 933-9999
ve Bourbonnais IL 60914   Home: (815) 933-1929

xcept Thu & Fri till 8.
7. Proceed north on Rte 50. At third light, turn left.

Bradford
(Map 1, page 24)

The Booksmith   **Antique Mall**
At Spoon River Antique Mall, 111 West Main Street   Mall: (309) 897-7010
Mailing address: 313 East Main Street Bradford IL 61421   Day: (309) 672-5920
    Eve: (309) 897-8342

Collection:	General stock.
# of Vols:	3,500
Hours:	Mon-Sat 9-5. Sun 11-4.
Credit Cards:	No
Travel:	Rte 40 exit off I-80. Proceed south on Rte 40 which becomes Main St in Bradford.
Owner:	Steve Smith
Year Estab:	1993
Comments:	Also displays at Illinois Antique Center, Back Door Antiques and Black Bird Books, all in Peoria. See below.

Carbondale
(Map 1, page 24)

Book World   **Open Shop**
823 South Illinois Avenue 62901   (618) 549-5122

Collection:	General stock of paperback and hardcover and ephemera.
# of Vols:	20,000
Specialties:	Military; film; science fiction.
Hours:	Mon-Sat 10-5.
Services:	Accepts want lists, mail order.
Travel:	On Rte 51.
Owner:	Tom North
Year Estab:	1978
Comments:	Stock is approximately 75% paperback.

(Carbondale)

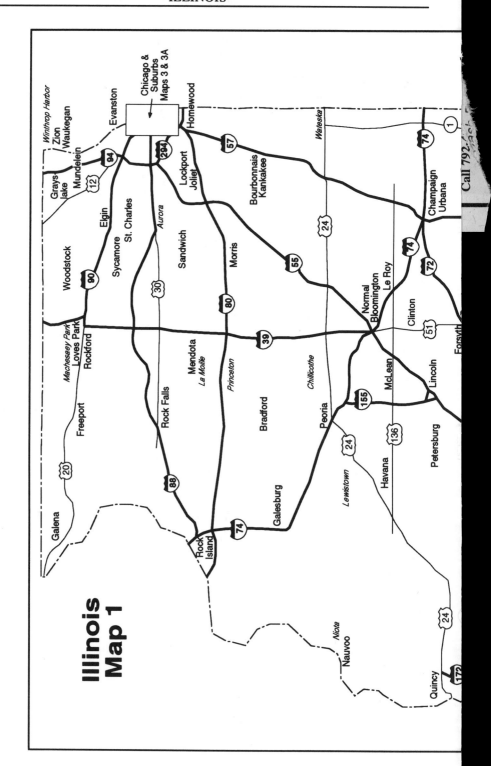

Illinois
Map 1

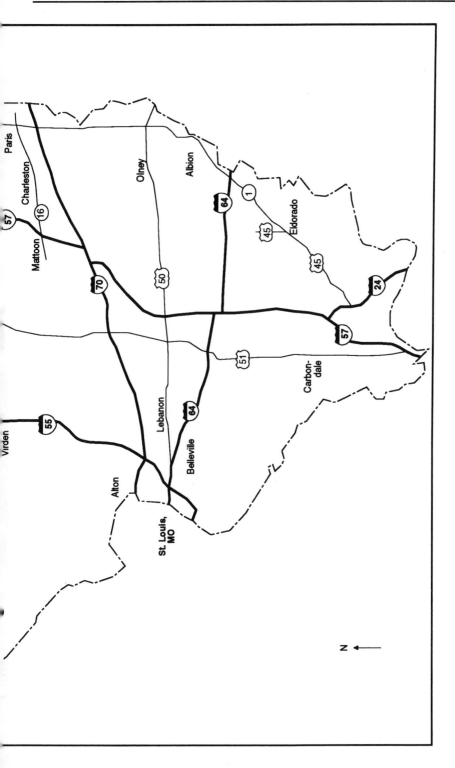

Choice Books   **By Appointment**
718 North Billy Bryan Street 62901   (618) 529-1979

Collection:	General stock.
# of Vols:	8,000+
Specialties:	History; Civil War; southern Illinois.
Credit Cards:	No
Owner:	Charles R. Feirich

Champaign
(Map 1, page 24 & Map 2, page 26)

Babbitt's Books   **Open Shop**
614 East Green Street 61820   (217) 352-7524
                                    E-mail: babbittc@soltec.com

Collection:	General stock of hardcover and paperback and some remainders.
# of Vols:	70,000
Specialties:	Literary criticism.
Hours:	Mon-Sat 10-6. Sun 12-5.
Services:	Search service.
Travel:	Neil St exit off I-74. Proceed south on Neil, then left on Green. Shop is about six blocks ahead.
Credit Cards:	Yes
Owner:	Brian Simpson
Year Estab:	1995
Comments:	A bi-level shop that is somewhat deceiving as its second level is two to three times the size of the first floor display space. Many of the books, particularly those in scholarly subjects, are titles one would expect to find close to a university. There were, however, plenty of titles covering the more popular subject areas. Lots of paperbacks, and in some areas, paperbacks and hardcovers were intershelved. If you're planning a visit, expect to stay for a while. The owner also operates a shop under the same name in Normal. See below.

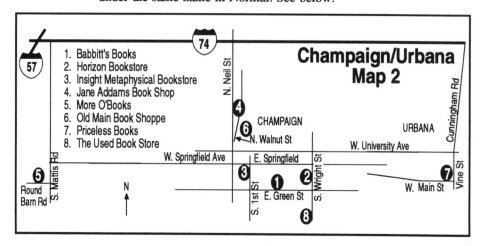

Horizon Bookstore
603 South Wright Street 61820

Collection:	General stock of mostly new and some used.
# of Vols:	6,500
Hours:	Mon-Fri 10-6. Sat 10-5.
Credit Cards:	Yes
Owner:	Dale Tolliver
Year Estab:	1976
Comments:	Primarily an academic bookstore. Approximately 15% of the stock is used, 75% of which is paperback.

Insight Metaphysical Bookstore
505 South First Street 61820

Collection:	Specialty new and some used paperback and hardcover.
# of Vols:	8,000-10,000
Specialties:	Metaphysics; astrology; UFOs.
Hours:	Mon 6-9pm. Tue-Fri 10-6. Sat 10-4.
Services:	Accepts want lists, mail order.
Owner:	Jack & Mary Jane Tuttle
Year Estab:	1987

Jane Addams Book Shop
208 North Neil 61820

Collection:	General stock and ephemera.
# of Vols:	70,000
Specialties:	Children's; art; women's studies; mystery and detective; cookbooks; social sciences; original Raggedy Ann/Andy watercolors.
Hours:	Mon-Sat 10-5, except Fri till 8. Sun 12-4.
Services:	Search service, accepts want lists, mail order.
Travel:	Neil St south exit off I-74. Proceed south to downtown.
Credit Cards:	Yes
Owner:	Flora Faraci
Year Estab:	1984
Comments:	A real winner, with books of every category and covering every period, including antiquarian. After you've visited the first floor and gone on to the second floor mezzanine, you have a real treat waiting for you on the third floor which contains several smaller rooms, each filled with quality books. The specialties listed above are well represented and from what we could see, the prices placed on each book were carefully arrived at. You get what you pay for.

More O'Books
1914D Round Barn Road 61821

Collection:	General stock of mostly paperback.
# of Vols:	25,000

(Champaign)

Specialties:	Science fiction.
Hours:	Mon-Fri 10-7. Sat 10-5. Sun 12-5.
Services:	Search service.
Travel:	University Ave exit off I-57. Proceed east on University, then right on Mattis, right on Springfield and first left on Round Barn Rd.
Credit Cards:	Yes
Owner:	Deb Morrow
Year Estab:	1994
Comments:	Predominately paperback with some hardcover volumes (mostly newer items) in the shop's specialty and in some miscellaneous subject areas. If you're a sci fi fan, you'll meet a kindred spirit here. Don't look for rare titles. The owner operates a second, similar but slightly smaller, store in Charleston. See below.

Old Main Book Shoppe   **Open Shop**
116 North Walnut Street 61820   Tel & Fax: (217) 355-6400
Web page: www.oldmain.com   E-mail: oldmain@prairienet.org

Collection:	Specialty books. Also ephemera and records.
# of Vols:	20,000
Specialties:	Civil War; children's; Abraham Lincoln; Africa; art; photography.
Hours:	Mon-Thu 10-5:30. Fri& Sat 10-7.
Services:	Appraisals, search service, mail order, accepts want lists.
Travel:	Neil St exit off I-74. Proceed south on Neil to downtown, then east on University and left on Walnut.
Credit Cards:	Yes
Owner:	Steve Kysar
Year Estab:	1980

Stonehill's Books   **By Appointment**
2606 Nottingham Court South 61821   Tel & Fax: (217) 359-5289
                                           E-mail: shbook@worldnet.att.net

Collection:	Specialty books and ephemera.
# of Vols:	10,000+
Specialties:	Children's; pop-ups and moveables; illustrated; Americana.
Services:	Appraisals, search service, accepts want lists, mail order.
Credit Cards:	Yes
Owner:	Allan L. Steinberg
Year Estab:	1976

The Used Book Store   **Open Shop**
1001 South Wright Street 61820   (217) 344-4707

Collection:	General stock of paperback and hardcover.
# of Vols:	15,000
Hours:	Sep-May: Mon-Fri 10:30-4:30. Sat 12-2. Jun-Aug: Mon-Fri 11-3.
Services:	Search service, accepts want lists, mail order.

Travel:	Two blocks south of Green St in university campus area. The shop is located in the basement of the YMCA/YWCA building.
Credit Cards:	No
Owner:	Kelly Mickey, Manager
Year Estab:	1970
Comments:	A combination of scholarly titles and more popular items in mixed condition, with an emphasis on the word "mixed." At the time of our visit, while the books were organized by category, there were few if any labels on the shelves and lots of books were scattered here and there. One should not expect to find a gold (or even silver) mine here.

Charleston
(Map 1, page 24)

More O'Books　　　　　　　　　　　　　　　　　　　**Open Shop**
904 East Lincoln 61920　　　　　　　　　　　　　　　(217) 345-3430
　　　　　　　　　　　　　　　　　　　　　　　　　　(888) 230-3430

Collection:	General stock of mostly paperback.
# of Vols:	10,000
Hours:	Mon-Fri 10-7. Sat 10-5. Sun 1-5.

Chicago
(Map 3, page 31 and Map 3A, page 34)

Abraham Lincoln Book Shop　　　　　　　　　　　　**Open Shop**
357 West Chicago Avenue 60610　　　　　　　　　　　(312) 944-3085
　　　　　　　　　　　　　　　　　　　　　　　　Fax: (312) 944-5549

Collection:	Specialty books, ephemera and memorabilia.
Specialties:	Abraham Lincoln; Civil War; military; autographs; photographs.
Hours:	Mon-Sat 9-5.
Services:	Appraisals, catalog, accepts want lists.
Travel:	Ohio St exit off I-90/94. Proceed east on Ohio, then left on Orleans and left on Chicago.
Credit Cards:	Yes
Owner:	Daniel R. Weinberg
Year Estab:	1938

After-Words　　　　　　　　　　　　　　　　　　　**Open Shop**
23 East Illinois Street 60611　　　　　　　　　　　　(312) 464-1110
Web page: www.abebooks.com\home\afterwords　　　Fax: (312) 464-1179
　　　　　　　　　　　　　　　　　　　E-mail: bdvorkin@aol.com

Collection:	General stock of used and new hardcover and paperback.
# of Vols:	50,000
Hours:	Mon-Fri 9-9, except Fri till 11. Sat 10am-11pm. Sun 12-7.
Services:	Accepts want lists, mail order.
Travel:	Exit 50B (Ohio St) off I-90/94. Proceed east on Ohio, then right on State St and first left on Illinois. Shop is 1/2 block ahead on right.
Credit Cards:	Yes

Owner:	Beverly Dvorkin
Year Estab:	1996
Comments:	A very pleasant shop with new books on the first floor and used books on the lower level. The condition of most of the used books is such that many of them could easily pass for new. A few oldies but the majority of the titles were fairly recent in vintage. Easy to browse.

The Antiquarian, Ltd.   **By Appointment**
1652 North Humboldt Boulevard 60647   Tel & Fax: (773) 235-5604

Collection:	Specialty
Specialties:	Early English literature; early English translations of Greek and Roman classics.
Services:	Catalog in planning stage.
Credit Cards:	No
Owner:	James Tenbroeck
Year Estab:	1990

The Armadillo's Pillow   **Open Shop**
6753 North Sheridan Road 60626   (773) 761-2558

Collection:	General stock of paperback and hardcover and ephemera.
# of Vols:	10,000
Specialties:	Pulps; literature; eastern and western philosophy.
Hours:	Tue-Fri 2-8. Sat 12-8. Sun 12-5.
Services:	Search service, accepts want lists.
Travel:	Sheridan Rd exit off Lake Shore Dr. Proceed east on Sheridan through Loyola campus. Shop is between Columbia & Pratt.
Credit Cards:	Yes
Owner:	Elizabeth Bremmel & Matt Ebert
Year Estab:	1995
Comments:	A relatively small rather crowded shop with a mix of paperbacks and mostly older hardcover books. A sharp eye could well discern a worthy find (we think we did) but the odds are not necessarily encouraging. We wish there had been a stool or small ladder to assist customers reach some of the higher shelves.

Beasley Books   **By Appointment**
1533 West Oakdale 60657   (773) 472-4528
Web page: www.abaa-booknet.com/usa/beasley/   Fax: (773) 472-7857
                                            E-mail: beasley@mcs.com

Collection:	Specialty
# of Vols:	4,500
Specialties:	Modern first editions; black literature and history; jazz and blues; radical literature; detective; psychiatry.
Services:	Catalog, accepts want lists.
Credit Cards:	Yes
Owner:	Elizabeth & Paul Garon
Year Estab:	1979

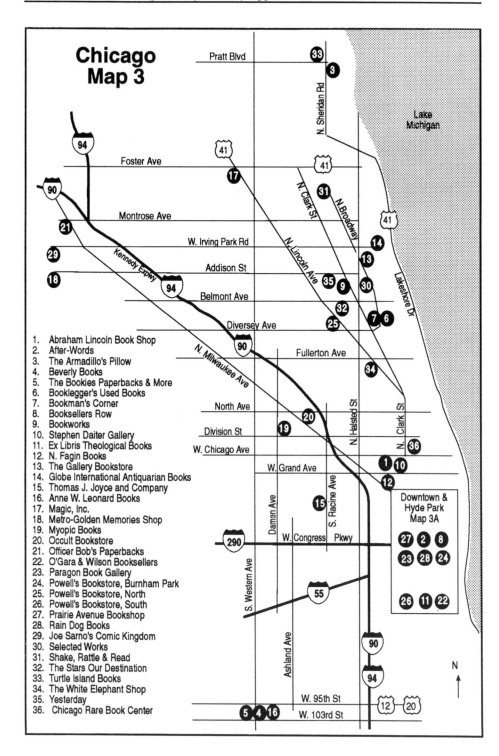

Chicago Map 3

1. Abraham Lincoln Book Shop
2. After-Words
3. The Armadillo's Pillow
4. Beverly Books
5. The Bookies Paperbacks & More
6. Booklegger's Used Books
7. Bookman's Corner
8. Booksellers Row
9. Bookworks
10. Stephen Daiter Gallery
11. Ex Libris Theological Books
12. N. Fagin Books
13. The Gallery Bookstore
14. Globe International Antiquarian Books
15. Thomas J. Joyce and Company
16. Anne W. Leonard Books
17. Magic, Inc.
18. Metro-Golden Memories Shop
19. Myopic Books
20. Occult Bookstore
21. Officer Bob's Paperbacks
22. O'Gara & Wilson Booksellers
23. Paragon Book Gallery
24. Powell's Bookstore, Burnham Park
25. Powell's Bookstore, North
26. Powell's Bookstore, South
27. Prairie Avenue Bookshop
28. Rain Dog Books
29. Joe Sarno's Comic Kingdom
30. Selected Works
31. Shake, Rattle & Read
32. The Stars Our Destination
33. Turtle Island Books
34. The White Elephant Shop
35. Yesterday
36. Chicago Rare Book Center

Pratt Blvd

Lake Michigan

Foster Ave

Montrose Ave

W. Irving Park Rd

Addison St

Belmont Ave

Diversey Ave

Fullerton Ave

North Ave

Division St

W. Chicago Ave

W. Grand Ave

W. Congress Pkwy

W. 95th St

W. 103rd St

N. Sheridan Rd

N. Clark St

N. Broadway

N. Lincoln Ave

Lakeshore Dr

Kennedy Expwy

N. Milwaukee Ave

N. Halsted St

N. Clark St

S. Racine Ave

Damen Ave

S. Western Ave

Ashland Ave

Downtown & Hyde Park Map 3A

N

(Chicago)

Beverly Books   **Open Shop**
9915 South Walden Parkway 60643   (773) 239-7760
                                          E-mail: simmons@insnet.com

Collection:	General stock of mostly hardcover.
# of Vols:	11,000
Specialties:	Philosophy; European history.
Hours:	Mon-Thu 10-7. Fri 11-9. Sat & Sun 10-6.
Services:	Search service, accepts want lists, mail order
Travel:	95th St exit off I-90/94. Proceed west on 95th St, then left on Ashland, right on 99th St and left on Walden Pkwy.
Credit Cards:	No
Owner:	Charles J. Simmons
Year Estab:	1997

Bibliodisia Books   **By Appointment**
4454 South Francisco Street 60632   (773) 247-7816
                                          E-mail: bibliodi@interloc.com

Collection:	General stock.
# of Vols:	4,000
Specialties:	Chicago; Illinois; American history and literature (in first editions); private press; fine bindings; genre fiction.
Services:	Appraisals, search service, accepts want lists, mail order.
Credit Cards:	No
Owner:	Carlos & Ofelia Martinez
Year Estab:	1994

The Bookies Paperbacks & More   **Open Shop**
2419 West 103rd Street 60655   (773) 239-1110

Collection:	General stock of paperback and hardcover.
# of Vols:	45,000
Hours:	Mon-Thu 10-7. Fri 10-6. Sat 10-5. Sun 11-3.
Travel:	Between Western & Kedzie.
Credit Cards:	No
Comments:	Stock is approximately 75% paperback.

Booklegger's Used Books   **Open Shop**
2935 North Broadway 60657   (773) 404-8780
Web page: www.bookleggers.com   E-mail: bookleggers@aol.com

Collection:	General stock of mostly hardcover and CDs.
# of Vols:	10,000
Specialties:	Philosophy; literature; art; architecture; photography; cooking.
Hours:	Daily 12-8. Hours change seasonally.
Services:	Appraisals
Travel:	Belmont exit off I-90/94. Proceed east on Belmont, then south on Broadway for about three blocks.

Credit Cards:　No
Owner:　Lawrence Van De Carr
Year Estab:　1979
Comments:　Most of the books we saw were of an earlier vintage. Most subjects were covered and a visitor who takes the time to browse may well find a gem.

Bookman's Corner　　　　　　　　　　　　　　　　　　　**Open Shop**
2959 North Clark Street 60657　　　　　　　　　　　　　(773) 929-8298

Collection:　General stock of hardcover and paperback.
# of Vols:　25,000
Hours:　Mon-Fri 12-7. Sat 12-8. Sun 12-6.
Travel:　Between Oakdale and Wellington.
Credit Cards:　Yes
Owner:　John Chandler
Year Estab:　1975
Comments:　A mixed bag, both in terms of vintage and condition, with the emphasis being on slightly older volumes, more than a few of which have seen better days. The aisles were extremely narrow and in some areas one might hesitate to wander too deeply for fear of being crushed by bookcases on both sides. While this layout provides the owner with an ability to display more books, unfortunately it makes it more difficult for the browser to view the books with any degree of comfort. Regardless of the shop's ambience, or lack thereof, as we have said previously, if you're patient, you may certainly find a long sought after item here.

Booksellers Row　　　　　　　　　　　　　　　　　　　**Open Shop**
408 South Michigan Avenue 60605　　　　　　　　　　　(312) 427-4242

Collection:　General stock of mostly used hardcover and paperback and ephemera.
# of Vols:　30,000
Specialties:　Black studies; art; literature.
Hours:　Mon-Thu 10:30-8:30. Fri & Sat 10:30-9:30. Sun 11:30-7:30.
Travel:　Chicago/Loop exit off I-90/94. Exit ramp becomes Congress Pkwy. Continue to Michigan Ave. Shop is between Congress & Van Buren. The entrance is through the lobby of the Fine Arts Building.
Credit Cards:　Yes
Owner:　Howard Cohen & Alison James
Year Estab:　1978
Comments:　A book traveler's delight in that one can find books of every type in both hardcover and paperback, from recent publications to much older items. The tri-level shop is not huge and so the selection is limited but there are enough interesting titles to whet one's appetite.

Bookworks　　　　　　　　　　　　　　　　　　　　　**Open Shop**
3444 North Clark 60657　　　　　　　　　　　　　　　(773) 871-5318
　　　　　　　　　　　　　　　　　　　　　　　　Fax: (773) 871-2924
　　　　　　　　　　　　　　　　　E-mail: bookwks@aol.com
Collection:　General stock of hardcover and paperback, ephemera and records.

Downtown Chicago Hyde Park Area Map 3A

2. After-Words
8. Booksellers Row
11. Ex Libris Theological Books
22. O'Gara & Wilson Booksellers
23. Paragon Book Gallery
24. Powell's Bookstore, Burnham Park
26. Powell's Bookstore, South
27. Prairie Avenue Bookshop
28. Rain Dog Books

# of Vols:	40,000
Hours:	Mon-Thu 12-10. Fri & Sat 12-11. Sun 12-6.
Services:	Accepts want lists.
Travel:	Addison exit off I-90/94. Proceed east to Clark, then right on Clark (at Wrigley Field). Shop is two blocks ahead. Limited parking is available in the rear.
Credit Cards:	Yes
Owner:	Bob Roschke & Ronda Pilon
Year Estab:	1984
Comments:	Well organized. Well stocked. The hardcover items in most areas were in quite good condition and were most reasonably priced. A nice place to shop. As befits the shop's location, we noted a strong Chicago/Illinois section.

Richard Cady-Antiquarian Bookseller   **By Appointment**
3323 North Paulina, #5H   60657   (773) 244-1361
                                                              E-mail: Rcadia@aol.com

Collection:	General stock.
# of Vols:	2,000-3,000
Specialties:	English and American literary first editions; literary autographs and manuscripts; fine bindings; books on books; illustrated; the "eighteen-nineties" in England and America.
Services:	Appraisals
Year Estab:	1980

Stephen Daiter Gallery   **Open Shop**
311 West Superior, #404   60610   (312) 787-3350
                                                              Fax: (312) 787-3354

Collection:	Specialty books and ephemera.
# of Vols:	3,500

Specialties: Photography; art and design (20th century).
Hours: Fri & Sat 11-6. Other times by appointment.
Services: Ohio St exit off I-90/94. Proceed east on Ohio then left on Orleans and right on Superior.

Les Enluminures Ltd.   **By Appointment**
2970 North Lake Shore Drive, Ste 11B   60657   (773) 929-5986
Fax: (773) 528-3976

Collection: Specialty
Specialties: Antiquarian, from medieval to 19th century; manuscripts.
Services: Appraisals, catalog, search service, accepts want lists.
Credit Cards: Yes
Owner: Sandra Hindman
Year Estab: 1976

Ex Libris Theological Books   **Open Shop**
1340 East 55th Street   60615   (773) 955-3456
Fax: (773) 955-4116

Collection: Specialty
# of Vols: 40,000+
Specialties: Religion (scholarly).
Hours: Mon-Fri 12-6. Sat 12-5.
Services: Accepts want lists.
Travel: In Hyde Park neighborhood.
Credit Cards: Yes
Owner: Wayne Bornholdt
Year Estab: 1982

N. Fagin Books   **Open Shop**
459 N. Milwaukee Avenue   60610   (312) 829-5252
E-mail: nfagbo@aol.com

Collection: Specialty used and some new hardcover and paperback and primitive artifacts.
# of Vols: 20,000
Specialties: Anthropology; archaeology; botany; ecology; ethnology; ethnographic art; zoology; geology.
Hours: Mon-Fri 10-5. Sat 10-3.
Services: Appraisals, search service, catalog, accepts want lists.
Travel: Just south of the intersection of Grand, Milwaukee and Halsted.
Credit Cards: Yes
Owner: Nancy L. Fagin

The Gallery Bookstore   **Open Shop**
3827 North Broadway   (773) 975-8200
Mailing address: 333 Charing Cross Elk Grove Village IL 60007

Collection: General stock of hardcover and paperback, records and ephemera.
# of Vols: 25,000
Specialties: Vintage paperbacks, magazines; pulps; mystery; science fiction; horror.

(Chicago)

Hours:	Mon-Fri 1-8. Sat 12-8. Sun 12-7. (See Comments)
Services:	Appraisals, search service, accepts want lists, mail order.
Travel:	Irving Park exit off Lake Shore Dr. Proceed west to Broadway, then south for two blocks.
Credit Cards:	Yes
Owner:	William C. Fiedler
Year Estab:	1927
Comments:	A crowded shop with books from floor to ceiling (a high one) and narrow aisles. Most of the titles were in the category one generally refers to as "popular culture" with an emphasis on the word "popular." The store's mystery, science fiction and horror collections are located on the second floor which is only open Saturday 1-8, Sunday 1-7 and weekdays by appointment.

Globe International Antiquarian Books

6005 West Irving Park Road 60613

Open Shop
(773) 282-3537

Collection:	Specialty. Mostly new and some used.
Specialties:	Polish books.
Hours:	Mon-Sat 10-8. Sun 11-5.

Thomas J. Joyce and Company

400 North Racine, #103A 60622

Open Shop
(312) 738-1933
Fax: (312) 243-6252

Collection:	Specialty
# of Vols:	8,000
Specialties:	First editions; Americana; Chicago; Illinois; private press; illustrated; Sherlock Holmes; law; medicine; fine bindings.
Hours:	Mon-Sat 10-5. A phone call in advance is recommended.
Services:	Appraisals, search service, catalog, accepts want lists.
Travel:	Eastbound on I-290: Racine Ave exit. Proceed north on Racine one mile (jog right at Madison St), then cross railroad tracks to building on left. From I-90/94 northbound: Randolph St exit. Turn left and proceed to third light, then right on Racine. Shop is about four blocks ahead.
Credit Cards:	Yes
Owner:	Thomas J. Joyce
Year Estab:	1975

Charles H. Kerr Co.

1740 West Greenleaf Avenue 60626

By Appointment
(773) 465-7774

Collection:	Specialty
Specialties:	Radicalism; history; socialism.
Services:	Accepts want lists, mail order.
Credit Cards:	Yes
Year Estab:	1886

Anne W. Leonard Books   **Open Shop**
1935 West 95th Street 60643   (773) 239-7768
                                                    E-mail: albooks@aol.com

Collection: General stock of hardcover and paperback.
# of Vols: 20,000
Hours: Mon-Fri 10-6. Sat 10-4. Sun 10-3.
Travel: 95th St exit off I-90/94. Proceed west on 95th St. Shop is between
                  Western and Ashland.
Credit Cards: No
Year Estab: 1986
Comments: A modest sized shop with an interesting selection of both hardcover
                  and paperback books. Many vintage items and quite reasonably priced.
                  The kind of place that Christopher Morely might have felt comfortable
                  visiting.

Magic, Inc.   **Open Shop**
5082 North Lincoln 60625   (773) 334-2855
                                                          Fax: (773) 334-7605
                                                    E-mail: magicinc@uss.net

Collection: Specialty. Mostly new and some used.
Specialties: Magic
Hours: Mon-Sat 10:30-5:30.
Services: Catalog
Travel: Two blocks south of Foster.
Credit Cards: Yes
Owner: Jay Marshall
Year Estab: 1926

March, Inc. (Movimiento Artistico Chicano)   **By Appointment**
PO Box 2890 60690   (773) 539-9638
                                                          Fax: (773) 539-0013

Collection: Specialty new and used books and journals.
# of Vols: 1,000
Specialties: U.S. Latino; Chicano (Mexican-American).
Services: Catalog, accepts want lists.
Credit Cards: No
Owner: Carlos Cumpián, Manager
Year Estab: 1984

Metro-Golden Memories Shop   **Open Shop**
5425 West Addison Street 60641   (800) 538-6675

Collection: Specialty
# of Vols: Limited used stock.
Specialties: Television; film; radio.
Hours: Mon-Sat 10-6. Sun 12-5.
Travel: Two miles west of I-90/94.
Credit Cards: Yes

(Chicago)

Owner:	Chuck Schaden
Year Estab:	1976
Comments:	Primarily a nostalgia shop with mostly new items and an emphasis on show business. The shop carries a small selection of used hardcover items.

Dorothy Meyer   **By Appointment**
10751 South Hoyne Avenue 60643   (773) 233-3368
                                                  Fax: (773) 233-3738
                                          E-mail: meyerbooks@icsp.net

Collection:	General stock.
# of Vols:	20,000
Specialties:	Children's illustrated; children's series.
Services:	Mail order.
Credit Cards:	Yes
Year Estab:	1987
Comments:	Also displays at Kankakee Antique Mall in Kankakee, IL, Mary's Antique Mall in Naperville, IL and Yesterday's Treasures Antique Mall in Chesterton, IN. Mall collections are general with an emphasis on children's illustrated and children's series books.

Monastery Hill Bindery   **By Appointment**
1751 West Belmont Avenue 60657   (773) 525-4126

Collection:	Specialty
Specialties:	Classical literature in fine bindings; illustrated; autographs.
Owner:	Blair Clark, President
Year Estab:	1868

Myopic Books   **Open Shop**
1726 West Division Street 60622   (773) 862-4882

Collection:	General stock of paperback and hardcover.
# of Vols:	70,000
Hours:	Mon-Sat 11am-1am. Sun 11am-10pm.
Travel:	Between Ashland and Damen.
Credit Cards:	Yes
Owner:	Joseph Judd
Year Estab:	1992
Comments:	Stock is approximately 70% paperback.

Ralph Newman Bibliopole Ltd.   **By Appointment**
175 East Delaware Place 60611   (312) 787-1860
                                                  Fax: (312) 787-9297

Collection:	Specialty
# of Vols:	25,000
Specialties:	Americana; Abraham Lincoln; Civil War; manuscripts.
Services:	Appraisals, catalog, accepts want lists.
Year Estab:	1938

Occult Bookstore   **Open Shop**
1561 North Milwaukee Avenue 60622   (312) 292-0995

Collection:	Specialty new and used hardcover and paperback.
Specialties:	Tarot; Kabbalah; magic; alchemy; astrology; free masonry.
Hours:	Mon-Thu 10:30-7. Fri & Sat 10:30-9. Sun 12-6.
Services:	Appraisals, catalog, accepts want lists.
Travel:	North Ave exit off I-90/94. Proceed west on North Ave to intersection of North/Damen/Milwaukee.

Officer Bob's Paperbacks   **Open Shop**
4340 North Milwaukee Avenue 60641   (773) 736-9522

Collection:	General stock of paperback and hardcover.
# of Vols:	25,000
Travel:	Lawrence Ave exit off I-90/94. Proceed west on Lawrence, then left on Milwaukee.
Credit Cards:	Yes
Owner:	Ann Samson
Year Estab:	1981

O'Gara & Wilson Booksellers   **Open Shop**
1448 East 57th Street 60637   (773) 363-0993
                                    E-mail: ogarawilson@worldnet.att.net

Collection:	General stock of hardcover and paperback.
# of Vols:	40,000+
Specialties:	History; philosophy; art; religion; humanities.
Hours:	Mon-Sat 9am-10pm. Sun 12-10.
Travel:	In Hyde Park neighborhood. 47th St exit off Lake Shore Dr. Proceed west one block, then south on Lake Park Ave and west on 57th St.
Credit Cards:	Yes
Owner:	Douglas Wilson
Year Estab:	1936
Comments:	Stock is approximately 60% hardcover.

Paragon Book Gallery   **Open Shop**
1507 South Michigan Avenue 60605   (312) 663-5155
Web page: www.paragonbook.com   Fax: (312) 663-5177
                                    E-mail: paragon@paragonbook.com

Collection:	Specialty used and new.
# of Vols:	30,000
Specialties:	Asia; art (Asian).
Hours:	Mon-Sat 9:30-5:30.
Services:	Search service, catalog, accepts want lists.
Credit Cards:	Yes
Owner:	Jeffrey Moy
Year Estab:	1991

(Chicago)

Powell's Bookstore, South   **Open Shop**
1501 East 57th Street 60637   (773) 955-7780
                                                    Fax: (773) 955-2967
                                          E-mail: orders@powellschicago.com

Collection:	General stock of new and used hardcover and paperback.
# of Vols:	100,000+
Specialties:	Philosophy; ancient history; art; architecture.
Hours:	Daily 9am-11pm.
Travel:	Located in Hyde Park neighborhood. 47th St exit off Lake Shore Dr. Proceed west one block then south on Lake Park Ave and right on 57th St.
Credit Cards:	Yes
Owner:	Bradley Jonas & Michael Powell, owners. Chelsea Nash, manager.
Year Estab:	1972
Comments:	Chicago's first Powell's and the store closest in ambience to a "traditional" used book store. The stock here, approximately 50% of which is used, is more scholarly oriented than the other locations given its proximity to the University of Chicago.

Powell's Bookstore, Burnham Park   **Open Shop**
828 South Wabash 60605   (312) 341-0748
                                                    Fax: (312) 341-1614

Collection:	General stock of remainders and used hardcover and paperback.
# of Vols:	100,000+
Hours:	Mon-Fri 10:30-6. Sat 10-6. Sun 12-5.
Travel:	Downtown, one block east of Michigan between 8th & 9th Streets.
Credit Cards:	Yes
Owner:	Sylvia Cave, Manager
Comments:	While there are some truly "used' books in this shop (older volumes of historical or bibliographic significance) one has to look carefully to find them. The vast majority of the stock consists of remainders which "ain't" necessarily bad considering that they are in universally wonderful condition and the buyer gets a fabulous discount off the original list price. After you've browsed the front section of the shop, don't miss row after row of bookshelves downstairs set up like a library warehouse—there are treasures galore at bargain prices.

Powell's Bookstore, North   **Open Shop**
2850 North Lincoln 60657   (773) 248-1444

Collection:	General stock of remainders and used hardcover and paperback.
# of Vols:	100,000+
Specialties:	Art; humanities.
Hours:	Sun-Fri 11-9. Sat 10-10.
Travel:	In Lakeview neighborhood between Oakdale and George.
Credit Cards:	Yes
Owner:	Mai Wagner, Manager

Comments: Spacious, wide aisles and attractive displays describe our initial impression to this third Powell's store in Chicago. Unlike the "traditional used book shop," this shop displays lots of remainders at bargain prices, but also carries plenty of used books, both paperbacks and hardcovers, on well marked shelves. Be sure to check out the separate rare book room located in the rear of the shop. Even if you don't see a used book you're interested in purchasing, the variety of the remainders makes the shop well worth a visit.

Prairie Avenue Bookshop   **Open Shop**
418 South Wabash Avenue 60605   (312) 922-8311
Web page: www.pabook.com   Fax: (312) 922-5184
      E-mail: beifrig@interaccess.com

Collection:	Specialty. Mostly new and some used.
Specialties:	Architecture
Hours:	Mon-Fri 9:30-5:30. Sat 10-4.
Services:	Catalog (primarily new books).
Credit Cards:	Yes
Owner:	Marilyn Hasbrouck

Rain Dog Books   **Open Shop**
404 South Michigan Avenue 60605   (312) 922-1200
Web page: www.raindogbooks.com   Fax: (312) 922-3182
      E-mail: raindog@raindogbooks.com

Collection:	General stock of mostly hardcover.
# of Vols:	15,000
Specialties:	First editions; art; philosophy; history; science.
Hours:	Mon-Sat 11-6. Sun 12-5.
Services:	Mail order.
Travel:	See Bookseller's Row above.
Credit Cards:	Yes
Owner:	Richard Vokoun
Year Estab:	1994
Comments:	An absolute Eden for the serious book person. Scholarly titles in every field from science to art to literary matters. If your tastes are erudite, once you arrive here you'll feel very much at home. Prices reflect the quality of the stock.

Ed Ripp: Bookseller   **By Appointment**
3719 North Fremont Street 60613   (773) 281-1451
      Fax: (773) 281-2988

Collection:	Specialty
# of Vols:	1,500
Specialties:	Art history; illustrated; artist monographs; Chicago art and artists; woodcut novels; decorative arts; photography; architecture; private press; books on books.
Services:	Appraisals, search service, accepts want lists, mail order.
Year Estab:	1991

(Chicago)

Bernie Rost-Books   **By Appointment**
2818 North Austin Avenue 60634   (773) 622-1256

Collection:	General stock.
# of Vols:	2,000-3,000
Specialties:	Illustrated; art; photography.
Year Estab:	1989

John Rybski, Bookseller   **By Appointment**
2319 West 47th Place 60609   (773) 847-5082
                                                                   Fax: (312) 847-6750
                                                                   E-mail: rybski@slash.net

Collection:	Specialty
# of Vols:	50,000
Specialties:	Americana; Civil War; military; business history; art; ethnic groups.
Services:	Catalog
Credit Cards:	Yes
Year Estab:	1968

Joe Sarno's Comic Kingdom   **Open Shop**
5941 West Irving Park Road 60634   (773) 545-2231

Collection:	Specialty used and new.
# of Vols:	50,000
Specialties:	Science fiction magazines (1930-1970); comics from 1933 to present.
Hours:	Tue-Sat 12-6.
Travel:	Irving Park exit off I-90/94. Proceed west on Irving Park.
Credit Cards:	Yes
Year Estab:	1971

Barry Scott   **By Appointment**
5805 South Dorchester Avenue 60637   (773) 324-9042
                                                                   Fax: (773) 324-9058
                                                                   E-mail: scotbook@interaccess.com

Collection:	Specialty
# of Vols:	500
Specialties:	History of science and medicine; literature; decorative arts; manuscripts; early printing; fine bindings.
Services:	Appraisals, occasional catalog, accepts want lists, mail order.
Credit Cards:	No
Year Estab:	1969

Selected Works   **Open Shop**
3510 North Broadway 60657   (773) 975-0002

Collection:	General stock of hardcover and paperback.
# of Vols:	30,000
Specialties:	Literature; philosophy; religion.
Hours:	Daily 12-9.

Travel:	Belmont or Irving Park Rd exits off I-90/94.
Credit Cards:	No
Owner:	Keith Peterson
Year Estab:	1984
Comments:	A very nice selection of hardcover volumes. Stronger in non fiction than fiction but an ample and well represented supply of the latter. The shelves were nicely labeled and the books attractively priced. The owner indicated to us that he would rather provide his customers with good reading copies than carry more expensive books.

Shake, Rattle & Read   **Open Shop**
4812 North Broadway 60640   (773) 334-5311

Collection:	General stock of paperback and hardcover.
# of Vols:	20,000
Hours:	Mon-Sat 11-6. Sun 12-6.
Travel:	Just north of Lawrence.
Credit Cards:	Yes
Owner:	Ric Addy
Year Estab:	1966
Comments:	Predominately paperback with some hardcover volumes, comic books and magazines. Don't look for a Hemingway first edition here.

The Stars Our Destination   **Open Shop**
1021 Belmont Avenue 60657   (773) 871-2722
Web page: www.sfbooks.com   Fax: (773) 871-6816
                                             E-mail: stars@sfbooks.com

Collection:	Specialty new and used.
Specialties:	Science fiction; fantasy; horror.
Hours:	Mon-Sat 11-9. Sun 12-6.
Services:	Catalog, accepts want lists.
Travel:	Southbound on I-90/94: Kimball exit. At first light, make left on Belmont. Shop is three miles ahead.
Credit Cards:	Yes
Owner:	Alice Bentley
Year Estab:	1988

Harry L. Stern, Ltd.   **By Appointment**
919 North Michigan Avenue, Ste. 2506 60611   (312) 337-1401
                                                 Fax: (312) 214-2510

Collection:	Specialty
Specialties:	Americana; maps; manuscripts; Renaissance.
Services:	Appraisals
Credit Cards:	No
Year Estab:	1975

(Chicago)

Helena Szépe, Books   **By Appointment**
1525 East 53rd St, Ste. 825 60615   (773) 684-5686
                                                   E-mail: szepe@interloc.com

Collection:	General stock.
# of Vols:	20,000
Specialties:	Art; architecture; early printing; science; European books.
Services:	Appraisals, catalog, accepts want lists.
Credit Cards:	Yes
Year Estab:	1980

Turtle Island Books   **Open Shop**
7001 Glenwood Avenue 60626   (773) 465-7212

Collection:	General stock of new and used hardcover and paperback.
# of Vols:	6,000
Specialties:	Magic; witchcraft; occult; metaphysics; astrology; psychology; philosophy; science fiction; mystery; eastern religions; art.
Hours:	Tue-Thu 11-7. Fri & Sat 11-8:30. Sun 12-6. Extended summer hours.
Travel:	At Lunt, one block west of Sheridan Rd. Between Devon and Touhy Aves.
Credit Cards:	No
Owner:	Warren & Violet Engelberg
Year Estab:	1992
Comments:	Stock is approximately 50% used.

The White Elephant Shop   **Open Shop**
2380 North Lincoln Avenue 60614   (773) 281-3747

Collection:	General stock of hardcover and paperback.
Hours:	Mon-Sat 10-5. Sun 11-4.
Travel:	Fullerton exit off Lake Shore Dr. West on Fullerton. Left on N. Lincoln.
Credit Cards:	Yes
Comments:	Non profit shop. All books are donated.

Yesterday   **Open Shop**
1143 West Addison Street 60613   (773) 248-8087

Collection:	Specialty books and ephemera.
# of Vols:	500
Specialties:	Magazines; newspapers; movie posters; sports memorabilia; comics.
Hours:	Mon-Sat 1-7. Sun 2-6.
Services:	Accepts want lists, mail order.
Travel:	In Lakeview neighborhood, one block west of Wrigley Field.
Credit Cards:	No
Owner:	Tom Boyle
Year Estab:	1976

Note: See page 94 for an additional Open Shop in Chicago.

Chicago Heights
(Map 4, page 66)

Gift Music Book & Collectibles   **Open Shop**
2501 Chicago Road 60411   (708) 754-4387

Collection:	General stock of hardcover and ephemera.
# of Vols:	50,000
Hours:	Mon, Tue, Fri 11-6. Wed, Thu, Sat 10-12. Best to call ahead.
Services:	Mail order, search service.
Travel:	Halsted exit off I-80. Proceed south on Rte 1 (Halsted) for several miles.
Credit Cards:	Yes
Owner:	Joe Schulte
Year Estab:	1989
Comments:	A non profit shop. The books are donated and purchased.

Chillicothe
(Map 1, page 24)

The American Botanist, Booksellers   **By Appointment**
1103 West Truitt   (309) 274-5254
Mailing address: PO Box 532 Chillicothe IL 61523   Fax: (309) 274-6143
E-mail: agbook2mtco.com

Collection:	Specialty
# of Vols:	3,000
Specialties:	Agriculture; horticulture; olericulture and their histories.
Services:	Appraisals, search service, catalog, accepts want lists.
Credit Cards:	Yes
Owner:	Keith Crotz
Year Estab:	1983
Comments:	Overnight accommodations are available for dealers. Call ahead.

Clinton
(Map 1, page 24)

Clinton Antique Mall   **Antique Mall**
Junction Bypass Rte 51 & Rte 54   (217) 935-8846

Hours:	Mon-Sat 10-5. Sun 12-5.

Decatur
(Map 1, page 24)

Novel Ideas   **Open Shop**
217 East Wood Street 62521   (217) 429-1995
Web page: www.abebooks.com   Fax: (217) 249-2081
E-mail: kdsoman@aol.com

Collection:	General stock.
# of Vols:	7,500
Specialties:	History
Hours:	Tue-Sat 10-6.

Services:	Appraisals, search service, mail order, book repairs.
Travel:	Exit 141 off I-72. Proceed south on Bus Rte 51 (which becomes North Main St) to downtown. Turn left on Wood.
Credit Cards:	Yes
Owner:	Kim Soman
Year Estab:	1995
Comments:	An attractive shop that sells exclusively hardcover volumes of mixed vintage. Most of the books we saw were in quite good condition and reasonably priced. The modest size of the shop's collection did not allow for much depth in most subject areas. The shop also sells gift items.

Deerfield
(Map 4, page 66)

Norma Adler   **By Appointment**
59 Eastwood Drive 60015   (847) 945-8575

Collection:	General stock.
# of Vols:	1,500
Specialties:	Modern literary first editions (American).
Services:	Search service, accepts want lists, mail order.
Credit Cards:	No
Year Estab:	1977

Bookman Extraordinaire   **By Appointment**
PO Box 676 60015   (847) 945-2957
                                                                    Fax: (847) 498-4655
                                                                E-mail: ed@justdoit.net

Collection:	General stock.
# of Vols:	8,000
Specialties:	Color plates; A&C Black books; fine bindings; fore-edge paintings; children's; travel; Limited Editions Club.
Services:	Appraisals, search service, accepts want lists.
Credit Cards:	Yes
Owner:	Edward Halpern
Year Estab:	1990

Eldorado
(Map 1, page 24)

Books & Things   **Open Shop**
Route 45   (618) 273-9550
Mailing address: 1023 1st Street Eldorado IL 62960

Collection:	General stock of mostly paperback.
# of Vols:	250,000
Hours:	Tue-Sat 10-4.
Travel:	On Rte 45, one half mile south of Rte 142.
Credit Cards:	No
Year Estab:	1976

Comments: Like those early Spanish explorers, we too traveled miles (and hours) off the beaten path hoping to find a city with, if not gold, then at least wonderful books. And, like those same explorers, we came up empty handed. What we did find was an establishment that, in addition to thousands and thousands of paperbacks, sells used clothing, bric a brac, records and other assorted items. While the shop did carry a few thousand older hardcover volumes, most were in rather mixed condition and hardly, at least in our humble opinion, deserving the time spent seeking the elusive "pot of gold."

Elgin
(Map 1, page 24)

Reader's Haven Paperback Books   **Open Shop**
815 St. Charles Street 60120   (847) 697-2526

Collection:	General stock of paperback and hardcover.
# of Vols:	60,000
Hours:	Tue-Sat 10-5, except Thu till 7.
Travel:	Rte 25 south exit off Rte 20. Proceed south on Rte 25 for one block to first light.
Credit Cards:	Yes
Year Estab:	1976
Comments:	Stock is approximately 70% paperback.

Elk Grove Village
(Map 4, page 66)

Edwin Schaeffer   **Antique Mall**
At Antiques Mart of Elk Grove Village, 1170 W. Devon Ave.   Mall: (847) 895-8900
Mailing address: PO Box 379523 Chicago IL 60637   Home: (773) 324-2640
                                                E-mail: win@alumni.princeton.edu

Collection:	General stock.
# of Vols:	3,000 (See Comments)
Specialties:	Military; archeology; ancient history; American and political history.
Hours:	Mon-Fri 11-7. Sat & Sun 10-5.
Travel:	Thorndale Rd exit off I-290. Proceed west on Thorndale, then right on Rohling. Shop is 1/2 mile ahead in a shopping center at corner of Rohling and West Devon.
Owner:	Win Schaeffer
Comments:	An additional 7,000-8,000 volumes are not on display.

Elmhurst
(Map 4, page 66)

Thrifty Scholar   **Open Shop**
142 North York Road 60126   (630) 834-7056

Collection:	General stock of mostly new and some used.
# of Vols:	25,000

Hours:	Mon-Sat 10-9:30. Sun 12-6.
Travel:	In center of downtown, between St. Charles and North Ave.
Year Estab:	1994
Comments:	Stock is approximately 20% used, most of which is hardcover.

Wilder Books   **By Appointment**
PO Box 762 60126   (630) 834-8529
                                                        Fax: (630) 834-5641

Collection:	General stock.
# of Vols:	2,000-3,000
Specialties:	Literature; autographs; manuscripts; old photography; first editions; Americana; illustrated; black studies.
Services:	Catalog, accepts want lists.
Credit Cards:	No
Owner:	Bob Fiene
Year Estab:	1981

Evanston
(Map 5, page 49 & Map 1, page 24)

The Aleph Bookshop   **Open Shop**
831 Main Street 60202   (847) 869-6410
                                                             Fax: (847) 328-1146

Collection:	Specialty paperback and hardcover.
# of Vols:	3,000+
Specialties:	Science fiction; fantasy; horror; first editions.
Hours:	Tue-Sat 11-6, except Thu till 9. Sun 11-5.
Services:	Appraisals, catalog, accepts want lists.
Travel:	From Chicago, proceed north on Lake Shore Dr to Sheridan Rd, then continue north on Sheridan to Evanston. Left on Main St. The shop shares space with Chicago Historical Bookworks (see below).
Credit Cards:	Yes
Owner:	Kenan, Carol & Tiger Heise
Year Estab:	1985
Comments:	A healthy collection in the specialties listed above. There are more paperback than hardcover BUT many of the hardcover titles go well beyond the typical Stephen King, Dean Koontz selections into more of the vintage titles. If this is your cup of tea, you should find some items of interest here.

Alkahest Bookshop   **Open Shop**
1814 Central Street 60201   (847) 475-0990
                                                   E-mail: alkabook@aol.com

Collection:	General stock.
# of Vols:	5,000+
Specialties:	Art; Americana.
Hours:	Tue-Sat 11-5.
Services:	Search service, catalog, accepts want lists.

Travel:	Old Orchard exit off I-94. Proceed east on Old Orchard, then north (left) on Crawford for one block. At light, turn east (right) on Central. Shop is about 1½ miles ahead.
Credit Cards:	Yes
Owner:	David Harmon & Pat Martinak
Year Estab:	1984
Comments:	A corner shop with an excellent selection of books, particularly in the areas identified above as specialties. The books we saw were in very good to better condition. Prices were, in most cases, "on target" and in a few instances slightly higher. But then sometimes one has to pay a few dollars more to get a book not easily found elsewhere.

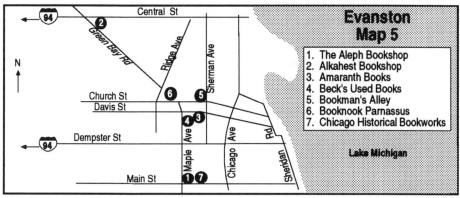

Amaranth Books
Open Shop
828 Davis Street 60201
(847) 328-2939

Collection:	General stock of hardcover and paperback.
# of Vols:	15,000
Hours:	Mon-Sat 11-5:30. Sun 1-5.
Services:	Catalog, accepts want lists.
Travel:	Dempster Ave exit off I-94. Proceed east on Dempster, then north on Chicago and left on Davis. Shop is at corner of Benson St.
Credit Cards:	Yes
Owner:	Joseph Warnick
Year Estab:	1985
Comments:	A quality shop with nice titles, mostly in good condition and reasonably priced.

Beck's Used Books
Open Shop
1583 Maple Avenue 60201
(847) 869-6099

Collection:	General stock.
# of Vols:	2,000
Hours:	See Comments.
Travel:	See Amaranth above.
Credit Cards:	No
Year Estab:	1980

(Evanston)

Comments: You're on your own when it comes to this shop. When we tried to
                  contact the owner to update his listing, the answering machine message
                  indicated that the owner was indeed still selling books—in addition to
                  operating a lawn and yard business. Perhaps because our calls (several
                  of them) were made during the spring/summer season, the message
                  never included the hours the shop was open. So, if you find yourself in
                  Evanston and have some free time, you may want to be guided by the
                  following comments which are based on our earlier visit to the shop.
                      We can't recall ever referring to a used book shop as "a hole in the
                  wall" and perhaps it's unfair to classify this shop in such terms.
                  The phrase occurred to us in describing this shop only because of
                  the absence of an appropriate sign out front identifying it as a used
                  bookstore, the size of the shop, the age and condition of the books
                  we saw inside and the general sense of disorderliness. The above
                  word picture notwithstanding, the shop does carry a modest stock
                  of used books, and in the book hunting game, one never knows
                  where a long sought after item may turn up.

Booklady   **By Appointment**
400 Main Street, #2C 60202   (847) 869-1385
Web page: www.abebooks.com   E-mail: bookladyA1@aol.com

Collection: Specialty
# of Vols: 10,000
Specialties: Local history and other non fiction.
Services: Search service, accepts want lists, mail order.
Credit Cards: No
Owner: Sue E. Holbert
Year Estab: 1994

Bookman's Alley   **Open Shop**
1712 (rear) Sherman Avenue 60201   (847) 869-6999

Collection: General stock.
# of Vols: 50,000
Specialties: Art; literature; American history.
Hours: Mon 12-7. Tue & Wed 12-8. Thu 12-9. Fri 12-6. Sat 10:30-6. Sun 12-6.
Services: Appraisals, mail order.
Travel: See Amaranth above.
Credit Cards: No
Owner: Roger Carlson
Year Estab: 1981
Comments: If you're looking for ambience in a bookstore, this store gets an A+
                  rating. The book collection is tastefully integrated in this meandering
                  shop with period clothing, antiques, fresh flowers and plants and other
                  objet d'art, giving each section a mood appropriate to the contents of the
                  books. The books themselves, almost universally in excellent condition,

run the gamut from rare to collectible to more ordinary and are priced, as one might suspect, considering their condition, appropriately.

Chicago Historical Bookworks   **Open Shop**
831 Main Street 60202   (847) 869-6410
Web page: www.books.msg.net   Fax: (847) 328-1146

Collection:	Specialty new and used.
Specialties:	Chicago; Midwest; Civil War; first editions; Lakeside Classics.
Hours:	Tue-Sat 11-6, except Thu till 9. Sun 11-5.
Services:	Appraisals, catalog, accepts want lists.
Travel:	Shares space with The Aleph Bookshop. See above.
Credit Cards:	Yes
Owner:	Kenan, Carol & Tiger Heise
Year Estab:	1985
Comments:	The owner, an author and expert on the history of Chicago, stocks a healthy variety of used and some new books (mostly hardcover but a few paperbacks) dealing with the windy city. Reasonably priced.

Hamill & Barker Antiquarian Booksellers   **By Appointment**
1719 Howard Street 60202   (847) 475-1724
                                                                     Fax: (847) 475-5846

Collection:	Specialty
Specialties:	Incunabula; early printing; medicine; science; literature; Americana.
Services:	Appraisals, catalog, accepts want lists.
Credit Cards:	Yes
Owner:	Terence A. Tanner
Year Estab:	1928

Phyllis Tholin, Books   **By Appointment**
824 Ridge Terrace 60201   (847) 475-1174
                                                              E-mail: r-tholin@nwu.edu

Collection:	General stock.
# of Vols:	10,000
Specialties:	Women's history and literature; Chicago; Methodist history.
Services:	Catalog, accepts want lists.
Credit Cards:	No
Year Estab:	1981

Note: See page 94 for an additional open shop in Evanston.

Forest Park
(Map 4, page 66)

Bookends and Fine Collectables   **By Appointment**
516 Elgin Avenue 60130   (708) 771-7721

Collection:	Specialty
# of Vols:	2,000-4,000
Specialties:	Art; architecture; antiques; general illustrated non fiction; nautical; railroads.

Services: Accepts want lists, mail order.
Credit Cards: No
Owner: Daniel A.D. Jones
Year Estab: 1990

Flying Moose Books, Ltd.   **Open Shop**
7510 West Madison 60130   (708) 366-4209

Collection: General stock of hardcover and paperback.
# of Vols: 15,000+
Hours: Wed-Sat 10-5. Other times by appointment.
Services: Search service, accepts want lists.
Travel: Eastbound on I-290: Des Plaines exit. Proceed north on Des Plaines,
                  then right on Madison. Westbound on I-290: Harlem Ave exit. Proceed
                  north on Rte 43 then left on Madison.
Credit Cards: No
Owner: Don Grazulis, president
Year Estab: 1995
Comments: We returned to this shop after 3½ years to be greeted by several changes,
                  including a new store name and a new owner. The shop now carries a
                  mix of hardcover books (some that could be considered collectible) and
                  paperbacks in varying condition, which, had a buyer been interested in
                  purchasing, could have been had at a 50% discount as the store was
                  having a sale at the time of our visit. At other times, we might have
                  questioned some of the prices. The success of the sale might also have
                  been responsible for our impression that there were somewhat fewer
                  volumes on hand than the number cited above. Clearly this could change
                  by the time of your visit.

Forsyth
(Map 1, page 24)

Old Book Barn   **Open Shop**
Route 51 North, Box 500 62535   (217) 875-0222
Web page: www.prairieghosts.com   Fax: (217) 877-9211
                                           E-mail: ttaylor@prairieghosts.com
Collection: General stock of mostly used paperback and hardcover.
# of Vols: 200,000+
Specialties: Romance
Hours: Mon-Sat 9-6. Sun 12-5.
Services: Mail order.
Travel: Exit 141 (Rte 51) off I-72. Proceed north on Rte 51 for two miles. Shop
                  is on the right at the intersection of Rte 51 and Shafer St. Look for a
                  large green metal building.
Credit Cards: Yes
Owner: Troy Taylor
Year Estab: 1981
Comments: This extremely large shop provides the browser with an opportunity to
                  be amused while searching for books as several sections have been

decorated to create an atmosphere that blends in with the subject matter displayed, i.e., the travel/adventure section, sports a cot covered with mosquito netting, pictures with African scenes and the taped sounds of jungle noises. The entertainment, horror and children's sections are similarly decorated with appropriate "paraphernalia." As for the books, the majority of them are of fairly recent vintage and many are remainders that are generally attractively priced. There's also a "vintage book room" that has older (although not necessarily rare) books. The store also has plenty of paperbacks in the usual subjects. While this is a place where the general browser could spend a good deal of time, those looking for antiquarian, rare or truly scholarly books are not likely to find them here. Dealers may want to check on the store's discount policy (which is not necessarily consistent with the general trend). The owner recently opened a second shop in Alton. See Riverboat Molly's above.

White Chapel Productions   **Open Shop**
Route 51 North, Box 11 62535   (217) 875-2366
Web page: www.prairieghosts.com   Fax: (217) 877-9211
                                                E-mail: ttaylor@prairieghosts.com

Collection:	Specialty. Mostly new and some used.
Specialties:	Supernatural; ghosts; local history.
Hours:	Mon-Sat 9-6. Sun 12-5.
Services:	Catalog
Travel:	Located within the Old Book Barn. See above.
Credit Cards:	Yes
Owner:	Troy Taylor

Freeport
(Map 1, page 24)

Dr. J's Books   **Open Shop**
214 West Main Street 61032   Tel & Fax: (815) 235-4535

Collection:	General stock, ephemera, postcards and records.
# of Vols:	20,000
Hours:	Mon-Sat 11-6.
Services:	Appraisals, accepts want lists.
Travel:	Bus Rte 20 (Galena St) to downtown intersection of Main and Galena. From Rte 26, proceed into town to Lincoln St, then east on Lincoln which becomes Main.
Credit Cards:	Yes
Owner:	Steve Jennings
Year Estab:	1988
Comments:	The entrance to this shop is filled with displays of baseball cards, coins, stamps and hobby-like materials. Once beyond the entrance, though, you'll find a rabbit warren of rooms, each containing several stacks of hardcover books, mostly of an older variety, in both fiction and non

fiction. Prices for a few of the items we pulled out appeared to be a bit higher than we've seen elsewhere for the same title and few of the titles could, in our judgement, be categorized as truly difficult to find.

Half Price Used Book Store   **Open Shop**
521 West Galena Avenue 61032   (815) 235-1544

Collection: General stock of mostly paperback.
# of Vols: 20,000
Hours: Tue-Sat 10-6.

Bob Rund-Books   **By Appointment**
2520 Stephenson Circle 61032   (815) 233-0488

Collection: General stock.
# of Vols: 15,000
Specialties: Americana
Services: Appraisals, search service, accepts want lists, mail order.
Credit Cards: No
Year Estab: 1965

Galena
(Map 1, page 24)

Main Street Fine Books & Manuscripts   **Open Shop**
206 North Main Street 61036   (815) 777-3749
Web page: www.wcinet.com/msfbooks   Fax: (8150 777-8950
                                              E-mail: msfb@galenalink.com

Collection: General stock.
# of Vols: 15,000-20,000
Specialties: Civil War; Ulysses Grant; Abraham Lincoln; autographs.
Hours: Daily 10-5.
Services: Appraisals, catalog, accepts want lists.
Travel: Rte 20 intersects Main St.
Credit Cards: Yes
Owner: William & Yolanda Butts
Year Estab: 1990
Comments: One simply has to walk into this shop to know that the owners care very much about the books they select and display; books not wearing dust jackets were meticulously protected with plastic covers. The subjects identified above as specialties were well represented and if these areas are close to your heart, there's little question but that you'll find one or more titles here to tempt you. At the time of our visit, the shop also displayed a collection of vintage paperbacks.

Peace of the Past   **Open Shop**
408 South Main Street 61036   (815) 777-2738
                                              E-mail: peace@galenalink.com

Collection: General stock.
# of Vols: 25,000

Specialties:	Children's
Hours:	Apr-Dec: Daily 10-5. Jan-Mar: Fri-Sun 10-5 and by appointment.
Services:	Accepts want lists.
Travel:	See Main Street Fine Books above.
Credit Cards:	Yes
Owner:	William & Jody Karberg
Year Estab:	1990
Comments:	The shop also sells antiques and collectibles.

Galesburg
(Map 1, page 24)

General Store Antiques
940 East North Street 61401

Open Shop
(309) 342-2926

Collection:	General stock.
# of Vols:	300
Hours:	Tue-Sat 10-4:30.

3R's HoneyBee Bookshoppe
68 South Seminary Street 61401

Open Shop
(309) 342-2994
E-mail: honeybee@misslink.net

Collection:	General stock.
# of Vols:	10,000
Specialties:	Illinois; modern first editions.
Hours:	Mon, Wed, Fri Sat 10-5. Tue & Thu 11-5.
Services:	Search service, accepts want lists, mail order.
Travel:	Galesburg exit of I-74. Proceed west on East Main St, then left on Seminary.
Credit Cards:	No
Owner:	Helen Masters
Year Estab:	1991
Comments:	Our apologies to our readers and the owner of this shop. We were on our way to Galesburg when we learned that the bridge crossing the Illinois River was out of service and that the wait for the alternate ferry was such that it would make us late for an appointment we had later that afternoon. Thus, we'll have to leave our observations of this shop to another edition and hope in the interim that our readers will fill us in on what we missed.

Glen Ellyn
(Map 4, page 66)

Four Seasons Books
677 Roosevelt Road 60137

Open Shop
(630) 469-1415

Collection:	General stock of paperback and hardcover.
# of Vols:	45,000
Hours:	Mon-Fri 11-8. Sat 10-8.

Travel:	Roosevelt Rd exit off I-355. Proceed west on Roosevelt Rd.
Credit Cards:	Yes
Year Estab:	1996
Comments:	Stock is approximately 70% paperback.

Glencoe
(Map 4, page 66)

Kenneth Nebenzahl, Inc.　　　　　　　　　　　　　　**By Appointment**
PO Box 370 60022　　　　　　　　　　　　　　　　　　(708) 835-0515

Collection:	Specialty
# of Vols:	5,000
Specialties:	Americana; history of travel and exploration; cartography.
Services:	Accepts want lists, mail order.
Credit Cards:	No
Year Estab:	1956

Grayslake
(Map 1, page 24)

The Book Stop　　　　　　　　　　　　　　　　　　　**Open Shop**
138 Centre Street 60030　　　　　　　　　　　　　　(847) 223-2665
　　　　　　　　　　　　　　　　　　　E-mail: pcmattes@aol.com

Collection:	General stock of mostly used hardcover and paperback.
# of Vols:	10,000-15,000
Specialties:	Literature; history; metaphysics; science fiction; romance.
Hours:	Mon-Fri 12-8. Sat 10-5. Occasional Sundays.
Services:	Search service.
Travel:	Grand Ave exit off I-294. Proceed west on Grand Ave (Rte 132), then left (south) on Rte 45 and right on Centre. Shop is in downtown.
Credit Cards:	Yes
Owner:	Patricia C. Mattes
Year Estab:	1993
Comments:	A modest sized shop selling mostly used paperbacks and hardcover books, the majority of which appeared to be of fairly recent vintage. Reasonably priced. While we were unable to spot any truly rare items, the turnover in the book world is such that you may well have better luck.

Havana
(Map 1, page 24)

The Neverending Story　　　　　　　　　　　　　　**Open Shop**
219 West Main Street 62644　　　　　　　　　　　　(309) 543-3475

Collection:	General stock of hardcover and paperback.
# of Vols:	100,000+ (See Commemts)
Hours:	Mon-Fri, except closed Tue, 10-6. Sat 9-6. Sun 12-5.
Services:	Search service, accepts want lists, mail order.
Travel:	Located in downtown.

Credit Cards:	Yes
Owner:	Dan Pitcher & Lynn Coots
Year Estab:	1991
Comments:	A shop that sells crafts, antiques and collectibles as well as paperback and hardcover books that are intershelved. The majority of the hardcover books we saw were reading copies, most reasonably priced, with a few older editions and some vintage mysteries and collectibles. While not great in number, there were enough books here to satisfy the casual browser. The number of books on display at the time of our visit was considerably less than the number cited above.

Highland Park
(Map 4, page 66)

Graton & Graton   **By Appointment**
1601 Oakwood Avenue, #109 60035   Tel & Fax: (847) 432-4722

Collection:	Specialty
Specialties:	Illuminated manuscripts; antique maps; antiquarian.
Services:	Accepts want lists.
Credit Cards:	Yes
Owner:	Waldo & Marilyn Graton
Year Estab:	1979

ORT Alley Bookstore   **Open Shop**
800 Central Avenue 60035   (847) 433-1172

Collection:	General stock of paperback and hardcover.
Hours:	Mon-Sat 9-4:30.
Travel:	Old Deerfield Rd exit off Rte 41. Proceed east on Deerfield. When road splits, take left fork onto Central.
Comments:	Operated by a non profit group. All books are donated.

Frank S. Pollack   **By Appointment**
1214 Green Bay Road 60035   (847) 433-2213
Fax: (312) 372-8343
E-mail: FPollack@compuserve.com

Collection:	Specialty
# of Vols:	3,000
Specialties:	Mystery; detective; modern literature.
Services:	Appraisals, search service, catalog, accepts want lists.
Credit Cards:	Yes
Year Estab:	1986

George Ritzlin Maps & Books   **Open Shop**
469 Roger Williams Avenue 60035   (847) 433-2627
Fax: (847) 433-6389

Collection:	Specialty books, maps and prints.
Specialties:	Antique maps and atlases; cartographic reference; medieval manuscript leaves; antique natural history prints; antique fashion plates.

Hours:	Wed, Thu, Fri 10-5. Sat 10-4. Other times by appointment.
Services:	Catalog
Travel:	Lake Cook Rd East exit off I-94. Proceed east on Lake Cook Rd, then north on Green Bay and east on Roger Williams.
Credit Cards:	Yes
Year Estab:	1976

Titles, Inc.   **Open Shop**
1931 Sheridan Road 60035   (847) 432-3690
                                                         Fax: (847) 432-3699
                                             E-mail: titlesbk@interloc.com

Collection:	Specialty
# of Vols:	5,000
Specialties:	Chicago; first editions; children's art; architecture; photography; books about books; Americana; fine bindings.
Hours:	Mon-Sat 10:30-5.
Services:	Search service
Travel:	When I-94 continues as Rte 41, exit at Central Ave East. Continue traveling east through Highland Park, then turn north on Sheridan and continue for one block.
Credit Cards:	No
Owner:	Florence Shay
Year Estab:	1974

Hinsdale
(Map 4, page 66)

Gemini Fine Books & Arts   **By Appointment**
917 Oakwood Terrace 60521   (630) 986-1478
Web page: www.tensornet.com/gemini   Fax: (630) 325-9127
                                            E-mail: gemini@tensornet.com

Collection:	Specialty books and original prints.
# of Vols:	5,000
Specialties:	Art reference (20th century); book with original graphics; livres d'artistes; modern first editions; Russian avant-garde.
Services:	Mail order.
Credit Cards:	No
Owner:	Arik Verezhensky
Year Estab:	1986
Comments:	Also books signed by artists.

Homewood
(Map 1, page 24)

Autumn Leaves Books   **Open Shop**
18029 Dixie Highway 60430   (708) 922-3522
                                                         Fax: (708) 922-3590
                                            E-mail: autumnlv@interloc.com

Collection:	General stock of mostly hardcover.

# of Vols:	5,000+
Specialties:	Modern first editions; older fiction.
Hours:	Mon-Sat 10-7.
Services:	Search service, accepts want lists, mail order.
Travel:	Halsted exit off I-80. Proceed south on Halsted, then right on Ridge and right on Dixie Hwy.
Credit Cards:	Yes
Owner:	Charles & Darlene Spohrer
Year Estab:	1997

Joliet
(Map 1, page 24)

Book Market Paperback Sales　　　　　　　　　　　**Open Shop**
1157 West Jefferson Street 60435　　　　　　　　　　(815) 744-4240

Collection:	General stock of mostly paperback.
# of Vols:	100,000
Hours:	Mon-Fri 10-6. Sat 10-5.

River Gallery　　　　　　　　　　　　　　　　　　**Open Shop**
61 West Clinton Street 60432　　　　　　　　　　　　(815) 722-5996
　　　　　　　　　　　　　　　　　　　　　　　Fax: (815) 722-5408

Collection:	Specialty
# of Vols:	200-500
Specialties:	Antiquarian; antique maps.
Hours:	Mon-Fri 10;30-5:30. Sat 10:30-3:30. (See Comments)
Travel:	Center St exit off I-80. Follow signs to Harrah's Casino. Shop is 1/2 block east of casino.
Credit Cards:	Yes
Owner:	Maureen Kahoun
Year Estab:	1994
Comments:	Shop is an art gallery, framing and gift shop. Antique maps are on display but books can only be viewed by appointment.

Kankakee
(Map 1, page 24)

Kankakee Antique Mall　　　　　　　　　　　　　**Antique Mall**
145 South Schuyler Avenue 60901　　　　　　　　　　(815) 937-4957

Hours:	Daily 10-6.
Travel:	Exit 312 off I-57. Proceed west on Court for one mile.

Kenilworth
(Map 4, page 66)

Ann Dumler Children's Books　　　　　　　　　**By Appointment**
645 Melrose 60043　　　　　　　　　　　　　　　　(847) 251-2034
　　　　　　　　　　　　　　　　　　　　　　　Fax: (847) 251-2044

Collection:	Specialty

Specialties:	Children's; illustrated.
Services:	Catalog, accepts want lists.
Credit Cards:	No
Year Estab:	1981

Joe Girardi   **By Appointment**
707 Kent Road 60043   (847) 251-3227
                                                     Fax: (847) 256-3862

Collection:	General stock.
# of Vols:	10,000
Services:	Mail order, accepts want lists.
Credit Cards:	No
Year Estab:	1989

Kay's Treasured Kookbooks   **By Appointment**
PO Box 17 60043   (847) 256-4459

Collection:	Specialty
# of Vols:	3,000+
Specialties:	Cookbooks
Services:	Search service, accepts want lists, mail order.
Credit Cards:	No
Owner:	Kay Sullivan
Year Estab:	1983

La Grange
(Map 4, page 66)

Legibus   **By Appointment**
PO Box 809 60525   (708) 352-3039
Web page: www.legibus.com   E-mail: drbryant@poboxes.com

Collection:	Specialty books and manuscripts.
Specialties:	Law (5th-17th century).
Services:	Appraisals, accepts want lists.
Credit Cards:	No
Owner:	David R. Bryant
Year Estab:	1996

John Wm. Martin—Bookseller   **By Appointment**
231 South La Grange Road 60525   (708) 352-8115

Collection:	Specialty
# of Vols:	10,000
Specialties:	British literature (18th-20th centuries); American literature (19th & 20th centuries); first editions; literary criticism; books on books.
Services:	Appraisals, catalog, accepts want lists.
Credit Cards:	No
Year Estab:	1973
Comments:	The dealer also operates an open shop in La Grange. See Twice Read Books below.

Twice Read Books   **Open Shop**
124 Calendar Court   (708) 354-2665
Mailing address: 231 South La Grange Road La Grange IL 60525

Collection:	General stock.
# of Vols:	20,000+
Specialties:	American history; European history; military; cookbooks; religion; philosophy.
Hours:	Mon-Fri 1-7. Sat 10-5:30.
Services:	Accepts want lists, mail order.
Travel:	Mannheim exit off I-290. Proceed south on Rte 45 (La Grange Rd). After crossing the railroad tracks, turn right on Burlington, then left on Ashland. Shop is at the corner of Ashland and Calendar.
Credit Cards:	No
Owner:	John Wm. Martin
Year Estab:	1980
Comments:	This shop makes maximum use of its limited space. While most subjects are covered, the areas listed above get a bit more shelf space. We also noted some interesting first edition Wodehouse items but these could be long gone by the time you visit the shop. If you don't spot the titles you're looking for in the shop, ask the owner for a chance to visit his "by appointment" location where his better, collectible quality items can be found. (See John Wm. Martin—Bookseller above).

La Moille
(Map 1, page 24)

Pine Stock Books and Antiques   **By Appointment**
Route 34   (815) 539-6630
Mailing address: Route 1, Box 55 La Moille IL 61330

Collection:	General stock and ephemera.
# of Vols:	1,000+
Specialties:	Agriculture
Credit Cards:	No
Owner:	Dawn Bauer
Year Estab:	1990

Le Roy
(Map 1, page 24)

Maddie's Book Nook   **Open Shop**
218 East Center Street   (309) 962-2213
Mailing address: PO Box 126 Downs IL 61736

Collection:	General stock of primarily paperback.
Hours:	Mon-Sat 9-5.

Lebanon
(Map 1, page 24)

The Peddler's Books & Things   **Open Shop**
209 West St. Louis Street 62254   (618) 537-4026
Web page: www.abebooks.com   E-mail: gejo@webtv.net

Collection: General stock and ephemera.
# of Vols: 45,000
Hours: Thu-Mon 10-4:30. Tue & Wed by chance or appointment.
Travel: Lebanon exit off I-64. Proceed north on Rte 4 to second stop sign in
                   Lebanon, then left on West St. Louis St.
Credit Cards: No
Owner: John Sweeney
Year Estab: 1991

Lewistown
(Map 1, page 24)

Neuman's Oak Point Books   **By Appointment**
PO Box 69 61542   (309) 547-2168
                                                 E-mail: ken16309@aol.com

Collection: Specialty. Mostly used and some new. Also related collectibles.
# of Vols: 1,500
Specialties: Guns; hunting.
Services: Appraisals, search service, catalog, accepts want lists.
Credit Cards: Yes
Owner: Kenneth Neuman
Year Estab: 1982

Lincoln
(Map 1, page 24)

Babbitt's Books   **Open Shop**
At Prairie Years, 121 Kickapoo Street 62656   (217) 732-9216

Collection: General stock of hardcover and paperback.
# of Vols: 2,000
Hours: Mon-Fri 9-6. Sat 9-4. Sun 1-4.
Travel: Mason City/Lincoln exit off I-55. Proceed east on Woodlawn Rd, then
                   right on Kickapoo.
Credit Cards: Yes
Year Estab: 1996
Comments: A satellite location located within a "new" book store. See also Babbitt's
                   Books in Normal and Champaign.

Yesteryear Books   **Antique Mall**
At D & G Mall, 123 Kickapoo Street   Mall: (217) 735-9500
Mailing address: PO Box 625 Lincoln IL 62656   Home: (217) 732-6474
                                                 E-mail: rweimer@ccaonline.com

Collection: General stock.

# of Vols:	2,000
Specialties:	Western Americana; Native Americans; black studies; Abraham Lincoln; medicine; children's.
Services:	Appraisals, accepts want lists, mail order.
Travel:	See Babbitt's Books above.
Credit Cards:	No
Owner:	Robert & Patsy Weimer
Year Estab:	1970

Lisle
(Map 4, page 66)

Bookstores of America　　　　　　　　　　　　　　　　　**Open Shop**
4714 Main Street 60532　　　　　　　　　　　　　　　　(630) 969-3639

Collection:	General stock of hardcover and paperback.
# of Vols:	25,000
Hours:	Mon-Sat 11-9. Sun 2-5.
Services:	Accepts want lists.
Travel:	From I-88 eastbound: Naperville Rd exit. Proceed south on Naperville, east on Ogden Ave (Rte 34) and right on Main. From I-88 westbound: Rte 53 exit. Proceed south on Rte 53, then east on Rte 34 and right on Main.
Credit Cards:	Yes
Owner:	David N. Holcomb
Year Estab:	1994
Comments:	After making several disappointing stops earlier in the day (we shall keep the names of these stores to ourselves in order to protect the guilty), we were pleased toward the end of the day to visit this most pleasant shop. The books, almost all of which were in very good condition sporting dust jackets, were attractively displayed. Some paperbacks were intershelved with the hardcover volumes. Prices were, in our judgement, real bargains. While there may not have been quite as many books on display as cited above, the subjects available for perusal ranged from the quite serious to a substantial mystery collection. We left with three titles and felt quite satisfied.

Lockport
(Map 1, page 24)

Frank G. Bezak - Bookseller　　　　　　　　　　　　　　**Antique Mall**
At Station House Antique Mall, 12305 West 159th Street 60441　(708) 301-9404

Collection:	Specialty
Specialties:	Children's; children's series.
Hours:	Daily 10-6, except Thu till 8.
Services:	Accepts want lists.
Travel:	3.5 miles west of La Grange Rd (Rte 45).
Credit Cards:	No

Long Grove
(Map 4, page 66)

Especially Maine Antique   **Open Shop**
231 Robert Parker Coffin Road 60047   (847) 634-3512

Collection:	General stock.
# of Vols:	400-500
Hours:	Mon-Sat 10-5. Sun 12-5.
Travel:	From Rte 83, turn west on Robert Parker Coffin Rd.
Comments:	Two stores, next to each other, each with a modest selection of used books and antiques.

Loves Park
(Map 1, page 24)

Tomorrow is Yesterday   **Open Shop**
5600 North 2nd Street 61111   (815) 633-0356

Collection:	General stock new and mostly paperback used.
Hours:	Mon-Fri 9-9. Sat 9-6. Sun 12-5.

Machesaey Park
(Map 1, page 24)

Gerald Rilling   **By Appointment**
1315 Ryan Street 61115   (815) 654-0389
                                                          Fax: (815) 633-2361
                                                  E-mail: eafricbk@ix.netcom.com

Collection:	Specialty
# of Vols:	500
Specialties:	Eastern Africa.
Services:	Catalog, accepts want lists.
Credit Cards:	No
Year Estab:	1975

Mattoon
(Map 1, page 24)

The Book Nook   **Open Shop**
1612 Broadway Avenue 61938   (217) 234-2277
                                                  E-mail: gunner1@ccipost.net

Collection:	General stock of mostly paperback.
# of Vols:	100,000
Hours:	Mon-Fri 8:30-5. Sat 9-2.
Travel:	Exit 190 off I-57. Stay on Rte 16 west (which becomes Charleston Ave in Mattoon). Turn north on 16th St and west on Broadway.
Credit Cards:	No
Year Estab:	1983

Comments: While both front windows of this shop contained displays of hardcover books (fairly new popular titles), the vast majority of the books inside the shop were paperbacks, all carefully labeled in terms of subject matter. There were some older hardcover items in glass cases to the right of the entry and a scattering of hardcover volumes elsewhere but these could not have numbered more than a couple of thousand, if that many.

McLean
(Map 1, page 24)

Puffabelly Station   **Open Shop**
Route 136   (309) 874-3161
Mailing address: PO Box 257 McLean IL 61754   E-mail: BooksAngel@aol.com

Collection: General stock.
# of Vols: 4,000-5,000
Specialties: Children's
Hours: Wed-Sun 10-6. Mon & Tue by chance.
Services: Search service, accepts want lists, mail order.
Travel: On Rte 136, two blocks west of I-55. Shop is just behind the hedge.
Credit Cards: Yes
Owner: Angel Shoemaker
Year Estab: 1972
Comments: Most of the books we saw were older volumes, not always in the best condition. The books were attractively displayed together with the shop's antiques and collectibles but their number did not offer depth in any area.

Mendota
(Map 1, page 24)

Little Shop on the Prairie   **Open Shop**
702 Illinois Avenue, Box 565   61342   (815) 538-4408
     (888) 240-5351
     E-mail: littleshop@softfarm.com
Collection: General stock of hardcover and paperback and ephemera.
# of Vols: 4,000-5,000
Hours: Mon-Sat 9-5 and other times by appointment.
Services: Search service, accepts want lists, mail order.
Travel: Rte 34 exit off I-39. Proceed west on Rte 34 for four miles, then right on Illinois.
Credit Cards: Yes
Owner: Nan Peterson
Year Estab: 1988
Comments: If you like antiques and don't mind spending a bit more for some items than you might elsewhere, this is certainly a pleasant enough shop to visit with lots of old books, magazines and some comics as well as bric a brac, vintage clothing and a second floor filled with paperbacks.

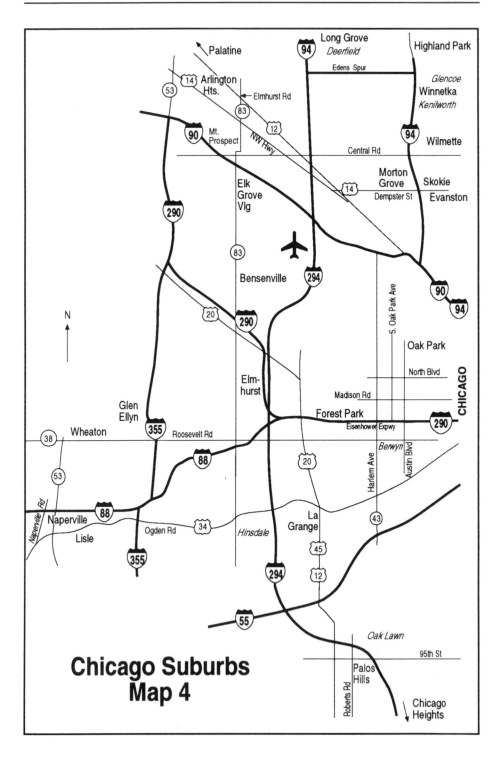

Chicago Suburbs
Map 4

Morris
(Map 1, page 24)

Books 'N' Bits   **Open Shop**
621 Liberty Street 60450   (815) 942-2525

Collection:	General stock of hardcover and paperback.
# of Vols:	5,000+
Hours:	Tue, Wed, Fri 10-5. Thu 10-6. Sat 10-4.
Travel:	Morris exit off I-80. Proceed north on Rte 47, right on North St and right on Liberty. Shop is across from library.
Year Estab:	1995
Comments:	Stock is evenly mixed between hardcover and paperback.

Morton Grove
(Map 4, page 66)

Magazine Memories   **Open Shop**
6006 Dempster 60053   (847) 470-9444

Collection:	Specialty
# of Vols:	100,000
Specialties:	Magazines (popular) from 1840; newspapers (from 17th century); posters.
Hours:	Mon-Fri 11-7. Sat 10-5.
Travel:	Dempster exit off I-94. Proceed west on Dempster for six blocks.
Credit Cards:	Yes
Owner:	Robert M. Katzman
Year Estab:	1960's

Mount Prospect
(Map 4, page 66)

Hooked On History   *** Open Shop**
15 North Elmhurst Avenue 60056   (847) 255-2340
                                                          Fax: (847) 255-9233
                                                       E-mail: histor1@ibm.net

Collection:	Specialty
# of Vols:	5,000
Specialties:	Civil War; Western Americana; American Revolution; presidents; Mexican War; World War I & II; War of 1812; Spanish American War; French & Indian War.
Hours: *	Hours vary so best to call ahead and make an appointment.
Services:	Search service, catalog, accepts want lists.
Travel:	Call for directions.
Credit Cards:	Yes
Owner:	Bruce Herrick
Year Estab:	1988

Jack's Used Books   **Open Shop**
718 East Northwest Highway 60056   (847) 398-7767

Collection:	General stock.

# of Vols:	30,000
Specialties:	Modern first editions; mystery; horror; Stephen King (first editions).
Hours:	Mon-Sat 9-5.
Services:	Appraisals, search service, accepts want lists, mail order.
Travel:	Seven blocks southeast of Rte 83 on Northwest Hwy (Rte 14).
Credit Cards:	Yes
Owner:	Jack Huggard
Year Estab:	1975
Comments:	This shop has a very good collection of hardcover volumes. Indeed, we saw quite a few titles in various subject areas not seen elsewhere. For the most part, the books were in good condition. At the time of our visit, volumes considered "special" in terms of value (some first editions and some signed) were shelved behind protective plastic sheeting although we have seen many of the same titles elsewhere on general shelves. While we like the books we saw in this establishment, we do believe that they were a bit pricey.

Mundelein
(Map 1, page 24)

Blake's Book Nook   **Open Shop**
525 North Lake Street 60060   (847) 949-7570

Collection:	General stock of mostly paperback.
# of Vols:	50,000
Hours:	Daily 11-6.

Naperville
(Map 4, page 66)

Books & Bytes   **Open Shop**
815 East Ogden Avenue 60563   (630) 416-0102
Web page: www.bytes.com   Fax: (630) 416-0375
                                                            E-mail: order@bytes.com

Collection:	Specialty. New and recently out of print.
Specialties:	Computers
Hours:	Mon-Fri 9-9. Sat 10-6. Sun 11-6.
Services:	Mail order.
Credit Cards:	Yes
Year Estab:	1987

Bookzeller   **Open Shop**
202 South Main Street 60540   (630) 637-0200
                                                                Fax: (630) 637-0441
                                                        E-mail: bookzeller@ntsource.com

Collection:	General stock of mostly used hardcover and paperback.
# of Vols:	40,000
Specialties:	American history; military; literature; poetry; philosophy; new age.
Hours:	Mon-Thu 11-10. Fri 11-11. Sat 10-11. Sun 11-9. Open later in summer.

Services:	Search service.
Travel:	Naperville Rd exit off I-88. Proceed south on Naperville Rd, then west on Ogden, south on Washington and west on Jefferson. Shop is just off the corner of Jefferson and Main in the basement.
Credit Cards:	Yes
Owner:	Lee Mathers
Year Estab:	1994
Comments:	A nice shop with a healthy selection of books in almost every subject area. While there were as many paperbacks as hardcover volumes (perhaps even a few more), the hardcover titles were most respectable and impressive. We saw some rare items and some first editions. This is a place where the knowledgeable buyer who is willing to take the time should certainly enjoy the visit.

Mary's Antique Mall   **Antique Mall**
34 West Jefferson 60540   (630) 717-8899

Hours:	Mon-Sat 10-5. Sun 12-4.

Nauvoo
(Map 1, page 24)

Old House Bookstore   **Open Shop**
1250 Mulholland 62354   Tel & Fax: (217) 453-2069

Collection:	Specialty
Specialties:	Midwest; Western Americana; local history; hunting; guns; Mormons.
Hours:	Mon-Sat 8:30-4:30, except closed Wed afternoon.
Travel:	On Rte 96, in downtown Nauvoo.
Credit Cards:	Yes
Owner:	Estel Neff
Year Estab:	1989

Niota
(Map 1, page 24)

Green Hat Bookstore   **By Appointment**
Box 80 62358   (217) 755-4322

Collection:	General stock.
# of Vols:	15,000+
Services:	Accepts want lists, mail order.
Owner:	Norma J. Teesdale
Year Estab:	1990

Normal
(Map 1, page 24)

Babbitt's Books   **Open Shop**
104 North Street 61761   (309) 454-7393
                                                    E-mail: babbitts@ice.net

Collection:	General stock of hardcover and paperback and ephemera.

# of Vols:	50,000
Hours:	Mon-Thu 10-8. Fri & Sat 10-6. Sun 12-5.
Services:	Search service, accepts want lists, mail order.
Travel:	Normal exit (Rte 51) off I-55/I-74. Proceed south on Rte 51, then east on College, south on Broadway and east on North.
Credit Cards:	Yes
Owner:	Brian Simpson
Year Estab:	1990
Comments:	If, after following the above travel directions through Normal's one way street pattern you've located this shop, give yourself an "A" in geography. Once you've arrived, you'll discover the trip was worth your effort. The shop has a great balance (we think) between newer used and vintage used items and the selection in both categories is quite good. The books are in good condition and prices are on target. In addition to a fine fiction section (separated into modern and vintage), there's a separate small room devoted to literary criticism. The shop sponsors readings and other literary events. The owner operates a second shop in Champaign and has a small selection on display in a "new" bookstore in Lincoln.

Oak Lawn
(Map 4, page 66)

Bits & Pieces of History   **By Appointment**
11012 South Cicero 60453   (708) 423-5966
                                                        Fax: (708) 423-5968

Collection:	Specialty books and memorabilia.
# of Vols:	1,500
Specialties:	Civil War; Western Americana.
Services:	Accepts want lists, mail order.
Credit Cards:	No
Owner:	John McGuire
Year Estab:	1960's

Oak Park
(Map 4, page 66)

Armchair Books   **Open Shop**
819 South Oak Park Avenue 60304   (708) 383-3338

Collection:	General stock of hardcover and paperback and jazz CDs and videos.
# of Vols:	20,000
Specialties:	Music; performing arts; humanities.
Hours:	Mon-Fri, except closed Wed, 11:30-7. Sat 10:30-5:30. Sun 11-4.
Services:	Accepts want lists, mail order. Also sponsors special events.
Travel:	Austin or Harlem exits off I-290. From Austin, proceed west on Jackson (from Harlem, proceed east on Jackson) to Oak Park Ave. Turn south on Oak Park.
Credit Cards:	No

Owner:	Larry Leonard
Year Estab:	1993
Comments:	A mix of hardcover and paperback books with most of the hardcover items being reading copies in mixed condition and of mixed vintage. Except for the specialties listed above, the balance of the stock offered little of an unusual nature.

The Booksmith **Open Shop**
108 South Marion Street 60302 (708) 383-8734
E-mail: booksmith@aol.com

Collection:	General stock of hardcover and paperback.
# of Vols:	15,000
Specialties:	Literature; poetry.
Hours:	Tue, Wed, Fri 11-6. Thu 11-7. Sat 10-4.
Services:	Appraisals, accepts want lists, lists, mail order.
Travel:	Harlem Ave exit off I-290. Proceed north on Harlem for about one mile, then east on South Blvd for two blocks and south on Marion. Shop is just ahead.
Credit Cards:	No
Owner:	Tom O'Brien
Year Estab:	1979
Comments:	The shop offers a mostly hardcover collection in mixed condition, along with the usual assortment of paperbacks. While there may well have been some winners among the hardcover titles, I confess to being too weary and frustrated (no fault of the owner's) by our adventures earlier that day to have carefully browsed all the titles on the shelves.

Joyce Klein (Little Treasures) **Antique Mall**
At Antiques, Etc., 125 North Marion Street 60301 (708) 386-9194

Collection:	Specialty with some general stock.
Specialties:	Cookbooks
Hours:	Mon-Fri 11-6, except Mon & Thu till 8. Sat 11-5. Sun 11-5.
Travel:	Harlem Ave exit off I-290. Proceed north on Harlem, then east on Westgate for one block to Marion (a pedestrian mall at this point).
Credit Cards:	Yes
Year Estab:	1970's

The Old Bookseller **Open Shop**
808 Harrison 60304 (815) 545-7585

Collection:	General stock of mostly hardcover.
# of Vols:	8,000
Hours:	Sat only 9-5:30.
Travel:	Austin Ave exit off I-290. Proceed north on Austin, then west on Harrison.
Credit Cards:	No
Owner:	Brian W. Burhoe & Charles J. Shields
Year Estab:	1974

(Oak Park)

Comments:	As the shop is only open on Saturdays, the owner has thoughtfully placed a note on the front door suggesting that if you see an item of interest displayed in the window, you should slip a piece of paper through the mail slot indicating the title as well as your name and phone number and he'll hold the book for you. When we were able to visit the shop on our earlier trip to Oak Park we noted: A fairly small selection of mostly reading copies with a few older items in sight. Nothing unusual. Looking through the store window some 3½ years later, the above comments appeared to remain applicable.

Persistence Of Memory   **Open Shop**
1016 North Boulevard 60301   Tel & Fax: (708) 660-0122
E-mail: persistm@interloc.com

Collection:	General stock of mostly hardcover.
# of Vols:	5,000
Hours:	Mon-Sat 11:30-6. Sun by chance or appointment.
Services:	Appraisals, search service, accepts want lists.
Travel:	Harlem Ave exit off I-290. Proceed north on Harlem Ave to North Blvd (first block after crossing train viaduct), then right on North. Shop is 1½ blocks ahead on left. Access is from the parking lot.
Credit Cards:	Yes
Owner:	John E. Montes
Year Estab:	1989
Comments:	Bookstores don't necessarily have to be large or have enormous numbers of books for them to be worth a visit. This rather modest shop provided me with two hardcover titles, both of which were priced very reasonably. Most of stock here appeared to be reading copies and of rather good quality.

Bernard Wheel   **By Appointment**
834 Wenonah Avenue 60304   (708) 386-4974

Collection:	Specialty
# of Vols:	5,000
Specialties:	Esperanto language; interlinguistics.
Services:	Search service, catalog, accepts want lists.
Credit Cards:	No
Year Estab:	1977

Olney
(Map 1, page 24)

D & E Books & More   **Open Shop**
423 South Whittle 62450   (618) 392-6615

Collection:	General stock of mostly paperback.
# of Vols:	8,000
Hours:	Mon-Sat 9:30-5.

Palatine
(Map 4, page 66)

Top Shelf Books   **Open Shop**
47 East Northwest Highway 60067   (847) 705-9940

Collection:	General stock of used and new paperback and hardcover.
# of Vols:	40,000
Hours:	Mon-Fri 10-6, except Thu till 8. Sat 10-5.
Travel:	On Rte 14 between Plum Grove and Benton. Shop is on the left in the Palatine Centre shopping center (just after Rte 53).
Credit Cards:	Yes
Owner:	Sandy Redding
Year Estab:	1992
Comments:	A combination new/used book store with an adjoining gift shop. The majority of the used books we saw were paperbacks and the hardcover items appeared to be of fairly recent vintage and in generally good condition. While a pleasant enough shop to visit, it did not appear to be one that would offer many surprises to the used book aficionado.

Palos Hills
(Map 4, page 66)

Palos Books   **Open Shop**
10303 South Roberts Road 60465   (708) 430-5977
                                                                 Fax: (708) 430-5978

Collection:	General stock of hardcover and paperback.
# of Vols:	30,000
Specialties:	First editions; children's; religion; science fiction; sports; history; military.
Hours:	Mon-Fri 10-8. Sat 10-6. Sun 12-5.
Services:	Appraisals, search service, accepts want lists, mail order.
Travel:	95th St exit off I-294. Proceed west on 95th St to Roberts Rd, then south on Roberts to 103rd St.
Credit Cards:	No
Owner:	Martin Singer
Year Estab:	1992
Comments:	If it's still around at the time of your visit, you may be greeted by a beautiful white cat with long (and at the time of our visit) shedding hair. The store offers an even mix of hardcover and paperback books. Most of the hardcover items we saw were in relatively good condition and displayed along the side, front and back walls with a few more intershelved with the paperbacks that took up the middle of the shop. We wish the shelves had been more clearly labeled but patience would certainly help any browser figure out where things are. Most of the titles we saw were familiar faces. If there were some rarities, unfortunately, we missed them, although there was a shelf marked "Collectibles."

Paris
(Map 1, page 24)

The Book Shelf   **Open Shop**
130 North Main 61944   (217) 465-2665
Web page: www.thebookshelf.com   Fax: (217) 463-1094
                                          E-mail: damita@thebookshelf.com

Collection:	General stock of paperback and hardcover.
# of Vols:	72,000
Specialties:	Romance
Hours:	Mon-Sat 10-5 and other times by appointment.
Travel:	Marshall/Paris exit off I-70. Proceed north on Rte 1 for about 15 miles. Shop is located at northeast corner of the square.
Credit Cards:	Yes
Owner:	Damita Lewis
Year Estab:	1986
Comments:	Stock is approximately 85% paperback.

History Hardbacks   **By Appointment**
310 Monterey Street 61944   (217) 463-4555

Collection:	Specialty
# of Vols:	5,000
Specialties:	Abraham Lincoln; Civil War; military.
Services:	Catalog, accepts want lists.
Credit Cards:	No
Owner:	Chuck Hand
Year Estab:	1988

Peoria
(Map 1, page 24)

Back Door Antiques   **Antique Mall**
725 SW Washington Street 61602   (309) 637-3446

Hours:	Mon-Fri 11-4:30. Sat 9-5. Sun 12-5
Travel:	Washington St exit off I-74. Proceed south on Washington. Parking and entrance is in the alley.

Black Bird Books   **Open Shop**
915 Western 61604   (309) 672-6455
                                          E-mail: blackbrd@concentric.net

Collection:	General stock of hardcover and paperback.
# of Vols:	20,000+
Specialties:	Phillip Jose Farmer; counter culture.
Hours:	Wed-Sun 12-6.
Services:	Search service, accepts want lists, mail order.
Travel:	University exit off I-74. Proceed south on University. At second set of lights, turn right on Main St. Shop is in a shopping center about five blocks away at the point where the street curves.

Credit Cards: No
Owner: Joel & Denise Johnson
Year Estab: 1997
Comments: A modest sized shop with a good collection of hardcover volumes, most of which were in better than average condition and reasonably priced. Worth a visit.

Book Court **Open Shop**
1125 West Lake Avenue 61614 (309) 686-7000
Web page: www.lakeview-museum.org Fax: (309) 686-0280
E-mail: lvmstaff@lakeview-museum.org

Collection: General stock of hardcover and paperback and magazines.
# of Vols: 3,300
Hours: Mon-Sat 10-5, except Wed till 8. Sun 1-5.
Travel: University St exit off I-74. Proceed north on University, then right on Lake and left into the museum parking lot.
Credit Cards: Yes
Owner: Lakeview Museum of Arts & Sciences
Year Estab: 1965
Comments: A non profit shop. All books are donated.

Books From The Past **Antique Mall**
At Illinois Antique Center, 308 SW Commercial Mall: (309) 673-3354
Mailing address: 817 N. Rebecca Pl. Peoria IL 61606 Home: (309) 673-0584

Collection: General stock.
# of Vols: 2,500+
Hours: Mon-Sat 9-5. Sun 12-5.
Services: Accepts want lists.
Travel: Washington St exit off I-74. Proceed south on Washington then left on Liberty to Commercial.
Credit Cards: Yes
Owner: Paul & Sharon Trower
Year Estab: 1986
Comments: A display of mostly older volumes, some of historical interest, at reasonable prices. For the most part, the books on display here were a "level above" those we have usually (but not always) seen in multi dealer antique malls. An additional 8,000-10,000 books are located in the dealer's home. The dealer also displays at Black Bird Books.

The Mystery Nook **Antique Mall**
At Illinois Antique Center 308 SW Commercial 61602 (309) 673-3354
Home: (309) 685-3840

Collection: Specialty. Mostly used hardcover and paperback.
# of Vols: 8,000
Specialties: Mystery; true crime; biographies of mystery authors; espionage; children's mysteries; signed first editions.

Hours:	Mon-Sat 9-5. Sun 12-5.
Services:	Search service, catalog, accepts want lists.
Travel:	See Books From The Past above.
Credit Cards:	Yes
Owner:	Kathy Miller & Joyce Welsch
Year Estab:	1991
Comments:	We saw more used mystery hardcover titles here than we've seen in most shops under the "mystery" heading and certainly more used hardcovers than is often the case in combination new/used mystery specialty shops. There wasn't a lot of depth to the collection but a reasonable sampling and a combination of older and more recent items. As the owners' entire collection is not on display, we suggest a call to the home number if you don't see what you're looking for at the mall.

Second Chance Books   **Open Shop**
3223 North Prospect Road 61603   (309) 688-5851

| *Collection:* | General stock of mostly paperback. |
| *Hours:* | Mon-Fri 10-6. Sat 10-4. |

Petersburg
(Map 1, page 24)

The Village Reader   **Antique Mall**
At Petersburg Peddlers, 113 South 7th   Mall: (217) 632-2628
Mailing address: c/o B. Vanderveen, 12443 N. Route 97 Havana IL 62644
                                    Home: (309) 543-3834 or (309) 546-2368

Collection:	General stock of mostly hardcover.
Hours:	Tue-Sun 10-5.
Services:	Accepts want lists, mail order.
Travel:	On the square, one block west of Rte 97.
Credit Cards:	Yes
Owner:	B. Vanderveen & Judy Hurdle
Year Estab:	1989
Comments:	Additional stock is located at owners' homes.

Princeton
(Map 1, page 24)

Village Books   **By Appointment**
223 Park Avenue West 61356   (815) 872-1511
                                          E-mail: vilbks@ramp.net

Collection:	General stock.
# of Vols:	5,000
Specialties:	Needlecrafts; children's; modern first editions.
Services:	Search service, accepts want lists, mail order.
Credit Cards:	No
Owner:	Laura Prendergast
Year Estab:	1966

Quincy
(Map 1, page 24)

The Book Stop   **Open Shop**
418 North 24th Street 62301   (217) 228-1486
                             E-mail: bookstop@golden.adams.net

Collection:	General stock of hardcover and paperback.
# of Vols:	30,000
Hours:	Mon-Sat 10-6.
Services:	Search service, accepts want lists, mail order.
Travel:	Rte 104 exit off I-172. Proceed west on Rte 104 (Broadway) for about three miles, then right on 24th St. Shop is one half block ahead on right.
Credit Cards:	Yes
Owner:	Doug & Robin Alexander
Year Estab:	1995
Comments:	Stock is evenly mixed between hardcover and paperback.

Rock Falls
(Map 1, page 24)

The Bookstore   **Open Shop**
111 West 2nd Street 61071   (815) 626-8560

Collection:	General stock of mostly used paperback and hardcover, comics and greeting cards.
# of Vols:	50,000+
Hours:	Mon-Sat 10-5, except Wed & Sat 10-2.
Services:	Accepts want lists, mail order.
Travel:	Rte 40 exit off I-88. Proceed north on Rte 40 for about one mile, then west on 2nd St. Shop is 1/2 block ahead on south side of street.
Credit Cards:	No
Owner:	Vingene (Bud) & Wanda Martens
Year Estab:	1983
Comments:	Used stock is 65% paperback.

Rock Island
(Map 1, page 24)

Book Keeper Paperback Exchange   **Open Shop**
2608 21st Avenue 61201   (309) 788-6410

Collection:	General stock mostly paperback.
# of Vols:	15,000+
Hours:	Mon-Sat 9-5. Sun by appointment.

Rockford
(Map 1, page 24)

Book Stall Of Rockford   **Open Shop**
1032 Crosby Street 61107   (815) 963-1671

Collection:	General stock and ephemera.
# of Vols:	15,000
Specialties:	History; technology; art.
Hours:	Tue & Fri 5:30-8:30. Sat 10-5.
Services:	Appraisals, mail order.
Travel:	Bus Rte 20 (State St) exit off I-90. Proceed on State St to 1100 East State block, then right on Longwood St then left on Crosby.
Credit Cards:	Yes
Owner:	Karl Moehling & John Peterson
Year Estab:	1980
Comments:	If you can arrange a visit to this bi-level shop during its rather limited hours, you'll find a collection of older books with some interesting titles. If you can't get to the shop, we suggest you visit the State Street Antique Mall (see below) where the owners have a large booth with even more interesting titles.

State Street Antique Malls   **Open Shop**
5411 East State Street 61108   (815) 229-4004

Hours:	Daily 10-9.
Travel:	At corner of New Towne Drive. The entrance to the antique mall is located in the rear lower level of a 3 story brick building.

Toad Hall Books & Records   **Open Shop**
2106 Broadway 61104   (815) 226-1259
                                                           (815) 399-4644
                                                      Fax: (815) 226-9887

Collection:	General stock of mostly hardcover, ephemera and records.
# of Vols:	40,000+
Specialties:	Science fiction; vintage paperbacks, children's; music; art; military; local history; signed; first editions; cookbooks; E.R. Burroughs; magazines; photoplay editions.
Hours:	Sun-Thu, except closed Tue, 12-7. Fri & Sat 10-7.
Services:	Catalog, accepts want lists.
Travel:	State St (Bus Rte 20) exit off I-90. Proceed west on State St, then left at first light on Bell School Rd and right on Newburgh (which becomes Broadway). Shop is at 17th St.
Credit Cards:	Yes
Owner:	Larry & Beverly Mason
Year Estab:	1972
Comments:	If your interest is in popular culture, you'll enjoy browsing this shop which stocks an interesting combination of books, records (lots of jazz), magazines, comics and ephemera. Even if you're interests are more serious, you may want to browse the more general stock.

Saint Charles
(Map 1, page 24)

The Book Rack **Open Shop**
At Piano Factory Mall, 410 South 1st Street 60174 (630) 513-5787
Fax: (630) 513-0883

Collection:	General stock of used and new paperback and hardcover.
# of Vols:	53,000+
Hours:	Mon-Fri 10-9. Sat 10-6. Sun 11-5.
Travel:	From the north: Rte 59 exit off I-90. Proceed south on Rte 59, then west on Rte 64 and south on Rte 25. Right on Illinois St. Cross the Fox River, then first left after river on 1st St. Mall is ahead on left.
Credit Cards:	Yes
Year Estab:	1992
Comments:	Located in an indoor shopping mall, this is a combination new/used hardcover/paperback shop with most of the used books (about 70% of the collection) being of fairly recent vintage and in good condition. Few surprises. This is not a place where you're likely to find many rarities.

Riverside Antiques **Antique Mall**
410 South First Street 60174 (630) 377-7730

Hours:	Mon-Sat 10-6. Sun 11-5.
Travel:	In Piano Factory Mall. See The Book Rack above.

Sandwich
(Map 1, page 24)

Paperback Encore **Open Shop**
1 North Main Street 60548 (815) 786-8175

Collection:	General stock of mostly paperback.
# of Vols:	150,000
Hours:	Mon-Fri 9:30-6. Sat 9:30-5. Closed first week in May.
Travel:	Rte 34 goes through town and becomes Church St. Turn north on Main. Shop is just over the railroad tracks.
Year Estab:	1976
Comments:	Overwhelmingly paperback with perhaps 2,000-3,000 hardcover volumes, including several shelves of Reader's Digest volumes, most of which are located in the rear of the shop. If you're looking for inexpensive paperbacks, you may have found your paradise.

Skokie
(Map 4, page 66)

Articles of War **Open Shop**
8806 Bronx Avenue 60077 (847) 674-7445
Fax: (847) 674-7449

Collection:	Specialty new and used.
# of Vols:	15,000+

Specialties:	Military; aviation history; naval history; Civil War; Western Americana.
Hours:	Tue, Wed, Fri 11-6. Thu 11-9. Sat 10-5.
Services:	Search service, catalog, accepts want lists.
Travel:	Dempster exit off I-94. Proceed east on Dempster for four lights, then north on Bronx. Shop is second store from corner.
Credit Cards:	Yes
Owner:	Robert Ruman
Year Estab:	1971

Historical Newspapers   **By Appointment**
9850 Kedvale 60076   (847) 676-9850

Collection:	Specialty
Specialties:	Newspapers from 1690-1948; autographs; documents (including special collection relating to George Washington and Abraham Lincoln); maps; engravings.
Services:	Catalog
Credit Cards:	No
Owner:	Steve & Linda Alsberg
Year Estab:	1973

Springfield
(Map 1, page 24)

Epperson Books, Etc.   **Open Shop**
401 Highland 62704   (217) 528-9296

Collection:	General stock of primarily paperback.
# of Vols:	30,000
Hours:	Daily, except closed Wed, 10-6.

Prairie Archives, Booksellers   **Open Shop**
522 East Adams 62701   (217) 522-9742
                                                                (217) 522-9753
                                               E-mail: prairiea@midwest.net

Collection:	General stock, ephemera and records.
# of Vols:	75,000
Specialties:	Abraham Lincoln; Illinois; Vachel Lindsay.
Hours:	Mon-Sat 10-5.
Services:	Appraisals, search service, subject lists, accepts want lists.
Travel:	Clearlake Ave exit off I-55. Follow signs to downtown. Shop is just south of the old State Capitol.
Credit Cards:	Yes
Owner:	John Paul
Year Estab:	1971
Comments:	An attractive shop with books in most areas of interest. Most of the books we saw were in very good condition and reasonably priced. In addition to the book collection, the shop also sells old records and ephemera. Well worth a visit.

Sycamore
(Map 1, page 24)

Storey Book Antiques & Books   **Open Shop**
1325 East State Street 60178   (815) 895-5910

Collection:	General stock.
# of Vols:	6,000
Specialties:	Christmas
Hours:	Weekend afternoons (except Jan & Feb). Other times by chance.
Travel:	On Rte 64.
Credit Cards:	No
Owner:	Jean A. Larkin
Year Estab:	1972

Urbana
(Map 1, page 24 and Map 2, page 26)

Priceless Books   **Open Shop**
108A West Main Street 61801   (217) 344-4037

Collection:	General stock of hardcover and paperback and records.
# of Vols:	34,000
Specialties:	Performing arts; humanities.
Hours:	Mon-Fri 10-7. Sat 10-5. Sun 12-5.
Services:	Search service, mail order.
Travel:	Cunningham Rd exit off I-74. Follow signs to downtown. After Cunningham becomes Vine St, turn right on Main.
Credit Cards:	Yes
Owner:	Leslie Troutman, Michael Vaillancourt & William Thornhill
Year Estab:	1993
Comments:	A mix of hardcover and paperback books with the hardcover volumes in generally quite good condition. (The books look as though they've been carefully selected.) Considering the shop's proximity to several other good sized shops in the immediate region, certainly worth a visit.

Virden
(Map 1, page 24)

Books on the Square   **Open Shop**
153 East Jackson Street 62690   (217) 965-5443
                                               E-mail: bksonsqr@ctllc.com

Collection:	General stock.
# of Vols:	10,000
Specialties:	Illinois; Abraham Lincoln; Civil War; vintage paperbacks.
Hours:	Mon-Sat 9-6. Sun and evenings by appointment.
Services:	Accepts want lists.
Travel:	Rte 104 exit off I-55. Proceed west on Rte 104, then south on Rte 4 to Virden. Shop is on the north side of the square.
Credit Cards:	No

Owner:	John & Jeannie Alexander
Year Estab:	1993
Comments:	One of those shops that, while small in size and a bit off the beaten path, does have a nice selection of hardcover books in good condition and at quite reasonable prices. We were delighted to have found the shop and even to have made a purchase here. We wish our readers equal good fortune.

Wateska
(Map 1, page 24)

Dale St. Peter Books   **By Appointment**
315 East Lincoln 60970   (815) 432-4437
E-mail: dalebren@capstonebank.com

Collection:	General stock.
# of Vols:	20,000
Specialties:	Children's; military.
Services:	Accepts want lists, mail order.
Credit Cards:	Yes
Year Estab:	1982

Waukegan
(Map 1, page 24)

ICS Used Book Store   **Open Shop**
808 West Glen Flora Avenue 60085   (847) 244-7676

Collection:	General stock of hardcover and paperback.
# of Vols:	10,000-20,000
Hours:	Mon-Sat 10-4.
Travel:	From Grand Ave (Rte 132) eastbound, turn north on Lewis and east on Glen Flora.
Year Estab:	1970's
Comments:	Stock is approximately 70% hardcover. All books are donated.

Waukegan Bridge Center   **By Appointment**
927 Grand Avenue 60085   (847) 662-7204
E-mail: FutileWill@aol.com

Collection:	Specialty books and magazines.
# of Vols:	5,000
Specialties:	Bridge and other card games; chess; backgammon and other indoor games; playing cards.
Services:	Search service, catalog, accepts want lists.
Credit Cards:	No
Owner:	William F. & Marianne M. Sachen
Year Estab:	1972

Wheaton
(Map 4, page 66)

Richard Owen Roberts, Booksellers **Open Shop**
123-145 North Washington (630) 752-4122
Mailing address: PO Box 21 Wheaton IL 60189 Fax: (630) 653-8616
E-mail: roberts@juno.com

Collection:	General stock.
# of Vols:	150,000
Specialties:	Religion; biography; history; philosophy; psychology; bibles.
Hours:	Mon-Fri 9-6. Sat 10-4.
Services:	Appraisals, search service, catalog, accepts want lists, book binding.
Travel:	On west side of Wheaton College, 1/4 mile north of Rte 38 (Roosevelt Rd). Proceeding westbound on Rte 38, turn right on Washington.
Credit Cards:	Yes
Year Estab:	1961
Comments:	If you're interested in acquiring books in the theological realm, you should enjoy a visit to this establishment where 70% or more of the stock is in the shop's specialty area (mostly, but not exclusively, Protestant). The general stock is less distinguished in terms of quality and/ or quantity although we did see many antiquarian items, not all of a religious bent, (e.g., a five volume biography of William Wilberforce, an 18th century British politician). Indeed, we were told that some of the books date back to the 16th century (and we can believe it). The entire collection is catalogued so if you're unable to visit, a phone call or written communication should be able to tell you if the shop has the volume you're looking for.

Wheaton Antique Mall **Antique Mall**
1621 North Main 60187 (630) 653-7400

Hours:	Mon-Sat 10-5, except Thu till 8. Sun 12-5.
Travel:	Naperville Rd exit off I-88. Proceed north on Naperville Rd, then left on Roosevelt for one block and right at light on Main St. Continue through downtown area.

Wilmette
(Map 4, page 66)

Heritage Trail Mall **Antique Mall**
410 Ridge Road 60091 (847) 256-6208

Hours:	Mon-Sat 10-5:30. Sun 12-5.
Travel:	Lake St exit off I-94. Proceed east on Lake then right on Ridge.

Winnetka
(Map 4, page 66)

Scotland Yard Books
556 Green Bay Road 60093

Open Shop
(847) 446-2214
Fax: (847) 446-2210

Collection: Specialty. Mostly new and some used (primarily paperback.)
# of Vols: 200+ (used)
Specialties: Mystery
Hours: Mon-Sat 9:30-5.

Winthrop Harbor
(Map 1, page 24)

Leekley Books
PO Box 337 60096

By Appointment
(847) 872-2311
E-mail: bleekley@juno.com

Collection: General stock.
# of Vols: 5,000+
Services: Mail order.
Credit Cards: No
Owner: Brian Leekley
Year Estab: 1961

Woodstock
(Map 1, page 24)

Heartland Books
126 North Benton Street 60098

Open Shop
Tel & Fax: (815) 338-5272
E-mail: hartland@interloc.com

Collection: General stock of mostly hardcover.
# of Vols: 10,000
Specialties: Mystery; literature; Western Americana; religion; cookbooks; Civil War; history.
Hours: Tue-Sat 11-5. Sun 12-4.
Services: Search service, catalog in planning stage, accepts want lists.
Travel: Woodstock exit off I-90. Proceed north on Rte 47 to Rte 120, following signs to stay on Rte 120. After crossing railroad tracks, make immediate left turn and proceed one block to street running from train depot to town square. Turn right onto square. Coming off square, turn right on Benton.
Credit Cards: Yes
Owner: Jim Bykowski
Year Estab: 1986
Comments: A shop that has changed ownership and location since our earlier visit 3½ years ago. The shop continues to impress us as one that has a respectable collection in the areas identified above as specialties. We particularly liked the mystery section because, in addition to the usual titles of the past dozen or so years, there was a nice selection of vintage items.

Zion
(Map 1, page 24)

Galaxy Of Books   **Open Shop**
1908 Sheridan Road   (847) 872-3313
Mailing address: PO Box 153 Zion IL 60099   E-mail: MSGALAXYBK@juno.com

Collection:	General stock of paperback and hardcover.
# of Vols:	6,000+ (hardcover)
Specialties:	Military; hunting; fishing; natural history; metaphysics.
Hours:	Tue-Fri 12-7. Sat 10-5. Sun by appointment.
Services:	Accepts want lists.
Travel:	Rte 173 exit off I-94. Proceed east on Rte 173, then left on Sheridan Rd.
Credit Cards:	No
Owner:	Eileen Donohue
Year Estab:	1976
Comments:	The shop carries mostly paperbacks, plenty of comics and a very modest collection of hardcover titles consisting of recently published titles, mostly fiction. If you happen to be heading this way, it can't hurt to stop. If you're headed in another direction, though, we don't advise a side trip. Note: If you don't see what you're looking for, you may want to ask as, at least at the time of our visit, only a portion of the hardcover stock, located to the rear of the retail shop, was accessible to the general public.

Mail Order Dealers

Aah! Rare Chicago   (847) 657-7944
1324 Oxford Lane Glenview 60025   Fax: (773) 880-3839
                                                                                      E-mail: jconway@nwu.edu

Collection:	Specialty books and related ephemera.
# of Vols:	4,000
Specialties:	Chicago; Chicago authors.
Services:	Accepts want lists, catalog.
Credit Cards:	No
Year Estab:	1996

Allison's Signed Books & Autographs   (630) 637-8285
415 Westglen Drive Naperville 60565   Fax: (630) 637-9872

Collection:	Specialty
# of Vols:	8,500
Specialties:	Signed modern first editions.
Services:	Catalog, accepts want lists.
Credit Cards:	No
Owner:	Derrick and Vicki Allison
Year Estab:	1992

Americas Antiquarium   (773) 506-8438
1941 West Balmoral, #2R Chicago 60640

Collection:	General stock.
# of Vols:	5,000+
Specialties:	Western Americana; travel and exploration; early maps; autographs; Lakeside Classics.
Services:	Appraisals, accepts want lists.
Credit Cards:	Yes
Owner:	Kurt Gippert
Year Estab:	1989
Comments:	Collection may be viewed by appointment.

Ancient Society Books   (309) 836-3811
3100 West Adams Road Macomb 61455

Collection:	Specialty books and periodicals.
# of Vols:	4,000 (books) 10,000 (periodicals)
Specialties:	Archeology; anthropology. (Worldwide, but specializing in New World.)
Services:	Catalog, accepts want lists.
Credit Cards:	No
Owner:	Lawrence A. Conrad
Year Estab:	1990

Bank Lane Books   (847) 733-1680
PO Box 6292 Evanston 60204   Fax: (847) 733-1681
                                      E-mail: rhh@interaccess.com

Collection:	General stock.
Specialties:	Art
Services:	Catalog (on line).
Credit Cards:	No
Year Estab:	1986
Owner:	Randy Hudson

Richard S. Barnes & Co.   (847) 869-2272
1745 Hinman Avenue Evanston 60201

Collection:	General stock.
Specialties:	Scholarly; art; children's; history.
Services:	Appraisals, accepts want lists.
Credit Cards:	No
Year Estab:	1953

Beadsman Books   (847) 696-3790
1206 Carol Street Park Ridge 60008

Collection:	Specialty books and ephemera.
# of Vols:	5,000
Specialties:	Medieval studies; religion (Catholicism); Mariology; signed books.
Services:	Search service, catalog, accepts want lists.
Credit Cards:	No

Owner: Steve Wagner
Year Estab: 1995

Books & Beyond (773) 472-9500
3952 North Southport Avenue Chicago 60613 E-mail: reviews@enteract.com

Collection: Specialty
# of Vols: 3,000+
Specialties: First editions only (fiction and non fiction).
Services: Catalog, accepts want lists.
Credit Cards: No
Owner: Lynne Sinton
Year Estab: 1982

Robert S. Brooks, Bookseller (847) 866-7175
824 Gaffield Evanston 60201 Fax: (847) 866-7266
E-mail: bobsshop@interloc.com

Collection: General stock.
Specialties: Baedekers; children's series; Sherlock Holmes; Folio Society; Chicago; Lakeside classics; first editions.
Services: Search service, accepts want lists.
Credit Cards: No
Year Estab: 1993

Thomas W. Burrows, Bookseller (630) 960-1028
PO Box 400 Downers Grove 60515

Collection: Specialty
# of Vols: 30,000+
Specialties: Scholarly books in literature; humanities; religion.
Services: Search service, accepts want lists, catalog.
Credit Cards: No
Year Estab: 1971

Casterbridge Books (312) 294-0055
720 South Dearborn, Ste 601 Chicago 60605

Collection: Specialty
Specialties: 19th & 20th century literature and poetry; literary periodicals.
Services: Appraisals, search service, catalog, accepts want lists.
Credit Cards: No
Owner: Peter Lennon
Year Estab: 1990

Chicago Book Mart (630) 879-6097
PO Box 595 Batavia 60510

Collection: General stock.
# of Vols: 2,000-3,000
Services: Search service, accepts want lists.
Owner: Josephine Bray
Year Estab: 1983

Gerald J. Cielec-Books (773) 235-2326
2248 North Kedvale Avenue Chicago 60639

Collection:	General stock.
# of Vols:	2,000
Specialties:	Americana; art; photography.
Services:	Catalog
Credit Cards:	No
Year Estab:	1977

Estate Books (708) 547-6239
5827 Burr Oak Berkeley 60163

Collection:	General stock.
# of Vols:	5,000
Specialties:	Children's; Civil War; Western Americana; Jesse Stuart.
Services:	Catalog, accepts want lists.
Credit Cards:	No
Owner:	Rose Lasley
Year Estab:	1975

First Impressions (815) 462-0900
PO Box 889 Orland Park 60462 E-mail: firstimp@interloc.com

Collection:	General stock.
# of Vols:	5,000
Specialties:	Modern first editions.
Credit Cards:	No
Owner:	Anthony Polito
Year Estab:	1990

The Fisherman's Bookshelf (708) 771-9076
PO Box 5513 River Forest 60305 Fax: (708) 771-9061

Collection:	Specialty. Mostly used.
# of Vols:	1,000-2,000
Specialties:	Fishing
Services:	Appraisals, search service, catalog, accepts want lists.
Credit Cards:	No
Owner:	Bob Andersen
Year Estab:	1986

D. J. Flynn-Books (847) 234-1146
421 East Westleigh Road Lake Forest 60045 Fax: (847) 234-1633

Collection:	General stock.
# of Vols:	8,000
Specialties:	Fore-edge paintings.
Services:	Search service.
Credit Cards:	No
Owner:	Doris J. Flynn
Year Estab:	1975

Gerhart's Rare & Out-of-Print Automobile Books   Tel & Fax: (708) 445-0498
PO Box 3164 Oak Park 60303

Collection:	Specialty books and ephemera.
# of Vols:	700
Specialties:	Automotive; automotive travel (pre-1930).
Services:	Appraisals, catalog, accepts want lists.
Credit Cards:	No
Year Estab:	1994

Ginkgo Leaf Press   (773) 989-2200
1759 Rosehill Drive Chicago 60660   Fax: (773) 989-7599
E-mail: kroomers@interaccess.com

Collection:	Specialty
# of Vols:	4,000
Specialties:	African American literature, poetry and history; arts and crafts; books on books.
Services:	Search service, catalog, accepts want lists.
Credit Cards:	Yes
Owner:	Charles Kroon

Good Books

2456 Devonshire Road Springfield 62703

Collection:	Specialty new and used. Mostly hardcover.
# of Vols:	4,000
Specialties:	Religion, theology, church history.
Services:	Catalog, accepts want lists.
Credit Cards:	No
Owner:	Curt Daniel
Year Estab:	1983
Comments:	Stock is evenly mixed between new and used books.

The Illuminated Eye   (217) 525-2041
540 West Carpenter Street Springfield 62702   E-mail: iebooks@aol.com

Collection:	General stock.
Services:	Search service.
Credit Cards:	No
Owner:	Ross & Julie Hulvey
Year Estab:	1990

Jane Austen Books   (312) 266-0080
860 North Lake Shore, #21J Chicago 60611   E-mail: JABooks@aol.com

Collection:	Specialty. Mostly used.
# of Vols:	5,000
Specialties:	Jane Austen (books by and about); English history (Regency period); female writers before and shortly after Jane Austen.
Services:	Catalog
Credit Cards:	Yes

Owner: Patricia Latkin
Year Estab: 1992

Dorothy V. Keck Out-of-Print Books   (217) 428-5100
1360 West Riverview Decatur 62522

Collection: General stock.
# of Vols: 8,000
Services: Search service, accepts want lists.
Credit Cards: No
Year Estab: 1969

Ashley Kennedy   (847) 475-2481
PO Box 191 Evanston 60204

Collection: Specialty
# of Vols: 500-1,000
Specialties: Vintage technology.
Services: Accepts want lists.
Credit Cards: No
Year Estab: 1966

Barry A. Klaung   (815) 395-9581
923 15th Street Rockford 61104

Collection: General stock.
# of Vols: 1,000
Specialties: Emphasis on modern first editions.
Credit Cards: No
Year Estab: 1998

Gail Klemm-Books   Tel & Fax: (847) 398-2625
204 West Saint James St. Arlington Heights 60004

Collection: Specialty
# of Vols: 10,000-12,000
Specialties: Children's
Services: Appraisals, search service, accepts want lists.
Credit Cards: No
Year Estab: 1967

Klimas Books   (630) 393-3939
PO Box 622 Warrenville 60555   Fax: (630) 393-4949
                                          E-mail: klimasbooks@worldnet.att.net
Collection: Specialty
# of Vols: 20,000
Specialties: Scholarly, with an emphasis on philosophy; law; economics; science.
Services: Catalog
Owner: Rick Klimas

Larry Laws   (773) 477-9247
831 Cornelia Chicago 60657
Collection: General stock of new and used books and theatrical ephemera.

# of Vols:	3,000
Specialties:	Theater; dance; film; U.S. paper money; erotica; Third Reich; fairs and expositions; sheet music.
Services:	Search service, accepts want lists.
Credit Cards:	No
Year Estab:	1975

Left Bank Bookstall   (708) 383-4700
PO Box 3516 Oak Park 60303   Fax: (708) 383-7857
                              E-mail: leftbank@ripco.com

Collection:	General stock and ephemera.
# of Vols:	5,000
Specialties:	History; Americana; regional Americana.
Services:	Search service, catalog, accepts want lists.
Credit Cards:	Yes
Owner:	Carole Goodwin & Carol Zientek
Year Estab:	1978

Madigan's Books   (217) 345-3657
PO Box 62 Charleston 61920   E-mail: mmadigan@advant.com
Web page: www.advant.com/madigan

Collection:	Specialty
# of Vols:	3,000
Specialties:	Genealogy; local history.
Services:	Accepts want lists, catalog.
Credit Cards:	Yes
Owner:	Matt Madigan
Year Estab:	1986
Comments:	Collection may also be viewed by appointment.

Anthony Maita   (847) 998-9804
813 Greenwood Road Glenview 60025

Collection:	Specialty
# of Vols:	5,000
Specialties:	U.S. Marine Corps.
Services:	Catalog, accepts want lists.
Credit Cards:	No
Year Estab:	1985

Martinton Book Co.   Tel & Fax: (815) 486-7252
2516 N2400 East Road Martinton 60951   E-mail: martinbk@interloc.com

Collection:	General stock.
# of Vols:	10,000
Specialties:	Science; technology; books about books.
Credit Cards:	Yes
Owner:	Leonard Hoffnung
Year Estab:	1977

McNeilly Books (708) 848-6178
309 South Scoville Ave. Oak Park 60302 E-mail: David_A_McNeilly@msn.com

Collection: General stock.
# of Vols: 4,000
Specialties: Modern first editions; children's (modern); military.
Services: Search service, accepts want lists.
Credit Cards: No
Owner: David McNeilly
Year Estab: 1997

David Meyer Magic Books (708) 757-4950
PO Box 427 Glenwood 60425

Collection: Specialty
# of Vols: 5,000
Specialties: Magic; gambling; Punch & Judy; puppetry; automata; confidence methods (con games).
Services: Catalog, accepts want lists.
Credit Cards: No
Year Estab: 1976

Montagnana Books (847) 864-5991
1615 Cleveland Street Evanston 60202 Fax: (847) 864-6064
Web page: http://home.earthlink.net/~montagnana/
E-mail: montagnana@earthlink.net

Collection: Specialty books, magazines and autographs
# of Vols: 1,000-1,500
Specialties: Music (violins).
Services: Appraisals, catalog.
Credit Cards: Yes
Owner: David Sanders
Year Estab: 1989

National Law Resource (312) 382-3822
328 South Jefferson Street Chicago 60661 (800) 886-1800
Fax: (312) 382-0323

Collection: Specialty
# of Vols: 500,000
Specialties: Law
Services: Appraisals, search service, accepts want lists.
Credit Cards: Yes
Year Estab: 1980

Plain Tales Books (847) 253-1472
PO Box 1691 Arlington Heights 60006 E-mail: plaintales@earthlink.net

Collection: Specialty
# of Vols: 2,000
Specialties: Modern first editions; travel; cookbooks.

Credit Cards: No
Owner: Thomas Zimmerman
Year Estab: 1984

Rhythm & Views Tel & Fax: (773) 227-4178
2322 North Spaulding Chicago 60647

Collection: Specialty books and ephemera.
# of Vols: 2,000-3,000
Specialties: Music (with focus on jazz and blues); performing arts; art; technology (with emphasis on inventions); photography.
Services: Appraisals in jazz and photography only, sheet music auction catalogs.
Credit Cards: No
Owner: Joe Cavalier & Maurene Sherlock
Year Estab: 1983
Comments: Collection may also be viewed by appointment

Paul Rohe Books (847) 491-9132
2339 Hastings Avenue Evanston 60201

Collection: General stock.
# of Vols: 5,000
Specialties: First editions; signed; American and British literature pre-1950.
Services: Accepts want lists.
Credit Cards: Yes
Year Estab: 1977

M. Sand Books Tel & Fax: (630) 964-5526
900 Ogden Ave., #119 Downers Grove 60515 E-mail: msandbks@worldnet.att.net

Collection: General stock of mostly used hardcover.
# of Vols: 750
Specialties: Mystery; science fiction; modern first editions.
Services: Appraisals, search service, catalog, accepts want lists.
Credit Cards: No
Owner: Sandra Kral
Year Estab: 1996

Stan Stites Books (217) 935-2093
816 West South Street Clinton 61727 Fax: (217) 935-2247
E-mail: stanbks@jwbank.net

Collection: General stock.
# of Vols: 15,000
Specialties: Literature; Americana; maps.
Services: Appraisals, accepts want lists.
Credit Cards: Yes
Year Estab: 1984

Uncle Buck's Mysteries Tel & Fax: (618) 397-3568
390 Oak Hill Drive Belleville 62223 E-mail: unclebuck@peaknet.net

Collection: General stock of mostly used and some new.

# of Vols:	30,000
Specialties:	Mystery
Services:	Appraisals, search service, catalog, accepts want lists.
Credit Cards:	Yes
Owner:	Roger Wuller
Year Estab:	1988

Weidler Book Source   (309) 853-4160
726 Henry Street Kewanee 61443

Collection:	General stock.
# of Vols:	5,000
Specialties:	Civil War; Western Americana; children's.
Services:	Search service, accepts want lists.
Credit Cards:	No
Owner:	Verne Weidler
Year Estab:	1977

Robert Williams Bound To Please Books   (309) 534-8249
2615 170th Avenue Preemption 61276   E-mail: bookman@netins.net
Web page: www.abebooks.com/home/SERIESBKS/

Collection:	General stock and ephemera.
# of Vols:	10,000
Specialties:	Children's series; children's illustrated; Frank Baum; Americana; maga-zines.
Services:	Search service, catalog, accepts want lists.
Credit Cards:	No
Year Estab:	1991

World Exonumia Press   (815) 226-0771
PO Box 4143CAN Rockford 61110   Fax: (815) 397-7662
                                                  E-mail: hartzog@execpc.com

Collection:	Specialty
# of Vols:	4,000+
Specialties:	Tokens and medals.
Services:	Appraisals, search service, catalog, accepts want lists.
Credit Cards:	Yes
Owner:	Rich Hartzog
Year Estab:	1972

<hr>

Late addtions to Open Shop Listings

Reopening: **Booknook Parnassus**
            2000 Maple Street, Evanston 60201 (847) 475-3445
            We enjoyed this shop on our earlier visit to Evanston and were glad to
            learn that it has reopened after a temporary closing.
New listing: **Chicago Rare Book Center**
            56 West Maple Street, Chicago 60610 (312) 988-7246
            Between Clark & Dearborn, two blocks south of Division.
            A group shop opening in September '98.

INDIANA

Alphabetical Listing By Dealer

The Abstract	108	The Busy Hermit	126
Americana Books	104	Campfire Books	130
Antiquarian Book Company	106	Caveat Emptor	102
Antique Avenue Mall	125	Cedars of Lebanon Antiques	116
Arnn' Antiques	108	Chapter III Used Bookstore	117
Autonomy House Publications	130	Cherished Again Antique Mall	105
AC Books	103	Chuck's Books	114
B & W Booksellers	125	Circle City Antiquarian Books	110
Barely Used Books	102	Columbus Antique Mall	104
Bartholomew Books	118	Corner Cupboard Cookbooks	130
Between The Lines	130	The Corner Shop	123
Bob The Bookseller	127	Country Bookshelf	103
The Book Broker	105	Crunk & Wagley's	116
Book Center	119	Don's Books	113
The Book Inn Bed & Breakfast	125	Downtown Antique Mall	111
Book Nook	121	DreamWeaver Books	107
The Book Nook	123	Earl Plaza Books	115
Book Nook & Unique Gift Shop	120	Emmenegger Books	124
Bookcellar	101	Erasmus Books	126
Bookmark	105	Forest Park Books	105
Books, Antiques & More	109	Fountain Of Mystery Books	111
Books Unlimited	108	J.E. Frazier	131
The Booksellers Shoppe	119	Gateway Collectibles	118
Bookshelf	101	The Gentlemen Soldier	122
The Bookstack	104	Golden Raintree Books	120
The Bookworm	129	Good News Books	124
Broad Ripple Bookshop	109	Granny's Trunk	101
Buck Creek Books	114	The Griffin Building Antique Mall	104
Bullfrog Books	110	The Griffon	127

Half Price Books	107, 111, 111	Pandora's Books	127
History Makers Rare Find Gallery	111	The Paperback Peddlar	117
Hourglass Collectibles & Antiques	113	Paperback-Comic Paradise	124
Hyde Brothers Booksellers	106	Eleanor Pasotti	131
HIS Used Christian Book Shop	120	Pendleton Antique Mall	123
Idlewood Rare Books	116	Mark Razor	131
Orval J. Imel	112	Reading Room Books	129
Jackie's Book Store	120	Remarkable Book Shop	118
JB Books-Records	106	Stephen Rose Fine Arts	112
Jefferson Street Book Sellers	127	Sam's Half Price Book Store	101
JW Books	131	P.R. Schwan, Bookseller	121
Kokomo North Drive In Flea Market	114	Shuman's Antiques & Books	115
Leonard's Antiques and Books	115	Flo Silver Books	132
Lost N' Found Books	131	Trails' End Books	112
Meridian Street Books	116	Treasure Trove Antique Mall	121
Midnight Bookman	129	Verl's Books	132
Mighty Fine Books	117	Wabash River Books	128
Miles Books	107	White Rabbit Used Books	119
Mostly Books	122	J.F. Whyland Books	113
Mr. Books!	123	Wik's Books & Treasures	122
Mudpies	121	Wallace M. Wojtkowski, Bookseller	128
New Concept Book Store	128	Ye Olde Genealogie Shoppe	112
Noblesville Antique Mall	122	Yesterday's Books	132
Old Time Flea Market	104	Yesterday's Treasures Antique Mall	103

Alphabetical Listing By Location

Location	Dealer	Page
Anderson	Granny's Trunk	101
Angola	Sam's Half Price Book Store	101
Batesville	Bookshelf	101
Bloomington	Between The Lines	130
	Bookcellar	101
	Caveat Emptor	102
	J.E. Frazier	131
Carmel	Barely Used Books	102
Chesterton	Country Bookshelf	103
	Yesterday's Treasures Antique Mall	103
Columbus	AC Books	103
	Columbus Antique Mall	104
	Old Time Flea Market	104
Corydon	The Griffin Building Antique Mall	104
Decatur	Americana Books	104
Elkhart	The Bookstack	104
Evansville	The Book Broker	105
	Campfire Books	130
Fort Wayne	Bookmark	105
	Cherished Again Antique Mall	105
	Forest Park Books	105
	Hyde Brothers Booksellers	106
	JB Books-Records	106
Grabill	Antiquarian Book Company	106
Greenwood	Half Price Books, Records, Magazines	107
Hagerstown	DreamWeaver Books	107
Highland	Miles Books	107
Indianapolis	The Abstract	108
	Arnn' Antiques	108
	Books, Antiques & More	109
	Books Unlimited	108
	Broad Ripple Bookshop	109
	Bullfrog Books	110
	Circle City Antiquarian Books	110
	Downtown Antique Mall	111
	Fountain Of Mystery Books	111
	Half Price Books, Records, Magazines	111
	Half Price Books, Records, Magazines	111
	History Makers Rare Find Gallery	111
	Orval J. Imel	112
	Lost N' Found Books	131
	Eleanor Pasotti	131
	Stephen Rose Fine Arts	112
	Flo Silver Books	132

Indianapolis	Trails' End Books	112
	Verl's Books	132
	Ye Olde Genealogie Shoppe	112
Jeffersonville	J.F. Whyland Books	113
Jolietville	Hourglass Collectibles & Antiques	113
Kokomo	Don's Books	113
	Kokomo North Drive In Flea Market	114
La Porte	Chuck's Books	114
Lafayette	Buck Creek Books	114
	Earl Plaza Books	115
	Leonard's Antiques and Books	115
	Shuman's Antiques & Books	115
Lebanon	Cedars of Lebanon Antiques	116
	Idlewood Rare Books	116
	Meridian Street Books	116
Leo	Crunk & Wagley's	116
Madison	Mighty Fine Books	117
Marion	Chapter III Used Bookstore	117
	The Paperback Peddlar	117
Martinsville	Gateway Collectibles	118
Merrillville	Remarkable Book Shop	118
Mishawaka	Bartholomew Books	118
Monticello	Autonomy House Publications	130
Muncie	Book Center	119
	White Rabbit Used Books	119
Nappanee	The Booksellers Shoppe	119
Nashville	HIS Used Christian Book Shop	120
New Castle	Book Nook & Unique Gift Shop	120
	Jackie's Book Store	120
New Harmony	Golden Raintree Books	120
	Mudpies	121
	P.R. Schwan, Bookseller	121
	Treasure Trove Antique Mall	121
Newburgh	Book Nook	121
Noblesville	The Gentlemen Soldier	122
	JW Books	131
	Noblesville Antique Mall	122
North Judson	Wik's Books & Treasures	122
North Manchester	Mostly Books	122
North Vernon	The Book Nook	123
Pendleton	Pendleton Antique Mall	123
Peru	Mr. Books!	123
Portland	The Corner Shop	123
Richmond	Emmenegger Books	124
	Paperback-Comic Paradise	124
	Yesterday's Books	132

Rossville	Good News Books	124
Scottsburg	B & W Booksellers	125
South Bend	Antique Avenue Mall	125
	The Book Inn Bed & Breakfast	125
	The Busy Hermit	126
	Erasmus Books	126
	The Griffon	127
	Jefferson Street Book Sellers	127
	Pandora's Books	127
Terre Haute	Bob The Bookseller	127
	New Concept Book Store	128
	Wabash River Books	128
Valparaiso	Wallace M. Wojtkowski, Bookseller	128
Wabash	Reading Room Books	129
Wadesville	Mark Razor	131
Wanatah	The Bookworm	129
West Lafayette	Midnight Bookman	129
Zionsville	Corner Cupboard Cookbooks	130

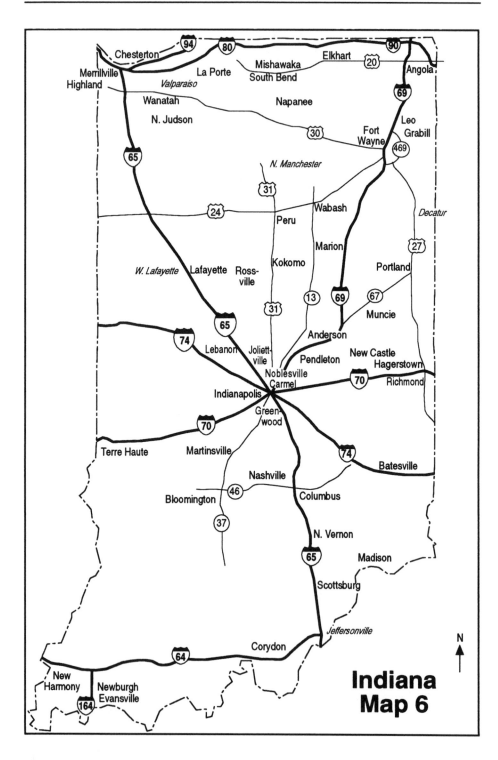

Indiana
Map 6

Anderson
(Map 6, page 100)

Granny's Trunk **Antique Mall**
At Anderson Antique Mall, 1407 Main Street Mall: (765) 622-9517
Mailing address: 2315 Fowler Anderson IN 46012 Home: (765) 642-1263
E-mail: vel5@juno.com

Collection:	General stock.
# of Vols:	15,000
Specialties:	Children's series; technical; religion; technical.
Hours:	Mon-Sat 10-5. Sun 12-5.
Services:	Accepts want lists.
Travel:	Exit 22 off I-69. Proceed north on Pendleton Ave, then east on Rte 32 to Main. Shop is at corner of 14th & Main.
Credit Cards:	No
Owner:	Velma & Dick Milliron
Year Estab:	1993

Angola
(Map 6, page 100)

Sam's Half Price Book Store **Open Shop**
206 West Maumee Street 46703 (219) 665-2392

Collection:	General stock of mostly paperback.
# of Vols:	35,000-40,000
Hours:	Mon-Sat 10-6.

Batesville
(Map 6, page 100)

Bookshelf **Open Shop**
101 North Walnut Street 47006 (812) 934-5800

Collection:	General stock of mostly used paperback and new books.
# of Vols:	100,000 (used)
Hours:	10-5 Mon-Thu 10-5. Fri 10-6. Sat 10-3.

Bloomington
(Map 6, page 100)

Bloomington Antique Mall **Antique Mall**
311 West 7th Street 47401 (812) 332-2290

Hours:	Mon-Sat 10-5. Sun 12-5.
Travel:	Rte 37 to College Ave. Proceed south on College, then right on 7th.

Bookcellar **Open Shop**
322 East Kirkwood Avenue 47408 (812) 331-1781
Web page: www.kiva.net/~rarebook E-mail: rarebook@kiva.net

Collection:	General stock of hardcover and paperback and records.

# of Vols:	50,000
Specialties:	Philosophy; linguistics; religion.
Hours:	Mon-Sat 11-7.
Travel:	College Ave exit off Rte 37. Proceed south on Rte 37, then west on 5th/ Kirkwood and right on Grant. Shop is in basement of Kirkwood Manor.
Credit Cards:	Yes
Owner:	Hans van der Genugten & James D. Williams
Year Estab:	1989
Comments:	Corridor after corridor is filled with quality titles of a mostly (but not exclusively) scholarly bent. If you're looking for an esoteric volume that may have eluded you, there's a better than average chance you may find it here.

Caveat Emptor   **Open Shop**
112 North Walnut Street 47404   (812) 332-9995

Collection:	General stock.
# of Vols:	50,000
Specialties:	Scholarly; history; biography; politics.
Hours:	Mon-Sat 11-9. Sun 12-5.
Services:	Appraisals, search service, accepts want lists, mail order.
Travel:	Bloomington exit off Rte 37. Proceed on College to Kirkwood/5th St, then left on Kirkwood and right on Walnut. Shop is on the east side of Courthouse Square between Kirkwood and 6th St.
Credit Cards:	Yes
Owner:	Janis Starcs & Donald R. Wilds
Year Estab:	1971
Comments:	This shop maintains a very nice balance between scholarly volumes (this is, after all a university town) and popular culture subjects. We spent a lot of time browsing here and could have remained even longer.

Carmel
(Map 6, page 100)

Barely Used Books   **Open Shop**
616 Station Drive 46032   (317) 843-1855

Collection:	General stock of paperback and hardcover and records.
# of Vols:	40,000
Hours:	Mon-Fri 10-6. Sat 10-6. Sun 12-5.
Services:	Search service, accepts want lists, mail order.
Travel:	Five miles north of I-465 on Rte 431 (Keystone Ave) at 116th St. Shop is in Merchants' Square, on the north side of the parking lot.
Credit Cards:	Yes
Owner:	Larry Miller
Year Estab:	1987
Comments:	A better than average "mall" book shop with typical rows of paper-backs down the center aisle and hardcovers along the side and rear walls. At the time of our visit, we saw several shelves of Indiana books

and a larger than average science fiction and mystery section with mostly recent titles (as is the case with the majority of the remaining hardcover stock). The books were in generally good condition and reasonably priced and the owner had thoughtfully provided lots of chairs for his customers' comfort and convenience.

Chesterton
(Map 6, page 100)

Country Bookshelf   **Open Shop**
933 North Calumet Road 46304   (219) 926-4694

Collection:	General stock.
# of Vols:	7,000
Specialties:	Children's; Indiana.
Hours:	Wed and Fri-Mon 1-5.
Services:	Search service, accepts want lists, mail order.
Travel:	From I-80/I-90. After toll plaza, at light, turn south on Rte 49, then make first possible left after light on N. Calumet. Shop is the third house on the left.
Credit Cards:	No
Owner:	Virginia McLean
Year Estab:	1971
Comments:	A modest collection of mostly older titles on the first floor and in the basement of the dealer's home. Interspersed with the older volumes were several almost brand new titles in varying categories. No great depth in the general stock areas but certainly lots of subjects and authors.

Yesterday's Treasures Antique Mall   **Antique Mall**
700 West Broadway 46304   (219) 926-2268

Hours:	Mon-Sat 10-5. Sun 12-5.
Travel:	Exit 26A off I-94. Proceed south on Rte 49 to first light, then right on Indian Boundary, left on Calumet and right on Broadway.

Columbus
(Map 6, page 100)

AC Books   **Open Shop**
1871 State Street 47201   (812) 372-0929

Collection:	General stock of mostly paperback.
# of Vols:	50,000
Specialties:	Children's; McGuffy readers; Civil War; history; westerns.
Hours:	Mon-Fri 10-4:30, Sat 10-2:30. (See Comments)
Services:	Accepts want lists, mail order.
Travel:	Rte 46 exit off I-65. Proceed east on Rte 46 then right on Rte 7 which is State St.
Credit Cards:	No
Owner:	Sam Knoy

Year Estab: 1977
Comments: In addition to this predominately paperback shop, the owner exhibits his hardcover books at a number of nearby locations (see below).

Columbus Antique Mall   **Antique Mall**
1235 Jackson Street 47201   (812) 375-2904
Hours: Daily 10:30-5:30.

Old Time Flea Market   **Flea Market**
Route 46

Hours: Apr-Oct: Sat & Sun 9-5.
Travel: Rte 46 exit off I-69. Proceed west on Rte 46 for about 10 miles.

Corydon
(Map 6, page 100)

The Griffin Building Antique Mall   **Antique Mall**
113 East Beaver Street 47112   (812) 738-3302

Hours: Mon-Sat 10-5. Sun 1-5.
Travel: Corydon exit off I-64. Proceed south on Rte 135, then left on Rte 62 to downtown, right at light and left on Beaver.

Decatur
(Map 6, page 100)

Americana Books   **By Appointment**
506 North 10th Street   (219) 728-2810
Mailing address: PO Box 14 Decatur IN 46733   Fax: (219) 724-9755
                                                 E-mail: amerbook@interloc.com
Collection: General stock of hardcover, vintage paperbacks and ephemera.
# of Vols: 8,000
Specialties: Modern first editions; vintage paperbacks; photographic ephemera. Also publishes books about Gene Stratton Porter.
Hours: Closed Nov-Mar.
Services: Search service, accepts want lists, mail order.
Credit Cards: Yes
Owner: David G. MacLean
Year Estab: 1956

Elkhart
(Map 6, page 100)

The Bookstack   **Open Shop**
112 West Lexington Avenue 46516   (219) 293-3815
                                                              (800) 386-7501
                                                 E-mail: bookstak@interloc.com
Collection: General stock of hardback and paperback, comics and records.
# of Vols: 28,000

Specialties:	Hunting; fishing; natural history; Civil War; cookbooks.
Hours:	Mon-Sat 10-5:30, except Thu till 8.
Services:	Appraisals, search service, accepts want lists, mail order.
Travel:	Three miles south of I-80/I-90 in downtown.
Credit Cards:	Yes
Owner:	Charles & Judith Brothers
Year Estab:	1975
Comments:	Quite a nice establishment, with books in every category. The books were in generally good condition, of mixed vintage, and reasonably priced. The selection of books ranged from scholarly titles to popular culture. Many were of collectible quality.

Evansville
(Map 6, page 100)

The Book Broker   **Open Shop**
2127 South Weinbach 47714   (812) 479-5647

Collection:	General stock of paperback, hardcover, magazines and comics.
# of Vols:	150,000
Hours:	Mon-Fri 10-9. Sat 10-7. Sun 12-5.
Travel:	Rte 41 exit off I-64. Proceed south on Rte 41, then east on Covert and south on Weinbach. Shop is in the Fairlawn Shopping Center.
Credit Cards:	Yes
Year Estab:	1975
Comments:	Stock is approximately 70% paperback.

Fort Wayne
(Map 6, page 100)

Bookmark   **Open Shop**
3420 North Anthony Boulevard 46805   (219) 484-2665

Collection:	General stock of mostly paperback.
# of Vols:	10,000+
Hours:	Mon-Thu 10-7. Fri 10-6. Sat 10-5.

Cherished Again Antique Mall   **Antique Mall**
230 East Collins Road   (219) 484-4534

Hours:	Mon, Wed, Fri, Sat 9-5. Tue & Thu 9-8.
Travel:	Coldwater exit off I-69. Proceed east on Coldwater, then right on Collins.

Forest Park Books   **By Appointment**
1909 Florida Drive 46805   (219) 424-6777
Web page: www.abebooks.com   E-mail: sirromkaj@fwi.com

Collection:	General stock.
# of Vols:	5,000
Specialties:	Americana, especially in series (WPA guides, rivers and Lakeside Classics); American artists and illustrators.

Owner: L.M. Morris
Year Estab: 1970

Hyde Brothers Booksellers   **Open Shop**
1428 Wells Street 46808   (219) 424-0197
Web page: http://interloc.com/~hydebros/   (800) 264-6369
                                          E-mail: hydebros@worldnet.att.net

Collection: General stock of paperback and hardcover.
# of Vols: 100,000
Specialties: Indiana; natural history; history; religion; science fiction; mystery;
                literature.
Hours: Mon-Sat 11-6. Sun 1-5.
Services: Appraisals, search service, accepts want lists.
Travel: Exit 112 off I-69. Proceed south on Rte 27. Once Clinton (Rte 27
                south) becomes one way, turn right on State, then left at next light on
                Wells. Shop is about eight blocks ahead. Parking is available in rear.
Credit Cards: Yes
Owner: Joel & Samuel Hyde
Year Estab: 1992
Comments: We visited this shop late in the day and regretted not having more time
                to browse. What we did see were very strong collections in the special-
                ties listed above. We also saw enough titles of collectible quality to
                make us feel that unless your interests are extremely esoteric, you
                should be able to find titles here that will be of interest to you. Prices
                were quite reasonable.

JB Books-Records   **Flea Market**
At Ft. Wayne Flea Market S. Hanna & Hwy 27 South   Home: (219) 424-4383

Collection: General stock of hardcover and paperback.
# of Vols: 20,000 (hardcover)
Hours: Fri 12-6. Sat & Sun 10-6. (Year-round)
Travel: Rte 27 exit off Rte 469. Proceed north on Rte 27 for about four miles.
Owner: John G. & Loretta Buckles

Grabill
(Map 6, page 100)

Antiquarian Book Company   **Antique Mall**
At Country Shops, 13756 State Street   Mall: (219) 627-6315
Mailing address: PO Box 686 Auburn IN 46706   Home: (219) 925-4560
                                                       Fax: (219) 925-4563

Collection: General stock, maps and prints.
# of Vols: 2,000
Specialties: Gene Stratton Porter; Indiana history and authors.
Hours: Mon-Sat 9-5. Sun 12-5.
Services: Mail order
Travel: Exit 116 off I-69. Proceed east on Rte 1 to 4-way stop at Leo. Turn
                right and proceed two miles.

Credit Cards: Yes
Owner: Barbara Clark Smith
Year Estab: 1989

Greenwood
(Map 6, page 100)

Half Price Books, Records, Magazines   **Open Shop**
844 North US 31 46142   (317) 889-1076
                                                      Fax: (317) 889-1081

Collection: General stock of new and used hardback and paperback.
# of Vols: 150,000+
Hours: Mon-Sat 9-9. Sun 11-7.
Travel: From I-465, proceed south on Rte 31. Shop is on Rte 31, west of Greenwood Mall.

Hagerstown
(Map 6, page 100)

DreamWeaver Books   **Open Shop**
65 West Main Street 47346   Tel & Fax: (765) 489-6212

Collection: General stock of hardcover and paperback.
# of Vols: 15,000
Specialties: Vintage paperbacks; pulps; history; modern first editions; cookbooks.
Hours: Tue & Wed 10-5. Thu-Sat 10-8. Call for Sunday hours.
Services: Appraisals, search service, accepts want lists, mail order.
Travel: Rte 1 exit off I-70. Proceed north on Rte 1 for about 3.3 miles to flashing red light, then left on Rte 38 and proceed to Hagerstown. Shop is across from post office.
Credit Cards: No
Owner: Janice E. Pentecost
Year Estab: 1996
Comments: A mix of hardcover and paperback books with most of the hardcover items being in good condition. Titles ranged from older collectibles to more recent best sellers. In addition to the specialties listed above we noted a strong selection of children's series books. An added bonus: if you're visiting this shop around dinner time, the owner might suggest that you treat yourself to the well known smorgasbord restaurant just down the block.

Highland
(Map 6, page 100)

Miles Books   **Open Shop**
2820 Highway Avenue 46322   (219) 838-8700

Collection: General stock of hardcover and paperback.
# of Vols: 40,000

Hours:	Mon-Fri 9:30-6, except Thu till 8. Sat 9:30-5.
Services:	Search service, accepts want lists, mail order.
Travel:	Exit 3 (Kennedy Ave) off I-94. Proceed south on Kennedy for five lights, then left on Highway Ave. Shop is just ahead on south side.
Credit Cards:	Yes
Owner:	Jim Roumbos
Year Estab:	1984
Comments:	A potpourri of some new and used books, both paperback and hardcover, with an emphasis on the "used." Plenty of interesting hardcover titles to peruse, some quite recent, several older volumes. One problem which created a challenge for the browser, but which could be corrected by the time you visit, is that the shelves were not labeled and in more than one instance, we saw books on some shelves that had little relationship to others on the same shelf. Reasonably priced.

Indianapolis
(Map 6, page 100 & Map 7, page 110)

The Abstract   **Open Shop**
4850 West Mooresville Road 46221   (317) 856-3710
E-mail: abstract@interloc.com

Collection:	General stock.
# of Vols:	14,000
Hours:	Tue 10-6 and Sun 1-4. Other times by appointment or chance.
Services:	Search service, accepts want lists, mail order.
Travel:	Kentucky Ave (Rte 67) exit off I-465. Proceed north on Kentucky Ave, then right on Lynhurst and left at second stop sign. The shop, about three blocks ahead on the right, is located behind the owner's home.
Credit Cards:	Yes
Owner:	Leonard G. Koerber
Year Estab:	1985
Comments:	While the collection here is modest in size, we spotted several titles of an unusual nature and feel that book aficionados would find a stop here to their advantage.

Arnn'Antiques   **Antique Mall**
At Manor House, 5454 US 31 South 46227   (317) 782-1358

Hours:	Mon-Fri 10-6. Sat 10-8. Sun 12-5.
Travel:	Exit 2B off I-465. Proceed south on Rte 31 for 1/2 mile. Shop is on the right.
Owner:	Sammye Arnn Baker & Helen Arnn

Books Unlimited   **Open Shop**
922 East Washington Street 46202   (317) 634-0949

Collection:	General stock of paperback and hardcover.
# of Vols:	5,000
Hours:	Mon-Sat 9-6.

Services:	Appraisals, search service, accepts want lists, mail order.
Travel:	Market St exit off I-65. Proceed on Market to Washington, then right on Washington. Look for a small one story concrete block building.
Credit Cards:	Yes
Owner:	James Ware
Year Estab:	1979
Comments:	In addition to selling girlie magazines, *Time/Life* books, book club editions and paperbacks, the shop also has a few thousand hardcover titles, few of which caught our eye in terms of true collectibility.

Books, Antiques & More
1048 Virginia Avenue 46203

Open Shop
(317) 636-1595

Collection:	General stock of hardcover and paperback and ephemera.
# of Vols:	20,000 (hardcover)
Hours:	Mon-Sat 10-6. Sun 12-5.
Services:	Appraisals, accepts want lists, mail order.
Travel:	South from Chicago: Exit 110A (East St) exit off I-65. Left on East St and proceed for two blocks to Morris. Left on Morris and proceed five blocks to Shelby, then left on Shelby. At fountain, take left fork, and proceed on Virginia for one block. Shop is about 10 doors from fountain.
Credit Cards:	No
Owner:	Carrie Walker
Year Estab:	1986
Comments:	A traditional used book shop in both the positive and negative sense: the shop has a large collection (for its size) of hardcover volumes, the aisles are narrow, there are books in the aisles, and the books on the shelves, representing many time periods, did not, at the time of our visit, have the look of having been carefully culled. The bottom line is that a visitor stopping here may, depending on the time he or she has to spend, walk away with some prize finds or be disappointed.

Broad Ripple Bookshop
6407 Ferguson Street 46220

Open Shop
(317) 259-1980
E-mail: broadrip@interloc.com

Collection:	General stock of mostly hardcover.
# of Vols:	35,000
Specialties:	Civil War; Americana; natural history; modern first editions; art.
Hours:	Tue-Fri 11-6. Sat 11-5.
Services:	Appraisals, accepts want lists, mail order.
Travel:	Meridian St exit off I-465. Proceed south on Meridian, then left on 91st, right on College and left on 65th St. Continue on 65th St for two blocks, then right on Ferguson.
Credit Cards:	Yes
Owner:	June H. Sublett
Year Estab:	1975
Comments:	A bi-level shop with mixed vintage volumes in mixed condition and a good selection for someone who has seen all of the usual stuff.

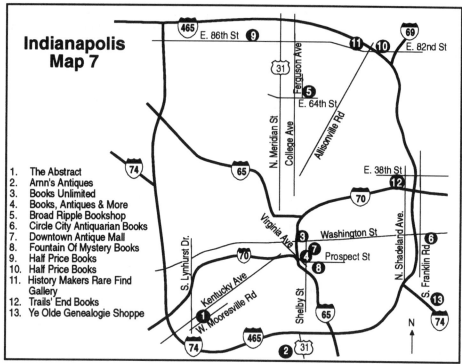

Indianapolis Map 7

1. The Abstract
2. Arnn's Antiques
3. Books Unlimited
4. Books, Antiques & More
5. Broad Ripple Bookshop
6. Circle City Antiquarian Books
7. Downtown Antique Mall
8. Fountain Of Mystery Books
9. Half Price Books
10. Half Price Books
11. History Makers Rare Find Gallery
12. Trails' End Books
13. Ye Olde Genealogie Shoppe

Bullfrog Books
9144 Aintree Drive 46250

By Appointment
(317) 595-9238

Collection:	Specialty
# of Vols:	10,000
Specialties:	Games and puzzles; recreational mathematics, recreational linguistics; physical sciences; mathematics.
Services:	Appraisals, search service, catalog, accepts want lists.
Credit Cards:	Yes
Owner:	Jeremiah Farrell
Year Estab:	1993

Circle City Antiquarian Books
45 South Franklin Road 46219

Open Shop
(317) 898-1724
E-mail: circlecitybooks@webtv.net

Collection:	General stock of mostly hardcover.
# of Vols:	15,000
Specialties:	Americana; children's illustrated; children's series; natural history.
Hours:	Mon, Tue, Thu-Sat 11-6. Other times by appointment.
Services:	Appraisals, search service, accepts want lists, mail order.
Travel:	Washington St exit off I-465. Proceed east on Washington for one block, then right on Franklin. Shop is just ahead on left.
Credit Cards:	Yes
Owner:	Don Prescott & John Mullins

Year Estab: 1997
Comments: A bi-level group shop with something for almost everyone. We saw
                  some very common items as well as some very unusual titles. (If you're
                  into entomology, we saw an entire series of books with each volume
                  devoted to a specific insect.) Lots of fiction. Lots of children's books.
                  Plenty of older items. If you're patient, who knows what you'll find.

Downtown Antique Mall   **Antique Mall**
1044 Virginia Avenue 46203   (317) 635-5336
Hours: Mon-Sat 10-6. Sun 12-5.
Travel: See Books, Antiques & More above.

Fountain Of Mystery Books   **Open Shop**
1119 Prospect Street 46203   (317) 635-2583

Collection: Specialty. Mostly used paperback.
# of Vols: 40,000
Specialties: Mystery; true crime; science fiction.
Hours: Thu-Sat 12-4.
Services: Accepts want lists, mail order.
Travel: See Books, Antiques & More above.
Credit Cards: Yes
Owner: Winona M. Eads
Year Estab: 1985

Half Price Books, Records, Magazines   **Open Shop**
1551 West 86th Street 46260   (317) 824-9002
                                                                Fax: (317) 842-9004
Collection: General stock of new and used hardback and paperback.
Hours: Mon-Sat 9-9. Sun 11-7.
Services: Mail order.
Travel: Meridan exit off I-465 North. Proceed south on Meridan, then west on
                  86th and left on Ditch Rd. Shop is in Northbrook Shopping Center.

Half Price Books, Records, Magazines   **Open Shop**
8316 Castleton Corner 46250   (317) 577-0410
                                                                Fax: (317) 577-0320
Collection: General stock new and used hardcover and paperback.
Hours: Mon-Sat 9-9. Sun 11-7.
Services: Mail order.
Travel: Allisonville exit off I-465. Proceed north on Allisonville, then right on
                  86th St and right on Castleton. Shop is two blocks ahead on right in
                  Castleton Corner Shopping Center.

History Makers Rare Find Gallery   **Open Shop**
4040 East 82nd Street 46250   (317) 842-5828
Web page: www.historymaker.com   Fax: (317) 842-5845
                                                             E-mail: steven@indy.net
Collection: Specialty documents.

(Indianapolis)

# of Vols:	6,000
Specialties:	Signed documents from 16th century to present, including presidents, Civil War and pop icons.
Hours:	Mon-Thu 10-5. Fri & Sat 10-2.
Services:	Appraisals, search service, catalog, accepts want lists.
Travel:	Keystone exit off I-465. Proceed south on Keystone, then left on 82nd St.
Credit Cards:	Yes
Owner:	Steve Nowlin
Year Estab:	1983

Orval J. Imel   By Appointment
424 East Vermont Street 46202   (317) 638-2618

Collection:	Specialty
Specialties:	*National Geographic*. Magazines and related materials..
Services:	Mail order.

Stephen Rose Fine Arts   By Appointment
212 East 10th Street   Office: (317) 822-0989
Mailing address: PO Box 55701 Indianapolis IN 46205   Home: (317) 926-6031
                                               Fax: (317) 925-0783
                                        E-mail: roseart@indy.com

Collection:	Specialty
# of Vols:	2,000
Specialties:	Photography; art; design.
Services:	Appraisals, catalog, accepts want lists.
Credit Cards:	Yes
Year Estab:	1977

Trails' End Books   Antique Mall
At Shadeland Antique Mall, 3444 N. Shadeland Avenue   Mall: (317) 542-7283
Mailing address: 911 N. Sadlier Dr. Indianapolis IN 46219   Home: (317) 359-1513

Collection:	General stock and ephemera.
# of Vols:	10,000
Specialties:	Indiana; art; photography; cookbooks; children's.
Hours:	Daily 10-6.
Services:	Mail order.
Travel:	Exit 89 (Shadeland) off I-70. Proceed north on Shadeland for 1½ miles.
Credit Cards:	Yes
Owner:	Anna K. & Michael J. Griffin
Year Estab:	1985

Ye Olde Genealogie Shoppe   Open Shop
9605 Vandergriff Road   (317) 862-3330
Mailing address: PO Box 39128 Indianapolis IN 46239

Collection:	Specialty

Specialties:	Genealogy; local history.
Hours:	Mon-Sat 9-3:30 but a call ahead on Sat.
Services:	Mail order.
Travel:	Post Rd exit off I-74. Proceed south on Post, then left on Northeastern. Proceed two blocks to Vandergriff, then go over I-74 overpass to sixth house on right.
Credit Cards:	Yes
Owner:	Ray Gooldy
Year Estab:	1975

Jeffersonville
(Map 6, page 100)

J.F. Whyland Books
409 Chippewa Drive 47130

By Appointment
(812) 282-0264

Collection:	Specialty
# of Vols:	2,000
Specialties:	Modern first editions.
Services:	Catalog, accepts want lists.
Credit Cards:	Yes
Owner:	Jon Whyland
Year Estab:	1991

Jolietville
(Map 6, page 100)

Hourglass Collectibles & Antiques
Highway 32

Antique Mall
Home: (317) 896-3292

Collection:	General stock of hardcover and paperback.
# of Vols:	10,000
Hours:	Mon 12-6. Thu-Sat 9-5. Sun 12-4.
Travel:	Five miles west of Rte 31.
Credit Cards:	No
Owner:	Don & Maggie Smith
Comments:	Stock is evenly divided between hardcover and paperback. The books, which sell for 50¢ apiece, are not sorted by category.

Kokomo
(Map 6, page 100)

Don's Books
815 North Washington Street 46901

Open Shop
(765) 459-4901

Collection:	General stock of paperback and hardcover.
# of Vols:	70,000
Hours:	Mon-Sat 10-5.
Services:	Accepts want lists.
Travel:	Jefferson St exit off Rte 31. Proceed west on Jefferson, then right on Washington.

Credit Cards: Yes
Owner: Donald L. Zewtz
Year Estab: 1995
Comments: Stock is approximately 70% paperback.

Kokomo North Drive In Flea Market
Route 31

Hours: Sat & Sun 8-5.
Travel: On Rte 31, seven miles north of Kokomo.
Comments: Don's Books (see above) displays 12,000 volumes, 60% of which are
                  paperback.

La Porte
(Map 6, page 100)

Chuck's Books
701 Michigan Avenue 46350

Open Shop
(219) 324-4734
(888) 690-4734

Collection: General stock of mostly hardcover.
# of Vols: 30,000
Specialties: Indiana; modern first editions.
Hours: Mon-Sat 10-5.
Services: Appraisals, accepts want lists.
Travel: Rte 35 exit off I-94. Proceed south on Rte 35, left on Rte 2 (Lincolnway).
                  and right on Michigan. From IN toll road: La Porte exit. Proceed south
                  on Rte 39, then left on Rte 35, left on Rte 2 and right on Michigan.
Credit Cards: Yes
Owner: Charles De Armond
Year Estab: 1981
Comments: The shop offers a mix of mostly older hardcover books and a back
                  room completely filled with paperbacks. We spotted quite a few gems
                  on the shelves, particularly in the area of vintage mystery. A discern-
                  ing buyer could easily make several purchases here at what we believe
                  to be bargain prices.

Lafayette
(Map 6, page 100)

Buck Creek Books
838 Main Street 47901
Web page: www.gklink.com/bcb

Open Shop
(765) 742-6618
E-mail: bcb@wcic.org

Collection: General stock of hardcover and paperback.
# of Vols: 40,000
Specialties: Vintage paperbacks.
Hours: Mon-Sat 10-6.
Services: Appraisals, search service, catalog, accepts want lists.
Travel: Exit 26 off I-65. Proceed west on Rte 26 which becomes South St.
                  Continue on South, then right on Main.

Credit Cards:	Yes
Owner:	Nancy Mancing
Year Estab:	1989
Comments:	This shop has a lot going for it. In addition to the hardcover items in good condition located on the first floor, there's a second floor with four rooms of books, including a kitchen filled with cookbooks and a separate area for women's studies. We've seen many shops claiming to have vintage paperbacks and usually find only a shelf or two. However, this shop's claim to being a specialist in the field is well deserved as the collection, off limits to the casual browser at the time of our visit, really does represent some of the scarcest vintage paperbacks we've seen. A shop well worth visiting.

Earl Plaza Books   **Open Shop**
402 North Earl Avenue 47904   (765) 448-1305

Collection:	General stock of mostly used paperback and hardcover.
# of Vols:	150,000
Hours:	Mon-Sat 9-7.
Travel:	From intersection of Rtes 52 & 26, proceed west on Rte 26 one block, then right on Earl Ave. Shop is in shopping center.
Credit Cards:	Yes
Owner:	James Atkins
Year Estab:	1977

Leonard's Antiques and Books   **Open Shop**
1324 North 14th Street 47904   (765) 742-8668
Web page: www.leonards.lafayette.in.us   E-mail: leonards@carlnet.org

Collection:	Specialty books and ephemera.
# of Vols:	3,000
Specialties:	Life sciences; technology; American history; travel; fine arts.
Hours:	Mon-Fri 1-7. Sat 10-5.
Services:	Appraisals, search service, accepts want lists, mail order, bookbinding
Travel:	Rte 25 exit off I-65. Proceed south on Rte 25, then right on Greenbush then a quick left on 14th.
Credit Cards:	Yes
Owner:	Eric Haley
Year Estab:	1972

Shuman's Antiques & Books   **Open Shop**
828 Main Street 47901   (765) 420-7479

Collection:	General stock of mostly hardcover.
# of Vols:	2,000
Hours:	Mon-Sat 10-5.
Services:	Accepts want lists, mail order.
Travel:	Rte 26 exit off I-65. Proceed west on Rte 26, then north on 9th St and west on Main.
Credit Cards:	Yes

Owner: John & Sharon Shuman
Year Estab: 1996

Lebanon
(Map 6, page 100)

Cedars of Lebanon Antiques   **Antique Mall**
126 West Washington Street 46052   (765) 827-809

Hours: Mon-Sat 10-5. Sun 12-5.
Travel: Any Lebanon exit off I-65. Follow signs to downtown. Shop is on the
                square.

Idlewood Rare Books   **By Appointment**
6420 West 50 South 46052   (765) 483-0072
                                                   Fax: (765) 483-9772

Collection: Specialty
Specialties: Literary first editions; children's; illustrated; private press; Indiana
                authors and history.
Services: Appraisals, catalog.
Credit Cards: No
Owner: Thomas Budd
Year Estab: 1995

Meridian Street Books   **Open Shop**
126 South Meridian Street 46052   (765) 482-4882

Collection: General stock of mostly hardcover and ephemera.
# of Vols: 19,000
Specialties: Religion; Indiana; military.
Hours: Mon-Sat 9:30-5.
Services: Appraisals, search service, accepts want lists, mail order.
Travel: Exit 139 off I-65. Proceed east on Rte 32. Right at first light, then first
                left on Meridian.
Credit Cards: Yes
Owner: Jon D. & Susan Mason
Year Estab: 1995
Comments: A modest sized shop with an interesting selection of hardcover books
                and some paperbacks. Most of the books we saw were in good condi-
                tion. Several collectibles were on hand. The dealers previously owned
                Mason's Rare & Used Books in Wabash, IN and Chambersburg, PA.

Leo
(Map 6, page 100)

Crunk & Wagley's   **Open Shop**
At Olde Churche Shoppes, Main St at the River   Shop: (219) 627-8627
Mailing address: PO Box 355 Woodburn IN 46797   Home: (219) 632-4765

Collection: General stock of mostly hardcover.
Hours: Mon-Sat 10-5.
# of Vols: 3,000

Travel:	Dupont Rd exit off I-69. Proceed east on Dupont which becomes Rte 1. Continue on Rte 1 into Leo. One block after the 4-way stop, turn right on Main St. Shop is one block ahead.
Credit Cards:	Yes
Owner:	Doreen Crunk
Year Estab:	1995

Madision
(Map 6, page 100)

Mighty Fine Books   **Antique Mall**
At Jefferson Street Antique Mall, 200 Jefferson Street   Mall: (812) 265-6464
Mailing address: 1231 S. Adams Versailles 47042   Home: (812) 689-3782
                                                        E-mail: geberhar@seidata.com

Collection:	General stock and ephemera.
Specialties:	Non fiction; local history; World War II, signed; travel.
# of Vols:	2,000+
Hours:	Tue-Sat 10-6. Sun 12-5.
Travel:	In downtown, two blocks south of intersection of Rtes 421 & 56.
Services:	Search service, mail order.
Owner:	Galen Eberhart
Year Estab:	1992

Marion
(Map 6, page 100)

Chapter III Used Bookstore   **Open Shop**
122-124 East 5th Street 46953   (765) 664-1071

Collection:	General stock of hardcover and paperback.
# of Vols:	20,000
Hours:	Mon-Sat 10-5:30.
Services:	Search service, accepts want lists, mail order.
Travel:	Marion exit off I-69. Proceed west on Rte 18, then left on Branson and right on 5th St.
Credit Cards:	Yes
Owner:	Carolyn A. Sager
Year Estab:	1978
Comments:	A nice sized collection of mixed vintage books in mixed condition. During our visit we noted strong cookbook and mystery sections, lots of technical titles and some collectibles and magazines. The books were inexpensively priced with a reasonable chance that there might be a hidden gem among the more ordinary items.

The Paperback Peddler   **Open Shop**
4711 South Adams Street 46953   (765) 677-1644

Collection:	General stock of mostly paperback.
# of Vols:	40,000

Hours:	Mon-Sat 10-6. Sun 12-5.
Travel:	Exit 59 off I-69. Proceed west on Rte 35 north, then north on Rte 15. Shop is about two miles ahead on right.
Owner:	Janie Hayde
Year Estab:	1997
Comments:	On the way to this shop I asked my partner why we were visiting a store whose name clearly indicated the type of stock we were likely to find there. The answer I received was that we had been assured that the store had a respectable number of hardcover volumes on hand. What we found when we arrived was an overwhelmingly paperback shop. Far be it from me to question the respectability of the hardcover volumes (perhaps 2,000-3,000) that were scattered around the outer edges of the shop (mostly mystery, science fiction, etc.). I guess it all depends on how much time you have and how you're willing to spend it while on the road.

Martinsville
(Map 6, page 100)

Gateway Collectibles   **Open Shop**
96 East Morgan 46151   (765) 342-8983

Collection:	General stock.
# of Vols:	4,000+
Specialties:	Indiana
Hours:	Tue-Sat 9-5.
Travel:	On the northeast corner of the square.
Year Estab:	1989

Merrillville
(Map 6, page 100)

Remarkable Book Shop   **Open Shop**
7227 Taft Street 46410   (219) 738-2084

Collection:	General stock of mostly paperback.
# of Vols:	20,000
Hours:	Mon, Tue, Wed 10-5:30. Thu & Fri 10-6. Sat 10-4.

Mishawaka
(Map 6, page 100)

Bartholomew Books   **Open Shop**
302 West 3rd Street 46544   (219) 257-8137

Collection:	General stock of paperback and hardcover.
# of Vols:	15,000
Hours:	Mon-Sat 10-4.
Travel:	In downtown, two blocks west of Main St.
Credit Cards:	Yes
Year Estab:	1994
Comments:	Stock is approximately 60% paperback.

Muncie
(Map 6, page 100)

Book Center   **Open Shop**
2901 North Broadway 47303   (765) 288-4065

Collection:	General stock of mostly paperback and some hardcover.
# of Vols:	150,000+
Hours:	Mon-Sat 9-5. Sun 12-5.
Travel:	Rte 332 (McGalliard Rd) exit off I-69. Proceed east on McGalliard, then right on Broadway.
Credit Cards:	No
Owner:	Larry Swhier
Year Estab:	1974
Comments:	This shop is large, in fact, very large, with between 80%-90% of the stock consisting of paperbacks and a few thousand hardcover volumes scattered throughout the shop in various categories. With the exception of some old Muncie city directories and two glass cases at the front of the shop displaying some collectible items, most of the hardcover stock fell into the newer, more popular category.

White Rabbit Used Books   **Open Shop**
1604 University 47303   (765) 282-8978

Collection:	General stock of paperback and hardcover and ephemera.
# of Vols:	5,000-8,000
Specialties:	Science fiction; horror; occult; new age.
Hours:	Mon-Sat 11-8. Sun 12-6.
Services:	Appraisals, accepts want lists, mail order.
Travel:	From downtown, proceed west on Rte 32. Left at third light on Jackson St, then right on Dill St. Shop is at corner of Dill and University.
Credit Cards:	No
Owner:	Derek Edwards
Year Estab:	1990
Comments:	Stock is evenly divided between paperback and hardcover.

Nappanee
(Map 6, page 100)

The Booksellers Shoppe   **Open Shop**
162½ East Market Street 46550   (219) 875-8330

Collection:	General stock of mostly used hardcover.
# of Vols:	7,500
Specialties:	Religion; science fiction; politics (conservative).
Hours:	Mon & Thu 10-5. Tue, Wed, Fri 9:30-5. Sat 9-1.
Travel:	In downtown, just east of Rte 19. Market St is Rte 6.
Credit Cards:	No
Owner:	Medford Caudill
Year Estab:	1996

Comments: A relatively small shop with books in mixed condition. If you know
what you're looking for you might want to call ahead to see if the book
is in stock as browsing should not require a lengthy visit.

Nashville
(Map 6, page 100)

HIS Used Christian Book Shop   **Open Shop**
66 East Main Street, Box 365 47448   (812) 988-4873

Collection: Specialty. Mostly used and some new.
# of Vols: 10,000
Specialties: Religion (Christian).
Hours: Mon-Sat 10-5. Sun 12:30-5.
Services: Accepts up to three or four specific wants.
Travel: Rte 46 (Columbus) exit off I-65. Proceed west on Rte 46 for 16 miles to
Nashville. Turn right at light at edge of village and continue for three
blocks to the courthouse, then turn right.
Credit Cards: Yes
Owner: Dan Sparks & Connie Steininger
Year Estab: 1978

New Castle
(Map 6, page 100)

Book Nook & Unique Gift Shop   **Open Shop**
1327 South 18th Street 47362   (765) 521-2188

Collection: General stock of mostly paperback.
# of Vols: 30,000
Hours: Mon-Fri 9-6. Sat 9-4.

Jackie's Book Store   **Open Shop**
208 South 14th Street 47362   (765) 529-2808

Collection: General stock of mostly paperback and comics.
# of Vols: 10,000
Hours: Mon-Sat 10-6. Sun 1-5.

New Harmony
(Map 6, page 100)

Golden Raintree Books   **Open Shop**
507 Main Street   (812) 682-3725
Mailing address: PO Box 629 New Harmony IN 47631   E-mail: rainbooks@aol.com

Collection: General stock of mostly used hardcover.
# of Vols: 10,000
Specialties: Regional; utopian societies.
Hours: Tue-Sat 10-5.
Services: Search service, accepts want lists, mail order.

Travel:	Rte 1 (Grayville) exit off I-64. Proceed south on Rte 1 for six miles to Crossville, then continue east on Rte 14 for five miles. After crossing the toll bridge, shop is two doors from the light at intersection of Rtes 66 & 69 (Main St).
Credit Cards:	Yes
Owner:	Robert J. Brooks
Year Estab:	1987
Comments:	An oasis in an area otherwise barren of "quality" used books. This shop has a little bit of everything: new books, some remainders, a few paperbacks and a most respectable collection of hardcover volumes representing several periods and including some antiquarian and collectible items. Worth a visit.

Mudpies   **Open Shop**
509 Main Street   (812) 682-3723
Mailing address: PO Box 629 New Harmony IN 47631

Collection:	General stock of mostly new and some used books.
# of Vols:	2,000
Hours:	Tue-Sat 10-5.
Travel:	See Golden Raintree Books above.
Credit Cards:	Yes
Owner:	Arlene E. Porter
Year Estab:	1991

P.R. Schwan, Bookseller   **By Appointment**
802 East Granary 47631   (812) 682-3022
E-mail: prschwan@interloc.com

Collection:	General stock.
# of Vols:	3,500
Specialties:	Cookbooks; nautical; aviation.
Services:	Search service.
Credit Cards:	No
Owner:	Carol Schwan
Year Estab:	1988
Comments:	Also displays at Treasure Troves Antique Mall. See below.

Treasure Trove Antique Mall   **Antique Mall**
414 Main Street   (812) 682-4112

Hours:	Mon-Sat 10-5. Sun 12-5. Closes one hour earlier in winter.
Travel:	Poseyville exit off I-64. Follow signs to downtown.

Newburgh
(Map 6, page 100)

Book Nook   **Open Shop**
109 State Street 47630   (812) 858-1707

Collection:	General stock paperback and hardcover.

# of Vols:	15,000
Hours:	Tue-Sat 10-5. Sun 1-5.
Year Estab:	1996
Comments:	Stock is approximately 70% paperback.

Noblesville
(Map 6, page 100)

The Gentlemen Soldier   **Open Shop**
876 Logan Street 46060   (317) 776-8790
                                      E-mail: dwha1863@aol.com

Collection:	Specialty
Specialties:	Antiquarian; private press, first editions; illustrated; fine bindings.
Hours:	Tue-Sat 10-5:30. Sun 1-5.
Services:	Appraisals, search service, accepts want lists, mail order.
Travel:	In downtown, opposite the courthouse, on north side of square.
Credit Cards:	Yes
Owner:	Duane W.H. Arnold
Year Estab:	1998
Comments:	Also sells pre-World War I military collectibles.

Noblesville Antique Mall   **Antique Mall**
20 North 9th Street   (317) 773-5095

Hours:	Mon-Sat 9-6. Sun 12-6.

North Judson
(Map 6, page 100)

Wik's Books & Treasures   **Open Shop**
201 Lane Street 46366   (219) 896-3273

Collection:	General stock of paperback and hardcover.
Hours:	Mon-Sat 10-6. Best to call ahead.
Travel:	One block north of intersection of Rtes 10 & 39.
Comments:	Stock is approximately 75% paperback.

North Manchester
(Map 6, page 100)

Mostly Books   **By Appointment**
PO Box 43 North Manchester IN 46962   (219) 982-1800

Comments:	Shortly before we embarked on our Midwest tour we contacted this shop to confirm travel directions. When we arrived in town, however, we found a sign on the window indicating that the shop was in the process of moving. Several unanswered phone messages later, we are unable to provide our readers with more updated information on the dealer's current status or collection.

North Vernon
(Map 6, page 100)

The Book Nook
604 South State Street 47265

Open Shop
(812) 346-5505
Fax: (812) 346-7226

Collection: General stock of mostly paperback.
Hours: Mon-Sat 10-10. Sun 12-10.

Pendleton
(Map 6, page 100)

Pendleton Antique Mall
123 West State Street 46064

Antique Mall
(765) 778-2303

Hours: Mon-Sat 10-5. Sun 1-5.
Travel: Either Pendleton exit off I-69. Follow signs to downtown.

Peru
(Map 6, page 100)

Mr. Books!
At Peru Antique Mall, 21 Main Street 46970

Antique Mall
(765) 473-8179

Collection: General stock of hardcover and paperback.
# of Vols: 10,000
Hours: Mon-Sat, except closed Wed, 10-5. Sun 1-5.
Services: Search service, accepts want lists, mail order.
Travel: Located in downtown, across from the Miami County Courthouse.
Credit Cards: No
Owner: F. I. Chagnon
Year Estab: 1990
Comments: A larger display than typically found in an antique mall, the shelves here contained a mix of mostly vintage titles and some collectibles. With the exception of the children's section, most subjects were not represented in any great depth. The shop also displayed a few collectible comics and magazines. If you or your companion enjoy visiting antique malls, you might find this shop of interest.

Portland
(Map 6, page 100)

The Corner Shop
116 East Water Street 47371

Open Shop
(219) 726-4090

Collection: General stock of hardcover and paperback.
# of Vols: 20,000+
Specialties: Mystery; adventure.
Hours: Mon-Fri 8-5. Sat 8-12.
Services: Search service, accepts want lists, mail order.
Travel: On Rte 26, 1/2 block east of intersection with Rte 27 at south end of business district.

Credit Cards:	No
Owner:	Margaret Cheeseman
Year Estab:	1981
Comments:	In our travels, we've seen books displayed in a variety of settings; this shop shares space with a plumbing supply outlet. Most of the books we saw (both hardcover and paperback) were older reading copies. We did spot several collectibles and the shop also carries some ephemera. If you're an inveterate browser, don't miss the books in the second room (which is not heated in the winter).

Richmond
(Map 6, page 100)

Emmenegger Books **By Appointment**
2023 Boston Pike 47374 (765) 935-6293

Collection:	General stock and ephemera.
# of Vols:	10,000
Services:	Accepts want lists, mail order.
Credit Cards:	No
Owner:	Marian & Gene Emmenegger
Year Estab:	1985

Paperback-Comic Paradise **Open Shop**
750 North 10th Street 47374 (765) 962-5875

Collection:	General stock of mostly paperback.
# of Vols:	50,000
Hours:	Mon-Sat 10-6.

Rossville
(Map 6, page 100)

Good News Books **Open Shop**
22 North Plank Street (765) 379-3938
Mailing address: PO Box 527 Rossville IN 46065

Collection:	General stock of mostly hardcover.
# of Vols:	10,000+
Specialties:	Children's series; turn of the century romance; religion; Indiana history and authors.
Hours:	Mon-Sat 10-4.
Services:	Search service, accepts want lists, mail order.
Travel:	Rte 26 to Rossville, then north on Rte 421.
Credit Cards:	No
Owner:	Ken & Jan Jones
Year Estab:	1975
Comments:	Although the shop clearly identifies itself on the outside sign and on the business card as a "Christian" book shop, visitors will find the shop also offers books in many other categories. The children's section is

strong and there are plenty of items that one would find in any general book shop. Unfortunately, too many of the books in the areas not identified as specialties were in only fair condition. Also, we noted items that were priced much higher than we felt they should be considering their condition. Translation: the items might have been worth the priced asked had they been in pristine condition.

Scottsburg
(Map 6, page 100)

B & W Booksellers **Open Shop**
503 East McClain Avenue 47170 (812) 752-6858

Collection:	General stock of mostly paperback.
# of Vols:	100,000+
Hours:	Mon-Sat 9-5. Sun 11-4.
Travel:	Scottsburg exit off I-65. Proceed east on Rte 56 (McClain). Shop is on east side of town.
Credit Cards:	No
Owner:	Bill Lewis
Year Estab:	1987
Comments:	I really don't always want to be correct when I predict that a shop with a large number of volumes (100,000 in this case) is more likely to be overwhelmingly paperback. Unfortunately, however, I am more often right than not and was again in the case of this shop. Yes, there were some hardcover books. Indeed, if one walked around the shop's two rooms, one could find hardcover books in both, shelved horizontally rather than in the more traditional vertical manner. Ninety nine percent of what we saw were reading copies of recent vintage, heavy in fiction. Need we say more.

South Bend
(Map 6, page 100)

Antique Avenue Mall **Antique Mall**
52345 US 31 North (Rte 933) 46637 (219) 272-2558

Hours:	Mon-Sat 10-6. Sun 11-6.
Travel:	Exit 77 off I-80/I-90 Proceed north on Rte 31. Shop is two miles ahead.

The Book Inn Bed & Breakfast **Open Shop**
508 West Washington Street 46601 (219) 288-1990

Collection:	General stock of hardcover and paperback.
# of Vols:	10,000
Hours:	Daily 11-7 but a call ahead is advised.
Travel:	Exit 77 off I-80/I-90 Proceed south on Rte 31/33, then west on Washington.
Credit Cards:	Yes
Owner:	Peggy Livingston

(South Bend)

Year Estab:	1989
Comments:	If you like B & Bs, you'll love the Book Inn, located in an elegantly restored 19th century residence. The rooms, named after well known writers of the gentler gender, are tastefully decorated in a book lover's mode. Of course, you don't have to stay the night to see the books, but if you do, the owner will encourage you to take some of the books to your room so you can decide at a more leisurely pace whether you want to take them home with you. The books, located throughout the house but mostly in the basement, are a mix of general fiction and period non fiction. While a collection this size does not have great depth, we did spot some interesting titles and the atmosphere is such that you should enjoy your visit.

The Busy Hermit   **Antique Mall**
At Unique Antique Mall, 50981 US 33 North   Mall: (219) 271-1799
Mailing address: 6234 Brush Lake Rd Eau Claire MI 49111   Home: (616) 782-6728

Collection:	General stock.
# of Vols:	1,500
Hours:	Daily 10-5.
Services:	Accepts want lists, mail order.
Travel:	Exit 77 off I-80/I-90 Proceed north on Rte 31/33 for about three miles.
Credit Cards:	Yes
Owner:	Mary Ann Steimle
Year Estab:	1982
Comments:	Additional stock is available on a by appointment basis at the owner's home in Eau Claire, MI.

Erasmus Books   **Open Shop**
1027 East Wayne Street 46617   (219) 232-8444

Collection:	General stock of mostly hardcover.
# of Vols:	30,000
Hours:	Tue-Sun 12-6.
Services:	Appraisals, search service, accepts want lists, mail order.
Travel:	Notre Dame exit off I-80/I-90. Proceed south on Rte 31/33 to downtown. At library, turn east on Western Ave and proceed across river to third light, then right on Eddy St and right on Wayne. Shop is just ahead.
Credit Cards:	No
Owner:	Philip Schatz & William Storey
Year Estab:	1980
Comments:	Carefully selected for their good condition, most of the volumes in this bi-level shop were of a scholarly nature, aimed, we assume, at the local university community. Even the quality of the fiction collection was above average. At the time of our visit, the shop's paperbacks and hardcover items a bit closer to the popular culture vein were located in the basement.

The Griffon   **Open Shop**
121 West Colfax Street 46601   (219) 287-5533
                                                            E-mail: griffonb@aol.com

Collection:	Specialty new and used, hardcover and paperback.
# of Vols:	10,000 (used)
Specialties:	Science fiction; fantasy; mystery; literature (in original language and in translation); history; philosophy; religion.
Hours:	Mon-Thu 10-5:30. Fri & Sat 10-7.
Services:	Appraisals, accepts want lists, mail order.
Travel:	Proceeding south on Rte 31, turn east on Colfax.
Credit Cards:	Yes
Owner:	Sarah Bird & Ken Peczkowski
Year Estab:	1976
Comments:	Stock is approximately 50% hardcover.

Jefferson Street Book Sellers   **Open Shop**
501 West Jefferson Boulevard 46601 (See Comments)   (219) 234-3860
                                                          E-mail: jeffstbks@aol.com

Collection:	General stock.
# of Vols:	20,000+
Specialties:	Aviation
Hours:	Tue, Wed, Thu 11-1. Sat & Sun 10-5. Other times by appointment.
Services:	Search service, accepts want lists, mail order.
Credit Cards:	No
Owner:	Patrick Doyle
Year Estab:	1997
Comments:	At press time, the owner was in the process of closing down his current location and looking for new space in South Bend. Travelers are advised to call the above number for the latest information.

Pandora's Books   **Open Shop**
808 Howard Street 46617   (219) 233-2342

Collection:	General stock of mostly paperback.
Hours:	Mon-Sat 10-5. Sun 9-3.

Terre Haute
(Map 6, page 100)

Bob The Bookseller   **Open Shop**
1634 North 3rd Street 47804   (812) 232-0925
                                                        E-mail: bucfan@earthlink.net

Collection:	General stock of paperback and hardback.
# of Vols:	10,000
Hours:	Tue-Thu 10-6. Fri 12-8. Sat 12-5.
Services:	Accepts want lists, mail order.
Travel:	On Rte 41, three miles north of I-70.
Credit Cards:	Yes

Owner:	Bob Orlandini
Year Estab:	1995
Comments:	Stock is approximately 70% paperback.

New Concept Book Store   **Open Shop**
3726 South US Highway 41 47802   (812) 232-2363

Collection:	General stock mostly used paperback.
# of Vols:	10,000
Hours:	Mon-Sat 10-8. Sun 12:30-5.

Wabash River Books   **Open Shop**
2612 South 7th Street 47807   (812) 234-7999
E-mail: matreshka@aol.com

Collection:	General stock.
# of Vols:	12,000
Specialties:	Emphasis on nonfiction; biography; history.
Hours:	Tue-Sat 12-6. Sun (winter only): 12-4 but best to call ahead.
Services:	Search service, accepts want lists, mail order.
Travel:	Rte 41 exit off I-70. Proceed north on Rte 41 to first light then right on Margaret Ave and left on 7th St. Shop is two blocks ahead.
Credit Cards:	Yes
Owner:	Tim Kelley
Year Estab:	1996
Comments:	Had we travelled to Terre Haute a week or two later than we actually did, we would have been able to visit this shop at its current location. All was not lost, however, as we did get to meet the owner and view his collection at his previous location. What we saw was a nice selection of primarily hardcover books in generally good condition with an emphasis on non fiction but also a respectable fiction collection. The books were well chosen (the owner, a former scout, knows his books) and the prices were most reasonable. We assume you'll find more of the same at the new location.

Valparaiso
(Map 6, page 100)

Wallace M. Wojtkowski, Bookseller   **By Appointment**
2005 Clover Lane 46385   (219) 464-9061

Collection:	General stock.
# of Vols:	5,000
Specialties:	Modern first editions.
Services:	Accepts want lists, mail order.
Credit Cards:	No
Year Estab:	1976

Wabash
(Map 6, page 100)

Reading Room Books
264 South Wabash Street 46992

Open Shop
(219) 563-6421
(800) 563-6422
E-mail: spearltd@interloc.com

Collection:	General stock of hardcover and paperback.
# of Vols:	50,000+
Hours:	Tue-Sat 9-5.
Services:	Accepts want lists, search service.
Travel:	In downtown, on Rtes 15 & 13.
Credit Cards:	Yes
Year Estab:	1973
Comments:	At the time of our visit, the shop had recently changed hands and the new owner was in the process of fixing up the store and weeding and reorganizing the collection. What we saw was a large collection of mostly hardcover books. The bad news is that many of the books were in only fair condition. The good news was that hidden on some of the shelves were a goodly share of collectible items that, had they been in much better condition, would have sold for a much higher price. It is quite possible that by the time you read this, the shop may have changed its appearance and/or some scouts may have made off with any hidden treasures before your arrival.

Wanatah
(Map 6, page 100)

The Bookworm
305B East Railroad 46390

Open Shop
(219) 733-2119

Collection:	General stock.
# of Vols:	4,000
Hours:	Mon-Fri 12-3. Sat 10-5.
Travel:	From intersection of Rtes 421 and 30, proceed west on Rte 30 to Main St, then left at railroad. Shop is three blocks ahead.
Credit Cards:	No
Owner:	Laurie Koselke
Year Estab:	1976

West Lafayette
(Map 6, page 100)

Midnight Bookman
237 Schilling 47906

By Appointment
(765) 743-1790
E-mail: posey2@gte.net

Collection:	General stock of hardcover and paperback and some ephemera.

# of Vols:	12,000
Specialties:	Books on books; bibliography; printing; private press; Bruce Rogers.
Services:	Catalog, search service.
Credit Cards:	No
Owner:	Edwin D. Posey
Year Estab:	1968

Mail Order Dealers

Autonomy House Publications   (219) 583-6465
417 North Main Street Monticello 47960

Collection:	Specialty
# of Vols:	2,000
Specialties:	Antique stove manufacturer's catalogs and cookbooks (pre 1935).
Credit Cards:	No
Owner:	Clifford Boram
Year Estab:	1982

Between The Lines   (812) 332-4440
PO Box 1818 Bloomington 47402   E-mail: betweenl@bluemarble.net

Collection:	General stock of mostly hardcover.
# of Vols:	50,000
Specialties:	Scholarly; humanities; university press.
Services:	Search service, accepts want lists.
Credit Cards:	Yes
Owner:	Danna D'Esopo Jackson
Year Estab:	1981

Campfire Books   (812) 425-8549
6016 Sarbeth Evansville 47712   Fax: (812) 425-3776

Collection:	Specialty
# of Vols:	2,500
Specialties:	Hunting; fishing; guns; Alaska.
Services:	Search service, catalog, accepts want lists.
Credit Cards:	Yes
Owner:	Jerry Madden
Year Estab:	1980

Corner Cupboard Cookbooks   (317) 872-4319
PO Box 171 Zionsville 46077

Collection:	Specialty new and used.
# of Vols:	2,000
Specialties:	Cookbooks

Services:	Catalog, accepts want lists.
Credit Cards:	Yes
Owner:	Helen Jump
Year Estab:	1976
Comments:	Stock is approximately 35% used.

J.E. Frazier (812) 339-4970
4180 North Baugh Road Bloomington 47408

Collection:	General stock.
# of Vols:	5,000
Services:	Search service, accepts want lists.
Credit Cards:	No
Owner:	James E. Frazier
Year Estab:	1983

JW Books (317) 773-7037
2008 Walnut Way Noblesville 46060   E-mail: jwielinski@ameritech.net

Collection:	Specialty
# of Vols:	3,000
Specialties:	Children's
Credit Cards:	No
Owner:	John Wielinski
Year Estab:	1994
Comments:	Also displays at Circle City Books in Indianapolis.

Lost N' Found Books Tel & Fax: (317) 297-2760
3214 Columbine Court Indianapolis 46224   E-mail: lostnfnd@interloc.com

Collection:	Specialty
Specialties:	Children's illustrated.
Services:	Search service, accepts want lists.
Credit Cards:	No
Owner:	Linda Lengerich
Year Estab:	1994

Eleanor Pasotti
5939 Evanston Avenue Indianapolis 46220

Collection:	General stock.
# of Vols:	3,000
Specialties:	Children's
Year Estab:	1979

Mark Razor (812) 985-5550
10441 Highway 66 Wadesville 47638   E-mail: mrazor.ucs@smtp.us.edu

Collection:	General stock.
# of Vols:	3,000+
Services:	Accepts want lists.
Credit Cards:	No
Year Estab:	1994

Flo Silver Books   Tel & Fax: (317) 255-5118
8442 Oakwood Court North Indianapolis 46260   E-mail: Flosilver@aol.com

Collection:	Specialty
# of Vols:	2,000
Specialties:	Latin America; pre-Columbian art; archaeology; early travel; Indians; natural history of Mexico, South and Central America.
Services:	Catalog
Credit Cards:	No
Year Estab:	1987

Verl's Books   (317) 243-0557
611 Prairie Depot Indianapolis 46241   E-mail: VerlWise@aol.com
                              Web page: http://members.aol.com/VerlWise/index.html

Collection:	Specialty
# of Vols:	600
Specialties:	Booth Tarkington; Kurt Vonnegut.
Services:	Accepts want lists.
Credit Cards:	No
Owner:	Verl Wisehart
Year Estab:	1994

Yesterday's Books   (765) 966-3056
3868 Turner Road Richmond 47374   E-mail: yestrBooks@worldnet.att.net

Collection:	General stock.
# of Vols:	12,000
Services:	Accepts want lists.
Credit Cards:	No
Owner:	Bob & Becky Scott
Year Estab:	1981
Comments:	Also display at Noblesville Antique Mall in Noblesville.

Ex Libris
Frederick Eugene Hartnell

IOWA

Alphabetical Listing By Dealer

A & M Booksellers	142	Iowa Book & Supply Co.	147
Anni's Antiques & Books	150	Jim's Books	142
Antique America	141	Kanesville Kollectibles	140
Karl M. Armens - Books	145	The Legacy Company	150
Avatar Books	141	The Library	151
Banowetz Antique Mall	148	Mike Maddigan	139
Big Table Books	137	Majestic Lion Antique Center	143
The Bookery	145	Murphy-Brookfield Books	147
Books N Stuff	149	Murray's Antiques	143
Books on the Sun Porch	149	Natural History Books	151
Bought Again Books	138	Northside Book Market	147
Broken Kettle Books	144	Gil O'Gara Antiquarian	151
C & D Woods Books	140	Pella Books	151
Camp Pope Bookshop	146	Gerald Pettinger	152
Chessco	150	John Quinn, Bookseller	152
Counterpoint Used Books	146	Read Books	139
Ted Danielson	150	Second Storey Bookshop	137
D.R. Doerres Rendezvous Trader	150	Slightly Read	145
Excellence in Books	148	Source Book Store	141
Fireside Books	137	Dennis Sutterer Books	143
Fostoria Trading Post	145	Tall Ships Books	152
Gateways Books	139	Timber City Books	152
Gilgen's Consignment Furnishings	139	Tri-State Indep.Blind Soc. Bookstore	144
Good Question	150	Upstart Crow Books	143
Half Price Books	140	The Way Station	140
Handled With Care	138	Well Read Books	144
Haunted Bookshop On The Creek	146	Windy Hill Books	137
Hawk Hollow	138	Yesterday's Treasures	148

Alphabetical Listing By Location

Location	Dealer	Page
Ames	Big Table Books	137
	Fireside Books	137
	Second Storey Bookshop	137
	Windy Hill Books	137
Bellevue	Hawk Hollow	138
Burlington	Handled With Care	138
Cedar Falls	Bought Again Books	138
	Ted Danielson	150
	Gateways Books	139
	Gilgen's Consignment Furnishings	139
	John Quinn, Bookseller	152
Cedar Rapids	Mike Maddigan	139
	Read Books	139
	Tall Ships Books	152
Clive	Half Price Books, Records, Magazines	140
Colesburg	Anni's Antiques & Books	150
Council Bluffs	C & D Woods Books	140
	Kanesville Kollectibles	140
	The Way Station	140
Davenport	Antique America	141
	Avatar Books	141
	Chessco	150
	Source Book Store	141
Des Moines	A & M Booksellers	142
	Jim's Books	142
	The Library	151
	Majestic Lion Antique Center	143
	Murray's Antiques	143
	Gil O'Gara Antiquarian	151
	Dennis Sutterer Books	143
	Upstart Crow Books	143
	Well Read Books	144
Dubuque	Tri-State Independent Blind Society Used Bookstore	144
Fairfield	Broken Kettle Books	144
Fostoria	Fostoria Trading Post	145
Grinnell	Slightly Read	145
Iowa City	Karl M. Armens - Books	145
	The Bookery	145
	Camp Pope Bookshop	146
	Counterpoint Used Books	146
	Haunted Bookshop On The Creek	146
	Iowa Book & Supply Co.	147
	The Legacy Company	150

Iowa City	Murphy-Brookfield Books	147
	Natural History Books	151
	Northside Book Market	147
Lamoni	Yesterday's Treasures	148
Maquoketa	Banowetz Antique Mall	148
	Timber City Books	152
Marion	Excellence in Books	148
Osceola	Books N Stuff	149
Pella	Pella Books	151
Russell	Gerald Pettinger	152
Sioux City	Books on the Sun Porch	149
Vinton	Good Question	150
Wilton	D.R. Doerres Rendezvous Trader	150

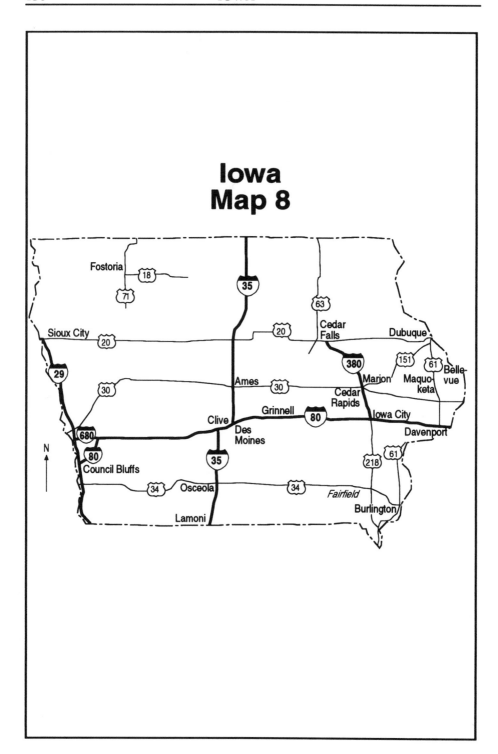

Ames
(Map 8, page 136)

Big Table Books   **Open Shop**
330 Main Street 50010   (515) 232-8976

Collection: General stock new and used paperback and hardcover.
# of Vols: 1,000-2,000 (used)
Hours: Mon 9-7. Tue-Fri 9-6. Sat 9-7. Sun 11-4.
Comments: Used stock is approximately 70% paperback.

Fireside Books   **Open Shop**
405 Kellogg Avenue 50010   (515) 232-6609

Collection: General stock of paperback and hardcover.
# of Vols: 22,000
Hours: Mon-Fri 10-8. Sat 10-6.
Travel: 13th St exit off I-35. Proceed west on 13th St, then south (left) on Duff,
                  right (just before railroad tracks) on Main and right on Kellogg.
Credit Cards: Yes
Year Estab: 1997
Owners: Christopher & Cathy Nelson
Comments: As evidence of the volatility of the used book business, not long after
                  we visited this shop, and just two weeks before going to press, we learned
                  that the shop's original owner had sold the business, taking with her a
                  portion of the stock we had viewed, and that the new owners had changed
                  the store name. Regrettably, we could not return to Ames to give you an
                  update on the "new" store, which, we were advised, would have a stock
                  that was approximately 70% paperback.

Second Storey Bookshop   **By Appointment**
915 Gaskill Drive 50014   (515) 296-2615

Collection: Specialty
# of Vols: 5,000
Specialties: Modern literature (western novels and Americana); poetry.
Services: Appraisals, accepts want lists, mail order.
Credit Cards: No
Owner: Henry A. Campbell
Year Estab: 1991

Windy Hill Books   **By Appointment**
2439 Ridgetop Circle   50014   (800) 522-8385
Web page: www.abebooks.com/home/windyhillbooks

Collection: Specialty
# of vols: 8,000
Specialties: Children's
Services: Occasional catalog.
Credit Cards: Yes
Owner: Dana Richardson
Year Estab: 1993

Bellevue
(Map 8, page 136)

Hawk Hollow   **Open Shop**
106 South Riverview Drive 52031   Tel & Fax: (319) 872-5467

Collection:	General stock of hardcover and paperback.
# of Vols:	4,000
Hours:	Daily 9-5.
Travel:	On Rte 52.
Credit Cards:	Yes
Owner:	C. Hawks
Year Estab:	1983

Burlington
(Map 8, page 136)

Handled With Care   **Open Shop**
419 Jefferson Street 52601   (319) 754-1121

Collection:	General stock of paperback and hardcover.
# of Vols:	12,000
Hours:	Mon-Sat 9:30-5.
Travel:	Central or Main St exit off Rte 34. Proceed to downtown.
Credit Cards:	Yes
Comments:	Stock is approximately 75% paperback.

Cedar Falls
(Map 8, page 136)

Bought Again Books   **Open Shop**
909 West 23rd Street 50613   (319) 266-7115
                                                            (888) 396-6354
                                                        Fax: (319) 268-2245
                                                  E-mail: bagain@interloc.com

Collection:	General stock of mostly used hardcover.
# of Vols:	20,000
Specialties:	Iowa
Hours:	Mon-Sat 10-5.
Services:	Search service.
Travel:	Westbound on Rte 218 (from Waterloo): Main St exit off Rte 218, then south on Main, west on 18th St, south on College and west on 23rd St. Shop is at northeast corner of University of Northern Iowa campus.
Credit Cards:	Yes
Owner:	Bob Neymeyer
Year Estab:	1991
Comments:	An unpretentious bi-level shop. The majority of the books were reading copies, plus several interesting sets, some fine bindings and, should anyone be interested, an entire wall filled with a legal library which, we were advised, could be acquired very very inexpensively.

Gateways Books **Open Shop**
109 East 2nd Street 50613 (319) 277-3973

Collection:	General stock of mostly used paperback.
# of Vols:	4,000+
Hours:	Mon, Tue Fri 10:30-5:30. Wed & Thu 10;30-7. Sat 9-4.

Gilgen's Consignment Furnishings **Open Shop**
115 West 16th Street 50613 (319) 266-5152

Collection:	General stock of hardcover and paperback.
# of Vols:	2,000+
Hours:	Mon-Fri 10-7. Sat 10-5.
Travel:	Between Main and Washington Street.
Comments:	Stock is evenly divided between hardcover and paperback.

Cedar Rapids
(Map 8, page 136)

Mike Maddigan **By Appointment**
1741 4th Avenue, SE (319) 362-3483
Mailing address: PO Box 824 Cedar Rapids IA 52406

Collection:	General stock.
# of Vols:	1,000
Specialties:	Wizard of Oz; Frank Baum; Midwest/Plains states; Americana.
Services:	Appraisals, search service, accepts want lists, mail order.
Credit Cards:	No
Year Estab:	1971

Read Books **Open Shop**
215 2nd Street SE 52401 (319) 363-2065

Collection:	General stock of hardcover and paperback.
# of Vols:	50,000-60,000
Hours:	Mon-Sat 10-7. Sun 12-5.
Travel:	From I-380 southbound: 1st St east exit. Left at bottom of ramp and proceed east on 1st St. Left at light on 1st Ave, then right on 2nd St. From I-380 northbound: 1st St west exit. At bottom of ramp, go through light, cross bridge and turn right on 1st St. Proceed east on 1st St as above.
Services:	Mail order.
Credit Cards:	No
Owner:	David Cochran
Year Estab:	1988
Comments:	Most of the books we saw during our visit (a portion of the stock was in storage) were in relatively good condition and were of a more recent vintage. The shop also carries lots of *Time/Life* series. If you live in Cedar Rapids and this is the only open shop you can buy used books from, the prices might not offend you. If, on the other hand, you were a regular visitor to used books shops, you would find that in most cases, prices were higher here than elsewhere.

Clive
(Map 8, page 136 & Map 9, page 142)

Half Price Books, Records, Magazines   **Open Shop**
8801 University Avenue, Ste. 25 50325   (515) 224-4429
Collection: General stock of new and used hardcover and paperback.
Hours: Mon-Sat 9-9. Sun 10-6.
Travel: 22nd St exit off I-235. Proceed north on 22nd St to University, then left
                 on University. Shop is located in a strip mall.

Council Bluffs
(Map 8, page 136)

C & D Woods Books   **By Appointment**
210 Meadow Lane 51503   (712) 322-0169
Web page: www.abebooks.com   E-mail: woodsbooks@worldnet.att.net
Collection: General stock.
# of Vols: 5,000
Services: Accepts want lists, mail order.
Credit Cards: Yes
Owner: Dorothy Woods
Year Estab: 1990

Kanesville Kollectibles   **Open Shop**
530 4th Street 51503   (712) 328-8731
Collection: General stock of paperback and some hardcover.
# of Vols: 15,000
Hours: Mon-Sat 10-5.
Travel: In Haymarket Square.
Credit Cards: Yes
Owner: Tim Behrens
Year Estab: 1978
Comments: Stock is approximately 70% paperback.

The Way Station   **Open Shop**
2800 West Broadway, Bay 6 51501   (712) 325-8226
Collection: General stock of new and used.
# of Vols: 12,000
Specialties: Science fiction; fantasy.
Hours: Tue-Thu 4:30-8. Fri 4:30-9. Sat 12-9. Sun 1-5.
Travel: 25th St exit off I-29. Proceed to Broadway, then left on Broadway.
Credit Cards: No
Year Estab: 1990
Comments: Stock is approximately 70% paperback.

Davenport
(Map 8, page 136)

Antique America   **Antique Mall**
702 West 76th Street 52806   (319) 386-3430

Hours: Mon-Sat 10-6. Sun 11-6.
Travel: Exit 295A off I-80. Proceed south on Rte 61 (Brady St South), then right
                  on 65th St and right on Business Park. Mall is about one mile ahead.

Avatar Books   **Open Shop**
2218 East 11th Street 52803   (319) 322-4159

Collection: General stock of hardcover and paperback.
# of Vols: 20,000
Hours: Mon-Sat 10:30-5.
Services: Appraisals, search service, accepts want lists.
Travel: Rte 61 exit off I-80. Proceed south on Rte 61 to Rte 67 (River Dr), then
                  east on Rte 67, left on Mound and right on 11th. Shop is 1½ blocks
                  ahead across from park.
Credit Cards: Yes
Owner: Phyllis & Richard Erickson
Year Estab: 1981
Comments: We visited the owners of this shop at their former location and were
                  impressed by the quality of their books, their taste in selecting stock and
                  the manner in which the books were displayed. These are features which
                  usually go along with any move. However, we would be delighted to
                  hear from any of our readers to determine how the new location stacks
                  up to the previous one.

Source Book Store   **Open Shop**
232 West 3rd Street 52801   (319) 324-8941

Collection: General stock, records and magazines.
# of Vols: 100,000-125,000
Specialties: Mississippi River; chiropractic.
Hours: Mon-Fri 9:30-5:30. Sat 9:30-5.
Travel: Rte 61 exit off I-80. Proceed south on Rte 61 which becomes Harrison St
                  in downtown Davenport, then left on 3rd St.
Credit Cards: Yes
Owner: Virginia S. Pekios
Year Estab: 1939
Comments: Regrettably, we did not have the time to stop in Davenport on our return
                  trip to Iowa to see if the following comments, based on our earlier visit,
                  were still valid.
                  A nice shop to visit if you like old books. The collection is large. As
                  a matter of fact, the collection is very large. While the books are
                  organized and the shelves are labeled, the labels could be a bit clearer.
                  The books are of mixed vintage and in mixed condition and almost
                  every subject area is covered. While there are several lighting fix-

tures in the shop's basement (as large an area as the first floor), if you're planning to stay down there a while, we suggest you bring a flashlight for additional illumination. If you're not turned off by the condition of some of the books or occasional organizational problems, and if you're patient enough, you may find some very interesting titles to add to your collection.

Des Moines
(Map 8, page 136 & Map 9, page 142)

A & M Booksellers   **Open Shop**
2716½ Ingersoll Avenue 50312   (515) 244-4944

Collection:	General stock.
# of Vols:	4,000
Hours:	Mon-Fri 11-6. Sat 10-4. Best to call ahead.
Services:	Accepts want lists.
Travel:	Proceeding east (toward downtown) on I-235: 35th St exit. Proceed south on 35th St, then left (south) on Ingersoll. Westbound on I-235: 31st St exit. Proceed south on 31st St, then left on Ingersoll.
Credit Cards:	Yes
Owner:	Randy Mouchka
Year Estab:	1995
Comments:	A rather small shop that should not require a great deal of time to browse. The shop does, however, contain some interesting items and more than a few hard to find titles. Some first editions and a few, but not many, paperbacks. If you don't see what you're looking for, ask, as not all the stock is displayed in the shop.

Jim's Books   **Open Shop**
3510 University Avenue 50311   (515) 255-0316

Collection:	General stock of mostly paperback.
Hours:	Mon-Sat 9-4.

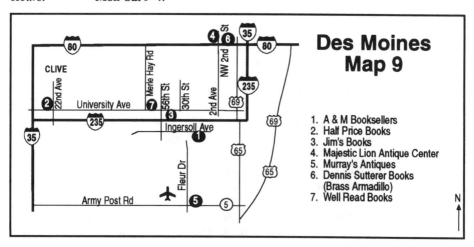

Des Moines Map 9

1. A & M Booksellers
2. Half Price Books
3. Jim's Books
4. Majestic Lion Antique Center
5. Murray's Antiques
6. Dennis Sutterer Books (Brass Armadillo)
7. Well Read Books

Majestic Lion Antique Center   **Antique Mall**
5048 NW 2nd Street 50313   (515) 282-5466

Hours:	Daily 9-7.
Travel:	At exit 135 off I-80.

Murray's Antiques   **Open Shop**
1805 Army Post Road 50315   (515) 285-8840

Collection:	General stock and ephemera.
# of Vols:	4,000-5,000
Hours:	Tue-Sat 10-5.
Travel:	Northbound on I-35: Rte 5 exit. Proceed east on Rte 5 (Army Post Rd) for about seven miles. Shop is just east of the airport. From I-80 westbound: Rte 65/69 exit (Des Moines bypass). Proceed south on Rte 65/69 to Indianola/Rte 65/69 exit, then continue north on Rte 65/69. At first light turn left on Rte 5 (Army Post Rd.)
Credit Cards:	No
Owner:	Irene Murray
Year Estab:	1971
Comments:	A combination antiques/collectibles shop and used book store located in a former private residence. (The books are located on the second level.) An interesting selection of both older books and newer items, quite reasonably priced, plus lots of ephemera, old magazines, prints and pulps. If you're a nostalgia buff, you should enjoy your visit here.

Dennis Sutterer Books   **Antique Mall**
At Brass Armadillo, 701 NE 50th Avenue   Mall: (515) 244-2140
Mailing address: 512 South 2nd Street Grimes IA 50111   Home: (515) 986-3639

Collection:	General stock.
Specialties:	Agriculture; automobiles; engineering; Western Americana; golf; esoteric religion; first editions (fiction). See Comments below.
Hours:	Daily 9-9.
Year Estab:	1994
Comments:	Also displays at Majestic Lion in Des Moines (with specialties in agriculture; automobiles, engineering), Yesterday's Treasures in Lamoni, IA (with specialties in esoteric religion and first edition fiction) and the Brass Armadillo in Omaha, NE (with specialties in western non fiction and golf).

Upstart Crow Books   **By Appointment**
1325 41st Street 50311   (515) 255-4901

Collection:	Specialty
# of Vols:	4,000-5,000
Specialties:	Philosophy; literature; poetry; art; history; Renaissance; music; first editions; criticism.
Services:	Appraisals, search service, accepts want lists, mail order.
Credit Cards:	No
Year Estab:	1994

Owner:	David & Karen Thuente
Comments:	Also displays at Books Revisited in Saint Cloud, MN. See below.

Well Read Books   **Open Shop**
5737 University 50311   (515) 274-0100
E-mail: dashace@aol.com

Collection:	General stock of mostly hardcover.
# of Vols:	20,000
Hours:	Tue-Sat 10-6. Sun 12:30-5. Other times by chance or appointment.
Services:	Mail order.
Travel:	From I-235: 56th or 63rd St exits. From either exit, turn north and proceed four blocks to University. From 56th St, turn west on University and continue for two blocks. From I-80: Merle Hay exit. Turn south and continue on Merle Hay to the end. Shop is at corner of Merle Hay and University.
Credit Cards:	No
Owner:	Dennis Ashby
Year Estab:	1998
Comments:	A modest sized shop with an assortment of fairly common titles (with perhaps some exceptions). Mostly older books in mixed condition. Plenty of religious titles, discarded textbooks and other miscellaneous items.

Dubuque
(Map 8, page 136)

Tri-State Independent Blind Society Used Bookstore   **Open Shop**
3333 Asbury Road 52002   (319) 556-8746
Fax: (319) 556-3592

Collection:	General stock of paperback and hardcover.
# of Vols:	100,000+
Hours:	Mon-Fri 9-4:30. Sat 9-1.
Travel:	From Rte 20, turn north on Wacker Dr, then left on John F. Kennedy Rd. At third light turn left on Asbury.
Credit Cards:	No
Year Estab:	1973
Comments:	Stock is approximately 70% paperback. All books are donated.

Fairfield
(Map 8, page 136)

Broken Kettle Books   **By Appointment**
702 East Madison Avenue 52556   (515) 472-8643

Collection:	General stock.
# of Vols:	40,000
Specialties:	Trade catalogs.
Services:	Search service, accepts want lists, subject lists, mail order.
Owner:	Eldon Bryant
Year Estab:	1959

Fostoria
(Map 8, page 136)

Fostoria Trading Post
14 Highway Avenue SW 51340

Open Shop
(712) 264-8918
E-mail: books@ncn.net

Collection:	General stock of paperback and hardcover.
# of Vols:	2,000
Specialties:	Computers; romance.
Hours:	Tue-Sat 11-4, except Thu till 8.
Travel:	Rte 71 to Fostoria. Turn west on Main St, then west on Highway Ave. Shop is on right.
Credit Cards:	Yes
Owner:	Emily G. Boetel
Year Estab:	1997

Grinnell
(Map 8, page 136)

Slightly Read
928 Main Street 50112

Open Shop
(515) 236-0541

Collection:	General stock of mostly used paperback.
Hours:	Mon-Fri 9-5:30, except Thu till 8. Sat 9-5.

Iowa City
(Map 8, page 136)

Karl M. Armens–Books
740 Juniper Drive 52245

By Appointment
(319) 337-7755

Collection:	General stock.
# of Vols:	20,000
Specialties:	Literary first editions; Western Americana; mystery; detective; science fiction; fantasy.
Services:	Appraisals, accepts want lists, mail order.
Credit Cards:	No
Year Estab:	1973
Comments:	Much of the stock consists of first editions.

The Bookery
523 Iowa Avenue 52240

Open Shop
(319) 351-3510
E-mail: jolin9@prodigy.net

Collection:	General stock of mostly hardcover.
# of Vols:	30,000-35,000
Specialties:	Children's; military; oriental philosophy; history.
Hours:	Mon-Sat 10-5:30. Sun by appointment.
Services:	Appraisals, search service, accepts want lists, mail order, book repair and binding.

(Iowa City)

Travel:	Dubuque St exit off I-80. Proceed south on Dubuque, then left on Iowa Ave. Shop is 1½ blocks ahead on right. Parking is available in the rear.
Credit Cards:	Yes
Owner:	Joe & Linda Michaud
Year Estab:	1986
Comments:	Located in a private residence, the books in this bi-level shop were attractively displayed on well labeled shelves. The majority of the books were in good condition and moderately priced. In addition to the specialties listed above we noted some first editions, fine leather bindings, a separate antiquarian section and some unusual titles. Most subjects were represented. Paperbacks were located on the lower level.

Camp Pope Bookshop   By Appointment
1117 East Davenport Street   (319) 351-2407
Mailing address: PO Box 2232 Iowa City IA 52244
Web page: http://members.aol.com/ckenyoncpb   E-mail: ckenyoncpb@aol.com

Collection:	Specialty
# of Vols:	500+
Specialties:	Civil War, especially Iowa, Missouri and the trans-Mississippi.
Services:	Catalog, accepts want lists. Also publishes reprints dealing with above specialty.
Credit Cards:	Yes
Owner:	W. Clark Kenyon
Year Estab:	1988

Counterpoint Used Books   Open Shop
114 South Linn Street 52240   (319) 354-3413

Collection:	General stock of hardcover and paperback.
# of Vols:	10,000
Specialties:	Scholarly
Hours:	Mon-Sat 11-6. Sun 12-5.
Services:	Accepts want lists, mail order.
Travel:	Dubuque St exit off I-80. Proceed south on Dubuque to Washington, then left on Washington for one block and right on Linn.
Credit Cards:	No
Owner:	William Boatman
Year Estab:	1993
Comments:	Most, but clearly not all, of the books we saw would fall into the "reading copy" category. At the time of our visit, the biography section was among the shop's stronger areas but because of the modest size of the collection, the section did not have depth.

Haunted Bookshop On The Creek   Open Shop
520 East Washington 52240   (319) 337-2996
E-mail: haunted@soli.inav.net

Collection:	General stock of paperback and hardcover.

# of Vols:	30,000
Specialties:	Literature; biography; mystery; poetry; drama; religion.
Hours:	Mon-Fri 11-6. Sat 10-6. Sun 12-5.
Services:	Search service, mail order.
Travel:	Dubuque St exit off I-80. Proceed south on Dubuque to Washington then left on Washington.
Credit Cards:	Yes
Owner:	Howard L. Zimmon & Kristin Garnant
Year Estab:	1978
Comments:	Located in a private residence with lots of interesting nooks and crannies on the first floor and a basement offering a mix of paperbacks and hardcover titles. We would categorize a majority of the hardcover volumes as being more modern than antiquarian. The shelves were well labeled and the books attractively displayed. Certainly worth a browse.

Iowa Book & Supply Co. | Open Shop

8 South Clinton Street
(319) 337-4188
Mailing address: PO Box 2030 Iowa City IA 52244

Collection:	General stock paperback and hardcover.
# of Vols:	40,000
Hours:	Mon-Fri. 9-6. Sat 10-6. Sun 12-5.
Travel:	Across from old Capital Building.
Comments:	A college bookstore with a general used book section that is 80% paperback.

Murphy-Brookfield Books | Open Shop

219 North Gilbert Street 52245
(319) 338-3077

Collection:	General stock.
# of Vols:	50,000
Hours:	Mon-Sat 11-6.
Services:	Accepts want lists, mail order.
Travel:	Dubuque St exit off I-80. Proceed south on Dubuque, then east on Bloomington. Shop is at corner of Bloomington and Gilbert. Parking is available in rear.
Credit Cards:	Yes
Owner:	Jane Murphy & Mark Brookfield
Year Estab:	1980
Comments:	A solid selection of scholarly books in most areas. Both the main level and the second floor are filled with books that would be of interest to the serious reader. The books were in excellent condition and could supplement many a university library. If your interests are more mundane, stay away.

Northside Book Market | Open Shop

203 North Linn Street 52245
(319) 466-9330

Collection:	General stock of paperback and hardcover and records.
# of Vols:	15,000

Hours:	Mon-Sat 10-8. Sun 12-5. Longer hours in summer.
Travel:	Eastbound on I-80: Dubuque St exit. Proceed south on Dubuque, then left on Jefferson and left on Linn.
Credit Cards:	Yes
Owner:	Jan Williams
Year Estab:	1997
Comments:	Stock is approximately 70% paperback.

Lamoni
(Map 8, page 136)

Yesterday's Treasures   **Antique Mall**
108 North Linden Street 50140   (515) 784-7658

Hours:	Mon-Sat 10-5. Sun 1-4.
Travel:	Exit 4 off I-35. Proceed west on Rte 69 (Main St) for about two miles, then right on Linden.

Maquoketa
(Map 8, page 136)

Banowetz Antique Mall   **Antique Mall**
122 Mackensey Drive 52060   (319) 652-6226

Hours:	Mon-Sat 9-5. Sun 10-5.
Travel:	At intersection of Rts 61 and 64.

Marion
(Map 8, page 136)

Excellence in Books   **Antique Mall**
At Sanctuary Antique Center, 801 10th Street 52302   (319) 377-7753
E-mail: excelbks@interloc.com

Collection:	General stock.
# of Vols:	10,000+
Specialties:	Wizard of Oz; Iowa; natural science; Western Americana.
Hours:	Mon-Sat 10-5. Sun 12-4.
Services:	Appraisals
Travel:	Exit 24B off I-380. Proceed east on Blair Ferry Rd to 7th Ave, then continue on 7th Ave to 10th St. Left on 10th St. Shop is two blocks ahead in a former church.
Credit Cards:	Yes
Owner:	Gary L. Wallin
Year Estab:	1989
Comments:	Unlike most used book booths in multi dealer antique malls, the selection here, both in terms of size and quality, is more like a separate small to modest sized book shop. Most of the books are located on the lower level with a selection of better books upstairs.

Osceola
(Map 8, page 136)

Books N Stuff   **Open Shop**
130 South Fillmore Street 50213   Day: (515) 342-6496
                                               Eve: (515) 342-7256
                                   E-mail: bksnstff@pionet.net

Collection:	General stock of hardcover and paperback.
# of Vols:	60,000+ (See Comments)
Hours:	Mon-Sat 9-5.
Services:	Search service, accepts want lists, mail order.
Travel:	From I-35, proceed east on Rte 34, then north Rte 69 to square. Continue around square.
Credit Cards:	No
Owner:	Delores Hardy
Year Estab:	1993
Comments:	Overwhelmingly paperback with a few book club hardcover editions and some other reading copies of books you won't have trouble finding elsewhere. The above comments were written a few minutes after leaving the shop. Once we arrived home, however, we received an e-mail message from the owner who was not in the store at the time of our visit. In her message, she advised us that of the 60,000+ volumes in her collection, only about 25,000 were on display at the store; the remaining 40,000+ were at home "in boxes and on a few shelves." One assumes that these are the books she is listing on-line. We leave it up to our readers to decide whether they want to browse this shop in person or on line.

Sioux City
(Map 8, page 136)

Books on the Sun Porch   **Antique Mall**
At Old Town Antiques and Collectibles, 1024 4th Street   (712) 255-0841
Mailing address: Timberlane, #11, RR #5 Sioux City IA 51108
                                       E-mail: cyschatz@aol.com

Collection:	General stock of mostly used hardcover and paperback.
# of Vols:	6,000
Specialties:	Arkham House; first editions; Frank Baum; children's; history; regional authors; Little golden Books; Gene Stratton Porter; John Steinbeck; school books.
Hours:	Mon-Sat 9-5. Other times by appointment.
Services:	Appraisals, search service, accepts want lists, mail order.
Travel:	Nebraska St exit off I-29. Proceed east on Nebraska, then north on Virginia and right on 4th.
Credit Cards:	Yes
Owner:	Janice K. Schatz
Year Estab:	1994
Comments:	Used stock is evenly divided between hardcover and paperback.

Mail Order Dealers

Anni's Antiques & Books (319) 856-3115
321 New Street Colesburg 52035 E-mail: lwaterman@mwci.net

Collection:	General stock.
# of Vols:	2,000-3,000
Specialties:	Pre-1900 German material in all subject areas.
Credit Cards:	Yes
Owner:	Anni Waterman
Year Estab:	1973

Chessco (319) 323-1226
PO Box 8 Davenport 52805 E-mail: tpiWchewsco.com
Web page: www.chessco.com

Collection:	Specialty new and used.
Specialties:	Chess

Ted Danielson (319) 987-2280
8204 Waverly Road Cedar Falls 50613

Collection:	General stock and ephemera.
# of Vols:	2,000
Credit Cards:	No
Year Estab:	1993

D.R. Doerres Rendezvous Trader (319) 732-2874
PO Box 676 Wilton 52778 E-mail: ddoerres@netins.net

Collection:	Specialty
Specialties:	Western Americana; fur trade; French & Indian War; Lakeside Classics.
Year Estab:	1969

Good Question (319) 472-2067
PO Box 841 Vinton 52349

Collection:	Specialty
# of Vols:	2,000+
Specialties:	Philosophy; social sciences.
Services:	Catalog
Owner:	Thom Carlson
Year Estab:	1992

The Legacy Company (319) 337-9914
PO Box 1303 Iowa City 52244

Collection:	Specialty
Specialties:	Literary first editions; art; architecture; photography; Americana; manuscripts.
Services:	Appraisals, catalog, accepts want lists, collection development.
Credit Cards:	No
Owner:	Dr. John Mullen
Year Estab:	1974

The Library
PO Box 37 Des Moines 50301

(515) 262-6714
Fax: (515) 263-8116

Collection:	Specialty
# of Vols:	26,000 (See Comments)
Specialties:	Antiques; collectibles; decorative arts; nostalgia.
Services:	Accepts want lists.
Credit Cards:	Yes
Owner:	Nancy Johnson
Year Estab:	1977
Comments:	Most of inventory consists of in-print titles and includes privately published books, museum and historical society presses and both English and foreign language imports.

Natural History Books
1025 Keokuk Street Iowa City 52240
Web page: www.avalon.net/~nathist

(319) 354-9088
Fax: (319) 354-0844
E-mail: nathist@avalon.net

Collection:	Specialty books and ephemera.
# of Vols:	1,500
Specialties:	Ornithology; herpetology; mammalogy; naturalist travels; botany; Darwin; Wallace; other natural history. Emphasis is on antiquarian and color plate books.
Services:	Appraisals, search service, catalog, accepts want lists.
Credit Cards:	Yes
Owner:	Noriko I. Ciochon
Year Estab:	1985

Gil O'Gara Antiquarian
PO Box 36172 Des Moines 50315

(515) 287-0404

Collection:	Specialty
# of Vols:	2,000
Specialties:	Children's series; film.
Services:	Appraisals, search service, catalog, accepts want lists, publishes *Yellowback Library* newsletter dealing with children's series books.
Credit Cards:	No
Year Estab:	1981

Pella Books
PO Box 229 Pella 50219

(515) 628-6868
E-mail: postalfr@se-iowa.net

Collection:	General stock of paperback and hardcover.
# of Vols:	10,000
Specialties:	Literature; history; religion; chess; games; mystery.
Services:	Search service, accepts want lists.
Owner:	Alfred Post
Year Estab:	1998

Gerald Pettinger   (515) 535-2239
Route 2, Box 125 Russell 50238

Collection:	Specialty. Mostly used.
# of Vols:	2,000
Specialties:	Hunting; fishing; guns; natural history.
Services:	Appraisals, search service, catalog, accepts want lists.
Credit Cards:	Yes
Year Estab:	1976

John Quinn, Bookseller   (319) 268-0902
PO Box 847 Cedar Falls 50613   Fax: (319) 277-3457
                                          E-mail: scholar@cfu-cybernet.net

Collection:	Specialty
# of Vols:	10,000
Specialties:	Literary criticism; first editions; British and American literature; black studies.
Credit Cards:	No
Year Estab:	1996

Tall Ships Books   (319) 396-2549
PO Box 8027 Cedar Rapids 52408   Fax: (319) 396-6572
Web page: www.tallshipsbooks.com   E-mail: tallshipsbooks.merritt@cedar-rapids.net

Collection:	Specialty used and new hardcover and paperback.
Specialties:	Nautical fiction.
Services:	Accepts want lists, trade-ins, consignments.
Credit Cards:	No
Owner:	Rich Merritt
Year Estab:	1994

Timber City Books   (319) 652-5694
PO Box 1076 Maquoketa 52060
Web page: www.clinton.net/~tcbooks   E-mail: tcbooks@caves.net

Collection:	General stock of hardcover and paperback and magazines.
# of Vols:	20,000
Specialties:	History; paleontology; science fiction; fantasy; mystery.
Services:	Search service, catalog, accepts want lists.
Credit Cards:	No
Owner:	David L. Rosheim
Year Estab:	1992
Comments:	Also displays at Banowetz Antique Mall in Maquoketa.

Ex Libris
Frederick Eugene Hartnell

KENTUCKY

Alphabetical Listing By Dealer

A Likely Story	173	John Dinsmore & Associates	166
A Reader's Corner	169	Evans Firearms and Archery	166
Morgan Adams Books	164	Footnotes Bookshop	178
All Booked Up	169	For The Love Of Books	160
Arbor Antique Service	178	Cynthia K. Fowler Books	170
Armchair Adventures	160	David R. Friedlander, Antiques	170
Robert L. Barth, Bookseller	178	Georgetown Antique Mall	162
Bison Books	173	Glover's Bookery	167
Black Swan Books	165	Goff's Florist & Trading Post	175
Blenheim Books	175	Great Escape	171
The Book Barn	161	Harry's Books	176
The Book Barn	164	Timothy Hawley Books	178
Book Exchange Used Book Store	165	Historic Danville Antique Mall	161
The Book Gallery	165	Legacy Books	179
The Book Inn	158	Mac Neil's Books and Records	171
Book Inn	158	Moneytree Book Warehouse	174
Book Lady	164	Mostly Baseball	179
Books Are Everything	178	Donald S. Mull - Books	172
Books are R's	162	The Mt. Sterling Rebel	174
Books For Sense	161	Old Army Books	167
The Bookstore	163	Olde Book Shoppe	157
Bookworm Book Store	175	Once Again Gently Used Books	172
Boulands Booksellers	174	Pac-Rats	157
Box of Rocks	157	Paperback Exchange	176
Caraway Book Company	166	Paterson-Ford Booksellers	172
Cherie's Books	177	Pennyroyal Books	163
Children's Planet	170	Philatelic Bibliopole	179
The Cookbook Cottage	170	Poor Richard's Books	162
Creatures of Habit	174	Proud Mary's Booksellers	176

Radcliff Antique Mall	175	T & S Books	160
J. Sampson Antiques & Books	163	TJ's Consignment	158
Mike Sarki, Rogue Books	179	True Treasures	161
Schenk Enterprises	163	Twice Sold Tales	157
Don Smith's Nat'l. Geog. Magazines	179	Twice Told Books	172
Sqecial Media	168	Unique Thrift Stores	173
The Sporting Horse Gallery	168	Woodland Park Bookstore	168
Raymond M. Sutton, Jr. Books	177		

Alphabetical Listing By Location

Location	Dealer	Page
Anchorage	Mike Sarki, Rogue Books	179
Berea	Twice Sold Tales	157
Bowling Green	Box of Rocks	157
	Pac-Rats	157
Cadiz	Olde Book Shoppe	157
Campbellsville	TJ's Consignment	158
Clarkson	Book Inn	158
Corbin	The Book Inn	158
Covington	Armchair Adventures	160
	For The Love Of Books	160
	T & S Books	160
Crestwood	The Book Barn	161
Danville	Historic Danville Antique Mall	161
Edgewood	Robert L. Barth, Bookseller	178
Florence	True Treasures	161
Fort Thomas	Mostly Baseball	179
Frankfort	Books For Sense	161
	Poor Richard's Books	162
Georgetown	Georgetown Antique Mall	162
Harrodsburg	Books are R's	162
	J. Sampson Antiques & Books	163
Hazard	Schenk Enterprises	163
Hopkinsville	Pennyroyal Books	163
Horse Cave	The Bookstore	163
Jeffersontown	Book Lady	164
La Grange	The Book Barn	164
Lexington	Morgan Adams Books	164
	Black Swan Books	165
	Book Exchange Used Book Store	165
	The Book Gallery	165
	Caraway Book Company	166
	John Dinsmore & Associates, Booksellers	166
	Evans Firearms and Archery	166
	Footnotes Bookshop	178
	Glover's Bookery	167
	Old Army Books	167
	Sqecial Media	168
	The Sporting Horse Gallery	168
	Woodland Park Bookstore	168
Louisville	A Reader's Corner	169
	All Booked Up	169
	Children's Planet	170
	The Cookbook Cottage	170
	Cynthia K. Fowler Books	170

Louisville	David R. Friedlander, Antiques	170
	Great Escape	171
	Timothy Hawley Books	178
	Legacy Books	179
	Mac Neil's Books and Records	171
	Donald S. Mull - Books	172
	Once Again Gently Used Books	172
	Paterson-Ford Booksellers	172
	Philatelic Bibliopole	179
	Don Smith's National Geographic Magazines	179
	Twice Told Books	172
	Unique Thrift Stores	173
Maysville	A Likely Story	173
Mount Sterling	Bison Books	173
	The Mt. Sterling Rebel	174
Owensboro	Moneytree Book Warehouse	174
Paducah	Boulands Booksellers	174
	Creatures of Habit	174
Pikeville	Goff's Florist & Trading Post	175
Prospect	Blenheim Books	175
Radcliff	Bookworm Book Store	175
	Radcliff Antique Mall	175
Richmond	Books Are Everything	178
	Harry's Books	176
	Paperback Exchange	176
Shelbyville	Proud Mary's Booksellers	176
Somerset	Arbor Antique Service	178
Waynesburg	Cherie's Books	177
Williamsburg	Raymond M. Sutton, Jr. Books	177

Berea
(Map 10, page 159)

Twice Sold Tales   **Open Shop**

At Something Olde Antique Mall, 437 Chestnut Street   Mall: (606) 986-6057
Mailing address: 102 Peachbloom Circle Berea KY 40403   Home: (606) 986-2605
                                                       Fax: (606) 985-9493
                                  E-mail: harryrobie@kih.net

Collection:	General stock of mostly hardcover.
# of Vols:	35,000+
Specialties:	Regional Americana; Pacific Rim; scholarly; fiction.
Hours:	Mon-Sat 10-6. Sun 1-5.
Services:	Accepts want lists, mail order.
Travel:	Exit 76 off I-75. Proceed east on Chestnut St for about half a mile to downtown. Shop is on the second floor.
Credit Cards:	Yes
Owner:	Harry Robie
Year Estab:	1992
Comments:	For collectible quality books, or other information about the books, contact the owner at the home phone number.

Bowling Green
(Map 10, page 159)

Box of Rocks   **Open Shop**

917 Broadway Avenue 42101   (502) 793-9743

Collection:	Specialty. Mostly used paperback.
# of Vols:	1,500
Specialties:	Science fiction; horror; classics.
Hours:	Mon-Sat 10:30-9. Sun 12-7.
Comments:	Stock is approximately 75% paperback.

Pac-Rats   **Open Shop**

1051 Bryant Way 42103   (502) 782-8092

Collection:	Specialty
# of Vols:	500-1,000
Specialties:	Science fiction; horror.
Hours:	Mon-Sat 10-9. Sun 1-6.
Comments:	Primarily a comics and game shop with a limited collection of mostly paperback copies of more recent titles.

Cadiz
(Map 10, page 159)

Olde Book Shoppe   **Open Shop**

13 Marion Street 42211   (502) 522-6484

Collection:	General stock of paperback and hardcover.

# of Vols:	10,000+
Hours:	Mon-Wed and Fri & Sat 10-5.
Travel:	Cadiz exit off I-24. Proceed west on Rte 68 to Bus 68 bypass. At blinking light in middle of town, turn right on Marion. Shop is just ahead on left.
Credit Cards:	No
Year Estab:	1992
Comments:	Stock is approximately 60% paperback.

Campbellsville
(Map 10, page 159)

TJ's Consignment **Open Shop**
203 West Broadway 42718 (502) 465-7710

Collection:	General stock of paperback and hardcover.
Hours:	Mon-Fri 9-5.

Clarkson
(Map 10, page 159)

Book Inn **Open Shop**
112 Peonia Road 42726 (502) 242-4099

Collection:	General stock of mostly used paperback.
# of Vols:	10,000 (used)
Hours:	Mon-Fri 10-5. Sat 10-2.

Corbin
(Map 10, page 159)

The Book Inn **Open Shop**
213 Center Street (606) 523-2665
Mailing address: PO Box 21 Corbin KY 40702 E-mail: bookinn@2geton.net

Collection:	General stock.
# of Vols:	3,500+
Hours:	Thu & Fri 10-6. Sat 10-3. Other times by appointment.
Services:	Search service, accepts want lists, mail order.
Travel:	Exit 29 off I-75. Proceed south on Rte 25E for about 1½ miles, then right at first light. Continue south on Rte 25W. At overpass, veer left, go under overpass and continue to light. Shop is in the Poynter Building on second floor.
Credit Cards:	No
Owner:	Cathy Prewitt & Jan Bolding
Year Estab:	1995

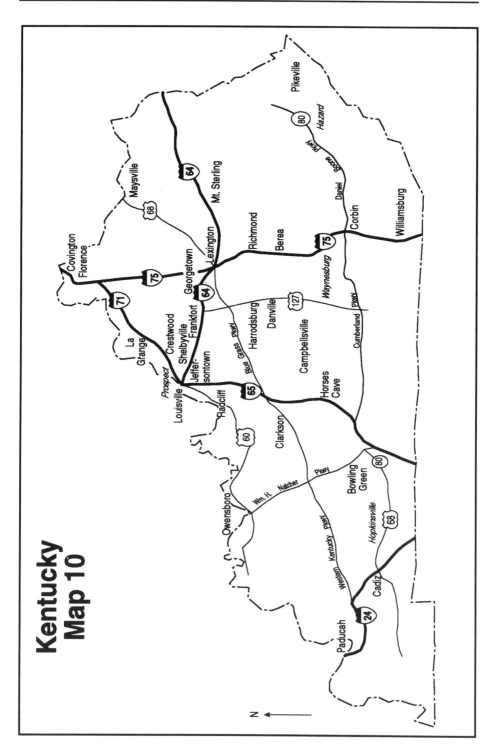

Kentucky
Map 10

Covington

(Map 10, page 159 & Map 26, page 368)

Armchair Adventures   **Open Shop**
1545 Scott Street   Shop: (606) 261-6435
Mailing address: 7229 Longwood Ct. Cincinnati OH 45239   Home: (513) 521-0517

Collection:	Specialty
# of Vols:	3,500
Specialties:	Children's illustrated; fantasy; science fiction; Frank Baum; Seckatary Hawkins.
Hours:	Wed & Sat 2-6 and other times by appointment.
Services:	Accepts want lists, mail order.
Travel:	Located above T & S Books. (See below.) If T & S is closed, check for a separate side entrance.
Credit Cards:	No
Owner:	Russ Bernard
Year Estab:	1988
Comments:	Located on the second floor of another book store, a visit here gives you two for the price of one (see T & S Books below). The shop carries a strong selection in the specialities listed above. If you have particular interests, be sure to ask the owner as he may have access to what you're looking for in a spot not immediately visible to the browser.

For The Love Of Books   **Open Shop**
4331 Winston Avenue 41015   (606) 261-5515

Collection:	General stock of hardcover and paperback.
# of Vols:	35,000
Hours:	Mon-Fri 10-8, except Mon till 7. Sat 10-6. Sun 12-5.
Services:	Appraisals, search service, mail order.
Travel:	Rte 16 exit off I-275. Proceed north on Rte 16 (Winston Ave) for one mile. Shop is on left in Latonia Centre Shopping Center.
Credit Cards:	Yes
Owner:	Daniel O'Connor
Year Estab:	1991
Comments:	The layout here was typical of many used book shops located in shopping malls with paperbacks in the center aisles and hardcovers along the side and rear walls. The hardcover volumes were in generally good condition and covered a range of subject areas. While depth was lacking, there were certainly some interesting titles available at fairly reasonable prices.

T & S Books   **By Appointment**
1545 Scott Boulevard   Tel & Fax: (606) 261-6435
Mailing address: PO Box 14077 Covington KY 41014   E-mail: tnsbooks@one.net
Web page: www.abebooks.com/home/tandsbooks

Collection:	General stock.
# of Vols:	40,000

Specialties:	Local history; Civil War; river boats and rivermen.
Services:	Accepts want lists.
Credit Cards:	Yes
Owner:	Dan Nagle
Year Estab:	1978
Comments:	Although we generally do not visit "by appointment" dealers when researching our guides, we were fortunate to have visited this dealer on our earlier trip when he maintained an open shop. At that time we noted: A nice collection of mixed vintage hardcovers in almost every subject area and titles not generally seen elsewhere. Prices were fair and the owners are "real" book people.

Crestwood
(Map 10, page 159)

The Book Barn　　　　　　　　　　　　　　　　　　　　　**Open Shop**
6103 Crestwood Station 40014　　　　　　　　　　　　　　(502) 241-4700

Collection:	General stock of mostly paperback.
Hours:	Mon-Fri 10-8. Sat 10-6.

Danville
(Map 10, page 159)

Historic Danville Antique Mall　　　　　　　　　　　　　**Antique Mall**
158 North 3rd Street 40422　　　　　　　　　　　　　　　(606) 236-3026

Hours:	Tue-Sat 10-5. Sun 1:30-5.

Florence
(Map 10, page 159)

True Treasures　　　　　　　　　　　　　　　　　　　　**Open Shop**
165 Lloyd Avenue 41042　　　　　　　　　　　　　　　　(606) 371-0068
　　　　　　　　　　　　　　　　　　　　　E-mail: sofiet3@fuse.net

Collection:	General stock of paperback and hardcover.
# of Vols:	18,000
Hours:	Mon-Fri 11-7. Sat 10:30-6.
Services:	Search service, mail order.
Travel:	Turfway Rd exit off I-75. Turn right on Turfway Rd and continue to Lloyd Ave. Shop is at corner of Turfway and Lloyd.
Credit Cards:	Yes
Year Estab:	1996
Comments:	Stock is approximately 70% paperback.

Frankfort
(Map 10, page 159)

Books For Sense　　　　　　　　　　　　　　　　　　　**Open Shop**
1187 US Highway 127 South 40601　　　　　　　　　　　　(502) 223-6974

Collection:	General stock of mostly paperback.

| *# of Vols:* | 30,000 |
| *Hours:* | Mon-Fri 10-8. Sat 10-6. Sun 1-5. |

Poor Richard's Books   **Open Shop**
233 West Broadway 40601   (502) 223-8018

Collection:	General stock of new and used hardcover and paperback.
# of Vols:	75,000
Specialties:	Kentucky
Hours:	Mon-Fri 9:30-6. Sat 9:30-5:30. Sun 1-5.
Travel:	From 1-64 westbound: Rte 60 exit. Proceed west on Rte 60 for about five miles, then left on Broadway. From I-64 Eastbound: Rte 127 exit. Proceed north on Rte 127 for about three miles, then right on Wilkinson Blvd (Rte 421) immediately after the bridge and left on Broadway.
Credit Cards:	Yes
Owner:	Richard & Elizabeth Taylor
Year Estab:	1979
Comments:	If you're looking for volume you won't be disappointed if you decide to stop here. While most of the front of the shop is filled with new books, there were hardcover volumes toward the rear of the first floor and the entire second floor of the shop (if it doesn't collapse by dent of its weight) is filled with older used books. We saw many items that would certainly fit the "antiquarian" definition and many that were just old. Condition varied from quite good to fair to "in need of first aid." We suspect that more knowledgeable book people than we could probably select several titles and walk away with some finds. It's too bad that the lighting on the second floor and the way some of the books were displayed were not more conducive to browsing.

Georgetown
(Map 10, page 159)

Georgetown Antique Mall   **Antique Mall**
124 West Main Street   (502) 863-9033

| *Hours:* | Mon-Sat 10-5. Sun 1-5. |
| *Travel:* | Downtown |

Harrodsburg
(Map 10, page 159)

Books are R's   **Open Shop**
1028 North College Street, #1 40330   (606) 734-0678

Collection:	General stock of paperback and hardcover.
# of Vols:	21,000
Hours:	Mon-Sat 10-6.
Travel:	Located on Rte 127 in a small strip shopping area.
Credit Cards:	Yes
Year Estab:	1992
Comments:	Stock is approximately 75% paperback.

J. Sampson Antiques & Books   **Open Shop**
107 South Main Street 40330   (606) 734-7829

Collection:	General stock.
# of Vols:	8,000-10,000
Specialties:	Kentucky
Hours:	Mon-Sat 10-5. Sun 1:30-5. (Jan-Mar: closed Wed.)
Services:	Appraisals, search service, accepts want lists, mail order.
Travel:	Rte 127 to Harrodsburg. Turn east on Lexington, then right on Main.
Credit Cards:	Yes
Owner:	Jerry Sampson
Year Estab:	1990
Comments:	Looking for old books? Not necessarily good books, but books that have been around for a while in someone's attic and have not seen the best of care? You'll find them here, at least several thousand of them. Very few of the books had dust jackets. Very few were in particularly good condition.

Hazard
(Map 10, page 159)

Schenk Enterprises   **By Appointment**
5841A Lotts Creek Road 41701   (606) 785-4225

Collection:	General stock mostly hardcover.
# of Vols:	2,000+
Specialties:	Eastern philosophy; philosophy; mystery; "coffee table" books.
Services:	Mail order.
Owner:	Richard Schenk

Hopkinsville
(Map 10, page 159)

Pennyroyal Books   **By Appointment**
112 Cox Mill Court 42240   (502) 885-1532
                                                        Fax: (502) 885-5272

Collection:	General stock.
Specialties:	History; genealogy.
Services:	Mail order.
Owner:	D. D. Cayce
Year Estab:	1963

Horse Cave
(Map 10, page 159)

The Bookstore   **Open Shop**
111 Water Street   (502) 786-3084
Mailing address: PO Box 73 Horse Cave KY 42749   Fax: (502) 786-3085
                                                E-mail: matera@screc.blue.net

Collection:	General stock of hardcover and paperback.

# of Vols:	21,000+
Hours:	Mon-Sat 7am-8pm. Sun 11:30-5. (Mid June-Oct: Tue-Sat till 10pm.)
Services:	Search service, accepts want lists, mail order.
Travel:	Exit 58 off I-65. Proceed east on Rte 218. Shop is at intersection of Rtes 31 West and 218.
Credit Cards:	Yes
Owner:	Ann & Jerry Matera, owners. Tom Chaney, manager
Year Estab:	1994
Comments:	Stock is evenly divided between hardcover and paperback. The shop also serves breakfast, lunch and dinner.

Jeffersontown
(Map 10, page 159)

Book Lady   **Open Shop**
9908 Taylorsville Road 40299   (502) 266-8831

Collection:	General stock of mostly paperback.
# of Vols:	15,000
Hours:	Tue-Sat 10-5.

La Grange
(Map 10, page 159)

The Book Barn   **Open Shop**
127 East Main Street 40031   (502) 222-0918

Collection:	General stock of mostly paperback.
Hours:	Mon-Fri 10-7. Sat 10-5.

Lexington
(Map 10, page 159 & Map 11, page 167)

Morgan Adams Books   **Open Shop**
1439 Leestown Road 40511   (606) 252-3612

Collection:	General stock of hardcover and paperback.
# of Vols:	50,000
Specialties:	Literature; science fiction; mystery; children's; self help; business; cookbooks; how-to books.
Hours:	Mon-Sat 10-6. Sun 1-5.
Services:	Search service, accepts want lists.
Travel:	Between intersections of Burke (Lisle) Rd and Forbes Rd. Leestown Rd is an extension of West Main St.
Credit Cards:	Yes
Owner:	David, Mary E. & Morgan Adams
Year Estab:	1990
Comments:	A fair sized collection of mostly recent used items in mixed condition. More reading copies than truly rare or collectible titles, although one never knows what may show up in the future.

Black Swan Books   **Open Shop**
505 East Maxwell Street   Tel & Fax: (606) 252-7255
Mailing address: PO Box 22804 Lexington KY 40522   E-mail: bswan@mis.net

Collection:	General stock.
# of Vols:	45,000
Specialties:	Kentucky; military; horses; modern first editions; literature; American history; Civil War.
Hours:	Mon-Sat 11-5:30.
Services:	Appraisals, search service, catalog, accepts want lists.
Travel:	Rte 60 exit off I-75 south. Proceed west on Rte 60 (Winchester Rd) for about 3-4 miles, then left on Walton Ave and proceed to dead end. Right on Main St. At second set of lights turn left on Woodland Ave, then left on Maxwell. Shop is just ahead on left.
Credit Cards:	Yes
Owner:	Michael Courtney
Year Estab:	1984
Comments:	We liked this shop the first time we visited it 3½ years earlier and discovered on our return to Lexington that a very good store could become even better. The shop had more than doubled in the intervening years and, at the time of our visit, the owner was in the process of stocking some additional new space which should be ready by the time this book is in print. The shop continues to offer very fine books, most in excellent condition, in almost every subject imaginable. The shelves are well labeled and the quality of the titles (both common and uncommon) is such that discriminating book people should find this shop an absolute pleasure to visit.

Book Exchange Used Book Store   **Open Shop**
867 East High Street 40502   (606) 266-4212

Collection:	General stock of mostly paperback.
Hours:	Tue 12-5. Wed & Thu 10-6. Fri & Sat 12-5.

The Book Gallery   **Open Shop**
3250 Nicholasville Road 40503   (606) 272-1094
                                                        Fax: (606) 281-1533
                                              E-mail: bgallery@lex.infi.net

Collection:	General stock.
# of Vols:	18,500
Specialties:	Modern first editions; Native Americans; cookbooks; history; American history.
Hours:	Mon-Sat 10-7. Sun 1-5.
Services:	Search service, accepts want lists, mail order.
Travel:	Nicholasville Rd (Rte 27) off Rte 4 (New Circle Rd). Proceed south on Rte 27 and make very first left (Canary Rd) and then an immediate right into Crossroads Plaza. The shop is in the building just ahead, on the lower level.

Credit Cards: Yes
Owner: Bruce & Deborah Knox
Year Estab: 1996
Comments: Easy to miss because of its lower level location off to the side of a
                   shopping center but a most pleasant store to visit. The floor is plushly
                   carpeted, a rest room is available to the public, tables and chairs and
                   coffee and cookies are there for the visitor's comfort and the owner is
                   most gracious. Besides all that, the books on display, the vast majority
                   of which are hardcover volumes in quite good condition, offer many
                   pleasant surprises. In addition to more common recent fiction and first
                   editions, one can also find many antiquarian and collectible items,
                   some displayed behind glass. Whether or not you make a purchase
                   here, you should certainly enjoy your visit.

Caraway Book Company   By Appointment
3516 Castlegate Wynd 40502   (606) 266-9412

Collection: General stock.
# of Vols: 10,000
Specialties: Children's
Services: Accepts want lists.
Credit Cards: No
Owner: Herbert Regenstreif
Year Estab: 1984

John Dinsmore & Associates, Booksellers   By Appointment
1037 Castleton Way South 40517   Tel & Fax: (606) 271-8042
Web page: www.autobahn.mb.ca/~parker/jda/   E-mail: dinsmorej@uky.campus.mci.net

Collection: Specialty
# of Vols: 1,000
Specialties: Modern first editions; private press; jazz; art (modern American); ar-
                   chitecture; humanities periodicals; New York City; beat generation.
Services: Catalog, accepts want lists.
Credit Cards: No
Year Estab: 1991

Evans Firearms & Archery   Open Shop
117 Southland Drive 40503   Tel & Fax: (606) 277-7770
                                                           E-mail: jpe111@gte.net

Collection: Specialty new and used.
# of Vols: 200
Specialties: Guns; hunting; archery; woodworking; metalworking.
Hours: Mon-Fri 10-6. Sat 10-5. Later hours in fall.
Travel: Rte 27 (Nicholasville Rd) exit off New Circle Rd. Proceed north on
                   Nicholasville for about one mile, then left on Southland.
Owner: Jay Evans
Comments: Shop also sells guns and archery equipment.

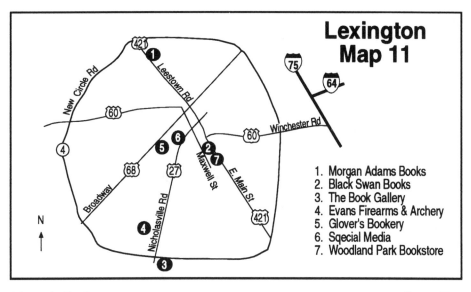

Lexington Map 11

1. Morgan Adams Books
2. Black Swan Books
3. The Book Gallery
4. Evans Firearms & Archery
5. Glover's Bookery
6. Sqecial Media
7. Woodland Park Bookstore

Glover's Bookery   **Open Shop**
862 South Broadway 40504   (606) 253-0614
                                         E-mail: bookery@ix.netcom.com

Collection:	General stock.
# of Vols:	60,000
Specialties:	Americana; Kentucky; horses; caves; Civil War; World War II.
Hours:	Mon-Sat 10-6.
Services:	Appraisals, search service, catalog, accepts want lists.
Travel:	Rte 68 exit off I-75 or I-64. Proceed west on Rte 68 through Lexington. Shop is on Rte 68, one mile west of downtown and 1½ blocks after railroad overpass.
Credit Cards:	Yes
Owner:	John & Carey Glover
Year Estab:	1978
Comments:	The specialties listed above are represented in reasonable depth by some very fine and unusual titles. We also noted a nice fiction section and some interesting genealogical volumes. If you're planning a visit to Lexington, you'll definitely want to stop here. The owner also displays at antique malls in Georgetown and Danville. See above.

Old Army Books   **By Appointment**
PO Box 24652 40524   (606) 273-5614
Web page: www.sonic.net/~bstone/oldarmy/   E-mail: bhalsted@lex.infi.net

Collection:	Specialty
# of Vols:	5,000
Specialties:	Military
Services:	Appraisals, search service, catalog, accepts want lists.
Credit Cards:	Yes

(Lexington)

Owner:	Bruce Halsted
Year Estab:	1989

Sqecial Media   **Open Shop**
371 South Limestone Street 40508   (606) 255-4316

Collection:	Specialty. Mostly new and some used.
Specialties:	Metaphysics; magic; astrology; eastern philosophy; hypnotism; beat poetry and literature; women's studies.
Hours:	Mon-Sat 10-8. Sun 12-6.
Travel:	Follow signs to Univ. of Kentucky. Shop is 1/2 block north of Euclid.
Credit Cards:	Yes
Year Estab:	1972

The Sporting Horse Gallery   **By Appointment**
PO Box 12601 40511   Tel & Fax: (606) 293-6421
                                                       E-mail: horsebks@aol.com

Collection:	Specialty books and ephemera.
# of Vols:	4,000+
Specialties:	Horses; livestock; farrier; veterinary; agriculture.
Credit Cards:	Yes
Owner:	Wayne G. Hipsley
Year Estab:	1987

Woodland Park Bookstore   **Open Shop**
700 East Main Street 40502   Tel & Fax: (606) 252-5854
Web page: www.woodbook.com   E-mail: woodbook@lex.infi.net

Collection:	General stock, maps and ephemera.
# of Vols:	30,000
Hours:	Mon-Sat 10-8. Sun 12-5.
Services:	Appraisals, search service, catalog, accepts want lists.
Travel:	Rte 60 exit off I-75 south. Proceed west on Rte 60 (Winchester Rd) for about 3-4 miles, then left on Walton and left on Main.
Credit Cards:	Yes
Owner:	Diana Rice Turnbull
Year Estab:	1985
Comments:	The early bird does not necessarily get the worm. We arrived at this shop before noon on a Sunday in June, having been advised that the shop hours were as stated above. (There were no hours posted on the window or door.) A large sandwich sign outside the shop indicated that a sale was on. By 12:35pm the shop was still not open and our lack of patience was such that we decided to move on. We had nice things to say about this shop during our earlier visit to Lexington and had hoped to be able to reconfirm those observations at the shop's new location. Should you find the shop open when you're in the Lexington area and have a chance to visit, we would be happy to have your views. After our earlier visit 3½ years ago we noted:

A showcase, not only for its fine books, almost all of which were in good to excellent condition, but also for its display (for sale) of original art, maps, etc. The shop has a large enough collection, particularly in subjects related to history, to make it worth a visit. The books we saw were priced "at value."

Louisville
(Map 10, page 159 & Map 12, page 171)

A Reader's Corner   **Open Shop**
115 Wiltshire 40207   Tel & Fax: (502) 897-5578
                                                 E-mail: tim_fout@ntr.net

Collection:	General stock of hardcover and paperback.
# of Vols:	15,000
Specialties:	Religion (Catholic and other denominations); philosophy; cookbooks.
Hours:	Mon-Fri 11-7. Sat 10-7. Sun 1-5.
Services:	Search service, accepts want lists, mail order.
Travel:	Exit 18B (Breckenridge Lane) off I-264. Proceed north on Breckenridge, then left on Willis and right on Wiltshire.
Credit Cards:	Yes
Owner:	Tim Fout
Year Estab:	1997
Comments:	A relatively new shop that shows promise with a nice balance between its hardcover and paperback books. Most of the books we saw were in good condition and appeared to have been carefully selected. Many subjects were represented and the books ranged from older (some collectible) volumes to more recent titles. We hope that unlike us, you do not get "lost in Louisville" while in the process of finding this place. (Our advice when crossing the city from one book neighborhood to another is to avoid shortcuts and stay on the major roads.)

All Booked Up   **Open Shop**
1555 Bardstown Road 40205   (502) 459-6348

Collection:	General stock of hardcover and paperback.
# of Vols:	35,000-40,000
Specialties:	Kentucky; children's.
Hours:	Tue-Sat 10-7. Sun 12-5.
Services:	Appraisals, search service, accepts want lists, mail order.
Travel:	Grinstead Dr exit off I-64. Proceed south on Grinstead, then left on Bardstown. Shop is 3/4 of mile ahead on right.
Credit Cards:	Yes
Owner:	Richard E. Young
Year Estab:	1992
Comments:	A bi-level shop with class. The books were in good condition, of mixed vintage and very reasonably priced.

(Louisville)

Children's Planet   **Open Shop**
1341 Bardstown Road 40204   (502) 458-7018
Web page: www.children'splanet.com   Fax: (502) 458-6943
                                                                   E-mail: cplanet@aye.net

Collection:	Specialty
# of Vols:	4,000
Specialties:	Children's
Hours:	Mon-Sat 11-5.
Services:	Appraisals, search service, accepts want lists, mail order.
Travel:	Eastern Pkwy exit off I-65. Proceed east on Eastern Pkwy, then left on Bardstown. Shop is three blocks ahead on right. From I-64: Grinstead Dr exit. West on Grinstead, then south on Bardstown.
Credit Cards:	Yes
Owner:	David R. & Mary Friedlander
Year Estab:	1996
Comments:	A visit to this shop is like a trip backwards in time that children of all ages should find fascinating. In addition to the many children's books displayed throughout the shop, there are several rooms of children's toys and games that will take the visitor back to happier times. If you're a children's book enthusiast or a nostalgia buff, you should definitely plan to stop here.

The Cookbook Cottage   **By Appointment**
1279 Bardstown Road 40204   (502) 458-5227
Collection: Specialty

Specialties:	Cookbooks
Services:	Appraisals, search service, catalog, accepts want lists.
Credit Cards:	Yes
Owner:	Stephen Lee
Year Estab:	1986

Cynthia K. Fowler Books   **By Appointment**
1723 Tyler Parkway 40204   (502) 458-2784

Collection:	Specialty
# of Vols:	1,000
Specialties:	Children's; children's illustrated. (Mainly 20th century collectible first editions. No series.)
Services:	Catalog, accepts want lists.
Year Estab:	1983

David R. Friedlander, Antiques   **Open Shop**
1341 Bardstown Road 40204   (502) 458-7586
Web page: www.children'splanet.com   E-mail: cplanet@aye.net

Collection:	General stock.
# of Vols:	300-500

Hours:	Mon-Sat 9-5:30.
Services:	Catalog, accepts want lists.
Travel:	See Children's Planet above.
Credit Cards:	Yes
Owner:	David R. & Mary Friedlander
Year Estab:	1973
Comments:	A limited selection of books without any major discernible theme. However, the proprietor owns a second establishment, almost immediately next door, which any collector or dealer of children's books should definitely visit. (See Children's Planet above.)

Great Escape   **Open Shop**
2433 Bardstown Road 40205   (502) 456-2216

Collection:	Specialty paperbacks.
# of Vols:	200
Specialties:	Science fiction.
Hours:	Mon-Sat 10-9. Sun 1-6.
Comments:	Shop also sells comics, videos, toys, etc.

Mac Neil's Books and Records   **Flea Market**
At Derby Park Traders Circle, 2900 South 7th Street Road   (502) 448-5253

Collection:	General stock of hardcover and paperback.
Hours:	Sat & Sun 9-5.
Comments:	Also displays at Radcliff Antique Mall. See below.

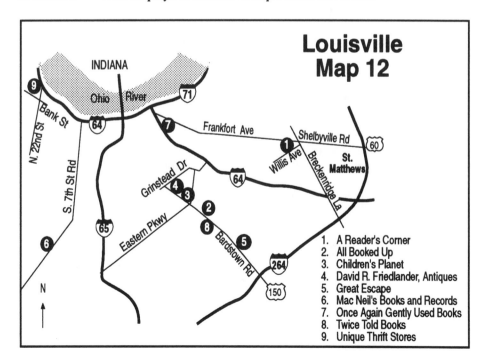

Louisville
Map 12

1. A Reader's Corner
2. All Booked Up
3. Children's Planet
4. David R. Friedlander, Antiques
5. Great Escape
6. Mac Neil's Books and Records
7. Once Again Gently Used Books
8. Twice Told Books
9. Unique Thrift Stores

(Louisville)

Donald S. Mull - Books
1706 Girard Drive 40222

By Appointment
(502) 426-2947

Collection:	Specialty
# of Vols:	5,000
Specialties:	Civil War; Kentucky; Americana.
Services:	Appraisals, accepts want lists.
Credit Cards:	No
Year Estab:	1983

Once Again Gently Used Books
2210 Frankfort Avenue 40206

Open Shop
(502) 893-0582

Collection:	General stock of paperback and some hardcover.
# of Vols:	37,000+
Specialties:	Mystery
Hours:	Tue-Fri 11-5. Sat 9:30-4.
Services:	Accepts want lists, mail order.
Travel:	Grinstead Dr exit off I-64. Proceed east on Grinstead for one block, then left on Peterson and left on Frankfort. Shop is about four blocks ahead.
Credit Cards:	Yes
Owner:	Jean McDonald
Year Estab:	1989
Comments:	A small shop with a preponderance of paperbacks and some hardcover volumes. The strongest hardcover section was mystery and most of these titles were of fairly recent vintage.

Paterson-Ford Booksellers
85 Breckenridge Square 40220
Web page: www. pfbooks.com

By Appointment
Tel & Fax: (502) 458-2438
E-mail: joni@pfbooks.com

Collection:	Specialty
# of Vols:	10,000-12,000
Specialties:	Scotland; Britain; animals.
Services:	Appraisals, search service, catalog, accepts want lists.
Credit Cards:	Yes
Owner:	Joni Margill Paterson & David W. Ford
Year Estab:	1995

Twice Told Books
1578 Bardstown Road 40205

Open Shop
(502) 458-7420
E-mail: twicetol@iglou.com

Collection:	General stock of mostly hardcover and records (jazz).
# of Vols:	30,000
Specialties:	Modern first editions; Civil War; Kentucky; Southern Americana.
Hours:	Mon-Sat 11-7. Sun 12-6. Longer hours in summer.
Services:	Accepts want lists.

Travel:	Bardstown exit off I-264. Proceed north on Bardstown.
Credit Cards:	Yes
Owner:	Harold Maier
Year Estab:	1984
Comments:	A nice shop with a good sized collection of mixed vintage books in mixed condition with an emphasis on reading copies. Most subjects were covered. With another used book dealer just a block away, the shop is definitely worth visiting.

Unique Thrift Stores   **Open Shop**
617 Carter Street 40212   (502) 772-9304

Collection:	General stock of paperback and hardcover.
# of Vols:	1,000-2,000
Hours:	Mon-Sat 9-9.
Travel:	22nd St exit off I-64. Proceed west on Portland to first parking lot on the right.
Comments:	Stock is approximately 60% paperback.

Maysville
(Map 10, page 159)

A Likely Story   **Open Shop**
15 West 2nd Street 41056   (606) 564-9370
                                                              E-mail: alstory@ntr.net

Collection:	General stock mostly hardcover.
# of Vols:	20,000
Hours:	Mon-Fri 9:30-5. Sat 10-4.
Services:	Search service, accepts want lists, mail order.
Travel:	Located in downtown historic district.
Credit Cards:	Yes
Owner:	Susan Wills
Year Estab:	1993

Mount Sterling
(Map 10, page 159)

Bison Books   **Open Shop**
32 East Main Street 40353   (606) 497-2188
                                                              Fax: (606) 497-2185
                                                       E-mail: bisonbks@interloc.com

Collection:	General stock of mostly used hardcover.
# of Vols:	20,000
Hours:	Mon-Fri 10-5. Sat 10-2.
Services:	Search service, accepts want lists.
Travel:	Exit 110 off I-64. Proceed south on Rte 11 for about two miles, then left on Rte 60. Shop is seventh shop on Main Street.
Credit Cards:	No
Owner:	Liz Mandrell

Year Estab: 1996
Comments: You know that a book dealer takes her business seriously when, despite
               the fact that had just been bitten by a dog and was told that she required
               shots, she remained open so that we could visit her shop. What we saw
               was a spacious, attractively decorated store with a modest selection of
               hardcover books representing several subject areas. The majority of the
               books were reading copies that were quite reasonably priced. We made
               a purchase and might have made more were it not for the fact that the
               owner had to get to the hospital and we didn't want to be responsible
               for her injury becoming any more serious than it was.

The Mt. Sterling Rebel   **By Appointment**
PO Box 481 40353   (606) 498-5821

Collection: Specialty
# of Vols: 2,000
Specialties: Civil War.
Services: Catalog, appraisals.
Credit Cards: Yes
Year Estab: 1978

Owensboro
(Map 10, page 159)

Moneytree Book Warehouse   **Open Shop**
1421 Triplett Street 42303   (502) 684-0000

Collection: General stock of mostly paperback.
# of Vols: 10,000
Hours: Mon-Sat 9-9. Sun 12-9.

Paducah
(Map 10, page 159)

Boulands Booksellers   **Open Shop**
2225 Broadway 42001   (502) 443-0805

Collection: General stock of paperback and hardcover.
# of Vols: 15,000 (hardcover)
Hours: Mon-Thu 9:30-5:30. Fri & Sat 9:30-8.
Travel: Bus Rte 60 exit off I-24. Proceed east on Bus Rte 60, then south on
                 28th St and east on Broadway.
Credit Cards: Yes
Year Estab: 1997
Comments: The owner operates a second store in Popular Bluff, MO. See below.

Creatures of Habit   **Open Shop**
406 Broadway Street 42001   (502) 442-2923

Collection: General stock.
# of Vols: 2,000

Hours:	Mon-Sat 10-5.
Travel:	Exit 7 off I-24. Follow downtown loop to Broadway. Shop is at the intersection of the loop and Broadway, on the right.
Credit Cards:	Yes
Owner:	Natalya Haden & Jack Cody
Year Estab:	1986
Comments:	Shop also sells antiques and collectibles.

Pikeville
(Map 10, page 159)

Goff's Florist & Trading Post   **Open Shop**
Highway 119   (606) 432-8142
Mailing address: PO Box 198 Raccoon KY 41557

Collection:	General stock of mostly used paperback.
Hours:	Daily 9-5.

Prospect
(Map 10, page 159)

Blenheim Books   **By Appointment**
8001 Harrods Landing 40059   (502) 228-8774
                                                     Fax: (502) 228-7558
                                                     cbronte@iglou.com

Collection:	Specialty books and ephemera.
# of Vols:	3,000
Specialties:	Bronte sisters; Jane Austen; Winston Churchill; C. S. Lewis; Inklings; W. Woolf; literature (19th & 20th century).
Services:	Appraisals, catalog, accepts want lists, mail order.
Credit Cards:	Yes
Owner:	R. Alan Fitch
Year Estab:	1994

Radcliff
(Map 10, page 159)

Bookworm Book Store   **Open Shop**
853 North Dixie Highway 40160   (502) 351-6777

Collection:	General stock of mostly paperback.
# of Vols:	30,000
Hours:	Mon-Sat 10-5.

Radcliff Antique Mall   **Antique Mall**
509 South Dixie Highway 40160   (502) 351-5155

Hours:	Daily 9-5.
Travel:	Located on Rte 31W.

Richmond
(Map 10, page 159)

Harry's Books   **Open Shop**
805 East Main Street 40475   (606) 623-2370

Collection:	General stock of mostly hardcover.
# of Vols:	50,000
Specialties:	Kentucky; Civil War.
Hours:	Mon-Sat 9-5 but best to call ahead.
Travel:	Exit 90A off I-75. Continue south on Bus Rte 421/25. Shop is on left, just after crossing the railroad tracks.
Credit Cards:	Yes
Owner:	Harry Revel
Year Estab:	1990
Comments:	The problem for the browser is that the books are packed to the ceiling (and we mean literally to quite a high ceiling) and many are just too high to view. Also, few if any of the shelves are labeled. Without the owner's guidance directing the visitor to the areas of the visitor's interest, browsing would require a greater investment of time than we believe is appropriate for this establishment.

Paperback Exchange   **Open Shop**
200 West Irvine Street 40475   (606) 624-9921

Collection:	General stock of mostly paperback.
# of Vols:	15,000
Hours:	Mon-Sat, except closed Wed, 10-5.

Shelbyville
(Map 10, page 159)

Proud Mary's Booksellers   **Open Shop**
617 Main Street 40065   (800) 760-3313
Web page: www.proudmarys.com   (502) 647-3313
                                                          E-mail: proudmarys@ka.net

Collection:	General stock of mostly used hardcover.
# of Vols:	30,000
Specialties:	Military; world history; Kentucky.
Hours:	Tue-Sat 9-5. Mon by chance.
Services:	Appraisals, search service, accepts want lists, subject lists.
Travel:	Eastbound on I-64: Take first Shelbyville exit, then follow signs to Rte 60. Right on Rte 60. Shop is about three miles ahead in downtown, 1/2 block past 7th St. Westbound on I-64: Take first Shelbyville exit and follow signs to Rte 60. Turn left on Rte 60 which is Main St.
Credit Cards:	Yes
Owner:	Mary Potter, president

Year Estab: 1995
Comments: A very nice shop with a good selection of books, mostly hardcover. Strong in the subjects listed above as specialties. Most of the books we saw were in quite good condition; a few older items were worn. Our only caveat would be that several of the books we were familiar with were priced a tad higher here than similar items in the same condition seen elsewhere.

Waynesburg
(Map 10, page 159)

Cherie's Books   **By Appointment**
600 Shake Rag Road 40489   (606) 365-1050
                                                                      Fax: (606) 365-4849
                                                                  E-mail: cherie@mis.net

Collection: General stock.
# of Vols: 18,000
Specialties: Homeschooling
Services: Mail order, search service, accepts want lists.
Credit Cards: No
Owner: Cherie Carroll
Year Estab: 1997

Williamsburg
(Map 10, page 159)

Raymond M. Sutton, Jr. Books   **Open Shop**
430 Main Street   (606) 549-3464
Mailing address: PO Box 330 Williamsburg KY 40769   Fax: (606) 549-3469
                                                              E-mail: suttonbks@2geton.net

Collection: Specialty
# of Vols: 7,500
Specialties: Natural history; gardening.
Hours: Mon-Fri 9-6. Other times by appointment.
Services: Catalog, accepts want lists.
Travel: From I-75, follow signs to downtown.
Credit Cards: Yes
Year Estab: 1986

Mail Order Dealers

Arbor Antique Service
Sept-Apr: 400 Clements Avenue Somerset KY 42501   (606) 679-2979
May-Aug: PO Box 84 Newcastle ME 04553   (207) 563-1616

Collection:	General stock and ephemera.
Services:	Search service, accepts want lists.
Credit Cards:	No
Owner:	Sherry W. Hughes
Year Estab:	1986

Robert L. Barth, Bookseller   (606) 344-0043
3122 Royal Windsor Drive Edgewood 41017

Collection:	Specialty new and used
# of Vols:	5,000
Specialties:	Poetry (20th century).
Services:	Catalog, accepts want lists.
Credit Cards:	No
Year Estab:	1988

Books Are Everything   (606) 624-9176
302 Martin Drive Richmond 40475   Fax: (606) 623-9354
Web page: www.booksareeverything.com   E-mail: holland@zeus.chapel1.com

Collection:	General stock of all paperback.
# of Vols:	500,000+
Specialties:	Vintage paperbacks (1938-1978).
Services:	Appraisals, occasional catalog, accepts want lists, search service.
Credit Cards:	Yes
Owner:	R.C. Holland
Year Estab:	1978

Footnotes Bookshop   (606) 266-5414
2000 St. Christopher Drive Lexington 40502   E-mail: clauson@iglou.com

Collection:	Specialty
# of Vols:	3,000
Specialties:	Religion; philosophy; history; political science; government.
Credit Cards:	No
Owner:	Marc C. Clauson
Year Estab:	1997

Tim Hawley Books   (502) 451-3021
915 South Third Street Louisville 40203

Collection:	Specialty
# of Vols:	5,000
Specialties:	Books on books; printing and typography; fine printing; private press.
Services:	Catalog
Year Estab:	1984

Legacy Books Tel & Fax: (502) 499-9563
3019 Kaye Lawn Drive Louisville 40220 E-mail: legacybooks@iglou.com

Collection: General stock.
# of Vols: 10,000
Specialties: Kentucky; local history and fiction; Civil War; genealogy; Americana.
Services: Appraisals, search service, accepts want lists.
Credit Cards: No
Owner: Larry Dean
Year Estab: 1984
Comments: Collection may also be viewed by appointment,.

Mostly Baseball (606) 441-8646
8010 Nob Hill Drive Fort Thomas 41075

Collection: Specialty books and ephemera.
# of Vols: 2,000
Specialties: Baseball; sports.
Services: Catalog, accepts want lists.
Credit Cards: No
Owner: Richard D. Miller
Year Estab: 1990

Philatelic Bibliopole (502) 451-0317
PO Box 36006 Louisville 40233 Fax: (502) 459-8538
Web page: www.pbbooks.com E-mail: pbbooks@ibm.net

Collection: Specialty
Specialties: Philately
Services: Appraisals, search service, catalog, accepts want lists.
Credit Cards: No
Owner: Leonard H. Hartmann
Year Estab: 1965

Mike Sarki, Rogue Books (502) 245-4155
1403 Evergreen Road Anchorage 40223 E-mail: rogue@jcc-uky.campus.mci.net
Web page: www.autobahn.mb.ca/~parker/rouge/

Collection: Specialty
# of Vols: 1,000
Specialties: Poetry; new fiction.
Services: Catalog, accepts want lists.
Credit Cards: No
Year Estab: 1995

Don Smith's National Geographic Magazines (502) 366-7504
3930 Rankin Street Louisville 40214

Collection: Specialty
Specialties: *National Geographic.* Magazines and related matter.
Services: Appraisals. Also publishes a price guide booklet.
Credit Cards: No
Year Estab: 1969

Is the owner of this store trying to cool off some "hot" books?

Ex Libris
Frederick Eugene Hartnell

MICHIGAN

Alphabetical Listing By Dealer

Acorn Books	247	George Barry, Books	255
Afro Sol	222	Thomas C. Bayer	255
All Star Book Store	250	Becky's Main Street Books	230
Andrews & Rose Booksellers	232	Beulahland	222
Angling Book Hunter	229	Bibliotective	234
Another Look Books	248	Bicentennial Book Shop	223
Antiquarian Prints & Maps	236	Big Bang Books	255
Antique Connection	242	Big Book Store	206
Antique Enterprises	206	Bohling Book Company	255
Antique Mall of Ann Arbor	195	The Book Barn	220, 226
Antique Market of Williamston	252	Book Beat	235
Apparitions Comics & Books	224	The Book Bin	229
Arbor Books	195	The Book Devil	223
Arcadia Books	212	Book Exchange	242
Archives Book Shop	210	Book Exchange/Kazoo Books	224
Argos Book Shop	216	Book Gallery	217
Arnold's Of Michigan	228	The Book Nook	215
Artesian Wells Antique Mall	204	Book Nook	204
Artis Books & Antiques	195	Book Nook	205
Aunt Agatha's	195	The Book Shop	230
Aurora Books	230	The Book Stop	238
Avalon Books	245	The Book Worm	244
Avalon Bookshop	239	Bookmark Book Exchange	251
A-albionic Research	255	Bookop Shop	256
James M. Babcock, Bookseller	220	Books & Beyond	205
Backroom Bargains Used Bookstore	225	Books 'N' Things	256
Backroom MultiEntertainment	222	Books Abound	213
Backroom Obsessions	228	The Books Connection	246
Baker Book House	217	Books Connection	227
Balcony Books	221	Books Connection	247

Books Et Cetra	241	Galerie De Boicourt	251
Books In General	196	La Galerie	245
Boyne Country Books	203	Sam Gatteno Books	219
Branchwater Books & Ephemera	256	Thatcher C. Goetz, Books	216
Browns Family Bookstore	245	Graham Books	211
Capital City Comics & Books	226	John M. Gram	239
Carol's Paperbacks Plus	213	Grant's Book Store	218
A. Casperson Books	232	Great Midwestern Antique Emporium	250
Ralph A. Casperson Books	233	Green Gryphon Books	212
The Cellar Book Shop	207	Gunnerman Books	257
The Christensen Gallery	235	GT Motors	226
Classic Book Shop	242	H & B Booksellers	202
Albert G. Clegg, Bookseller	212	Harley's Antique Mall	193
Cliff's Engraving & Gifts	237	Hartfield Fine and Rare Books	197
The Cottage Book Shop	216	Ken Hebenstreit, Bookseller	243
The Country Tutor School Books	225	Hidden Room Book Shoppe	246
Crazy Barb's Paperback Exchange	251	Highwood Bookshop	248
Cross Street Book Shop	252	Hill Shop Paperbacks	214
Curious Book Shop	210	Michael A. Hogle Company	236
A. Dalrymple, Bookseller	256	Honeycomb Books & Records	251
Dann Collectibles	239	Huizinga's Books	209
David's Books	196	Ice Cream & Dreams	232
Dawn Treader Book Shop	196	Jack's Corner Bookstore	238
Deadly Passions Bookshop	224	Jane's Books & Etc.	218
Deux Amasse Books	241	Jay's African-American Books	207
Dog Ears Used Books	234	Jelly Bean's Used Book Exchange	244
Dolce Books Gifts Cards	193	Jellybean's Collectibles	215
John B. Doukas	256	Jellybean's Used Books	215, 237
Dove Booksellers	227	Jillson's Nauticals & Antiques	201
Dunes Antique Center	245	Jim's Books	257
Dusty Tome Used Book Store	206	John Paul II Bookstore	219
Milton F. Ehlert - Books	217	Lucetta A. Johnson	194
84 Charing Cross, EH?	231	Kaleidoscope Books & Collectibles	198
ETBooks	221	Keramos	257
Exnowski Enterprises	250	John K. King Books	207
FBS	252	John King Books North	214
The Fine Books Company	240	Knightsbridge Antique Mall	234
Else Fine Books	206	Known Books	248
First Edition Bookstore	231	Kregel Bookstore	218
First Edition Too Bookstore	203	Krickett's Bookshop	200
Jackie Foote Used Books	256	Kruklitis' Latvian Bookstore	258
Forgotten Lore	257	L & M Antiques	248
Four Score Books and Ect.	257	Lantern Enterprises	226
Fourth Street Book Shop	242	Leaves of Grass Books	198
Sheila Frank, Bookseller	217	Margaret Lee Antiques and Bookseller	236
Freddie The Bookie	252	Liberty Antique Mall	208
Friends Book Cellar	223	Library Bookstore	214
Friends of the Library Book Shop	197	Lindsay Chess Supplies	253

Links To The Past	249	Revolution Books	208
Looking Glass Books	227	Wm. M. Ripley Rare Books	198
Lowry's Books	249	Romeo Antique Mall	241
Mackinaw Book Company	222	Royal Oak Books	244
C. MacNeill Bookdealer	201	L.A. Rubin Rare Books	202
Mad Hatter Collectible Books	258	Russian Language Specialties	246
Magina Books	227	P.C. Schmidt, Bookseller	211
Mail Order Mysteries	258	The Science Bookshelf	260
Marion The Antiquarian Librarian	200	Second Story Used Books	211
Mary Ann's Books	258	Shaw's Books	219
Maxey's Discount Bookstore	244	J.E. Sheldon Fine Books	260
Mayflower Bookshop	201	Shirley's Book Services	236
McDonnell House Antiques	247	Silver Hills Antique Mall	229
Memory Lane Antique Mall	233	Sleepy Hollow Bookshop	230
Metropolis Art Books	208	Snowbound Books	229
Michiana Antique Mall	233	Something Wicked This Way Comes	225
Michiana Antiques & Books	194	Art Spindler	260
Miller's Antiques	240	Talponia Books Limited	193
James A. Monnig, Bookseller	258	Taylor Search Service	260
Morrie's Books	213	Tecumseh Antique Mall II	249
Mossback Books	208	Tomes & Treasures	194
My Wife's Books	240	Topaz-Mineral Exploration	261
David Netzorg	259	Treasures From The Castle	261
North Wind Books	209	Used Books	238
Novel Exchange Two	205	Patrick Vargo, Antiquarian Books	202
Old Horizons Book Shoppe	204	Volume I Books	220
Olympia Books & Prints	209	Water Tower Antiques	222
Out-of-the-Way Books	205	Dale Weber Books	261
Paperback Trader	251	Weekend Bookman	253
Paperbacks and Things	251	Richard Wertz, Bookseller	261
Barbara Parks - Books	243	West Side Book Shop	199
Peninsula Books	250	David L. White - Books	261
Peripatetic Bibliophile	218	White Raven Books	254
Phoenix Bookshop	243	Jett W. Whitehead - Rare Books	201
Pickers Antique Mall	233	The Wilderness Collection	262
Pineberry Collections	200	Win's Books	262
Pisces and Capricorn Books	193	The Wine And Food Library	199
Geraldine Powers	259	Pat & Bill Wisney-Books	262
Michael G. Price	259	Wooden Spoon Books	199
Prints Ancient & Modern	211	Wooten's Books	203
Quest Antiques-Books-Collectibles	259	Timothy B. Wuchter	262
Read It Again Books	234	Yesterday's Books	247
Red Flannel Antique Co. & Books	204	Yesterday's Books	237
Reformation Heritage Books	259	Yorty's Half-Priced Books of Mich.	241
Russell S. Rein, Books & Records	253	J.D. Zucatti, Bookseller	244
Rereadables	260		

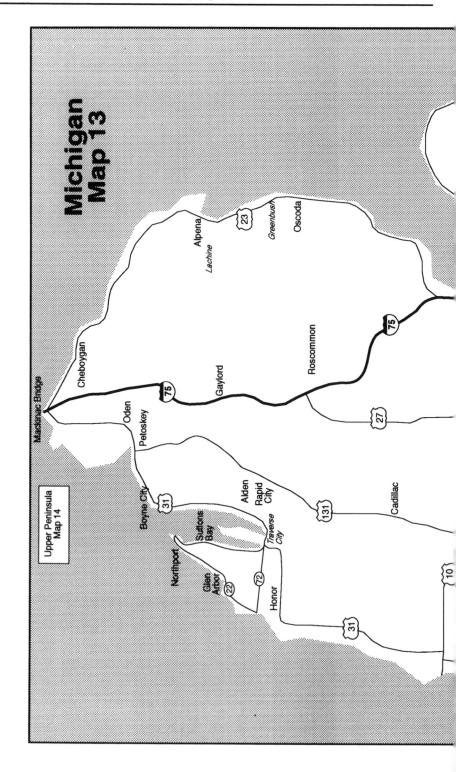

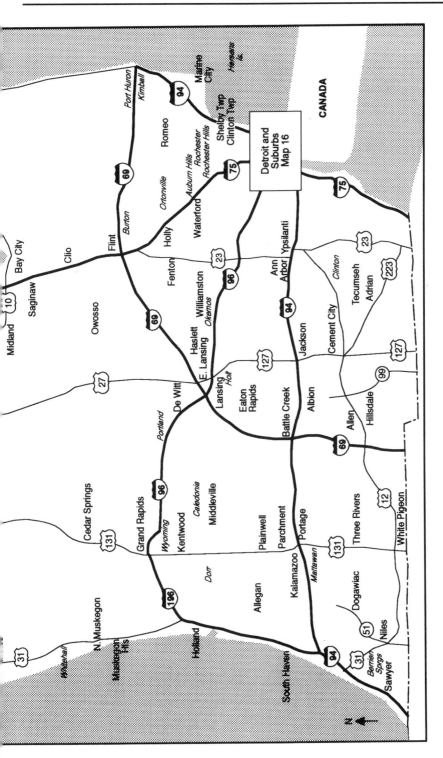

Alphabetical Listing By Location

Location	Dealer	Page
Adrian	Bookop Shop	256
	Dolce Books Gifts Cards	193
Albion	Harley's Antique Mall	193
	Pisces and Capricorn Books	193
Alden	Talponia Books Limited	193
Allegan	Lucetta A. Johnson	194
Allen	Michiana Antiques & Books	194
	Tomes & Treasures	194
Alpena	Artis Books & Antiques	195
Ann Arbor	Antique Mall of Ann Arbor	195
	Arbor Books	195
	Aunt Agatha's	195
	Books In General	196
	David's Books	196
	Dawn Treader Book Shop	196
	The Friends of the Library Book Shop	197
	Hartfield Fine and Rare Books	197
	Kaleidoscope Books & Collectibles	198
	Keramos	257
	Leaves of Grass Books	198
	Mail Order Mysteries	258
	Wm. M. Ripley Rare Books	198
	The Science Bookshelf	260
	J.E. Sheldon Fine Books	260
	West Side Book Shop	199
	The Wine And Food Library	199
	Wooden Spoon Books	199
Auburn Hills	Marion The Antiquarian Librarian	200
Battle Creek	Krickett's Bookshop	200
Bay City	Pineberry Collections	200
	Jett W. Whitehead - Rare Books	201
Berkley	C. MacNeill Bookdealer	201
	Mayflower Bookshop	201
Berrien Springs	Jillson's Nauticals & Antiques	201
Big Rapids	H & B Booksellers	202
Birmingham	A. Dalrymple, Bookseller	256
	L.A. Rubin Rare Books	202
	Patrick Vargo, Antiquarian Books	202
Boyne City	Boyne Country Books	203
Branch	Branchwater Books & Ephemera	256
Brevort	First Edition Too Bookstore	203
Brighton	Quest Antiques-Books-Collectibles	259
Burton	Wooten's Books	203
Cadillac	Book Nook	204

Caledonia	Old Horizons Book Shoppe	204
Cedar Springs	Red Flannel Antique Co. & Books	204
Cement City	Artesian Wells Antique Mall	204
Cheboygan	Book Nook	205
Clinton	Out-of-the-Way Books	205
Clinton Township	Books & Beyond	205
	Novel Exchange Two	205
Clio	Dusty Tome Used Book Store	206
Coopersville	David L. White - Books	261
Dearborn	Else Fine Books	206
Decatur	Bohling Book Company	255
Detroit	Antique Enterprises	206
	Big Book Store	206
	The Cellar Book Shop	207
	Jay's African-American Books and Posters	207
	John K. King Books	207
	Metropolis Art Books	208
	James A. Monnig, Bookseller	258
	Mossback Books	208
	David Netzorg	259
	Revolution Books	208
DeWitt	Liberty Antique Mall	208
Dorr	Huizinga's Books	209
Dowagiac	Olympia Books & Prints	209
Eagle Harbor	North Wind Books	209
East Lansing	Archives Book Shop	210
	Curious Book Shop	210
	Graham Books	211
	Kruklitis' Latvian Bookstore	258
	Prints Ancient & Modern	211
	P.C. Schmidt, Bookseller	211
Eastpointe	Second Story Used Books	211
Eaton Rapids	Arcadia Books	212
	Albert G. Clegg, Bookseller	212
Escanaba	Green Gryphon Books	212
Farmington	Books Abound	213
Farmington Hills	Morrie's Books	213
Fenton	Carol's Paperbacks Plus	213
	Rereadables	260
Ferndale	A-albionic Research	255
	John King Books North	214
	Library Bookstore	214
Flint	Hill Shop Paperbacks	214
	Jellybean's Collectibles	215
	Jellybean's Used Books	215
	Richard Wertz, Bookseller	261

Gaylord	The Book Nook	215
Glen Arbor	The Cottage Book Shop	216
Goetzville	Thatcher C. Goetz, Books	216
Grand Haven	Topaz-Mineral Exploration	261
Grand Rapids	Argos Book Shop	216
	Baker Book House	217
	Book Gallery	217
	Milton F. Ehlert - Books	217
	Sheila Frank, Bookseller	217
	Grant's Book Store	218
	Jane's Books & Etc.	218
	Kregel Bookstore	218
	Reformation Heritage Books	259
Greenbush	Peripatetic Bibliophile	218
Grosse Pointe	Sam Gatteno Books	219
Grosse Pointe Park	Mad Hatter Collectible Books	258
	Shaw's Books	219
Hamtramck	John Paul II Bookstore	219
Harsens Island	James M. Babcock, Bookseller	220
Haslett	The Book Barn	220
Hillsdale	Thomas C. Bayer	255
	Volume I Books	220
Holland	ETBooks	221
Holly	Balcony Books	221
	Water Tower Antiques	222
Holt	Mackinaw Book Company	222
Honor	Beulahland	222
Houghton	Backroom MultiEntertainment	222
Inkster	Afro Sol	222
Jackson	The Book Devil	223
	Books 'N' Things	256
	Friends Book Cellar	223
Kalamazoo	Bicentennial Book Shop	223
	Book Exchange/Kazoo Books	224
	Deadly Passions Bookshop	224
	John B. Doukas	256
Kentwood	Apparitions Comics & Books	224
Kimball	The Country Tutor School Books	225
L'Anse	Backroom Bargains Used Bookstore	225
Lachine	Something Wicked This Way Comes	225
Lansing	The Book Barn	226
	Capital City Comics & Books	226
	GT Motors	226
	Lantern Enterprises	226
	Looking Glass Books	227
Lawton	The Wilderness Collection	262

Lincoln Park	Magina Books	227
Livonia	Books Connection	227
	Dove Booksellers	227
Marine City	Arnold's Of Michigan Antiquarian Booksellers	228
Marquette	Backroom Obsessions	228
	Snowbound Books	229
Mattawan	Angling Book Hunter	229
Mears	Silver Hills Antique Mall	229
Melvindale	The Book Bin	229
Menominee	Aurora Books	230
Merrill	Four Score Books and Ect.	257
Michigan Center	Michael G. Price	259
Middleville	Becky's Main Street Books	230
Midland	The Book Shop	230
	Sleepy Hollow Bookshop	230
Munising	84 Charing Cross, EH?	231
Muskegon Heights	First Edition Bookstore	231
Newberry	Ice Cream & Dreams	232
Niles	Andrews & Rose Booksellers	232
	A. Casperson Books	232
	Ralph A. Casperson Books	233
	Michiana Antique Mall	233
	Pickers Antique Mall	233
North Muskegon	Memory Lane Antique Mall	233
Northport	Dog Ears Used Books	234
Northville	Knightsbridge Antique Mall	234
Novi	Read It Again Books	234
Oak Park	Bibliotective	234
	Book Beat	235
Oden	The Christensen Gallery	235
Okemos	Michael A. Hogle Company	236
	Shirley's Book Services	236
Orchard Lake	Antiquarian Prints & Maps	236
Ortonville	Margaret Lee Antiques and Bookseller	236
Oscoda	Cliff's Engraving & Gifts	237
Owosso	Gunnerman Books	257
	Jellybean's Used Books	237
	Jim's Books	257
	Win's Books	262
Parchment	Yesterday's Books	237
Pelkie	Timothy B. Wuchter	262
Petoskey	The Book Stop	238
Plainwell	Used Books	238
Plymouth	Jack's Corner Bookstore	238
Pontiac	Forgotten Lore	257
Port Huron	John M. Gram	239

Portage	Avalon Bookshop	239
	Big Bang Books	255
	Dann Collectibles	239
Portland	My Wife's Books	240
Rapid City	Miller's Antiques	240
Rochester	The Fine Books Company	240
	Dale Weber Books	261
Rochester Hills	Deux Amasse Books	241
	Treasures From The Castle	261
Romeo	Books Et Cetra	241
	Romeo Antique Mall	241
Roscommon	Yorty's Half-Priced Books of Michigan	241
Rosebush	Pat & Bill Wisney-Books	262
Royal Oak	Antique Connection	242
	George Barry, Books	255
	Book Exchange	242
	Classic Book Shop	242
	Fourth Street Book Shop	242
	Ken Hebenstreit, Bookseller	243
	Barbara Parks - Books	243
	Phoenix Bookshop	243
	Geraldine Powers	259
	Royal Oak Books	244
Saginaw	The Book Worm	244
	Jelly Bean's Used Book & Record Exchange	244
	Maxey's Discount Bookstore	244
	J.D. Zucatti, Bookseller	244
Saint Clair Shores	Browns Family Bookstore	245
	Art Spindler	260
Sault Ste. Marie	La Galerie	245
Sawyer	Dunes Antique Center	245
Shelby Township	Avalon Books	245
	The Books Connection	246
South Haven	Hidden Room Book Shoppe	246
	Russian Language Specialties	246
Southfield	Books Connection	247
	Mary Ann's Books	258
	McDonnell House Antiques	247
	Yesterday's Books	247
Sterling Heights	Acorn Books	247
Suttons Bay	Highwood Bookshop	248
	Known Books	248
Taylor	Another Look Books	248
Tecumseh	L & M Antiques	248
	Tecumseh Antique Mall II	249
Three Rivers	Links To The Past	249

Three Rivers	Lowry's Books	249
Traverse City	Peninsula Books	250
Warren	All Star Book Store	250
	Exnowski Enterprises	250
Waterford	The Great Midwestern Antique Emporium	250
	Honeycomb Books & Records	251
	Paperback Trader	251
Wayne	Crazy Barb's Paperback Exchange	251
West Bloomfield	Galerie De Boicourt	251
West Branch	Jackie Foote Used Books	256
Westland	Paperbacks and Things	251
	Taylor Search Service	260
White Pigeon	Bookmark Book Exchange	251
Whitehall	Freddie The Bookie	252
Williamston	Antique Market of Williamston	252
Wyoming	FBS	252
Ypsilanti	Cross Street Book Shop	252
	Lindsay Chess Supplies	253
	Russell S. Rein, Books & Records	253
	Weekend Bookman	253
	White Raven Books	254

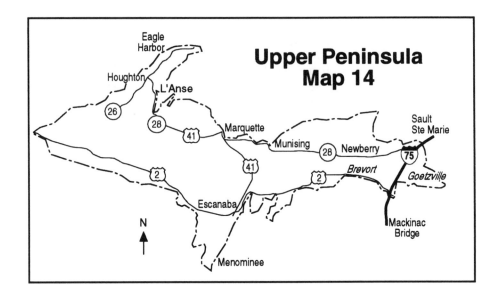

Upper Peninsula
Map 14

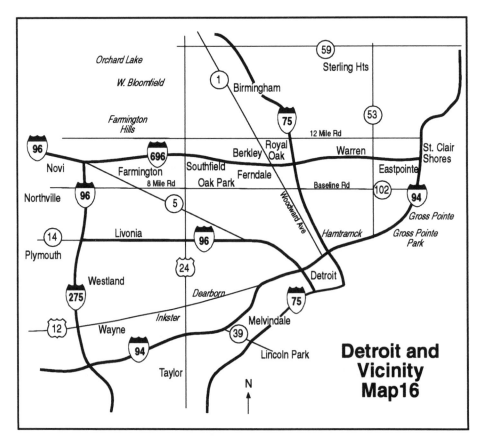

Detroit and
Vicinity
Map16

Adrian
(Map 13, page 184)

Dolcé Books Gifts Cards
111 East Maumee Street 49221

Open Shop
(517) 265-9152

Collection: General of mostly paperback.
# of Vols: 2,000+
Hours: Mon-Fri 9-8. Sat 9-4.

Albion
(Map 13, page 184)

Harley's Antique Mall
13789 Donovan Road 49224

Antique Mall
(517) 531-5300

Hours: Daily 10-8.
Travel: Located just off exit 127 off I-94. Proceed south on Concord then west on Donovan.

Pisces and Capricorn Books
501 Fitch
Mailing address: PO Box 478 Albion MI 49224

By Appointment
(517) 629-3267

Collection: Specialty
Specialties: Hunting; fishing; Notable Trials Series of British trials.
Services: Appraisals, accepts want lists, search service, mail order.
Credit Cards: No
Owner: Joe Wilcox
Year Estab: 1975

Alden
(Map 13, page 184)

Talponia Books Limited
10545 Coy Street
Mailing address: PO Box 36 Alden MI 49612

Open Shop
(616) 331-6324

Collection: General stock.
# of Vols: 20,000
Specialties: Great Lakes; children's; modern first editions.
Hours: May-Nov: Daily 10-6.
Services: Search service, accepts want lists, mail order.
Travel: From Rte 72, proceed north on Rte 597 (Rapid City/Alden Hwy which becomes Rte 593) for approximately eight miles to Alden. Shop is located in a former grist mill.
Credit Cards: Yes
Owner: Dr. & Mrs. John Esslinger
Year Estab: 1988
Comments: Most of the books were in good condition and several of the titles would definitely fall into the rare or collectible category with more

than a few first editions on hand. The owners, a charming couple who clearly have a romance with books, are most gracious. While some of the titles clearly deserve the prices being asked, we did spot several volumes that we felt were overpriced.

Allegan
(Map 13, page 184)

Lucetta A. Johnson   **Antique Mall**
At Water Street Antique Mall, 420 Water Street   (616) 673-4356
Mailing address: PO Box 68 Allegan MI 49010

Hours: Jan-Mar: Fri-Mon 10-5. Apr-Dec: Daily, except closed Thu, 10-5.
Travel: In downtown.

Allen
(Map 13, page 184)

Michiana Antiques & Books   **Antique Mall**
100-104 West Chicago, Box 28 49227   (517) 869-2132

Collection: General stock and ephemera.
# of Vols: 100,000
Specialties: Americana; world fairs; children's; local history.
Hours: Mon-Fri 11-4. Sat & Sun 11-5.
Services: Appraisals, search service, accepts want lists, mail order.
Travel: Exit 13 off I-69. Proceed east on Rte 12 for 12 miles.
Credit Cards: Yes
Owner: Bill & Eva Pengelly & Betty Dobson
Year Estab: 1965
Comments: The majority of the books on hand in this antique/collectibles shop are located in the basement with additional displays of bargain books located upstairs and in an outside shed on the street. A few items can also be found in glass display cases mixed in among the antiques. While the selection is broad in terms of subject area and you may be able to find an unusual item you've been looking for here, unfortunately, the majority of the books were in mixed condition. An additional 10,000 volumes can be viewed next door at the Old Book Shop, 108 West Chicago St, on a by appointment or chance basis. The dealer also displays at Harley's Antique Mall in Albion. See above.

Tomes & Treasures   **Antique Mall**
At Old Allen Township Hall Shops, 114 W. Chicago 49227   Mall: (517) 869-2575
                                                            Home: (517) 688-9673

Collection: General stock.
# of Vols: 10,000
Hours: Daily 10-5.
Travel: On Rte 12, in heart of downtown.
Owner: Robert C. Warner

Comments: Most of the volumes we saw here were of a nondescript nature: some fiction and biography, a few reference works and a miscellaneous mix of other titles. If you're an optimist, or interested in antiques, you might stop by; otherwise, keep driving. The dealer also displays at the Artesian Wells Antique Mall in Cement City. See below.

Alpena
(Map 13, page 184)

Artis Books & Antiques   **Open Shop**
201 North Second Avenue 49707   (517) 354-3401

Collection: General stock of new and used hardcover and paperback.
# of Vols: 14,000
Specialties: Michigan; Great Lakes; fishing; hunting; outdoors; Alaska; Arctic.
Hours: Mon-Fri 9-5+. Sat 10-5+. Sun by chance or appointment.
Services: Appraisals, catalogs.
Travel: One block from Rte 23.
Credit Cards: Yes
Owner: Thomas R. McKeever
Year Estab: 1978

Ann Arbor
(Map 15, page 197 & Map 13, page 184)

Antique Mall of Ann Arbor   **Antique Mall**
2739 Plymouth Road 48105   (734) 663-8200

Hours: Daily 11-7.
Travel: Exit 41 off Rte 23. Proceed west one mile on Plymouth Rd.

Arbor Books   **By Appointment**
1610 Charlton Street 48103   (734) 668-8443
                                                  E-mail: arborbks@mail.ic.net

Collection: General stock.
# of Vols: 2,000
Specialties: Modern first editions.
Services: Appraisals, search service, accepts want lists, mail order.
Credit Cards: No
Owner: Don Kramb
Year Estab: 1993

Aunt Agatha's   **Open Shop**
213 South Fourth Avenue 48104   (734) 769-1114
                                          E-mail: auntagathas@mailexcite.com

Collection: Specialty used and new paperback and hardcover.
# of Vols: 20,000+
Specialties: Mystery; true crime.
Hours: Mon-Thu 11-7. Fri & Sat 11-8. Sun 12-5.
Services: Accepts want lists.

Travel:	State St exit off I-94. Proceed north on State, then left on Liberty and right on Fourth. Shop is between Liberty and Washington.
Credit Cards:	Yes
Owner:	Jamie & Robin Agnew
Year Estab:	1992
Comments:	Stock is approximately 70% used, 90% of which is paperback.

Books In General   **Open Shop**
332 South State Street 48104   (734) 769-1250

Collection:	General stock.
# of Vols:	15,000-20,000
Specialties:	Science; technology; humanities; scholarly.
Hours:	Mon-Sat 10-7. Sun 12-5.
Services:	Accepts want lists.
Travel:	See Aunt Agatha's above. Shop in located on second floor.
Credit Cards:	Yes
Owner:	Paul Spater
Year Estab:	1990
Comments:	A neat, well organized shop with a selection of books in excellent condition. The majority of the titles would certainly fall into the category of serious or scholarly. The shop also has a good selection of general literature. Don't look for a cookbook or mystery section here. The books are very reasonably priced and the owner more than willing to be of assistance in any way possible.

David's Books   **Open Shop**
622 East Liberty Street 48104   (734) 665-8017
                                           E-mail: davidsbook@aol.com

Collection:	General stock of hardcover and paperback.
# of Vols:	30,000
Hours:	Mon-Sat 9:30-9. Sun 12-8.
Services:	Search service, accepts want lists, mail order.
Travel:	See Aunt Agatha's above. Shop is upstairs.
Credit Cards:	Yes
Owner:	Ed Koster
Year Estab:	1979
Comments:	Well worth the climb. The shop offers a large selection of books, mostly hardcover but with a fair share of paperbacks, with a heavy emphasis on the kinds of scholarly titles one would expect to find in a university town. In addition to the serious titles, the shop also has a good selection of fiction and popular titles.

Dawn Treader Book Shop   **Open Shop**
514 East Liberty Street 48104   (734) 995-1008
Web page: www.dawntreader.com   E-mail: gillmore@ameritech.net

Collection:	General stock of hardcover and paperback.
# of Vols:	75,000

Specialties:	Science fiction; first editions; foreign language books; mystery; fantasy; philosophy.
Hours:	Mon-Thu 11-8. Fri & Sat 11-9. Sun 11-6.
Services:	Appraisals, search service, occasional catalog, accepts want lists, book binding.
Travel:	See Aunt Agatha's above. Shop is between Maynard & Thompson.
Credit Cards:	Yes
Owner:	Bill Gillmore
Year Estab:	1978
Comments:	A truly fabulous shop with something for everyone. Our mouths watered as we examined rare signed first editions by well known writers. We were further impressed by the scope and variety of the books found here ranging from scholarly and technical volumes to general literature with a particularly strong emphasis on science fiction and horror. Whether you're a high brow, a general devotee of good literature or someone into a particular technical area, you should find something to delight you here. A map of the store layout is available.

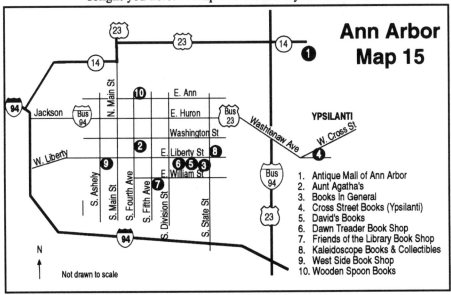

Ann Arbor Map 15

YPSILANTI

1. Antique Mall of Ann Arbor
2. Aunt Agatha's
3. Books In General
4. Cross Street Books (Ypsilanti)
5. David's Books
6. Dawn Treader Book Shop
7. Friends of the Library Book Shop
8. Kaleidoscope Books & Collectibles
9. West Side Book Shop
10. Wooden Spoon Books

N

Not drawn to scale

The Friends of the Library Book Shop   **Open Shop**
343 South Fifth Street 48104   (734) 994-2333

Hours:	Sept-Apr Sat 10-4. Sun 1:30-4:30
Travel:	See Aunt Agatha's above. Shop is at corner of Fifth and William, on the lower level of the public library.

Hartfield Fine and Rare Books   **By Appointment**
117 Dixboro Road 48105   (734) 662-6035
                                                                        Fax: (734) 971-4212

Collection:	Specialty

(Ann Arbor)

# of Vols:	8,000
Specialties:	English literature before 1800; Samuel Johnson; fore-edge paintings.
Services:	Appraisals, catalog.
Credit Cards:	No
Owner:	Ruth Iglehart
Year Estab:	1971

Kaleidoscope Books & Collectibles   Open Shop
217 South State Street 48104   (734) 995-9887
E-mail: BookScene@aol.com

Collection:	General stock of hardcover and paperback and ephemera.
# of Vols:	50,000
Specialties:	Children's; children's series; science fiction; mystery; vintage paperbacks; pulps.
Hours:	Mon-Wed 10-6. Thu-Sat 10-8. Sun 1-5.
Travel:	See Aunt Agatha's above.
Services:	Search service, accepts want lists, mail order.
Credit Cards:	Yes
Owner:	Jeff Pickell
Year Estab:	1990
Comments:	No matter what your age, if you have memories of "the good old days" you're likely to enjoy a visit to this nostalgia shop. And you may even be able to find a collectible or two of interest in the form of a book, magazine, comic book, poster, toy or record. On the other hand, if you're looking for antiquarian, rare or scholarly books, we suggest you look elsewhere in Ann Arbor.

Leaves of Grass Books   By Appointment
2433 Whitmore Lake Road 48105   (734) 995-2300

Collection:	General stock.
# of Vols:	20,000
Specialties:	Literature; Americana; books on books.
Services:	Appraisals, catalog, accepts want lists.
Credit Cards:	No
Owner:	Tom Nicely
Year Estab:	1973

Wm. M. Ripley Rare Books   By Appointment
1341 Dixboro Road 48105   (734) 995-5370
Web page: www.sayyestomichigan.com/rarebooks   Fax: (734) 995-7076
E-mail: ripley@mich.com

Collection:	General stock.
# of Vols:	5,000
Specialties:	Literature (20th century).
Services:	Accepts want lists, mail order.
Year Estab:	1993

West Side Book Shop   **Open Shop**
113 West Liberty 48104   (734) 995-1891

Collection:	General stock of mostly hardcover and original photography.
# of Vols:	20,000
Specialties:	Travel; exploration; literary first editions; books on books; natural history.
Hours:	Mon 11-6. Tue-Sat 11-10. Sun 1-5.
Travel:	See Wooden Porch below. Shop is just west of S. Main St.
Services:	Appraisals, catalog, accepts want lists.
Credit Cards:	Yes
Owner:	Jay Platt
Year Estab:	1975
Comments:	A typical university town used book shop with an emphasis on scholarly titles. Most of the books we saw were in good to excellent condition and many of the titles unusual.

The Wine And Food Library   **By Appointment**
1207 West Madison Street 48103   Tel & Fax: (734) 663-4894

Collection:	Specialty books and ephemera.
# of Vols:	20,000
Specialties:	Cookbooks; wine and other beverages; hotels and restaurants; culinary history.
Services:	Appraisals, search service, catalog, accepts wants lists, collection development.
Credit Cards:	No
Owner:	Jan Longone
Year Estab:	1972

Wooden Spoon Books   **Open Shop**
200 North Fourth Avenue 48104   (734) 769-4775
                                              E-mail: wspoonbks@provide.net

Collection:	General stock of mostly hardcover and records (jazz).
# of Vols:	40,000
Specialties:	Literary criticism; cookbooks; radical politics; labor history; African American history and literature.
Hours:	Mon-Sat 10-8. Sun 12-6.
Travel:	Exit 172 off I-94. Proceed east on Jackson (Bus Rte I-94), which becomes Huron, for about three miles, then north on Fourth Ave.
Credit Cards:	Yes
Owner:	Richard Wunsch
Year Estab:	1968
Comments:	A good sized shop with an excellent mix of older volumes in varying condition. In addition to the above specialities, the shop is strong in political science and has a healthy representation in most other areas in both serious and popular subjects. While the books could hardly be classified as being in pristine condition, the prices were most reasonable.

Auburn Hills
(Map 13, page 184)

Marion The Antiquarian Librarian   **By Appointment**
3668 South Shimmons Circle 48326   (248) 373-8414

Collection:	General stock.
# of Vols:	5,000
Specialties:	Art; architecture; illustrated; first editions.
Services:	Search service, mail order.
Credit Cards:	Yes
Owner:	Marion E. Brodie
Year Estab:	1971

Battle Creek
(Map 13, page 184)

Krickett's Bookshop   **Open Shop**
69 Calhoun Street 49017   (616) 962-2495

Collection:	General stock of paperback and hardcover.
# of Vols:	30,000 hardcover. (See Comments)
Hours:	Wed-Sat 11-5 but best to call ahead.
Travel:	Rte 66 exit off I-94. Proceed north on Rte 66, left on Freemont and left on Calhoun. Shop is about two blocks ahead on the right.
Credit Cards:	No
Owner:	Paul Ronning
Year Estab:	1975
Comments:	Don't be intimidated by the very large number of paperbacks, and even comic material. Also, don't be put off by the large number of book club items you're likely to see. After a little searching, you should come across shelf after shelf of hardcover volumes. At the time of our visit, the hardcover stock was particularly strong in fiction, from the classics and modern fiction to mystery and everything inbetween. The books were in mixed condition and most reasonably priced. Note: Not all the hardcover stock is displayed.

Bay City
(Map 13, page 184)

Pineberry Collections   **Antique Mall**
At Bay City Antiques Center, 1010 North Water St.   Mall: (517) 893-1116
Mailing address: 4651 Jacob Road Cass City MI 48726   Home: (517) 673-4731

Collection:	General stock.
Hours:	Mon-Sat 10-5, except Fri till 8. Sun 12-5.
Services:	Mail order, accepts want lists.
Owner:	Dee Smith
Year Estab:	1986

Jett W. Whitehead - Rare Books
1412 Center Avenue 48708

By Appointment
(517) 892-0719
Fax: (517) 892-9445

Collection:	Specialty
# of Vols:	5,000
Specialties:	Poetry (20th century), including first editions, limited editions, signed and association copies and broadsides.
Services:	Appraisals, catalog, search service, accepts want lists.
Year Estab:	1991

Berkley
(Map 16, page 192)

C. MacNeill Bookdealer
3165 12 Mile Road 48072

Open Shop
(248) 543-1177

Collection:	General stock of hardcover and paperback.
# of Vols:	30,000
Hours:	Tue-Sat 11-7. Sun 12-4. Closed Sun in summer.
Services:	Accepts want lists, mail order.
Travel:	One mile west of Woodward Ave (Rte 1) between Greenfield & Coolidge. Parking is available in the rear.
Credit Cards:	No
Year Estab:	1992
Comments:	We hope that the owner is in attendance when you visit this shop. His knowledge of the book trade and the quality of his stock should quickly overcome any preconception book people may have regarding the "typical" book dealer (if there is such a thing). We believe that you'll be pleasantly surprised. The stock is eclectic, well cared for and most reasonably priced.

Mayflower Bookshop
2645 West 12 Mile Road 48072

Open Shop
(248) 547-8227

Collection:	Specialty new and used.
Specialties:	Metaphysics; astrology; esoteric sciences; healing.
Hours:	Tue-Sat 10-6, except Fri till 7.
Services:	Mail order.
Travel:	One block west of Coolidge.
Credit Cards:	Yes
Owner:	Robert Thibodeau
Year Estab:	1972

Berrien Springs
(Map 13, page 184)

Jillson's Nauticals & Antiques
8798 Elizabeth Drive 49103

By Appointment
(616) 471-5006
E-mail: jna1898@qtm.net

Collection:	Specialty books and ephemera.

# of Vols:	1,000
Specialties:	Nautical, Great Lakes; lighthouses; life saving; Spanish American War; naval.
Services:	Accepts want lists, mail order.
Owner:	Ron & Kathy Jillson
Year Estab:	1987

Big Rapids
(Map 13, page 184)

H & B Booksellers   **Open Shop**
205 Maple Street 49307   (616) 592-0879
E-mail: habinc@netonecom.net

Collection:	General stock of mostly hardcover.
# of Vols:	30,000
Specialties:	Biography; first editions; Western Americana; European history; military.
Hours:	Tue-Fri 12-5. Sat 10-5.
Services:	Search service, accepts want lists.
Travel:	Big Rapids exit off Rte 131. Shop is in downtown, at corner of Michigan and Maple St (Rte 20). Parking is available in the rear.
Credit Cards:	Yes
Owner:	Hal & Barbara Palmer
Year Estab:	1994
Comments:	An attractive shop that should satisfy the browsing tastes of most book travelers. The books range from reading copies of fairly recent vintage to older and often quite interesting and unusual titles. The shop also offers a bit of ephemera and some paperbacks and less expensive fiction on a mezzanine level. The books are priced to sell. A most pleasant shop to browse.

Birmingham
(Map 16, page 192)

L.A. Rubin Rare Books   **By Appointment**
PO Box 31 48012

Collection:	Specialty
Specialties:	Fine bindings; illustrated classics; art reference.
Services:	Collection development
Year Estab:	1965

Patrick Vargo, Antiquarian Books   **Open Shop**
725 South Adams, Ste. L-85 48009   (248) 647-0135
Web page: www.vargobooks.com   Fax: (248) 647-0136
E-mail: patvargo@vargobooks.com

Collection:	Specialty
# of Vols:	10,000
Specialties:	Fine bindings.

Hours:	Mon-Fri 11-3:30. Sat 10-5.
Services:	Appraisals, search service, catalog, accepts want lists.
Travel:	Woodward Ave exit off I-696. Proceed north on Woodward, then right on Adams. Shop is in South Adams Square Shopping Center.
Credit Cards:	Yes
Year Estab:	1988

Boyne City
(Map 13, page 184)

Boyne Country Books   **Open Shop**
125 Water Street 49712   (616) 582-3180

Collection:	General stock of new and mostly paperback used.
# of Vols:	5,000 (used)
Hours:	Mon-Thu 9-6. Fri & Sat 9-9. Sun 11-5. Memorial Day to Labor Day: Daily 9am-10pm.

Brevort
(Map 14, page 192)

First Edition Too Bookstore   **By Appointment**
461 Worth Road   (906) 292-5513
Mailing address: 461 Worth Road   Moran 49760

Collection:	General stock of hardcover and paperback and ephemera.
# of Vols:	12,000
Specialties:	Great Lakes; Michigan.
Hours:	May-Sept or Oct. Other times by chance.
Services:	Appraisals, search service, accepts want lists, mail order.
Credit Cards:	Yes
Owner:	Mary Carney
Year Estab:	1979

Burton
(Map 13, page 184)

Wooten's Books   **By Appointment**
G-3311 Cheyenne 48529   (810) 744-1987
                                                 E-mail: magicbook@aol.com

Collection:	General stock.
# of Vols:	8,000
Specialties:	Children's; conjuring; history; illustrated.
Credit Cards:	Yes
Owner:	Richard & Mary Ann Wooten
Year Estab:	1980
Comments:	We visited these dealers on our earlier trip to Michigan when they maintained an open shop and noted at the time:
	If you enjoy the sight of quality books and would like an opportunity to chat with two knowledgeable book people, stop at this shop,

located behind the owners' home. We saw interesting and rare items in the owners' areas of specialization and the general collection, while small, is worth a careful study.

Cadillac
(Map 13, page 184)

Book Nook   **Open Shop**
120 East Pine Street 49601   (616) 775-8171

Collection: General stock of mostly paperback.
Hours: Mon-Sat 9:30-5.

Caledonia
(Map 13, page 184)

Old Horizons Book Shoppe   **By Appointment**
7079 Hammond Avenue, SE 49316   (616) 698-5098

Collection: General stock of paperback and hardcover.
# of Vols: 12,000
Specialties: Mystery; westerns.
Services: Search service, accepts want lists, mail order.
Credit Cards: No
Owner: Danell Griffith
Year Estab: 1989
Comments: Stock is approximately 65% paperback.

Cedar Springs
(Map 13, page 184)

Red Flannel Antique Co. & Books   **Open Shop**
128 North Main Street   (616) 696-9599
Mailing address: 4540 Bailey Road Coral MI 49322   (616) 354-6354

Collection: General stock and ephemera.
# of Vols: 3,000 (See Comments)
Hours: Mon-Sat 10-5. Sun by chance or appointment.
Services: Search service, accepts want lists, mail order.
Travel: Rte 46 exit off Rte 131. Proceed east on Rte 46 to Main St.
Credit Cards: No
Owner: Judith Rogers
Year Estab: 1970
Comments: An additional 4,000 books are in storage.

Cement City
(Map 13, page 184)

Artesian Wells Antique Mall   **Antique Mall**
18707 West Toledo Road 49233   (517) 437-7422

Hours: Daily 10-6.
Travel: Located at junction of Rtes 127 and 12.

Cheboygan
(Map 13, page 184)

Book Nook **Open Shop**
232 North Main Street 49721 (616) 627-1010

Collection:	General stock of paperback and hardcover.
# of Vols:	7,000+
Hours:	Mon-Sat 10-5. Extended hours (including Sun) during summer.
Travel:	Exit 326 off I-75. Proceed east on Levering State Rd, then right at first light on Main. Shop is at next light in a complex of stores.
Comments:	Stock is approximately 75% paperback.

Clinton
(Map 13, page 184)

Out-of-the-Way Books **By Appointment**
317 Clark, #D 49236 (517) 456-7273
E-mail: outofway@interloc.com

Collection:	General stock.
# of Vols:	5,000
Specialties:	Travel
Services:	Accepts want lists, mail order.
Credit Cards:	Yes
Owner:	Mike Gajda
Year Estab:	1992
Comments:	Also displays at L & M Antiques and Tecumseh Antique Mall II, both in Tecumseh. See below.

Clinton Township
(Map 13, page 184)

Books & Beyond **Open Shop**
20666 Hall Road 48038 (810) 468-6023

Collection:	General stock of paperback and hardcover.
# of Vols:	3,000
Hours:	Mon-Sat 10-6.
Travel:	On Rte 59, four miles west of I-94.
Year Estab:	1996
Comments:	Stock is approximately 75% paperback.

Novel Exchange Two **Open Shop**
41972 Hayes Road 48038 (810) 228-2226

Collection:	General stock of mostly used paperback.
Hours:	Mon-Sat, except closed Wed, 10-6.

Clio
(Map 13, page 184)

Dusty Tome Used Book Store
107 West Vienna Street 48420

Open Shop
(810) 686-5517

Collection:	General stock of mostly paperback.
# of Vols:	10,000
Hours:	Mon-Thu 10:30-5. Fri 12-5. Sat 10-4.

Dearborn
(Map 16, page 192)

Else Fine Books
PO Box 43 48121

By Appointment
(313) 582-1080
Fax: (313) 584-1591
E-mail: elsefine@compuserve.com

Collection:	Specialty
# of Vols:	10,000
Specialties:	Modern literary first editions; first editions of mystery; detective; science fiction; fantasy; horror.
Services:	Catalog, accepts want lists.
Credit Cards:	Yes
Owner:	Louise Oberschmidt & Allen M. Hemlock
Year Estab:	1983

Detroit
(Map 16, page 192)

Antique Enterprises
At L & L Books 66 Penobscot
Mailing address: 9200 Dwight Ave Detroit MI 48214

Open Shop
Shop: (313) 963-8672
Home: (313) 822-4412

Collection:	General stock.
# of Vols:	10,000
Specialties:	Vintage paperbacks.
Hours:	Mon-Fri 9-6.
Services:	Appraisals, accepts want lists, mail order.
Travel:	Downtown, one block from Lodge Fwy and Woodward, in a "new" bookstore.
Credit Cards:	Yes
Owner:	Harry Letzmann
Comments:	Only a portion of the collection is on display. Additional books can be viewed by appointment.

Big Book Store
5911 Cass Avenue 48202

Open Shop
(313) 831-8511

Collection:	General stock of mostly paperback and some hardcover.
# of Vols:	50,000
Specialties:	Magazines (popular titles from 1970's and up and adult publications).

Hours:	Mon-Sat 9:30-5:30.
Services:	Accepts want lists.
Travel:	On campus of Wayne State University.
Credit Cards:	Yes
Owner:	John K. King
Year Estab:	1930

The Cellar Book Shop   **By Appointment**
18090 Wyoming 48221   Tel & Fax: (313) 861-1776
E-mail: cellarbook@aol.com

Collection:	Specialty new and used.
# of Vols:	10,000
Specialties:	Southeast Asia; Pacific Islands.
Services:	Catalog, accepts want lists.
Credit Cards:	Yes
Owner:	Petra F. Netzorg
Year Estab:	1946

Jay's African-American Books and Posters   **By Appointment**
1519 Chateaufort 48207   (313) 568-7732

Collection:	Specialty
# of Vols:	1,000
Specialties:	African American authors; black studies.
Services:	Accepts want lists, mail order.
Credit Cards:	No
Owner:	Jay C. Levine
Year Estab:	1993

John K. King Books   **Open Shop**
901 West Lafayette Boulevard 48226   (313) 961-0622
(313) 963-9138

Collection:	General stock.
# of Vols:	1 million
Specialties:	Americana; literature; Michigan; military; automotive.
Hours:	Mon-Sat 9:30-5:30.
Services:	Appraisals, search service, catalog, accepts want lists.
Travel:	Howard exit off southbound Rte 10 (Lodge Fwy), where Rte 10 inter-sects with I-75. Shop is 1/2 block from exit ramp. On site parking is available.
Credit Cards:	Yes
Year Estab:	1965
Comments:	Once we overcame our paranoia about venturing into "downtown De-troit" and found this establishment just off the freeway exit and with easy on site parking, we thoroughly enjoyed the opportunity to browse four floors of books representing every conceivable category. A com-puter printout of the shop's exhaustive subject categories (including one for "coffee table" books) and their locations is conveniently lo-

cated on each floor and the aisles and shelves are clearly marked. Needless to say, the selection here in every category was large, large, large. Perhaps the best part of our visit (in addition to finding titles to purchase) was the fact that the books were priced attractively. Be sure to arrive early and plan to stay late. Also, depending on your interests, you may want to request an opportunity to visit the shop's rare book room; even these books were reasonably priced. A "must" for any visitor to the Detroit area.

Metropolis Art Books   **By Appointment**
950 West Fort Street   Tel & Fax: (313) 961-5140
Mailing address: 901 West Lafayette Boulevard Detroit MI 48226
                                                 E-mail: metropolis@ameritech.net

Collection:	Specialty
# of Vols:	12,000
Specialties:	Fine art; decorative arts; photography.
Services:	Catalog, accepts want lists.
Credit Cards:	No
Owner:	Laurie Margot Ross
Year Estab:	1985

Mossback Books   **By Appointment**
16215 Warwick Road 48219   (313) 255-5663
                                                 E-mail: mossbakbk@gatecom.com

Collection:	General stock and ephemera.
# of Vols:	7,500
Specialties:	Americana; technical; medicine.
Services:	Appraisals, accepts want lists, mail order.
Credit Cards:	No
Year Estab:	1992
Comments:	Also displays at the Knightsbridge Antique Mall in Northville. See below.

Revolution Books   **Open Shop**
406 West Willis Street 48201   (313) 833-7310

Collection:	Specialty. Mostly new and some used.
Specialties:	Radical studies.
Hours:	Call for hours.
Comments:	A volunteer run shop. All used books are donated and profits are used to further the organization's political goals.

DeWitt
(Map 13, page 184)

Liberty Antique Mall   **Antique Mall**
1161 East Clark Road, #310 48820   (517) 669-4050

Hours:	Mon-Sat 10-9. Sun 12-5.
Travel:	Exit 87 off I-69.

Dorr
(Map 13, page 184)

Huizinga's Books   **By Appointment**
3916 18th Street 49323   (616) 681-9554
                                                       Fax: (619) 681-2901
                                                     E-mail: kjhuiz@aol.com

Collection: General stock.
# of Vols: 2,000+
Specialties: Religion with emphasis on Reformed and Presbyterian.
Services: Search service, accepts want lists, mail order.
Credit Cards: No
Owner: Ken Huizinga
Year Estab: 1996

Dowagiac
(Map 13, page 184)

Olympia Books & Prints   **Open Shop**
208 South Front Street 49047   (616) 782-3443

Collection: General stock of hardcover and paperback.
# of Vols: 30,000
Hours: Tue-Fri 10:30-4:30. Sat 10-3. Mon by chance.
Services: Search service, accepts want lists.
Travel: Dowagiac exit off I-94. Proceed south on Rte 51 to Dowagiac, then
                    continue straight to South Front.
Credit Cards: Yes
Owner: Paul & Karen Pugh
Year Estab: 1987
Comments: A modest sized shop with a fair collection of books in mixed condition
                    and representing mixed vintages. Prices quite reasonable.

Eagle Harbor
(Map 14, page 192)

North Wind Books   **Open Shop**
HC1, Box 190 49950   (906) 289-4911
Mailing address: Winter: 12 Ridge Lane Nantucket MA 02554
Web page: www.northwinbooks.com   Fax: (906) 289-4949
                                                     E-mail: pvanpelt@up.net

Collection: Specialty. Mostly new and some used.
# of Vols: 3,000
Specialties: Upper Midwest; Great Lakes.
Hours: Late May-Oct only: Jul & Aug: Daily 10-5. Other times: Tue-Sat 10-5.
                    Sun 1-5. Remainder of year, via mail or internet from Massachusetts
                    address, or by phone at (508) 325-9944, Fax: (508) 325-8944.
Services: Catalog
Travel: From Houghton, continue north on Rte 41 for about 35 miles. Left on

Rte 26 through Eagle River and Eagle Harbor, then left on Marina Rd. Continue for 1/2 mile.

Credit Cards: Yes
Owner: Patricia Van Pelt
Year Estab: 1991

East Lansing
(Map 13, page 184)

Archives Book Shop   **Open Shop**
517 West Grand River 48823   (517) 332-8444
                                                         Fax: (517) 332-1998
                                            E-mail: archivbk@interloc.com

Collection: Specialty, ephemera, prints and maps
# of Vols: 100,000
Specialties: Fine bindings; sets; first editions; antiquarian; signed; association copies; manuscripts.
Hours: Mon-Sat 11-6. Sun 12-5. Evenings by appointment.
Services: Appraisals, search service, catalog, accepts want lists.
Travel: Grand River Rd (Rte 43) exit off Rte 127. Proceed east on Grand River.
Credit Cards: Yes
Owner: Ray Walsh, owner. Dawn Martin, manager.
Year Estab: 1987
Comments: A good sized shop that carries an interesting mix of hardcover titles, many that could be considered hard to find, and a good share of collectibles. Definitely worth a visit. The owner operates a second shop in East Lansing, the Curious Book Shop. See below.

Curious Book Shop   **Open Shop**
307 East Grand River 48823   (517) 332-0112
Web page: www.interloc.com/~curious1   Fax: (517) 332-1915
                                            E-mail: curious1@interloc.com

Collection: General stock of hardcover and paperback and ephemera.
# of Vols: 100,000
Specialties: Science fiction; pulps; sports; magazines; mystery; children's; Michigan; history.
Hours: Mon-Fri 10-8. Sat 10-6. Sun 12-5.
Services: Appraisals, search service, accepts want lists, catalog.
Travel: See Archives. Continue east on Grand River Rd for six blocks. Shop is across from Michigan State University campus.
Credit Cards: Yes
Owner: Ray Walsh
Year Estab: 1969
Comments: There are books of every variety in this tri-level shop, most of them in very good condition. So even if you're not into any of the specialties listed above, you might easily find titles of interest here. If, of course, you're a devotee of any of the shop's specialty areas, you're in for a real treat since in both the number and variety of titles, the selections

in these areas offer a great deal to choose from. Be sure to visit the basement as well as the second floor. The owner also displays at the Antique Market of Williamston in Williamston. See below.

Graham Books   **By Appointment**
335 Wildwood Drive 48823   (517) 337-7290
                                                             Fax: (517) 337-0072
                                              E-mail: kwilcox@sojourn.com

Collection:	General stock.
# of Vols:	10,000
Specialties:	See Comments.
Services:	Appraisals, occasional lists, accepts want lists, mail order.
Credit Cards:	No
Owner:	Kent Wilcox & Donna Graham
Year Estab:	1974
Comments:	The owners describe their specialty as "collectible quality books starting at $50."

Prints Ancient & Modern   **Open Shop**
300 M.A.C. 48823   (517) 337-6366

Collection:	Specialty
Specialties:	Maps; prints (mostly European); botanicals.
Hours:	Mon-Wed 10-6. Thu-Fri 10-9. Sat 10-6. Sun 12-5.
Services:	Appraisals, search service, accepts want lists.
Travel:	Exit 127 off I-496, then first exit onto Michigan Ave. Proceed east on Michigan Ave for about for two miles, then left on M.A.C. Shop is two blocks ahead in building that also houses the Marriott Hotel.
Credit Cards:	Yes
Owner:	Bill Hankins
Year Estab:	1984

P.C. Schmidt, Bookseller   **By Appointment**
1016 Gainsborough Drive 48823   (517) 332-0580

Collection:	General stock of hardcover and paperback.
# of Vols:	40,000
Specialties:	Modern literature; science fiction; mystery.
Services:	Appraisals, search service, catalog, accepts want lists.
Credit Cards:	No
Year Estab:	1994
Comments:	Stock is approximately 70% hardcover.

Eastpointe
(Map 16, page 192)

Second Story Used Books   **Open Shop**
17920 East 10 Mile Road 48021   (810) 773-6440

Collection:	General stock of mostly paperback.

# of Vols:	50,000+
Hours:	Mon-Sat 10-8. Sun 10-5.

Eaton Rapids
(Map 13, page 184)

Arcadia Books
715 Goodrich Street 48827

Open Shop
(517) 663-4316
E-mail: vicolan@aol.ciom

Collection:	General stock.
# of Vols:	20,000
Hours:	Tue-Sat 1-6.
Travel:	From Rte 50/99, proceed east on Main, then left on Plain and right on Goodrich.
Credit Cards:	No
Owner:	Victor Colthorp
Year Estab:	1997
Comments:	At the time of our visit, there were considerably fewer books on display than noted above and the owner indicated that he still had many many more books to unpack. Most of what we saw were hardcover books with dust jackets in generally good condition. Perhaps by the time you visit, more books will be on display.

Albert G. Clegg, Bookseller
PO Box 306 48827

By Appointment
(517) 663-8428
Fax: (517) 663-1023

Collection:	Specialty
# of Vols:	10,000
Specialties:	Geology; hydrology; paleontology; chemistry.
Services:	Appraisals, catalog, accepts want lists.
Credit Cards:	No
Year Estab:	1962

Escanaba
(Map 14, page 192)

Green Gryphon Books
1100 Ludington, Ste 204 49829

Open Shop
(906) 789-2160
E-mail: grngryphon@aol.com

Collection:	General stock of paperback and hardcover.
Specialties:	Regional history; local authors; science fiction; mystery.
Hours:	Mon-Fri 9:30-6. Sat 9:30-5 (except till 4 Jan-Apr).
Services:	Appraisals, search service, accepts want lists, mail order, book repair.
Travel:	From Rte 2/Rte 35, go east on Ludington St. Shop is at corner of 11th St.
Credit Cards:	Yes
Owner:	Sherry Stegner
Year Estab:	1996
Comments:	Stock is approximately 75% paperback.

Farmington
(Map 16, page 192)

Books Abound   **Open Shop**
33336 Grand River 48336   Tel & Fax: (248) 477-8777
                                          E-mail: bkabound@interloc.com

Collection:	General stock of used and new hardcover and paperback.
# of Vols:	20,000
Hours:	Mon-Sat 10-9.
Travel:	8 Mile Rd exit off I-275. Proceed east on 8 Mile, then north on Farmington to Grand River. Make first right turn on Grand River and proceed into the alley parking lot.
Services:	Search service.
Credit Cards:	Yes
Owner:	Skip Rosenthal
Year Estab:	1980
Comments:	A neat little shop which, even though it sells some new books, does have a nice selection of used volumes, about evenly divided between hardcover and paperback, including quite a few in the areas of biography, literature and the arts.

Farmington Hills
(Map 16, page 192)

Morrie's Books   **By Appointment**
29734 Nova Woods 48331   (248) 788-9808
                                          E-mail: morriebk@oeonline.com

Collection:	General stock and ephemera.
# of Vols:	40,000
Specialties:	Art; cookbooks; Judaica; biography.
Services:	Search service, accepts want lists, mail order.
Credit Cards:	No
Owner:	Morris Cooper
Year Estab:	1991
Comments:	Also displays at the Antique Mall of Ann Arbor in Ann Arbor, Countryside Crafts and Antique Mall in Livonia and Knightsbridge Antiques Mall in Northville.

Fenton
(Map 13, page 184)

Carol's Paperbacks Plus   **Open Shop**
1443 North Leroy Street 48430   (810) 629-0050

Collection:	General stock mostly used paperback.
# of Vols:	20,000+
Hours:	Mon-Fri 10-8. Sat 10-6. Sun 12-5.

Ferndale
(Map 16, page 192)

John King Books North   **Open Shop**
22524 Woodward Avenue* 48220   (248) 548-9050
                                                    Fax: (313) 963-9138

Collection:	General stock of mostly hardcover and some paperback.
# of Vols:	60,000
Specialties:	Michigan; Detroit; automobiles; military.
Hours:	Mon-Fri 11-7. Sat 10-6. Sun 12-5.
Services:	Appraisals, search service, accepts want lists.
Travel:	Located between 8 Mile Rd and I-696.
Credit Cards:	Yes
Owner:	John King
Year Estab:	1988
Comments:	Unlike its vast parent establishment (see above), this much smaller shop takes on more of the traditional used book store appearance, but with the same kind of careful labeling of shelves found in the main location. You can obviously browse this store more quickly, and if you're looking for a special title, the manager will be more than glad to check if the main store has a copy. That's service! Prices were quite reasonable.

* *At the same location as in the previous edition (Woodward Ave was renumbered).*

Library Bookstore   **Open Shop**
169 West Nine Mile Road 48220   (248) 545-4300

Collection:	General stock of hardcover and paperback.
# of Vols:	30,000
Hours:	Mon-Sat 10-7, except Thu till 9. Sun 12-5.
Services:	Appraisals, accepts want lists.
Travel:	One mile south of I-696, in first block west of Woodward. Parking is available in rear.
Credit Cards:	Yes
Owner:	M. Sempliner
Year Estab:	1979
Comments:	An interesting mix of vintage paperbacks, traditional paperbacks and hardcover titles, most of fairly recent vintage. The shop is one that you can be in and out of in a short time, either spotting books in your areas of interest or seeing nothing and exiting quickly. Most items we saw were very reasonably priced.

Flint
(Map 13, page 184)

Hill Shop Paperbacks   **Open Shop**
4617 Fenton Road 48507   (810) 767-4351

Collection:	General stock of mostly paperback.

# of Vols:	40,000
Hours:	Mon-Sat 10-5.

Jellybean's Collectibles   **Open Shop**
730 South Dort Highway 48506   (810) 239-8808

Collection:	General stock of hardcover, paperback, records and comics.
# of Vols:	150,000
Specialties:	First editions; signed; antiquarian.
Hours:	Tue-Sat 11-5.
Travel:	Dort exit off I-69. Proceed north on Dort for 1/4 mile.
Credit Cards:	Yes
Owner:	Ron Samek
Year Estab:	1974
Comments:	A large store with a heavy concentration of comic books, records, magazines, paperbacks as well as hardcover books. At the time of our visit, the owner showed us several back rooms filled to the brim with cartons of books that he is hoping will one day be displayed and available for sale. While the shop's emphasis seems to be collectibles and nostalgia, other fields are represented. It's not always easy to determine the rational behind a shop's pricing practices and this becomes even more difficult when the stock is determined by the seller to have "collectible" value.

Jellybean's Used Books   **Open Shop**
5401-G Fenton Road 48507   (810) 233-4555

Collection:	General stock of mostly paperback, videos and CDs.
# of Vols:	200,000
Hours:	Mon-Sat 10-6. Most Sun 11-5.
Comments:	Better hardcover items are located at the owner's second shop in Flint. See above.

Gaylord
(Map 13, page 184)

The Book Nook   **Open Shop**
132 West Main Street 49735

Collection:	General stock of new and used??? (See Comments)
Comments:	If you find yourself in the "upper reaches of the lower peninsula," you may want to check this one out. We heard about a possible shop in Gaylord from a reader, and with the help of a "new" book store in town, confirmed the fact that indeed there was a store selling new and used books in Gaylord. As the "new" store also told us that the "used" store did not have a phone, we sent a letter to the shop asking the owner to get in touch with us. Alas, we haven't heard back. So, you're on your own here. If you do visit, let us know what you find.

Glen Arbor
(Map 13, page 184)

The Cottage Book Shop   **Open Shop**
Lake Street   Tel & Fax: (616) 334-4223
Mailing address: PO Box 115 Glen Arbor MI 49636   E-mail: siepker@aol.com

Collection:	General stock of mostly new.
# of Vols:	8,000
Hours:	May-Dec: Daily 10-5:00. Jan-Apr: by appointment or chance.
Travel:	Just south of Rte 22.
Comments:	Stock is approximately 90% new.

Goetzville
(Map 14, page 192)

Thatcher C. Goetz, Books   **By Appointment**
PO Box 267 49736   (906) 297-5912

Collection:	Specialty
# of Vols:	3,000+
Specialties:	Michigan; Great Lakes; Western Americana; Americana.
Services:	Appraisals, search service (Michigan items only), accepts want lists, mail order.
Credit Cards:	No
Year Estab:	1974

Grand Rapids
(Map 13, page 184)

Argos Book Shop   **Open Shop**
1405 Robinson Road SE 49506   (616) 454-0111
                                                   Fax: (616) 454-0736

Collection:	General stock of paperback and hardcover, comics, games.
# of Vols:	20,000-30,000
Specialties:	Michigan
Hours:	Mon-Sat 10-6, except Fri till 8. Sun 12-5.
Services:	Appraisals, search service, accepts want lists, mail order.
Travel:	Fuller exit off Rte 196. Proceed south on Fuller for about 1½-2 miles, then left on Lake. Shop is at the "Y" intersection where Robinson intersects with Lake Dr.
Credit Cards:	Yes
Owner:	Ray Walsh
Year Estab:	1975
Comments:	Once you get past the comic books and science fiction paperbacks that proliferate in the large entry room, there is indeed a room to the left that contains several long rows of traditional hardcover used stock in a wide range of subject categories. While few titles appeared to be truly rare, the selection was large enough to offer the possibility of a find in your area of interest should you be both patient and lucky.

Baker Book House
2768 East Paris 49546

Open Shop
(616) 957-3110
Fax: (616) 957-0965
E-mail: used.books@bakerbooks.com

Collection:	Specialty new and used.
# of Vols:	30,000
Specialties:	Religion
Hours:	Mon-Fri 8:30-9. Sat 9-5.
Services:	Accepts want lists, mail order.
Travel:	28th St exit off I-96. Proceed west on 28th St for approximately two miles, then right on East Paris.
Credit Cards:	Yes
Owner:	Gary Popma
Year Estab:	1939
Comments:	Stock is approximately 25% used.

Book Gallery
1206 Leonard NW 49504

Open Shop
(616) 459-4944

Collection:	General stock of hardcover and paperback.
# of Vols:	75,000
Hours:	Tue-Fri 10-9. Sat 8-6. Call for vacation hours in Feb.
Services:	Search service, mail order.
Travel:	Leonard St exit off Rte 131. Proceed west for one mile.
Credit Cards:	Yes
Owner:	John & Alex Rau
Year Estab:	1985
Comments:	This shop makes good use of its relatively small size by its placement of shelving and the creation of a series of alcoves. The shop is strong in both the occult and philosophy. The hardcover volumes were in good to better condition and most had dust jackets. The window sign that reads: "Used & Rare" does not exaggerate in terms of the phrase "rare." A back room stocks a typical selection of paperbacks.

Milton F. Ehlert - Books
2017 Chesaning SE 49506

By Appointment
(616) 241-4759

Collection:	General stock.
# of Vols:	2,000
Specialties:	Military; modern first editions; Michigan; illustrated; Horatio Alger.
Services:	Accepts want lists, mail order.
Credit Cards:	No
Year Estab:	1987

Sheila Frank, Bookseller
2929 Beechwood SE 49506

By Appointment
(616) 949-0510
Summer only: (616) 672-7883
E-mail: sfrank@iserv.net

Collection:	General stock.

# of Vols:	5,000+
Specialties:	Women's studies; children's; modern first editions on writing, theater, Michigan.
Hours:	Available Sept-June, and July & August by special arrangement.
Services:	Search service, accepts want lists, mail order.
Credit Cards:	No
Year Estab:	1994

Grant's Book Store   **Open Shop**
601 Bridge Street NW 49504   (616) 458-6580

Collection:	General stock of hardcover and paperback.
# of Vols:	2,000-3,000
Hours:	Mon-Fri 9-5. Sat 10-3.
Services:	Appraisals, accepts want lists.
Travel:	Exit 85A off Rte 131 northbound. At exit, cross Fulton St and proceed north on Scribner, then turn left on Bridge.
Owner:	Terry Kirkwood
Year Estab:	1959

Jane's Books & Etc.   **By Appointment**
2715 East Beltline NE 49525   Tel & Fax: (616) 363-4303
                                         E-mail: createhack@aol.com

Collection:	General stock.
Credit Cards:	No
Owner:	Jane Hackbardt
Year Estab:	1997
Comments:	Also displays at Silver Hills Antique mall in Mears. See below.

Kregel Bookstore   **Open Shop**
525 Eastern Avenue SE   (616) 459-9444
Mailing address: PO Box 2607 Grand Rapids MI 49501   Fax: (888) 873-2665
Web page: www.kregel.com   E-mail: usedbooks@kregel.com

Collection:	Specialty
# of Vols:	200,000
Specialties:	Religion
Hours:	Mon-Fri 9-5.
Services:	Appraisals, catalog, accepts want lists.
Travel:	One mile east of US 131.
Credit Cards:	Yes
Year Estab:	1919

Greenbush
(Map 13, page 184)

Peripatetic Bibliophile   **By Appointment**
3261 South US 23 48738   (517) 739-0041

Collection:	General stock.
# of Vols:	13,000

Specialties:	Private press, limited editions, modern fiction.
Services:	Catalog, accepts want lists.
Credit Cards:	No
Owner:	Elizabeth P. Walker
Year Estab:	1991

Grosse Pointe
(Map 16, page 192)

Sam Gatteno Books   **By Appointment**
542 Lakeland 48230   (313) 885-2254
E-mail: sgatteno@worldnet.att.net

Collection:	Specialty
# of Vols:	3,000+
Specialties:	Illuminated manuscripts; manuscripts; incunabula; early printed books; books on books; T. F. Dibdin; color plate books; fine bindings; illustrated.
Services:	Appraisals, accepts want lists, mail order.
Credit Cards:	Yes
Year Estab:	1995

Grosse Pointe Park
(Map 16, page 192)

Shaw's Books   **By Appointment**
14932 Kercheval Avenue 48230   (313) 824-0816
(313) 824-4932

Collection:	General stock and ephemera.
# of Vols:	20,000
Specialties:	Nautical; sports; automobiles; military; hunting; fishing; Americana; antiques; natural history; performing arts; Great Lakes; medicine; golf; autographs; art; fine bindings; Michigan; books on books; travel; Limited Editions Club.
Services:	Appraisals, accepts want lists, mail order.
Credit Cards:	No
Owner:	Henry Zuchowski
Year Estab:	1986

Hamtramck
(Map 16, page 192)

John Paul II Bookstore   **By Appointment**
10304 Joseph Campau 48212   Tel & Fax: (313) 873-3588

Collection:	General stock.
# of Vols:	10,000
Specialties:	Religion
Owner:	Cliff Poshadlo, Jr.
Year Estab:	1984

Harsens Island
(Map 16, page 192)

James M. Babcock, Bookseller   **By Appointment**
PO Box 28004 48028   (810) 748-9779
                                            E-mail: jbiibook@industrynet.net

Collection:	General stock and autographs.
# of Vols:	5,000
Services:	Appraisals, catalog, accepts want lists.
Credit Cards:	Yes
Year Estab:	1972

Haslett
(Map 13, page 184)

The Book Barn   **Open Shop**
1673 Haslett Road 48840   (517) 339-9140

Collection:	General stock of mostly used paperback.
Hours:	Mon-Fri 10-8:30. Sat 10-6. Sun 12-5.
Comments:	It should probably be against the booksellers Code of Ethics to name a shop "Book Barn" when the shop is located in a shopping center; to us, at least, the term "book barn" denotes a building located in a rustic setting. The used books in this shop are primarily paperback with a very modest sized collection of used hardcover books of very recent vintage. The owner operates a similar "Book Barn" in Lansing. See below.

Hillsdale
(Map 13, page 184)

Volume I Books   **Open Shop**
1 Union Street 49242   (517) 437-2228
Web page: www.abebooks.com/home/Volume1books/   (800) 694-8717
                                                    Fax: (517) 437-7923
                                            E-mail: volume1book@dmci.net

Collection:	General stock of mostly hardcover and ephemera.
# of Vols:	50,000+
Specialties:	Labor; cookbooks; children's; history; socialism.
Hours:	Mon-Sat 10-6. Other times by appointment.
Services:	Appraisals, search service, catalog, accepts want lists.
Travel:	From north: From Rte 12 in Jonesville, proceed south on Rte 99 to Hillsdale. At the City Hall, bear right and continue on Rte 99 for 1/2 a block, then turn left and left again on Union. From south: Exit 2 off I-80/I-90. Proceed north on Ohio Rte 15 which turns into Michigan Rte 99. In Hillsdale, turn right just before post office. From west; Exit 13 off I-69. Proceed east on Rte 12 to Jonesville, then south on Rte 12.
Credit Cards:	Yes
Owner:	Richard Wunsch & Aimee England
Year Estab:	1983

Comments: A bit of a distance from the main highways, this bi-level shop is like an oasis that carries a good sized selection of hardcover books in most subject areas. Reasonably priced and easy to browse. The owners also display at the Artesian Wells Antique Mall in Cement City, MI and the Pioneer Antique Mall in Pioneer, OH.

Holland
(Map 13, page 184)

ET Books   **Antique Mall**
At Tulip City Antique Mall, 3500 US Highway 31   Mall: (616) 786-4424
Mailing address: PO Box 1702 Holland MI 49422   Home: (616) 396-1817
                                                              E-mail: etbooks@macatawa.org

Collection: General stock and ephemera.
# of Vols: 2,000
Specialties: Michigan; Americana; Western art (by mail only).
Hours: Mon-Sat 10-6. Sun 12-6.
Services: Search service, accepts want lists, mail order.
Travel: On Rte 31, five miles north of I-96.
Credit Cards: Yes
Owner: Eileen Talamantez
Year Estab: 1987

Holly
(Map 13, page 184)

Balcony Books   **Open Shop**
214 South Broad Street 48442   (248) 634-1400

Collection: General stock.
# of Vols: 5,000-10,000
Specialties: Civil War (books and relics); military; history; Napoleon (books and documents).
Hours: Thu-Sat 10:30-5. Sun 1-5.
Travel: Exit 98 off I-75. Proceed west on Holly Rd into Holly, then left on Broad St. Shop is one block ahead on right.
Credit Cards: Yes
Owner: E. Raskin & J. Hilty
Year Estab: 1973
Comments: If you're in love with the past, you'll enjoy a visit to this combination antique/book shop. The specialties listed above are well represented (there's a separate room set aside just for Napoleon related titles) with both ordinary and unusual titles. Prices for the scarcer and truly rare books were "on target," or so it seemed to us. Even if you don't make a purchase here, you should enjoy feasting your eyes on some unusual antique pieces, e.g., a room built to accommodate exquisitely carved medieval Spanish doors.

Water Tower Antiques	**Antique Mall**
310 South Broad Street 48442	(248) 634-3500

Hours: Tue-Thu 10-5. Fri 10-7. Sat 10-5. Sun 12-5.

Holt
(Map 13, page 184)

Mackinaw Book Company	**By Appointment**
1953 Chestnut 48842	(517) 694-2516

Collection: General stock.
# of Vols: 1,000
Specialties: Nautical; history.
Services: Catalog, accepts want lists.
Credit Cards: No
Owner: Mike Russell

Honor
(Map 13, page 184)

Beulahland	**Open Shop**
9780 Honor Highway	Tel & Fax: (616) 325-5483

Mailing address: 8062 Lincoln Road Beulah MI 49617

Collection: General stock of mostly hardcover.
# of Vols: 30,000
Specialties: Military
Hours: Mon-Sat 9:30-5:30, plus Tue 7pm-10pm. Also, Jul & Aug: Sun 1-5.
Services: Accepts want lists, mail order.
Travel: On Rte 31, one mile west of Honor or four miles northeast of Beulah.
Credit Cards: Yes
Owner: William E. Tompkins
Year Estab: 1979

Houghton
(Map 14, page 192)

Backroom MultiEntertainment	**Open Shop**
109 Shelden Avenue 49931	(906) 482-0637
	Fax: (906) 482-0054

Collection: General stock of mostly paperback, records, CDs and videos
# of Vols: 40,000+
Hours: Daily 11am-10pm.

Inkster
(Map 16, page 192)

Afro Sol	**By Appointment**
1072 Magnolia	(313) 278-5781
Mailing address: PO Box 624 Inkster MI 48141	Fax: (313) 592-1864

Collection: General stock of mostly hardcover.

# of Vols:	8,000
Specialties:	Buffalo soldiers; magazines (*Time, Newsweek*).
Services:	Search service, accepts want lists, mail order.
Credit Cards:	No
Owner:	Mel Turner
Year Estab:	1984

Jackson
(Map 13, page 184)

The Book Devil   **By Appointment**
518 20th Street 49203   (517) 796-1645

Collection:	General stock of hardcover and paperback.
# of Vols:	9,000
Services:	Appraisals, accepts want lists, mail order.
Credit Cards:	No
Owner:	Ed Richardson
Year Estab:	1977
Comments:	Stock is approximately 70% hardcover.

Friends Book Cellar   **Open Shop**
290 West Michigan Avenue 49201   (517) 782-5617

Collection:	General stock of hardcover and paperback.
Hours:	Tue & Thu 11-3 and Thu only 7-8:30.
Travel:	Rte 138 (West Ave) exit off I-94. Proceed south on West, then left on Michigan.
Comments:	A non-profit shop operated by the Friends of the Jackson Public Library.

Kalamazoo
(Map 13, page 184)

Bicentennial Book Shop   **Open Shop**
820 South Westnedge Avenue 49008   (616) 345-5987
                                                                Fax: (616) 345-3030
                                                                E-mail: ztkh10A@prodigy.com

Collection:	General stock, magazines and ephemera.
# of Vols:	40,000
Specialties:	Sports; literature; Americana; children's.
Hours:	Mon-Fri 10-5:30. Sat 10-4.
Services:	Appraisals, search service, accepts want lists, mail order.
Travel:	Exit 76B (Westnedge) off I-94. Proceed north on Westnedge for about two miles. When Westnedge becomes one way, continue on Park, then left on Vine and left on Westnedge. Shop is on the right.
Credit Cards:	No
Owner:	Vaughan & Michael Baber
Year Estab:	1975

Comments: A rather nice shop with a good sized collection of books shelved from floor to ceiling in almost every category. The condition of the books varied but most were in good to better condition. We saw quite a few titles that we believe are in the hard to find and/or rare category. Prices were generally moderate with bargains to be had if you know what you're looking for.

Book Exchange/Kazoo Books   **Open Shop**
407 North Clarendon Street 49006   (616) 385-2665
Web page: www.iserv.net/~bookex   Fax: (616) 385-5786
                                                     E-mail: bookex@iserv.net

Collection: General stock of paperback and hardcover.
# of Vols: 60,000
Hours: Mon-Sat 10-6.
Services: Search service, accepts want lists, mail order.
Travel: Exit 38 off Rte 131. Proceed east on West Main (Rte 43), then left on Clarendon. Shop is about 2½ miles ahead, on the left on the corner. (Note: At the time of our visit, we were traveling west on Rte 43 and there was no sign for Clarendon Rd on the north side of the street.)
Credit Cards: Yes
Owner: James & Gloria Tiller
Year Estab: 1988
Comments: Located in what was once a private home, this overwhelmingly paperback shop does carry some hardcover volumes consisting of both recent and older fiction and non fiction. The owner advised us that he will be expanding the shop and so more hardcover titles may be available for browsing at a future time. During our visit, however, we were overwhelmed by the much higher number of paperbacks on display which clearly meets the needs and desires of this shop's customers.

Deadly Passions Bookshop   **Open Shop**
157 South Kalamazoo Mall 49007   (616) 383-4402
                                                          Fax: (616) 383-4403

Collection: Specialty. Mostly new.
Specialties: Mystery, science fiction; fantasy.
Hours: Mon-Fri 10-5:15, except Thu till 7. Sat 10-5. Sun 12-4.
Services: Search service, accepts want lists, mail order.
Travel: On the mall in downtown.
Credit Cards: Yes
Owner: Jim Huang & Jennie Jacobson
Year Estab: 1992

Kentwood
(Map 13, page 184)

Apparitions Comics & Books   **Open Shop**
2757 Ridgemoor Drive SE 49512   (616) 940-2025

Collection: General stock of hardcover and paperback.

# of Vols:	1,000+
Specialties:	Science fiction; fantasy.
Hours:	Mon-Sat 10-7. Sun 12-5.
Travel:	East Beltline exit off I-96. Proceed south on East Beltline, then right on 28th St and right on Ridgemoor.
Comments:	Stock is evenly divided between hardcover and paperback.

Kimball
(Map 13, page 184)

The Country Tutor School Books   **By Appointment**
4765 West Water Street 48074   (810) 984-3076

Collection:	Specialty books and ephemera.
Specialties:	School books.
Services:	Search service.
Credit Cards:	No
Owner:	Dr. Francine Fisher
Year Estab:	1988

Lachine
(Map 13, page 184)

Something Wicked This Way Comes   **By Appointment**
PO Box 55 49753   (517) 379-3646
Web page: http://members.tripod.com/~mcalevy/home   (517) 379-2100
E-mail: something_wicked_@yahoo.com

Collection:	Specialty paperback and hardcover.
Specialties:	Mystery; thrillers.
Services:	Search service, accepts want lists, mail order.
Credit Cards:	No
Owner:	Andrea Shull
Year Estab:	1996
Comments:	Stock is approximately 60% paperback.

L'Anse
(Map 14, page 192)

Backroom Bargains Used Bookstore   **Open Shop**
US 41 South at Dynamite Hill Road   (906) 524-7677
(877) 325-5764

Collection:	General stock of paperback and hardcover.
# of Vols:	20,000
Hours:	Mon-Sat 11-7. Summer only: Also Sun 11-5.
Travel:	On Rte 41, just east of L'Anse.
Comments:	Stock is approximately 65% paperback. The hardcover volumes are described by the owner as: "25¢ bargains or non fiction."

Lansing
(Map 13, page 184)

The Book Barn   **Open Shop**
5429 West Saginaw 48917   (517) 321-7703

Collection:	General stock of mostly paperback used and new.
Hours:	Mon-Fri 10-8:30. Sat 10-6. Sun 12-5.
Comments:	See comments for the shop's sister store in Haslett.

Capital City Comics & Books   **Open Shop**
2004 East Michigan Avenue 48912   (517) 485-0416
Web page: www.mindspring.com/~capitalcity/   Fax: (517) 485-0981
                                        E-mail: capitalcity@mindspring.com

Collection:	General stock of mostly used paperback and hardcover.
# of Vols:	10,000 (used hardcover)
Specialties:	Comics (collectible).
Hours:	Mon-Fri 10-7. Sat 10-6. Sun 12-6.
Travel:	Michigan Ave exit off Rte 127. Proceed west on Michigan.
Credit Cards:	Yes
Owner:	Stephen Jahner & Bill Dutcher
Year Estab:	1970

GT Motors   **Open Shop**
816 East Howe Avenue 48906   (517) 485-6815

Collection:	Specialty new and used books and magazines.
# of Vols:	6,000
Specialties:	Motorcycles
Hours:	Tue-Fri 11-6, except Thu till 9. Sat 9-3. A call ahead is advised if planning a visit on Fri or Sat.
Services:	Appraisals, search service, accepts want lists, mail order.
Travel:	One block east of Rte 27.
Credit Cards:	Yes
Owner:	L.E. Klein
Year Estab:	1972

Lantern Enterprises   **Antique Mall**
At Mid-Michigan Mega Mall, 15487 US 27   Mall: (517) 487-3275
Mailing address: 315 Orchard Street East Lansing MI 48823   Home: (517) 332-5976
                                                     Fax: (517) 353-0638
                                        E-mail: mattson@pilot.msu.edu

Collection:	Specialty
Specialties:	Music; children's; sheet music; Michigan.
Hours:	Daily 11-6, except Thu till 8:30.
Services:	Accepts want lists.
Travel:	Exit 87 off I-69. Proceed south on Rte 27 for two miles.
Owner:	Jeremy Mattson
Year Estab:	1986

Looking Glass Books   **Antique Mall**
At Mid-Michigan Mega Mall, 15487 US 27   Mall: (517) 487-3275
Mailing address: PO Box 575 DeWitt MI 48820   Home: (517) 224-1784

Collection:	General stock and ephemera.
# of Vols:	10,000
Specialties:	Children's; nature.
Hours:	Daily 11-6, except Thu till 8:30.
Services:	Search service, accepts want lists.
Travel:	See Lantern Enterprises above.
Credit Cards:	Yes
Owner:	Caroline deMauriac
Year Estab:	1994
Comments:	Collection may also be viewed by appointment.

Lincoln Park
(Map 16, page 192)

Magina Books   **Open Shop**
2311 Fort Street 48146   (313) 928-7177
E-mail: maginabk@interloc.com

Collection:	General stock of hardcover and paperback.
# of Vols:	50,000
Specialties:	Automobiles; military; cookbooks.
Hours:	Tue-Sat 10-5.
Services:	Accepts want lists.
Travel:	Southfield Rd exit off I-75. Proceed east on Southfield (Rte 39), then south on Fort St. Shop is about six blocks ahead.
Credit Cards:	Yes
Owner:	Steve Magina
Year Estab:	1948
Comments:	Some interesting collectibles which were attractively displayed along with some new titles, remainders and a collection of mixed vintage hardcover volumes. Since the owner has a sharp eye for books, you could find an item or two of interest while browsing here.

Livonia
(Map 16, page 192)

Books Connection   **Open Shop**
19043 Middlebelt Road 48152   (248) 471-4742

Collection:	General stock of mostly used paperback.
# of Vols:	5,000-10,000 (used)
Hours:	Mon-Fri 10-9. Sat 10-8. Sun 11-5.

Dove Booksellers   **Open Shop**
30633 Schoolcraft Road, Ste. C 48150   (734) 522-7440
Web page: www.dovebook.com   Fax: (734) 522-7441
E-mail: dovebook@ix.netcom.com

Collection:	Specialty used and new.

Specialties:	Biblical studies; ancient history.
Hours:	Mon-Fri 10-5. Sat 11-3.
Services:	Search service, catalog, accepts want lists.
Travel:	Located on the service drive of I-96 between Middlebelt and Merriman Rds. Entrance to book shop is located on southwest corner of building.
Credit Cards:	Yes
Owner:	Jeffrey Ball & John Marine
Year Estab:	1985
Comments:	Stock is approximately 60% used.

Marine City
(Map 13, page 184)

Arnold's Of Michigan Antiquarian Booksellers   **Open Shop**
218 South Water Street 48039   (810) 765-1350
                                                            Fax: (810) 765-7914
                                          E-mail: arnoldbk@ees.eesc.com

Collection:	General stock and nautical ephemera.
# of Vols:	20,000
Specialties:	Great Lakes; shipping; cookbooks; Michigan.
Hours:	Tue-Fri 10-5. Sat 10-4. Sun 12-4 and by appointment, except closed Sun from Jan 1st to last Sun in Feb.
Services:	Appraisals, search service, catalog, accepts want lists.
Travel:	Eastbound on I-94 to 26 Mile Rd. Right on 26 Mile Rd and proceed to end. Turn right, then first left on West Blvd. Left at first light and proceed about 3/4 mile to St. Clair River. Turn right. Shop is two blocks ahead.
Credit Cards:	Yes
Owner:	Judith A. Herba
Year Estab:	1931
Comments:	A book buyer's find. While the shop is not overly large, the stock is generally of high quality and the culinary section is exceptionally strong. Most of the books were in very good condition and prices were extremely reasonable. The owner is a charmer.

Marquette
(Map 14, page 192)

Backroom Obsessions   **Open Shop**
215 Front Street   (906) 226-6660

Collection:	General stock of paperback and hardcover.
# of Vols:	10,000
Hours:	Mon-Sat 11-7.
Travel:	Downtown exit off Rte 28/41. Shop is just under the railroad bridge.
Comments:	Stock is approximately 75% paperback.

Snowbound Books   **Open Shop**
118 North Third Street 49855   (906) 228-4448
                                               E-mail: snowboun@interloc.com

Collection:	General stock of mostly used hardcover and paperback.
# of Vols:	26,000
Specialties:	Local history; Robert Traver.
Hours:	Mon-Fri 9:30-6. Sat 9:30-5.
Services:	Search service, accepts want lists, mail order.
Travel:	Rte 41 to downtown. Left on Washington, then right on Third.
Credit Cards:	Yes
Owner:	Ray Nurmi
Year Estab:	1984
Comments:	A very pleasant little shop that makes excellent use of its space and which displays hardcovers and paperbacks in the same category together on well labeled shelves. Books are attractively priced. In addition to the more common titles one generally sees, we saw several older volumes and sets, again attractively priced.

Mattawan
(Map 13, page 184)

Angling Book Hunter   **By Appointment**
PO Box 145 49071   (616) 668-4222

Collection:	Specialty
Specialties:	Fishing; hunting; nature.
Services:	Catalog, accepts want lists.
Credit Cards:	No
Owner:	Tom Coles
Year Estab:	1982

Mears
(Map 13, page 184)

Silver Hills Antique Mall   **Antique Mall**
6780 West Fox Road 49436   (616) 873-3905

Hours:	May 15th-Labor Day only: Thu-Mon 11-5. Tue & Wed by chance.
Travel:	Northbound from Muskegon: Hart exit off Rte 31. Turn left and follow signs to mall.

Melvindale
(Map 16, page 192)

The Book Bin   **Open Shop**
18643 Allen Road 48122   (313) 386-9499

Collection:	General stock of mostly paperback.
# of Vols:	20,000
Hours:	Mon-Fri 11-5. Sat 12-5.

Menominee
(Map 14, page 192)

Aurora Books   **Open Shop**
625 First Street 49858   (906) 863-5266
                                                   E-mail: aurora@mari.net

Collection:	General stock of mostly used hardcover and paperback.
# of Vols:	8,000 (used)
Hours:	Mon-Fri 9:30-6. Sat 9:30-5. Sun (July only)
Services:	Search service, accepts want lists, mail order.
Travel:	From Rte 41, proceed east on 10th Ave, then right on First St.
Credit Cards:	Yes
Owner:	Linda Murto & Ross Parcels
Year Estab:	1995
Comments:	Stock is evenly mixed between hardcover and paperback.

Middleville
(Map 13, page 184)

Becky's Main Street Books   **Open Shop**
101 East Main Street   (616) 795-8800
Mailing address: PO Box 392 Middleville MI 49333

Collection:	General stock of mostly paperback.
# of Vols:	40,000+
Hours:	Tue-Sat 10-5.
Travel:	From Rte 37, turn east at Middleville traffic light and proceed two blocks over bridge. Shop is first building on left.
Credit Cards:	No
Owner:	Becky Bell
Year Estab:	1994
Comments:	Overwhelmingly paperback with the hardcover books on hand being primarily older but run of the mill titles in mixed condition. Unfortunately, older does not necessarily mean rare or collectible.

Midland
(Map 13, page 184)

The Book Shop   **Open Shop**
1001 East Carpenter Street 48640   (517) 835-1000

Collection:	General stock of mostly paperback.
# of Vols:	5,000-10,000
Hours:	Mon-Sat 12-6.

Sleepy Hollow Bookshop   **Open Shop**
22 Ashman Circle 48640   (517) 832-7065
                                              E-mail: sleepybk@interloc.com

Collection:	General stock of hardcover and paperback.
# of Vols:	20,000-30,000

Hours:	Mon-Wed 10-6. Thu 10-8. Fri & Sat 10-5. Best to call ahead, especially if coming from a distance.
Travel:	Eastman exit off Rte 10. Head into town. After about two miles, turn left on Saginaw and continue for about two miles to the circle (marked by a flag in the center of the road). Shop is visible from Saginaw on the right. Veer right onto Jefferson Rd for store's parking lot.
Credit Cards:	Yes
Owner:	Andrew Halldorson
Year Estab:	1996
Comments:	While this shop carries a slightly higher ratio of paperbacks to hardcover books, the hardcover volumes we did see ran the gamut from recent fiction to vintage items, mostly in reading copy condition. At the time of our visit, the owner advised us that some of his better stock was located elsewhere. That, of course, could change, as you read this.

Munising
(Map 14, page 192)

84 Charing Cross, EH?   **Open Shop**
102 East Munising Avenue 49862   (906) 387-3937
Web page: www.84cc.com   Fax: (906) 387-2649
                                                                              E-mail: 84char@up.net

Collection:	General stock, prints and ephemera.
# of Vols:	35,000+
Specialties:	Americana; children's; mining; geology; signed.
Hours:	Jul & Aug: Mon-Sat 9-9. Sun 12-5. Remainder of year: Daily 10-5. A call ahead is advised on snow days.
Services:	Appraisals, search service, accepts want lists, mail order.
Travel:	On Rte 28 at corner of Elm Street.
Credit Cards:	Yes
Owner:	Sandra & Jeffrey Inskeep-Fox
Year Estab:	1988
Comments:	An absolutely delightful shop providing three floors of enjoyable browsing and an excellent stock of used, rare and antiquarian titles. Moderately priced. The shop also displays some vintage paperbacks, maps, prints and ephemera (and a fabulous collection of Mickey Mouse memorabilia which we suspect is not for sale.) If you visit anywhere on the Upper Peninsula, you should certainly stop here. The owner also displays at a multi dealer antique mall in Sault Ste. Marie. See below.

Muskegon Heights
(Map 13, page 184)

First Edition Bookstore   **Open Shop**
7 Center Street 49444   (616) 733-2176

Collection:	General stock of used and new hardcover and paperback.
# of Vols:	15,000-20,000 (used)

Hours:	Mon-Fri 7:45-6, except Fri till 7. Sat 8-6. Sun: Labor Day-Memorial Day: 8-4. Memorial Day-Labor Day: 8-1.
Services:	Appraisals, search service.
Travel:	Sherman Blvd exit off Rte 31. Proceed west on Sherman, then south on Peck for two blocks and left on Center St. Shop is just ahead on right.
Credit Cards:	Yes
Owner:	Mary Carney
Year Estab:	1979
Comments:	This shop sells newspapers, new magazines and some new books as well as used paperbacks and a modest collection of used hardcover books in a variety of subject areas. Most of the used volumes we saw were in mixed condition and fairly reasonably priced. A few more expensive items were displayed behind glass and there were some signed volumes on hand. The owner operates a second by appointment shop in Brevort on the Upper Peninsula.

Newberry
(Map 14, page 192)

Ice Cream & Dreams   **Open Shop**
1100 Newberry Avenue 49868   (906) 293-3668

Collection:	General stock of mostly paperback.
# of Vols:	5,000
Hours:	Mon-Sat 11-5.

Niles
(Map 13, page 184)

Andrews & Rose Booksellers   **Open Shop**
105 East Main Street 49120   (616) 683-4251
E-mail: anrbooks@interloc.com

Collection:	General stock.
# of Vols:	18,000
Hours:	Mon-Sat 12-6.
Services:	Appraisals, search service.
Travel:	In downtown, on Bus Rtes 12 & 31.
Credit Cards:	Yes
Owner:	Eimi Andrews-Rose & Jim Rose
Year Estab:	1975
Comments:	Rather a neat shop with books carefully selected by the owners for their condition. While many subjects were covered, few sections were represented in any depth. Prices were moderate.

A. Casperson Books   **Antique Mall**
At Four Flags Antique Mall, 218 North Second Street   Mall: (616) 683-6681
Mailing address: 1900 Platt Street Niles MI 49120   Home: (616) 683-2851
E-mail: casperbook@aol.com

Collection:	General stock and ephemera.
# of Vols:	6,000

Hours:	Mon-Fri 10-5. Sat & Sun 12-6.
Services:	Search service, accepts want lists, mail order.
Travel:	In downtown Niles, just off Main St.
Credit Cards:	Yes
Year Estab:	1995
Comments:	Also displays at Pickers Antique Mall in Niles.

Ralph A. Casperson Books   **Open Shop**
1303 Buchanan Rd   (616) 683-2888
Mailing address: PO Box 634 Niles MI 49120   (888) 612-5774
                                                          Fax: (616) 683-4067
                                                   E-mail: caspersons@aol.com

Collection:	General stock and ephemera.
# of Vols:	100,000
Hours:	Sat & Sun 12-6. Other times by appointment or chance.
Travel:	From I-80/I-90: Rte 31 bypass exit. Proceed north on bypass to exit 5, then turn right and proceed two miles. Shop is on north side of road behind the owner's home. From I-94: Decatur/Dowagiac exit. Proceed south on Rte 51 to Main St in Niles. Turn right through town to first street past bridge, then turn left and proceed one block to Grant. Right on Grant and continue for 1/2 mile.
Credit Cards:	Yes
Year Estab:	1970
Comments:	This may not be the largest used book store in Michigan but it is certainly one of the finest AND well worth a pilgrimage to Niles. The books, located in two separate buildings, are meticulously organized, are in almost universally excellent condition and are reasonably priced. We cannot think of a subject in which a true collector would not find a few treasures.

Michiana Antique Mall   **Antique Mall**
2423 South 11th Street 49120   (616) 684-7001

Hours:	Daily 10-6.
Travel:	Roseland exit off I-80/I-90. Proceed north on Rte 31. Mall is on Rte 31. (Do not take Rte 31 bypass.)

Pickers Antique Mall   **Antique Mall**
2809 South 11th Street 49120   (616) 683-6644

Hours:	Mon-Fri 10-6. Sat & Sun 10-6.
Travel:	Approximately 1/4 mile north of Michigan/Indiana state line.

North Muskegon
(Map 13, page 184)

Memory Lane Antique Mall   **Antique Mall**
2073 Holton Road 49445   (616) 744-8510

Hours:	Daily 10-6.

Travel: Fremont/N. Muskegon exit off Rte 31. Proceed west on Rte 120, then
                   right on Roberts and right into first shopping center.

Northville
(Map 16, page 192)

Knightsbridge Antique Mall   **Antique Mall**
42305 West 7 Mile Road   (248) 344-7200

Hours: Daily 11-6, except Wed to 8.
Travel: Two miles east of Rte 275.

Northport
(Map 13, page 184)

Dog Ears Used Books   **Open Shop**
Corner of Mill & Nagonaba Streets   Home: 616) 256-7745
Mailing address: PO Box 865 Leland MI 49654   E-mail: pjgg@netonecom.net

Collection: General stock of hardcover and paperback.
# of Vols: 6,000
Hours: Memorial Day-Labor Day: Daily 1-5. Sept-Oct: Sat & Sun 1-5.
Credit Cards: No
Owner: Pamela Grath
Year Estab: 1993

Novi
(Map 16, page 192)

Read It Again Books   **Open Shop**
39733 Grand River Avenue 48375   (248) 474-6066
                                                            Fax: (248) 474-6746
                                                    E-mail: maryreader@aol.com

Collection: General stock of paperback and hardcover.
# of Vols: 30,000-40,000
Hours: Mon-Fri 10-8. Sat 10-6. Sun 11-4.
Services: Accepts want lists, mail order.
Travel: 8 Mile Rd exit off I-275. Proceed west on 8 Mile, then north on Haggerty
                   Rd and west on Grand River. Shop is in Pheasant Run Plaza.
Credit Cards: Yes
Owner: Mary Mansour
Year Estab: 1995
Comments: Stock is approximately 70% paperback.

Oak Park
(Map 16, page 192)

Bibliotective   **By Appointment**
21861 Stratford   (248) 968-2437
Mailing address: PO Box 47347 Oak Park MI 48237

Collection: General stock.

# of Vols:	3,500
Specialties:	Mystery; detective; Sherlock Holmes; American almanacs.
Services:	Appraisals, search service, catalog, accepts want lists.
Credit Cards:	No
Owner:	William A. Rothman
Year Estab:	1989

Book Beat   **Open Shop**
26010 Greenfield 48237   (248) 968-1190
Fax: (248) 968-3102
E-mail: BookBeat@aol.com

Collection:	General stock of mostly new and some used hardcover and paperback.
# of Vols:	50,000 (combined)
Specialties:	Photography; art; children's; modern first editions.
Hours:	Mon-Sat 10-9. Sun 11-6.
Services:	Appraisals, search service.
Travel:	Greenfield exit off I-696. Located between 10 and 11 Mile Rd in Lincoln Shopping Center.
Credit Cards:	Yes
Owner:	Cary Loren
Year Estab:	1982
Comments:	Approximately 20% of the stock consists of used books with a heavy emphasis on photography and art. Collectible quality titles were located behind the front counter and in glass display cases. If you don't see what you want, ask for it.

Oden
(Map 13, page 184)

The Christensen Gallery   **Open Shop**
4265 US 31 North   (616) 348-3618
Mailing address: PO Box 354 Oden MI 49764

Collection:	General stock.
# of Vols:	4,000
Specialties:	Literature; baseball.
Hours:	Jun-Aug: Daily 10-6. Rest of year: Mon-Sat 12-5 or by appointment.
Services:	Accepts want lists.
Travel:	Located on Rte 31, six miles north of Petoskey. Shop is on the left.
Credit Cards:	No
Owner:	Ken Christensen
Year Estab:	1991
Comments:	When we stopped by this shop on our earlier visit to Michigan, we saw perhaps 500-1,000 hardcover volumes of fairly common variety. Since then, the owner has added to his stock. While we did not have a chance to revisit the shop when researching this edition, if you're on your way to the Upper Peninsula, or find yourself otherwise in the neighborhood, you might want to stop in for a visit. The shop also features an art gallery and sells antiques.

Okemos
(Map 13, page 184)

Michael A. Hogle Company
PO Box 82 48805

By Appointment
(517) 347-2433
E-mail: hogle.mike@acd.net

Collection:	Specialty
# of Vols:	800
Specialties:	Civil War; Abraham Lincoln.
Services:	Appraisals, search service, accepts want lists, mail order.
Credit Cards:	Yes
Year Estab:	1979

Shirley's Book Services
4330 Hulett Road 48864

By Appointment
(517) 347-4841
(517) 349-2314
E-mail: shirleys@interloc.com

Collection:	General stock.
# of Vols:	10,000+
Specialties:	Michigan; cooking; children's; antiques.
Services:	Appraisals, search service, mail order.
Credit Cards:	No
Owner:	Shirley Sliker
Year Estab:	1987

Orchard Lake
(Map 16, page 192)

Antiquarian Prints & Maps
4082 Hardwood Drive 48323

By Appointment
(248) 682-2189

Collection:	Specialty
Specialties:	Maps
Credit Cards:	No
Owner:	Rosalie Alexander
Year Estab:	1987

Ortonville
(Map 13, page 184)

Margaret Lee Antiques and Bookseller
1910 Kent Road 48462

By Appointment
Tel & Fax: (248) 627-2375
E-mail: mlee@tln.lib.mi.us

Collection:	General stock.
# of Vols:	3,000
Specialties:	Maritime; submarines; diving; children's; maps; cookbooks.
Services:	Search service, catalog, accepts want lists.
Credit Cards:	Yes
Year Estab:	1984

Oscoda
(Map 13, page 184)

Cliff's Engraving & Gifts   **Open Shop**
329 South State Street 48750   (517) 739-9569
Web page: www.cliffsenvgraving/oscoda.net   E-mail: mcarraway@i-star.com

Collection:	General stock of paperback and hardcover.
# of Vols:	120,000
Hours:	Mon-Fri 10-5. Sat 11-2.
Travel:	State St is Rte 23.
Credit Cards:	Yes
Year Estab:	1982
Comments:	Stock is approximately 70% paperback.

Owosso
(Map 13, page 184)

Jellybean's Used Books   **Open Shop**
2256 East Main 48867   (517) 725-6949
                                                   E-mail: jellybella@aol.com

Collection:	General stock of paperback and hardcover.
# of Vols:	500,000
Hours:	Mon-Sat 10-6.
Owner:	Ron Samek
Comments:	Stock is approximately 80% paperback.

Parchment
(Map 13, page 184)

Yesterday's Books   **Open Shop**
239 South Riverview Drive 49004   (616) 345-1011
                                                   E-mail: yesbooks@aol.com

Collection:	General stock of hardcover and paperback.
# of Vols:	8,000
Specialties:	Americana; Michigan; hunting; fishing; children's; magazines.
Hours:	Mon-Sat 10-5:30. Sun by appointment.
Services:	Appraisals, search service, accepts want lists.
Travel:	Sprinkle Rd exit off I-94. Proceed north on Sprinkle for about eight miles, then west on G Ave and left on Riverview. Shop is one mile ahead.
Credit Cards:	No
Owner:	Bob & Sue Rozankovich
Year Estab:	1978
Comments:	It's probably just an accident that this shop is located in the town of Parchment touted as the "Paper City" since a goodly portion of the stock consists of ephemera. The rest of the collection is a mix of paperbacks and hardcover volumes of varying degrees of age and interests. If you're into collectibles, you might well spot something to tickle your fancy.

Petoskey
(Map 13, page 184)

The Book Stop   **Open Shop**
301 West Mitchell 49770   (616) 347-4400

Collection:	General stock of paperback and hardcover.
# of Vols:	15,000
Specialties:	Michigan
Hours:	Mon-Sat 8-5:30.
Services:	Mail order.
Travel:	On Rte 31, five blocks north of intersection of Rtes 31 & 131.
Credit Cards:	No
Owner:	Diane Halford
Year Estab:	1975
Comments:	A mostly paperback shop with an assortment of hardcover books. While the shop does have several books in the specialty area listed above, from what we could see the selection was not particularly large. Many of the other books consisted of newer fiction, library discards, book club items, etc. Certainly not in the rare or antiquarian category.

Plainwell
(Map 13, page 184)

Used Books   **Open Shop**
138 South Main Street 49080   (616) 685-9114

Collection:	General stock of primarily paperback.
# of Vols:	18,000
Hours:	Tue-Fri 11-3. Sat 12-4.

Plymouth
(Map 16, page 192)

Jack's Corner Bookstore   **Open Shop**
583 West Ann Arbor Trail 48170   (734) 455-2373

Collection:	General stock.
# of Vols:	11,000
Specialties:	Children's
Hours:	Mon-Sat 10:30-5.
Services:	Accepts want lists.
Travel:	Ann Arbor Rd exit off I-275. Proceed west on Ann Arbor Rd, then north on Main St and right on Ann Arbor Trail.
Credit Cards:	Yes
Owner:	Jack Gunsaulus
Year Estab:	1989
Comments:	A small shop loaded with mostly older books that clearly fit the "vintage" category. While several subjects are represented, the owner's specialty should not be overlooked. Considering the age of the stock,

condition was generally good and prices reasonable. A downside for book hunters who want to eyeball as many titles as possible are the piles of books on the floor stacked against the bookcases. The shop also sells collectibles and Victorian jewelry.

Port Huron
(Map 13, page 184)

John M. Gram   **By Appointment**
2026 Military   (810) 987-4886
Mailing address: PO Box 611941 Port Huron MI 48061

Collection:	General stock.
# of Vols:	5,000
Specialties:	Americana; archaeology; Michigan; military; French Canadiana.
Services:	Accepts want lists, mail order.
Credit Cards:	No
Year Estab:	1988

Portage
(Map 13, page 184)

Avalon Bookshop   **Open Shop**
8314 Portage Road 49002   (616) 329-1952

Collection:	General stock of paperback and hardcover.
# of Vols:	27,000
Hours:	Tue-Sat 11-7:30.
Travel:	Portage Rd exit off I-94. Proceed south on Portage.
Credit Cards:	No
Owner:	Daryl Longman
Year Estab:	1985
Comments:	A neat little shop with a modest sized collection that consists of a majority of paperbacks and a reasonable number of hardcover volumes, mostly of recent vintage. We saw plenty of mystery and fiction, some biography and a few other subjects but little that we would categorize as rare or unusual.

Dann Collectibles   **By Appointment**
1918 Greenbriar Drive   (616) 345-1459
Mailing address: PO Box 1268 Portage MI 49081

Collection:	General stock and ephemera.
# of Vols:	1,000
Specialties:	Americana (17th & 18th century); women's studies; children's; N.C. Wyeth.
Services:	Accepts want lists.
Credit Cards:	No
Owner:	Ray & Margaret Dann
Year Estab:	1995

Portland
(Map 13, page 184)

My Wife's Books   **By Appointment**
650 Riverside Drive 48875   (517) 647-7620
E-mail: wifesbooks@voyager.net

Collection:	General stock.
# of Vols:	4,000
Specialties:	Military
Services:	Accepts want lists, mail order.
Credit Cards:	No
Owner:	Bruce Werner
Year Estab:	1992

Rapid City
(Map 13, page 184)

Miller's Antiques   **Open Shop**
Harrison Street   (616) 331-6104
Mailing address: PO Box 69 Rapid City MI 49676

Collection:	General stock.
# of Vols:	10,000
Specialties:	Non fiction; military; sporting; history.
Hours:	May-Oct: Daily 10-5.
Travel:	From Rte 72, turn north on Rapid City Rd. Once in Rapid City, turn left on Harrison. Shop is just ahead on the left.
Credit Cards:	No
Owner:	Stuart & Isabella Miller
Year Estab:	1969
Comments:	If you're looking for older books you'll find lots to choose from here. If you're looking for books in good condition, we're afraid this shop may not be for you.

Rochester
(Map 13, page 184)

The Fine Books Company   **By Appointment**
781 East Snell 48306   (248) 651-8799
Fax: (248) 651-6542
E-mail: finebook@mich.com

Collection:	Specialty
# of Vols:	10,000
Specialties:	19th & 20th century English and American literary first editions; science fiction; mystery; detective; children's; illustrated; selected nonfiction.
Services:	Appraisals, catalog, accepts want lists.
Credit Cards:	No
Owner:	David Aronovitz
Year Estab:	1981

Rochester Hills
(Map 13, page 184)

Deux Amasse Books   **By Appointment**
169 Grosse Pines Court 48309   (248) 610-3647
E-mail: 103643.477@compuserve.com

Collection:	General stock.
# of Vols:	7,500+
Specialties:	Archaeology; Egypt; Near and Far East; art; travel.
Services:	Accepts want lists, mail order.
Credit Cards:	No
Owner:	Thomas & Dorothy Van Leeuwen
Year Estab:	1991

Romeo
(Map 13, page 184)

Books Et Cetra   **By Appointment**
101 South Main   (810) 752-3443
Mailing address: PO Box 551 Romeo MI 48065

Collection:	General stock.
# of Vols:	7,000
Specialties:	Romance novels (1870-1900).
Services:	Search service, accepts want lists, mail order.
Credit Cards:	No
Year Estab:	1992

Romeo Antique Mall   **Antique Mall**
218 North Main Street   (810) 752-6440

Hours:	Daily 10-5.
Travel:	At intersection of Rte 53 (Van Dyke) and 32 Mile Rd.

Roscommon
(Map 13, page 184)

Yorty's Half-Priced Books of Michigan   **Open Shop**
103 Yorty Drive (Higgins Lake) 48653   (517) 821-9242

Collection:	General stock of hardcover and paperback and ephemera.
# of Vols:	25,000
Specialties:	Gladys Taber; James Oliver Curwood; Grace Livingstone Hill; Gene Stratton Porter, Edgar Rice Burroughs; Michigan; Civil War; Joseph Lincoln; medicine.
Hours:	Apr 1-Nov 1: Mon-Sat 12-5 but a call ahead is preferred.
Services:	Appraisals, accepts want lists; mail order.
Travel:	Higgins Lake State Park exit off Rte 27. Proceed east on Rte 104 for two miles, then north on Rte 202 for two miles and east on Rte 100 for one mile to shopping center.

Credit Cards: Yes
Owner: Rollin & Ethel Yorty
Year Estab: 1940
Comments: Taking our own advice, we called ahead before heading north to visit
                   this shop and were told that the shop would not be open on the day of
                   our planned visit.

Royal Oak
(Map 16, page 192)

Antique Connection   **Antique Mall**
710 East 11 Mile Road 48067   (248) 542-5042

Hours: Tue-Sun 10-5.
Travel: Downtown, five blocks east of Main St.

Book Exchange   **Open Shop**
1600 Rochester Road 48067   (248) 542-0717

Collection: General stock of mostly used paperback and hardcover.
Hours: Daily except closed Wed, 10-6.
Travel: 12 Mile Rd exit off I-75. West on 12 Mile Rd, then left on Rochester.
Comments: Stock is approximately 75% used, 75% of which is paperback.

Classic Book Shop   **Open Shop**
32336 Woodward Avenue * 48073   (248) 549-0220

Collection: General stock of hardcover and paperback.
# of Vols: 40,000
Specialties: Art
Hours: Mon-Sat 11-7. Sun 12-5.
Services: Search service, accepts want lists.
Travel: Four miles north of I-696, between Normandy & 14 Mile Rd.
Credit Cards: Yes
Owner: Bill Gillmore
Year Estab: 1988
Comments: A sister shop to Ann Arbor's Dawn Treader. Most of the books we saw
                   were in good to excellent condition and priced quite reasonably. Many
                   of the titles would fit into the collectible category and indeed there were
                   intriguing displays throughout the store that would tempt anyone with
                   a taste for nostalgia to think about making a purchase. The store also
                   has some modern first editions and more than a few scholarly items.
*At the same location as in the previous edition (Woodward Ave was renumbered).

Fourth Street Book Shop   **Open Shop**
327 East Fourth Street 48067   (248) 544-3373
Web page: abebooks.com/home/BRBOOKS   E-mail: brbooks@globalbiz.net

Collection: Specialty
# of Vols: 20,000
Specialties: Military; Americana.

Hours:	Wed-Sat 11-7.
Services:	Search service, catalog, accepts want lists.
Travel:	Three blocks south of 11 Mile Rd and east of Woodward.
Credit Cards:	Yes
Owner:	Brian Russell
Year Estab:	1977

Ken Hebenstreit, Bookseller   **By Appointment**
813 North Washington Avenue 48067   (248) 548-5460
Web page: www.abebooks.com/home/kenbooks   E-mail: KHBooks@ibm.net

Collection:	Specialty
# of Vols:	5,000
Specialties:	Mystery; detective; suspense; horror; modern first editions; literature; fantasy.
Services:	Catalog, search service, accepts want lists.
Credit Cards:	No
Owner:	Ken Hebenstreit & Sharlan Douglas
Year Estab:	1995

Barbara Parks—Books   **By Appointment**
932 Amelia Street 48073   (248) 588-8773

Collection:	General stock and ephemera.
# of Vols:	9,200+
Specialties:	Americana; cookbooks; children's; black studies; women's studies.
Services:	Appraisals; search service, accepts want lists, mail order.
Credit Cards:	No
Year Estab:	1980
Comments:	Also displays at the Antique Connection in Royal Oak and antique malls in Northville and Romeo.

Phoenix Bookshop   **Open Shop**
32184 Woodward Avenue *   48073   (248) 549-8876

Collection:	General stock of hardcover and paperback.
# of Vols:	27,000
Hours:	Mon-Fri 11-7. Sat 11-6. Sun 12-5.
Services:	Accepts want lists, mail order.
Travel:	Woodward Ave exit off I-696. Proceed north on Woodward. Shop is between Normandy & 14 Mile Rd.
Credit Cards:	Yes
Owner:	Cheryl Ward
Year Estab:	1986
Comments:	A nice selection consisting of both hardcover books and paperbacks. We spotted more than a few unusual titles along with the "usual suspects." We also purchased a few which always leaves us feeling good about our stop. Of course, we can't guarantee that you'll have the same success.

*At the same location as in the previous edition (Woodward Ave was renumbered).

Royal Oak Books   **Open Shop**
28806 Woodward Avenue * 48067   (248) 545-6510

Collection:	General stock of mostly hardcover.
# of Vols:	40,000
Specialties:	History; religion.
Hours:	Mon-Sat 10-7. Sun 12-5.
Travel:	One block south of 12 Mile Rd.
Credit Cards:	Yes
Owner:	Edward & Patricia Jonas
Year Estab:	1980
Comments:	An interesting shop with a collection of mixed vintage hardcover items, including some unusual titles but few if any truly antiquarian volumes. Worth a visit, particularly as there are so many other used book dealers nearby.

*At the same location as in the previous edition (Woodward Ave was renumbered).

Saginaw
(Map 13, page 184)

The Book Worm   **Open Shop**
7871 Gratiot Square 48609   (517) 781-1155

Collection:	General stock of primarily paperback.
Hours:	Tue-Sat 10-6.

Jelly Bean's Used Book & Record Exchange   **Open Shop**
7886 Gratiot Road 48609   (517) 781-0881

Collection:	General stock of paperback and hardcover.
# of Vols:	10,000
Hours:	Mon-Sat 10-6.
Travel:	On Rte 46 in Shields, just west of Saginaw.
Owner:	Barbara Barnett
Year Estab:	1988

Maxey's Discount Bookstore   **Open Shop**
3647 Bay Road 48603   (517) 790-0114

Collection:	General stock of primarily paperback.
Hours:	Tue-Fri 10:30-6. Sat 10:30-4.

J.D. Zucatti, Bookseller   **Open Shop**
122 North Michigan Avenue 48602   (517) 790-1776
                                                                Fax: (517) 790-3150
                                                  E-mail: zbooks@concentric.net

Collection:	General stock of paperback and hardcover.
# of Vols:	30,000+
Specialties:	Science fiction; mystery.
Hours:	Mon-Sat 11-7.
Services:	Search service, accepts want lists.

Travel:	Exit 149B (Holland Ave) off I-75. Proceed west on Holland/Remington for about five miles, then turn south (left) on North Michigan Ave. Shop is about two miles ahead on left.
Credit Cards:	Yes
Owner:	Joe Zucatti
Year Estab:	1993
Comments:	A good sized shop with an interesting mix of both hardcover books and paperbacks. Most of the hardcover volumes would be considered reading copies. Prices are extremely reasonable.

Saint Clair Shores
(Map 16, page 192)

Browns Family Bookstore   **Open Shop**
27309 Harper Avenue 48081   (810) 773-7370

Collection:	General stock of mostly used paperback and hardcover.
# of Vols:	89,000
Hours:	Mon-Sat 10-6.
Travel:	10 Mile Rd exit off I-94. Proceed east on 10 Mile, then north on Harper.
Credit Cards:	Yes
Year Estab:	1992
Comments:	If you're heavily into paperbacks, you might find an item of interest here. On the other hand, if you're looking for hardcover volumes of any consequence. . .while there are a few on hand. . .

Sault Ste. Marie
(Map 14, page 192)

La Galerie   **Antique Mall**
1420 Ashmun Street 49783   (906) 635-1044

Hours:	Mon-Sat 10-5. Sun 12-4.
Travel:	Bus Rte 75 off I-75. Proceed north on Bus Rte 75 to 6th Ave.

Sawyer
(Map 13, page 184)

Dunes Antique Center   **Antique Mall**
12825 Red Arrow Highway 49125   (616) 426-4043

Hours:	Mon, Wed, Thu, Fri, Sat 10-6. Sun 11-6. Summer: Also Tue 10-6.
Travel:	Exit 12 off I-94. Proceed west on Sawyer Rd for one block, then right on Red Arrow Hwy.

Shelby Township
(Map 13, page 184)

Avalon Books   **Open Shop**
48538 Van Dyke 48317   Tel & Fax: (810) 731-7444

Collection:	General stock of paperback, hardcover and comics.

# of Vols:	25,000
Hours:	Tue-Sat 12-8.
Services:	Accepts want lists.
Travel:	Van Dyke exit off I-696. Proceed north on Van Dyke for about 10 miles. Shop is located in Regency Square shopping center.
Credit Cards:	Yes
Owner:	Lynn Noyes
Year Estab:	1992
Comments:	This shop offers a combination of paperbacks, *Dungeon and Dragon* materials, a selection of new and recent hardcover publications in the fantasy/horror/science fiction genre and some general used hardcover titles (clearly in the minority).

The Books Connection   **Open Shop**
52924 Van Dyke 48316   (810) 731-6601

Collection:	General stock of mostly used paperback.
# of Vols:	10,000 (used)
Hours:	Mon-Fri 10-6. Sat 10-4:30.

South Haven
(Map 13, page 184)

Hidden Room Book Shoppe   **Open Shop**
518 Phoenix 49090   (616) 637-7222

Collection:	General stock.
# of Vols:	25,000
Specialties:	Maritime
Hours:	May-Aug: Daily 10-5. Sep-Dec: Daily, except closed Wed, 10-5. Jan-Apr: Fri-Mon 10-5.
Travel:	Located on the main street of town.
Credit Cards:	No
Owner:	Nancy L. Phillips
Year Estab:	1985
Comments:	Yes, there is a "hidden room" located in the rear of the shop that is used primarily to display children's and maritime books. One half of the shop is set aside for antiques and collectibles, while the other half is divided into a series of book alcoves containing a mix of newer fiction and vintage titles, all in quite good condition. We found the books to be reasonably priced.

Russian Language Specialties   **By Appointment**
PO Box 305 49090   (616) 639-8310

Collection:	Specialty new and used.
# of Vols:	25,000
Specialties:	Russian language only.
Services:	Appraisals, catalog, accepts want lists.
Credit Cards:	No

Owner:	LeRoy Wolins
Year Estab:	1960

Southfield
(Map 16, page 192)

Books Connection
29211 Southfield Road 48076

Open Shop
(248) 559-3780

Collection:	General stock new and mostly paperback used.
# of Vols:	25,000 (used)
Hours:	Mon-Fri 10-7. Sat 10-5. Sun 12-5.

McDonnell House Antiques
19860 West 12 Mile Road 48076

Open Shop
(248) 559-9120

Collection:	General stock.
# of Vols:	400
Hours:	Mon-Sat 10-5.
Travel:	Evergreen exit off I-696. Proceed north on Evergreen then east on 12 Mile Rd.
Credit Cards:	Yes
Year Estab:	1991
Comments:	Shop also sells antiques.

Yesterday's Books
25625 Southfield Road 48075

By Appointment
(248) 557-7099
Fax: (248) 559-7371
E-mail: lbwbooks@aol.com

Collection:	Specialty
Specialties:	First editions; 20th century literature; mystery; science fiction; horror.
Services:	Appraisals, catalog, accepts want lists.
Credit Cards:	Yes
Owner:	Lois Wodika
Year Estab:	1980

Sterling Heights
(Map 16, page 192)

Acorn Books
3645 East 15 Mile Road 48310

Open Shop
(810) 795-2700

Collection:	General stock of paperback and hardcover.
# of Vols:	10,000 (hardcover)
Specialties:	Children's series; mystery; science fiction; science; technology.
Hours:	Mon-Sat 10-9. Sun 12-5.
Services:	Appraisals, accepts want lists, search service, mail order.
Travel:	Located in a shopping center at the northwest corner of 15 Mile Rd and Ryan Rd.
Credit Cards:	Yes
Owner:	Jim Deak

Year Estab: 1991
Comments: Far more paperbacks than hardcover books and few of the hardcover
                  titles we saw would fall into the collectible category. Generally, a shop
                  offering neighborhood residents reading copies.

Suttons Bay
(Map 13, page 184)

Highwood Bookshop   **By Appointment**
13801 East Shady Lane Road 49682   (616) 271-3898

Collection: Specialty new and used books and magazines.
# of Vols: 10,000
Specialties: Hunting; fishing; guns.
Services: Accepts want lists, mail order.
Credit Cards: Yes
Owner: Lewis L. Razek
Year Estab: 1974

Known Books   **Open Shop**
119½ St. Josephs Avenue   (616) 271-6483
Mailing address: PO Box 251 Suttons Bay MI 49682
Web page: www.known.com   E-mail: known@traverse.com

Collection: General stock of mostly hardcover used and new.
# of Vols: 5,000 (used)
Hours: Mon-Sat 10-5:30. Evenings and Sun by chance.
Travel: On Rte 22, 15 miles north of Traverse City.
Credit Cards: Yes
Owner: Cheryl C. Cigan
Year Estab: 1997

Taylor
(Map 16, page 192)

Another Look Books   **Open Shop**
22263 Goddard Road 48180   (313) 374-5665

Collection: General stock of paperback and hardcover.
# of Vols: 50,000+
Hours: Mon-Sat 10-6, except Fri 12-8.
Year Estab: 1995
Comments: Stock is approximately 75% paperback.

Tecumseh
(Map 13, page 184)

L & M Antiques   **Antique Mall**
7811 West Chicago Boulevard 49286   (517) 423-7346

Hours: Tue-Sun 12-5.
Travel: Located on Rte 50.

Tecumseh Antique Mall II   **Antique Mall**
1111 West Chicago Boulevard 49286   (517) 423-6082

Hours: Mon-Sat 10-5. Sun 12-5.
Travel: On Rte 50.

Three Rivers
(Map 13, page 184)

Links To The Past   **Open Shop**
52631 US 131 North 49093   (616) 279-7310

Collection: General stock of hardcover and paperback.
# of Vols: 30,000
Specialties: Children's; Gene Stratton Porter; Gladys Taber; Harold Bell Wright.
Hours: Mon-Sat, except closed Wed, 10-6. Sun 11-5. Closed major holidays.
Services: Accepts want lists, mail order.
Travel: Located on east side of Rte 131, six miles north of Three Rivers.
Credit Cards: No
Owner: Pamela K. Blackburn
Comments: When you first enter this shop you may suspect it will be just another
                "mixed bag" of paperbacks and recent bestsellers. The further back
                into the cavernous building you go, however, the more fascinated
                you're likely to be with the selection of books in almost every cat-
                egory. As the sign outside suggests, there's much more inside than
                immediately meets your eye.

Lowry's Books   **Open Shop**
22 North Main Street 49093   (616) 273-7323

Collection: General stock of used and new hardcover and paperback.
# of Vols: 40,000 (used)
Specialties: Military; religion; regional; biography.
Hours: Mon-Wed 10-6. Thu & Fri 10-8. Sat 10-7. Sun 11-5.
Services: Search service, accepts want lists, mail order.
Travel: From Rte 131, take Bus Rte 131 into downtown where it becomes
                Main St.
Credit Cards: Yes
Owner: Tom Lowry
Year Estab: 1993
Comments: A combination shop, offering some new books (mostly up front), paper-
                backs and used hardcover volumes of varying time periods. While the
                selection of hardcovers was mixed, we saw more interesting older titles
                than one usually spots in a new/used shop. Even though the selection
                here is small, since there is another used book shop in town, we cer-
                tainly think it worth the few extra minutes it would take to visit here.

Traverse City
(Map 13, page 184)

Peninsula Books   **By Appointment**
451 North Madison 49684   (616) 941-2032
                                                      Fax: (616) 941-1787
                                             E-mail: penbooks@traverse.com

Collection: General stock.
# of Vols: 10,000
Specialties: Michigan; Great Lakes; Americana; Midwest; travel; exploration.
Services: Appraisals, search service, catalog, accepts want lists.
Credit Cards: Yes
Owner: Guy A. Wood
Year Estab: 1985

Warren
(Map 16, page 192)

All Star Book Store   **Open Shop**
21747 Van Dyke Avenue 48089   (810) 758-4780

Collection: General stock of paperback and hardcover.
# of Vols: 20,000
Hours: Mon-Sat 12-7.
Travel: Van Dyke exit off I-696. Proceed south on Van Dyke for 2½ miles.
Credit Cards: No
Year Estab: 1977
Comments: Stock is approximately 75% paperback.

Exnowski Enterprises   **By Appointment**
31512 Reid 48092   (810) 264-1686

Collection: Specialty
# of Vols: 7,000
Specialties: Native Americans; Americana; Teutonic history, mythology and lit-
                  erature; aviation; ethnic history.
Services: Appraisals, search service, catalog, accepts want lists.
Credit Cards: No
Owner: Eugene Exnowski
Year Estab: 1974

Waterford
(Map 13, page 184)

The Great Midwestern Antique Emporium   **Antique Mall**
5233 Dixie Highway 48329   (248) 623-7460

Hours: Tue-Sun 10-5.
Travel: Dixie Hwy exit off I-75. Proceed south on Dixie Hwy.

Honeycomb Books & Records
1052 West Huron 48328

Open Shop
(248) 681-6615

Collection:	General stock of mostly paperback.
# of Vols:	35,000
Hours:	Mon-Fri 10-6. Sat 10-5:30.

Paperback Trader
6486 Williams Lake Road 48329

Open Shop
(248) 623-3070

Collection:	General stock of mostly paperback.
# of Vols:	50,000
Hours:	Mon-Sat 10-7. Sun 12-5.

Wayne
(Map 16, page 192)

Crazy Barb's Paperback Exchange
3127 South Wayne Road 48184

Open Shop
(313) 728-6663

Collection:	General stock of mostly paperback.
# of Vols:	100,000
Hours:	Mon-Sat 9:30-6.

West Bloomfield
(Map 16, page 192)

Galerie De Boicourt
6136 Westbrooke Drive 48322

By Appointment
(248) 788-9253

Collection:	Specialty new and out of print.
Specialties:	Art (including folk art); antiques; textiles.
Services:	Search service, catalog, accept want lists.
Credit Cards:	No
Owner:	Eva M. Boicourt
Year Estab:	1966

Westland
(Map 16, page 192)

Paperbacks and Things
8044 North Wayne Road 48185

Open Shop
Tel & Fax: (313) 522-8018

Collection:	General stock of mostly paperback.
# of Vols:	35,000
Hours:	Mon-Sat 9:30-8:30.

White Pigeon
(Map 13, page 184)

Bookmark Book Exchange
69464 South Kalamazoo Street 49099

Open Shop
(616) 483-7709

Collection:	General stock of mostly paperback.

# of Vols: 100,000
Hours: Tue-Sat 9:30-6.

Whitehall
(Map 13, page 184)

Freddie The Bookie   **By Appointment**
1003 South Mears Avenue 49461   (616) 894-2212

Collection: General stock.
# of Vols: 5,000
Specialties: Military; prisoners of war; Holocaust; black studies; Alaska; cookbooks.
Services: Accepts want lists, mail order.
Credit Cards: No
Owner: Fred M. Wacholz
Year Estab: 1992
Comments: Also displays at Memory Lane Antique Mall in N. Muskegon. See above.

Williamston
(Map 13, page 184)

Antique Market of Williamston   **Antique Mall**
2992 Williamston Road   (517) 655-1350

Hours: Daily 10-6.
Travel: Exit 117 off I-96. Proceed north on Williamston Rd for 1/3 mile.

Wyoming
(Map 13, page 184)

FBS   **By Appointment**
1540 Pinnacle East SW 49509   (616) 249-9291
                                                         Fax: (616) 249-8406

Collection: Specialty
Specialties: Religion, with emphasis on Puritans, Presbyterian and Reformed.
Services: Catalog, accepts want lists.
Credit Cards: No
Year Estab: 1978

Ypsilanti
(Map 15, page 197 & Map 13, page 184)

Cross Street Book Shop   **Open Shop**
523 West Cross Street 48197   (734) 484-3000

Collection: General stock of paperback and hardcover.
# of Vols: 25,000
Specialties: Black studies; music; modern first editions; art; science; technology.
Hours: Mon-Fri 11-8. Sat 12-8. Sun 1-5.
Services: Appraisals, search service, catalog, accepts want lists.

Travel:	Exit 183 off I-94. Proceed north on Huron St. After passing through downtown, the left lane forks onto West Cross St (Rte 17). Shop is located immediately after second light.
Credit Cards:	Yes
Owner:	Sheridan Settler
Year Estab:	1993
Comments:	Reminiscent in some ways of what some of the old New York City Fourth Avenue book stores used to look like (except they didn't carry paperbacks) with books on the floor in the aisles and a dealer struggling to keep up with the volume. Hardcover and paperback titles were intershelved and most subject areas were covered. While this may not be one of the neatest shops we've visited, the books are organized by subject and perhaps because of the shop's crowded appearance, we felt it would be possible for you to find an item or two of interest here.

Lindsay Chess Supplies   **By Appointment**
4171 Woodcreek Drive 48197   (734) 434-6123
Web page: fplindsay@aol.com

Collection:	Specialty used and new.
# of Vols:	4,000
Specialties:	Chess
Services:	On line catalog.
Credit Cards:	Yes
Owner:	Fred Lindsay
Year Estab:	1974
Comments:	Stock is approximately 65% used.

Russell S. Rein, Books & Records   **By Appointment**
522 Maulbetsch Street 48197   (734) 434-2968
                                                   E-mail: Ypsi-Slim@juno.com

Collection:	General stock, ephemera and records.
# of Vols:	3,500+
Specialties:	Early automobile travel; U.S. highways and related ephemera (maps, travel guides, postcards, etc.); petroleum.
Services:	Accepts want lists, mail order.
Credit Cards:	No
Year Estab:	1978
Comments:	Also displays a general stock at Harley's Antique Mall in Albion.

Weekend Bookman   **By Appointment**
PO Box 980464 48198   (734) 482-1760

Collection:	General stock.
# of Vols:	10,000
Specialties:	Americana
Services:	Accepts want lists, mail order.
Credit Cards:	No
Owner:	Bob Maday

Owner: Bob Maday
Year Estab: 1981

White Raven Books
PO Box 980469 48198

By Appointment
(734) 485-3770

Collection: General stock.
# of Vols: 2,000
Specialties: Art; architecture; books on books; gardening; signed.
Services: Accepts want lists, mail order.
Credit Cards: Yes
Owner: C. Hedger & Colin Breed
Year Estab: 1994

They say, "You can't take it with you." While that may
apply to money, it certainly doesn't apply to books.

A-albionic Research   Fax: (313) 885-1181
PO Box 20273 Ferndale 48220

Collection:	Specialty
Specialties:	Conspiracy; ruling class; radicalism; secret societies; super-rich biography; assassinations; occult; new age.
Services:	Search service, catalog.
Credit Cards:	Yes
Year Estab:	1984

George Barry, Books   Tel & Fax: (248) 548-6434
321 Ninth Street Royal Oak 48067   E-mail: gbbooks@mich.com
Web page: www.abebooks.com

Collection:	General stock.
# of Vols:	10,000
Specialties:	Mythology; folklore; illustrated.
Services:	Appraisals, accepts want lists, search service.
Credit Cards:	No
Year Estab:	1988

Thomas C. Bayer   (517) 439-4134
85 Reading Avenue Hillsdale 49242   Fax: (517) 439-5661

Collection:	Specialty used and new.
# of Vols:	10,000
Specialties:	Science; technology; natural history.
Services:	Catalog, accepts want lists.
Credit Cards:	No
Year Estab:	1987
Comments:	Books of interest primarily to academics and research institutions.

Big Bang Books   (616) 345-9501
1830 Greenbriar Drive Portage 49024

Collection:	General stock of mostly paperbacks.
# of Vols:	40,000
Specialties:	Vintage paperbacks; mystery; science fiction.
Services:	Search service, accepts want lists.
Credit Cards:	No
Owner:	Jim Combs
Year Estab:	1992

Bohling Book Company   (616) 423-8786
PO Box 204 Decatur 49045   Fax: (616) 423-6146
                                               E-mail: bohlings@mich.com

Collection:	Specialty
# of Vols:	8,500
Specialties:	Midwestern Americana; Western Americana; railroads and related land promotional materials designed to induce tourism and immigration.
Services:	Lists

Credit Cards: Yes
Owner: Curt & Lynnette Bohling
Year Estab: 1976

Bookop Shop   (517) 423-4467
64 Swan Lake Drive Adrian 49221

Collection: General stock.
# of Vols: 8,000-10,000
Specialties: Children's; children's illustrated; cookbooks.
Services: Accepts want lists.
Credit Cards: No
Owner: Alice & John Nolan
Year Estab: 1974

Books 'N' Things   (517) 750-4332
6844 West Michigan Avenue Jackson 49201

Collection: General stock of new and used.
Services: Appraisals, search service, accepts want lists.
Owner: Leonard "Joe" McManus
Year Estab: 1979

Branchwater Books & Ephemera   Tel & Fax: (616) 898-2286
Route 1, Box 468 Branch 49402   E-mail: rdj@carrinter.net

Collection: Specialty books and ephemera.
Specialties: Historical ephemera; technology (pre turn of the century).
Services: Appraisals, accepts want lists.
Credit Cards: No
Owner: Roger D. Jones
Year Estab: 1977

A. Dalrymple, Bookseller   (248) 649-2149
1791 Graefield Birmingham 48009

Collection: Specialty
# of Vols: 8,000
Specialties: Children's; illustrated moveables; pop-ups.
Services: Accepts want lists.
Credit Cards: No
Owner: Alex & Dolores Dalrymple
Year Estab: 1984

John B. Doukas   (616) 342-8155
132 North Kalamazoo Mall, #2 Kalamazoo 49007

Collection: Specialty
Specialties: Greece & Rome; antiquarian.

Jackie Foote Used Books   (517) 345-4384
PO Box 331 West Branch 48661

Collection: General stock.
# of Vols: 2,000

Specialties:	First editions.
Services:	Accepts want lists, lists.
Credit Cards:	No
Year Estab:	1986

Forgotten Lore (248) 334-9739
670 East Mansfield Avenue Pontiac 48340

Collection:	Specialty
# of Vols:	300
Specialties:	Philately
Services:	Accepts want lists.
Owner:	Glenn Robinson
Year Estab:	1984

Four Score Books and Ect. (517) 643-5368
PO Box 415 Merrill 48637

Collection:	Specialty books and prints.
Specialties:	Civil War; American Revolution; general stock of other historical periods.
Services:	Catalog, accepts want lists.
Credit Cards:	No
Owner:	James & Kathy Maxson
Year Estab:	1988
Comments:	Also does reenactments and historical encampments.

Gunnerman Books (517) 729-7018
PO Box 217 Owosso 48867   Fax: (517) 725-9391
E-mail: gunnermanbks@webtv.net

Collection:	Specialty. Mostly used.
# of Vols:	1,600
Specialties:	Hunting
Services:	Appraisals, search service, catalog, accepts want lists.
Credit Cards:	Yes
Owner:	Carol Barnes
Year Estab:	1977

Jim's Books (517) 723-5586
280 East Riley Road Owosso 48867

Collection:	General stock.
# of Vols:	3,500
Specialties:	Gene Stratton Porter; Zane Grey; children's; James Oliver Curwood.
Services:	Appraisals, search service, accepts want lists.
Credit Cards:	Yes
Owner:	James VanPelt
Year Estab:	1983

Keramos Tel & Fax: (734) 439-1300
PO Box 7500 Ann Arbor 48107

Collection:	Specialty. Mostly used.

# of Vols:	10,000
Specialties:	Oriental art; Asia; ceramics.
Services:	Accepts want lists, subject lists.
Credit Cards:	No
Year Estab:	1976

Kruklitis' Latvian Bookstore   (517) 332-1206
511 Charles Street East Lansing 48823

Collection:	Specialty new and used.
Specialties:	Latvia.
Services:	Catalog, appraisals.
Owner:	Robert Kruklitis

Mad Hatter Collectible Books   (313) 882-6206
16635 East Jefferson Grosse Pointe Park 48230

Collection:	General stock.
# of Vols:	1,000-2,000
Specialties:	Children's
Services:	Accepts want lists.
Credit Cards:	No
Owner:	Kay Mackay
Year Estab:	1982

Mail Order Mysteries   (734) 665-5813
1313 Henry Street Ann Arbor 48104

Collection:	Specialty
# of Vols:	4,000
Specialties:	Mystery
Services:	Search service, catalog, accepts want lists.
Credit Cards:	No
Owner:	Judith A. Steeh
Year Estab:	1992

Mary Ann's Books   (248) 615-8944
28475 Greenfield, #213 Southfield 48076

Collection:	Specialty. Mostly used hardcover.
# of Vols:	700
Specialties:	Baseball; football, basketball; hockey; fighting.
Services:	Catalog (please send large SASE).
Credit Cards:	No
Year Estab:	1998

James A. Monnig, Bookseller   (313) 882-7240
5295 Ashley Detroit 48236   E-mail: bookjim@juno.com

Collection:	Specialty
# of Vols:	2,500
Specialties:	Cookbooks
Services:	Accepts want lists.

Credit Cards: No
Year Estab: 1974

David Netzorg (313) 272-1454
18090 Wyoming Detroit 48221 E-mail: dnetzorg@compuserve.com
Collection: General stock.
# of Vols: 2,000
Specialties: Folk songs and ballads; statistics; old technology.
Services: Search service, catalog, accepts want lists.
Credit Cards: Yes
Year Estab: 1966

Geraldine Powers (248) 549-5126
4216 Mandalay Street Royal Oak 48073
Collection: General stock.
# of Vols: 3,000
Services: Accepts want lists.
Credit Cards: No
Year Estab: 1988

Michael G. Price (517) 764-4517
PO Box 468 Michigan Center 49254 E-mail: mgprice@sojourn.com
Collection: General stock and ephemera.
Specialties: Asia
Services: Accepts want lists.
Credit Cards: No
Year Estab: 1980

Quest Antiques-Books-Collectibles (517) 546-6416
PO Box 670 Brighton 48116 E-mail: questabc@interloc.com
Collection: Specialty
# of Vols: 3,000-4,000
Specialties: Geology; mining; natural sciences.
Services: Catalog
Credit Cards: No
Owner: Loyal Suntken
Year Estab: 1994

Reformation Heritage Books (616) 977-0599
2919 Leonard, NE Grand Rapids 49525 Fax: (616) 977-0889
Web page: www.heritagebooks.org E-mail: jrbeeke@aol.com
Collection: Specialty new and used.
Specialties: Puritan
Services: Catalog, accepts want lists.
Credit Cards: Yes
Owner: Dr. J. R. Beeke
Year Estab: 1994
Comments: Stock is approximately 85% new.

Rereadables
6060 Bullard Road Fenton 48430
Web page: www.rereadables.com

Tel & Fax: (810) 632-9566
E-mail: knovak@htonline.com

Collection:	General stock of mostly paperback.
# of Vols:	10,000
Credit Cards:	Yes
Owner:	Katherine Novak
Year Estab:	1997

The Science Bookshelf
525 Fourth Street Ann Arbor 48103

(734) 665-0537
Fax: (734) 930-0450

Collection:	General stock.
Specialties:	Science; osteopathy; mystery; medicine.
Services:	Search service, accepts want lists.
Owner:	C.A. Hough
Year Estab:	1981

J. E. Sheldon Fine Books
1126 South Seventh Street Ann Arbor 48103

(734) 998-0604

Collection:	General stock.
# of Vols:	6,000
Specialties:	Books on books; Michigan; occult; J. Gruelle; palmistry.
Services:	Appraisals, accepts want lists.
Credit Cards:	No
Owner:	Julie Ellen Sheldon
Year Estab:	1974
Comments:	Also displays at Wooden Spoon in Ann Arbor.

Art Spindler
33340 Jefferson Avenue Saint Clair Shores 48082

(810) 293-2483
Fax: (810) 293-2002
E-mail: aspindle@aol.com

Collection:	General stock
# of Vols:	8,000
Specialties:	Automotive; nautical.
Services:	Automotive only: appraisals, search service, accepts want lists, catalog.
Credit Cards:	No
Year Estab:	1993

Taylor Search Service
PO Box 85396 Westland 48185
Web page: www.golfmystery.com

(313) 326-0700
Fax: (313) 326-6980
E-mail: ttbooks@aol.com

Collection:	Specialty
# of Vols:	3,000
Specialties:	Golf; P.G. Wodehouse; weaving; mystery; Allan Eckert.
Services:	Accepts want lists.
Credit Cards:	No
Year Estab:	1979

Topaz-Mineral Exploration (616) 842-3506
1605 Hillcrest Grand Haven 49417

Collection:	Specialty books and ephemera.
Specialties:	Geology; Michigan; exploration; archaeology; maps.
Services:	Appraisals, catalog, accepts want lists.
Credit Cards:	No
Owner:	Thomas M. Bee
Year Estab:	1977

Treasures From The Castle (248) 651-7317
1720 North Livernois Rochester Hills 48306 E-mail: treasure3@juno.com

Collection:	Specialty
# of Vols:	4,000
Specialties:	Children's
Services:	Search service, catalog (by subscription), accepts want lists.
Credit Cards:	Yes
Owner:	Connie Castle
Year Estab:	1979

Dale Weber Books (248) 651-3177
5740 Livernois Rochester 48306 Fax: (248) 651-3774
E-mail: weber521@msn.com

Collection:	General stock.
# of Vols:	3,000
Specialties:	Roycroft Press; Edgar Allan Poe; Agatha Christie; Winston Churchill; Stephen King.
Credit Cards:	No
Owner:	Dale & Phyllis Weber
Year Estab:	1970

Richard Wertz, Bookseller (810) 767-3630
Rosehaven Manor 3900 Hammerberg Road, #121 Flint 48507
E-mail: wertzbook@aol.com

Collection:	General stock and ephemera.
# of Vols:	2,000
Specialties:	Michigan
Year Estab:	1980

David L. White—Books (616) 837-6053
PO Box 61 Coopersville 49404 E-mail: whitebks@interloc.com

Collection:	Specialty
# of Vols:	1,000
Specialties:	Michigan and northern fiction and authors including James Oliver Curwood, Stewart Edward White, James B. Hendry, George Marsh, Rex Beach.
Services:	Appraisals, accepts want lists, search service.
Credit Cards:	Yes
Year Estab:	1993

The Wilderness Collection   (616) 624-4410
716 Delaware Court Lawton 49065   Fax: (616) 624-5309
                                                 E-mail: wilcobooks@aol.com

Collection:	Specialty used and new.
# of Vols:	2,000
Specialties:	Canoes and kayaks.
Services:	Catalog, accepts want lists.
Credit Cards:	No
Owner:	Jerry Cassell & Marriane McArthur
Year Estab:	1992

Win's Books   (517) 725-9974
1102 North Ball Street Owosso 48867

Collection:	Specialty
# of Vols:	2,000-3,000
Specialties:	Gene Stratton Porter; Zane Grey; Gladys Taber; Harold Bell Wright; James Oliver Curwood; James Whitcomb Riley.
Hours:	Available for business from May 1st-Oct 31st.
Services:	Accepts want lists.
Credit Cards:	No
Owner:	Winston R. Reynolds
Year Estab:	1970

Pat & Bill Wisney—Books   (517) 433-2119
PO Box 5 Rosebush MI 48878

Collection:	General stock and ephemera.
# of Vols:	4,000
Specialties:	Michigan; Americana.
Services:	Accepts want lists.
Credit Cards:	No
Year Estab:	1981

Timothy B. Wuchter   (906) 353-7846
HC 01, Box 291 Pelkie 49958   E-mail: tbw@up.net

Collection:	Specialty books and ephemera.
# of Vols:	10,000
Specialties:	Rivers of America Series; Series Americana; Federal Writer's Project; signed literary first editions; Americana.
Services:	Search service, catalog, accepts want lists.
Credit Cards:	No
Year Estab:	1990

MINNESOTA

Alphabetical Listing By Dealer

A Novel Place	288	Books Unlimited	299
A Williams Books	278	Booksmart	279
A-Z Collectables	299	Calhoun Book Store	302
ABC Collectables	301	Canal Park Antique Center	273
Robert C. Alexander Books	301	Carlson Book	273
Ally Press	301	Cash Coin Connection	302
American Gothic Antique Mall	296	Chapman Street Books	275
Arch Books	301	China Book Gallery	302
The Artique	270	Classic Arms Books	291
As Time Goes By	286	The Constant Reader	269
E.J. Bankey	301	Country Comfort Antiques and Books	299
Barnes & Noble	290	Cummings Books	279
Bee Creek Books	302	Dan's Books	288
Bev's Book Nook	288	Dinkytown Antiquarian Bookstore	280
Biermaier's B. H. Books	278	Dreamhaven	280
Big League Company	272	Earthly Remains	276
Blue Leaf Books	299	The Extraordinary Bookseller	290
Book & Cover	289	Fact and Fiction	296
The Book Bin	272	Felicitas Cookbooks	296
The Book House in Dinkytown	278	Fireproof Books	303
The Book House on Grand	292	Friends of Mpls Pub Lib Book Shop	280
The Book Trader	279	Gabriel's Bookstore	274
The Bookcase	287	Gregory and Beverly Gamradt	303
Bookdales	289	H.M. George Books	280
Bookery	269	Betsy Gerboth	303
Books Bound	273	Great Books	288
Books of Choice	302	Green Lion Books	292
Books of Olde Towne Square	271	Half Price Books	293
Books Revisited	291	Half Price Books	277

Half Price Books	292	Once Read Reads	276
Half Price Books	270	Once Upon A Crime	284
Harold's Book Shop	293	Orr Books	285
Hazen's Books, Records & Antiques	289	The Out-of-Print Book Shoppe	285
Heartland Plus	275	Oxcart Trail Books	295
Peter M. Holmes Fine Books	281	Paperback Writer	285
Theodore J. Holston Jr., Bookseller	303	PDW Books	304
Hopkins Antique Mall	276	Richard G. Peterson, Bookseller	304
Arthur Hudgins	293	Philco Books	304
Hymie's Vintage Records Etc.	281	Plunkett/Higgins Books	270
Impact Books	271	Remember When	272
J O'Donoghue Books	270	Robbin's Bookworm	289
Kisselburg Military Books	303	Duane Robeck- Bookseller	305
Ladybug Books	276	Rulon-Miller Books	305
Lancaster & Simpson	304	S & S Books	305
James & Mary Laurie, Booksellers	281	S & S Booksellers	305
Leipold's of Excelsior	275	St. Croix Antiquarian Booksellers	297
Lien's Book Shop	283	Sauk River Books	291
Little Professor Book Center	286	Science Book Service	306
Loome Theological Booksellers	296	Second Look Books	275
Barb Mader - Books	293	Dale Seppa	306
Magers & Quinn Booksellers	283	Seven Gables Books & Antiques	287
Magus Books	283	Sixth Chamber Used Books	294
Mary Twyce Books & Paper	300	Snowy Egret Books	295
Melvin McCosh, Bookseller	304	Station 17 Books	285
Midtown Book Center	297	Stillwater Children's Books	298
Midway Bookstore	294	Terrace Horticultural Books	285
The Mill Antiques	297	Turnabout Books	295
Minnehaha Books	284	Uncle Edgar's Mystery Bookstore	286
Nicollet Book Store	284	Uncle Hugo's Sci Fiction Bookstore	286
North Woods Books	274	Vikingland Book Trader	269
Northern Lights Books	298	T.E. Warth, Esq., Automotive Books	277
Notting Hill Books	294	Wild Rumpus	286
Old Town Books	274	Wind River Used Books	277

Alphabetical Listing By Location

Location	Dealer	Page
Albert Lea	Bookery	269
	The Constant Reader	269
Alexandria	Vikingland Book Trader	269
Anoka	The Artique	270
	J O'Donoghue Books	270
Apple Valley	Half Price Books, Records, Magazines	270
Austin	Plunkett/Higgins Books	270
Big Lake	Books of Olde Towne Square	271
Bird Island	Impact Books	271
Bloomington	Books of Choice	302
	Betsy Gerboth	303
Coon Rapids	The Book Bin	272
Detroit Lakes	Remember When	272
Duluth	Big League Company	272
	Books Bound	273
	Canal Park Antique Center	273
	Carlson Book	273
	Gabriel's Bookstore	274
	North Woods Books	274
	Old Town Books	274
	Philco Books	304
	Second Look Books	275
Eagan	S & S Booksellers	305
Edina	E.J. Bankey	301
	Calhoun Book Store	302
Ely	Chapman Street Books	275
Excelsior	Theodore J. Holston Jr., Bookseller	303
	Leipold's of Excelsior	275
	Melvin McCosh, Bookseller	304
Hill City	Heartland Plus	275
Hopkins	Hopkins Antique Mall	276
Lino Lakes	Lancaster & Simpson	304
Mankato	Earthly Remains	276
	Once Read Reads	276
Maple Lake	Ladybug Books	276
Maplewood	Half Price Books, Records, Magazines	277
Marine on St. Croix	T.E. Warth, Esq., Automotive Books	277
Marshall	Wind River Used Books	277
Mendota Heights	A Williams Books	278
Minneapolis	Arch Books	301
	Biermaier's B. H. Books	278
	The Book House in Dinkytown	278
	The Book Trader	279
	Booksmart	279

Minneapolis	Cummings Books	279
	Dinkytown Antiquarian Bookstore	280
	Dreamhaven	280
	Friends of the Mpls Pub Lib Book Shop	280
	Gregory and Beverly Gamradt, Books on the Orient	303
	H.M. George Books	280
	Peter M. Holmes Fine Books	281
	Hymie's Vintage Records Etc.	281
	James & Mary Laurie, Booksellers	281
	Lien's Book Shop	283
	Magers & Quinn Booksellers	283
	Magus Books	283
	Minnehaha Books	284
	Nicollet Book Store	284
	Once Upon A Crime	284
	Orr Books	285
	The Out-of-Print Book Shoppe	285
	Paperback Writer	285
	PDW Books	304
	Richard G. Peterson, Bookseller	304
	Station 17 Books	285
	Terrace Horticultural Books	285
	Uncle Edgar's Mystery Bookstore	286
	Uncle Hugo's Science Fiction Bookstore	286
	Wild Rumpus	286
Minnetonka	Fireproof Books	303
North Oaks	Little Professor Book Center	286
Northfield	As Time Goes By	286
	The Bookcase	287
	Seven Gables Books & Antiques	287
Osseo	A Novel Place	288
	Dan's Books	288
Perham	Bev's Book Nook	288
Plato	China Book Gallery	302
Plymouth	Great Books	288
Richfield	Bookdales	289
	Hazen's Books, Records & Antiques	289
Robbinsdale	Robbin's Bookworm	289
Rochester	Book & Cover	289
	The Extraordinary Bookseller	290
Roseville	Barnes & Noble	290
Saint Cloud	Books Revisited	291
	Classic Arms Books	291
	Sauk River Books	291
Saint Louis Park	Half Price Books, Records, Magazines	292

Saint Paul	ABC Collectables	301
	Robert C. Alexander Books	301
	Ally Press	301
	The Book House on Grand	292
	Green Lion Books	292
	Half Price Books, Records, Magazines	293
	Harold's Book Shop	293
	Arthur Hudgins	293
	Barb Mader - Books	293
	Midway Bookstore	294
	Notting Hill Books	294
	Duane Robeck- Bookseller	305
	Rulon-Miller Books	305
	S & S Books	305
	Science Book Service	306
	Sixth Chamber Used Books	294
	Snowy Egret Books	295
Sartell	Cash Coin Connection	302
Sauk Rapids	Oxcart Trail Books	295
South Saint Paul	Turnabout Books	295
Spring Grove	Bee Creek Books	302
Stillwater	American Gothic Antique Mall	296
	Fact and Fiction	296
	Felicitas Cookbooks	296
	Kisselburg Military Books	303
	Loome Theological Booksellers	296
	Midtown Book Center	297
	The Mill Antiques	297
	St. Croix Antiquarian Booksellers	297
	Stillwater Children's Books	298
Thief River Falls	Northern Lights Books	298
Virginia	Dale Seppa	306
Winona	A-Z Collectables	299
	Blue Leaf Books	299
	Books Unlimited	299
	Country Comfort Antiques and Books	299
	Mary Twyce Books & Paper	300

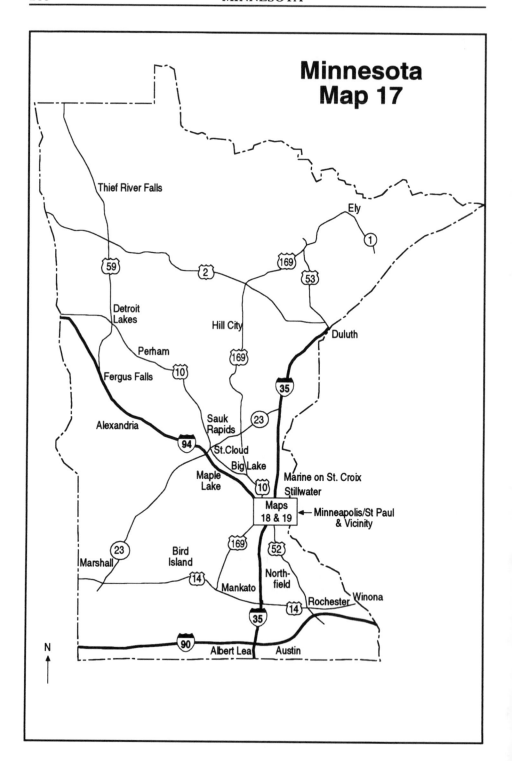

Minnesota
Map 17

Thief River Falls

Ely

59

2

169

53

1

Detroit Lakes

Hill City

Duluth

Perham

169

Fergus Falls

10

Alexandria

Sauk Rapids

23

35

94

St.Cloud

Big Lake

Maple Lake

10

Marine on St. Croix

Stillwater

Maps 18 & 19 ← Minneapolis/St Paul & Vicinity

23

Marshall

Bird Island

169

52

14

Mankato

North-field

Rochester

Winona

14

35

N

90

Albert Lea

Austin

Albert Lea
(Map 17, page 268)

Bookery   **Open Shop**
1030 South Broadway Avenue 56007   (507) 373-0242

Collection: General stock of mostly used paperback.
# of Vols: 100,000
Hours: Mon-Fri 10-6. Sat 10-4.

The Constant Reader   **Open Shop**
238 Broadway 56007   (507) 373-6512

Collection: General stock of used and new paperback and hardcover.
# of Vols: 20,000 (used)
Hours: Mon-Fri 9:30-6, except Thu till 8. Sat 9:30-4.
Services: Mail order.
Travel: Albert Lea exit off I-35. Proceed to Main St. Shop is three doors from
                   corner of Main and Broadway.
Credit Cards: Yes
Owner: Grace Haukoos
Year Estab: 1987
Comments: Most of the used books in this combination new/used shop are in such
                   good condition that unless one looks very closely it's not always easy
                   to distinguish the previously owned volumes from the new ones. Of
                   course, this correctly implies that the majority of the used items are of
                   recent vintage.

Alexandria
(Map 17, page 268)

Vikingland Book Trader   **Open Shop**
605 Broadway 56308   Tel & Fax: (320) 762-8722

Collection: General stock of hardcover and paperback.
# of Vols: 30,000
Hours: Mon-Sat 10-5, except Thu till 7. Sun 12-4.
Services: Appraisals, search service, accepts want lists, mail order.
Travel: Exit 103 off I-94. Proceed north on Rte 29 to center of town. Shop is
                   between 6th & 7th Ave.
Credit Cards: Yes
Owner: Chuck Crane
Year Estab: 1995
Comments: One of those shops with hardcover books along the side and rear walls
                   and paperbacks taking up the center aisles. The majority of the hard-
                   cover volumes we saw were mostly of recent vintage with some no-
                   table exceptions. There were some modern firsts and a few signed
                   editions. Reasonably priced.

Anoka
(Map 18, page 290)

The Artique
203 Jackson Street

Antique Mall
(612) 506-0562

Hours:	Mon-Sat 10-6. Sun 12-5.
Travel:	From Minneapolis: Rte 10 to Main St exit in Anoka. Proceed east on Main, then north on 2nd. Shop is at corner of 2nd and Jackson.

J O'Donoghue Books
1926 2nd Avenue South 55303

Open Shop
(612) 427-4320

Collection:	General stock of hardcover and paperback.
# of Vols:	35,000
Specialties:	Children's series; mystery; science fiction.
Hours:	Mon-Thu 10-8. Fri & Sat 10-5:30. Jan & Feb: 10-5:30 except, Thu till 8.
Services:	Accepts want lists.
Travel:	Ferry St exit off Rte 10. If westbound on Rte 10, then left on Ferry, left on Main St and right on 2nd Ave.
Credit Cards:	Yes
Owner:	Jean O'Donoghue
Year Estab:	1972
Comments:	We were impressed by the many shelves of mixed vintage mysteries, including some rare and interesting titles along with more common ones. The rest of the shop displays a mix of used paperback and hardcover items as well as some newer titles. If you're a mystery fan, we suggest you stop. If you're looking for something more esoteric, the odds of finding your wants here may not be worth the gamble.

Apple Valley
(Map 18, page 290)

Half Price Books, Records, Magazines
7600 West 150th Street 55124

Open Shop
(612) 431-0749

Collection:	General stock of hardcover and paperback, remainders and magazines.
Hours:	Mon-Sat 9-9. Sun 10-6.
Travel:	Cedar Ave exit off I-35E. Proceed south on Cedar then west on Rte 42. Shop is in mall at southwest corner of intersection of Cedar and Rte 42.

Austin
(Map 17, page 268)

Plunkett/Higgins Books
209 Third Avenue, NW 55912

Open Shop
Shop: (507) 437-8161
Home: (507) 433-2039

Collection:	General stock of mostly hardcover, ephemera, prints and maps.
# of Vols:	15,000+
Specialties:	Vintage paperbacks; pulps; sheet music; magazines.
Hours:	Fri & Sat 11-6:30. Sun 12-5. Other times by appointment.

Services:	Mail order.
Travel:	Oakland Ave exit off I-90. Proceed on Oakland to 4th St NW. Left on 4th St then right on 3rd Ave NW. Shop is two blocks ahead on right.
Credit Cards:	No
Owner:	Roger Plunkett & Bud Higgins
Year Estab:	1993
Comments:	Located in three small rooms in a brick office building, the shop offers a mix of mostly older hardcover volumes, paperbacks, pulp magazines, sheet music and other assorted ephemera and some popular old magazines, including film and photography. Organization is not necessarily one of the shop's strong points. However, with a bit of patience and some direction from the owners, it may well be possible to find items of interest to you here. What you don't see in the "open" portion of the shop is supplemented by additional books and magazines stored in the basement.

Big Lake
(Map 17, page 268)

Books of Olde Towne Square　　　　　　　　　　　**Open Shop**
160 North Lake Street　　　　　　　　　　　　　　　(612) 263-1130
Mailing address: PO Box 628 Big Lake MN 55309　　Fax: (612) 261-2839
　　　　　　　　　　　　　　　　　　　　　E-mail: tjt@sherbtel.net

Collection:	General stock of hardcover and paperback.
# of Vols:	45,000
Hours:	Tue-Sat 10-6, expect Thu till 9.
Services:	Appraisals, search service, accepts want lists, mail order.
Travel:	In downtown, at junction of Rte 10 & Rte 25. Shop is located on northwest corner in a former school building.
Credit Cards:	Yes
Owner:	Linda Havrilla & Corrine Jacobson
Year Estab:	1992
Comments:	Most of the hardcover volumes we saw were of fairly recent vintage with a few old timers and even some collectibles hiding on the shelves. Quite reasonably priced.

Bird Island
(Map 17, page 268)

Impact Books　　　　　　　　　　　　　　　　　**Open Shop**
Basement of Bleasener's, Main Street　　　　　　　(320) 365-3615
Mailing address: 550 Oak Avenue Bird Island MN 55310

Collection:	General stock of mostly hardcover.
# of Vols:	3,000
Specialties:	Modern first editions.
Hours:	Mon-Fri 9-5.
Travel:	1/2 block off Rte 212.
Credit Cards:	No

Owner:	Paul Heyl
Year Estab:	1983
Comments:	Located on the premises of a facility that provides services for brain injured people. Ask for access to the books.

Coon Rapids
(Map 18, page 290)

The Book Bin   **Open Shop**
125 85th Ave NW 55433   (612) 784-5958

Collection:	General stock of paperback and hardcover.
# of Vols:	50,000
Hours:	Mon-Fri 10-8. Sat 10-6. Sun 12-5.
Services:	Accepts want lists.
Travel:	University north exit (Rte 47) off I-694. Proceed north on University for three miles, then left on 85th Ave. Shop is in the Springbrook Mall on the right.
Credit Cards:	Yes
Owner:	Michael & Catherine Schmit
Year Estab:	1990
Comments:	We all have our biases and we'll admit that book stores in malls make us apprehensive. However, this shop, regardless of its location, does indeed stock rare and antiquarian items along with a good selection of more recent vintage hardcover volumes and a healthy selection of paperbacks. In our opinion, worth a visit.

Detroit Lakes
(Map 17, page 268)

Remember When   **Open Shop**
107 Pioneer 56561   (218) 847-2535

Collection:	General stock of hardcover and paperback.
Hours:	Mon-Sat 12-4. (See Comments)
Travel:	On Rte 10 in downtown.
Comments:	Before heading off to visit this shop, we suggest a phone call as, at press time, the owner was uncertain as to whether she would be remaining in business.

Duluth
(Map 17, page 268)

Big League Company   **Open Shop**
314 East Superior Street 55802   (218) 722-1275

Collection:	General collection of hardcover and paperback.
# of Vols:	5,000
Specialties:	Sports; military; science fiction.
Hours:	Mon-Sat 9-5.
Services:	Catalog, accepts want lists.

Travel:	In downtown. Lake Ave exit off I-35. Proceed north on Lake Ave, then east on Superior.
Credit Cards:	Yes
Owner:	Kent L. Henricksen
Year Estab:	1970
Comments:	A combination used book, antiques/collectibles and sports memorabilia shop.

Books Bound   Open Shop
2109 East Superior Street 55812   (218) 722-1419
E-mail: dbjoralt@computerpro.com

Collection:	General stock of mostly hardcover.
# of Vols:	15,000
Specialties:	Children's; regional.
Hours:	Mon-Fri 11-6. Sat 10-5.
Services:	Search service, accepts want lists, mail order, book binding.
Travel:	21st Ave east exit off I-35. Proceed on 21st St for three blocks, then right on Superior.
Credit Cards:	No
Owner:	Don Bjoralt
Year Estab:	1987
Comments:	At the time of our visit 3 ½ years ago, the owner was in the process of expanding his collection to include a series of rooms on the second floor and we commented that if the books displayed in this new space were as attractive and in as good condition as those we saw on the first floor, the visitor would be in for quite a treat. While we didn't have the time to revisit this shop on our most trip to Minnesota to confirm our earlier observations, we suspect that the loss was ours.

Canal Park Antique Center   Antique Mall
310 Lake Avenue South 55802   (218) 720-3940

Hours:	Mon-Sat 10-6. Sun 12-5.
Travel:	Lake Ave South exit off I-35. If Northbound on I-35, turn right on Lake Ave South, then right at first light and left at next light continuing on Lake Ave.

Carlson Book   Open Shop
206 East Superior Street 55802   (218) 722-8447

Collection:	General stock of hardcover and paperback.
# of Vols:	100,000 (hardcover)
Hours:	Mon-Sat 10am-11pm. Sun 12-10.
Travel:	Lake Ave exit off I-35. Proceed north on Lake, then right on Superior.
Credit Cards:	No
Owner:	Bob Carlson
Year Estab:	1979
Comments:	We almost made the mistake of passing this shop by because of the profusion of magazines in the shop's large window. However, once

(Duluth)

you've gone beyond the front entrance, packed tightly with magazines and paperbacks, you'll find long rows (and narrow aisles) devoted to hardcover titles in most subject areas. The good news is that there are some better and more unusual titles to be found of the shelves. The bad news is that the place is so crowded with books strewn in almost all the aisles that it may be very difficult to locate the few gems that are on the premises. Condition of the books varied from newer items with their dust jackets in tact to much older worn items with rather loose bindings. On balance, the question is just how patient you are as a browser.

Gabriel's Bookstore   **Open Shop**
4915 East Superior Street 55804   (218) 525-7542

Collection:	General stock of hardcover and paperback and records.
# of Vols:	60,000
Hours:	Mon-Sat 10-5. First Sun of the month 9-3.
Travel:	London Rd exit off I-35. Make left on 47th Ave and proceed east for one block, then right on Superior.
Credit Cards:	No
Owner:	St. Michael's Parish
Year Estab:	1985
Comments:	A non profit operation operated for the benefit of St. Michael's school. Stock is evenly divided between hardcover and paperback.

North Woods Books   **By Appointment**
5400 London Road   55804   (218) 525-7218

Collection:	General stock.
# of Vols:	20,000 (See Comments)
Specialties:	Natural history; regional Americana; sports.
Services:	Appraisals, accepts want lists, mail order.
Owner:	Kay & Mark Kilen
Year Estab:	1984
Comments:	A portion of the stock is on display at Old Town Books and two other antique malls downtown. See below.

Old Town Books   **Open Shop**
102 East Superior Street 55802   (218) 722-5426

Collection:	General stock.
# of Vols:	5,000-10,000
Specialties:	Children's; illustrated.
Hours:	Mon-Sat 10-5. Sun 11-5.
Services:	Accepts want lists, mail order.
Travel:	Lake Ave exit off I-35. Proceed north on Lake Ave, then east on Superior for one block.
Credit Cards:	Yes
Year Estab:	1996
Comments:	A group shop.

Second Look Books   **Open Shop**
1925 West Superior Street 55806   (218) 723-1366

Collection: General stock of mostly paperback.
# of Vols: 23,000
Hours: Tue-Sat 9-5.

Ely
(Map 17, page 268)

Chapman Street Books   **Open Shop**
139 East Chapman Street 55731   (218) 365-2212

Collection: General stock of hardcover and paperback.
# of Vols: 50,000
Specialties: Nature; outdoor living; literary classics.
Hours: Tue-Fri 10-6. Sat 11-5.
Travel: Downtown
Credit Cards: No
Owner: Gwen A. Derr
Year Estab: 1998
Comments: Stock is approximately 60% hardcover. Formerly owned Second Story
                 Books in Minneapolis.

Excelsior
(Map 18, page 290)

Leipold's of Excelsior   **Open Shop**
239 Water Street 55331   (612) 474-5880

Collection: Specialty books and ephemera.
# of Vols: 2,000+ (See Comments)
Specialties: Minnesota; children's; children's series; old novels; cookbooks; fish-
                 ing; hunting; poetry.
Hours: Mon-Fri 9:30-7. Sat 10-5. Sun 1-4.
Services: Accepts want lists, mail order.
Travel: Rte 7 west from Minneapolis to Rte 19. Proceed north on Rte 19 for 1½
                 blocks to light, then right on Water.
Credit Cards: Yes
Owner: Darel & LaVerna Leipold
Year Estab: 1971
Comments: If you don't see what you're looking for ask as only a portion of the
                 collection is on display at any given time.

Hill City
(Map 17, page 268)

Heartland Plus   **Open Shop**
140 Linden Avenue   (218) 697-2786
Mailing address: PO Box 68 Hill City MN 55748

Collection: General stock of paperback and hardcover.

# of Vols:	1,000
Hours:	Daily. Hours vary.
Comments:	Stock is approximately 65% paperback.

Hopkins
(Map 18, page 290)

Hopkins Antique Mall   **Antique Mall**
1008 Main Street 55343   (612) 931-9748

Hours: Mon-Sat 11-6. Sun 11-5.

Mankato
(Map 17, page 268)

Earthly Remains   **Antique Mall**
731 South Front Street 56001   (507) 388-5063

Hours: Mon-Sat 10-5.
Travel: Three blocks south of the downtown civic center.

Once Read Reads   **Open Shop**
629 South Front Street 56001   (507) 388-8144

Collection:	General stock of paperback and hardcover.
# of Vols:	4,000
Specialties:	Minnesota
Hours:	Mon-Sat 10-5.
Travel:	Proceed on Madison St (Rtes 60/14) to river. Left on Riverfront Dr, then left on Warren and right on South Front.
Credit Cards:	No
Owner:	Mark Hustad
Year Estab:	1975
Comments:	A mostly paperback shop with a scattering of used hardcover titles. We saw some older volumes in mixed condition and a few titles that might be considered collectible. However, unless you have lots of spare time, we're not sure that a side trip to this community will bring you the books you're looking for.

Maple Lake
(Map 17, page 268)

Ladybug Books   **Open Shop**
63 Birch Avenue South   (320) 963-6010
Mailing address: PO Box 340 Maple Lake MN 55358   E-mail: oldtimes@lkdllink.net

Collection:	General stock of hardcover and paperback and ephemera.
# of Vols:	5,000
Hours:	Tue-Sat 10-5. Other times by appointment.
Services:	Search service, accepts want lists, mail order.
Travel:	Located on Rte 55.

Credit Cards:	No
Owner:	David Christenson, Mary Durben & Tom Ratzloff
Comments:	Stock is approximately 70% hardcover. The store has a 19th century letterpress printing shop on premises.

Maplewood
(Map 18, page 290)

Half Price Books, Records, Magazines **Open Shop**
1731-A Beam Avenue 55109 (651) 773-0631

Collection:	General stock of new and used paperback and hardcover.
Hours:	Mon-Sat 9-9. Sun 10-6.
Travel:	White Bear Rd exit off I-694. Proceed south on White Bear, then west on Beam. Shop is next to the Maplewood Mall.

Marine on St. Croix
(Map 17, page 268)

T.E. Warth, Esq., Automotive Books **Open Shop**
At Lumberyard Shops 55047 (651) 433-5744
Mailing address: PO Box 253 Marine on St. Croix MN 55047 Fax: (651) 433-5012

Collection:	Specialty
# of Vols:	12,000
Specialties:	Automobiles, including motorcycles, trucks, tractors and models. No manuals or sales literature.
Hours:	Wed 9-4. Other times by appointment or chance.
Services:	Appraisals, search service, catalog, accepts want lists.
Travel:	Rte 95 to Marine. Proceed one block east to Main St, then turn left and proceed one block. Shop is next to post office.
Credit Cards:	Yes
Owner:	Thomas Warth
Year Estab:	1986

Marshall
(Map 17, page 268)

Wind River Used Books **Open Shop**
126 North 3rd Street 56258 (507) 537-9809

Collection:	General stock of paperback and hardcover.
# of Vols:	14,000
Hours:	Mon-Fri 10-5:30, except Thu till 7. Sat 10-5.
Travel:	From Rte 59 (Main St in downtown Marshall), turn east on 3rd St. Shop is across from public library and post office.
Credit Cards:	No
Owner:	Shirley K. Hazen
Year Estab:	1993
Comments:	Stock is approximately 75% paperback.

Mendota Heights
(Map 18, page 290)

A Williams Books
1664 Celia Road 55118

Collection:	Specialty
Specialties:	Magazines
Services:	Appraisals, accepts want lists, mail order.
Credit Cards:	No
Owner:	Leon G. Williams
Year Estab:	1978

Minneapolis
(Map 19, page 282 & Map 17, page 268)

Biermaier's B. H. Books
809 4th Street SE 55414

Open Shop
(612) 378-0129

Collection:	General stock.
# of Vols:	100,000
Specialties:	Art; literature.
Hours:	Tue-Sat 11-5:30.
Services:	Search service, mail order.
Travel:	Exit 18 off I-35W. Southbound, turn west on 4th St. Northbound, proceed straight ahead on frontage road for one block, then left on 4th St. Shop is between 8th Ave SE and I-35W.
Credit Cards:	No
Owner:	William Biermaier
Year Estab:	1972
Comments:	In addition to the shop's strong esoteric collection of scholarly books, there's a good representation of mystery and even a nice section on the occult. The books are generally in very good condition and moderately priced. Definitely worth a visit.

The Book House in Dinkytown
429 SE 14th Avenue 55414

Open Shop
(612) 331-1430

Collection:	General stock.
# of Vols:	150,000
Specialties:	Science; social sciences; literature; scholarly.
Hours:	Mon-Sat 10am-11pm. Sun 12-6:30.
Services:	Mail order.
Travel:	Westbound on I-94: University Ave exit. Proceed west (left) on University. When road veers to the right, continue on 4th St SE, then right on 14th Ave SE. Shop is one block ahead. Eastbound on I-94: exit at I-35W north, then follow directions under Cummings Books. See below.
Credit Cards:	Yes
Owner:	Kristen Eide-Tollefson, proprietor

Year Estab:	1976
Comments:	Within walking distance of the University campus, the stock in this bi-level shop is reflective of both scholarly interests and the interests of young America. The books we saw were of mix of scholarly trade paperbacks and hardcover and most were in good condition and very reasonably priced. The stock was large enough to make this visit worth your while. Note that some shelves are double stacked so when you find a section of interest to you, be certain to check the back row.

The Book Trader **Open Shop**
5344 34th Avenue South 55417 (612) 721-5526

Collection:	General stock of paperback and hardcover.
# of Vols:	100,000 (See Comments)
Specialties:	Military; Civil War.
Hours:	Mon-Fri 11-7. Sat 10-6.
Services:	Accepts want lists, mail order.
Travel:	Rte 62 exit off I-35W. Proceed east on Rte 62, then north on 34th Ave.
Credit Cards:	Yes
Owner:	Lynn Budach-Murray
Year Estab:	1988
Comments:	Not the neatest shop we've ever visited. The proportion of paperback to hardcover, at least at the time of our visit, was roughly ten to one and the 10% hardcover volumes were of a general nature with no one subject area standing out in terms of importance. Although we did not stop to count, we saw fewer books on display than indicated above.

Booksmart **Open Shop**
2919 Hennepin Avenue South 55408 (612) 823-5612

Collection:	General stock of hardcover and paperback and some remainders.
# of Vols:	50,000
Hours:	Daily 9-midnight.
Travel:	In "uptown," at intersection of Hennepin and Lagoon, one block north of Lake.
Credit Cards:	Yes
Owner:	Cheapo Records
Comments:	Located immediately behind a record/CD shop, this large store offers mostly popular hardcover and paperback titles (intershelved) of recent vintage. Several tables in the front of the store displayed new arrivals by the day of the week they arrived in the shop. Prices seemed most reasonable. This is not a location where one is likely to find many vintage or truly rare items.

Cummings Books **Open Shop**
318 14th Avenue SE 55414 (612) 331-1424
E-mail: aldine@pioneerplanet.infi.net

Collection:	General stock of hardcover and paperback.
# of Vols:	50,000-60,000+
Hours:	Mon-Thu 10-7. Fri & Sat 10-9. Sun 12-5.

(Minneapolis)

Travel:	University/4th St SE exit off I-35W. Proceed east on University then left on 14th Ave SE. From I-94, see Book House in Dinkytown above.
Credit Cards:	Yes
Owner:	James Cummings, Jr.
Year Estab:	1997
Comments:	A bi-level shop with a very nice selection of mostly hardcover volumes ranging from scholarly to the more popular. The shelves were well labeled. The vast majority of the books we saw were in very good to excellent condition and reasonably priced.

Dinkytown Antiquarian Bookstore   **By Appointment**
1316 SE 4th Street 55414   (612) 378-1286

Collection:	General stock.
Specialties:	Literary first editions; westerns.
Services:	Appraisals, catalog, accepts want lists.
Credit Cards:	No
Owner:	Larry Dingman
Year Estab:	1974

Dreamhaven   **Open Shop**
912 West Lake Street 55408   (612) 823-6161
Web page: www.visi.com/~dreamhvn/   Mail order: (612) 823-6070
                                                             Fax: (612) 823-6062
                                                E-mail: dreamhvn@visi.com

Collection:	Specialty new and used.
Specialties:	Science fiction; horror; fantasy; vintage paperbacks.
Hours:	Mon-Fri 11-8. Sat 11-6. Sun 12-5.
Services:	Appraisals, search service, catalog, accepts want lists.
Travel:	Northbound on I-35W: Lake St exit. Proceed west on Lake. Shop is between Bryant and Colfax. Free parking behind store.
Credit Cards:	Yes
Owner:	Greg Ketter
Year Estab:	1981

Friends of the Mpls. Public Library Book Shop   **Open Shop**
300 Nicollet Mall 55401   (612) 630-6177

Collection:	General stock of hardcover and paperback.
Hours:	Mon, Wed, Fri 10-3. Tue & Thu 10-7. Sat 10-3:30.
Travel:	5th St exit off I-94. Proceed to Marquette, then north to 3rd St and west to Hennepin.
Year Estab:	1983

H.M. George Books   **By Appointment**
6912 Hickory Drive 55432   (612) 571-5789

Collection:	Specialty
# of Vols:	5,000

Specialties: Children's; photography; modern first editions; signed editions; Midwest authors.
Services: Accepts want lists, search service, mail order.
Credit Cards: No
Year Estab: 1992

Peter M. Holmes Fine Books **By Appointment**
3112 Fremont Avenue South 55408 (612) 827-0461
Fax: (612) 824-5743
E-mail: hlmsbook@millcomm.com

Collection: Specialty new and used.
# of Vols: 1,200
Specialties: Napoleon
Services: Appraisals, search service, accepts want lists, catalog.
Credit Cards: Yes
Year Estab: 1988

Hymie's Vintage Records Etc. **Open Shop**
3318 East Lake Street 55406 (612) 729-8890

Collection: General stock of mostly paperback.
# of Vols: 2,000
Specialties: Vintage paperbacks.
Hours: Mon-Sat 11:30-7.
Travel: Riverside Ave exit off I-94. Proceed southeast on Riverside, south on 31st Ave and east on Lake. Shop is two blocks ahead.
Owner: Hymie Peterson
Comments: A shop offering mostly LPs with fewer than 50-60 hardcover volumes and a thousand or so vintage paperbacks.

James & Mary Laurie, Booksellers **Open Shop**
921 Nicollet Mall 55402 (612) 338-1114
(800) 774-1114
Fax: (612) 338-3665
E-mail: lauriebk@mail.winternet.com

Collection: General stock of mostly hardcover, prints and records.
# of Vols: 75,000+
Specialties: Literature; first editions; early science and medicine; Western Americana; private press; maps; art; architecture; photography.
Hours: Mon-Sat 10-6. Sun 12-5. Longer hours in summer.
Services: Appraisals, search service, catalog, accepts want lists.
Travel: In downtown, on Nicollet pedestrian mall, between 9th & 10th Sts. Westbound on I-94: 11th St exit. Proceed on 11th St, then right on Marquette and park between 9th & 10th Sts. Eastbound on I-94: 7th St exit. Proceed on 7th St which becomes 10th St, then left on Marquette. From I-35W (north or southbound): 11th St exit. Continue on 11th St to Marquette, then right on Marquette.
Credit Cards: Yes
Year Estab: 1973

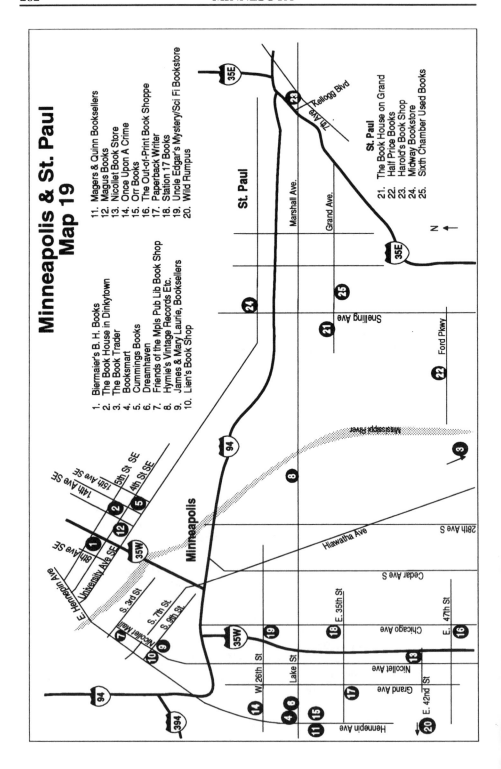

Minneapolis & St. Paul
Map 19

1. Biermaier's B. H. Books
2. The Book House in Dinkytown
3. The Book Trader
4. Booksmart
5. Cummings Books
6. Dreamhaven
7. Friends of the Mpls Pub Lib Book Shop
8. Hymie's Vintage Records Etc.
9. James & Mary Laurie, Booksellers
10. Lien's Book Shop
11. Magers & Quinn Booksellers
12. Magus Books
13. Nicollet Book Store
14. Once Upon A Crime
15. Orr Books
16. The Out-of-Print Book Shoppe
17. Paperback Writer
18. Station 17 Books
19. Uncle Edgar's Mystery/Sci Fi Bookstore
20. Wild Rumpus

St. Paul
21. The Book House on Grand
22. Half Price Books
23. Harold's Book Shop
24. Midway Bookstore
25. Sixth Chamber Used Books

Comments: Considering our several treks to thousands of book stores across the
                 nation, there are only a handful that, in our judgment, provide the visitor
                 with the volume, scope and quality that is available for viewing at this
                 tri-level location. While no one can guarantee that the book you're
                 looking for will be on hand at the time of your visit, we can certainly
                 certify that your visit here will be a rewarding one if you're any kind of
                 serious book person. The shop is well organized. Occasionally pricey.

Lien's Book Shop   **Open Shop**
57 South 9th Street 55402   (612) 332-7081
Web page: www.liens/old/book.com   Fax: (612) 321-9597
                                                                          E-mail: lien@pro-ns.net

Collection: General stock.
# of Vols: 50,000
Specialties: American history.
Hours: Mon-Sat 10-5:30. Summer only: 5pm closing on Mon.
Services: Catalog (Americana only), accepts want lists, book restoration.
Travel: In downtown, between Nicollet & LaSalle, 1/4 block from Nicollet
                 pedestrian mall.
Credit Cards: Yes
Owner: Leland N. Lien
Year Estab: 1972
Comments: A "must see" shop in the heart of downtown. All three levels of this
                 long established shop offer quality titles. In addition to the shop's
                 strength in history, we noted a fine fiction section, many older sets and
                 some very attractive items in the arts. The owner is clearly selective in
                 his book buying choices.

Magers & Quinn Booksellers   **Open Shop**
3038 Hennepin Avenue South 55408   (612) 822-4611
Collection: General stock of hardcover and paperback.
# of Vols: 100,000+
Hours: Mon-Thu 10-10. Fri 10am-11pm. Sat 9am-11pm. Sun 11-10.
Services: Accepts want lists, mail order.
Travel: From downtown or I-94, take Hennepin Ave south to Lake St. Shop is
                 just south of intersection of Hennepin and Lake.
Credit Cards: Yes
Owner: Dennis Magers
Year Estab: 1994
Comments: How could I not say something nice about a shop that had a half dozen
                 books I was able to purchase (and, had we had more time, I might have
                 purchased more). Easy to browse, spacious, well organized, books in
                 excellent condition, treasures behind glass. Don't miss it.

Magus Books   **Open Shop**
1316 SE 4th Street 55414   (612) 379-7669
Web page: www.magusbooks.com   E-mail: store@magusbooks.com
Collection: General stock of new and used paperback and hardcover.

(Minneapolis)

# of Vols:	3,000+ (used)
Specialties:	Occult; metaphysics.
Hours:	Mon-Fri 9-9. Sat 10-6. Sun 12-6.
Travel:	University/4th St exit off I-35W. Proceed east on University, then left on 13th Ave SE. Shop is one block ahead in the Dinkytown Mall.
Credit Cards:	Yes
Owner:	Roger Williamson
Year Estab:	1992
Comments:	Used stock is evenly divided between hardcover and paperback.

Minnehaha Books   **By Appointment**
4901 39th Avenue South 55417   (612) 722-3630
                                                       Fax:(612) 721-7082
                                      E-mail: clarkhan@interloc.com

Collection:	General stock.
# of Vols:	25,000
Specialties:	Literature; history; theology; reference.
Services:	Accepts want lists, mail order.
Credit Cards:	Yes
Owner:	Clark B. Hansen
Year Estab:	1973

Nicollet Book Store   **Open Shop**
4237 Nicollet Avenue 55409   (612) 822-5226

Collection:	General stock of mostly hardcover.
# of Vols:	5,000
Hours:	Tue-Sun 12-5.
Services:	Accepts want lists.
Travel:	46th St exit off I-35W. Proceed west on 46th St, then north on Nicollet.
Credit Cards:	Yes
Owner:	Karen Hallinan
Year Estab:	1994

Once Upon A Crime   **Open Shop**
604 West 26th Street 55405   (612) 870-3785

Collection:	Specialty new and used hardcover and paperback.
Specialties:	Mystery.
Hours:	Mon-Fri 11-5, except Wed till 7. Sat 10-6. Sun 12-5.
Services:	Appraisals, catalog.
Travel:	Lyndale Ave exit off I-94. Proceed south on Lyndale for 1/2 mile to 26th, then east on 26th St for 1/2 mile.
Credit Cards:	Yes
Owner:	Steven Stilwell
Year Estab:	1987
Comments:	Stock is 40% used, 70% of which is hardcover. Used books are in an annex.

Orr Books   **Open Shop**
3043 Hennepin Avenue 55408   (612) 823-2408

Collection:	General stock of mostly new books and mostly paperback used.
# of Vols:	1,000 (used)
Hours:	Mon-Fri 9:30-9. Sat 9:30-6. Sun 12-6.
Travel:	Across the street from Magers & Quinn. See above.
Credit Cards:	Yes

The Out-of-Print Book Shoppe   **Open Shop**
4756 Chicago Avenue 55407   (612) 823-1006

Collection:	General stock of mostly hardcover.
# of Vols:	30,000
Specialties:	Religion; philosophy.
Hours:	Tue-Sat 11-4:30.
Services:	Appraisals, search service, accepts want lists.
Travel:	46th St exit off I-35W. Proceed east on 46th St, then right on Chicago. Shop is at intersection of 48th St and Chicago.
Credit Cards:	No
Owner:	Russell & Thelma Peterson
Year Estab:	1989
Comments:	Unless you have a major interest in one of the shop's specialties listed above, we doubt if the other books on display would be enough of an enticement to bring you here.

Paperback Writer   **Open Shop**
3544½ Grand Avenue South 55408   (612) 824-3157

Collection:	General stock of paperback and hardcover, and videos.
# of Vols:	20,000
Hours:	Mon-Sat 9:30-8:30. Sun 12-5:30.
Travel:	35th st exit off I-35W. Proceed west on 35th, then left on Grand.
Comments:	Stock is approximately 60% paperback.

Station 17 Books   **Open Shop**
821 East 35th Street 55407   (612) 825-9662

Collection:	General stock of mostly used paperback.
# of Vols:	30,000
Hours:	Tue & Thu 5-9. Sat 10-5.
Comments:	Stock is approximately 80% used, 85% of which is paperback.

Terrace Horticultural Books   **By Appointment**
908 East River Terrace 55414   (612) 332-1821
Web page: www.bibliofind.com/terracehorticultural.html

                               E-mail: terrace@winternet.com

Collection:	Specialty books, magazines and ephemera.
# of Vols:	6,000
Specialties:	Gardening; agriculture; herbs; landscaping.
Services:	Appraisals, search service, accepts want lists, mail order.
Credit Cards:	No

Owner:	Kent R. Petterson
Year Estab:	1992
Comments:	Also displays at the Midtown Book Center in Stillwater.

Uncle Edgar's Mystery Bookstore   **Open Shop**
Uncle Hugo's Science Fiction Bookstore   (612) 824-6347   (612) 824-9984
2684 Chicago Avenue, South 55407   Fax: (612) 827-6394
                                                    E-mail: unclehugo@aol.com

Collection:	Specialty new and used, hardcover and paperback.
# of Vols:	15,000 (used)
Specialties:	Mystery; suspense fiction; science fiction; fantasy.
Hours:	Mon-Fri 10-8. Sat 10-6. Sun 12-5.
Services:	Accepts want lists, mail order.
Travel:	31st St exit off I-35W. Proceed east on 31st St, then north on Chicago.
Credit Cards:	Yes
Owner:	Don Blyly
Year Estab:	1980
Comments:	If you're either a mystery or sci fi fan, a visit here would be like going to your favorite amusement park, playground or candy store. While the vast majority of the books are paperback, both sections of the store do have used hardcover items as well as new hardcover books and trade paperbacks. Fun to visit, but only if you're an addict.

Wild Rumpus   **Open Shop**
2720 West 43rd Street 55410   (612) 920-5005

Collection:	Children's. Primarily new.
# of Vols:	500+ (used)
Specialties:	Children's
Hours:	Mon-Fri 10-8. Sat 10-5. M
Comments:	Primarily a new bookstore with a section of "recycled" books.

North Oaks
(Map 18, page 290)

Little Professor Book Center   **Open Shop**
125 Village Center Drive 55127   (651) 486-8880

Collection:	General stock of new and used paperback and hardcover.
# of Vols:	30,000 (used)
Hours:	Mon-Fri 10-8. Sat 10-5. Sun 12-5.
Travel:	In shopping center, at intersection of Rtes 96 and 49.
Comments:	Used stock is approximately 80% paperback.

Northfield
(Map 17, page 268)

As Time Goes By   **Open Shop**
425 Division Street 55057   (507) 645-6700

Collection:	General stock of hardcover and paperback.
# of Vols:	20,000

Specialties:	Literature; children's; science fiction; fantasy; mystery; religion; Minnesota.
Hours:	Mon-Sat 10-6.
Services:	Appraisals, search service, accepts want lists, mail order.
Travel:	Exit 69 (Rte 19) off I-35. Follow signs to Northfield. Left on Division.
Credit Cards:	Yes
Owner:	Richard A. Waters
Year Estab:	1995
Comments:	While the shop is modest in size, it has a nice selection of hardcover books, most of which are in quite good condition and are reasonably priced. Considering the fact that another used bookstore is located just a few doors down from this establishment, giving the browser two stops for price of one, and also considering that the stores are located in the historic town celebrated in western lore for its famous bank robbery, a stop in Northfield could be a pleasant experience.

The Bookcase   **Open Shop**
409 Division Street 55057   (507) 645-5580
                                      E-mail: thebookcase@microassist.com

Collection:	General stock of mostly hardcover.
# of Vols:	25,000
Specialties:	Cookbooks; Minnesota; children's; religion; Jesse James; modern first editions.
Hours:	Mon-Sat 10-6. Sun 1-4.
Services:	Search service, accepts want lists, mail order.
Travel:	See As Time Goes By above.
Credit Cards:	Yes
Owner:	Gary Morstad
Year Estab:	1989
Comments:	The books are attractively displayed and are in good to very good condition. Most subject areas are covered. If you're looking for titles related to the region, there's an excellent chance you'll find items of interest here. The owner clearly displays good taste in his selection of volumes.

Seven Gables Books & Antiques   **Open Shop**
313 Washington 55057   (507) 645-8572

Collection:	General stock and ephemera.
# of Vols:	5,000
Specialties:	Dogs; cats; children's.
Hours:	Wed & Sat 10-6. Thu 10-9.
Services:	Catalog
Travel:	Rte 19 into Northfield. After light at intersection of Rtes 19 & 3, proceed three blocks and turn left on Washington.
Credit Cards:	No
Owner:	Joy Ganyo
Year Estab:	1985

Comments: Once we reached the second floor of this shop and made our way
                 through each of the small, quite crowded and often cluttered rooms, it
                 became clear why the shop is called Seven Gables Books (although the
                 owner claims that there are actually eight gables—and a hawthorn tree
                 in front). Shops that combine antiques and books often offer a chal-
                 lenge to the visitor and this one is no exception. The owner has so
                 much material to display that it often becomes difficult to navigate the
                 narrow aisles and low ceilings. Most of the books we saw were older
                 and more than a few were unusual. If you don't mind the adventure and
                 you have time and patience, you could leave this shop pleased to have
                 made a purchase (as we were).

Osseo
(Map 18, page 290)

A Novel Place   **Open Shop**
311A Central Avenue 55369   (612) 424-4122
                                                        Fax: (612) 494-0772

Collection: General stock of mostly paperback.
# of Vols: 100,000
Hours: Tue, Wed, Fri 10-6. Thu 1-7. Sat 9-3.

Dan's Books   **By Appointment**
132 2nd Avenue NE 55369   (612) 424-5854
                                          E-mail: dansbooks@wavetech.net

Collection: Specialty books and some magazines.
# of Vols: 2,000
Specialties: Children's series; children's; boy scouts; Whitman 2300 series; sports;
                 illustrated.
Services: Accepts want lists.
Owner: Dan Richie
Year Estab: 1992
Comments: Also displays at The Artique in Anoka. See above.

Perham
(Map 17, page 268)

Bev's Book Nook   **Open Shop**
235 West Main Street 56573   (218) 346-2556

Collection: General stock of new and mostly paperback used.
# of Vols: 20,000 (used)
Hours: May-Oct: Mon-Fri 9:30-5:30. Sat 9:30-3. Nov-Apr: Mon-Fri 10-5.
                 Sat 10-3.

Plymouth
(Map 18, page 290)

Great Books   **Open Shop**
Four Seasons Mall   (612) 559-1471
Mailing address: 4152 Lancaster Lane Plymouth MN 55441

Collection:	General stock of mostly paperback.
# of Vols:	30,000
Specialties:	Vintage paperbacks.
Hours:	Tue-Fri 10-6:30, except Wed till 7:30. Sat 12-5.

Richfield
(Map 18, page 290)

Bookdales   **Open Shop**
406 West 65th. Street 55423   (612) 861-3303
E-mail: bookdales@aol.com

Collection:	General stock.
# of Vols:	30,000+
Specialties:	Modern first editions; mystery; illustrated; children's; Minnesota; cookbooks.
Hours:	Tue-Sat 10-5.
Services:	Catalog, accepts want lists, search service.
Travel:	Lyndale exit off I-35W. Go south for three blocks, then left on 65th St.
Credit Cards:	Yes
Owner:	David & Joyce Dale
Year Estab:	1974
Comments:	It appears as though every volume on the shelves of this shop was selected with the utmost care for condition, appearance and desirability. Prices, considering the quality of the stock, are most reasonable.

Hazen's Books, Records & Antiques   **Antique Mall**
At Spider Web Antiques, 6525 Penn Avenue South 55423   Mall: (612) 798-1862
Home: (612) 721-3854

Collection:	General stock of hardcover and paperback.
Hours:	Mon-Fri 10-6. Sat & Sun 10-5.
Owner:	Kent Hazen
Year Estab:	1985
Comments:	Also displays at the New Hopkins Mall in Hopkins. See above.

Robbinsdale
(Map 18, page 290)

Robbin's Bookworm   **Open Shop**
3919 West Broadway 55422   (612) 533-2733

Collection:	General stock of mostly paperback.
# of Vols:	10,000
Hours:	Thu-Sat 10-5.

Rochester
(Map 17, page 268)

Book & Cover   **Antique Mall**
At Broadway Antiques, 324 South Broadway 55904   (507) 288-5678

Hours:	Mon-Sat 10-6. Sun 11-4.

The Extraordinary Bookseller   **Open Shop**
113 North Broadway 55906   (507) 289-2407

Collection: General stock of hardcover and paperback.
# of Vols: 5,000
Hours: Jul-Sep: Mon-Sat 11-8. Sun 12-5. Rest of year: Mon-Sat 11-6:30. Sun
                  12-5.
Travel: Rte 63 exit off I-90. Proceed north on Rte 63 (which becomes Broad-
                  way). Shop is between 1st & 2nd St, just after Center St.
Credit Cards: Yes
Owner: Stephen W. Plunkett
Year Estab: 1993
Comments: In addition to comics, the shop stocks paperbacks and some hardcover
                  volumes of mixed vintage. We were not able to discern any out of the
                  ordinary titles.

Roseville
(Map 18, page 290)

Barnes & Noble   **Open Shop**
2100 Snelling Avenue North 55113   (651) 639-9256

Collection: General stock of new and used hardcover and paperback.
# of Vols: 30,000-40,000 (used)
Hours: Mon-Thu 9am-11pm. Fri & Sat 9am-midnight. Sun 9-9.
Travel: One block south of intersection of Rte 36 and Snelling Ave.

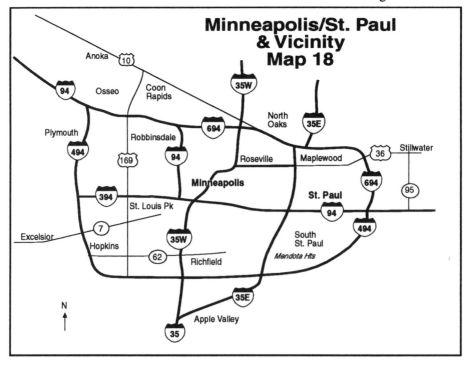

Saint Cloud
(Map 17, page 268)

Books Revisited   **Open Shop**
607 West St. Germain Street 56301   (320) 259-7959
                                              E-mail: books@cloudnet.com

Collection:	General stock hardcover and paperback.
# of Vols:	60,000
Specialties:	Military; sports; literature; regional titles.
Hours:	Mon-Sat 10-6.
Services:	Appraisals, search service, accepts want lists, mail order.
Travel:	Exit 171 off I-94. Proceed to downtown.
Credit Cards:	Yes
Owner:	Jon V. Lee
Year Estab:	1991
Comments:	A most attractive group shop that is a pleasure to browse and that offers books in almost every category. In addition to more modern hardcover titles, almost universally with dust jackets, one can find fine bindings, older sets, vintage titles, a wide assortment of children's books and even a section of paperbacks. We enjoyed our visit here and trust you will.

Classic Arms Books   **Open Shop**
At Books Revisited, 607 West St. Germain   Shop: (320) 259-7959
Mailing address: 2665 32nd St., SE Saint Cloud MN 56304 Home: (320) 255-1870
                                              E-mail: classbk@cloudnet.com

Collection:	Specialty
# of Vols:	3,000
Specialties:	Big game hunting; hunting; exploration; fishing; military.
Services:	Catalog
Credit Cards:	Yes
Owner:	Kenneth P. Czech
Year Estab:	1990

Sauk River Books   **By Appointment**
4031 County Road 134 56303   (320) 255-0295

Collection:	General stock.
# of Vols:	20,000
Services:	Accepts want lists, mail order.
Credit Cards:	No
Owner:	Jerry Hansen
Year Estab:	1992
Comments:	After visiting this dealer on our earlier trip to Minnesota (when he maintained an open shop) we had the following comments: A real book barn, meticulously remodeled by a bookman who builds his own shelves and fills them with a carefully selected attractive stock. While only a small portion of the titles we saw would be classified as esoteric, almost all of the books were in

excellent condition and priced as reading copies although many of them, we feel, would sell at much higher prices in shops that enjoy more traffic.

Saint Louis Park
(Map 18, page 290)

Half Price Books, Records, Magazines   **Open Shop**
5011 Excelsior Boulevard 55416   (612) 922-2414
                                                        Fax: (612) 922-3499

Collection:	General stock of used paperback and hardcover and new.
Hours:	Mon-Sat 9-9. Sun 10-6.
Travel:	Excelsior Blvd exit off Rte 100. Proceed east on Excelsior to Miracle Mile Shopping Center.

Saint Paul
(Map 19, page 282 & Map 17, page 268)

The Book House on Grand   **Open Shop**
1665 Grand Avenue 55105   Tel & Fax: (651) 699-3998
                                             E-mail: grandbks@interloc.com

Collection:	General stock of paperback and hardcover.
# of Vols:	50,000
Specialties:	Psychology; Judaica; poetry; cultural studies.
Hours:	Mon-Fri 11:30-8. Sat & Sun 12-7.
Services:	Subject lists; accepts want lists, mail order.
Travel:	See Sixth Chamber Used Books below. At Grand, turn west. Shop is 1½ blocks ahead.
Credit Cards:	Yes
Owner:	Kimberly Koch
Year Estab:	1993
Comments:	The books we saw here, both hardcover and paperback, were in generally mixed condition and, in addition to the specialties listed above, covered other subjects reflective of the shop's proximity to a local university. We wish we could have spent a few more minutes browsing, but nature's call and the kind suggestion of the owner that we find relief in the restaurant next door (as she had no facilities) slowed us down somewhat.

Green Lion Books   **By Appointment**
2402 University Ave West, Ste. 409 55114   (651) 644-9070
                                                        Fax: (651) 646-5591

Collection:	Specialty paperbacks.
# of Vols:	120,000
Specialties:	Vintage paperbacks; science fiction; horror; mystery; westerns.
Services:	Appraisals, search service, accepts want lists, mail order.
Credit Cards:	Yes

Owner: Linda Goodman
Year Estab: 1979

Half Price Books, Records, Magazines   Open Shop
2041 Ford Parkway   55116   (651) 699-1391
     Fax: (651) 699-1448

Collection: General stock of new and used hardcover and paperback.
# of Vols: 50,000+
Hours: Mon-Sat 9-9. Sun 10-6.
Travel: Snelling Ave exit off I-94. Proceed south on Snelling, then right on Ford Pkwy. Shop is about seven blocks ahead.

Harold's Book Shop   Open Shop
186 West 7th Street   55102   (651) 222-4524

Collection: General stock.
# of Vols: 30,000
Specialties: Film; occult; Minnesota.
Hours: Mon-Fri 10:30-5. Sat 9:30-5.
Travel: One half block from Civic Center. Marion St exit off I-94 eastbound. Proceed on Marion to intersection of Kellogg & 7th St, then west on 7th. Shop is 1/2 block ahead.
Credit Cards: Yes
Owner: Ted Henry
Year Estab: 1949
Comments: A neat little bi-level shop with a great selection of books on film as well as film posters, all on the second floor. Prices are reasonable and the books are generally in good condition.

Arthur Hudgins   By Appointment
8-B Irvine Park   55102   (651) 222-6461
     E-mail: hudginsbks@aol.com

Collection: General stock.
# of Vols: 6,000-7,000
Specialties: Literature (19th & 20th century).
Services: Mail order, accepts want lists.
Credit Cards: No
Year Estab: 1994

Barb Mader—Books   By Appointment
1759 Grand Avenue, #301   55105   (651) 690-2439
Web page: www.abebooks.com/home/BMader   E-mail: yanis001@tc.umn.edu

Collection: Specialty
# of Vols: 1,500
Specialties: Children's; Minnesota authors.
Services: Search service, catalog, accepts want lists.
Credit Cards: No
Year Estab: 1994
Comments: Also displays at As Time Goes By in Northfield. See above.

(St. Paul)

Midway Bookstore   **Open Shop**
1579 University Avenue 55104   (651) 644-7605

Collection:	General stock of hardcover and paperback and magazines.
# of Vols:	50,000+
Specialties:	Art; illustrated; literature; world history; American history; military; photography; books on books; fantasy; science fiction; children's.
Hours:	Mon-Fri 10-9. Sat 10-7. Sun 12-7.
Services:	Appraisals, accepts want lists, mail order.
Travel:	Snelling Ave exit off I-94. Proceed north for two blocks.
Credit Cards:	Yes
Owner:	Tom & Kathy Stransky
Year Estab:	1965
Comments:	It's always a pleasant surprise to find that a shop with a sign outside that reads "Books & Comics" has a substantial collection of hardcover books. This tri-level shop stocks a fair share of scholarly titles but also has particularly strong sections in film, theater and the arts as well as a good biography section. The shop also carries comics, pulps, Big Little Books and other collectibles.

Notting Hill Books   **By Appointment**
826 James Avenue 55102   (651) 227-2435
                                              E-mail: NHBBooks@aol.com

Collection:	Specialty
# of Vols:	2,500
Specialties:	Poetry (British and American); literature; humanities; religion (Catholic); homeschooling.
Services:	Accepts want lists, mail order.
Owner:	Joseph Michalak, Jr.
Year Estab:	1995

Sixth Chamber Used Books   **Open Shop**
1332 Grand Avenue 55105   Tel & Fax: (651) 690-9463
Web page: www.sixthchamber.com   E-mail: chamber6@sprynet.com

Collection:	General stock of hardcover and paperback.
# of Vols:	36,000
Hours:	Mon-Sat 11-9. Sun 12-5.
Travel:	From I-94 eastbound: Snelling Ave exit. Proceed south on Snelling then east on Grand. From I-94 westbound: Hamline exit. Proceed south on Hamline then east on Grand.
Credit Cards:	Yes
Owner:	James T. Williams
Year Estab:	1995
Comments:	An interesting shop with good books in most categories. Perhaps because of the shop's closeness to a university, some of the books appear to reflect student and professional interests although there are plenty of popular titles as well. Reasonably priced.

Snowy Egret Books   **By Appointment**
1237 Carroll Avenue 55104

Collection:	Specialty
# of Vols:	6,000+
Specialties:	Ornithology; natural history; nature; entomology; zoology; marine sciences; wildlife art; journals.
Services:	Catalog, accepts want lists, search service.
Credit Cards:	Yes
Owner:	Ernest d'Anjou
Year Estab:	1994

Sauk Rapids
(Map 17, page 268)

Oxcart Trail Books   **Open Shop**
107 Benton Drive South 56379   (320) 202-7878
Web page: www.netlink.com/~oxcart/   E-mail: oxcart@netlink.com

Collection:	General stock of hardcover and paperback.
# of Vols:	20,000
Hours:	Mon-Fri 12-5:30. Sat 10-4. Other times by appointment.
Services:	Accepts want lists.
Travel:	Benton Dr exit off Rte 10. Proceed towards Sauk Rapids. Shop is near intersection of Benton Dr and 1st Street South (where bridge crosses Mississippi River).
Year Estab:	1973
Credit Cards:	No
Owner:	Lynn A. Machula
Year Estab:	1996
Comments:	A mix of paperback and hardcover books with the hardcover items, for the most part, rather ordinary and not particularly in the best condition. We did see a shelf marked "First Editions" which may mean different things to different book people. Perhaps a more discerning eye would have been more impressed. The shop also has a large selection of yo yos for sale.

South Saint Paul
(Map 18, page 290)

Turnabout Books   **Open Shop**
708 Southview Boulevard 55075   Tel & Fax: (651) 552-8718
E-mail: booklady01@aol.com

Collection:	General stock of paperback and hardcover.
# of Vols:	40,000
Specialties:	Mystery; modern first editions; vintage paperbacks; cookbooks; children's.
Hours:	Mon-Fri 10-6. Sat 10-5. Extended hours during spring and summer.
Services:	Accepts want lists, mail order.

Travel:	Fifth/Seventh Ave exit off I-494. Proceed north on 7th Ave to Southview Blvd. Shop is at intersection of 7th and Southview.
Credit Cards:	Yes
Owner:	Lowell & Grace Johnson
Year Estab:	1993
Comments:	Stock is approximately 75% paperback.

Stillwater
(Map 17, page 268 & Map 18, page 290)

American Gothic Antique Mall   **Antique Mall**
208 South Main Street, 2nd Fl.   (651) 439-7709

Hours:	Daily 10-6, except till 9 on Fri & Sat.

Fact and Fiction   **By Appointment**
6311 St. Croix Trail North 55082   (651) 439-7498
                                    E-mail: bjeanne@aol.com

Collection:	Specialty
# of Vols:	3,500
Specialties:	Children's
Credit Cards:	No
Owner:	Barbara & Mike McGuire
Year Estab:	1995
Comments:	Also displays at the American Gothic Antique Mall. See above.

Felicitas Cookbooks   **Open Shop**
At Midtown Book Center, 301 South Main Street   (651) 430-0306
Mailing address: 1219 N. William St. Stillwater MN 55082   Fax: (651) 439-8504
Web page: www.booktown.com   E-mail: gvyx39@prodigy.com

Collection:	Specialty
# of Vols:	1,200
Specialties:	Cookbooks
Hours:	Mon-Thu 10-5. Fri & Sat 10-8. Sun 11-6.
Services:	Search service, accepts want lists, mail order.
Credit Cards:	Yes
Owner:	Felicity M. Loome
Year Estab:	1996

Loome Theological Booksellers   **Open Shop**
320 North Fourth Street 55082   (651) 430-1092
Web page: www.booktown.com   Fax: (651) 439-8504
                                    E-mail: gvyx39A@prodigy.com

Collection:	Specialty
# of Vols:	225,000+
Specialties:	Theology, philosophy, religion and all related areas including Graeco-Roman, medieval, missiology, ecclesiastical music, art and architecture, etc.
Hours:	Mon-Sat 9-5.

Services:	Appraisals, search service, catalog, accepts want lists.
Travel:	From Main St, turn left on Myrtle, then right on 4th St. The shop is located in a former church.
Credit Cards:	Yes
Owner:	Thomas M. Loome
Year Estab:	1980
Comments:	A most appropriate settings for a dealer who specializes in used, rare and truly antiquarian religious materials. The owner's assertion that his is the largest such collection in an English speaking country would not be challenged by us. One does not have to be deeply religious (although it wouldn't hurt) to appreciate the beauty of the setting (a former Swedish Covenant church) in which the collection is meticulously shelved. The owner displays an ecumenical spirit by carrying religious material of every faith with particular emphasis on the more traditional ones. Whether or not you make a purchase here, you will not soon forget your visit. Note: Although the focus of the collection is religion, because of its breath, it does contain books that in a non specialty shop might be found in other subject headings, e.g., Americana, art, architecture, music, etc.

Midtown Book Center   **Open Shop**
301 South Main Street 55082   (651) 430-0732
Web page: www.booktown.com   For Book Info: (6510 430-0808
                                                      Fax: (651) 430-2450
                                          E-mail: grgoodmn@msn.com

Collection:	General stock.
# of Vols:	18,000
Specialties:	Children's; gardening; cookbooks; philosophy; literature; antiques and collectibles.
Hours:	Mon-Thu 10-5. Fri & Sat 10-8. Sun 11-6.
Travel:	Rte 95 exit off I-94. Proceed north on Rte 95 to Main St.
Credit Cards:	Yes
Owner:	Gary Goodman & Thomas M. Loome
Year Estab:	1996
Comments:	A small group shop located in the front left corner of a multi dealer antique mall. The selections are nice but limited. As the shop is located directly across from one of Minnesota's premier book dealers (one that you won't want to miss), a stop here won't take you far afield.

The Mill Antiques   **Antique Mall**
410 North Main Street 55082   (651) 430-1816
Hours: Daily 10-6.

St. Croix Antiquarian Booksellers   **Open Shop**
232 South Main Street 55082   (651) 430-0732
Web page: www.booktown.com   Fax: (651) 430-2450
                                          E-mail: grgoodmn@msn.com

Collection:	General stock.

# of Vols:	120,000
Specialties:	Hunting; fishing; art; architecture; philosophy; children's; Western Americana; literature; literary criticism.
Hours:	Mon-Thu 10-7. Fri & Sat 10-10. Sun 12-9.
Services:	Appraisals, search service, catalog, accepts want lists.
Travel:	Rte 95 exit off I-94. Proceed north on Rte 95 to Main St.
Credit Cards:	Yes
Owner:	Gary Goodman & Thomas M. Loome
Year Estab:	1990
Comments:	No matter what your interests, they should be satisfied in this large, highly organized shop. The collection is particularly strong in history, both American and European, but the areas listed above as specialties are certainly well represented. The books we saw were in excellent condition and ran the gamut from antiquarian to rare and scholarly. We returned to this shop some 3½ years after penning the above comments only to find ourselves once more in awe of both the shop's organization and the quality of the books on hand. The shop continues to be an absolute winner.

Stillwater Children's Books   **Open Shop**
At Midtown Book Center, 301 South Main Street   (651) 430-0306
Mailing address: 1219 N. William St. Stillwater MN 55082   Fax: (651) 439-8504
Web page: www.booktown.com   E-mail: gvyx39A@prodigy.com

Collection:	Specialty
# of Vols:	2,000
Specialties:	Children's; children's series; children's illustrated.
Hours:	Mon-Thu 10-5. Fri & Sat 10-8. Sun 11-6.
Services:	Search service, accepts want lists, mail order.
Credit Cards:	Yes
Owner:	Thomas Noah Loome
Year Estab:	1996

Thief River Falls
(Map 17, page 268)

Northern Lights Books   **Open Shop**
208 Labree Avenue North 56701   (218) 681-8242

Collection:	General stock of paperback and hardcover.
# of Vols:	10,000
Hours:	Mon-Sat 10-5:30, except Thu till 8:30.
Travel:	One block east of Main St.
Credit Cards:	No
Year Estab:	1988
Comments:	Stock is approximately 70% paperback.

Winona
(Map 17, page 268)

A-Z Collectables **Open Shop**
158 Main Street, Lower Level 55987 (507) 454-0366

Collection:	General stock.
# of Vols:	3,000
Specialties:	Children's; military.
Hours:	Mon-Fri 11-5. Sun 12-4. Other times by chance.
Travel:	Around the corner from Country Comfort. See below.
Services:	Accepts want lists, mail order.
Credit Cards:	No
Owner:	Neil Hunt
Year Estab:	1993
Comments:	Primarily reading copies. The shop also sells a variety of nostalgia collectibles.

Blue Leaf Books **Antique Mall**
At RD Cone Antique Mall, 66 East Street Mall: (507) 453-0445
Mailing address: 211 West 7th Street Winona MN 55987 Home: (507) 454-6564

Collection:	General collection of hardcover and paperback.
# of Vols:	8,000
Hours:	Mon-Fri, except closed Tue, 10-5. Sat 10-4. Sun 12-4.
Travel:	At corner of Lafayette & 2nd St.
Comments:	Stock is 70% hardcover.

Books Unlimited **Open Shop**
160 Johnson Street 55987 (507) 454-2723

Collection:	General stock of hardcover and paperback and magazines.
# of Vols:	2,000-3,000
Hours:	Mon-Fri 9-5. Sat & Sun 12-4.
Travel:	Huff St exit off Rte 61. Proceed north on Huff, then right on 4th St and left on Johnson.
Comments:	A non profit shop operated by the Winona County Historical Society. All books are donated.

Country Comfort Antiques and Books **Open Shop**
79 West 3rd Street 55987 (507) 452-7044
Web page: www.countrycomfortantiques.com
E-mail: antiques@countrycomfortantiques.com

Collection:	General stock.
# of Vols:	10,000
Specialties:	Modern first editions; Western Americana; Minnesota; Wisconsin; children's; beat generation; counter culture; Native Americans; black studies; art; fine bindings.
Hours:	Mon-Sat 10-5. Sun 12-4.
Services:	Appraisals, search service, accepts want lists.

Travel:	Huff St exit off Rte 61. Proceed north on Huff to downtown, then right on 3rd St.
Credit Cards:	Yes
Owner:	Jane Beseler & John Campbell
Year Estab:	1985
Comments:	Books and antiques under the same roof BUT with a difference. The books here are of higher quality than are usually found in such combination shops. We saw a nice selection of first editions along with books focusing on Minnesota as well as lots of history, classical literature, etc. Prices reflect the quality of the books.

Mary Twyce Books & Paper   By Appointment

601 East Fifth Street   (507) 454-4412
Mailing address: 364 West Wabasha Street Winona MN 55987   (507) 452-7296

Collection:	General stock and ephemera.
Specialties:	Children's series; children's; Wisconsin; Minnesota.
Services:	Search service, accepts want lists, mail order.
Credit Cards:	No
Owner:	Mary Pendelton
Year Estab:	1969

*Even in the most remote jungle, a book can be a
comforting companion under a mosquito net.*

ABC Collectables   (651) 771-6960
508 East Ivy Avenue Saint Paul 55101   Fax: (651) 772-8356
                                                       E-mail: dbesky@aol.com

Collection:	General stock.
# of Vols:	15,000
Specialties:	Children's (including foreign language children's); Presidents; natural history; sports; biography; first editions; reference.
Services:	Search service, accepts want lists.
Credit Cards:	Yes
Owner:	Don Besky
Year Estab:	1994
Comments:	Also displays at Books Revisited in St. Cloud. Collection can be viewed by appointment.

Robert C. Alexander Books   (651) 483-6177
20 Hay Camp Road Saint Paul 55127

Collection:	General stock (non fiction only).
# of Vols:	14,000
Services:	Occasional catalog, search service, accepts want lists.
Credit Cards:	No
Year Estab:	1992

Ally Press   Tel & Fax: (651) 291-2652
524 Orleans Street Saint Paul 55107   (800) 729-3002
Web page: www.catalog.com/ally   E-mail: pferoe@pclink.com

Collection:	Specialty new and used, paperback and hardcover, and some general stock.
Specialties:	Robert Bly; poetry; psychology (Jungian); mythopoetic; men's works.
Credit Cards:	No
Year Estab:	1985

Arch Books   (612) 927-0298
PO Box 24642 Minneapolis 55424   E-mail: archbooks@archbooks.com
Web page: www.archbooks.com

Collection:	Specialty
# of Vols:	60,000
Specialties:	Children's; illustrated; books about children's books, authors and illustrators.
Services:	Appraisals, search service, accepts want lists.
Credit Cards:	Yes
Owner:	Ruth P. Hendrickson
Year Estab:	1980

E.J. Bankey   (612) 941-6384
5515 West 70th Street Edina 55439

Collection:	General stock.
# of Vols:	3,000
Specialties:	Children's

Services: Accepts want lists.
Credit Cards: No
Year Estab: 1986

Bee Creek Books   (507) 498-3346
Route 1, Box 157A Spring Grove 55974   Fax: (507) 498-5366
                                            E-mail: beecreek@means.net

Collection: Specialty books and ephemera.
# of Vols: 5,000
Specialties: Grand Canyon; Colorado River and plateau; Baja California; deserts
                 (U.S.); angling; U.S. government publications (pre-1880).
Services: Appraisals, search service, catalog, accepts want lists.
Credit Cards: No
Owner: Clement David Hellyer & Gloria Penrose
Year Estab: 1978

Books of Choice   (651) 227-7363
8500 Normandale Lake Blvd, #140 Bloomington 55437   Fax: (612) 921-8369

Collection: Specialty
Specialties: Modern first editions; black literature.
Services: Catalog, accepts want lists.
Credit Cards: No
Owner: Bill Stevens
Year Estab: 1992

Calhoun Book Store   Tel & Fax: (612) 920-2507
PO Box 24552 Edina 55424   E-mail: calhounbk@aol.com

Collection: Specialty
# of Vols: 25,000
Specialties: University press books.
Credit Cards: No
Owner: Virginia Lou Seay
Year Estab: 1961

Cash Coin Connection   (320) 393-3148
PO Box 122 Sartell 56377
Web page: www.geocities.com/eureka/plaza/2835

Collection: Specialty used and new hardcover and paperback.
# of Vols: 1,000
Specialties: Numismatics
Credit Cards: Yes
Owner: John K. Kallman
Year Estab: 1985
Comments: Stock is approximately 75% used.

China Book Gallery   (612) 926-6887
PO Box 181 Plato 55370   Fax: (320) 238-2591
                                       E-mail: jcavanaugh@usinternet.com

Collection: General stock.

# of Vols:	100,000+
Specialties:	China; Japan; India.
Services:	Appraisals, catalog, accepts want lists.
Credit Cards:	No
Owner:	Jerome Cavanaugh
Year Estab:	1974

Fireproof Books (612) 546-7033
13958 Oakland Place Minnetonka 55305

Collection:	Specialty
# of Vols:	1,500
Specialties:	Modern first editions.
Services:	Search service, catalog, accepts want lists.
Credit Cards:	Yes
Owner:	Mark S. Larson
Year Estab:	1995

Gregory and Beverly Gamradt, Books on the Orient (612) 537-0359
PO Box 22694 Minneapolis 55422   Fax: (612) 536-0579
Web page: www.iglou.com/bcs/asianbook/   E-mail: gamra002@maroon.tc.umn.edu

Collection:	Specialty
# of Vols:	8,000
Specialties:	Tibet; Central Asia; Mongolia; China; Japan; Southeast Asia; South Asia; Middle East.
Services:	Search service, catalog, accepts want lists.
Credit Cards:	Yes
Year Estab:	1979

Betsy Gerboth (612) 829-0885
6800 W. Old Shakopee Rd., #223 Bloomington 55438   E-mail: begsjt19@idt.net

Collection:	General stock of mostly hardcover.
Specialties:	Children's (1940's-1980's).
Services:	Search service.
Credit Cards:	No
Year Estab:	1996

Theodore J. Holston Jr., Bookseller (612) 474-5780
6400 Smithtown Road Excelsior 55331   Fax: (612) 401-9032

Collection:	Specialty
# of Vols:	3,000
Specialties:	Sports; big game hunting; natural history; guns; fishing; exploration, especially Africa, Asia, Arctic; mountaineering.
Services:	Search service, catalog, accepts want lists.
Credit Cards:	Yes
Year Estab:	1976

Kisselburg Military Books Tel & Fax: (651) 439-7013
5653 Memorial Avenue North Stillwater 55082

Collection:	Specialty

# of Vols:	10,000
Specialties:	Military; World War II.
Services:	Catalog, accepts want lists.
Credit Cards:	Yes
Owner:	Paul E. Kisselburg
Year Estab:	1993

Lancaster & Simpson   (651) 490-1132
6292 Red Maple Lane Lino Lakes 55014

Collection:	Specialty
# of Vols:	2,000
Specialties:	Agriculture; self-sufficiency; organic gardening.
Credit Cards:	No
Owner:	Gary S. Quam
Year Estab:	1984

Melvin McCosh, Bookseller   (612) 474-8084
26500 Edgewood Road Excelsior 55331

Collection:	General stock.
Specialties:	Literature; history; bibliography. (Scholarly and semi-scholarly).
Services:	Accepts want lists.
Credit Cards:	No
Year Estab:	1952

PDW Books   (612) 721-5996
3721 Minnehaha Avenue South Minneapolis 55406   Fax: (612) 721-9491
E-mail: pdw@visi.com

Collection:	Specialty used and new. Mostly hardcover.
# of Vols:	2,000-3,000
Specialties:	Supernatural literature; Arkham House; Ash-Tree Press.
Services:	Catalog, accepts want lists.
Credit Cards:	No
Owner:	Peder Wagtskjold
Year Estab:	1997

Richard G. Peterson, Bookseller   (612) 421-7148
PO Box 421053 Minneapolis 55442
Web page: www2.netcom.com/~brindia/india.html   E-mail: brindia@ix.netcom.com

Collection:	Specialty
# of Vols:	1,000
Specialties:	19th century British India; Rudyard Kipling.
Services:	Catalog, search service, accepts want lists.
Credit Cards:	No
Year Estab:	1992

Philco Books   (218) 729-8374
5025 Arrowhead Road Duluth 55811

Collection:	General stock of paperback and hardcover and ephemera.
# of Vols:	25,000

Specialties: Sports; military; mystery.
Services: Search service, catalog, accepts want lists.
Credit Cards: No
Owner: Phyllis Henricksen
Year Estab: 1972
Comments: Stock is approximately 60% paperback.

Duane Robeck-Bookseller (651) 489-3012
PO Box 7368 Saint Paul 55107

Collection: Specialty
# of Vols: 2,000
Specialties: Japan; Korea
Services: Catalog, accepts want lists.
Credit Cards: No
Year Estab: 1991

Rulon-Miller Books (800) 441-0076
400 Summit Avenue Saint Paul 55102 (612) 290-0700
Web page: www.rulon.com Fax: (612) 290-0646
E-mail: rulon@winternet.com

Collection: General stock.
# of Vols: 10,000
Specialties: Dictionaries; books on language.
Services: Appraisals, catalog.
Credit Cards: Yes
Owner: Robert Rulon-Miller, Jr.
Comments: Collection can also be viewed by appointment.

S & S Books (651) 645-5962
80 North Wilder Saint Paul 55104 E-mail: 102724.2170@compuserve.com

Collection: Specialty
# of Vols: 10,000
Specialties: Science fiction; fantasy; horror; mystery; detective; religion; occult.
Services: Search service, accepts want lists.
Credit Cards: No
Owner: Jack & Pat Sticha
Year Estab: 1971

S & S Booksellers (612) 882-0386
PO Box 22194 Eagan 55122 E-mail: sbooks777@aol.com

Collection: General stock.
# of Vols: 4,000
Specialties: Children's; illustrated.
Services: Appraisals, search service, accepts want lists.
Credit Cards: No
Owner: Shirley Smith
Year Estab: 1994
Comments: Also displays at The Mill Antiques in Stillwater. See above.

Science Book Service   (651) 633-0178
124 Windsor Court Saint Paul 55112   Fax: (651) 633-9171

Collection:	Specialty
# of Vols:	7,000
Specialties:	Physics; history of science; mathematics; technology; transportation; maritime; automobiles.
Services:	Catalog, accepts want lists.
Credit Cards:	No
Owner:	Helga Stuewer
Year Estab:	1976
Comments:	Also displays at Midtown Books in Stillwater. See above.

Dale Seppa   (218) 749-8108
103 Sixth Avenue North Virginia 55792   Fax:(218) 749-8145
                                            E-mail: seppa@rangenet.com

Collection:	Specialty new and used.
# of Vols:	5,000
Specialties:	Latin America, with an emphasis on South America; numismatics.
Services:	Appraisals and search service in specialty areas only, catalog (numismatics only), accepts want lists.
Credit Cards:	Yes
Year Estab:	1979
Comments:	Collection can also be viewed by appointment.

Ex Libris
Frederick Eugene Hartnell

MISSOURI

Alphabetical Listing By Dealer

A Better Book Store	313	The Book House	336
A Collector's Bookshop	334	The Book House	319
AJ'S Books & Crafts	317	Book Jungle	342
A-1 Book Exchange	330	The Book Rack	342
ABC Books	341	Books Galore	316
Acorn Books	315	Bouland Brother's Booksellers	331
Acorn #2	315	Phyllis Y. Brown	337
Adams Walls of Books	315	Brown's Books	330
Addison's Book Store	341	Byrd's Books & Collectibles	317
Americana Antiques	344	Bags End	333
A. Amitin's Book Shop	334	B. Caldwell - Bookseller	331
Antiquarium Books & Collectibles	322	Changing Hands Book Shoppe	324
Antique & Furniture Mall	318	Clues! Mystery Bookseller	324
Archer's Antiques & Books	331	Collector's Paradise	330
The Attic Trunk and Book Review	329	Columbia Books	316
The Avid Reader	335	Cordell-Wilson Booksellers	314
Bare Necessities	323	Deerlilly Farms	346
Bargain Books	332	Delmar Books	337
Becky Thatcher Book Shop	320	R. Dunaway, Bookseller	337
Bell's Books & Candles	346	Eddie's Books, Games and Gifts	325
Betty's Books and Collectible Comics	321	Encore Books of Harvester	332
Big Sleep Books	335	Fireside Bookstore	345
Bloomsday Books	324	Galey's Record Store	318
Blue Nile Books	329	Anthony Garnett Fine Books	338
The Book Barn	323	Glenn Books	325
The Book Barn	346	Grandview Book Gallery	319
Book Brokers Unlimited	335	Great Books	332
Book Brokers Unlimited	318	Greenfield Books	320
Book Haven	323	Greentrails Book Shop	314

Klaus Grunewald - Bookdealer	325	Overlord Military Collectibles	339
John Hajicek	346	Ozarks Antiques	330
Half Price Books of the Ozarks	342	Pam's Books	313
Half Price Used Books of the Ozarks	313	Paper Moone	333
Hammond's Books	338	Peddler's Wagon	347
Harrisonville Trade Fair	320	Dan Pekios Books	347
Hooked On Books	343	Prospero's Books	326
Eugene M. Hughes, Antiq. Bookseller	338	Purple Shamrock	348
Just Books	329	Queen City Books And Bargains	340
KD'S Books	329	Rare Christian Books	317
Keeper's Antique Mall	320	Reader's Heaven	322
L & B Bookstore	344	Red Bridge Books	327
Lasus Books	325	St. Marys Antique Mall	340
Left Bank Books	339	Rev. D.A. Schroeder	348
E. Llewellyn, Bookseller	346	Second-Hand Rows	318
M & M Books	345	Second Hand Stories	339
Marvelous Books	347	Shirley's Old Book Shop	344
Midge's Dollhouse & Antiques	321	Sign of Jonas Books	341
Monty's Book Swap	321	Spivey's Books, Old Maps, Fine Art	327
My Father's Books	326	Steel's Used Christian Books	328
Mythos Books	347	Swiss Village Book Store	340
Charles O'Dell-Paper Collectibles	332	Used Books & Unicorns	328
The Old Book Shop	321	Robert D. Wagner	330
The Open Book	343	WXICOF	348
The Open Book	320		

Alphabetical Listing By Location

Location	Dealer	Page
Arnold	Pam's Books	313
Ballwin	Marvelous Books	347
Belton	A Better Book Store	313
Branson	Half Price Used Books of the Ozarks	313
Cape Girardeau	Dan Pekios Books	347
Carthage	Cordell-Wilson Booksellers	314
Chesterfield	Greentrails Book Shop	314
Columbia	Acorn Books	315
	Acorn #2	315
	Adams Walls of Books	315
	Columbia Books	316
Crescent	Deerlilly Farms	346
DeSoto	Books Galore	316
Diamond	AJ'S Books & Crafts	317
Dixon	Rare Christian Books	317
Fairdealing	Byrd's Books & Collectibles	317
Farmington	Second-Hand Rows	318
Florissant	Book Brokers Unlimited	318
Fredericktown	Galey's Record Store	318
Grandview	Antique & Furniture Mall	318
	Grandview Book Gallery	319
Gray Summit	The Book House	319
Greenfield	Greenfield Books	320
Hannibal	Becky Thatcher Book Shop	320
	The Open Book	320
Harrisonville	Harrisonville Trade Fair	320
	Keeper's Antique Mall	320
High Ridge	Betty's Books and Collectible Comics	321
Holden	Midge's Dollhouse & Antiques	321
Independence	John Hajicek	346
	Monty's Book Swap	321
	The Old Book Shop	321
	Reader's Heaven	322
Jefferson City	Antiquarium Books & Collectibles	322
	Bare Necessities	323
Joplin	The Book Barn	323
	Book Haven	323
	Changing Hands Book Shoppe	324
Kansas City	Bloomsday Books	324
	Clues! Mystery Bookseller	324
	Eddie's Books, Games and Gifts	325
	Glenn Books	325
	Klaus Grunewald - Bookdealer	325
	Lasus Books	325

Kansas City	E. Llewellyn, Bookseller	346
	My Father's Books	326
	Prospero's Books	326
	Red Bridge Books	327
	Spivey's Books, Old Maps, Fine Art	327
	Steel's Used Christian Books	328
Kirksville	Used Books & Unicorns	328
Lake Ozark	Rev. D.A. Schroeder	348
Lamar	Peddler's Wagon	347
Lebanon	Blue Nile Books	329
Lee's Summit	KD'S Books	329
Mount Vernon	Just Books	329
Mountain View	The Attic Trunk and Book Review	329
New Bloomfield	Robert D. Wagner	330
Nixa	Brown's Books	330
Overland	A-1 Book Exchange	330
Ozark	Ozarks Antiques	330
Peculiar	Collector's Paradise	330
Pierce City	Archer's Antiques & Books	331
Poplar Bluff	Bouland Brother's Booksellers	331
	Mythos Books	347
Rocheport	B. Caldwell - Bookseller	331
	Charles O'Dell-Paper Collectibles	332
Rock Port	Great Books	332
Saint Charles	Bargain Books	332
	Encore Books of Harvester	332
Saint Joseph	Bags End	333
	Paper Moone	333
Saint Louis	A Collector's Bookshop	334
	A. Amitin's Book Shop	334
	The Avid Reader	335
	Big Sleep Books	335
	Book Brokers Unlimited	335
	The Book House	336
	Phyllis Y. Brown	337
	Delmar Books	337
	R. Dunaway, Bookseller	337
	Anthony Garnett Fine Books	338
	Hammond's Books	338
	Eugene M. Hughes, Antiquarian Bookseller	338
	Left Bank Books	339
	Overlord Military Collectibles	339
	Second Hand Stories	339
	Swiss Village Book Store	340
Saint Marys	St. Marys Antique Mall	340
Sedalia	Queen City Books And Bargains	340

Sedalia	Sign of Jonas Books	341
Springfield	ABC Books	341
	Addison's Book Store	341
	Book Jungle	342
	The Book Rack	342
	Half Price Books of the Ozarks	342
	Hooked On Books	343
	The Open Book	343
	Purple Shamrock	348
	Shirley's Old Book Shop	344
Sullivan	L & B Bookstore	344
Sycamore Hills	Bell's Books & Candles	346
Unionville	The Book Barn	346
Vienna	Americana Antiques	344
Webb City	Fireside Bookstore	345
	M & M Books	345
Wentzville	WXICOF	348

Missouri
Map 20

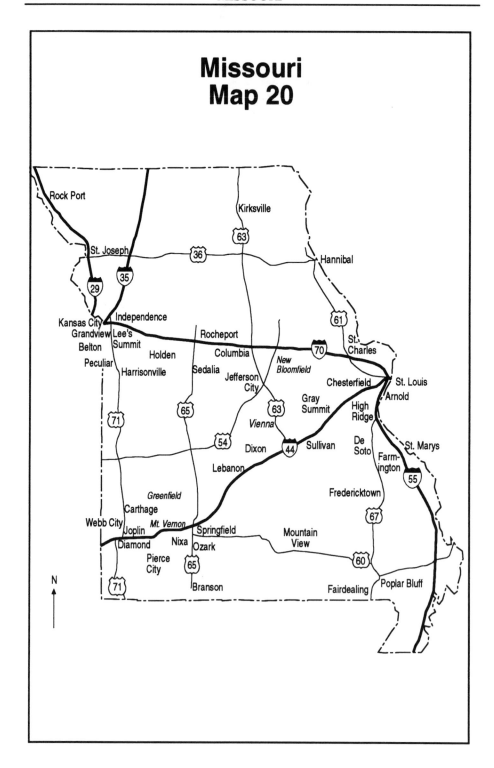

Rock Port

Kirksville

63

St. Joseph

36

Hannibal

35

29

61

Kansas City

Independence

Grandview

Lee's

Rocheport

St.

Summit

Charles

Belton

70

Peculiar

Holden

Columbia

New

Harrisonville

Sedalia

Bloomfield

Chesterfield

St. Louis

Jefferson

City

Gray

Arnold

Summit

High

71

65

63

Ridge

Vienna

De

St. Marys

54

Dixon

44

Sullivan

Soto

Farm-

Lebanon

ington

55

Greenfield

Fredericktown

Carthage

67

Webb City

Mt. Vernon

Joplin

Springfield

Mountain

Diamond

Nixa

View

Pierce

Ozark

60

City

65

N

71

Branson

Fairdealing

Poplar Bluff

Arnold

(Map 20, page 312)

Pam's Books   **Open Shop**
219 Arnold Crossroads 63010   (314) 282-2665

Collection: General stock of mostly paperback.
# of Vols: 15,000
Hours: Mon-Sat 10-7. Sun 1-5 but best to call ahead to verify.

Belton

(Map 20, page 312)

A Better Book Store   **Open Shop**
549 North Scott 64012   (816) 331-9166
Web page: www.kcnet.com/abet.com   E-mail: abetbook@kcnet.com

Collection: General stock of paperback and hardcover.
# of Vols: 8,000 (hardcover)
Hours: Mon-Fri 12:30-7. Sat 10-6. Sun by chance.
Services: Accepts want lists, mail order.
Travel: 155th St exit off Rte 71. Proceed west on 155th St for 1/2 block, then
                left on North Scott. Shop is about 1½ miles ahead in a small strip
                shopping center.
Credit Cards: Yes
Owner: David K. Varner
Year Estab: 1994
Comments: We returned to this shop some 3½ years after our first visit and found it
                to have fulfilled the positive expectations we had on our initial visit.
                While much of the stock consists of paperbacks, the side and rear walls
                contain a very nice selection of hardcover items, particularly strong in
                the areas of vintage mystery, science fiction and fantasy. We saw quite
                a few rare and certainly hard to find titles that collectors (or dealers) in
                these subjects would be tempted to purchase. The shop also carries
                pulp magazines and other interesting ephemera. Additional books are
                in storage and the owner displays at antique malls in Grandview, Pecu-
                liar and Harrisonville. (See other listings.)

Branson

(Map 20, page 312)

Half Price Used Books of the Ozarks   **Open Shop**
1819-B West Highway 76 65616   (417) 334-7970

Collection: General stock of paperback and hardcover.
# of Vols: 30,000-35,000
Hours: Mon-Sat 9-5.
Services: Accepts want lists.
Travel: Rte 76 exit off Rte 65. Proceed west on Rte 76 for about 1½ miles.

Credit Cards:	Yes
Owner:	Ron Sampson
Year Estab:	1990
Comments:	Stock is approximately 65% paperback.

Carthage
(Map 20, page 312)

Cordell-Wilson Booksellers   **Open Shop**
17665 Old 66 Boulevard 64836   (417) 358-9380
E-mail: cdwilson@getonthe.net

Collection:	General stock of used and new.
# of Vols:	30,000
Specialties:	Art; history; business biographies; true crime.
Hours:	Mon-Sat 10-10. Sun 12-5.
Services:	Search service, accepts want lists, mail order.
Travel:	Rte 71 exit off I-44. Proceed north to Carthage, staying on Alt (Bus) 71. In Carthage, exit at Central St and continue west on Rte 71, then Brooklyn Heights exit off Rte 71. Proceed east on Old 66 Blvd for 1/4 mile.
Owner:	Bennett Wilson & Curtis Cordell
Year Estab:	1995
Comments:	One's first impression upon entering this shop is that it sells only new books because the books all appear to be in such good condition (with shiny dust jackets) and there are multiple copies of so many of the titles. Upon closer observation, it's clear that many of the books are remainders while others have been simply carefully selected by the owners. The books are, for the most part, of fairly recent vintage and cover a wide range of subjects. A few collectibles, signed editions and older titles are displayed on open shelves and in glass cases in an adjoining room which serves primarily as a bar (and also sports a pool table). The shop also sells CDs and has a modest selection of paperbacks.

Chesterfield
(Map 20, page 312)

Greentrails Book Shop   **Open Shop**
14270 Ladue Road 63017   (314) 576-7758
Fax: (314) 576-1884

Collection:	General stock of mostly used paperback and hardcover.
# of Vols:	10,000 (used)
Hours:	Mon-Thu 9:30-7:30. Fri 9:30-6 (except in winter). Sun 11-5.
Travel:	Woods Mill North exit off Rte 40. Proceed north on Woods Mill, then west on Ladue. Shop is about one mile ahead in shopping center.
Credit Cards:	Yes
Year Estab:	1986
Comments:	Used stock is approximately 75% paperback.

Columbia
(Map 20, page 312)

Acorn Books   **Open Shop**
211 South Ninth Street 65201   (573) 449-8030

Collection:	General stock of mostly used paperback and hardcover.
# of Vols:	50,000
Specialties:	Art; women's studies; history; cooking; philosophy; poetry; nature; drama; fiction; antiques (at Acorn #2, see below).
Hours:	Mon-Fri 10-7. Sat 10-5. Sun 12-5.
Services:	Appraisals, search service, accepts want lists.
Travel:	Providence Rd exit off I-70. Proceed south on Providence, then east on Broadway and south on 9th. Shop is 2½ blocks ahead on right.
Credit Cards:	Yes
Owner:	Ken & Linda Green
Year Estab:	1986
Comments:	A shop containing more books that one would expect considering its size. The books are packed solidly with little wasted space. There's lots to see if you're patient and willing to spend the time. Most of the volumes we saw were in good condition. Prices varied from reasonable to "?" but you get what you pay for. The owners also display a general collection with an emphasis on Americana and antique reference at the Ice Chalet Antique Mall. See below.

Acorn #2   **Antique Mall**
At Ice Chalet Antique Mall, 3411 Old Highway 63 South   (573) 442-6893

Hours:	Mon-Sat 10-8. Sun 11-6.
Travel:	Exit 128A off I-70. Proceed south on Rte 63, then AC exit off Rte 63. Continue west on Old Rte 63.

Adams Walls of Books   **Open Shop**
214 North 8th Street   (573) 443-5350
Mailing address: 16 North Glenwood Columbia MO 65203

Collection:	General stock of hardcover and paperback.
# of Vols:	80,000+ (See Comments)
Specialties:	World War II; armor; Civil War; nature; Missouri.
Hours:	Mon-Sat 1-5:30.
Services:	Accepts want lists.
Travel:	Range Line exit off I-70. South on Range Line, then right on Rogers St and left on North 8th. Shop is two blocks ahead.
Credit Cards:	No
Owner:	I. C. Adams
Year Estab:	1945
Comments:	The sign on the front door reads: Come in and meet Ike Adams "The King of Klutter." After entering the shop, we would not take issue with the owner's assessment of his shop. The owner has been in business for over 50 years and has accumulated tens of thousands of books, ap-

proximately half of which are stored in a warehouse. If you plan to visit this shop, you may want to bring your own ladder as the shelves reach to the top of the building's 10 foot ceiling and the one ladder we saw during our visit looked a bit shaky. Surely, in a collection this large there may be some truly scarce items. However, with the shelves unmarked, the aisles narrow and the lighting marginal, we chose not to search as long as we might have. Note: If you're coming from a distance, we advise a call ahead as the shop is a one man operation and subject to unexpected closings.

Columbia Books   **Open Shop**
22 South 9th   (573) 449-7417
Mailing address: PO Box 27 Columbia MO 65205
Web page: www.abebooks.com   E-mail: COLBOOKS@interloc.com

Collection:	General stock of mostly used.
# of Vols:	60,000
Specialties:	Children's; illustrated; Missouri; art; gardening.
Hours:	Mon-Sat 9:30-7. Sun 12-4.
Services:	Appraisals, search service, mail order.
Travel:	See Acorn Books above.
Credit Cards:	Yes
Owner:	Annette Weaver
Year Estab:	1977
Comments:	An attractively decorated multi level shop that's easy to browse—and the books ain't bad either. Most of the volumes we saw were in quite good condition with solid selections in a wide range of subject areas. Whether or not you make a purchase here, you should certainly enjoy your visit. It doesn't hurt that another very good book store is located just a 1½ block away on the same street.

De Soto
(Map 20, page 312)

Books Galore   **Open Shop**
2116 Rock Road 63020   (314) 586-5243
Web page: www.books-galore.com   (888) 586-8220
                                          E-mail: info@books-galore.com

Collection:	General stock of mostly used hardcover and paperback.
# of Vols:	20,000
Specialties:	Radical studies (See Comments).
Hours:	Tue-Fri 10-6. Sat 10-4.
Services:	Mail order.
Travel:	Exit 174 off I-55. Proceed south on Rte 67, then west on Rte 110, left on Rte 21 and left on Rock Rd. Shop is just ahead on left in a small strip center.
Credit Cards:	Yes
Owner:	John Gilbert
Year Estab:	1997

Comments: The shop is modest in size, somewhat off the beaten path and at least 50% of its stock is paperback. However, the hardcover collection (about 4,000-5,000 volumes at the time of our visit) contained some interesting titles and were in quite good condition. We saw more than a few items worthy of consideration. If you're doing the St. Louis suburbs, you could do far worse. If you're interested in the shop's specialty (see above), call ahead as that collection is not on display at the store.

Diamond
(Map 20, page 312)

AJ'S Books & Crafts   **Open Shop**
200 North Jefferson Street 64840   (417) 325-5414

Collection: General stock of mostly paperback.
# of Vols: 15,000
Hours: Mon-Fri 9-7. Sat 10-5.

Dixon
(Map 20, page 312)

Rare Christian Books   **Open Shop**
19275 Highway 28 65459   Tel & Fax: (573) 336-7316
                                       E-mail: RCB@ctwok.com

Collection: Specialty new and used hardcover and paperback.
# of Vols: 50,000+
Specialties: Religion (Conservative Christian).
Hours: Mon-Sat 8-8. Best to call ahead.
Services: Search service, catalog ($5 per year for subscription), special sales.
Travel: Exit 163 off I-44. Proceed north on Rte 28 for about 3½ miles.
Credit Cards: Yes
Owner: Jack Morrison
Year Estab: 1981
Comments: Stock is approximately 50% used, 50% of which is hardcover.

Fairdealing
(Map 20, page 312)

Byrd's Books & Collectibles   **Open Shop**
HC 1 Box 717 63939   Tel & Fax: (573) 857-2727

Collection: General stock of mostly used paperback and hardcover and comics.
# of Vols: 20,000
Specialties: Children's; antiques; science fiction; horror.
Hours: Tue-Sat 9-5.
Services: Appraisals, search service, accepts want lists, mail order.
Travel: Rte 160, 12 miles west of Rte 67.
Credit Cards: No
Owner: James D. Byrd
Year Estab: 1991
Comments: Used stock is approximately 75% paperback.

Farmington
(Map 20, page 312)

Second-Hand Rows   **Open Shop**
738 Weber Road 63640   (573) 756-7006

Collection:	General stock of paperback and hardcover.
# of Vols:	30,000
Hours:	Tue, Thu, Fri 10-3. Sat 10-5.
Travel:	Karsch Blvd exit off Rte 67. Proceed east on Karsch to second light then left on Weber.
Credit Cards:	No
Owner:	Carolyn & Tim Murphy
Year Estab:	1993
Comments:	Stock is approximately 70% paperback.

Florissant
(Map 22, page 336)

Book Brokers Unlimited   **Open Shop**
12 Paddock Hills Plaza 63033   (314) 838-8111

Collection:	General stock of paperback and hardcover.
# of Vols:	25,000
Hours:	Mon-Sat 9-9. Sun 11-4:30.
Travel:	North Lindbergh exit off I-270. Proceed north on Lindbergh for about three miles. Shop is in Paddock Hills Plaza shopping center.
Credit Cards:	Yes
Owner:	Wesley & Carolyn Ginder
Year Estab:	1976
Comments:	A few hardcover books scattered among many paperbacks and magazines (new and used). If your time is limited, you could spend it more wisely checking some of our other listings in the St. Louis area.

Fredericktown
(Map 20, page 312)

Galey's Record Store   **Open Shop**
114 West Main Street 63645   (573) 783-6405

Collection:	General stock of mostly paperback.
# of Vols:	15,000-20,000
Hours:	Mon-Sat 10-6.

Grandview
(Map 20, page 312)

Antique & Furniture Mall   **Antique Mall**
12236 South 71 Highway 64030   (816) 761-2221

Hours:	Mon-Fri 10-8. Sat 10-7. Sun 12-6.

Grandview Book Gallery   **Open Shop**
820 Main Street 64030   (816) 763-1008

Collection:	General stock of hardcover and paperback, comics and magazines.
# of Vols:	8,000
Specialties:	Children's series; military; Western Americana; pulps; aviation; railroads; occult.
Hours:	Tue-Fri 12-6. Sat 11-5:30. Sun 12-4.
Services:	Accepts want lists, mail order.
Travel:	Main St exit off Rte 71. Proceed west on Main.
Credit Cards:	Yes
Owner:	Randal Hawkins
Year Estab:	1973
Comments:	If you're into children's series books or a fan of older horror, mystery, westerns and the like, your stay at this shop will be a lengthy one as you browse the titles and are amazed at the bargain prices being asked. The shop also carries more traditional hardcover items as well as comics, magazines and paperbacks.

Gray Summit
(Map 20, page 312)

The Book House   **Open Shop**
2980 Highway 100 West 63089   (314) 451-4491
Web page: www.findbooks.com   E-mail: bkhouse1@interloc.com

Collection:	General stock of hardcover and paperback.
# of Vols:	100,000+
Specialties:	History; art; children's; nature; illustrated.
Hours:	Mon-Thu 10:30-6:30. Fri & Sat 10:30-8. Sun 12-5.
Services:	Search service, mail order.
Travel:	Exit 253 (Gray Summit) exit off I-44. Turn south over highway then continue west on Rte 100 for 1/2 mile.
Credit Cards:	Yes
Owner:	Michelle Baron
Year Estab:	1997
Comments:	A real find and a most appropriate name for a shop that displays its collection on three floors of a former residence. The shop offers an assortment of books ranging from paperbacks in all subject areas to hard to find and occasionally rare collectibles, also in all subject areas. Prices are quite reasonable, particularly if you know your field. Where else could you shop for books and find rest rooms on all three levels plus plush carpeting on the first and second levels? In our view, well worth a visit. The owner operates a second shop in St. Louis.

Greenfield
(Map 20, page 312)

Greenfield Books   **By Appointment**
1 North Allison Street 65661   (417) 637-2665
                                                          Fax:(417) 637-5096
                                               E-mail: greenfld@interloc.com

Collection: Specialty
# of Vols: 1,500
Specialties: Polar; magic; occult; medicine; nautical; law.
Services: Appraisals, subject lists, accepts want lists.
Owner: Michael Park
Year Estab: 1992

Hannibal
(Map 20, page 312)

Becky Thatcher Book Shop   **Open Shop**
211 Hill Street 63401   (573) 221-0822

Collection: Specialty. Mostly new.
Specialties: Mark Twain.
Hours: Daily 8-5.
Services: Appraisals, accepts want lists.
Travel: From Rte 36, take Rte 79 south for two blocks, then left on Hill St.
Credit Cards: Yes
Owner: Frank North
Year Estab: 1971
Comments: Occasionally has out-of-print first editions of Mark Twain.

The Open Book   **Open Shop**
606 Mark Twain Avenue 63401   (573) 221-6449

Collection: General stock of mostly paperback.
# of Vols: 20,000
Hours: Mon-Sat 10-4, except Wed, till 7. Sun (Mem Day-Labor Day) 12-4.

Harrisonville
(Map 20, page 312)

Harrisonville Trade Fair   **Antique Mall**
2301 Commercial 64701   (816) 380-5413

Hours: Mon-Sat 10-5. Sun 12-5.
Travel: Southbound on Rte 71. Third Harrisonville exit. Turn left and cross the
                   viaduct. Shop is just ahead on left.

Keeper's Antique Mall   **Antique Mall**
801 South Commercial 64701   (816) 380-7175

Hours: Daily 9-6.
Travel: South on Rte 71. Second Harrisonville exit. After exit loops around to
                   stop sign, turn right and continue straight. Right at Commercial.

High Ridge
(Map 20, page 312)

Betty's Books and Collectible Comics   **Open Shop**
1520-B Gravois Road 63049   Tel & Fax; (314) 677-3197

Collection:	General stock of paperback and hardcover, and comics.
# of Vols:	50,000 (books)
Hours:	Mon-Fri 10-6. Sat 10-4.
Services:	Accepts want lists, mail order.
Travel:	Rte 30 exit off I-270. Proceed west on Rte 30 to Brennan. Left on Brennan and left on Gravois.
Credit Cards:	Yes
Year Estab:	1978
Comments:	Stock is approximately 70% paperback.

Holden
(Map 20, page 312)

Midge's Dollhouse & Antiques   **Open Shop**
1461 NW US Highway 50 64040   (816) 229-5154

Collection:	General stock and ephemera.
# of Vols:	3,000+
Specialties:	Religion (Christianity); older fiction; agriculture.
Hours:	Mon-Sat 10-5.
Services:	Accepts want lists, mail order.
Travel:	On Rte 50, 20 minutes east on Lee's Summit.
Credit Cards:	Yes
Owner:	Paul & Midge Myers
Year Estab:	1992

Independence
(Map 20, page 312 & Map 21, page 326)

Monty's Book Swap   **Open Shop**
9302 East 40 Highway 64052   (816) 737-1427

Collection:	General stock of mostly paperback.
# of Vols:	100,000+
Hours:	Mon-Sat 9-6.

The Old Book Shop   **Open Shop**
120 South Main Street 64050   (816) 252-1379
                          E-mail: oldbkshp@interloc.com

Collection:	General stock of hardcover and paperback.
# of Vols:	30,000
Specialties:	Harry Truman; railroads; children's; mystery; biography; Missouri Trail related; religion (RLDS).
Hours:	Mon-Sat 10-5. Most Sun 1-5. Closed major holidays.

Services:	Appraisals, search service, mail order.
Travel:	From I-435: east on Truman Rd, then south on Main. From I-70: north on Noland Rd, then west on Truman and south on Main.
Credit Cards:	Yes
Owner:	Barbara Young
Year Estab:	1990
Comments:	A delightful little shop divided into two rooms (Volume I and Volume II), each with a different focus and connected by a hallway. The books were in generally good condition, well organized and reasonably priced. Worth a visit, particularly since there is another small shop right around the corner. In addition to the specialties listed above, we noted some signed first editions.

Reader's Heaven
105 West Lexington 64050

Open Shop
(816) 254-7333

Collection:	General stock of mostly hardcover.
# of Vols:	10,000
Hours:	Mon & Wed-Sat 10-4.
Travel:	See above. Shop is around the corner.
Credit Cards:	No
Owner:	Dorothy J. Christina
Year Estab:	1992
Comments:	The books here are a trifle older (with exceptions) and we spotted many unusual and interesting titles with prices a bit below those that might be asked for the same volume elsewhere. While there were some common items, there were also some rather rare gems.

Jefferson City
(Map 20, page 312)

Antiquarium Books & Collectibles
504 East High Street 65101

Open Shop
(573) 636-8995

Collection:	General stock of paperback and hardcover and comics.
# of Vols:	20,000
Specialties:	Science fiction; mystery; Missouri; vintage paperbacks; pulps.
Hours:	Mon-Sat 12-5.
Services:	Accepts want lists; mail order.
Travel:	Rte 54 exit off I-70 westbound. Proceed south on Rte 54, then east on McCarty, north on Jackson and right on High. Shop is just ahead on the right.
Credit Cards:	Yes
Owner:	Tom Strong
Year Estab:	1991
Comments:	Heavily comic book oriented (both new and used) with lots of paperbacks. The hardcover books appeared to be stronger in the specialties listed above but even these categories lacked depth. Lots of "girlie" stuff as well.

Bare Necessities **By Appointment**
804 East High Street 65101 (573) 636-5509

Collection:	General stock of mostly hardcover and ephemera.
# of Vols:	4,000
Travel:	See Antiquarium Books above.
Services:	Appraisals, accepts want lists, mail order.
Credit Cards:	No
Owner:	Tom & Joan Benke
Year Estab:	1968
Comments:	A rather small collection (we saw only a few hundred volumes displayed) of older books, some magazines and other ephemera. Unless you plan to be in the Missouri state capital, you might be better off phoning to see if the owner has the titles you're looking for.

Joplin
(Map 20, page 312)

The Book Barn **Open Shop**
3128 Main Street 64804 (417) 782-2778
Fax: (417) 782-0024

Collection:	General stock of paperback and hardcover and comics.
# of Vols:	30,000
Hours:	Mon-Sat 9-8. Sun 12-6.
Services:	Accepts want lists.
Travel:	Main St exit off I-44. Proceed north on Main for one mile.
Credit Cards:	Yes
Owner:	Ron Erwin
Year Estab:	1980
Comments:	Several well spaced shelves down the center aisle containing paperbacks, a wide selection of comics, cassettes and CDs and a modest (probably less then 2,000 volumes) collection of used hardcover items along the rear wall and one side wall. The hardcover volumes were mainly reading copies along with some recent book club editions.

Book Haven **Open Shop**
1605 Main Street 64804 (417) 781-7756

Collection:	General stock of new and used paperback and hardcover.
# of Vols:	5,000 (used hardcover)
Hours:	Mon-Sat 9-5.
Travel:	Main St exit off I-44. Proceed north on Main to 16th.
Credit Cards:	No
Owner:	Joyce Bible
Year Estab:	1979
Comments:	Far more paperbacks than hardcover items. We noted little organization among the hardcover volumes, most of which were reading copies.

Changing Hands Book Shoppe
528 Virginia Avenue 64801

Open Shop
(417) 623-6699
Fax: (417) 624-4772

Collection:	General stock of mostly paperback.
# of Vols:	35,000+
Hours:	Mon-Sat 10-8.

Kansas City
(Map 20, page 312 & Map 21, page 326)

Bloomsday Books
6229 Brookside Boulevard 64113

Open Shop
(816) 523-6712
E-mail: tracen@ix.netcom.com

Collection:	General stock of mostly hardcover.
# of Vols:	40,000+
Specialties:	Irish literature; history; biography; writer biographies.
Hours:	Mon-Fri 7-7. Sat 9-6. Sun 10-5.
Travel:	63rd St exit off I-435. Proceed west on 63rd St for about eight miles to Brookside Blvd (not to be mistaken with Brookside Plaza which is the next street over). Right on Brookside. Shop is just ahead on left.
Credit Cards:	Yes
Owner:	Tom & Nancy Shawver
Year Estab:	1995
Comments:	An attractive shop with mostly hardcover volumes and several shelves of paperbacks. The vast majority of the hardcover items were in good to excellent condition. The subjects listed above as specialties were well represented and prices were reasonable. If you're a bread addict (as one of our team is), you may also find the adjoining bakery an additional motivation for a stop here. The shop also has a coffee bar.

Clues! Mystery Bookseller
At State Line Antique Mall, 4510 State Line Road
Mailing address: PO Box 5464 Kansas City MO 64131

Antique Mall
Mall: (913) 362-2002
Home: (816) 361-9151
Fax: (816) 361-6152
E-mail: clues2@ix.netcom.com

Collection:	Specialty paperback and hardcover. (All used)
# of Vols:	6,000 (See Comments)
Specialties:	Mystery; detective.
Hours:	Mon-Sat 10-5. Sun 12-5. Closed most holidays.
Services:	Accepts want lists, mail order.
Travel:	Exit 234 off I-35. Proceed south on Rainbow Blvd, then east on 43rd and south on State Line Rd.
Owner:	Karen Spengler
Year Estab:	1992
Comments:	If you don't see what you're looking for at the mall, call the owner directly as she has additional volumes in stock.

Eddie's Books, Games and Gifts   **Open Shop**
1509 NE Parvin Road 64116   (816) 455-5924

Collection:	General stock of primarily paperback.
Hours:	Mon-Sat 10-7.

Glenn Books   **By Appointment**
4503 Genessee Street, 2nd Fl. 64111   Tel & Fax: (816) 561-9989
                                                  E-mail: glennbks@interloc.com

Collection:	General stock.
# of Vols:	5,000
Specialties:	Americana; American and English literature; illustrated; private press; first editions.
Services:	Appraisals, catalog.
Credit Cards:	Yes
Owner:	Frederic & Carolyn Gilhousen
Year Estab:	1933
Comments:	The following comments are based on our earlier visit to these dealers when they maintained an open shop.
	If you love books, particularly older, rare, more interesting ones, be certain to visit here. The books on display at this shop should tempt even the most dedicated antiquarian. Whether it's a children's item you're looking for, a religious volume or one of the classics (during our visit, we spotted a $7,000 Nonesuch set of Charles Dickens), you are sure to see something here to make your mouth water. Prices reflect the value of the items on display.

Klaus Grunewald—Bookdealer   **By Appointment**
807 West 87 Terrace 64114   (816) 333-7799

Collection:	General stock.
# of Vols:	25,000
Specialties:	Philosophy; illustrated; Limited Editions Club; Kansas; Missouri.
Services:	Search service, catalog, accepts want lists.
Credit Cards:	No
Year Estab:	1972

Lasus Books   **Open Shop**
5312 NW 64th Street 64151   Tel & Fax: (816) 505-2665

Collection:	General stock of hardcover and paperback.
# of Vols:	55,000
Hours:	Mon-Fri 10-8. Sat 10-5. Sun: call for hours.
Services:	Appraisals, search service, accepts want lists.
Travel:	Just west of intersection of I-29 and 64th St. Shop is on the right.
Credit Cards:	No
Owner:	Gene Roberts
Year Estab:	1993

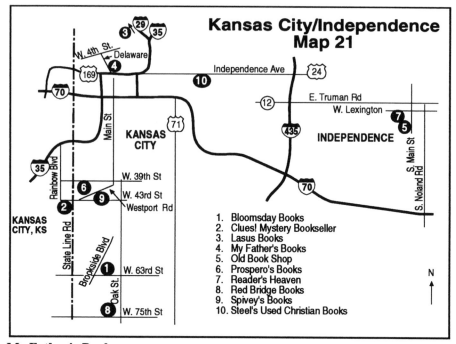

Kansas City/Independence Map 21

1. Bloomsday Books
2. Clues! Mystery Bookseller
3. Lasus Books
4. My Father's Books
5. Old Book Shop
6. Prospero's Books
7. Reader's Heaven
8. Red Bridge Books
9. Spivey's Books
10. Steel's Used Christian Books

My Father's Books   **Open Shop**
412-D Delaware 64105   (816) 221-1677

Collection:	General stock of hardcover and paperback.
# of Vols:	10,000 (See Comments)
Specialties:	Scholarly; history.
Hours:	Mon-Fri 10-6. Sat 10-7. Sun 11-3.
Services:	Accepts want lists.
Travel:	Broadway exit off I-70. Proceed north on Broadway, then right on 4th St, right at next street and left on 5th St. Shop is one block ahead on left.
Credit Cards:	Yes
Owner:	Herbert Kaufmann
Year Estab:	1995
Comments:	A spacious shop that, during the time of our visit, appeared understocked with lots of unused display space on its shelves. What we saw were a combination of hardcover books and trade paperbacks, mostly of recent vintage and a tad less attractive than remainders. In many cases, two or three copies of the same title were on display. If your time in Kansas City is limited, think about whether you want to spend it here.

Prospero's Books   **Open Shop**
1717 West 39th Street 64111   (816) 960-7202
Web page: www.prosbooks.com   E-mail: prosbooks@aol.com

Collection:	General stock of hardcover and paperback.
# of Vols:	20,000

Specialties:	Art; philosophy; literature; counter culture.
Hours:	Mon-Thu 10-10. Fri & Sat 10-midnight. Sun 9-6.
Services:	Search service, accepts want lists, catalog in planning stage.
Travel:	Rainbow/KU Medical Center exit off I-35. Proceed south on Rainbow, then left on 39th St. Shop is three blocks ahead.
Credit Cards:	Yes
Owner:	John Condra & Will Leathem
Year Estab:	1997
Comments:	A mix of hardcover and paperback with most of the hardcover books shelved along the side and rear walls and paperbacks down the center aisles. The majority of the items we saw would fit into the "popular culture" category. The books were in mixed condition and were reasonably priced.

Red Bridge Books   **Antique Mall/Open Shop**
At Waldo Antique Center, 230 West 75th Street 64131   (816) 942-0106

Collection:	General stock.
# of Vols:	15,000-20,000
Hours:	Wed-Sun 11-5.
Services:	Search service, mail order.
Travel:	75th St exit off Rte 71. Proceed west on 75th St. Shop is just before Wornell.
Credit Cards:	No
Owner:	Joan & Frank Hood
Year Estab:	1976
Comments:	A very pleasant surprise and far different from the kinds of books one generally finds in a multi dealer antique mall. The books are tightly packed (double shelved) in a series of several narrow aisles making it difficult to browse, particularly if one suffers from claustrophobia. That said, the titles and condition of the books, as well as their generally reasonable prices, makes this a shop worth visiting if you're in Kansas City or even near by.

Spivey's Books, Old Maps, Fine Art   **Open Shop**
825 Westport Road 64111   (816) 753-0520
                                                  E-mail: spiveybook@delphi.com

Collection:	General stock and prints.
# of Vols:	40,000
Specialties:	Military; Americana; maps; modern fiction.
Hours:	Mon-Fri 10-6. Sat 10-5. Sun by chance.
Services:	Appraisals, occasional catalog, accepts want lists, mail order.
Travel:	Westbound on I-70: Take I-35 south exit, then exit 1A off I-35. Proceed south on SW Trafficway for about one mile to Westport Rd (W. 43rd St) and made adjustments for traffic pattern. Eastbound on I-70: KU Medical Center exit. Proceed south on 7th St which becomes Rainbow Blvd. Continue south on Rainbow, then left on 43rd St which becomes Westport Rd.

Credit Cards:	Yes
Owner:	David Spivey
Year Estab:	1979
Comments:	If you're anywhere near Kansas City, this is a "must see" shop. In addition to a dazzling display of books attractively shelved and well cared for, the shop also sells prints (framed and unframed) and maps. The books, even the more collectible ones, are priced fairly and reasonably and the selection is generous. If you don't happen to see what you're looking for, try asking as the owner has more treasures in storage. An expansion to the building's second floor was in the works when we visited.

Since we made the above observations 3½ years ago, the owner has taken over the adjoining store and doubled his display space. We regret that we did not have time to visit the expanded shop when we returned to Kansas City.

Steel's Used Christian Books   **Open Shop**
3827 Independence Avenue 64124   (816) 483-2004
Web page: www.fathersbusiness.com/steels.htm   Fax:(81) 648-32448
                                                     E-mail: steelsbooks@juno.com

Collection:	Specialty
# of Vols:	90,000
Specialties:	Religion
Hours:	Mon-Sat 10-5:30, except Tue till 7.
Services:	Catalog, accepts want lists.
Travel:	Exit 24 off I-435. Proceed west on Rte 24 for 2½ miles.
Credit Cards:	Yes
Year Estab:	1972

*(Note: For more dealers across the river in Kansas City, Kansas, see **The Used Book Lover's Guide to the Central States**.)*

Kirksville
(Map 20, page 312)

Used Books & Unicorns   **Open Shop**
305 South Franklin Street 63501   (660) 627-1772

Collection:	General stock of hardcover and paperback.
Hours:	Mon-Fri 10-7. Sat 9-6. Sun 12-6.
Travel:	Jefferson Ave exit off Rte 63. Proceed west on Jefferson and south on Franklin.
Credit Cards:	No
Owner:	Dr. Shirley Morahan
Year Estab:	1986
Comments:	Despite several phone calls and messages left for the owner, we were unable to get an approximation of the size of this store's collection. About the only information we were given was that the books were evenly divided between hardcover and paperback.

Lebanon
(Map 20, page 312)

Blue Nile Books   **Antique Mall**
At Pleasant Memories Antique Mall, 25999 N. Highway 5   Mall: (816) 822-9588
Mailing address: 30641 Garrett Road Richland MO 65556   Home: (417) 532-6545

Collection:	General stock.
# of Vols:	1,000
Specialties:	Missouri Ozarks.
Hours:	Daily 10-5.
Credit Cards:	Yes
Owner:	Keith Park
Year Estab:	1995
Comments:	Also displays at Ozarks Antiques in Ozark. See below.

Lee's Summit
(Map 20, page 312)

KD'S Books   **Open Shop**
241 SE Main Street 64063   (816) 525-1366

Collection:	General stock of new and mostly paperback used.
Hours:	Mon-Fri 10-6. Sat 10-5.

Mount Vernon
(Map 20, page 312)

Just Books   **By Appointment**
RR 2, Box 214 65712   (417) 466-4282
                                                        E-mail: jusbooks@interloc.com

Collection:	General stock.
# of Vols:	2,000
Specialties:	Nautical; agriculture; gardening; homesteading.
Services:	Search service, catalog, accepts want lists.
Credit Cards:	No
Owner:	Paul Anthony
Year Estab:	1996

Mountain View
(Map 20, page 312)

The Attic Trunk and Book Review   **Open Shop**
120 North Elm Street 65548   (417) 934-2810

Collection:	General stock of mostly paperback.
# of Vols:	10,000
Hours:	Mon-Sat 9-5.

New Bloomfield
(Map 20, page 312)

Robert D. Wagner　　　　　　　　　　　　　　　**By Appointment**
417 Redwood Drive　65053　　　　　　　　　　　　(314) 491-3578

Collection:	General stock.
# of Vols:	2,000
Specialties:	House plants; horticulture.
Credit Cards:	No
Year Estab:	1972

Nixa
(Map 20, page 312)

Brown's Books　　　　　　　　　　　　　　　　　**Open Shop**
268 West Mt. Vernon　　　　　　　　　　　　　　(417) 725-4314
Mailing address: PO Box 874　Nixa　MO　65714

Collection:	General stock of paperback and hardcover.
# of Vols:	35,000
Hours:	Mon-Fri 10-5. Sat 10-4.
Travel:	Located at corner of Rtes 160 & 14 in shopping center.
Credit Cards:	No
Owner:	L.J. Brown
Year Estab:	1989
Comments:	Stock is approximately 70% paperback.

Overland
(Map 22, page 336)

A-1 Book Exchange　　　　　　　　　　　　　　**Open Shop**
10204 Page Avenue　63132　　　　　　　　　　　(314) 426-9088

Collection:	General stock of mostly paperback.
Hours:	Mon-Fri 10-8. Sat 10-6.

Ozark
(Map 20, page 312)

Ozarks Antiques　　　　　　　　　　　　　　　**Antique Mall**
200 South 20th Street　65721　　　　　　　　　　(417) 581-5233

Hours:	Mon-Fri 9-5. Sat 9-6.
Travel:	From Rte 65, proceed west on Rte 14, then right on South 20th St.

Peculiar
(Map 20, page 312)

Collector's Paradise　　　　　　　　　　　　　**Antique Mall**
232 C Highway　　　　　　　　　　　　　　　　(816) 779-6910

Hours:	Mon-Sat, except closed Wed, 10-5. Sun 11-5.

Pierce City
(Map 20, page 312)

Archer's Antiques & Books
119 West Commercial 65723
Web page: www.sofnet.com/archer

Open Shop
(417) 476-2951
(800) 299-3523
E-mail: jarcher@sofnet.com

Collection:	General stock.
# of Vols:	5,000
Specialties:	Children's (20th century); Harold Bell Wright.
Hours:	Mon-Sat 10-5. Sun 1-5.
Services:	Catalog, accepts want lists.
Travel:	Stotts City/Pierce City exit off I-44. Proceed south on Rte 97.
Credit Cards:	Yes
Comments:	If someday you should happen to be driving on Route 97 in Missouri and you have a lot of time on your hands, and, if you also have a penchant for older books that were not valuable when they were originally published and have not been maintained in very good condition, you might want to stop at this antique establishment to determine how much of your money you're willing to spend for such items.

Poplar Bluff
(Map 20, page 312)

Bouland Brother's Booksellers
2176 North Westwood Boulevard 63901

Open Shop
(573) 785-9067

Collection:	General stock of mostly used paperback and hardcover.
# of Vols:	18,000 (hardcover)
Hours:	Mon-Fri 10-6. Sat 9-6.
Services:	Search service, accepts want lists, mail order.
Travel:	Located on Rte 67.
Credit Cards:	Yes
Owner:	Michael Bouland
Year Estab:	1994
Comments:	The owner operates a second store in Paducah, KY. See above.

Rocheport
(Map 20, page 312)

B. Caldwell - Bookseller
Third & Clark Streets
Mailing address: PO Box 98 Rocheport MO 65279

Open Shop
(573) 698-2665

Collection:	General stock.
# of Vols:	8,000
Specialties:	Missouri; Southwest Americana; Americana; children's; first editions; art; military; history.
Hours:	Wed-Sat 10-5. Most Sun 1-5. Mon & Tue by chance or appointment.
Services:	Appraisals, limited search service, accepts want lists, mail order.

Travel:	Exit 115 off I-70. Proceed north to Rocheport for two miles. Shop is on lower level of the Schoolhouse B & B as one enters Rocheport.
Credit Cards:	Yes
Owner:	Bill S. Caldwell
Year Estab:	1985
Comments:	Regrettably, our itinerary brought us to Missouri when this dealer was out of town. Below are our observations from our earlier visit.
	We visited this dealer shortly before his move to Rocheport. If his new shop is anything like the one we visited, browsers should find it attractively decorated with nice books representing the specialties listed above and a kind of "odds & ends" collection of other titles. Limited in size but not in quality.

Charles O'Dell-Paper Collectibles   **Antique Mall**
At Farm Road Antiques 370 North Roby Farm Road   Mall: (573) 698-2206
Mailing address: 1904 Garden Drive Columbia MO 65202   Home: (573) 445-6467

Collection:	General stock, ephemera and magazines.
Hours:	Daily 10-5.
Travel:	At exit 115, off I-70. Proceed south on Roby Farm Rd.
Credit Cards:	Yes
Year Estab:	1992

Rock Port
(Map 20, page 312)

Great Books   **Open Shop**
400 South Main Street 64482   (660) 744-6457

Collection:	General stock of mostly paperback.
# of Vols:	20,000
Hours:	Mon-Sat 9-5, except Fri till 5:30. Sun 11-3:30.

Saint Charles
(Map 20, page 312)

Bargain Books   **Open Shop**
3010 North Hwy 94 63301   (314) 723-9598

Collection:	General stock of mostly used paperback.
Hours:	Mon-Thu 9:30-10. Fri & Sat 9:30-midnight. Sun 11-10.

Encore Books of Harvester   **Open Shop**
3970 Old Highway 94 South 63304   (314) 477-1554
                                                    E-mail: blodgett@interloc.com

Collection:	General stock of paperback and hardcover.
# of Vols:	18,000+
Hours:	Tue-Fri 10-7. Sat 10-5. Sun 12-5.
Services:	Search service, accepts want lists, mail order.
Travel:	Exit 228 (Rte 94) off I-70. Proceed south on Rte 94 West for about six miles, then left on Jungerman and continue up hill to Old Hwy 94 South. Turn left on Old Hwy 94 south. Shop is 1/2 block ahead.

Credit Cards:	No
Owner:	Elaine Blodgett & Lea Paul
Year Estab:	1997
Comments:	A modest sized bi-level shop that carries both hardcover and paperbacks books. Most of the books we saw were in good condition and quite reasonably priced.

Saint Joseph
(Map 20, page 312)

Bags End　　　　　　　　　　　　　　　　　　　　　　**By Appointment**
1023 Main Street 64501　　　　　　　　　　　　　　　　　(816) 364-1327

Collection:	General stock.
# of Vols:	3,000-5,000
Specialties:	Lafcadio Hearn; books about books; history; private press.
Services:	Appraisals, search service, catalog, accepts want lists.
Credit Cards:	No
Owner:	Marshall White
Year Estab:	1978

Paper Moone　　　　　　　　　　　　　　　　　　　　　　**Open Shop**
622 Francis 64501　　　　　　　　　　　　　Temporary: (816) 232-5652

Collection:	General stock of hardcover and paperback.
# of Vols:	24,000
Specialties:	Literary first editions; Americana; poetry.
Hours:	Mon-Sat 10-5. Sun by appointment.
Services:	Appraisals, search service, accepts want lists, mail order.
Travel:	Edmond St exit off I-229. Proceed on Edmond to 6th, then left on 6th and right on Francis.
Credit Cards:	No
Owner:	Hans Bremer
Year Estab:	1998 (See Comments)
Comments:	Shortly after visiting this shop, and just two weeks prior to going to press, we learned that Felix Street Antiquarian had changed hands and that the former manager had bought most of the stock and planned to reopen at a nearby location under the new name that appears above. We sincerely hope that the new owner will be able to maintain the shop in the same manner we saw when we visited and prepared the following comments.

Lots of book dealers use the word "antiquarian" on their signs; this shop uses it legitimately. In addition to some fine items that certainly meet the "antiquarian" definition (not only in terms of age but also in terms of quality) the shop has a large number of first editions as well as a general collection that should keep the average book browser happy. We recommend a stop. The shop also hosts readings and signings.

Saint Louis
(Map 20, page 312 & Map 22, page 336)

A Collector's Bookshop   **Open Shop**
6275 Delmar Boulevard University City 63130   Shop: (800) 721-6127
                                                            Office: (314) 721-6588
                                                               Fax: (314) 721-5315
                                      E-mail: ACollectorsBookshop@worldnett.att.net

Collection:	General stock of used and scholarly remainders.
# of Vols:	150,000+
Specialties:	History; art; science fiction; literary criticism.
Hours:	Mon-Thu 10-7. Fri & Sat 10-9. Sun 12-5. Longer hours May-Oct.
Services:	Appraisals
Travel:	Westbound on I-64/Rte 40: Clayton Rd/Skinker exit. Proceed right on Skinker and continue for about 1½ miles, then left on Delmar. Shop is 1¼ blocks ahead. Eastbound on I-64/Rte 40: McCausland exit. Left on McCausland, then left on Delmar. Shop is 1¼ blocks ahead.
Credit Cards:	Yes
Owner:	Sheldon Margulis
Year Estab:	1987
Comments:	This establishment has doubled in size since our last visit and continues to be a book lovers' delight, especially if their interests are in buying fairly recent editions (some remainders, some not), almost all in excellent condition and at bargain prices. You'll find books here that you might purchase elsewhere, in some cases directly from the publisher, at two to three times the price. The shop carries scholarly titles as well as popular items in almost every subject imaginable. If you're a volume buyer, ask to visit the warehouse. You won't find too many older volumes here but select dealers get to receive word when "oldies" of value are offered for sale via auction.

A. Amitin's Book Shop   **Open Shop**
1207 Washington Avenue 63103   (314) 421-9208
                                                                  (314) 421-2426
                                                            E-mail: eamitin@aol.com

Collection:	General stock of mostly hardcover.
# of Vols:	500,000
Specialties:	Regional; Civil War; signed.
Hours:	Mon-Fri 12-5. Sat 12:30-5. (See Note)
Services:	Subject lists.
Travel:	In downtown, just off 12th St. Five blocks west of Convention Center.
Owner:	Lawrence Amitin
Year Estab:	1929
Comments:	Impressions aren't always everything. Or are they? (We're not sure why this shop seemed to have bars on the inside of the front windows.) The first room one enters (at least when we visited) had books displayed on bookshelves but unfortunately, there were so many boxes of

books on the floor that in some sections we could not get near enough to the shelves to read the titles. Perhaps this was a temporary situation. The vast majority of the books in this huge shop are located in the room beyond the front area and reminded us of the basement of a major library that the public would not normally have access to. The books, in various stages of wear, were shelved from floor to ceiling and if you had time to wander down the many narrow aisles you could certainly spot labels indicating appropriate categories.

Note: Readers are advised to call ahead before visiting as the shop is for sale.

The Avid Reader   **Open Shop**
11029 Manchester Road 63122   (314) 821-4610
                                                        Fax: (314) 821-4311
                                      E-mail: gary.fishgall@gte.net

Collection:	General stock of hardcover and paperback.
# of Vols:	20,000
Hours:	Tue-Sat 10:30-7. Sun 12-6.
Travel:	From The Book House (see below) continue west on Manchester. Shop is three blocks west of Lindbergh.
Credit Cards:	Yes
Owner:	Gary Fishgall
Year Estab:	1998
Comments:	A new store scheduled to open in the summer of 1998. The stock is evenly divided between hardcover and paperback.

Big Sleep Books   **Open Shop**
229 North Euclid Avenue 63108   (314) 361-6100

Collection:	Specialty new and used.
Specialties:	Mystery; espionage; true crime.
Hours:	Mon-Sat 11-6. Sun 11-5.
Services:	Accepts want lists, mail order.
Travel:	In Central West End neighborhood. Kingshighway exit off I-64/Rte 40. Proceed north on Kingshighway, right on Lindell and left on Euclid.
Credit Cards:	Yes
Owner:	Helen Simpson
Year Estab:	1988
Comments:	A small shop with mostly new hardcover and paperback mysteries. The majority of the used books are paperback with anywhere from 100-200 used hardcover volumes. When we spotted a selection of detective book club editions (3 in 1) priced at $7.50 each, usually on sale elsewhere for $1-$3 each, we wondered about the shop's pricing policy.

Book Brokers Unlimited   **Open Shop**
12 Paddock Hills Plaza 63033   (314) 838-8111

Collection:	General stock of mostly paperback.
Hours:	Mon-Sat 9-9. Sun 11-4:30.

The Book House   **Open Shop**
9719 Manchester Road 63119   (314) 968-4491
Web page: www.findbooks.com   Fax: (314) 968-3318
                                                      E-mail: bkhouse1@interloc.com

Collection:	General stock of hardcover and paperback.
# of Vols:	100,000+
Specialties:	History; children's; art; first editions; illustrated.
Hours:	Mon-Fri 10:30-8. Sat 9:30-8. Sun 10:30-6:30.
Services:	Search service, mail order.
Travel:	McKnight Rd exit off I-64/Rte 40. Proceed south on McKnight, then right on Manchester. Shop is 1½ blocks ahead on right in a house set back from street.
Credit Cards:	Yes
Owner:	Michelle Baron
Year Estab:	1983
Comments:	The name of this shop is a literal description of what you'll find: a house with each room on the first and second floors (and the basement) filled with books, most of which are in good condition and of fairly recent vintage. Visitors to the second floor are advised not to miss any of the several gables but also to be careful of the low ceilings. The owner operates a second shop in Gray Summit. See above.

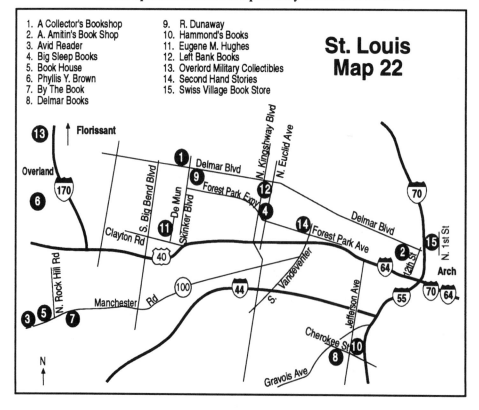

1. A Collector's Bookshop
2. A. Amitin's Book Shop
3. Avid Reader
4. Big Sleep Books
5. Book House
6. Phyllis Y. Brown
7. By The Book
8. Delmar Books
9. R. Dunaway
10. Hammond's Books
11. Eugene M. Hughes
12. Left Bank Books
13. Overlord Military Collectibles
14. Second Hand Stories
15. Swiss Village Book Store

St. Louis Map 22

Phyllis Y. Brown   **Open Shop**
At Ladue Galleries, 8811 Ladue Road   (314) 726-6166
Mailing address: 6325 Ellenwood Saint Louis MO 63105

Collection: Specialty
Specialties: Maps and prints.
Hours: Mon-Fri 10-8. Sat 10-7. Sun 11-5.
Travel: McKnight exit off I-64/Rte 40. North on McKnight then east on Ladue.
Year Estab: 1974

By The Book   **Open Shop**
9040 Manchester   63144   (314) 968-4255

Collection: General stock of hardcover and paperback.
# of Vols: 30,000+
Hours: Mon-Sat 10:30-6.
Services: Search service, accepts want lists.
Travel: Brentwood exit off I-170. Proceed south on Brentwood, then right on
                   Manchester.
Credit Cards: Yes
Year Estab: 1991

Delmar Books   **Open Shop**
2740 Cherokee Street 63118   (314) 664-7044

Collection: General stock of hardcover and paperback.
Hours: Sat 12-4. (See Comments)
Travel: See Hammond's Books below. Turn right on Cherokee.
Owner: Debra Cholak
Year Estab: 1994
Comments: Although we weren't able to contact this dealer, we were advised by
                   another dealer in the area that the shop is open on Saturdays and sells
                   inexpensive used books.

R. Dunaway, Bookseller   **Open Shop**
6138 Delmar Boulevard 63112   (314) 725-1581

Collection: General stock.
# of Vols: 10,000
Specialties: Literary criticism; Americana; fiction.
Hours: Mon-Sat 10-5:30.
Services: Appraisals, catalog, accepts want lists.
Travel: See A Collector's Bookshop above. Shop is just east of Skinker.
Credit Cards: No
Owner: Reginald P. Dunaway
Year Estab: 1965
Comments: You may have some initial difficulty spotting this storefront shop from
                   the street as there is no prominent sign on the door, in the window or
                   above the entrance indicating that a book dealer does business here.
                   However, after ringing the bell to gain entrance, you'll find a shop that

(St. Louis)

has a large collection of mostly scholarly volumes. The owner believes that his collection of books dealing with literary criticism may be the largest in the Midwest (or perhaps in the country). In addition to the scholarly titles, the shop also carries a more general collection of fiction. If you're visiting here, be prepared to wear your girdle as the space between some of the shelves is quite narrow.

Anthony Garnett Fine Books   **By Appointment**
PO Box 4918   63108   (314) 367-8080
                                                    Fax: (314) 361-3014

Collection: Specialty
# of Vols: 35,000
Specialties: English and American literature in first or scholarly editions; fine art; private press.
Services: Appraisals, accepts want lists, collection development.
Credit Cards: No
Year Estab: 1967

Hammond's Books   **Open Shop**
1939 Cherokee Street 63118   (314) 776-4737
                                                         (800) 776-4732
                                                    Fax: (314) 773-6340
                                              E-mail: hammonds@i1.net

Collection: General stock of mostly hardcover.
# of Vols: 80,000+ (See Comments)
Specialties: Art; architecture; history.
Hours: Tue-Sat 10-4.
Services: Appraisals, search service, catalog, accepts want lists.
Travel: Jefferson St exit off I-64/Rte 40. Proceed south on Jefferson, then left on Cherokee. Shop is located in the city's "Antique Row" neighborhood.
Credit Cards: Yes
Owner: Jovanka Hammond
Year Estab: 1980
Comments: A tightly packed bi-level shop. The majority of the items we saw were hardcover books in mixed condition ranging from fairly recent titles to old timers. Prices seemed slightly uneven. If you're looking for something unusual (not necessarily a rare or antiquarian title) it could turn up here. A portion of the collection is in storage.

Eugene M. Hughes, Antiquarian Bookseller   **Open Shop**
927 DeMun   (314) 727-9777
Mailing address: 3621 Jamieson Ave. St. Louis MO 63109 Fax: (314) 647-1751

Collection: General stock.
# of Vols: 4,000-5,000
Hours: Mon-Sat 12-5.

Services: Appraisals, catalog, accepts want lists.
Travel: Westbound on I-64/Rte 40: Clayton Rd exit. Proceed west on Clayton
                  for one block, then right on DeMun.
Credit Cards: Yes
Year Estab: 1978
Comments: Well worth the visit, particularly if your tastes are for truly antiquarian
                  and/or rare titles, many with attractive bindings. The shop is small.
                  The quality high. The selection not common. Don't come here if you're
                  looking for cookbooks or general fiction.

Left Bank Books   **Open Shop**
399 North Euclid Avenue 63108   (314) 367-6731

Collection: General stock of new and paperback and hardcover used.
# of Vols: 9,000 (used)
Hours: Mon-Sat 10-10. Sun 11-6.
Travel: In Central West End neighborhood. Kingshighway exit off I-64/Rte
                  40. Proceed north on Kingshighway, then right on McPherson. Shop is
                  at corner of McPherson and Euclid.
Credit Cards: Yes
Owner: Barry Leibman, Lisa Greening & Kris Kleindienst
Year Estab: 1969
Comments: Most of the stock in this shop consists of new books, cards, posters, etc.
                  focusing to some extent on the message implied in the shop's name.
                  The used books, located on the shop's lower level, run the gamut from
                  mystery, science fiction, general fiction and biography to other assorted
                  subjects. The majority of the books were of recent vintage, in good to
                  fair condition and could be considered reading copies. An interesting
                  shop to visit but not one that's likely to have many rare items.

Overlord Military Collectibles   **Open Shop**
3008 Woodson Road 63114   (314) 423-6644
Web page: www.overlordmilitary.com   E-mail: tpetruso@aol.com

Collection: Specialty books, ephemera, collectibles
# of Vols: 3,500
Specialties: Military
Hours: Tue-Sat 10-6.
Services: Appraisals, accepts want lists, mail order.
Travel: Airport exit off I-70. Proceed south on Woodson Rd for about two miles.
Credit Cards: Yes
Owner: Tony Petruso
Year Estab: 1986

Second Hand Stories   **Open Shop**
13 South Vandeventer 63108   (314) 533-5152
                                                E-mail: ourwrldtoo@aol.com

Collection: Specialty. Mostly new
# of Vols: 500
Specialties: Gay and lesbian.

Hours:	Mon-Sat 10-9:30. Sun 12-8.
Services:	Accepts want lists, mail order.
Travel:	Eastbound on I-64/Rte 40: Vandeventer exit. Proceed north on Vandeventer for about 1/2 mile. Westbound: Forest Park exit.
Credit Cards:	Yes
Owner:	William Cordes
Year Estab:	1992

Swiss Village Book Store   **Open Shop**
707 North First Street 63102   (314) 231-2782

Collection:	General stock of mostly hardcover.
# of Vols:	15,000-20,000
Specialties:	Civil War; Western Americana; presidents; Mississippi River; Mark Twain.
Hours:	Mon-Sat 10-8. Sun 12-7. Earlier closing in winter.
Services:	Appraisals, search service, occasional catalog, accepts want lists, mail order.
Travel:	In restored Laclede's Landing area, just north of the Arch. Follow signs for the Arch.
Credit Cards:	Yes
Owner:	John Stratton
Year Estab:	1978
Comments:	We were pleasantly surprised to find this "traditional" style used book shop on the upper level of a tourist/gift shop complex in a restored former tobacco warehouse along the banks of the Mississippi River. The books were in generally good condition and not "tourist priced." Translation: Reasonable prices for a good book in a good used book shop. Even if you don't buy a book here, you should enjoy walking around the riverfront and seeing the sights.

Saint Marys
(Map 20, page 312)

Saint Marys Antique Mall   **Antique Mall**
777 7th Street 63673   (573) 543-2800

Hours:	Daily 9-6.
Travel:	St. Marys exit off I-55. Proceed east on "Z" for 4½ miles to the end, then left on Rte 61N and left on 7th St.

Sedalia
(Map 20, page 312)

Queen City Books And Bargains   **Open Shop**
229 South Ohio 65301   (660) 827-0865

Collection:	General stock of mostly paperback.
# of Vols:	25,000
Hours:	Tue, Thu, Fri, Sat 12-5:30.

Sign of Jonas Books   **Antique Mall**
At Country Village Mall, 4005 South Limit Avenue   Mall: (660)827-2877
Mailing address: PO Box 3017 Sedalia MO 65302   Home: (660) 826-5668
                                                           E-mail: jonas@iland.net

Collection:	General stock and ephemera.
# of Vols:	2,000
Hours:	Mon-Sat 9-6. Sun 11-6.
Services:	Search service, accepts want lists, mail order.
Travel:	From intersection of Rtes 65 & 50, proceed north on Rte 50 for about three miles.
Credit Cards:	No
Owner:	Jerrie E. Jones
Year Estab:	1997

Springfield
(Map 20, page 312 & Map 23, page 342)

ABC Books   **Open Shop**
2109-J North Glenstone 65803   (417) 831-3523
Web page: www.intrcom/~biblebks/   (800) 326-3523
                                                           Fax: (417) 862-3660
                                                           E-mail: biblebks@intrcom.com

Collection:	General stock of hardcover and paperback.
# of Vols:	100,000+
Specialties:	Religion; Missouri; Star Trek; children's; cookbooks.
Hours:	Mon-Sat 9-8. Sun 1-5.
Services:	Appraisals, accepts want lists, mail order.
Travel:	Exit 80 off I-44. Proceed south on Glenstone (Bus Rte 65) for one mile. Shop is on the right, just south of Kearny.
Credit Cards:	Yes
Owner:	Gerard J. Flokstra, Jr.
Year Estab:	1964
Comments:	A fairly even mix of hardcover and paperback with a majority of the hardcover items being in the owner's major speciality (religion). We found the books to be very reasonable in terms of price although many were only in fair condition. Overall, we believe it's possible for someone with a sharp eye to find some bargains here.

Addison's Book Store   **Open Shop**
314 East Commercial Street 65803   (417) 862-8460

Collection:	General stock of hardcover and paperback.
# of Vols:	25,000
Hours:	Mon-Sat 9-4:30.
Travel:	Exit 80 off I-44. Proceed south on Glenstone, then east on Commercial.
Credit Cards:	No
Owner:	Richard Addison
Year Estab:	1938

Comments: A musty smelling shop with generally older books double shelved with no organizational pattern or attempt to alphabetize even the fiction section. Most of the books were very inexpensive. Despite the lack of organization, if you have a good idea of what you're looking for and don't mind the clutter or moving books from level to level, you could find some collectible or hard to locate titles at a very reasonable price.

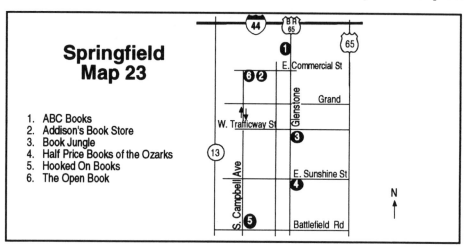

Springfield Map 23

1. ABC Books
2. Addison's Book Store
3. Book Jungle
4. Half Price Books of the Ozarks
5. Hooked On Books
6. The Open Book

Book Jungle   **Open Shop**
202 North Glenstone 65802   (417) 863-8645

Collection: General stock of primarily paperback and some hardcover.
# of Vols: 33,000
Specialties: Science fiction; fantasy.
Hours: Mon-Sat 10:30-6.
Travel: See ABC Books above. Continue south on Glenstone.
Credit Cards: No
Year Estab: 1991
Comments: Hardcover collection is non fiction, primarily history and how-to. Approximately one third of paperback stock is in specialty areas.

The Book Rack   **Open Shop**
300 West Olive 65806   (417) 865-4945

Collection: General stock of mostly paperback.
# of Vols: 50,000
Hours: Mon-Sat 9-5.

Half Price Books of the Ozarks   **Open Shop**
1950-O South Glenstone 65804   (417) 889-9042

Collection: General stock of paperback and hardcover.
# of Vols: 70,000
Specialties: Modern first editions; Civil War; history.

Hours:	Mon-Fri 9-6. Sat 9-5.
Services:	Search service, accepts want lists, mail order.
Travel:	See ABC Books above. The shop is just south of Sunrise, on the left, at the south end of the Plaza Shopping Center.
Credit Cards:	Yes
Owner:	Frank Clouse
Year Estab:	1986
Comments:	Yes, this shop does carry paperbacks but it also has a very good selection of hardcover items, including some antiquarian titles. Just as you think you've explored all the shop has to offer, you'll find another room and still another. The books are nicely shelved and with the exception of those older volumes which never did have dust jackets, most of the books we saw were in good condition and in their original dust jackets. The shop offers sufficient depth to satisfy most browsers.

Hooked On Books   **Open Shop**
2756 South Campbell 65807   (417) 882-3397
Web page: www.pcis.net/hookedonbooks   Fax: (417) 882-1537
                                  E-mail: hookedonbooks@pcis.net

Collection:	General stock of paperback and hardcover.
# of Vols:	50,000+
Specialties:	Classic literature; history; art; modern first editions; science fiction; mystery; cookbooks.
Hours:	Mon-Sat 9-6. Sun 1-5.
Services:	Search service, accepts want lists, mail order.
Travel:	Exit 80 off I-44. Proceed south on Glenstone, west on Battlefield, then north on Campbell for 1½ blocks to Village Shopping Center.
Credit Cards:	Yes
Owner:	Lavonne Foster
Year Estab:	1984
Comments:	This establishment provides a very good balance between its paperback and hardcover stock with enough hardcover items to easily fill a separate quality book shop. The collection has good books in most subject areas with particular strengths in the specializations listed above. Well worth a visit.

The Open Book   **Open Shop**
212 East Commercial Street 65803   (417) 831-2272

Collection:	General stock of paperback and hardcover.
# of Vols:	20,000
Specialties:	Vintage paperbacks.
Hours:	Mon-Sat 10-5.
Services:	Accepts want lists.
Travel:	See Addison's Book Store above.
Credit Cards:	No
Owner:	Carol Ebrite
Year Estab:	1993

Comments: A shop that intershelves its paperbacks and hardcover books. The
                books were in mixed condition, reading copies and some older titles
                that to some might be collectible. This is the kind of place that an
                occasional scout may enter and walk out of with a title or two to be
                sold to another book dealer.

Shirley's Old Book Shop   **By Appointment**
3237 East Berkely 65804   Shop: (417) 882-3734
                                                      Home: (417) 881-0319

Collection: General stock of paperback and hardcover.
# of Vols: 12,500
Specialties: Foreign languages; ESP; regional.
Services: Search service, accepts want lists, mail order.
Credit Cards: Yes
Owner: Sherlu R. Walpole
Year Estab: 1979

Sullivan
(Map 20, page 312)

L & B Bookstore   **Open Shop**
61 North Clark Street 63080   (573) 468-3948

Collection: General stock of mostly paperback.
# of Vols: 1 million (See Comments)
Hours: Mon-Sat 9-5.
Travel: Sullivan exit off I-44. East on Springfield then right on N. Clark.
Credit Cards: No
Owner: Joyce King
Year Estab: 1949
Comments: We can recall one or two other occasions when we were advised by a
                book dealer that they had "one million" books in stock; even if 90% of
                them were paperback, as 100,000 hardcover books would represent a
                substantial collection, we try to check out such shops when on the
                road. When we visited this shop, we found it indeed to be overwhelm-
                ingly paperback and the owner confirmed her estimate of one million
                books, telling us there were more books in the back room and in
                storage. We looked at the nominal number of hardcover books on the
                shelves and were not impressed. (We had been told over the phone that
                the collection was approximately 25% hardcover.) We also had trouble
                walking between the aisles. Need we say more. P.S. Don't bother
                bringing your calculator if you're planning to count up to one million.

Vienna
(Map 20, page 312)

Americana Antiques   * **By Appointment**
HCR 71, Box 16 65582   (573) 422-3505

Collection: General stock and ephemera.

# of Vols:	50,000
Specialties:	Missouri
*Hours:**	Open most weekends 10-6 (later in summer) and summer weekdays 6pm-8pm but best to call ahead.
Services:	Accepts want lists, mail order.
Travel:	On Rte 63, 1/2 mile north of intersection with Rte 42.
Credit Cards:	No
Owner:	John Viessman
Year Estab:	1970

Webb City
(Map 20, page 312)

Fireside Bookstore   **Open Shop**
2615 North Range Line Road 64870   (417) 782-1785

Collection:	General stock of paperback and hardcover.
# of Vols:	15,000
Hours:	Mon-Sat 10-6:30.
Travel:	Joplin exit off I-44. Proceed north on Range Line (Bus Rte 71).
Credit Cards:	No
Year Estab:	1996
Comments:	Stock is approximately 65% paperback.

M & M Books   **Open Shop**
906 West 5th Street   (417) 673-1486
Mailing address: PO Box 422 Webb City MO 64870

Collection:	General stock of paperback and hardcover.
# of Vols:	500,000+ (See Comments)
Hours:	Mon-Sat 8-5.
Services:	Appraisals, accepts want lists, mail order.
Travel:	Range Line Rd exit off I-44. Proceed north on Bus Rte 71 then right on W. 5th St.
Credit Cards:	No
Owner:	Martha Rutherford
Year Estab:	1962
Comments:	Located in what appeared to be a private residence, this extremely crowded shop has books galore; trying to view them, though, can be a problem as they're tightly packed and the aisles are very narrow. The shop has more paperbacks than hardcover books and the majority of hardcover items appeared to be fairly common and were in mixed condition. The owner indicates that she has additional books in a rear storage area (we saw perhaps 20,000 volumes in the store) and that if you call a day or two ahead of your planned visit, she'll make an effort to locate the books you're looking for. Our best guess is that if you're looking for a truly rare item, your chances of finding it here depend largely on your ability to locate a needle in the proverbial haystack.

Mail Order Dealers

Bell's Books & Candles   (314) 427-2374
2450 Ashland Avenue Sycamore Hills 63114

Collection:	Specialty
# of Vols:	20,000
Specialties:	American history; religion (Methodism); poetry; Heritage Press.
Services:	Accepts want lists.
Credit Cards:	No
Owner:	David H. Bell
Year Estab:	1970

The Book Barn   (660) 947-3585
1306 Union Unionville 63565   E-mail: klcasady@nemr.net
Web page: www.abebooks.com/home/BOOKBARN

Collection:	General stock of hardcover and paperback.
# of Vols:	5,000
Services:	Search service.
Credit Cards:	Yes
Owner:	Kari Casady
Year Estab:	1997

Deerlilly Farms   (314) 587-2665
389 Lewis Road Crescent 63025   Fax: (314) 587-9795
Web page: www.deerlilly.com   E-mail: deerlilly@usa.net

Collection:	Specialty new and used.
Specialties:	Cookbooks; gardening; fashion; country houses; decorative arts; biography as it relates to the above specialties.
Credit Cards:	Yes
Owner:	Lynn Hamilton
Year Estab:	1989
Comments:	Stock is approximately 60% new.

John Hajicek   (816) 220-3141
3514 Saddle Ridge Drive Independence 64057   (800) 862-5667
Web page: www.mormonism.com   Fax: (816) 220-3142
                                            E-mail: hajicek@mormonism.com

Collection:	General stock.
# of Vols:	15,000
Specialties:	Mormon Americana.
Services:	Appraisals, search service, catalog, accepts want lists.
Credit Cards:	No
Year Estab:	1980

E. Llewellyn, Bookseller   (816) 942-0259
9939 Walnut Drive, #101 Kansas City 64114

Collection:	General stock.

# of Vols:	10,000
Specialties:	Children's; illustrated.
Services:	Lists, accepts want lists (in specialty fields only).
Credit Cards:	No
Year Estab:	1977

Marvelous Books (314) 458-3301
PO Box 1510 Ballwin 63022
Fax: (314) 273-5452
E-mail: marvlous@interloc.com

Collection:	Specialty
# of Vols:	1,000
Specialties:	Children's; illustrated.
Services:	Appraisals, search service, catalog, accepts want lists.
Credit Cards:	Yes
Owner:	Dede Kern
Year Estab:	1974

Mythos Books (573) 785-7710
218 Hickory Meadow Lane Poplar Bluff 63901
E-mail: dwynn@ldd.net

Collection:	Specialty new and used, hardcover and paperback and ephemera.
# of Vols:	5,000
Specialties:	H.P. Lovecraft; horror; weird fiction; small press items.
Services:	Appraisals, search service, catalog, accepts want lists.
Credit Cards:	Yes
Owner:	David Wynn
Year Estab:	1995
Comments:	Collection may also be viewed by appointment.

Peddler's Wagon (417) 682-3734
PO Box 109 Lamar 64759

Collection:	Specialty books and magazines.
# of Vols:	7,500
Specialties:	Needlepoint and other needle arts; quilting; children's (20th century).
Services:	Search service, catalog, accepts want lists.
Credit Cards:	Yes
Owner:	Beverlee & Bob Reimers
Year Estab:	1985

Dan Pekios Books (573) 334-3856
1425 North Henderson Street Cape Girardeau 63701

Collection:	General stock of mostly hardcover.
# of Vols:	5,000
Services:	Accepts want lists.
Credit Cards:	No
Year Estab:	1985
Comments:	Also displays at St. Marys Antique Mall in St. Marys.

Purple Shamrock   (417) 831-3966
PO Box 3595 Springfield 65808   Fax: (417) 831-5518
                                                 E-mail: dbannigan@aol.com

Collection: Specialty new and used.
# of Vols: 3,000
Specialties: Dogs
Services: Accepts want lists.
Owner: Darcy Bannigan
Year Estab: 1973

Rev. D.A. Schroeder   (573) 302-0380
PO Box 1388 Lake Ozark 65049   Fax: (573) 302-1091
                                                  E-mail: oldbooks@juno.com

Collection: Specialty
Specialties: Religion (mostly pastoral helps, sermons, commentaries, reference
                   works, etc.).
Services: Catalog
Credit Cards: No
Year Estab: 1980

WXICOF   (314) 828-5100
914 Riske Lane Wentzville 63385   Fax: (314) 828-5431

Collection: Specialty new and used.
# of Vols: 7,500
Specialties: Natural history; animal breeding and raising; cookbooks; children's
                   titles dealing with animals and related subjects.
Services: Catalog
Credit Cards: Yes
Owner: Coreen Eaton
Year Estab: 1975
Comments: Stock is approximately 70% new.

Ex Libris
Frederick Eugene Hartnell

OHIO

Alphabetical Listing By Dealer

A Novel Idea	408	Matthew Bisiotti & Company	363
A Place in History	392	Bonnett's Book Store	387
A-1 Bookstore	367	The Book Beat	401
AAA I-70 Antique Mall	406	The Book Harbor	412
ABT Books	403	Book Outlet	389
Acorn Bookshop	382	Book Place	374
Admirable Books	394	The Book Shelf	399
After Five Booksellers	417	The Book Shop & Comic Stop	393
AJ's Books	400	The Book Shoppe	387
Alice's Book Shelf	391	The Book Store	393
All Things Victorian	374	Bookcase Coffeehouse	386
Almond Tree Antiques	359	Bookery Fantasy	390
Antiques at Hall House	396	Bookhaven of Springfield	406
Archer's Used And Rare Books	395	The Bookman Of Kent	417
Argonne Books	417	The Bookmark	411
Around About Books	411	Bookphil Out of Print & Signed	395
The Asphodel Book Shop	366	Books And More	408
Athens Book Center	363	Books and Things	359
Attenson's Coventry Antiq.& Books	381	Books In Stock	413
Augnat Book Exchange	386	Books N' Things	416
Avebury Books	365	Books Of The Ages	418
B & D Collectibles	411	Books on High	383
Barbie's Books	400	Books On Main	390
Bay Books	365	The Bookseller	359
Beechwold Books	383	Bookstore	367
Bell, Book & Candle Store	406	Bookworm & Bugjuice	418
Bible Scholar Books	417	Bookworm's Buffet	382
Bibliomania Book Store	417	The Bookworm	369
Bishop Of Books	407	Brad's Bookstore	398

Broadway Antique Mall	396	Hahn's House of Mystery	371
Browse Awhile Books	409	Half Price Books	371
Buckeye Bookshop	360	Half Price Books	384
Carol Butcher Books	418	Half Price Books	388
Candy Books	418	Half Price Books	405
Cap'n Books Treasure Chest	410	Half Price Books	371
Carpenter's Books	364	Half Price Books	399
Cattermole 20thC Children's Books	402	Half Price Books	384
Choir Loft Used Books	394	Half Price Books	384
Cindamar	402	Richard A. Hand, Bookseller	420
Circleback Books	369	Harry's Book Room	361
Cleveland Antiquarian Books	376	Susan Heller - Pages for Sages	377
Collector Book and Print Gallery	369	Hoffman's Bookshop	384
Collectors' Choice	403	Gordon W. Huber	420
Copperfield & Twist Bookstore	415	J.R. Huber, Bookseller	420
Country Closet	389	Invisible Ink: Books on Ghosts	420
Cover to Cover	364	Sheldon Jaffery: Books	377
Crossroad Rare Books & Bindery	397	Jeffrey's Antique Gallery	391
Dark Star Books & Comics	414	Junction Antique Mall	365
Dark Star Books & Comics	387	Kaldi's Coffeehouse & Bookstore	371
Mike DeBaptiste, Books	418	Peter Keisogloff Rare Books	377
Diane's Book Den	395	Kenyon College Bookstore	391
Dickens' Book Shop	396	Owen D. Kubik Fine Books	388
Discount Books	376	Tony Lamy, Bookseller	420
Dragon's Lair	387	Leyshon's Books Etc.	421
The Dust Jacket	370	The Library Friend's Shop	372
Duttenhofer's Books	370	The Literate Veteran	421
Charles David Dyer - Books	398	The Little Bookshop	412
Elegant Book & Map Co.	418	Little Journeys Bookshop	397
Enchanted Books, Antiques, Etc.	392	Little Professor Book Company	372
Bruce Ferrini Rare Books	361	Lofthouse Books	362
Fickes Crime Fiction	419	Loganberry Books	377
Fireside Book Company	383	The Looking Glass	414
C.H. Fischer, Books	419	Lyn's Books & Miniatures	415
Flea Market Books	394	Mac's Backs Paperbacks	381
Foul Play	412	Maggie McGiggles Antiques	399
W.K. Freedley's Books	410	Marrow of Tradition Books	361
Friends of the Library Bookstore	416	Medina Antique Mall	399
Frogtown Books	410	Jerry Merkel	421
Good Ol' Days Books	419	Miller's Antique Market	397
Goodwill Industries Book Store	361	A.A. Miran Arts and Books	421
Goodwill Industries Book Store	415	Munchkin Book Shop	408
Grand Antique Mall	370	Murder By The Book	421
D. Gratz, Books	419	Murder Is Served	388
Grave Matters - Mysteries	371	My Bookhouse	409
Grounds For Thought	366	Jeffrey Neumann	422

North Coast Americana	403	Second Hand Romance & More	373
North Coast Paper Mill	422	Second Shelf	388
Novelty Shop	405	Second Stage Books	396
Ohio Book Store	372	Significant Books	373
Ohio Valley Goodwill Industries	372	Six Steps Down Bookstore	379
Old Erie Street Bookstore	378	John Wallace Skinner Americana	379
Olde Pages Book Shoppe	389	Snowball Bookshop	364
Out of Print Books	378	Springfield Antiques Center	407
Owl Creek Books	422	Stagecoach Antiques	362
Kal Palnicki	422	Strange Birds Books	424
Paper Peddlers	406	Sunday Creek Books	363
Paragraphs Bookstore	401	Susie's	362
Mike Parise, Books	422	Sweet Caroline's	364
Pauper's Books	366	Tabula Rasa	425
Pioneer Antique Mall	403	Tally Ho Studios	425
Professional Book Service	423	Theron's Country Flea Market	382
Publix Books	423	Lila Trudel Books	425
R & K Book Exchange	423	Twice-Loved Books	415
R & R Books	423	Twice Told Tales	391
Ramtek International	424	The Village Bookshelf	398
Rare Book Store	379	Village Bookshop	414
The Rare Bookworm	424	Volunteers of America	386
R.D. Book Search	423	John Wade	425
Readers' Garden	393	West Hill Antiques	362
The Reading Doctor	401	Whimward Books	400
Regarding Books	424	White Cliffs of Dover Bookshop	405
ReReadables	399	Karen Wickliff Books	386
Philip Riggs, Books	373	Willisonian Institute	374
Robert Joseph Co.	373	Wonderland Books	381
Rowsburg Bookstore	404	Wood Stock	374
L.J. Ryan, Scholarly Books	385	The World of Books	413
Sandusky Street Books	388	Yannigan's	404
Joseph F. Scheetz Antiquarian Books	424	Ye Olde Book Shoppe	404
Science Book Service	401	John T. Zubal, Inc.	380

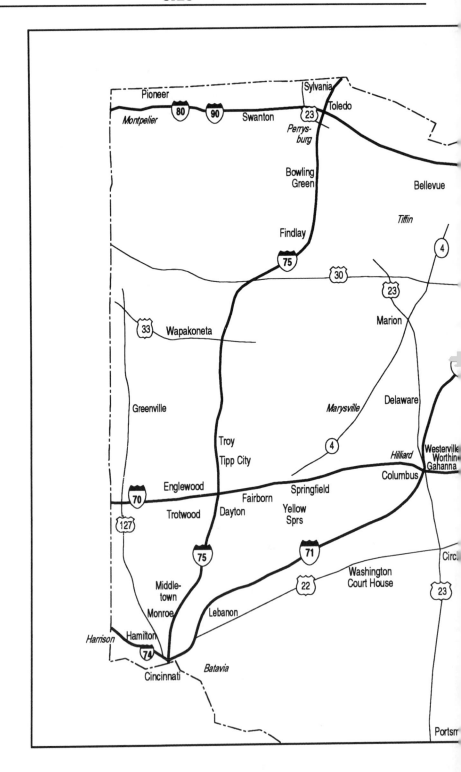

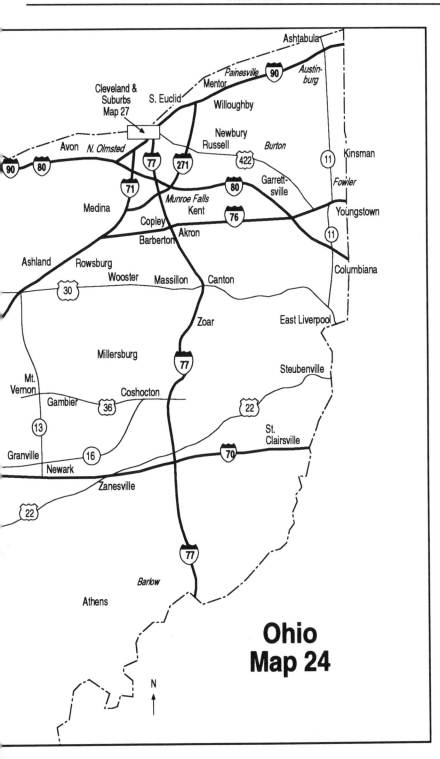

Ohio
Map 24

Alphabetical Listing By Location

Location	Dealer	Page
Akron	Almond Tree Antiques	359
	Books and Things	359
	The Bookseller	359
	Buckeye Bookshop	360
	Bruce Ferrini Rare Books	361
	Fickes Crime Fiction	419
	Goodwill Industries Book Store	361
	Harry's Book Room	361
	Marrow of Tradition Books & Fine Arts Gallery	361
	Stagecoach Antiques	362
	Tabula Rasa	425
	West Hill Antiques	362
Alliance	Bible Scholar Books (and Liberty Archives)	417
Ashland	Susie's	362
Ashtabula	Lofthouse Books	362
Athens	Athens Book Center	363
	Sunday Creek Books	363
Austinburg	Matthew Bisiotti & Company	363
Avon	Sweet Caroline's at the Williams House	364
Barberton	Snowball Bookshop	364
Barlow	Carpenter's Books	364
Batavia	Books Of The Ages	418
	Cover to Cover	364
Bay Village	Bay Books	365
Bellevue	Junction Antique Mall	365
Bluffton	D. Gratz, Books	419
Boardman	Joseph F. Scheetz Antiquarian Books	424
Bowling Green	Avebury Books	365
	Grounds For Thought	366
	Pauper's Books	366
Burton	The Asphodel Book Shop	366
Cambridge	Elegant Book & Map Co.	418
Campbell	Mike Parise, Books	422
Canton	A-1 Bookstore	367
	Tally Ho Studios	425
Cincinnati	Bookstore	367
	The Bookworm	369
	Circleback Books	369
	Collector Book and Print Gallery	369
	The Dust Jacket	370
	Duttenhofer's Books	370
	Grand Antique Mall	370
	Grave Matters - Mysteries	371
	Hahn's House of Mystery	371

Cincinnati	Half Price Books, Records, Magazines	371
	Kaldi's Coffeehouse & Bookstore	371
	Tony Lamy, Bookseller	420
	The Library Friend's Shop	372
	Little Professor Book Company	372
	Ohio Book Store	372
	Ohio Valley Goodwill Industries Tri-County Store	372
	Regarding Books	424
	Philip Riggs, Books	373
	Robert Joseph Co.	373
	Second Hand Romance & More	373
	Significant Books	373
	John Wade	425
	Willisonian Institute	374
	Wood Stock	374
Circleville	All Things Victorian	374
Cleveland	Book Place	374
	Bookworm & Bugjuice	418
	Cleveland Antiquarian Books	376
	Mike DeBaptiste, Books	418
	Discount Books	376
	Susan Heller - Pages for Sages	377
	Sheldon Jaffery: Books	377
	Peter Keisogloff Rare Books	377
	The Literate Veteran	421
	Loganberry Books	377
	Old Erie Street Bookstore	378
	Out of Print Books	378
	Publix Books	423
	Rare Book Store	379
	Six Steps Down Bookstore	379
	John Wallace Skinner Americana	379
	John T. Zubal, Inc.	380
Cleveland Heights	After Five Booksellers	417
	Attenson's Coventry Antiques & Books	381
	Mac's Backs Paperbacks	381
	Wonderland Books	381
Columbiana	Bookworm's Buffet	382
	Theron's Country Flea Market	382
Columbus	Acorn Bookshop	382
	Beechwold Books	383
	Books on High	383
	Fireside Book Company	383
	Half Price Books, Records, Magazines	384
	Hoffman's Bookshop	384
	Leyshon's Books Etc.	421

Columbus	A.A. Miran Arts and Books	421
	Kal Palnicki	422
	L.J. Ryan, Scholarly Books	385
	Volunteers of America	386
	Karen Wickliff Books	386
Copley	Augnat Book Exchange	386
Cortland	Argonne Books	417
Coshocton	Bookcase Coffeehouse	386
Cuyahoga Falls	Gordon W. Huber	420
Dayton	Bonnett's Book Store	387
	The Book Shoppe	387
	Dark Star Books & Comics	387
	Dragon's Lair	387
	Half Price Books, Records, Magazines	388
	Invisible Ink: Books on Ghosts & Hauntings	420
	Owen D. Kubik Fine Books	388
	Murder Is Served	388
	Professional Book Service	423
	R & R Books	423
	Second Shelf	388
Delaware	Sandusky Street Books	388
Doylestown	Good Ol' Days Books	419
East Liverpool	Country Closet	389
Englewood	Olde Pages Book Shoppe	389
Fairborn	Book Outlet	389
	Bookery Fantasy	390
Findlay	Books On Main	390
	Jeffrey's Antique Gallery	391
Fowler	Alice's Book Shelf	391
Gahanna	Twice Told Tales	391
Gambier	Kenyon College Bookstore	391
Garrettsville	Enchanted Books, Antiques, Etc.	392
Goshen	R.D. Book Search	423
Granville	A Place in History	392
	Readers' Garden	393
	The Book Store	393
Hamilton	The Book Shop & Comic Stop	393
	Choir Loft Used Books	394
Harrison	Flea Market Books	394
Hayesville	North Coast Paper Mill	422
Hilliard	Admirable Books	394
	Bookphil Out of Print & Signed	395
Hudson	C.H. Fischer, Books	419
Kent	Archer's Used And Rare Books	395
	The Bookman Of Kent	417
Kinsman	Diane's Book Den	395

Lakewood	Antiques at Hall House	396
	Second Stage Books	396
Lebanon	Broadway Antique Mall	396
	Dickens' Book Shop	396
	Miller's Antique Market	397
Lewis Center	Bibliomania Book Store	417
Lima	J.R. Huber, Bookseller	420
Mansfield	Crossroad Rare Books & Bindery	397
	Little Journeys Bookshop	397
Marion	Brad's Bookstore	398
Marysville	Charles David Dyer - Books	398
Massillon	The Village Bookshelf	398
Mayfield Heights	Half Price Books, Records, Magazines	399
Medina	The Book Shelf	399
	Medina Antique Mall	399
Mentor	Maggie McGiggles Antiques	399
	ReReadables	399
Middletown	Barbie's Books	400
Millersburg	AJ's Books	400
	Whimward Books	400
Monroe	The Book Beat	401
Montpelier	Science Book Service	401
Mount Vernon	Owl Creek Books	422
	Paragraphs Bookstore	401
Munroe Falls	The Reading Doctor	401
Newark	Cindamar	402
Newbury	Cattermole 20thC Children's Books	402
North Olmsted	ABT Books	403
Norton	Murder By The Book	421
Norwalk	Ramtek International	424
Norwood	Strange Birds Books	424
Painesville	North Coast Americana	403
Perrysburg	Collectors' Choice	403
Pioneer	Pioneer Antique Mall	403
Portsmouth	Ye Olde Book Shoppe	404
Rocky River	Yannigan's	404
Rowsburg	Rowsburg Bookstore	404
Russell	Novelty Shop	405
Saint Clairsville	White Cliffs of Dover Bookshop	405
Shaker Heights	Half Price Books, Records, Magazines	405
South Euclid	Paper Peddlers	406
Springfield	AAA I-70 Antique Mall	406
	Bell, Book & Candle Store	406
	Bookhaven of Springfield	406
	Springfield Antiques Center	407
Steubenville	Bishop Of Books	407

Struthers	R & K Book Exchange	423
Swanton	Munchkin Book Shop	408
	Lila Trudel Books	425
Sylvania	A Novel Idea	408
Tiffin	Books And More	408
	My Bookhouse	409
Tipp City	Browse Awhile Books	409
Toledo	W.K. Freedley's Books	410
	Frogtown Books	410
	The Rare Bookworm	424
Trotwood	Cap'n Books Treasure Chest	410
Troy	Around About Books	411
Wadsworth	Jeffrey Neumann	422
Wapakoneta	The Bookmark	411
Washington Court House	B & D Collectibles	411
Westerville	The Book Harbor	412
	Foul Play	412
	The Little Bookshop	412
Willoughby	The World of Books	413
Wooster	Books In Stock	413
Worthington	Candy Books	418
	The Looking Glass	414
	Village Bookshop	414
Xenia	Jerry Merkel	421
Yellow Springs	Dark Star Books & Comics	414
Youngstown	Carol Butcher Books	418
	Copperfield & Twist Bookstore	415
	Goodwill Industries Book Store	415
	Lyn's Books & Miniatures	415
	Twice-Loved Books	415
Zanesville	Friends of the Library Bookstore	416
	Richard A. Hand, Bookseller	420
Zoar	Books N' Things	416

Akron
(Map 25, page 360 & Map 24, page 352)

Almond Tree Antiques   **By Appointment**
1693 Brookwood Drive 44313   (330) 867-6889
                                                  E-mail: kovacja@sssnet.com

Collection:	General stock.
# of Vols:	500
Specialties:	Children's; cookbooks.
Services:	Accepts want lists, mail order.
Credit Cards:	No
Owner:	Maureen C. Kovach
Year Estab:	1970

Books and Things   **Open Shop**
500 West Exchange Street   (330) 434-2311
Mailing address: 576 Timothy Dr Tallmadge OH 44278   E-mail: rayff@aol.com

Collection:	General stock of hardcover and paperback.
# of Vols:	10,000
Specialties:	Mystery
Hours:	Wed-Fri 11-4. Sat 11-5.
Services:	Search service, accepts want lists.
Travel:	Main St/Broadway exit off I-77/I-76. Proceed north on Broadway to Exchange St, then left on Exchange. Shop is located in a former school.
Credit Cards:	No
Owner:	Ray Steinen
Year Estab:	1994
Comments:	Stock is evenly divided between hardcover and paperback.

The Bookseller   **Open Shop**
174 West Exchange Street 44302   (330) 762-3101
                                                        Fax: (330)762-4413
                                              E-mail: booklein@interloc.com

Collection:	General stock.
# of Vols:	20,000+
Specialties:	Ohio; aviation; military.
Hours:	Mon-Sat 10-5:30. Sun 1-5.
Services:	Appraisals, search service, catalog, accepts want lists.
Travel:	See Books & Things above. Shop is on left, just past Locust. Parking is available in the rear.
Credit Cards:	Yes
Owner:	Frank & Andrea Klein
Year Estab:	1946
Comments:	It was quite refreshing for us to return to this shop some 3½ years after it had suffered a terrible fire to find that "all is well in bookland." The shop houses a modest but significant collection of books in most subject areas. Prices are reasonable. The books are in good condition and the shop is easy to browse.

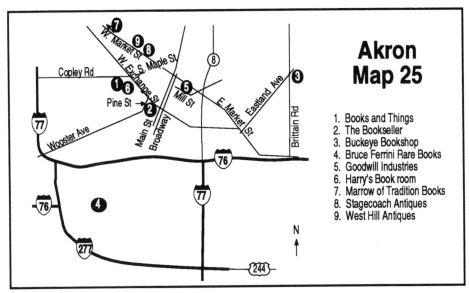

Akron Map 25

1. Books and Things
2. The Bookseller
3. Buckeye Bookshop
4. Bruce Ferrini Rare Books
5. Goodwill Industries
6. Harry's Book room
7. Marrow of Tradition Books
8. Stagecoach Antiques
9. West Hill Antiques

Buckeye Bookshop   **Open Shop**
795 Brittain Road 44305   (330) 794-2455
                                           E-mail: buckeye@raex.com

Collection:	General stock of hardcover and paperback.
# of Vols:	40,000
Specialties:	Modern first editions.
Hours:	Mon-Sat 11-7. Sun 1-4.
Services:	Accepts want lists, mail order.
Travel:	Eastbound on I-76: Exit 25B (Brittain Rd/General St) Follow sign for Brittain Rd, then proceed north on Brittain for 1½ miles. Westbound on I-76: Market St exit. Right on Market, left on General, right on Brittain Rd ramp. Continue on Brittain. From Rte 8 southbound: Tallmadge Ave exit. Left on Tallmadge, then south on Brittain.
Credit Cards:	Yes
Owner:	Bill Chappelear
Year Estab:	1989
Comments:	Unlike some used book shops that display their hardcover books along the side walls and fill the middle of the shop with paperbacks, this shop uses its side and back walls for paperbacks and its center space for hardcover books as well as some trade paperbacks. The vast majority of the titles we saw were in splendid condition, most with dust jackets. The store is well organized. Boxes on some of the top shelves are labeled with the names of popular authors suggesting that there is a sufficient supply of "back up" titles. The only downer from our perspective were the piles of books on the floor, some in front of some shelves and others in the front of the shop. There may well have been some wonderful books among those volumes but unfortunately, scanning for titles here would have been an almost impossible task.

Bruce Ferrini Rare Books

754 Kenmore Boulevard 44314
Web page: www.Ferrini.com

Open Shop
(330) 753-7447
Fax: (330) 753-2302
E-mail: Bruceferrini@msn.com

Collection:	Specialty
Specialties:	12th-16th century medieval and renaissance illuminated manuscripts.
Hours:	Mon-Fri 10-5. Sat 12-4. Other times by appointment.
Services:	Catalog
Travel:	Exit 19 (Kenmore Blvd) exit off I-76. Proceed east on Kenmore.
Credit Cards:	Yes
Year Estab:	1974

Goodwill Industries Book Store

185 East Mill Street 44308

Open Shop
(330) 762-8423

Collection:	General stock of hardcover and paperback.
Hours:	Mon-Sat 9:30-6, except Thu till 8. Sun 12-5.
Travel:	Main St/Broadway St exit off I-77/I-76. Proceed north on Broadway, then east on Mill. Shop is just south of Market St.
Comments:	Note: The telephone number listed above is for the main switchboard which will put the caller through to the bookstore.

Harry's Book Room

500 West Exchange Street 44302

Open Shop
(330) 434-2311

Collection:	General stock of mostly hardcover and records.
# of Vols:	15,000
Hours:	Wed-Sat 11-5.
Travel:	See Books & Things above.
Credit Cards:	No
Owner:	Harry Petri
Comments:	The collection includes a broad range of subjects although few are covered in any depth. The hardcover volumes were of mixed vintage and there were enough interesting titles to make a visit here worth your while. Prices were reasonable.

Marrow of Tradition Books & Fine Arts Gallery

1706 West Market Street 44313

Open Shop
(330) 864-8084
Fax: (330) 836-2525

Collection:	General stock of mostly new and some used paperback and hardcover.
# of Vols:	1,500 (used)
Specialties:	Africa; black studies; Caribbean literature.
Hours:	Mon-Fri 11-7. Sat 10-6.
Services:	Appraisals, search service.
Travel:	White Pond/Mull Ave exit off I-77. Proceed north on White Pond, east on Frank and left on Market.
Credit Cards:	Yes
Owner:	Nathan Oliver
Comments:	Shop also sells African masks, statuary, original art and fine art prints.

Stagecoach Antiques
449 West Market Street 44303

Collection:	General stock and magazines.
# of Vols:	2,000
Specialties:	Ohio
Hours:	Mon-Sat 10-6, except Mon till 8. Sun 12-5.
Services:	Search service, accepts want lists.
Travel:	Main St/Broadway exit off I-77/I-76. Proceed north on Main, then west on West Market. Shop is about 3/4 mile ahead on right.
Credit Cards:	Yes
Owner:	Leo Walter
Year Estab:	1959
Comments:	If you have a fondness for older volumes, and if condition is not that important to you, unlike other antique dealers who frequently over charge for such items, the owner of this establishment prices such volumes in the $1, $2 and $5 range.

West Hill Antiques
461 West Market Street 44303

Antique Mall
(330) 762-6633

Hours:	Mon-Fri 10-5. Sat 10-6. Sun 12-6.
Travel:	See Stagecoach Antiques above. Shop is between Aqueduct and Balch.

Ashland
(Map 24, page 352)

Susie's
59 South Street 44805

Open Shop
(419) 281-3685

Collection:	General stock of mostly used.
# of Vols:	1,000
Specialties:	History; royalty; nature.
Hours:	Mon 1-5. Tue-Sat 10-4, except Fri till 6:30.
Travel:	Rte 250 exit off I-71. Proceed west on Rte 250, then left on Walnut, right on Luther and right on South.
Credit Cards:	No
Year Estab:	1992
Comments:	Shop also sells antiques and gift items.

Ashtabula
(Map 24, page 352)

Lofthouse Books
4611 Main Avenue 44004
Web page: www.knownet.net/users/hloftus

Open Shop
Shop: (440) 992-1425
Home: (440) 969-1090
E-mail: hloftus@knownet.net

Collection:	General stock and ephemera.
# of Vols:	30,000
Hours:	Mon-Sat 11-5. Other times by chance or appointment.
Services:	Search service, accepts want lists, mail order.

Travel:	Rte 11 exit off I-90. Proceed north to Rte 20, then west on Rte 20 across viaduct bridge. After crossing bridge, turn left on Main Ave and continue to center of town.
Credit Cards:	No
Owner:	Sandi & Ed Loftus
Year Estab:	1989
Comments:	We noted the following after visiting this shop at its former location across the street (and under its former name, The Book Peddler). Any shop that provides us with an opportunity to part with a few dollars is always one that we feel is worth recommending to others. This shop was no exception. Modest in size, the shop offers a nice selection in almost every category in both newer and vintage books. Prices were very reasonable.

Athens
(Map 24, page 352)

Athens Book Center   **Open Shop**
747 East State Street 45701   (614) 592-4865

Collection:	General stock of new and used paperback and hardcover.
# of Vols:	5,000 (used)
Hours:	Mon-Sat 9:30-9. Sun 11-5:30.
Services:	Accepts want lists.
Travel:	From Columbus: East State St exit off Rte 33 south. Turn left. Shop is 1/2 mile ahead in Athens Mall.
Credit Cards:	Yes
Owner:	David & Paula Brennan
Year Estab:	1990
Comments:	Used stock is approximately 75% paperback.

Sunday Creek Books   **By Appointment**
PO Box 114 45701   (614) 593-8915

Collection:	General stock.
# of Vols:	12,000
Services:	Appraisals
Credit Cards:	No
Owner:	Jack & Barbara Matthews
Year Estab:	1979

Austinburg
(Map 24, page 352)

Matthew Bisiotti & Company   **By Appointment**
481 State Route 45 44010   (440) 275-1310
Web page: www.abebooks.com/home/DUKE333   Fax: (440) 275-3206
                                                        E-mail: mlb@ncweb.com

Collection:	Specialty
# of Vols:	3,000

Specialties:	Hunting; fishing; equestrian arts; book collecting.
Services:	Appraisals, catalog, search service, accepts want lists.
Credit Cards:	Yes
Year Estab:	1992

Avon
(Map 24, page 352)

Sweet Caroline's at the Williams House   **Antique Mall**
37300 Detroit Road 44011   (216) 934-4605

Hours:	Mon-Sat 10-5. Sun 12-5.
Travel:	Shop is located 1/4 mile west of intersection of Rte 254 & Rte 611.

Barberton
(Map 24, page 352)

Snowball Bookshop   **Open Shop**
564 West Tuscarawas Avenue 44203   (330) 745-9282
                                                    E-mail: booklady@webchamps.com

Collection:	General stock of hardcover and paperback.
# of Vols:	40,000
Specialties:	Religion; personal growth; cookbooks; mystery; romance; biography; science fiction.
Hours:	Mon-Sat 10-7. Sun by appointment.
Services:	Search service, accepts want lists, mail order.
Travel:	Barber Rd exit off Rte 224. Proceed south on Barber Rd for 2½ miles to dead end, then right on Lake, left on 6th St and left on Tuscarawas.
Credit Cards:	Yes
Owner:	Linda Snowball
Year Estab:	1995
Comments:	Stock is approximately 70% hardcover. Also sells book related gift items.

Barlow
(Map 24, page 352)

Carpenter's Books   **By Appointment**
Box 96, Route 550 45712   (614) 678-2602

Collection:	General stock.
# of Vols:	30,000+
Owner:	Glenn Carpenter
Year Estab:	1984

Batavia
(Map 24, page 352)

Cover to Cover   **By Appointment**
5499 Belfast Road 45103   (513) 625-2628
                                                                    Fax: (513) 625-2683
                                                    E-mail: metafouts@aol.com

Collection:	General stock.

# of Vols:	2,000
Services:	Appraisals, search service, accepts want lists, mail order.
Credit Cards:	No
Owner:	Meta Fouts
Year Estab:	1978

Bay Village
(Map 27, page 375)

Bay Books   **Open Shop**
27115 East Oviatt Road   Shop: (440) 892-9191
Mailing address: PO Box 40306 Bay Village OH 44140   Home: (440) 835-5444
Web page: www.abebooks.com   E-mail: baybooks@stratos.net

Collection:	Specialty and ephemera.
# of Vols:	23,000
Specialties:	Americana; architecture; art; photography; atlases; maps; Cleveland; natural history; Ohio; children's; amusements; transportation; travel; history; Western Reserve; trade catalogs.
Hours:	Tue & Wed 10-6. Thu & Fri 1-6. Sat 10-2. Best to call ahead if coming from a distance. Other times by chance or appointment.
Services:	Search service, accepts want lists.
Travel:	Rte 252 exit off I-90. Proceed north on Rte 252, west on Wolf, south on Dover Center and left on East Oviatt.
Credit Cards:	No
Owner:	David N. Harbaugh & Son
Year Estab:	1986
Comments:	A modest sized shop with a selection of books in mostly good condition. Reasonably priced. If you don't see a book that you're looking for, check with the owner as more than half of the stock is located a short distance away and arrangements can be made to bring other titles to the shop.

Bellevue
(Map 24, page 352)

Junction Antique Mall   **Antique Mall**
127 East Main Street 44811   (419) 483-8227

Hours:	Daily 10-6.
Travel:	On Rte 20 in downtown.

Bowling Green
(Map 24, page 352)

Avebury Books   **By Appointment**
PO Box 927 43402   (419) 352-0418
                                                      E-mail: ryan@tweney.com

Collection:	Specialty
# of Vols:	3,000
Specialties:	Science; technology; microscopy; transportation; medicine; psychology.
Services:	Appraisals, catalog, accepts want lists.

Credit Cards:	Yes
Owner:	Ryan D. Tweney & Karin G. Hubert
Year Estab:	1991

Grounds For Thought   **Open Shop**
174 South Main Street 43402   (419) 354-3266

Collection:	General stock of paperback and some hardcover.
# of Vols:	42,000
Specialties:	Mystery; science fiction; social sciences.
Hours:	Daily 7am-midnight.
Services:	Search service, accepts want lists, mail order.
Travel:	Bowling Green exit off I-75. Proceed west on Rte 64 north past Bowling Green State University, then left on Main.
Credit Cards:	Yes
Owner:	Kelly William Wicks
Year Estab:	1989
Comments:	If you're visiting this college town and want to stop for a quick snack, you might enjoy browsing this combination coffee shop/book store which, despite the fact that the overwhelming majority of its stock is paperback, does have a modest selection of mostly reading copy quality hardcover volumes.

Pauper's Books   **Open Shop**
206 North Main Street 43402   (419) 352-2163
Web page: www.wcnet.org/~paupers   E-mail: paupers@wcnet.org

Collection:	General stock of paperback and hardcover.
# of Vols:	110,000
Specialties:	Literature; environment; anarchism; cookbooks (vegetarian).
Hours:	Mon-Sat 10:30-7. Evenings (7:30-10) by chance.
Services:	Accepts want lists.
Travel:	See Grounds For Thought above. Turn right on Main.
Credit Cards:	Yes
Owner:	Shawn P. Wilbur
Year Estab:	1977
Comments:	The vast majority of the books we saw were paperbacks with only a smattering of hardcover volumes, mostly in the subjects listed above as specialties.

Burton
(Map 24, page 352)

The Asphodel Book Shop   **By Appointment**
17192 Ravenna Road 44021   (440) 834-4775

Collection:	Specialty
# of Vols:	6,000-7,000
Specialties:	Literary first editions.
Services:	Appraisals, catalog.

Credit Cards:	No
Owner:	James Lowell
Year Estab:	1963

Canton
(Map 24, page 352)

A-1 Bookstore   **Open Shop**
6067 Navarre Road, SW 44706   (330) 477-0908

Collection:	General stock of mostly used paperback and hardcover.
# of Vols:	20,000
Hours:	Mon-Sat 8-5:30.
Services:	Accepts want lists, mail order.
Travel:	Richville Dr (Rte 627) exit off Rte 30 West. Proceed south on Richville, then east at stop sign/blinker light.
Credit Cards:	No
Owner:	Ruth Braid
Year Estab:	1985
Comments:	If you require used auto parts you might want to browse this shop which is located adjacent to A-1 Used Auto Parts. In addition to a healthy supply of some very reasonably priced Harlequin romances, the shop carries lots of other used paperbacks and a handful of used hardcover volumes. On the other hand, if your car is running smoothly, we don't necessarily recommend a stop here.

Cincinnati
(Map 26, page 368 & Map 24, page 352)

Bookstore   **Open Shop**
454 West McMicken Street 45214   (513) 621-4865

Collection:	General stock.
# of Vols:	100,000
Hours:	Fri-Sun 2-6 (Call after 5pm).
Travel:	From Central Pkwy, turn north on Ravine, then west on McMicken.
Credit Cards:	No
Owner:	Tom Brengelman
Year Estab:	1979
Comments:	After making several wrong turns, we finally located this shop. As has occurred on more than one of our book hunting quests, we have occasionally had different opinions with regard to the desirability of leaving one's vehicle to visit a particular establishment. When we arrived here and one of us lacked the courage to make the visit, it was too late in the day for either of us to win an argument; thus our readers are the losers. We sincerely hope that those readers who are more willing to accept the challenge will share their impressions with us. We were advised by the owner that the stock, approximately 50% of which is paperback, is spread out over four floors.

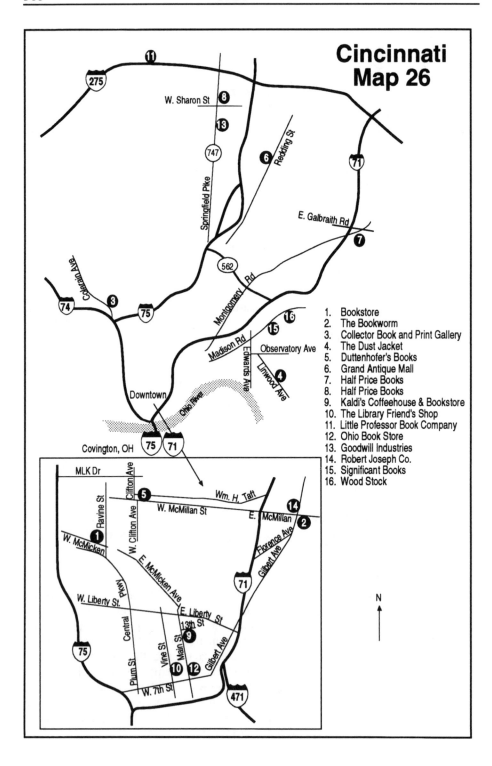

Cincinnati
Map 26

1. Bookstore
2. The Bookworm
3. Collector Book and Print Gallery
4. The Dust Jacket
5. Duttenhofer's Books
6. Grand Antique Mall
7. Half Price Books
8. Half Price Books
9. Kaldi's Coffeehouse & Bookstore
10. The Library Friend's Shop
11. Little Professor Book Company
12. Ohio Book Store
13. Goodwill Industries
14. Robert Joseph Co.
15. Significant Books
16. Wood Stock

The Bookworm
973 East McMillan Street 45206

Open Shop
(513) 221-5777

Collection:	General stock of hardcover and paperback.
# of Vols:	30,000
Specialties:	Black studies; occult; religion; health.
Hours:	Mon-Sat 11-6.
Services:	Search service, accepts want lists.
Travel:	From 1-71 northbound: Florence Ave exit. Proceed north on Florence, then left on Gilbert and right on McMillan. From I-71 southbound: Wm. H. Taft exit. Proceed 1/2 block to McMillan, then left on McMillan.
Credit Cards:	No
Year Estab:	1974
Comments:	Stock is approximately 50% paperback.

Circleback Books
707 Doepke Lane 45231

By Appointment
(513) 522-8421
E-mail: CircleBack@fuse.net

Collection:	Specialty
# of Vols:	8,000
Specialties:	Children's, including illustrated, prize winning authors, reference books about children's literature and history for children.
Services:	Occasional catalog, accepts want lists, mail order.
Owner:	Joyce Cauffield
Year Estab:	1992

Collector Book and Print Gallery
1801 Chase Avenue 45223

Open Shop
(513) 543-6600
(513) 385-7271

Collection:	Specialty hardcover and paperback books, ephemera and prints.
# of Vols:	10,000
Specialties:	Modern and hypermodern literature; regional history and literature; mystery; autographs; maps; lithographs, etchings.
Hours:	Wed, Sat & Sun 1-5.
Services:	Appraisals, search service, accepts want lists, mail order.
Travel:	Colerain Ave exit off I-74. Proceed west on Colerain (Rte 127 north), north on Florida, east on Chase. At corner of Chase and Kirby.
Credit Cards:	No
Owner:	Roger Stephens
Year Estab:	1993
Comments:	When we entered this shop, the owner advised us that he was in the process of "reorganizing" which may explain why we found it difficult to follow our usual procedure of walking around the shop viewing as many volumes as possible. In all honesty, we could not evaluate the hardcover collection as trying to maneuver through the aisles to view titles and examine condition presented too much of a challenge for this weary traveller. Should you have a chance to stop by once the shop has been "reorganized," please share your impressions with us.

(Cincinnati)

The Dust Jacket   **Open Shop**
3200 Linwood Avenue 45226   (513) 871-4224
                                              Fax: (513) 321-3862
                                          E-mail: dj3200@aol.com

Collection:	General stock.
# of Vols:	20,000
Specialties:	Modern first editions; history; military; natural history; fine bindings.
Hours:	Mon-Sat 11-5, except Wed & Thu till 8.
Services:	Appraisals, search service, mail order, accepts want lists.
Travel:	Exit 6 off I-71. Proceed southeast on Rte 561 for about two miles to Mt. Lookout Square.
Credit Cards:	Yes
Owner:	Sam Jenike & Phil Metz
Year Estab:	1980
Comments:	We were delighted to be able to visit this shop which we missed on our earlier visit to Cincinnati. The specialties listed above are represented by an assortment of outstanding titles, the vast majority of which were in excellent condition. Just walking from one section of the shop to another and viewing titles that are rarely seen in the average used book shop gives one a sense that this is a shop that appreciative book people will enjoy browsing. If after visiting this establishment you don't agree with us, we may consider giving up our book travels.

Duttenhofer's Books   **Open Shop**
214 West McMillan Street 45219   (513) 381-1340

Collection:	General stock of mostly hardcover.
# of Vols:	40,000
Specialties:	First editions; poetry.
Hours:	Mon-Fri 10-9. Sat 10-6. Sun 11-6.
Services:	Appraisals, accepts want lists, mail order, book bindery.
Travel:	Southbound on I-71: Wm.H.Taft exit. Proceed on Taft which becomes Calhoun and then dead ends at Clifton. Left on Clifton, then left on McMillan. From I-75 (either direction): Exit 3 (Hopple St). Proceed north on Hopple which becomes Martin Luther King, then right on Clifton. At dead end, turn left on McMillan.
Credit Cards:	Yes
Owner:	Russell J. Speidel
Year Estab:	1976
Comments:	A large bi-level shop with a healthy collection of good quality hardcover books. Well worth a visit.

Grand Antique Mall   **Antique Mall**
9701 Reading Road 45215   (513) 554-1919

Hours:	Mon-Sat 10-6. Sun 12-6.
Travel:	Exit 14 off I-75. Proceed east on Glendale-Milford Rd for about one mile, then right on Reading.

Grave Matters - Mysteries
PO Box 32192 45232
Web page: www.gravematters.com

By Appointment
(513) 242-7527
Fax: (513) 242-5115
E-mail: books@gravematters.com

Collection:	Specialty new and used, hardcover and paperback.
# of Vols:	20,000
Specialties:	Mystery; Sherlock Holmes; first editions; vintage paperbacks; mystery reference; pulps; magazines.
Services:	Catalog, accepts want lists.
Credit Cards:	Yes
Owner:	Alice Ann Carpenter & John Leininger
Year Estab:	1986

Hahn's House of Mystery
8414 Arundel Court 45231

By Appointment
(513) 521-4661
E-mail: mystbooks@fuse.net

Collection:	Specialty
# of Vols:	6,000
Specialties:	Mystery; hypermodern fiction; proofs; ARCS, signed. (Primarily first editions in collectible condition).
Services:	Accepts want lists.
Credit Cards:	No
Owner:	Robert C. Hahn
Year Estab:	1993

Half Price Books, Records, Magazines
11389 Princeton Road 45246

Open Shop
(513) 772-1511

Collection:	General stock of new and used paperback and hardcover.
Hours:	Mon-Sat 10-10. Sun 11-7.
Travel:	Exit 42 (Princeton Rd/Rte 747) off I-275. Proceed south on Princeton to the Gentry-Tricentre Shopping Center.

Half Price Books, Records, Magazines
8118 Montgomery Road 45236

Open Shop
(513) 891-7170

Collection:	General stock of new and used paperback and hardcover.
Hours:	Mon-Sat 10-10. Sun 11-7.
Travel:	Exit 12 (Montgomery Rd) off I-71. Proceed east on Montgomery to Kenwood Galleria shopping center.

Kaldi's Coffeehouse & Bookstore
1204 Main Street 45210

Open Shop
(513) 241-3070

Collection:	General stock of paperback and hardcover.
# of Vols:	20,000
Specialties:	Mystery; poetry.
Hours:	Mon-Fri 7am-1am, except Fri to 2am. Sat & Sun 10am-2am.
Travel:	Downtown, just north of 12th Street.
Credit Cards:	Yes

(Cincinnati)

Owner:	Sonya McDonnell & Michael Markiewicz
Year Estab:	1992
Comments:	A legitimate used book shop, not just a coffee house with some paperbacks. The stock is a combination of vintage paperbacks (several with the older, more popular, i.e., lurid covers) and mixed vintage hardcover volumes of every description. With some exceptions, the hardcover items were not necessarily shelved in any logical order, but there were some interesting and indeed some collectible titles. If the neighborhood doesn't intimidate you, you might stop by for a cup of java and a quick browse. The shop is also a full service restaurant that presents live music on weekends as well as poetry readings.

The Library Friend's Shop   **Open Shop**
800 Vine Street 45202   (513) 369-6920

Collection:	General stock of hardcover and paperback.
Hours:	Mon-Sat 10-4. Sun 1-4.
Travel:	Downtown, between 8th & 9th Sts. Entrance is from the public library.

Little Professor Book Company   **Open Shop**
1018 Forest Fair Drive 45240   (513) 671-9797

Collection:	General stock of mostly new.
# of Vols:	1,000 (used)
Hours:	Mon-Sat 10-9. Sun 12-5.
Comments:	Used books are ex library copies.

Ohio Book Store   **Open Shop**
726 Main Street 45202   (513) 621-5142
                                                          Fax: (513) 621-7941

Collection:	General stock.
# of Vols:	350,000
Specialties:	Ohio; Kentucky; history; Americana.
Hours:	Mon-Sat 9-4:45.
Services:	Appraisals, subject catalogs, book binding.
Travel:	7th St exit off I-75. Proceed to downtown. Shop is at corner of 8th St and Main.
Credit Cards:	Yes
Owner:	Jim Fallon
Year Estab:	1940
Comments:	Five stories high, this shop houses, without question, the city's largest collection of used books. Leave yourself plenty of time for browsing. Every subject area is covered and prices, we believe, are very reasonable.

Ohio Valley Goodwill Industries Tri-County Store   **Open Shop**
10600 Springfield Pike 45215   (513) 771-4804

Collection:	General stock of paperback and hardcover.
# of Vols:	500-1,000

Hours:	Mon-Sat 9:30-8. Sun 12-5:30.
Travel:	Rte 747 exit off I-275. Proceed south on Rte 747 for two miles.
Comments:	Smaller collections are available at other Goodwill stores in the city.

Philip Riggs, Books   **By Appointment**
5434 Cindy Lane 45239   (513) 541-4096

Collection:	Specialty books and ephemera.
# of Vols:	2,000
Specialties:	Hunting; fishing; guns; baseball.
Services:	Appraisals, search service, accepts want lists, mail order.
Credit Cards:	No
Year Estab:	1982

Robert Joseph Co.   **Open Shop**
2531 Gilbert Avenue 45206   (513) 559-1704

Collection:	General stock.
# of Vols:	100,000
Specialties:	Art; biography.
Hours:	Mon-Fri 9:30-3. Other times by appointment.
Services:	Appraisals, search service, accepts want lists, mail order.
Travel:	Northbound on I-71: Florence Ave exit. Continue uphill to first light, then left on Gilbert and left on Melrose. Shop is just ahead on second floor. Southbound on I-71: See The Bookworm above.
Credit Cards:	Yes
Owner:	Robert J. Fanning
Year Estab:	1990

Second Hand Romance & More   **Open Shop**
132 West Benson Street 45215   (513) 821-6695

Collection:	General stock of mostly paperback.
# of Vols:	8,000+
Hours:	Tue-Fri 11-6:30. Sat 9-4:30.

Significant Books   **Open Shop**
3053 Madison Road   (513) 321-7567
Mailing address: PO Box 9248 Cincinnati OH 45209   E-mail: signbook@iac.net
Web page: www.iac.net/~signbook

Collection:	General stock
# of Vols:	26,000+
Specialties:	Non fiction.
Hours:	Mon 12-6. Tue-Thu 12-9. Fri & Sat 12-6. Sun by chance or appointment.
Services:	Appraisals, search service.
Travel:	From I-71 southbound: Exit 6. Turn east and proceed to second light (Madison). Turn left. From I-71 northbound: Exit 6. Turn right at exit, left on Edward, right on Markbreit and left on Madison. Parking is available in rear.
Credit Cards:	Yes

Owner:	Bill & Carolyn Downing
Year Estab:	1978
Comments:	This shop is up one flight but the climb is worth it. The shop is also much larger than one's initial impression so give yourself time to meander through its many nooks and crannies. The shop offers a nice assortment of mixed vintage books in almost every category with many subjects represented by some fine titles. Reasonably priced.

Willisonian Institute **By Appointment**
1609 Chase Avenue 45223 (513) 542-5231

Collection:	General stock.
# of Vols:	5,000
Services:	Accepts want lists.
Credit Cards:	No
Owner:	David Willis
Year Estab:	1988

Wood Stock **Antique Mall**
At Duck Creek Mall, 3715 Madison Road Mall: (513) 321-0900
Mailing address: 4385 Antioch Rd New Vienna OH 45159 Home: (937) 987-2602

Collection:	General stock and ephemera.
Hours:	Mon-Sat 10-5. Sun 12-5.
Travel:	Ridge St exit off Rte 562 (Norwood Lateral). Proceed east on Ridge to Madison, then left on Madison.
Owner:	Wilma Wood

Circleville
(Map 24, page 352)

All Things Victorian **Open Shop**
424 South Court Street 43113 (614) 474-6257

Collection:	General stock.
# of Vols:	3,000
Specialties:	All non fiction.
Hours:	Mon-Fri 10-7. Weekends by appointment.
Travel:	Court St exit off Rte 23. Proceed east on Court St.
Credit Cards:	Yes
Owner:	Donna Brewer
Year Estab:	1978

Cleveland
(Map 27, page 375 & Map 24, page 352)

Book Place **Open Shop**
3853 Pearl Road 44109 (216) 398-1145

Collection:	General stock of mostly paperback.
# of Vols:	10,000
Hours:	Mon-Sat 11-6.

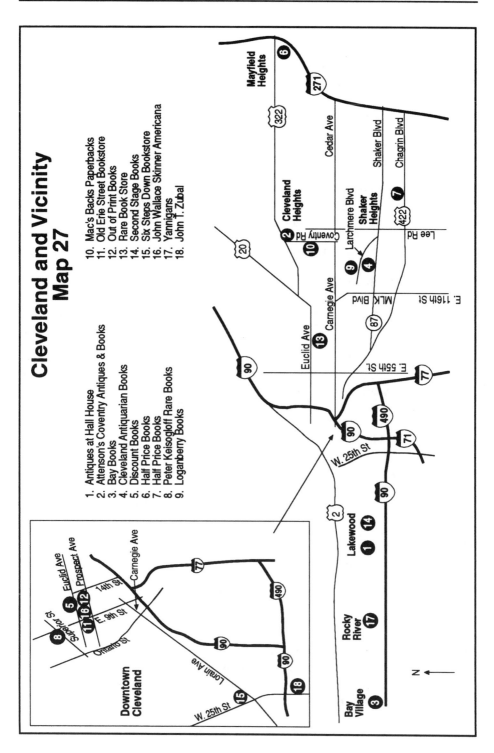

Cleveland and Vicinity
Map 27

1. Antiques at Hall House
2. Attenson's Coventry Antiques & Books
3. Bay Books
4. Cleveland Antiquarian Books
5. Discount Books
6. Half Price Books
7. Half Price Books
8. Peter Keisogloff Rare Books
9. Loganberry Books
10. Mac's Backs Paperbacks
11. Old Erie Street Bookstore
12. Out of Print Books
13. Rare Book Store
14. Second Stage Books
15. Six Steps Down Bookstore
16. John Wallace Skinner Americana
17. Yannigans
18. John T. Zubal

(Cleveland)

Cleveland Antiquarian Books   **Open Shop**
13127 Shaker Square 44120   (216) 229-2665
Web page: www.clevelandbooks.com   Fax: (216) 561-2771
                                      E-mail: antiquarian@clevelandbooks.com

Collection:	General stock, prints and ephemera.
# of Vols:	70,000
Specialties:	Fine bindings; sets; limited editions; art; architecture; oriental rugs; antiques; scholarly; children's; maps; autographs and manuscripts.
Hours:	Mon-Sat 10-8. Sun 12-6.
Services:	Appraisals, accepts want lists, mail order.
Travel:	From I-271: Chagrin Blvd exit. Turn right on Richmond, then left on Shaker Blvd. Continue to Shaker Sq. From I-71 or I-77: Proceed north to I-90, then east on I-90 to Carnegie exit. Right on Carnegie, then right on Stokes Blvd/Fairhill Blvd and right on Kemper/N. Moreland.
Credit Cards:	Yes
Owner:	William C. Chrisant
Year Estab:	1979
Comments:	For those of our readers who may be planning their own private libraries and would like some ideas on how to make the best use of wall space in an attractive and utilitarian manner, a visit here is a must. As for the books, if you're looking for paperbacks, last year's best sellers or exciting science fiction, forget it. This shop genuinely represents its name in that it houses a wonderful selection of antiquarian volumes along with a wide selection of books on every serious subject imaginable. Whether or not you make a purchase, you'll be pleased with the opportunity to have seen so many volumes in such good condition so well displayed.

Discount Books   **Open Shop**
1127 Euclid Avenue 44115   Shop: (216) 781-1666
                                                Main office: (216) 241-7640

Collection:	General stock of mostly used hardcover.
# of Vols:	40,000
Specialties:	Literature; poetry; art history; technology; medical; scholarly.
Hours:	Mon-Fri 12-4.
Travel:	East 9th St exit off I-90. Right on Carnegie, left on East 14th St, left on Euclid. Shop is two blocks ahead on right.
Credit Cards:	No
Owner:	John T. Zubal
Year Estab:	1993
Comments:	A nice place to buy books at bargain prices. While the volumes on display here are not always in the best condition, one can't really argue too much as they're priced almost universally at $3.97 each. We managed to pick up a couple of items that certainly would have cost us more elsewhere. The titles range from popular fiction to recent best sellers to some more unusual non fiction and vintage volumes.

Susan Heller—Pages for Sages
22611 Halburton Road 44122

By Appointment
(216) 283-2665
Fax: (216) 991-2665

Collection:	General stock.
# of Vols:	20,000+
Specialties:	Americana; art; signed; books on books; fine bindings; children's; literature; modern first editions; illustrated; sports; maritime; literature; Limited Edition Club; scholarly.
Services:	Appraisals, search service, catalog, accepts want lists.
Credit Cards:	Yes
Year Estab:	1976

Sheldon Jaffery: Books
3029 Prospect Avenue 44115

By Appointment
(216) 381-6324
Fax: (216) 382-0810
E-mail: srjaff@gateway.net

Collection:	Specialty
# of Vols:	3,000-5,000
Specialties:	Mystery; horror; supernatural; books on books; early printed books.
Services:	Accepts want lists.
Credit Cards:	No
Year Estab:	1982

Peter Keisogloff Rare Books
815 Superior Ave E, Ste 700 44114

Open Shop
(216) 621-3094
Fax: (216) 589-5810
E-mail: pkbooks@nacs.net

Collection:	Specialty
Specialties:	Artist's books; fine bindings; signed; limited editions; illustrated; books on books; mystery; first editions.
Hours:	Mon-Sat 10-4. Other times by appointment or chance.
Services:	Appraisals, catalog
Travel:	Downtown, near northeast corner of East 9th St and Superior Ave.
Credit Cards:	Yes
Year Estab:	1928

Loganberry Books
12633 Larchmere Boulevard 44120
Web page: www.logan.com/loganberry

Open Shop
(216) 795-9800
E-mail: harriett@logan.com

Collection:	General stock of mostly hardcover.
# of Vols:	10,000
Specialties:	Children's; illustrated; women's studies; fine art; performing arts.
Hours:	Mon-Sat 11-5. Sun 1-5. Other times by chance or appointment.
Services:	Catalog, accepts want lists.
Travel:	From downtown Cleveland, proceed east on Carnegie Blvd to Stokes Blvd/ Fairhill Rd. Right on Stokes and proceed up hill, then right on E. 127th St. At 'T' intersection, turn right on Larchmere. Shop is just ahead on right. From I-90, I-77 or I-71, take Carnegie exit. Proceed

(Cleveland)

	east on Carnegie and follow directions as above.
Credit Cards:	No
Owner:	Harriett Logan
Year Estab:	1994
Comments:	A class act and truly one of the shops the traveling book hunter should not miss. In addition to the fact that the books are attractively displayed (the shop shares space with a dealer in oriental rugs), one can find titles in every conceivable subject area and at generally reasonable prices. In addition to the specialties listed above, all of which are well represented, there are first editions, truly antiquarian items, fine bindings, etc. You name it and a representative title should be available.

Old Erie Street Bookstore   **Open Shop**
2128 East 9th Street 44115   (216) 575-0743
                                                         Fax: (216) 575-0733

Collection:	General stock mostly hardcover.
# of Vols:	25,000
Specialties:	Americana; fine art; military; fine printing; modern first editions; literature; fine bindings.
Hours:	Mon-Fri 9-6. Sat 9-4.
Services:	Appraisals, search service, catalog, accepts want lists.
Travel:	East 9th St exit off I-71. Proceed north on 9th St. Shop is between Huron and Bolivar.
Credit Cards:	Yes
Owner:	Mark Stueve, Owner. Dennis Milota, Manager
Year Estab:	1976
Comments:	A user friendly shop. In addition to the specialties noted above, the shop has a very strong collection of titles in the horror, fantasy, science fiction and popular culture genres.
	We revisited this shop 3½ years after making the above observation. The only additional comment we would make at this time is that the shop continues to be browser friendly, and in our opinion, is worth a visit.

Out of Print Books   **Open Shop**
1873 Prospect Avenue 44103   (216) 696-7045

Collection:	General stock.
# of Vols:	35,000
Specialties:	History; science.
Hours:	Mon-Sat 12-4. Best to call ahead. Other times by appointment.
Services:	Accepts want lists, mail order.
Travel:	21st St exit off I-71. Proceed west on 21st St, then left on Prospect. Shop is across from Cleveland State University Convocation Center.
Credit Cards:	No
Owner:	Donald Kapela
Year Estab:	1974

Comments: In addition to the books on display in the small front room, the owner has many more titles available for browsing in a second room. Most of the books we saw were in reasonably good condition and fairly priced. If the specialties listed above are of interest to you, you may well spot a book to your taste.

Rare Book Store   **Open Shop**
6820 Euclid Avenue 44103

Collection: ???
Travel: At corner of 69th Street.
Comments: We're frustrated at not being able to provide our readers with more information about this relatively new shop. The shop was closed when we passed it on our recent trip to Cleveland and when we returned home we were unable to get a telephone listing for the shop. The situation didn't improve when the owner did not return our Information Sheet. About all we can advise our readers is that they should possibly take the name of the store with the proverbial "grain of salt" as the sign on the building indicated that the books inside sold in the $2-$5 range.

Six Steps Down Bookstore   **Open Shop**
1921 West 25th Street 44113   (216) 566-8897
                                    E-mail: sixsteps@interloc.com

Collection: General stock of mostly used hardcover and paperback.
# of Vols: 70,000
Specialties: Women's studies; homosexuality; political theory; labor.
Hours: Mon-Sat 10-6. Sun 12-5.
Services: Accepts want lists, mail order.
Travel: West 25th St exit off I-90. Proceed north on 25th St. Shop is just north of Lorain.
Credit Cards: Yes
Owner: Mike O'Brien & Nancy Di Alesandro, Managers
Year Estab: 1977
Comments: If you're looking for reading copies in the subjects listed above at fairly reasonable prices, chances are good that you'll find copies to your liking here. The collection in strong in reference, language and non traditional subjects. Only a portion of the stock is on display. Note: The store is also known as the Bookstore on West 25th.

John Wallace Skinner Americana   **Open Shop**
812 Huron Road SE 44115   (216) 621-3764

Collection: Specialty books, ephemera and prints.
# of Vols: 500 (books)
Specialties: Americana; illustrated; Native American artifacts; Cleveland; maps.
Hours: Tue-Fri 11-4 but a call ahead is advised. Other times by appointment.
Services: Accepts want lists, mail order.
Travel: Around the corner from Old Erie Bookstore. See above.
Credit Cards: No

(Cleveland)

Year Estab:	1986
Comments:	Located on the third floor of an office building, the shop offers a very modest collection of books, together with prints, ephemera, artifacts and old bottles. If your interests are specific, you might want to call ahead to be sure the owner can help you.

John T. Zubal, Inc.   **By Appointment**
2969 West 25th Street 44113   (216) 241-7640
Web page: www.zubal.com   Fax: (216) 241-6966
                                                   E-mail: jzubal@zubal.com

Collection:	General stock.
# of Vols:	2 million +
Specialties:	Scholarly journals; government publications.
Services:	Appraisals, accepts want lists, auction catalogs.
Travel:	From I-90. West 25th St exit. Proceed south on 25th. From I-71. West 25th St exit. Proceed north on 25th. Shop is between Clark & I-90.
Credit Cards:	Yes
Year Estab:	1959
Comments:	When we last visited this shop (see our comments below) we weren't sure if it could get any better. But it has. During our most recent visit, we were escorted through the owner's latest addition—a huge building next door to the main warehouse with the capacity for housing an untold number of books. (The former site of a large commercial bakery, we were told that the staff uses bicycles to get from one part of the building to another; having visited the building, we can believe it.) Note: Although the shop has changed from an "open shop" to a "by appointment" basis, appointments are generally available weekdays during regular business hours.

Two multi-story warehouse like buildings with books in every conceivable category. The problem for the drop-in buyer is that while the staff knows where every subject category is located, we were advised that the locations are switched periodically and that none of the shelves or sections are marked for the convenience of visiting customers. Be that as it may, the sheer number of titles and the concentration on scholarly topics (as well as the more popular subjects) makes a visit to this establishment a must if you're a serious book person. Some sections are off limits to visitors, e.g., periodicals and the occult, but if you know what titles you're looking for a member of the staff will gladly assist. Unless your interests are very narrow, be prepared for a long visit. The owner operates a second smaller store downtown. See Discount Books above.

Cleveland Heights
(Map 27, page 375)

Attenson's Coventry Antiques & Books
1771-75 Coventry Road 44118

Open Shop
(216) 321-2515

Collection:	General stock.
# of Vols:	10,000
Hours:	Mon-Sat 11:30-5:30.
Travel:	Cedar Rd exit off I-271. Follow signs for Cedar at exit ramp. Right on Cedar and proceed west to Coventry, then north on Coventry to village business district.
Credit Cards:	Yes
Owner:	Stuart & Patricia Attenson
Year Estab:	1965
Comments:	At least 50% of the shop is devoted to antiques and collectibles with a majority of the book collection located in the basement and a few additional titles on the first floor. Most of the books were older but run of the mill items. There were, though, a few unusual titles that a truly discerning book hound might be able to spot.

Mac's Backs Paperbacks
1820 Coventry Road 44118

Open Shop
(216) 321-2665
Fax: (216) 321-7323

Collection:	General stock of mostly used paperback and hardcover.
# of Vols:	50,000
Hours:	Mon-Thu 10-9. Fri & Sat 10-10. Sun 11-6.
Services:	Search service, accepts want lists, mail order.
Travel:	From I-90: MLK exit. Proceed east on MLK, then right on Coventry. From I-271: Cedar exit. Proceed west on Cedar, then right on Coventry.
Credit Cards:	Yes
Owner:	James C. McSherry
Year Estab:	1978
Comments:	Stock is approximately 80% paperback.

Wonderland Books
1824 Wilton Road 44118

By Appointment
Tel & Fax: (216) 932-6471
E-mail: wondrlnd@interloc.com

Collection:	Specialty
# of Vols:	6,000
Specialties:	Children's; children's illustrated; pop-ups; Little Golden Books; Caldecott and Newberry medal books.
Services:	Appraisals, catalog, accepts want lists, search service.
Credit Cards:	No
Owner:	Larry Rakow
Year Estab:	1991

Columbiana
(Map 24, page 352)

Bookworm's Buffet
31 South Main Street 44408

Open Shop
(330) 482-0087
(800) 428-0087
Fax: (330) 482-0559
E-mail: bookworm@cboss.com

Collection:	General stock of mostly hardcover.
# of Vols:	25,000
Specialties:	Ohio
Hours:	Mon-Thu 9-7. Fri & Sat 9-5. Sun 12-5.
Services:	Appraisals, search service, catalog, accepts want lists.
Travel:	Exit 16 off I-76 (Ohio Tpk). Proceed south on Rte 7 for about one mile, then south on Rte 164 into town. Shop is one block after the circle.
Credit Cards:	Yes
Owner:	Jan H. & Naomi McPeek
Year Estab:	1984
Comments:	The collection was somewhat larger than it was at the time of our earlier visit and by all accounts should be larger still by the time our readers visit as the owners were in the process of opening a lower floor at the time we stopped by. Most of the books we saw were older and not always in the best condition. Prices vary and only the discerning buyer will be able to determine whether or not a particular book, considering its condition, is deserving of its asking price.

Theron's Country Flea Market
1641 Columbiana Lisbon Road 44408

Flea Market
(330) 482-4327

Hours:	Year-round: Sun 9-5.
Travel:	Leetonia Ave exit off Rte 11. Proceed east on Leetonia, south on Rte 440 and left on Columbiana-Lisbon Rd.

Columbus
(Map 28, page 385 & Map 24, page 352)

Acorn Bookshop
1464 West Fifth Avenue 43212

Open Shop
(614) 486-1860

Collection:	General stock of mostly hardcover.
# of Vols:	40,000
Specialties:	Natural history; science; aviation; military; science fiction.
Hours:	Tue-Fri 11-8. Sat 11-6. Sun 12-5.
Travel:	Eastbound: Grandview exit off I-70. Proceed north on Grandview for 1½ miles to Fifth. Shop is in a strip center at Fifth and Grandview. Southbound from I-270: Rte 315 south to Fifth then west on Fifth. Northbound and westbound: Rte 33 to Grandview, then north on Grandview to Fifth.
Credit Cards:	Yes
Owner:	Stuart Wheeler
Year Estab:	1992

Comments:	A premier shop that, as its business card reads, provides the browser with "fine used books: common, uncommon and collectible." After visiting the shop and admiring its spaciousness, organization, labeling and the quality of its books, we could not disagree at all with that claim. We saw some nice signed editions, many rarities, lots of antiquarian titles and a solid collection of just good used books. A pleasure to visit.

Beechwold Books   **By Appointment**
79 Westwood Road 43214   (614) 268-5725
                                             E-mail: beechbks@interloc.com

Collection:	General stock.
# of Vols:	8,000-10,000
Specialties:	Americana; music; press books.
Services:	Catalog, accepts want lists.
Credit Cards:	Yes
Owner:	Robert A. Tibbetts
Year Estab:	1958
Comments:	Also displays at Books on High. See below.

Books on High   **Open Shop**
3510 North High Street 43214   (614) 267-7774
                                             E-mail: bookhigh@interloc.com

Collection:	General stock of mostly hardcover and ephemera.
# of Vols:	25,000
Specialties:	Mystery; cookbooks; Americana; religion; philosophy; James Thurber; Modern Library; modern literature; first editions; children's; children's series; World War II; military aviation; Ohio.
Hours:	Mon-Thu 10:30-6. Fri & Sat 11-6.
Travel:	East North Broadway exit off I-71. Proceed west on East North Broadway, then north (right) on High St. Shop is two blocks ahead.
Credit Cards:	Yes
Owner:	Jay & Genie Hoster
Year Estab:	1995
Comments:	Based on our visit to this group shop shortly before the move to this new location, we have to believe that book people will be pleased with their stop here. Not only will they have a chance to view books displayed by several dealers at one time, but they'll also get to view quite a nice selection of collectible titles, signed editions and more than a few rarities. Sure, there are some paperbacks here and a reasonable share of recent best sellers, but the variety of other goodies, the space devoted to their display and the organization of the shop are such that we think you'll enjoy this visit.

Fireside Book Company   **Open Shop**
503 City Park Avenue 43215   (614) 621-1928
Web page: www.infinet.com/~fireside   E-mail: fireside@infinet.com

Collection:	General stock of mostly hardcover.
# of Vols:	15,000+

(Columbus)

Specialties:	Modern literature; history.
Hours:	Tue-Sat 11-7. Sun 12-5.
Services:	Search service, mail order.
Travel:	From I-71: Greenlawn exit. Proceed east on Greenlawn. At High St, jog right then left and continue to City Park. Turn left on City Park. From I-70: High St exit. Proceed to Third St, then south on Third, west on Blenkner for one block to City Park. Shop is located in German Village neighborhood.
Credit Cards:	Yes
Owner:	Jane Landwehr & Bryan Saums
Year Estab:	1993
Comments:	We would have liked this shop even if the owners hadn't commented on our both having slimmed down since our earlier visit 3½ years earlier. Not only were we able to make a very nice purchase, but we also viewed shelf after shelf filled with interesting titles in almost universally good to excellent condition throughout the shop's main level. The upper level offered a room filled with children's books and religious titles and a second room devoted to paperbacks. Book hunters with a sense of history and an appreciation for older things should also enjoy driving through the cobblestone streets of this attractively re-stored former German Village.

Half Price Books, Records, Magazines   **Open Shop**
2656 Brice Road 43068   (614) 755-4110

Collection:	General stock of new and used paperback and hardcover.
Hours:	Mon-Thu 10-10. Fri & Sat 10-11. Sun 10-8.
Travel:	Brice Rd exit off I-70. Proceed south on Brice. Shop is in the Brice Park Shopping Center.

Half Price Books, Records, Magazines   **Open Shop**
2660 Bethel Road 43220   (614) 457-6333

Collection:	General stock of new and used paperback and hardcover.
Hours:	Mon-Sat 10-10. Sun 11-7.
Travel:	Bethel Rd exit off Rte 315. Proceed west on Bethel to Sawmill. Shop is in the Carriage Place Shopping Center.

Half Price Books, Records, Magazines   **Open Shop**
1375 West Lane Avenue 43221   (614) 486-8765

Collection:	General stock of new and used hardcover and paperback.
Hours:	Mon-Sat 10am-11pm. Sun 10am-9pm.
Travel:	Lane Ave exit off Rte 315. Proceed west on Lane.

Hoffman's Bookshop   **Open Shop**
211 East Arcadia Avenue 43202   (614) 267-0203
                                                             Fax: (614) 267-7737
                                                   E-mail: hoffmans@interloc.com

Collection:	General stock and ephemera.

# of Vols:	15,000
Specialties:	Ohio; photography; James Thurber; Americana.
Hours:	Wed-Sat 11-5.
Services:	Appraisals, search service, catalog, accepts want lists.
Travel:	Hudson exit off I-71. Proceed west on Hudson, then north on Indianola and west on Arcadia.
Credit Cards:	Yes
Owner:	Ed & Tina Hoffman
Year Estab:	1982
Comments:	A mostly hardcover shop which also carries a healthy supply of ephemera (with a heavy emphasis on regional topics). Most of the books we saw were of mixed vintage and in generally good condition. The books were tightly packed requiring the browser to be careful in order not to risk missing an item of interest or value. If you don't spot an item you're looking for, ask, as the owner has a warehouse filled with additional books.

L.J. Ryan, Scholarly Books
PO Box 243 43216

By Appointment
(614) 252-4469

Collection:	Specialty
# of Vols:	10,000+
Specialties:	Religion; philosophy; social sciences; literature; Americana; international relations.
Services:	Accepts want lists, mail order.
Credit Cards:	No
Year Estab:	1972

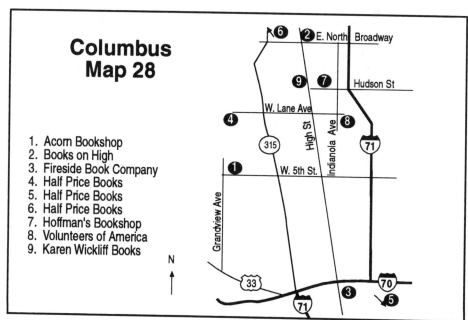

**Columbus
Map 28**

1. Acorn Bookshop
2. Books on High
3. Fireside Book Company
4. Half Price Books
5. Half Price Books
6. Half Price Books
7. Hoffman's Bookshop
8. Volunteers of America
9. Karen Wickliff Books

(Columbus)

Volunteers of America   **Open Shop**
2511 Summit Street 43202   (614) 262-3384

Collection:	General stock of hardcover and paperback.
# of Vols:	50,000
Hours:	Mon-Sat 5.
Travel:	Hudson St exit off I-71. Proceed west on Hudson for two blocks then left on Summit.
Credit Cards:	Yes
Comments:	Non profit shop. All books are donated. Stock is approximately 60% hardcover.

Karen Wickliff Books   **Open Shop**
2579 North High Street 43202   (614) 263-2903

Collection:	General stock.
# of Vols:	70,000
Specialties:	Fine art; literature; history; religion; children's; fine bindings; natural history; science; technology; folklore; archeology; medieval history.
Hours:	Mon-Sat 11:30-5:30. Other times by chance or appointment.
Travel:	Hudson St exit off I-71. Proceed west Hudson then right on High St. Shop is 1/2 block ahead on left.
Credit Cards:	No
Year Estab:	1972
Comments:	If you're looking for any of the specialties listed above, this shop is for you. In addition to these specialty areas, we were impressed with the general scope of the scholarly volumes on display. The size of the collection makes a visit here almost mandatory. If there are any negatives, it's with regard to some of the aisles which are piled high with books, perhaps newly acquired and not yet shelved, but nonetheless making browsing in some areas a real challenge. The owner operates a second shop in Springfield. See below.

Copley
(Map 24, page 352)

Augnat Book Exchange   **Open Shop**
3567 Copley Road 44321   (330) 666-2819

Collection:	General stock of mostly paperback.
# of Vols:	10,000
Hours:	Mon-Sat 10-5.

Coshocton
(Map 24, page 352)

Bookcase Coffeehouse   **Open Shop**
375 Downtowner Plaza 43812   (614) 623-2665

Collection:	General stock of paperback and hardcover.

# of Vols:	3,000+
Hours:	Tue-Thu 10-5:30. Fri & Sat 9-9.
Travel:	Coshocton exit off Rte 36. Right at end of exit ramp and continue on Chestnut St. Right on 2nd St and continue to Downtowner Plaza.
Credit Cards:	No
Year Estab:	1996
Comments:	Stock is approximately 60% paperback.

Dayton
(Map 24, page 352)

Bonnett's Book Store Open Shop
502 East Fifth Street 45402 (937) 228-1222

Collection:	General stock of mostly paperback.
Hours:	Mon-Sat 12-8.

The Book Shoppe Open Shop
2818 Wayne Avenue 45420 (937) 252-2276

Collection:	General stock.
# of Vols:	25,000+
Specialties:	Civil War; Ohio; genealogy.
Hours:	Wed-Fri 12-7. Sat 11-5. Other times by appointment.
Services:	Appraisals, accepts want lists, mail order.
Travel:	Rte 35 east exit off I-75. Proceed east on Rte 35, then south on Smithville and west on Wayne Ave.
Credit Cards:	Yes
Owner:	Don & Priscilla Leet
Year Estab:	1975
Comments:	For a shop that's not huge in size, this tri-level establishment contains a wealth of great titles in many fields. In addition to the specialties listed above, the owner displays a fine collection in mystery, horror and science fiction. In almost every other category we examined, there were titles of quality we had not seen elsewhere.

Dark Star Books & Comics Open Shop
1273 North Fairfield Road 45432 (937) 427-3213

Collection:	Specialty books, comics and games.
# of Vols:	1,500 (books)
Specialties:	Science fiction; fantasy; horror.
Hours:	Tue & Wed 2-7. Thu & Fri 12-7. Sat 11-7.
Comments:	A larger selection of books is available at the owner's second shop in Yellow Springs. See below.

Dragon's Lair Open Shop
110 West Fifth Street 45402 (937) 222-1479

Collection:	Specialty. Mostly used paperback and hardcover and comics.
# of Vols:	3,000+
Specialties:	Fantasy; science fiction; horror; mystery.

Hours:	Mon-Sat 10-6, except Thu till 8.
Travel:	Two blocks west of Main St.
Year Estab:	1974

Half Price Books, Records, Magazines   **Open Shop**
2090 Miamisburg-Centerville Rd. 45459   (937) 438-0249

Collection:	General stock of new and used paperback and hardcover.
Hours:	Mon-Sat 10-10. Sun 11-7.
Travel:	Miamisburg-Centerville Rd (Rte 725) exit off I-75. Proceed east on Miamisburg to South Towne Centre.

Owen D. Kubik Fine Books   **By Appointment**
3474 Clar Von Drive 45430   (937) 294-0253
                                        Fax: (937) 294-2690

Collection:	Specialty
# of Vols:	10,000
Specialties:	Military; historical fiction.
Services:	Appraisals, search service, catalog, accepts want lists.
Credit Cards:	Yes
Year Estab:	1986

Murder Is Served   **By Appointment**
5273 Bittersweet Drive 45429   Tel & Fax: (937) 438-0211
Fax: 5134380211
Web page: www.smt-inc.com/murder-is-served/

Collection:	Specialty
# of Vols:	4,000
Specialties:	Mystery; detective.
Services:	Catalog, accepts want lists.
Credit Cards:	No
Owner:	John W. Bierman
Year Estab:	1993

Second Shelf   **Open Shop**
2020 East 3rd Street 45403   (937) 252-4943

Collection:	General stock of paperback and hardcover.
# of Vols:	500-1,000
Hours:	Mon-Sat 9:30-4.
Travel:	At corner of Linden Ave.
Comments:	A non profit shop. All items are donated.

Delaware
(Map 24, page 352)

Sandusky Street Books   **Open Shop**
24 North Sandusky Street 43015   (614) 363-6285

| *Collection:* | General stock of paperback and hardcover. |

# of Vols:	15,000
Hours:	Mon-Sat 10-6.
Travel:	Rte 36/37 exit off I-71. Proceed west on Rte 36/37 to downtown.
Credit Cards:	Yes
Owner:	Trish Walker
Year Estab:	1997
Comments:	Stock is approximately 60% paperback.

East Liverpool
(Map 24, page 352)

Country Closet **Antique Mall**
At Pottery City Antique Mall, 409 Washington Street 43920 (330) 385-6933

Collection:	General stock.
Hours:	Sat 10-6. Sun 12-6.
Travel:	Downtown East Liverpool exit off Rte 11 southbound. Turn left at end of exit ramp. At top of overpass, turn right at light on 4th St. Mall is at corner of 4th & Washington.
Comments:	Also displays at Theron's Flea Market in Columbiana. See below.

Englewood
(Map 24, page 352)

Olde Pages Book Shoppe **Open Shop**
860 Union Road 45322 (937) 832-3022
(800) 887-2665
Fax: (937) 836-7407
E-mail: oldepages@aol.com

Collection:	General stock of paperback and hardcover.
# of Vols:	50,000
Hours:	Mon-Thu 10-8. Fri & Sat 10-6. Sun 12-5.
Services:	Search service, accepts want lists, mail order.
Travel:	Exit 29 off I-70. Proceed north on Rte 48, then left on Wenger Rd. At third light, turn right on Union. Shop is third driveway on right.
Credit Cards:	Yes
Owner:	Dee Dee Harrison
Year Estab:	1993
Comments:	Stock is approximately 70% paperback.

Fairborn
(Map 24, page 352)

Book Outlet **Open Shop**
8 West Main Street 45324 (937) 879-4444

Collection:	General stock of paperback and hardcover.
# of Vols:	35,000
Hours:	Mon-Sat 10-6.
Services:	Rte 235 exit off I-675. Turn west towards Fairborn, then left on Dayton

Dr and right on Main St.

Credit Cards: Yes
Owner: Allen Molnar
Year Estab: 1985
Comments: Stock is approximately 75% paperback.

Bookery Fantasy   **Open Shop**
16 West Main Street 45324   (937) 879-1408
Web page: www.bookeryfantasy.com   Fax: (937) 879-9327
                                          E-mail: bookeryfan@aol.com

Collection: Specialty books (mostly paperback) and ephemera.
# of Vols: 20,000
Specialties: Science fiction; pulps; comics (collectible); media.
Hours: Mon-Sat 11-7. Sun 12-5.
Services: Accepts want lists, mail order.
Travel: Just off Rte 444.
Credit Cards: Yes
Owner: Tim Cottrill
Year Estab: 1984

Findlay
(Map 24, page 352)

Books On Main   **Open Shop**
220 South Main Street 45840   (419) 424-3773
                                          E-mail: bksonmn@bright.net

Collection: General stock of mostly hardcover.
# of Vols: 25,000+
Specialties: Ohio; children's; Civil War; cookbooks.
Hours: Mon 12-8. Tue-Fri 9:30-5:30. Sat 9:30-4.
Services: Appraisals, search service, accepts want lists, mail order.
Travel: West Main Cross (Rte 12) east exit off I-75. Turn left at Main St (at the
                  courthouse). Shop is just ahead on left.
Credit Cards: Yes
Owner: Bob & Marjorie Weaver
Year Estab: 1993
Comments: Although conveniently located just off a heavily traveled interstate, a
                  visit to this shop necessitated a detour from our carefully constructed
                  itinerary and we wondered (and yes, argued) if the stock would be such
                  as to have made the trip worthwhile for us. I'm pleased to report that
                  the detour was well worth the effort. Indeed, I had to be forcibly
                  removed from the shop (while holding three volumes in my hand and
                  wanting to buy more) because we had an appointment later that day.
                  While many of the books we saw were reading copies, many more were
                  in quite good condition and most reasonably priced. The collection
                  offers more hardcovers than paperbacks and contains some pleasant
                  surprises.

Jeffrey's Antique Gallery   **Antique Mall**
11326 Township Road 99 45840   (419) 423-7500

Hours: Daily 10-6.
Travel: Located at exit 161 off I-75.

Fowler
(Map 24, page 352)

Alice's Book Shelf   **By Appointment**
5053 State Route 305   (330) 637-1766
Mailing address: PO Box 120 Fowler OH 44418

Collection: Specialty
# of Vols: 3,000
Specialties: Metaphysics; new age.
Services: Search service, accepts want lists, mail order.
Credit Cards: No
Owner: Alice Chipps
Year Estab: 1988

Gahanna
(Map 24, page 352)

Twice Told Tales   **Open Shop**
105 Town Street 43230   (614) 475-9707
                                                       E-mail: bottgc@msn.com

Collection: General stock of paperback and hardcover.
# of Vols: 20,000
Hours: Tue-Sat 10-6.
Travel: I-670 to Gahanna. Continue on Granville St, then left on High and first
                  possible right. Shop is located in an old barn.
Credit Cards: No
Owner: Gerard Bott
Year Estab: 1998
Comments: Stock is approximately 65% paperback.

Gambier
(Map 24, page 352)

Kenyon College Bookstore   **Open Shop**
106 Gaskin Avenue 43022   (740) 427-5633
Mailing address: PO Box 231 Gambier OH 43022   Fax: (740) 427-5618
                                                      E-mail: dailey@kenyon.edu
Collection: General stock of new and mostly hardcover used.
# of Vols: 12,000 (used)
Hours: Daily 7:30am-11pm.
Services: Search service, accepts want lists, mail order.
Travel: From Rte 13, continue on Rte 229. At "Gambier" sign, proceed up hill.
Credit Cards: Yes

Comments: If you've ever attended either your local library's annual book sale or the annual book sale put on by a college alumni group and wondered what it would be like to view the books before the mob arrived, you'll have this experience should you visit this shop. The multi purpose college shop offers used books of every vintage, both scholarly and popular, in generally mixed condition and at bargain prices. We know several major book dealers who visit the shop regularly, finding enough volumes to stock some of their own shelves. Like any other hit or miss proposition, your visit here may land you several winners or none at all. In any event, you'll rub elbows with the college crowd and have an opportunity to buy some Kenyon College souvenirs.

Garrettsville
(Map 24, page 352)

Enchanted Books, Antiques, Etc.   **Open Shop**
7971 State Street 44231   (330) 527-4556

Collection: General stock and ephemera.
# of Vols: 6,000
Specialties: Children's; cookbooks; Americana.
Hours: Tue, Wed, Sat & Sun 10-5 but a call ahead is advised. Other times by chance or appointment.
Services: Accepts want lists.
Travel: On Rte 82, 1/3 mile west of intersection of Rtes 82 & 88.
Credit Cards: No
Owner: Allene Daw Fodor
Year Estab: 1989
Comments: A combination of used hardcover books (admittedly a relatively small collection), old magazines, sheet music and other ephemera and miscellaneous non print collectibles. The books are located in the owner's home and in a barn behind the main house (which is closed on very cold winter days). This is not a shop you might want to drive miles to visit, but if you're in the neighborhood and decide to stop by, you may find an item of interest. At the time of our visit, the dealer's husband also treated us to a serenade on his accordion.

Granville
(Map 24, page 352)

A Place in History   **Open Shop**
130 North Prospect   (740) 587-2665
Mailing address: PO Box 132 Granville OH 43023

Collection: Specialty
# of Vols: 2,000
Specialties: History; biography; Civil War; political science; film; art; literature.
Hours: Tue-Fri 12-5. Sat 9-1.
Travel: On Rte 37, nine miles north of I-70. Shop is in downtown.

Credit Cards: Yes
Owner: Clarke L. Wilhelm
Year Estab: 1995

Readers' Garden   **Open Shop**
119 East Elm Street 43023   (740) 587-7744
        Fax: (740) 587-7745

Collection: General stock of mostly new and some used.
# of Vols: 5,000
Hours: Mon-Sat 10-5:30.
Travel: Granville exit off Rte 16. Proceed north on Rte 37 to downtown.
Credit Cards: Yes
Owner: Jo-Anne Geiger
Year Estab: 1998
Comments: Stock is approximately 20% used.

Greenville
(Map 24, page 352)

The Book Store   **Open Shop**
307 Pine Street 45331   (937) 548-7188

Collection: General stock of paperback and hardcover.
# of Vols: 30,000
Hours: Tue-Fri 11-5:30. Sat 10-4. Other times by appointment.
Services: Accepts want lists, mail order.
Travel: On Rte 49, seven blocks south of downtown.
Credit Cards: No
Owner: Pam Saively
Year Estab: 1985
Comments: One never knows what will turn up even in a shop that, like this one, carries predominately paperback books. One's initial instinct is to scan the hardcover books quickly and after viewing a number of common titles of no great distinction, assume that there's little of interest here. Adding to one's sense of frustration is the fact that the hardcover books are not organized into discernible categories or alphabetized. A less discriminating book person might even walk out of the shop without having spotted a half dozen or more titles in the Rivers of America Series, all with dust jackets and priced at less than half what we have seen these books sell for elsewhere. Of course, by the time this book is in print, those titles may have been gobbled up, but who knows—they may have been replaced by other winners.

Hamilton
(Map 24, page 352)

The Book Shop & Comic Stop   **Open Shop**
1018 Main Street 45013   (513) 887-2999

Collection: General stock of mostly paperback.

# of Vols:	20,000
Hours:	Tue-Fri 10-6. Sat 10-4.

Choir Loft Used Books   **Open Shop**
31 Millville-Oxford Road 45013   (513) 737-1880

Collection:	General stock and ephemera.
# of Vols:	5,000
Hours:	Thu-Sat 10:30-5.
Services:	Accepts want lists, mail order.
Travel:	From I-275 north of Cincinnati, proceed north on Rte 27 to Millville. Once in Millville, turn left at second light (continue on Rte 27). Shop is on left in a former church.
Credit Cards:	No
Owner:	M.J. Herr
Year Estab:	1995
Comments:	The shop also carries antiques, collectibles.

Harrison
(Map 24, page 352)

Flea Market Books   **By Appointment**
10452 Walking Fern Drive 45030   (513) 367-9536
Web page: http://fleamarketbooks.com   E-mail: fmb@fleamarketbooks.com

Collection:	General stock of paperback and hardcover.
# of Vols:	3,500
Specialties:	Science fiction; fantasy; romance; modern first editions; vintage paperbacks; show business.
Services:	Search service, accepts want lists, mail order.
Credit Cards:	Yes
Owner:	April Galt
Year Estab:	1997
Comments:	Stock is approximately 75% paperback.

Hilliard
(Map 24, page 352)

Admirable Books   **By Appointment**
3528 Mark Twain Drive 43026   (614) 777-9375
                                                          Fax: (614) 777-9376

Collection:	Specialty books and ephemera.
Specialties:	Mark Twain.
Services:	Appraisals, occasional catalog, search service, accepts want lists, mail order.
Credit Cards:	No
Owner:	Robert Slotta
Year Estab:	1991

Bookphil Out of Print & Signed | **By Appointment**
3987 Main Street 43026 | (614) 876-0442
Mailing address: PO Box 706 Hilliard OH 43026 | Fax: (614) 876-6403

E-mail: bookphil@interloc.com

Collection:	General stock.
# of Vols:	20,000+
Specialties:	Military; aviation; nautical; outdoors; literature; crime; espionage; National Geographic books.
Hours:	Not available in August.
Services:	Search service, computerized lists, mail order.
Credit Cards:	No
Owner:	Nelda Goddard
Year Estab:	1970

Kent
(Map 24, page 352)

Archer's Used And Rare Books | **Open Shop**
104 South Lincoln Street 44240 | (330) 673-0945

E-mail: archers@worldnet.att.net

Collection:	General stock of mostly hardcover and some paperback.
# of Vols:	25,000
Specialties:	Americana; baseball; botany; Ohio; true crime; music (blues, jazz, rock & roll).
Hours:	Mon-Fri 11-8. Sat 11-6.
Services:	Subject catalogs.
Travel:	Across from Kent State University. Park in lot on south side of Main St (Rte 59) between Willow and Lincoln.
Credit Cards:	Yes
Owner:	Paul Bauer
Year Estab:	1986
Comments:	A nice layout, neatly organized and easy to browse. The books are in generally good condition, of mixed vintage and reasonably priced. The basement offers a selection of paperbacks.

Kinsman
(Map 24, page 352)

Diane's Book Den | **Open Shop**
At Market Square, Routes 5 & 7 | (330) 876-3178
Mailing address: PO Box 381 Kinsman OH 44428 | Fax: (330) 876-5114

Collection:	General stock mostly used hardcover and paperback.
# of Vols:	25,000
Hours:	Mon-Sat 10-5. Sun 12-4.
Travel:	Rte 5 exit off Rte 11. Proceed east on Rte 5 until it joins with Rte 7 north. Shop is in town square, about one block after Rte 5 joins Rte 7.
Credit Cards:	No

Owner:	Diane Sutton
Year Estab:	1996
Comments:	Stock is approximately 75% hardcover.

Lakewood
(Map 27, page 375)

Antiques at Hall House   **Open Shop**
16906 Detroit Avenue 44107   (216) 228-4255
E-mail: pdbz04a@prodigy.com

Collection:	Specialty
# of Vols:	1,200-1,500
Specialties:	Children's series; antiques and collectibles; military (US).
Hours:	Wed-Sun 12-5.
Travel:	McKinley Ave exit off I-90. Proceed north one mile on McKinley, then right on Detroit. Shop is 1½ blocks ahead in a former residence.
Credit Cards:	Yes
Owner:	Don Fredgant
Year Estab:	1991

Second Stage Books   **Open Shop**
1386 Bonnieview Avenue 44107   (216) 226-9996

Collection:	General stock of paperback and hardcover.
# of Vols:	25,000
Specialties:	Vintage paperbacks; theater scripts.
Hours:	Wed-Fri 12-6. Sat 11-5. Sun 12-4.
Travel:	McKinley exit off I-90. Proceed north on McKinley, then right on Detroit and left on Bonnieview.
Credit Cards:	No
Owner:	Bill Modic
Year Estab:	1990
Comments:	A bi-level shop offering a mix of paperbacks and mostly hardcover reading copies. Some interesting titles but more very ordinary ones.

Lebanon
(Map 24, page 352)

Broadway Antique Mall   **Antique Mall**
15-17 South Broadway 45036   (513) 932-1410

Hours:	Mon-Sat 10-5. Sun 12-5.
Travel:	Lebanon exit off I-71. Proceed north on Rte 48 towards town, then left on South Broadway. From I-75: See Dickens' Book Shop below.

Dickens' Book Shop   **Open Shop**
26 South Broadway 45036   (513) 932-7001
Fax: (513) 932-4503
E-mail: bluesgene@your-net.com

Collection:	General stock of new and mostly hardcover used.

# of Vols:	6,000 (used)
Specialties:	Antiques; mystery; cookbooks.
Hours:	Mon-Thu 10-5. Fri & Sat 10-5:30. Sun 12-5.
Services:	Search service, mail order.
Travel:	Rte 63 exit off I-75. Proceed east on Rte 63 to downtown. Turn left on Broadway. From I-71: See Broadway Antique Mall above.
Credit Cards:	Yes
Owner:	Gene Jestice
Year Estab:	1987
Comments:	This store primarily offers new books although it has a section in the rear with perhaps 1,000-2,000 used books (hardcover volumes and trade paperbacks), most of which were reading copies of fairly recent vintage. If time is a factor in your book hunting travels, we suggest you exercise appropriate judgement.

Miller's Antique Market   **Antique Mall**
201 South Broadway 45036   (513) 932-8710

Hours:	Mon-Sat 10-5. Sun 12-5.
Travel:	See above Lebanon listings.

Mansfield
(Map 24, page 352)

Crossroad Rare Books & Bindery   **By Appointment**
1592 Timber Road 44905   (419) 589-2886
                                       E-mail: crossroadbooks@webtv.net

Collection:	General stock.
# of Vols:	8,000
Specialties:	Ohio; military; children's.
Services:	Appraisals, search service, accepts want lists, mail order.
Credit Cards:	No
Owner:	Helen Sackman
Year Estab:	1973

Little Journeys Bookshop   **Open Shop**
376 Park Avenue West 44906   (419) 522-2389
Web page: www.richnet.net/ljbooks   Fax: (419) 522-6019
                                        E-mail: alanewig@richnet.net

Collection:	General stock and ephemera.
# of Vols:	10,000
Specialties:	Local history; Americana; Louis Bromfield.
Hours:	Mon-Sat 11-6.
Services:	Search service, accepts want lists, catalog.
Travel:	Exit 176 off I-71. Proceed west on Rte 30, then Trimble Rd exit off Rte 30. Continue south on Trimble then east on Park Ave West.
Credit Cards:	Yes
Owner:	Alan Wigton

Year Estab: 1995
Comments: An interesting shop located in a former private residence. Strong in the
areas listed above as specialties, plus some other very nice titles, including more than a few collectibles and a nice selection of ephemera.
The majority of the books we saw were in quite good condition and
were reasonably priced. The kind of place where you might discover
an item you didn't even know you were looking for.

Marion
(Map 24, page 352)

Brad's Bookstore   **Open Shop**
219 North Main Street 43302   (614) 382-9671

Collection: General stock of mostly paperback and comics.
Hours: Jan-Apr: Wed-Sat 12-5. May-Dec: Tue-Sat 12-5.

Marysville
(Map 24, page 352)

Charles David Dyer - Books   **By Appointment**
13904 Fairway Drive 43040   (937) 644-0285

Collection: Specialty
Specialties: Mountaineering; arctic.
Services: Catalog, accepts want lists.
Credit Cards: No
Year Estab: 1983

Massillon
(Map 24, page 352)

The Village Bookshelf   **Open Shop**
746 Amherst Road, NE 44646   (330) 833-5666

Collection: General stock of mostly used paperback and hardcover.
# of Vols: 10,000
Specialties: Science fiction; fantasy; horror; mystery; Sherlock Holmes; vintage
paperbacks.
Hours: Mon-Sat 11-6, except Mon and Thu till 8:30.
Services: Appraisals
Travel: From Rte 21, proceed east on Cherry Rd, then north on Amherst for
about .1 mile.
Credit Cards: Yes
Owner: Roy K. Preece, Jr.
Year Estab: 1977
Comments: This shop offers lots of paperbacks and a couple of hundred hardcover
books of little distinction.

Mayfield Heights
(Map 27, page 375)

Half Price Books, Records, Magazines   **Open Shop**
1607 Golden Gate Plaza 44124   (440) 461-9222

Collection:	General stock of new and used hardcover and paperback.
Hours:	Mon-Sat 9-10. Sun 11-7.
Travel:	Mayfield Rd (Rte 322) exit off I-271. Proceed west on Mayfield and make first left into Golden Gate Shopping Center.

Medina
(Map 24, page 352)

The Book Shelf   **Open Shop**
1091 North Court 44256   (330) 725-3519

Collection:	General stock of paperback and hardcover.
# of Vols:	35,000
Hours:	Mon-Sat 10-8. Sun 12-5.
Travel:	Rte 18 exit off I-71. Proceed west on Rte 18 to Medina, then north on Rte 42. Shop is on the left in the Kmart Shopping Center.
Credit Cards:	Yes
Year Estab:	1996
Comments:	Certainly not all book stores located in shopping malls fit what we sometimes call the "usual" pattern: hardcover books that are former best sellers and/or book club editions along the side walls and mystery, romance and western paperbacks taking up all the space in the middle. For those of you "on the road," we should advise that this store does fit the "usual" pattern.

Medina Antique Mall   **Antique Mall**
2797 Medina Road 44256   (330) 722-0017

Hours:	Daily 10-6.
Travel:	Exit 218 off I-71. Proceed east on Rte 18.

Mentor
(Map 24, page 352)

Maggie McGiggles Antiques   **Open Shop**
8627 Mentor Avenue 44060   (440) 255-1623

Collection:	General stock.
# of Vols:	1,000
Hours:	Mon-Sun 11-5, except Tue till 6. Closed Thu and Sun during summer.
Travel:	See ReReadables below.

ReReadables   **Open Shop**
8674 Mentor Avenue 44060   (440) 255-4996

Collection:	General stock.
# of Vols:	10,000

Specialties:	Ohio; Civil War; biography; Americana.
Hours:	Tue & Thu 11-5. Sat 11-4.
Services:	Search service, accepts want lists.
Travel:	Rte 306 exit off Rte 90. Proceed north on Rte 306, then east on Rte 20. The shop is the last store in a long narrow building.
Credit Cards:	No
Owner:	Mary Ann Kern
Year Estab:	1980
Comments:	A modest sized shop with books in generally good condition, reasonably priced and representing a broad spectrum of subject areas. We saw some interesting titles during our visit which leads us to believe that this is a place that could well have a volume of interest to you.

Middletown
(Map 24, page 352)

Barbie's Books   **Open Shop**
1926 First Avenue 45044   (937) 422-2688

Collection:	General stock of hardcover and paperback.
# of Vols:	50,000
Hours:	Mon-Fri 12-5. Sat by appointment or chance.
Services:	Search service, accepts want lists, mail order.
Travel:	Exit 32 off I-75. Proceed west on Rte 122 to Middletown. Right on First St. Shop is two blocks ahead.
Credit Cards:	No
Owner:	Barbara Morelock
Year Estab:	1968
Comments:	We drove several miles out of our way to visit this shop based on the hours we had been given over the phone prior to our visit only to find the shop closed. Yes, we know that we advise our traveling readers to call ahead—and usually we do—but this time we goofed. Please don't make the same mistake. At the time of our visit, it appeared that the owner had only recently moved into this location and was still in the process of "settling in" as the store was in a state of disarray with boxes of books all over the floor and half empty shelves. The books we could see appeared to be older and in fair to mixed condition. Perhaps we "jumped the gun."

Millersburg
(Map 24, page 352)

AJ's Books & Whimward Books   **Antique Mall**
At Antique Emporium, 113 West Jackson Street 44654   (330) 674-0510

Collection:	General stock.
# of Vols:	2,000-3,000
Hours:	Daily 10-4. Longer hours in summer.
Travel:	At junction of Rtes 83 & 39.
Comments:	The stock of the two dealers is intermixed.

Monroe
(Map 24, page 352)

The Book Beat **Flea Market**
Buildings 9 & 10, Traders World Flea Market (937) 259-0577
Mailing address: 150 South Horton Street Dayton OH 45403

Collection:	General stock of hardcover and paperback.
# of Vols:	40,000-60,000
Hours:	Sat & Sun 9-5.
Travel:	Rte 63 exit off I-75. Proceed east on Rte 63 to Trader's World.
Year Estab:	1991
Comments:	We stumbled upon this modest sized collection located in a mammoth weekend shopper's market quite by chance. The books were mostly reading copies in good condition. Much to our surprise, and delight, we walked away with a very reasonably priced hard to find item in our field of interest.

Montpelier
(Map 24, page 352)

Science Book Service **By Appointment**
321 Iuka 43543 (419) 485-3602

Collection:	Specialty
# of Vols:	14,000
Specialties:	Science (physical and natural); creation/evolution; Jehovah's Witness and related cults.
Services:	Appraisals, accepts want lists, mail order.
Credit Cards:	No
Owner:	Dr. Gerald Bergman
Year Estab:	1971

Mount Vernon
(Map 24, page 352)

Paragraphs Bookstore **Open Shop**
515 North Sandusky Street 43050 (740) 392-9290

Collection:	General stock of mostly new and some used.
# of Vols:	60,000
Hours:	Mon-Sat 10-6.
Comments:	The stock is approximately 10% used, 70% of which is paperback.

Munroe Falls
(Map 24, page 352)

The Reading Doctor **By Appointment**
PO Box 351 44262 Tel & Fax: (330) 688-6273
  E-mail: readdoc@worldnet.att.net

Collection:	Specialty

# of Vols:	5,000
Specialties:	Children's; basal readers; aviation; nautical; military; World War II; Saalfield Press.
Services:	Search service, accepts want lists, mail order.
Credit Cards:	Yes
Owner:	V.Michael Lahey
Year Estab:	1994

Newark
(Map 24, page 352)

Cindamar   **Open Shop**
218 Granville Street 43055   (740) 345-6327

Collection:	General stock of hardcover and paperback.
# of Vols:	30,000
Specialties:	Children's; mystery; history; cookbooks; science fiction; esoterica.
Hours:	Tue-Fri 12-6. Sat 9-4.
Services:	Appraisals, accepts want lists.
Travel:	21st St exit off Rte 16. Proceed north on 21st St, then right on Granville St. Continue to 10th St. Shop is second building from 10th St.
Credit Cards:	No
Owner:	Stephanie L. Shaw
Year Estab:	1988
Comments:	If there's an inch of space that the owner of this shop has not been able to use effectively for the storage and display of books we would be quite surprised. Located in a former residence, every room (including the bathroom) has shelves displaying books of all kinds. The books on the first floor are evenly divided between hardcover volumes and paperbacks with most of the hardcover titles being reading copies, plus a few library discards and some older volumes. Children's books and French translations are located on the second floor. While it may be difficult to wend your way through the twists and turns of the shop's many sections, the possibility of discovering an unknown treasure here is certainly better than your chances of winning the powerball lottery. The owner notes that a portion of the collection is in storage in an adjacent garage.

Newbury
(Map 24, page 352)

Cattermole 20thC Children's Books   **Open Shop**
9880 Fairmount Road 44065   (440) 338-3253

Collection:	Specialty
# of Vols:	7,000
Specialties:	Children's fiction (after 1925). No series books.
Hours:	Tue-Sat 12-5. Other times by appointment.
Services:	Catalog
Travel:	Rte 306 exit off I-90. Proceed south on Rte 306 for 15 miles. Left on

Fairmount Rd and continue east for two miles. Shop driveway is on left, 1/3 mile past stop sign at Sperry Rd.

Credit Cards:	No
Owner:	Jane & Bill McCullam
Year Estab:	1987

North Olmsted
(Map 24, page 352)

ABT Books
6673 Chadbourne Drive   44070

By Appointment
(216) 235-2163

Collection:	Specialty
Specialties:	Aviation; railroads; gardening; cats.
Services:	Search service, catalog, accepts want lists.
Owner:	Dale & Lisa Abt
Year Estab:	1992

Painesville
(Map 24, page 352)

North Coast Americana
12154 State Route 608   44077

By Appointment
(440) 357-1690

Collection:	General stock and ephemera.
# of Vols:	1,000
Specialties:	Americana; nature; Native Americans; viewbooks.
Services:	Accepts want lists, search service, mail order.
Owner:	William Owen
Year Estab:	1990

Perrysburg
(Map 24, page 352)

Collectors' Choice
241543 North Dixie Highway   43551

By Appointment
(419) 872-2758

Collection:	General stock.
# of Vols:	6,000
Specialties:	John Steinbeck; children's; illustrated.
Services:	Appraisals, accepts want lists, occasional lists, mail order.
Credit Cards:	No
Owner:	Ronald Euton
Year Estab:	1976

Pioneer
(Map 24, page 352)

Pioneer Antique Mall
103 Baubice Street

Antique Mall
(419) 737-2341

Hours:	Mon-Sat 10-6. Sun 1-5.
Travel:	In downtown, across from public library.

Portsmouth
(Map 24, page 352)

Ye Olde Book Shoppe   **Open Shop**
1317 9th Street 45662   (614) 354-2960

Collection:	General stock of hardcover and paperback.
# of Vols:	2,000-3,000
Hours:	Mon-Sat 9:30-6.
Travel:	Eastbound on Rte 52, turn right on 9th.
Comments:	A non profit shop operated by Goodwill Industries.

Rocky River
(Map 27, page 275)

Yannigan's   **Open Shop**
19644 Center Ridge Road 44116   (440) 895-9880

Collection:	Specialty. New and used and memorabilia.
# of Vols:	300-500
Specialties:	Baseball
Hours:	Mon-Fri 11-7. Sat 10-6. Sun 12-5.
Services:	Search service, catalog, accepts want lists.
Travel:	Hilliard Rd exit off I-90. Proceed east on Hilliard Rd to first light, then right on Gasser and left at dead end on Center Ridge. Left at first light into Center Ridge Shopping Center.
Credit Cards:	Yes
Owner:	Richard E. Derby, Jr.
Year Estab:	1992

Rowsburg
(Map 24, page 352)

Rowsburg Bookstore   **Open Shop**
157 US 250 East   (419) 869-7697
Mailing address: 157 US Rte 250 Polk OH 44866   E-mail: rowsburg@interloc.com

Collection:	Specialty with limited general stock.
# of Vols:	16,000+
Specialties:	Americana (especially Ohio and local history); religion (scholarly); biblical; philosophy; scholarly books in any field.
Hours:	Wed-Sat 11-5. Sun 1-5.
Services:	Search service, mail order.
Travel:	Exit 186 off I-71. Proceed east on Rte 250 for six miles.
Credit Cards:	Yes
Owner:	Douglas Gunn
Year Estab:	1990
Comments:	We were fortunate to have visited this shop on our earlier visit to Ohio when it stocked a more general collection. Since then, the owner has decided to focus only on the specialties listed above. We suspect,

though, that our initial observations remain valid.

A very well organized collection in generally good condition. As can be deduced from the specialties listed above, this is a shop that deals with scholarly and serious items and indeed, most of the titles we saw clearly reflected this emphasis. Even the fiction collection reflects this focus. This is an easy shop to browse and a serious book person is likely to find items of interest here.

Russell
(Map 24, page 352)

Novelty Shop   **Open Shop**
14948 Chillicothe Road   (216) 338-5287
Mailing address: 4777 Dorshwood South Euclid OH 44121

Collection:	General stock.
# of Vols:	2,500
Specialties:	Children's illustrated; mystery.
Hours:	Thu-Sat 11-5. Sun 1-5.
Services:	Search service, accepts want lists.
Travel:	On Rte 306, just south of Rte 87. Shop is on second floor.
Credit Cards:	Yes
Owner:	Mike & Chris Franc
Year Estab:	1984

Saint Clairsville
(Map 24, page 352)

White Cliffs Bookshop   **Open Shop**
234 East Main Street 43950   (740) 695-8809
Fax: (740)695-7709
E-mail: mcmann@mindspring.com

Collection:	General stock of mostly hardcover.
# of Vols:	2,000
Specialties:	Literature; poetry; mystery. (More recent titles.)
Hours:	Tue-Fri 10-6:30. Other times by appointment.
Travel:	St. Clairsville exit of I-70. Shop is in center of town.
Services:	Appraisals, search service, catalog, accepts want lists.
Credit Cards:	No
Year Estab:	1997
Owner:	Richard G. McMann

Shaker Heights
(Map 27, page 375)

Half Price Books, Records, Magazines   **Open Shop**
20125 Van Aken Boulevard 44122   (216) 283-4420
Fax: (216) 283-6843

Collection:	General stock of new and used hardcover and paperback.

# of Vols:	100,000
Hours:	Mon-Sat 9am-10pm. Sun 12-7.
Travel:	Chagrin Blvd exit off I-271. Proceed west on Chagrin, right on Warrensville, left on Farnsleigh, then left into shopping center.
Credit Cards:	Yes
Year Estab:	1972
Comments:	With the understanding that both new and used stock changes according to local market conditions, we believe it is fair to describe the shops in the Half Price Books chain as being spacious, well organized, and carrying a large number of remainders in most fields with a strong emphasis in popular culture. The majority of the used books are paperback. While you're not likely to find truly rare items in one of these shops, you should be able to locate inexpensive copies of more popular books you may have been tempted to read.

South Euclid
(Map 24, page 352)

Paper Peddlers   **Open Shop**
4425 Mayfield Road 44121   (216) 382-6383

Collection:	General stock and ephemera.
# of Vols:	12,000
Specialties:	Children's; music; film; theater; magazines; sheet music.
Hours:	Most weekdays 1-6. Call ahead.
Travel:	Located on Rte 422 (Mayfield Rd), three miles west of I-271.
Credit Cards:	No
Owner:	Carole M. Lazarus
Year Estab:	1974

Springfield
(Map 24, page 352)

AAA I-70 Antique Mall   **Antique Mall**
4700 South Charleston Pike 45502   (937) 248-448

Hours:	Daily 10-6.
Travel:	At exit 59 off I-70.

Bell, Book & Candle Store   **Open Shop**
1335 West First Street 45504   (937) 322-4031

Collection:	General stock of mostly paperback.
# of Vols:	25,000
Hours:	Mon-Sat 10:30-5:30, except Wed 12-4.

Bookhaven of Springfield   **Open Shop**
1549 Commerce Road 45504   (937) 322-9021
                                            E-mail: alcove@icsnet1.com

Collection:	General stock of hardcover and paperback and records.
# of Vols:	45,000

Specialties:	History; religion; mystery; children's; fiction; cookbooks; technical.
Hours:	Mon-Fri 12-6. Sat 10:30-6.
Travel:	Exit 52B (Rte 68) off I-70. Proceed north on Rte 68 for one mile, then right on Rte 40 and left at first light on Bechtle. After crossing the railroad tracks, left at light on Commerce. Shop is just ahead on left.
Credit Cards:	No
Owner:	Karen Wickliff
Comments:	In addition to a generous selection of paperbacks, this shop has, what we believe to be, a very balanced selection of both modern and vintage hardcover items. We were particularly impressed with some of the older hardcover mysteries (not the more common titles) that were priced quite reasonably. If you like browsing, make sure that you get to the large back room (down a few steps) and keep your eyes peeled to each of the shelves lest you miss a real winner. The owner has a second shop in Columbus. See above.

Springfield Antiques Center   **Antique Mall**
1735 Titus Road   (937) 322-8868
Mailing address: PO Box 3028 Springfield OH 45501   Fax: (937) 322-8049

Hours:	Daily 10-6.
Travel:	Exit 59 off I-70.
Comments:	We acknowledge a slight antithesis towards used book dealer displays in antique malls. Notwithstanding this view, we stopped at two malls located next to one another off the same interstate exit. (See AAA I-70 Antique Mall above.) At the time of our visit, this mall had six to eight reasonable displays of used books ranging from common titles to interesting collectibles. If you're traveling and care to take a break from the usual book store environment, you might find it fun to wander the aisles here. The neighboring mall had at least three used book displays at the time of our visit.

Steubenville
(Map 24, page 352)

Bishop Of Books   **Open Shop**
328 Market Street 43952   (740) 283-2665
Mailing address: PO Box 579 Steubenville OH 43952   Fax: (740) 264-5120

Collection:	General stock of hardcover and paperback.
# of Vols:	30,000
Hours:	Mon-Sat 9-5.
Services:	Appraisals, search service, catalog, accepts want lists.
Travel:	Rte 7 to Washington St, then east on Washington for one short block, south on 3rd and west on Market.
Credit Cards:	No
Owner:	Roger Bertoia
Year Estab:	1987
Comments:	The good news is that this shop has a large stock of primarily hardcover

books ranging from book club editions to some hard to find items. Most of the books, even those with dust jackets, were of an earlier vintage. The bad news is that even though the books appear to be organized by category, as one wanders from shelf to shelf (particularly in the back room) and around each shelf, one finds a second or third section containing the same category of books seen elsewhere in the shop. This is a store that will require much patience to browse but if you know what you're looking for (and don't mind some of the organization problems), you could conceivably leave with several items purchased at bargain prices. If time is short, or you want to spare yourself a visit, we suggest you request a copy of the owner's catalog and do your browsing by mail.

Swanton
(Map 24, page 352)

Munchkin Book Shop
10435 Airport Highway 43558

Open Shop
(419) 865-1091

Collection:	General stock of mostly paperback.
# of Vols:	100,000+
Specialties:	Vintage paperbacks.
Hours:	Mon-Sat 11-5.

Sylvania
(Map 24, page 352)

A Novel Idea
5700 Monroe Street 43560

Open Shop
(419) 882-3939

Collection:	General stock of paperback and hardcover.
# of Vols:	36,000 (combined)
Specialties:	Mystery
Hours:	Mon-Wed 10-6. Thu 10-8. Fri & Sat 10-6.
Travel:	Sylvania/Monroe St exit off Rte 23. Proceed east on Monroe for 1½ miles. Shop is in Starlite Plaza.
Credit Cards:	No
Year Estab:	1989
Comments:	Stock is approximately 75% paperback.

Tiffin
(Map 24, page 352)

Books And More
113 East Perry Street 44883

By Appointment
(419) 448-1388
E-mail: jteeters@bpsom.com

Collection:	General stock of used and new.
# of Vols:	8,000
Services:	Appraisals, search service, accepts want lists, mail order.
Credit Cards:	Yes

Owner:	John D. Teeters
Year Estab:	1996
Comments:	Stock is approximately 60% used, most of which is hardcover.

My Bookhouse   **By Appointment**
27 South Sandusky Street 44883   (419) 447-9842
Web page: www.bright.net/~mybooks   E-mail: mybooks@bright.net

Collection:	General stock of mostly used.
# of Vols:	10,000
Specialties:	Children's; children's series; literary first editions; mystery; vintage paperbacks; history; art; photoplay editions.
Services:	Search service, catalog, accepts want lists.
Credit Cards:	No
Owner:	Cher Bibler
Year Estab:	1980
Comments:	Since our visit to this shop 3½ years ago, the owner has switched to a by appointment basis (at the same location) and has taken a booth at the Junction Antique Mall in Bellevue (see above). After our earlier visit we noted:
	A small shop with lots of mini rooms in which almost every inch of space is used to its maximum capacity. (The humor section is located in the bathroom.) Paperbacks and hardcover books are intershelved in some sections. In addition to the specialties listed above, the shop has enough off beat stock to make a visit here worthwhile.

Tipp City
(Map 24, page 352)

Browse Awhile Books   **Open Shop**
118 East Main Street 45371   (937) 667-7200
                                        E-mail: wiljones@mcione.com

Collection:	General stock of hardcover and paperback.
# of Vols:	100,000+
Specialties:	History
Hours:	Mon-Fri 12-6. Sat 12-4.
Services:	Appraisals, search service, accepts want lists.
Travel:	Exit 68 (Tipp City) off I-75. Proceed east on Rte 571 to downtown where Rte 571 becomes Main St.
Credit Cards:	Yes
Owner:	William A. Jones
Year Estab:	1981
Comments:	The shop has a mix of paperbacks (quite a large number) and hardcover books which fill a series of rooms to the rear of the shop. Most of the hardcover volumes were of fairly recent vintage and were in generally good condition. If you're an American history buff, you'll appreciate the connection between this city and the nickname "Tippacanoe."

Toledo
(Map 24, page 352)

W.K. Freedley's Books   **Open Shop**
3835 Rohr Drive 43613   (419) 472-9097

Collection:	General stock of mostly paperback.
# of Vols:	35,000
Hours:	Mon-Sat 11-6.

Frogtown Books   **Open Shop**
2131 North Reynolds Road 43615   (419) 531-8101
                                                            Fax: (419) 531-8139
                                                            E-mail: frogtown@toltbbs.com

Collection:	General stock of mostly hardcover.
# of Vols:	20,000
Specialties:	Illustrated; Harrison Fisher; Gone With The Wind; golf.
Hours:	Mon-Sat 10-7. Sun 12-5.
Services:	Appraisals, occasional catalog, mail order.
Travel:	From I-80/I-90: Exit 4/59: Proceed north on Reynolds (Rte 20) for about five miles. From I-475: Exit 8. Proceed east on Rte 2, then left on Reynolds.
Credit Cards:	Yes
Owner:	Pete & Cheryl Baughman
Year Estab:	1990
Comments:	The owners take great care to select and display books in excellent condition. Much of what we saw could easily fall into the collectible category. You would be missing something if you were anywhere near Toledo and didn't visit this shop. The owners also display at Jeffrey's Antique Gallery in Findlay. See above.

Trotwood
(Map 24, page 352)

Cap'n Books Treasure Chest   **Open Shop**
303 East Main Street 45426   (937) 854-2049

Collection:	General stock of paperback and hardcover.
# of Vols:	10,000
Hours:	Mon & Tue 9-5. Thu 9-4. Fri 12-7. Sat 9-6. EXCEPT Jun-Sept: Thu & Fri only.
Services:	Accepts want lists, mail order.
Travel:	Rte 49 exit off I-70. Proceed south on Rte 49, then right at light in Trotwood and left on Main.
Credit Cards:	No
Owner:	Sylvia Seitz
Year Estab:	1995
Comments:	Stock is approximately 70% paperback. Shop also sells gifts and greeting cards.

Troy
(Map 24, page 352)

Around About Books   **Open Shop**
8 West Main Street 45373   (937) 339-1707

Collection:	General stock of hardcover and paperback.
# of Vols:	70,000
Hours:	Mon-Sat 10-8. Sun 1-5.
Travel:	Exit 74A off I-75. Proceed east on Rte 41 South (Main St) for about two miles. Shop is one block before the traffic circle.
Credit Cards:	Yes
Owner:	Gary & Debbie Zuhl
Year Estab:	1992
Comments:	While this bi-level shop does have a heavy selection of paperbacks, the number of hardcover volumes on hand is quite respectable. Most of the hardcover books we saw were in good condition and of fairly recent vintage. Both levels are nicely carpeted and the shop is easy to browse. While this shop may be a fine source for recently out-of-print volumes, you're less likely to discover any rare or unusual titles on its shelves.

Wapakoneta
(Map 24, page 352)

The Bookmark   **Open Shop**
8 South Black Hoof Street 45895   (419) 738-4494

Collection:	General stock of hardcover and paperback.
# of Vols:	10,000
Hours:	Tue-Fri 10-6. Sat 10-2.
Services:	Appraisals, accepts want lists, mail order.
Travel:	Exit 111 off I-75. Proceed west on Pearl St, then right on Black Hoof.
Credit Cards:	No
Owner:	Charlotte Williams
Year Estab:	1995
Comments:	Stock is approximately 75% hardcover.

Washington Court House
(Map 24, page 352)

B & D Collectibles   **Open Shop**
143 North Main Street 43160   (740) 335-8417

Collection:	General stock and ephemera.
# of Vols:	4,000
Specialties:	*National Geographic.*
Hours:	Mon-Fri 10-5. Open most Sat 10-5 but best to call ahead.
Services:	Accepts want lists, mail order.
Travel:	Rte 35 exit off I-71. Proceed east on Rte 35 for about 10 miles. Shop is located in center of town across from courthouse.

Credit Cards:	Yes
Owner:	Bob & Doris Lutz
Year Estab:	1987
Comments:	Calling the shop "collectibles" rather than "book store" was probably a wise move on the part of the owners since more than half the stock (and more than half the space) in this shop is devoted to collectibles. The books on hand were mostly older and in mixed condition. Prices were quite reasonable. While you're not likely to find a rare or scholarly volume here, you could find something of nostalgic interest.

Westerville
(Map 24, page 352)

The Book Harbor   **Open Shop**
32 West College Avenue 43081   (614) 895-3788
E-mail: bookharbor@aol.com

Collection:	General stock of hardcover and paperback and ephemera.
# of Vols:	22,000
Specialties:	Mystery; Civil War; science fiction; film; television; illustrated; British history; Americana; military; crafts; Ohio.
Hours:	Mon-Wed & Fri 12-8. Sat 11-6. Sun 1-5. Closed Thu.
Services:	Search service, mail order.
Travel:	On Rte 3, two miles north of I-270. Turn west on College. Shop is in first house on right after stores.
Credit Cards:	Yes
Owner:	George Spurgeon
Year Estab:	1988
Comments:	This shop has a modest collection of mixed vintage books in mixed condition, a healthy supply of paperbacks and some collectible items in the specialties listed above.

Foul Play   **Open Shop**
27 East College Avenue 43081   (614) 818-2583

Collection:	Specialty new and mostly paperback used.
# of Vols:	25,000 (used)
Specialties:	Mystery; horror; science fiction; fantasy.
Hours:	Tue-Sat 10-6:30.
Services:	Accepts want lists, mail order.
Travel:	State St/Rte 3 exit off I-270. Proceed north on Rte 3, then east on College. Shop is 1/2 block ahead on right.
Credit Cards:	Yes
Owner:	John Cross
Comments:	Stock is approximately 60% used, most of which is paperback.

The Little Bookshop   **Open Shop**
58 East Main Street 43081   Store: (614) 899-1537
Home: (614) 882-1175

Collection:	General stock.

# of Vols:	10,000-15,000
Specialties:	Literature (modern); literary first editions; military; Western Americana; children's.
Hours:	Tue & Thu 12-8. Sat 12-5. Other times by appointment.
Services:	Appraisals, accepts want lists.
Travel:	Rte 3 exit off I-270. Proceed north on Rte 3 then right on Main.
Credit Cards:	No
Owner:	Bill Radloff
Year Estab:	1994
Comments:	Located in a former private home, we hope that the roadwork we encountered when visiting will be completed by the time you visit. Each room in the shop is packed to the hilt with an assortment of hardcover titles of mixed vintage. We spotted more than a fair share of truly collectible volumes, as well as some run of the mill titles. A heated garage to the rear of the residence houses the owner's military collection and other non fiction titles. Unless your tastes are very specific (in which case you may want to phone ahead to determine if the owner has something for you), you may well find your visit here to be worth your while.

Willoughby

(Map 24, page 352)

The World of Books   **Open Shop**
37231 Euclid Avenue 44094   (440) 951-1252

Collection:	General stock.
# of Vols:	30,000
Specialties:	Art; poetry; children's.
Hours:	Mon-Fri 2:30-6. Sat 10-6.
Services:	Appraisals
Travel:	Located on Rte 20 in Willoughby.
Credit Cards:	No
Owner:	Lynn M. Robinson
Year Estab:	1973
Comments:	A bi-level shop with mostly older volumes in mixed condition. The books were quite reasonably priced but few titles, except in the owner's areas of specialty, were truly unusual or difficult to find elsewhere.

Wooster

(Map 24, page 352)

Books In Stock   **Open Shop**
140 East Liberty Street 44691   (330) 262-2665

Collection:	General stock of paperbacks and hardcover.
# of Vols:	70,000
Hours:	Mon-Sat 8:30-9. Sun 1-5.
Services:	Appraisals, search service, accepts want lists, mail order.

Travel: Liberty St is the main street in downtown. Shop is 1/2 block east of
                     town square.
Credit Cards: No
Owner: Judi Stock
Year Estab: 1989
Comments: The majority of the stock in this bi-level shop was paperback with
                     most of the hardcover volumes consisting of reading copies of more
                     recent titles. The shelves are well labeled and there are several maps
                     posted around the shop to help visitors find the subject categories
                     they're looking for. The books were in generally good condition.

Worthington
(Map 24, page 352)

The Looking Glass   **By Appointment**
5584 Morning Street 43085   Tel & Fax: (614) 848-5600

Collection: General stock.
Specialties: Canadian authors; Nevil Shute; Loren Eiseley; mystery.
Services: Search service, catalog, accepts want lists.
Credit Cards: No
Year Estab: 1979

Village Bookshop   **Open Shop**
2424 West Dublin-Granville 43235   (614) 889-2674

Collection: General stock of new and hardcover used.
# of Vols: 1,000+ (used)
Hours: Daily 10-10.
Travel: Rte 161 exit off Rte 315. Proceed west on Rte 161 (Dublin-Granville
                     Rd). Shop is in an old church.

Yellow Springs
(Map 24, page 352)

Dark Star Books & Comics   **Open Shop**
237 Xenia Avenue 45387   (937) 767-9400
                                                          Fax: (937) 767-7926

Collection: Specialty
# of Vols: 20,000
Specialties: Science fiction; mystery.
Hours: Daily. Call for hours.
Services: Accepts want lists, mail order.
Travel: Rte 68 exit off I-70. Proceed south on Rte 68 to which becomes Xenia
                     Ave in Yellow Springs.
Credit Cards: Yes
Owner: Mary Alice Walker
Year Estab: 1982
Comments: The owner operates a second, smaller shop in Dayton. See below.

Youngstown
(Map 24, page 352)

Copperfield & Twist Bookstore   **Open Shop**
7050 Market Street, #102 44512   (330) 726-8175
                                                 E-mail: coppertwst@aol.com

Collection:	General stock.
# of Vols:	30,000
Specialties:	Mystery; modern first editions; military.
Hours:	Mon-Fri 10-7. Sat 10-5. Sun by appointment.
Services:	Appraisals, search service, accepts want lists, mail order.
Travel:	From I-76 (Ohio Tpk): Exit 16. Proceed north on Rte 7 (Market St) for three miles. From I-80 westbound: Rte 11 exit. Proceed south on Rte 11 to Canfield exit, then east on Rte 224 and left on Rte 7. Shop is one block ahead on left.
Credit Cards:	Yes
Owner:	Alan B. Cohen
Year Estab:	1995
Comments:	Most accommodating owners with an attractive and well organized shop. The books we saw were in good to excellent condition and consisted of both "old favorites" and a nice selection of unusual titles. Reasonably priced. Well worth a visit.

Goodwill Industries Book Store   **Open Shop**
7990 Boardman-Poland Road 44512   (330) 629-8822

Collection:	General stock of hardcover and paperback.
Hours:	Mon-Sat 10-8. Sun 12-5.
Travel:	Near Southern Blvd.

Lyn's Books & Miniatures   **Open Shop**
5370 Clarkins Drive, Ste 53 44515   (330) 799-1939

Collection:	General stock of primarily paperback.
# of Vols:	10,000
Hours:	Daily 10-5.

Twice-Loved Books   **Open Shop**
19 East Midlothian Boulevard 44507   (330) 783-2016
                                                 E-mail: twice@bright.net

Collection:	General stock of mostly used paperback and hardcover.
# of Vols:	60,000
Specialties:	Literature (avant garde); black studies; eastern and western spirituality; women's fiction.
Hours:	Mon-Fri 9-8. Sat 9-6. Sun 12-5.
Services:	Appraisals, search service, accepts want lists.
Travel:	Exit 9A off I-680. Proceed west on Midlothian Blvd (Rte 625) for two miles. Shop is on the left, just before the intersection of Market St and Midlothian.

Credit Cards: Yes
Owner: Peggy & Gary McKissick
Year Estab: 1982
Comments: We estimate that at least 50% of the books in this combination new/ used tri-level shop are paperback. Most of the used hardcover volumes we saw were of mixed vintage and in generally good condition and were intershelved with the new books by subject. We saw very few books that were underpriced.

Zanesville
(Map 24, page 352)

Friends of the Library Bookstore   **Open Shop**
220 North 5th Street 43701   (740) 452-4893

Hours: Tue & Sat 10-2.

Zoar
(Map 24, page 352)

Books N' Things   **Open Shop**
365 Main Street   (330) 874-3050
Mailing address: PO Box 471 Zoar OH 44697

Collection: General stock of mostly hardcover.
# of Vols: 10,000
Specialties: Children's
Hours: Tue-Sat 10-5. Sun 1-5.
Services: Accepts want lists.
Travel: Exit 93 off I-77. Proceed east on Rte 212 for two miles. Shop is at corner of 4th St, across from public garden.
Credit Cards: No
Owner: Colleen Taylor
Year Estab: 1980
Comments: A pleasant shop in an historic village with nice (but not rare) books of mixed vintage in many categories. Most of the hardcover volumes we saw were reading copies. The shop also sells some new children's books and has a tea room.

After Five Booksellers
991 Brunswick Road Cleveland Hts. OH 44112

(216) 851-4478
E-mail:afterfive@interloc.com

Collection:	General stock.
# of Vols:	4,000
Specialties:	Science; Ohio; non fiction.
Services:	Accepts want lists.
Credit Cards:	No
Owner:	Marianne & Robert Novak
Year Estab:	1990

Argonne Books
PO Box 516 Cortland 44410

(330) 637-9355
E-mail: Argonne2@aol.com

Collection:	Specialty
# of Vols:	1,500
Specialties:	World War I.
Services:	Search service, catalog, accepts want lists.
Year Estab:	1979

Bible Scholar Books (and Liberty Archives)
1395 Westwood Avenue Alliance 44601

(330) 821-9807

Collection:	Specialty
# of Vols:	3,000
Specialties:	Religion (Reformed and Evangelical theology); apologetics; philosophy; J. Gresham Machen; Patrick Henry.
Services:	Catalog, accepts want lists.
Credit Cards:	No
Owner:	Joel R. Parkinson
Year Estab:	1991

Bibliomania Book Store
6544 Columbus Pike Lewis Center 43035

(740) 548-5589
E-mail: franbooks@aol.com

Collection:	General stock.
# of Vols:	10,000
Specialties:	Modern first editions.
Services:	Search service, accepts want lists.
Credit Cards:	No
Owner:	Fran Chennells
Year Estab:	1978

The Bookman Of Kent
608 Fairchild Avenue Kent 44240

(330) 673-1894
E-mail: jimbest@sprintmail.com

Collection:	Specialty
# of Vols:	1,200+
Specialties:	Travel & exploration (pre-WW I); illustrated (pre-1860).
Services:	Appraisals, accepts want lists.
Credit Cards:	No
Owner:	Jim Best
Year Estab:	1981

Books Of The Ages   (513) 732-3456
4764 Silverwood Drive Batavia 45103

Collection:	Specialty
# of Vols:	2,000
Specialties:	Children's; illustrated; Tasha Tudor.
Services:	Catalog, accepts want lists.
Credit Cards:	No
Owner:	Gary J. Overmann
Year Estab:	1989

Bookworm & Bugjuice   (216) 398-9105
4403 Spokane Avenue Cleveland 44109   E-mail: bookworm@en.com

Collection:	General stock.
# of Vols:	6,000+
Specialties:	Fiction; science fiction; mystery.
Services:	Search service, accepts want lists.
Credit Cards:	No
Owner:	Kenneth Burington
Year Estab:	1992

Carol Butcher Books   (330) 793-6832
3955 New Road Youngstown 44515

Collection:	Specialty
Specialties:	Dogs; horses; hunting; Christianity.
Services:	Search service, catalog (excluding Christianity).
Credit Cards:	No
Year Estab:	1967
Comments:	Collection may also be viewed by appointment.

Candy Books   (614) 888-2659
263 Abbot Avenue Worthington 43085   E-mail: candybks@interloc.com

Collection:	General stock (Primarily non fiction).
# of Vols:	25,000
Specialties:	Military; cookbooks; biography; music; Judaica.
Services:	Occasional catalog, accepts want lists.
Credit Cards:	Yes
Owner:	Irene M. Candy
Year Estab:	1988

Mike DeBaptiste, Books   (216) 381-8092
4402 Prasse Road Cleveland 44121

Collection:	Specialty
# of Vols:	15,000
Specialties:	Children's series.
Services:	Search service, accepts want lists.
Credit Cards:	No
Year Estab:	1990

Elegant Book & Map Co.   (740) 432-4068
PO Box 1302 Cambridge 43725

Collection:	Specialty
# of Vols:	10,000
Specialties:	History; Americana; needlecrafts; maps; manufacturing/trades.
Services:	Accepts want lists.
Credit Cards:	No
Owner:	David Gander
Year Estab:	1988

Fickes Crime Fiction   (330) 773-4223
1471 Burkhardt Avenue   Akron 44301   Fax: (330) 773-4235
                                                    E-mail: fickes@sssnet.com

Collection:	Specialty
# of Vols:	8,000
Specialties:	Mystery; suspense; adventure.
Credit Cards:	No
Owner:	Patricia A. Fickes
Year Estab:	1983

C.H. Fischer, Books   (330) 650-4243
1668 Sapphire Drive Hudson 44236

Collection:	General stock.
# of Vols:	8,000
Specialties:	Natural history; Ohio.
Services:	Accepts want lists.
Credit Cards:	No
Year Estab:	1980

Good Ol' Days Books   (330) 658-2793
PO Box 264 Doylestown OH 44230

Collection:	Specialty
Specialties:	Boy scouts; girl scouts (official publications).
Services:	Appraisals, catalog.
Credit Cards:	No
Owner:	Cal Holden
Year Estab:	1985

D. Gratz, Books   (419) 358-7431
8990 Augsburger Road Bluffton 45817

Collection:	Specialty
Specialties:	Mennonite and Amish genealogy. (A few other genealogies are available).
Credit Cards:	No
Owner:	Delbert L. Gratz
Year Estab:	1955

Richard A. Hand, Bookseller   (740) 453-1732
280 East Highland Drive Zanesville 43701   E-mail: handbook@interloc.com

Collection:	Specialty
# of Vols:	700
Specialties:	Archeology (North, Central and South American).
Services:	Search service, catalog, accepts want lists.
Credit Cards:	No
Year Estab:	1986

Gordon W. Huber   (330) 923-6994
2767 8th Street Cuyahoga Falls 44221

Collection:	Specialty
# of Vols:	2,000
Specialties:	Children's series; mystery; science fiction; fantasy.
Services:	Accepts want lists.
Credit Cards:	No
Year Estab:	1979

J.R. Huber, Bookseller   (419) 999-4556
PO Box 8067 Lima 45805   E-mail: jrhuber@bright.net

Collection:	General stock.
Credit Cards:	No
Owner:	Ron & Cathy Huber
Year Estab:	1981
Comments:	Also displays at Jeffrey's Antique Gallery in Findlay and Springfield Antiques Center in Springfield. See above.

Invisible Ink: Books on Ghosts & Hauntings   (800) 314-4678
1811 Stonewood Drive Dayton 45432   Fax:(937) 320-1832
Web page: www.invink.com   E-mail: invisiblei@aol.com

Collection:	Specialty used and new.
# of Vols:	2,500
Specialties:	Ghosts; paranormal; supernatural; cryptozoology.
Services:	Accepts want lists.
Credit Cards:	Yes
Owner:	Chris Woodyard
Year Estab:	1989
Comments:	Stock is evenly divided between used and new.

Tony Lamy, Bookseller   (513) 821-5187
2809 Raleigh Lane Cincinnati 45215   E-mail: books@one.net

Collection:	Specialty
# of Vols:	2,000
Specialties:	Modern fiction; mystery.
Services:	Accepts want lists.
Credit Cards:	No
Year Estab:	1997

Leyshon's Books Etc.
PO Box 141133 Columbus 43214
Web page: railroadbooks.com

Tel & Fax: (614) 262-6120
E-mail: leyshonsbooksetc@worldnet.att.net

Collection:	Specialty
# of Vols:	2,000
Specialties:	Railroads, steamboats.
Services:	Search service, catalog, accepts want lists.
Credit Cards:	Yes
Owner:	Anna C. Leyshon
Year Estab:	1988

The Literate Veteran
1948 West 104th Street Cleveland 44102
Web page: www.abebooks.com

(216) 961-4757
E-mail: litveteran@stratos.net

Collection:	Specialty. Mostly used.
# of Vols:	2,000
Specialties:	Military
Services:	Search service, accepts want lists.
Credit Cards:	No
Owner:	Mike Vrabec
Year Estab:	1993

Jerry Merkel
2281 Spahr Road Xenia 45385

(937) 848-2359
E-mail: merkbook@sprynet.com

Collection:	General stock.
# of Vols:	5,000
Specialties:	Military; Americana; biography; scholarly books in all fields.
Services:	Appraisals, search service, accepts want lists.
Credit Cards:	No
Year Estab:	1973

A.A. Miran Arts and Books
921 Eastwind Drive Columbus 43081

Tel & Fax: (614) 224-6566
E-mail: miranbks@interloc.com

Collection:	General stock.
# of Vols:	30,000
Specialties:	Medicine
Credit Cards:	Yes
Owner:	Ivan Gilbert
Year Estab:	1975
Comments:	Collection can be viewed by appointment in a warehouse setting.

Murder By The Book
3300 Butternut Drive Norton 44203

(330) 706-0348

Collection:	Specialty
# of Vols:	1,000+
Specialties:	Sherlock Holmes; pulps; hardboiled.
Services:	Accepts want lists.

Credit Cards: No
Owner: Terry & Peg Sanford
Year Estab: 1982

Jeffrey Neumann
9960 Mount Eaton Road Wadsworth 44281

(216) 334-1784
E-mail: CNPI147@aol.com

Collection: Specialty books and ephemera.
# of Vols: 5,000
Specialties: Jehovah's Witness; Watchtower Society; International Bible Students.
Services: Appraisals, search service, accepts want lists.
Credit Cards: Yes
Year Estab: 1980

North Coast Paper Mill
PO Box 15 Hayesville 44838

Tel & Fax: (419) 994-5472

Collection: General stock.
# of Vols: 12,000-15,000
Specialties: Midwest Americana.
Services: Search service, accepts want lists, occasional catalog.
Credit Cards: No
Owner: Stewart Zody (contact person)
Year Estab: 1976

Owl Creek Books
235 Parrott Street Mount Vernon 43050

(740) 397-9337

Collection: General stock.
Services: Appraisals, search service, accepts want lists.
Credit Cards: No
Owner: B.K. Clinker
Year Estab: 1970

Kal Palnicki
PO Box 8063 Columbus 43201

(614) 421-0649
E-mail: kalpal@aol.com

Collection: General stock.
# of Vols: 10,000-15,000
Specialties: Emphasis on non fiction.
Services: Accepts want lists.
Credit Cards: No

Mike Parise, Books
410 McCartney Road Campbell 44405

(330) 743-0073
E-mail: mparise874@aol.com

Collection: Specialty
# of Vols: 3,000+
Specialties: Edgar Rice Burroughs; science fiction; photography.
Services: Appraisals, search service, accepts want lists, occasional catalog.
Credit Cards: No
Year Estab: 1974

Professional Book Service
PO Box 366 Dayton 45401

(937) 277-3079
Fax: (937) 275-5452
E-mail: 3626018@mcimail.com

Collection:	Specialty
# of Vols:	6,000
Specialties:	Law; medicine; science; music.
Services:	Appraisals, search service, catalog, accepts want lists.
Credit Cards:	Yes
Owner:	Gene Mayl
Year Estab:	1963

Publix Books
PO Box 181075 Cleveland 44118

(216) 249-2123
E-mail: publixbk@interloc.com

Collection:	General stock.
# of Vols:	6,000
Specialties:	English literature; history of medicine; natural history; cookbooks.
Services:	Appraisals, search service, catalog, accepts want lists.
Credit Cards:	No
Owner:	Wesley C. & Nina T. Williams
Year Estab:	1937

R & K Book Exchange
100 Snyder Avenue Struthers 44471

(330) 755-9094

Collection:	General stock.
# of Vols:	5,000
Credit Cards:	No
Owner:	Ruth A. Dunlap
Year Estab:	1992

R & R Books
3401 Dawnridge Drive Dayton 45414

(937) 454-0942

Collection:	Specialty
# of Vols:	3,000
Specialties:	Religion (primarily Protestant and Fundamental).
Services:	Catalog
Credit Cards:	No
Year Estab:	1992

R. D. Book Search
PO Box 71 Newtonsville OH 45158

Tel & Fax: (513) 625-8403
E-mail: rdbksrch@interloc.com

Collection:	Specialty
# of Vols:	1,000
Specialties:	Black literature; modern first editions; mystery; detective.
Services:	Search service, accepts want lists.
Credit Cards:	No
Owner:	Richard Dickson
Year Estab:	1991

Ramtek International
(419) 668-9640
6 Vinewood Drive Norwalk 44857

Collection:	Specialty. Mostly used and some new, paperback and hardcover.
Specialties:	Astrology, palmistry; occult; early science; technology; stamps; coins; marketing.
Services:	Search service.
Credit Cards:	No
Owner:	Dr. Richard P. Germann
Year Estab:	1948

The Rare Bookworm
(419) 472-0149

Collection:	Specialty
# of Vols:	1,000
Specialties:	Children's; homeschooling; first editions; poetry; basal readers; Little Golden Books.
Services:	Search service, accepts want lists.
Credit Cards:	No
Owner:	Liz Sullivan
Year Estab:	1990

Regarding Books
(See Comments) (513) 531-4717
E-mail: bkstrm@iac.net
6000 Ridge Road Cincinnati 45213
Web page: www.bookstream.com

Collection:	General stock of mostly hardcover.
# of Vols:	5,000
Specialties:	History
Owner:	Gladys & Bill Parker
Year Estab:	1994
Comments:	At press time the business was moving from the above location and the new address and phone number were not available. The e-mail address will remain the same.

Joseph F. Scheetz Antiquarian Books
(330) 758-0427
E-mail: scheetz@worldnet.att.net
6236 Foxridge Drive Boardman 44512

Collection:	General stock.
Credit Cards:	Yes
Year Estab:	1975

Strange Birds Books
(513) 631-3336
E-mail: strngbirds@aol.com
PO Box 12639 Norwood OH 45212

Collection:	Specialty paperback and hardcover.
# of Vols:	15,000
Specialties:	Mystery and detective.
Services:	Search service, catalog, accepts want lists.
Credit Cards:	Yes
Owner:	Ken Hughes
Year Estab:	1992

Tabula Rasa (330) 836-8851
985 West Exchange Street Akron 44302 E-mail: sarex@raex.com
Web page: http://www.raex.com/tabula.html

Collection:	Specialty books (mostly hardcover) and ephemera.
# of Vols:	5,000+
Specialties:	Science fiction; fantasy; fin de siecle literature and history.
Services:	Search service, catalog, accepts want lists.
Credit Cards:	No
Owner:	Karl E. Ziellenbach
Year Estab:	1994

Tally Ho Studios Tel & Fax: (330) 452-4488
639 Park Avenue, SW Canton 44706

Collection:	General stock, collectibles and ephemera.
# of Vols:	10,000
Specialties:	Film; magazines; television; science fiction.
Services:	Accepts want lists.
Credit Cards:	Yes
Owner:	Darlene Parsons
Year Estab:	1972

Lila Trudel Books Tel & Fax: (419) 826-8071
405 Dodge Street Swanton 43558 E-mail: booksIt@aol.com

Collection:	Specialty
Specialties:	Horses, especially standardbred and some thoroughbred.
Year Estab:	1985

John Wade (513) 661-2890
PO Box 11560 Cincinnati 45211 E-mail: chipande@aol.com

Collection:	General stock and ephemera.
# of Vols:	3,000-4,000
Specialties:	Modern first editions; Americana; illustrated; children's; early printed books.
Services:	Appraisals for institutions, accepts want lists.
Credit Cards:	No
Year Estab:	1979
Comments:	Also displays at the Duck Creek Antique Mall and Grand Antique Mall in Cincinnati and Circle City Books in Indianapolis, IN.

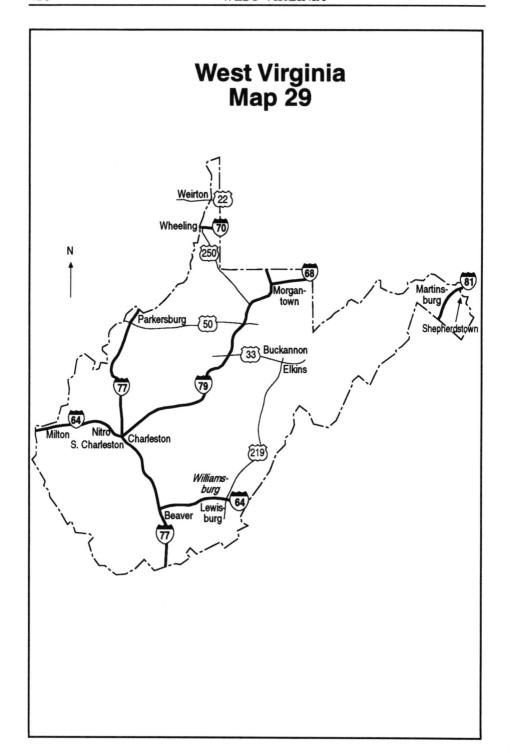

West Virginia
Map 29

Ex Libris
Frederick Eugene Hartnell

WEST VIRGINIA

Alphabetical Listing By Dealer

Bittersweet Books & Antiques	428	Paradox Book Store	432
The Book Store	431	Shepherdstown Book Shop	431
Books Books Books	429	Southwood Books	428
Books USA	432	Stilwell Book Shop	430
The Bookstore	428	Stroud Booksellers	433
The Bookstore	427	T & C Book Exchange	427
Patrick Cummings Books	433	Trans Allegheny Books	430
Four Seasons Books	431	Trans Allegheny Books	427
Mountain Heritage Books	433	Treasures Galore	429
Nailler Books	429	C.E. Turley	430
Olde Kilbourn Mill	428	Unicorn, Ltd.	433
Page Turners	427		

Alphabetical Listing By Location

Location	Dealer	Page
Beaver	T & C Book Exchange	427
Bruceton Mills	Unicorn, Ltd.	433
Buckhannon	The Bookstore	427
Charleston	Page Turners	427
	Trans Allegheny Books	427
Elkins	Bittersweet Books & Antiques	428
Lewisburg	The Bookstore	428
Martinsburg	Olde Kilbourn Mill	428
	Southwood Books	428
Milton	Treasures Galore	429
Morgantown	Books Books Books	429
	Nailler Books	429
	Stilwell Book Shop	430
Nitro	C.E. Turley	430
Parkersburg	Trans Allegheny Books	430
Saint Marys	Mountain Heritage Books	433
Shepherdstown	Four Seasons Books	431
	Shepherdstown Book Shop	431
South Charleston	The Book Store	431
Vienna	Patrick Cummings Books	433
Weirton	Books USA	432
Wheeling	Paradox Book Store	432
Williamsburg	Stroud Booksellers	433

Beaver
(Map 29, page 426)

T & C Book Exchange   **Open Shop**
Ritter Drive (Route 19)   25813   (304) 253-1878

Collection: General stock of mostly paperback.
# of Vols: 50,000
Hours: Mon-Sat 9-4.

Buckhannon
(Map 29, page 426)

The Bookstore   **Open Shop**
15 East Main Street   26201   (304) 472-1840

Collection: General stock of new and mostly hardcover used.
# of Vols: 1,500 (used)
Hours: Mon-Thu 9-6. Fri & Sat 8-8. Sun 8-1.
Travel: Exit 99 off I-79. Proceed east on Rte 33 to Buckhannon.
Credit Cards: Yes
Owner: Mike Oldiker

Charleston
(Map 29, page 426)

Page Turners   **Open Shop**
3410 Noyes Avenue   25304   (304) 342-2090

Collection: General stock of mostly paperback.
# of Vols: 5,000
Hours: Tue-Fri 11-6. Sat 11-4.

Trans Allegheny Books   **Open Shop**
118 Capital Street   Charleston 25301   (304) 346-0551
Web page: www.transabooks.com   Fax: (304) 345-0911
                                              E-mail:tabooks@westco.net

Collection: General stock of hardcover and paperback.
# of Vols: 50,000
Specialties: Appalachia
Hours: Tue- Sat 10-6. Other times by appointment.
Services: Appraisals, search service, mail order.
Travel: Virginia St exit off I-64. Proceed east on Virginia, then left on Capital.
Credit Cards: Yes
Owner: Joseph Sakach
Year Estab: 1988
Comments: We visited this shop 3½ years ago when it was located a few doors
                  away and at the time made the following observations:
                  Unlike its sister store in Parkersburg (see below), the mix of books
                  on display here shows a greater emphasis towards items of slightly
                  more recent vintage. Most subjects are represented with some rare

and unusual items in a glass display case at the front entrance.
Prices were reasonable and the books in good condition.

Elkins
(Map 29, page 426)

Bittersweet Books & Antiques   **Open Shop**
212 Davis Avenue   (304) 636-6338
Mailing address: PO Box 1248 Elkins 26241   (800) 417-6338

Collection:	General stock and ephemera.
# of Vols:	4,000-5,000
Hours:	Mon-Sat 10-5. Sun and evenings by chance or appointment.
Services:	Appraisals, mail order.
Travel:	In center of downtown.
Credit Cards:	No
Owner:	Sandra Marshall
Year Estab:	1989

Lewisburg
(Map 29, page 426)

The Bookstore   **Open Shop**
104 South Jefferson 24901   E-mail: dfife@wise.wnpb.wvnet.edu
Web page: www.abebooks.com/hp/bookstore

Collection:	General stock of hardcover and paperback.
# of Vols:	2,000-5,000
Specialties:	History; Civil War; non fiction.
Hours:	Mon-Sat 10-5. Sun by chance.
Travel:	Lewisburg exit off I-64. Shop is in downtown.
Credit Cards:	No
Owner:	Darlene Fife & Robert Head
Year Estab:	1977

Martinsburg
(Map 29, page 426)

Olde Kilbourn Mill   **Antique Mall**
616 John Street   (304) 262-4500

Hours:	Daily, except closed Wed, 10-6.
Travel:	Exit 13 (King St) off I-81. Proceed east on King to downtown. Right on Winchester and right on John.

Southwood Books   **Open Shop**
139 South Queen Street 25401   (304) 263-6358
Web page: www.martinsburg.com/southwood/swood.html

                                        E-mail: mrice15603@erols.com

Collection:	General stock of hardcover and paperback.
# of Vols:	50,000
Hours:	Mon-Sat 10-5.

Services:	Search service, accepts want lists, mail order.
Travel:	Exit 15 off I-81. Proceed east on King St into Martinsburg. Turn north (left) on Queen. Shop is just ahead on left.
Credit Cards:	Yes
Owner:	Frances J. Rice
Year Estab:	1988
Comments:	Also displays at the Olde Kilbourn Mill. See above.

Milton
(Map 29, page 426)

Treasures Galore   **Flea Market**
In Milton Flea Market, Route 60   Market: (304) 743-9471
Mailing address: PO Box 492 Milton 25541   Home: (304) 743-6218

Collection:	General stock of mostly paperback.
# of Vols:	35,000
Hours:	Fri 8-4. Sat & Sat 8-5.

Morgantown
(Map 29, page 426)

Books Books Books   **Open Shop**
198 Foundry Street   (304) 296-4808
Mailing address: PO Box 875 Morgantown 26507

Collection:	General stock of hardcover and paperback and ephemera.
# of Vols:	75,000+
Specialties:	West Virginia; Civil War; first editions.
Hours:	Mon-Fri 10-6. Sat 10-4. Sun 12-4.
Services:	Appraisals, search service, accepts want lists, mail order.
Travel:	From I-79: Exit 152. Proceed north on Rte 19 for three miles. When Rte 19 veers left, proceed straight, following sign to business district. Proceed one short block then right on High. Shop is a few blocks ahead. From I-68: Exit 1. Proceed north on Rte 119 for 3½ miles. Right on Foundry St. Shop is across from post office.
Credit Cards:	Yes
Owner:	Gail Martin, owner. Ann Stewart Plein, manager.
Year Estab:	1980
Comments:	If you enjoy books, you should enjoy visiting this shop which has a little bit of everything. On the entry level, browsers can find signed copies and first editions as well as older books covering every conceivable subject displayed on well labeled shelves. Mystery, science fiction and other fiction titles (basically reading copies) are located on the basement level together with paperbacks and foreign languages titles. Prices are very reasonable.

Nailler Books   **By Appointment**
249 Dormont Street 26505   (304) 292-1926
                                             E-mail: jrnailler@labs.net

Collection:	Specialty

# of Vols:	8,000
Specialties:	Mystery; modern fiction.
Services:	Appraisals, search service, accepts want lists, mail order.
Credit Cards:	No
Owner:	Elaine & Jody Nailler
Year Estab:	1996

Stilwell Book Shop   **Open Shop**
150 Pleasant Street   Morgantown 26505   (304) 296-6378

Collection:	General stock of new and used hardcover and paperback.
# of Vols:	5,000 (used)
Hours:	Mon-Fri 10-5:30. Sat 10-4.
Travel:	See Books Books Books above. Shop is one block away.
Credit Cards:	Yes
Owner:	Geoffrey George
Year Estab:	1973
Comments:	A small shop that intershelves its new and used paperbacks and hardcover volumes. Most of the used items were of fairly recent vintage. The shop also offers the browser an opportunity to enjoy a cup of coffee, or more, in an adjoining cafe. At the time of our visit, we saw fewer used books than suggested above.

Nitro
(Map 29, page 426)

C.E. Turley   **Antique Mall**
At Somewhere In Time Antique Mall,   21st Street   Mall: (304) 755-0734
Mailing address: PO Box 206 Milton 25541   Home: (304) 743-4155

Collection:	General stock.
# of Vols:	6,000
Specialties:	Civil War; West Virginia; genealogy.
Hours:	Fri-Sun 8-5. Mon & Tue 9-5. Thu 12-8.
Travel:	Exit 45 off I-64. Left on Rte 25 and go one mile, then left on 21st St.
Year Estab:	1985

Parkersburg
(Map 29, page 426)

Trans Allegheny Books   **Open Shop**
725 Green Street   26101   Tel & Fax: (304) 422-4499
Web page: www.transabooks.com   E-mail: tabooks@westco.net

Collection:	General stock of hardcover and paperback.
# of Vols:	30,000+
Hours:	Mon-Sat 10-6. Other time by appointment.
Services:	Appraisals, search service, accepts want lists, mail order.
Travel:	Rte 50 exit off I-77. Proceed west on Rte 50 which becomes 7th St in Parkersburg. When the traffic pattern becomes one way, continue on 8th St for another block then turn left on Green.

Credit Cards: Yes
Owner: Joseph Sakach
Year Estab: 1985
Comments: Located in a former Carnegie Library built in 1905, this shop has retained much of the original library's aura and detail. In fact, if you want to see all the books the shop has to offer, you'll need to be nimble enough to climb the attractive winding metal staircase that provides access to three floors of narrow stacks. Browsing the volumes located in several large rooms on the second floor is considerably easier (and less of a challenge). Posted maps denote locations of the various subjects. A large number of the books were of an older vintage. The collection is certainly large enough and varied enough to be worth a visit.

Shepherdstown
(Map 29, page 426)

Four Seasons Books   **Open Shop**
116 West German Street   (304) 876-3486
Mailing address: PO Box 70 Shepherdstown 25443   Fax: (304) 876-1376
                                          E-mail: fourseas@interloc.com

Collection: General stock of mostly new and some used.
Hours: Mon-Thu 10-6. Fri 10-8. Sat 10-6. Sun 12-5.
Travel: Exit 16E exit off I-81. Proceed east on Rte 45 which becomes German St in downtown.
Credit Cards: Yes
Owner: Ruth & Mike Raubertas
Year Estab: 1991
Comments: Stock is approximately 20% used, 50% of which is hardcover.

Shepherdstown Book Shop   **Open Shop**
121 East German Street   (304) 876-9491
Mailing address: PO Box 276   25443

Collection: General stock of paperback and hardcover.
# of Vols: 5,000
Hours: Mon, Thu, Fri 12:30-4:30. Sat 11-7. Sun 12-5.
Travel: See Four Seasons Books above.
Owner: Ted Harris
Comments: Stock is approximately 70% paperback.

South Charleston
(Map 29, page 426)

The Book Store   **Open Shop**
4522 MacCorkle Avenue SW   25309   (304) 766-6526

Collection: General stock of paperback and hardcover.
# of Vols: 18,000

Hours:	Tue-Fri 10-6. Sat 11-5.
Services:	Accepts want lists.
Travel:	MacCorkle Ave exit off I-64. Proceed west on MacCorkle. Shop is about one mile ahead on right.
Credit Cards:	No
Owner:	Marty Kemplin
Year Estab:	1992
Comments:	Stock is approximately 60% paperback.

Weirton
(Map 29, page 426)

Books USA   **Open Shop**
262 Three Springs Drive   26062   (304) 723-1364

Collection:	General stock of new and used paperback and hardcover.
# of Vols:	5,000-10,000 (used).
Hours:	Daily 10-9.
Travel:	Three Springs Dr exit off Rte 22. Proceed north on Three Springs Dr. Shop is just ahead, on left, in shopping center.
Comments:	Used stock is approximately 60% paperback.

Wheeling
(Map 29, page 426)

Paradox Book Store   **Open Shop**
2228 Market Street   26003

Collection:	General stock of hardcover and paperback.
# of Vols:	25,000
Hours:	Mon-Sat from "about" 10 or 11 to "about" 4-6.
Travel:	Adjoining the Central Market.
Credit Cards:	No
Owner:	Tom Stobart
Year Estab:	1974
Comments:	We were quite lucky when we arrived in Wheeling to find this shop open at 9:45 as the owner had earlier advised us by mail that his hours were somewhat flexible (see above), and we were not able to "phone ahead" as the shop does not have a phone. The shop itself offers an array of both paperback and hardcover volumes, most of which are reading copies in mixed condition. We saw very little that might be considered either rare or collectible. You can also buy back issues of *National Geographic* and *Playboy* here. The shop is small and quite crowded but clearly serves the needs of local folks who just want to read a good novel, mystery or how-to-do-it book. If you're into historic buildings, you should find the adjoining Central Market of interest.

Williamsburg
(Map 29, page 426)

Stroud Booksellers
HC 68, Box 94   24991

By Appointment
(304) 645-7169
Fax: (304) 645-4620
E-mail: oma00238@mail.wvnet.edu

Collection:	Specialty
# of Vols:	3,500
Specialties:	Primarily religion (antiquarian and 20th century scholarly works), including church history and the Reformation. Also some early printed books; agriculture; horticulture; railroads, West Virginia.
Services:	Appraisals, catalog.
Credit Cards:	Yes
Owner:	John Nathan Stroud
Year Estab:	1975

Mail Order Dealers

Patrick Cummings Books   (304) 295-7717
1317 - 20th Street Vienna 26105

Collection:	General stock
# of Vols:	10,000
Services:	Appraisals, accepts want lists, catalog.
Credit Cards:	No
Year Estab:	1985

Mountain Heritage Books   (304) 684-2529
101 Bryan Drive Saint Marys 26170   E-mail: billw@access.mountain.net

Collection:	Specialty
# of Vols:	5,000
Specialties:	West Virginia (primarily). Some Virginia and Ohio.
Services:	Catalog, accepts want lists.
Credit Cards:	No
Owner:	William D. White
Year Estab:	1993

Unicorn, Ltd.   (304) 379-8803
PO Box 397 Bruceton Mills 26525   Fax: (304) 379-8923
Web page: www.mountain.net/~unicorn   E-mail: unicorn@access.mountain.net

Collection:	Specialty
Specialties:	Vikings; Scotland; Celtic.
Services:	Search service, catalog, accepts want lists.
Credit Cards:	Yes
Owner:	Dr. William R. McLeod
Year Estab:	1979

It's a tight squeeze — but it's worth it.

Ex Libris
Frederick Eugene Hartnell

WISCONSIN

Alphabetical Listing By Dealer

A Good Book/The Mill Antiques	476
Aardvark Book Depot	477
Ace & Bubba Treasure Hunters	469
Alternate Realities	452
Amelia's Book House	448
John Angelos, Books	459
Antique Mall of Wisconsin Dells I	475
Antique Mall of Wisconsin Dells II	475
The Autograph Alcove	459
Avol's Bookstore	452
B & B Crafts	477
Badger Trading Co.	477
Baybury Books	447
Bayview Books	459
Bibliomanics	444
Blake Books	460
BNZ Enterprises	477
Book Boutique	471
The Book Nook	457
Book Nook	476
The Book Peddler	445
The Book Place	468
The Book Place	474
The Book Seller	461
Book Store	471
The Book Store	441
The Book Trader II	450
Bookcellar	474
Booked For Murder	452
The Bookplate	477
Books on the Rebound	471
Booksmith	467
Bookworks	453
BotanaBooks & Art	469
Buttons and Bows	444
Campus Antiques Mall	459
Casanova Books	443
Chequamegon Book & Coffee Co.	473
Constant Reader Book Shop	461
Crabbe Reader	471
Crossroad Books	445
James Cummings, Bookseller	450
Daltonbooks	467
Delavan Antique & Art Centre	444
Downtown Antiques Shop	472
Downtown Books Bought & Sold	461
Downtown Books Bought & Sold	461
Downtown Books Fine Arts Bookshop	462
Dusty Dreams Books	478
Raymond Dworczyk Rare Books	478
E-Z Reading	473
Et Al's Read & Unread Books	474
Fair Chase	451
Fireside Books	467
The Foundry Books	466
Fox River Antique Mall	441
Frugal Muse Books, Music & Video	453
W. Bruce Fye Antiq. Medical Books	478

Glaeve Gallery	454	Ottawa House Books	446
Gold Dog Books	474	O.Z. Enterprises	467
Half Price Books	462	Painted Lady Gallery	448
Half Price Books	454	Paper Mountain Books	479
Half Price Books	455	Paul's Book Store	455
Half Price Books	448	Picture That Antique Mall	442
Half Price Books	443	P.I.E.S.	479
Heirloom Books and Collectibles	478	Mike Plonsker Books	472
Historic Salem	475	Portage Antique Mall	469
T.S. Hotter Antiquarian Maps & Prints	443	Ravenswood Books	475
House of Scorpio	462	Recyled Books & Music	463
James Hyer, Bookseller	478	Remember When	449
Ingrid's Books and Antiques	462	Renaissance Book Shop	464
Knollwood Books	468	Renaissance Book Shop	464
Lake Geneva Antique Mall	451	Rib Mountain Antique Mall	470
Lakeshore Books	479	Ross & Haines Old Books Co.	449
Lakeview's Happy Tales Bookshop	458	St. Vincent De Paul Stores	456
Library Room Bookstore	443	School Days Antiques Mall	473
Louis & Clark Booksellers	479	Shakespeare's Books	456
Magnolia Books & Co.	449	Shenandoah Books, etc.	441
Main Street Galleries	446	Sign Of The Unicorn	451
Many Little Things Antique Mall	469	J.L. Skaggs	480
Maple Lawn Antiques	479	Margaret Soderberg, Bookseller	447
Martha Merrell's Bookstore	470	The Spring Green General Store	472
Materiality	442	Stony Hill Antiques	457
McDermott Books	455	Thimbleberry Used Books	458
Memories Antique Mall	441	Time Traveler Bookstore	465
Mineral Point Book Center	466	J. Tuttle Maritime Books	480
Mystery One Bookshop	463	20th Century Books	457
Noah's Ark	463	Untamed Shrew Books	480
North Gate Books	455	T.S. Vandoros Rare Books	458
October Books	441	What Goes Round	442
Old Bookshop of Rice Lake	470	The Winsted Shop	472
Old Delavan Book Co.	444	Wise Owl Books	451
On The Square Antique Mall	473	Wm Caxton Ltd	447
Andrew Oren Military Books	463	Wood Violet Books	480
Originals Mall of Antiques	468	Yesterdays Memories	465

Alphabetical Listing By Location

Location	Dealer	Page
Appleton	Badger Trading Co.	477
	The Book Store	441
	Fox River Antique Mall	441
	Memories Antique Mall	441
	October Books	441
	Shenandoah Books, etc.	441
Bayfield	What Goes Round	442
Beloit	Materiality	442
Berlin	Picture That Antique Mall	442
Brookfield	Casanova Books	443
	Half Price Books, Records, Magazines	443
Burlington	Library Room Bookstore	443
Cambridge	T.S. Hotter Antiquarian Maps & Prints	443
Delavan	Bibliomanics	444
	Buttons and Bows	444
	Delavan Antique & Art Centre	444
	Old Delavan Book Co.	444
Eau Claire	The Book Peddler	445
	Crossroad Books	445
	Main Street Galleries	446
	Ottawa House Books	446
	Margaret Soderberg, Bookseller	447
Ellison Bay	Wm Caxton Ltd	447
Ephraim	Baybury Books	447
Fond du Lac	Amelia's Book House	448
Green Bay	Heirloom Books and Collectibles	478
Greenfield	Half Price Books, Records, Magazines	448
Hartford	Painted Lady Gallery	448
Hayward	Remember When	449
Hudson	Magnolia Books & Co.	449
	Ross & Haines Old Books Co.	449
Knapp	James Cummings, Bookseller	450
La Crosse	The Book Trader II	450
Lake Delton	Wise Owl Books	451
Lake Geneva	Lake Geneva Antique Mall	451
	Sign Of The Unicorn	451
Lyndon Station	Fair Chase	451
Madison	Alternate Realities	452
	Avol's Bookstore	452
	Booked For Murder	452
	Bookworks	453
	Frugal Muse Books, Music & Video	453
	Glaeve Gallery	454
	Half Price Books, Records, Magazines	454

Madison	Half Price Books, Records, Magazines	455
	Louis & Clark Booksellers	479
	McDermott Books	455
	North Gate Books	455
	Paul's Book Store	455
	St. Vincent De Paul Stores	456
	Shakespeare's Books	456
	Stony Hill Antiques	457
	J. Tuttle Maritime Books	480
	20th Century Books	457
	Wood Violet Books	480
Manitowoc	The Book Nook	457
	Lakeshore Books	479
Markesan	Lakeview's Happy Tales Bookshop	458
Marshfield	W. Bruce Fye Antiquarian Medical Books	478
	Thimbleberry Used Books	458
Merrill	BNZ Enterprises	477
Middleton	T.S. Vandoros Rare Books	458
Milton	Campus Antiques Mall	459
	J.L. Skaggs	480
Milwaukee	John Angelos, Books	459
	The Autograph Alcove	459
	Bayview Books	459
	Blake Books	460
	The Book Seller	461
	Constant Reader Book Shop	461
	Downtown Books Bought & Sold	461
	Downtown Books Bought & Sold	461
	Downtown Books Fine Arts Bookshop	462
	Raymond Dworczyk Rare Books	478
	Half Price Books, Records, Magazines	462
	House of Scorpio	462
	Ingrid's Books and Antiques	462
	Mystery One Bookshop	463
	Noah's Ark	463
	Andrew Oren Military Books	463
	P.I.E.S. (Private Investigator Entertainment Service)	479
	Recyled Books & Music	463
	Renaissance Book Shop	464
	Renaissance Book Shop	464
	Time Traveler Bookstore	465
	Yesterdays Memories	465
Mineral Point	The Foundry Books	466
	Mineral Point Book Center	466
Monona	O.Z. Enterprises	467
Monroe	Fireside Books	467

Mosinee	Daltonbooks	467
Muskego	Maple Lawn Antiques	479
Oconomowoc	Booksmith	467
Oregon	Knollwood Books	468
Oshkosh	B & B Crafts	477
	The Book Place	468
	Originals Mall of Antiques	468
Osseo	Many Little Things Antique Mall	469
Platteville	Paper Mountain Books	479
Portage	Portage Antique Mall	469
Racine	Ace & Bubba Treasure Hunters	469
	BotanaBooks & Art	469
	Martha Merrell's Bookstore	470
Rib Mountain	Rib Mountain Antique Mall	470
Rice Lake	Old Bookshop of Rice Lake	470
River Falls	Books on the Rebound	471
Seymour	Crabbe Reader	471
Sheboygan	Book Boutique	471
	Book Store	471
	The Bookplate	477
Shorewood	Aardvark Book Depot	477
Spring Green	The Spring Green General Store	472
	The Winsted Shop	472
Stevens Point	Downtown Antiques Shop	472
	Dusty Dreams Books	478
	Mike Plonsker Books	472
Sturtevant	School Days Antiques Mall	473
Superior	E-Z Reading	473
Walworth	On The Square Antique Mall	473
Washburn	Chequamegon Book & Coffee Co.	473
Waterloo	James Hyer, Bookseller	478
	Untamed Shrew Books	480
Waukesha	The Book Place	474
Waupaca	Bookcellar	474
Wausau	Et Al's Read & Unread Books	474
	Gold Dog Books	474
West Salem	Historic Salem	475
Wisconsin Dells	Antique Mall of Wisconsin Dells I	475
	Antique Mall of Wisconsin Dells II	475
	Ravenswood Books	475
Wisconsin Rapids	Book Nook	476
Woodruff	A Good Book/The Mill Antiques	476

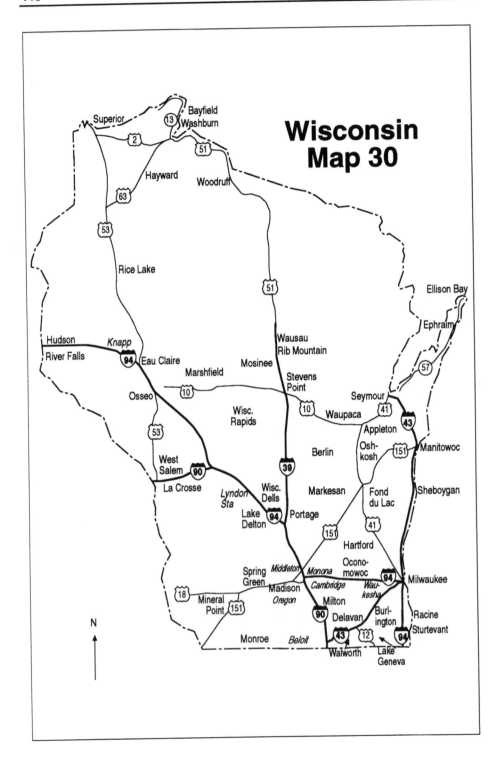

Wisconsin
Map 30

Appleton
(Map 30, page 440)

The Book Store
1033B West Northland Avenue 54914

Open Shop
(920) 734-8908

Collection:	General stock of mostly used paperback and hardcover.
# of Vols:	90,000
Hours:	Mon-Fri 9:30-8. Sat 10-5.
Travel:	Northland Ave exit off Rte 41. Proceed east on Northland.
Credit Cards:	Yes
Owner:	Susan Dobbe
Year Estab:	1977
Comments:	Stock is approximately 75% used, 75% of which is paperback.

Fox River Antique Mall
1074 South Van Dyke Road 54915

Antique Mall
(920) 731-9699

Hours:	Daily 10-6.
Travel:	College Ave exit off Rte 41. Proceed west on Rte 41, then left on Nicolet Blvd which runs into Van Dyke.

Memories Antique Mall
400 Randolph Drive 54915

Antique Mall
(920) 788-5553

Hours:	Daily 10-6, except Fri till 8.
Travel:	Exit 146 off Rte 41. Shop is at corner of Rte 41 and "N."

October Books
606 North Lawe Street 54911

Open Shop
(920) 735-0700

Collection:	General stock of mostly hardcover.
# of Vols:	5,000
Hours:	Mon-Fri 12-5.
Travel:	College Ave exit off Rte 41. Proceed east on College through downtown to Lawe, then north on Lawe. Shop is six blocks ahead.
Credit Cards:	No
Owner:	Doris Bauer
Year Estab:	1978

Shenandoah Books, etc.
133 East Wisconsin Avenue 54911

Open Shop
(920) 832-9525

Collection:	General stock.
# of Vols:	30,000
Specialties:	Native Americans.
Hours:	Mon-Wed 10-7. Thu 10-8. Fri 10-8. Sat 10-5. Sun 10-2.
Services:	Search service, accepts want lists, mail order.
Travel:	Wisconsin Ave exit off Rte 41. Proceed east on Wisconsin.
Credit Cards:	Yes
Owner:	Paul A. Skenandore
Year Estab:	1982

Comments: The owner's specialty, as stated above, is hardly coincidental as he is a proud Native American who also edits a newsletter on Indian affairs. The shop's general collection covers most areas and is larger than is immediately apparent as the books are double shelved. Their condition varies from fair to good and there's a sprinkling of paperbacks along with the hardcover choices. Prices are quite reasonable.

Bayfield
(Map 30, page 440)

What Goes Round   **Open Shop**
38 South 2nd Street   Store: (715) 779-5223
Mailing address: Box 163 Cornucopia WI 54827   Home: (715) 742-3220
                                              E-mail: spdwgr@win.bright.net

Collection: General stock of paperback and hardcover.
# of Vols: 15,000
Specialties: Americana; women's studies; metaphysics; nature; poetry; fiction; cookbooks.
Hours: May-Oct: Daily 10-6. Rest of year by appointment in Cornicopia.
Services: Accepts want lists, mail order.
Travel: Second St exit off Rte 13. Turn south on Second St.
Credit Cards: No
Owner: Stephen P. Dunker
Year Estab: 1986
Comments: As the owner was in the process of moving into this new location at the time our travels brought us to northern Wisconsin, we were not able to visit the shop. Approximately half of the stock is located in Cornucopia.

Beloit
(Map 30, page 440)

Materiality   **By Appointment**
11236 South County Road K 53511   (608) 365-3253
                                                      Fax: (608) 365-2589
                                              E-mail: ketcham@inwave.com

Collection: Specialty. Mostly hardcover.
# of Vols: 5,000
Specialties: History and preservation of material culture: art; technology, museums; art conservation.
Services: Accepts want lists, mail order.
Owner: Jane Ketcham
Year Estab: 1994

Berlin
(Map 30, page 440)

Picture That Antique Mall   **Antique Mall**
107 West Huron Street 54923   (920) 361-0255

Collection: General stock of mostly hardcover.

# of Vols:	500-1,000
Hours:	Mon-Sat 9:30-5. Sun (Mar-Dec) 11-4.
Travel:	Exit 91 off Rte 41. Proceed west on Hwy 91 which runs into Huron St.

Brookfield
(Map 32, page 460)

Casanova Books   **Open Shop**
13735 West Capitol Drive 53005   (414) 783-6456
Web page: www.casanovasadventures.com   Fax: (414) 783-6065
E-mail: cgimail@usa.anet

Collection:	Specialty. Mostly new.
# of Vols:	4,000
Specialties:	Military; sports cars; hunting; fishing; guns; stamps; coins; outdoors; photography; aviation.
Hours:	Daily 10-6.
Services:	Catalog, accepts want lists, mail order.
Travel:	Ten blocks west of Rte 45 at Capitol Dr.
Credit Cards:	Yes
Owner:	Jack Casanova
Year Estab:	1930

Half Price Books, Records, Magazines   **Open Shop**
16750B West Blue Mound Road 53005   (414) 789-0280
Fax: (414) 789-9809

Collection:	General stock of new and used paperback and hardcover.
Hours:	Mon-Sat 9-10. Sun 10-6.
Travel:	Moorland Rd exit off I-94. Proceed north on Moorland Rd, then west on Blue Mound. Shop is located in Brookfield Fashion Center.

Burlington

Library Room Bookstore   **Open Shop**
164 Commerce Street 53105   (414) 763-4690

Collection:	General stock of mostly paperback.
# of Vols:	10,000
Hours:	Tue-Fri 10-5. Sat 10-2.

Cambridge
(Map 30, page 440)

T.S. Hotter Antiquarian Maps & Prints   **By Appointment**
94 Water Street Rockdale 53523   (608) 423-9544

Collection:	Specialty
Specialties:	Maps; atlases; illustrated.
Services:	Appraisals, accepts want lists.
Credit Cards:	No
Owner:	Thomas J. Hotter
Year Estab:	1989

Delavan
(Map 30, page 440)

Bibliomanics   **Open Shop**
324 East Walworth Avenue   (414) 728-9933
Mailing address: PO Box 421 Delavan WI 53115   E-mail: grmosher@idcnet.com

Collection:	General stock of mostly hardcover and ephemera.
# of Vols:	20,000
Hours:	Mon-Fri 12-8. Sat 10-5. Sun 12-5.
Services:	Accepts want lists, mail order.
Travel:	Rte 50 exit off I-43. Proceed west on Rte 50, then west on Rte 11 (Walworth Ave) for four blocks. Shop is across from post office.
Credit Cards:	Yes
Owner:	Gerald R. Mosher
Year Estab:	1994
Comments:	This shop is quite aptly named as, in addition to its stock of used (mainly hardcover) books, it also carries an assortment of knic knacks, bookends, ties and throw pillows—all with book themes. It's the only book store we've ever visited that displays a casket with a number of used books (possibly favorites of the occupant) resting on its lid. The books we saw represented recent as well as vintage titles. There was also a fair share of ephemera. Certainly a fun place to browse, and for others in your party who may not be quite as addicted to the used book phenomena, the streets of this town are lined with antique shops and other specialty stores.

Buttons and Bows   **Open Shop**
312 East Walworth Avenue   (414) 728-6813

Collection:	General stock and ephemera.
# of Vols:	500-1,000
Hours:	Daily 11-5.
Comments:	If you're interested in older books, not necessarily in the best condition, and are willing to pay a few dollars more for them than you would in a typical used book store, this mostly antique/collectibles store is a place for you.

Delavan Antique & Art Centre   **Antique Mall**
230 East Walworth Avenue 53115   (414) 740-1400

Hours:	Mon-Thu 11-6. Fri & Sat 11-8. Sun 12-5.

Old Delavan Book Co.   **By Appointment**
67 East Walworth Avenue 53115   Tel & Fax: (414) 728-6988

Collection:	General stock.
Specialties:	Children's, including Little Golden Books and Volland; children's series; children's illustrated.
Services:	Appraisals, accepts want lists, mail order.
Owner:	Dorothy & Ed Chesko

Year Estab: 1974
Comments: Also displays in antique malls in Delavan, Lake Geneva and Walworth.

Eau Claire
(Map 30, page 440)

The Book Peddler   **Open Shop**
315 Graham Avenue 54701   (715) 832-8289
                                                E-mail: gtillema@werewolf.net

Collection: General stock of hardcover and paperback and records.
# of Vols: 160,000
Hours: Mon-Sat 10:30-6.
Services: Search service, mail order.
Travel: Bus Rte 12 to Barstow St. Turn left at 300 block, proceed one block, then left on Graham. Shop is just ahead on left.
Credit Cards: Yes
Owner: George A. Tillema
Year Estab: 1978
Comments: The largest used book shop in Eau Claire, this bi-level store offers a mix of paperbacks, hardcovers, collectibles (e.g., Little Big Books), hard to find items, library discards and book club editions. Both the age and condition of the books vary. Prices are extremely reasonable. As you enter the shop, pick up the handy map prepared by the thoughtful owner.

On a return visit some 3½ years after we noted the above, we found a larger percentage of paperbacks than we recalled from our earlier visit. However, the number of hardcover books, particularly on the second level, still offers the visiting book person a challenge in terms of selection. For those making a large purchase, the owner will offer a generous discount.

Crossroad Books   **Open Shop**
2529 East Clairemont Parkway 54701   (715) 831-9788
Web page: http://discover-net.net/~xroads/   E-mail: xroadsbk@interloc.com

Collection: General stock of paperback and hardcover.
# of Vols: 30,000
Hours: Mon-Fri 10:30-7, except Fri till 8. Sat 11-7.
Services: Search service, accepts want lists, mail order.
Travel: Rte 53 exit off I-94. Proceed north on Rte 53 then left into strip shopping center at intersection of Clairemont Pkwy (Rte 12).
Credit Cards: Yes
Owner: Mark Patterson & Sharon Ager
Year Estab: 1997
Comments: While this shop did have a slightly larger number of paperbacks than hardcover books, its hardcover titles were respectable enough and certainly interesting enough to merit a careful viewing. Most of the volumes we saw were in quite good condition and reasonably priced. We left the shop pleased with our purchase.

(Eau Claire)

Main Street Galleries   **Antique Mall**
306 Main Street 54701   (715) 832-2494
                                            E-mail: mgallery@execpc.com

Collection:	General stock and ephemera.
# of Vols:	8,000
Specialties:	Magazines
Hours:	Mon-Sat 10-5:30.
Services:	Accepts want lists, mail order.
Travel:	In heart of downtown. The books are located on the second floor.
Credit Cards:	Yes
Owner:	Hugh Passow
Comments:	Most of the books we saw were older volumes in mixed condition and most we would classify as common titles with a few Wisconsin books that would be of particular interest to local historians. The dealer also carries a large selection of magazines, records and ephemera.

Ottawa House Books   **Open Shop**
602 Water Street 54703   (715) 839-0600

Collection:	General stock of hardcover and paperback.
# of Vols:	15,000 (See Comments)
Hours:	Mon-Sat 9-5:30.
Services:	Accepts want lists, mail order.
Travel:	Rte 37 exit off I-94. Proceed north on Rte 37, then west on Rte 12 and south on Menomonie which becomes Water St. Shop is at corner of 6th & Water.
Owner:	Charles W. Vanden Breul
Year Estab:	1980
Comments:	After rereading the observations we made about this shop based on our earlier visit (see below), we thought the shop deserved a second look and so we stopped by at 4:30pm on a business Wednesday. The shop was not only closed but there was no sign on the window confirming the business hours that the owner had provided us with a short time before our trip. When we related our experience to other dealers in Eau Claire, we were told that the shop is open *but* on an erratic basis.

A modest collection of mostly hardcover books with some paperbacks in a dimly lit shop. We get the sense that the owner has not made the best use of either his floor or shelf space as many books that could have been shelved were lying flat on tables, stacked into piles making some of the titles difficult to view. According to the owner, only half his stock was on display at the shop. It may of course be that at the time of our visit the shop was being reorganized. The shelves were not as well labeled as they might have been. We did, however, see some unusual titles, and with two other book dealers in the same town, a stop here would not be out of order.

Margaret Soderberg, Bookseller   **By Appointment**
3530 Noble Drive 54703   (715) 833-9742
                                                      Fax: (715) 833-3533
                                            E-mail: MASBooks@aol.com

Collection:	General stock.
# of Vols:	4,000
Specialties:	Aviation history (non military); Scottish history and culture.
Services:	Search service, accepts want lists, mail order.
Credit Cards:	No
Year Estab:	1991
Comments:	Also displays at Many Little Things Antique Mall in Osseo.

Ellison Bay
(Map 30, page 440)

Wm Caxton Ltd   **Open Shop**
12037 Highway 42 54210   (920) 854-2955
                          E-mail: caxtonbooks@mail.doorcounty-wi.com

Collection:	General stock of mostly hardcover.
# of Vols:	100,000
Specialties:	Natural history; women's studies; philosophy; modern fiction; literature; literary criticism; anthropology; Native Americans.
Hours:	Jun-Oct: Mon-Sat 10-5. Sun 12-4. Nov-May: By chance or appointment. Often open weekends.
Services:	Appraisals, search service.
Travel:	In "downtown."
Credit Cards:	Yes
Owner:	Kubet Luchterhand
Year Estab:	1986
Comments:	We sometimes debate the wisdom of driving many miles to what on the map at least appears to be a remote and distant location for the purpose of visiting a used book shop. In this instance, the trip was well worth the extra miles. Not only does one get to visit a Class A book shop that sells quality books at very reasonable prices but one can also enjoy beautiful scenery, and if time allows, take advantage of the resort aspects of the region. The books were almost universally in excellent condition, covered most areas of interest and most categories were covered in some depth.

Ephraim
(Map 30, page 440)

Baybury Books   **Open Shop**
3058 Church Street   (920) 854-1933
Mailing address: PO Box 462 Ephraim WI 54211

Collection:	General stock.
# of Vols:	12,000

Hours:	Memorial Day through Oct: Mon-Sat, except closed Wed, 11-5.
Services:	Search service.
Travel:	Just off Rte 42 north. Located in center of town.
Credit Cards:	Yes
Owner:	Fred & Anne Schwartz
Year Estab:	1993

Fond du Lac
(Map 30, page 440)

Amelia's Book House   **Open Shop**
23 North Main Street 54935   (920) 921-4010
Web page: www.execpc.com/~gelly/   Fax: (920) 922-2829
                                                          E-mail: gelly@execpc.com

Collection:	General stock of hardcover and paperback.
# of Vols:	20,000
Specialties:	Science fiction; mystery; modern first editions; children's.
Hours:	Mon 10-2. Tue-Fri 10-5. Sat 10-2.
Services:	Accepts want lists, search service, mail order.
Travel:	Main St exit off I-41. Proceed north on Main for about three miles to center of town.
Credit Cards:	No
Owner:	Marcia Sturm & Lorraine Gelly
Year Estab:	1993
Comments:	An attractively decorated shop with three modest sized rooms displaying both hardcover and paperback books. Some older volumes. Some interesting titles. Reasonably priced. While we failed to spot any truly rare items, the titles on hand did suggest that the turnover one is likely to find here could well provide the traveling book hunter with a prize or two.

Greenfield
(Map 32, page 460)

Half Price Books, Records, Magazines   **Open Shop**
5032 South 74th Street 53220   (414) 281-0000
                                                             Fax: (414) 281-0383

Collection:	General stock of new and used hardcover, paperback and remainders.
# of Vols:	250,000
Hours:	Mon-Thu 9am-10pm. Fri & Sat 9am-11pm. Sun 9am-8pm.
Travel:	76th St exit off I-894. Proceed south on 76th St, then east on Edgerton to 74th St. Shop is in Stein Mart Plaza at Greenfield.

Hartford
(Map 30, page 440)

Painted Lady Gallery   **Open Shop**
100 North Main Street 53027   (414) 673-9000

Collection:	General stock of new and used hardcover and paperback.

# of Vols:	10,000 (used)
Hours:	Mon-Thu 10-6. Fri 10-8. Sat 10-4.
Travel:	Rte 60 exit off Rte 45. Proceed west on Rte 60 for about seven miles then north on Rte 83 for one block.
Credit Cards:	Yes
Owner:	Mary Jo Snedaker
Year Estab:	1990
Comments:	In addition to gift items and new books, the shop also sells used paperbacks and older hardcover books hardly in the best condition but not too expensively priced. Considering the shop's location, the traveling book person probably could spend his or her time more profitably elsewhere.

Hayward
(Map 30, page 440)

Remember When   **Open Shop**
10526 North Dakota   (715) 634-5282
Mailing address: PO Box 1094 Hayward WI 54843   Fax: (715) 634-9019
                                              E-mail: remwhen@win.bright.net

Collection:	General stock of paperback and hardcover.
# of Vols:	50,000 (See Comments)
Specialties:	Science fiction; fantasy; westerns; mystery.
Hours:	May-Oct Daily 9-5. Nov-Apr: Tue-Sat 9-5.
Services:	Search service, accepts want lists, mail order
Travel:	From Rte 63, turn west on Dakota.
Credit Cards:	Yes
Owner:	Kay McAllister
Year Estab:	1991
Comments:	A combination gift shop and used book store with a larger number of paperbacks than hardcover volumes. The hardcover items that we did see were a mix of recent fiction and some oldies. Prices varied from reasonable to "touristy." We didn't count them, but our estimate of the number of books on display would be about one half, or less, than the figure cited above.

Hudson
(Map 30, page 440)

Magnolia Books & Co.   **Open Shop**
221 Vine Street 54016   (715) 386-2309
                                                    Fax: (715) 386-2386

Collection:	General stock of mostly paperback.
Hours:	Mon-Fri 10-8. Sat 9:30-4. Sun: open seasonally.

Ross & Haines Old Books Co.   **Open Shop**
411 2nd Street   (715) 381-1955
Mailing address: 903 3rd Street Hudson WI 54016

Collection:	Specialty with small general stock.

# of Vols:	12,500+
Specialties:	Western Americana; military; American history; history.
Hours:	Mon-Sat 10-6. Sun 12-5.
Services:	Appraisals, accepts want lists, mail order.
Travel:	One mile north of I-94 at Wisconsin-Minnesota border.
Credit Cards:	Yes
Owner:	Steve Anderson
Year Estab:	1950

Knapp
(Map 30, page 440)

James Cummings, Bookseller   **By Appointment**
E544 US Highway 12 West 54749   (715) 665-2287

Collection:	Specialty
# of Vols:	80,000
Specialties:	Americana (19th century); religion; philosophy; literary biographies and criticism; scholarly books in the humanities; diaries.
Services:	Accepts want lists.
Credit Cards:	No
Year Estab:	1958
Comments:	While we did not visit this dealer, one of our loyal readers who travels frequently, advised us after visiting this establishment that it was a "real winner."

La Crosse
(Map 30, page 440)

The Book Trader II   **Open Shop**
1313 Redfield Street 54601   (608) 782-9752

Collection:	General stock of mostly paperback and some hardcover.
# of Vols:	100,000
Specialties:	Science fiction; fantasy; literature.
Hours:	Mon-Fri 10-6. Sat 10-4. Other times by appointment.
Services:	Accepts want lists, mail order, limited search service.
Travel:	Rte 53/35 exit off I-90. Proceed south on Rte 35 through town where it becomes George St/Lang Dr/West Ave. Left at Redfield. Shop is between 13th & 14th Sts.
Credit Cards:	No
Owner:	JoAnn Duckworth
Year Estab:	1977
Comments:	The shop does not exaggerate the number of books it has. Unfortunately, hardcover items represent only a fraction of the volumes and those few that we saw were, for the most part, very ordinary items not worthy of extraordinary travel.

Lake Delton
(Map 30, page 440)

Wise Owl Books   **Open Shop**
210 Burrit Street   (608) 254-2092
Mailing address: 210 West Adams, Box 377 Lake Delton WI 53940

Collection:	General stock and ephemera.
# of Vols:	12,000
Specialties:	Children's series; Wisconsin; Civil War; Americana; August Derleth.
Hours:	Mon-Sat 9-5. Sun 1-5. Ring the bell if the shop is closed.
Services:	Accepts want lists, mail order.
Travel:	Lake Delton exit off I-90. Proceed east on Rte 12, then left on Burrit.
Credit Cards:	No
Owner:	P.H. Seamans
Year Estab:	1970
Comments:	Located just a few miles away from Sauk City, the legendary home of Arkham House fame, the owner stocks a supply of non Arkham House August Derleth literature. The remainder of the collection consists of older books in mixed condition with little out of the ordinary. The collection is not very well organized.

Lake Geneva
(Map 30, page 440)

Lake Geneva Antique Mall   **Antique Mall**
829 Williams Street 53147   (414) 248-6345

Hours:	Daily 1-5, except Fri till 8.
Travel:	Rte 120 exit off Rte 12. South on Rte 120 (William St) for one mile.

Sign Of The Unicorn   **Open Shop**
233 Center Street 53147   (414) 248-1141

Collection:	General stock, maps and prints.
# of Vols:	300-400 (books)
Specialties:	Maps
Hours:	Mon-Sat 10-5. Sun 12-5.
Services:	Mail order.
Travel:	Rte 50 to downtown, then north on Center.
Credit Cards:	Yes
Owner:	Frank & Judy Scott
Year Estab:	1982

Lyndon Station
(Map 30, page 440)

Fair Chase   **By Appointment**
S1118 Highway HH 53944   Tel & Fax: (608) 524-9677

Collection:	Specialty. Mostly used and some new.
# of Vols:	2,000

Specialties: Big game hunting; wingshooting; guns; archery; record books.
Services: Appraisals, search service, catalog, accepts want lists.
Credit Cards: Yes
Owner: Carol Lueder
Year Estab: 1983

Madison
(Map 31, page 454 & Map 30, page 440)

Alternate Realities   **Open Shop**
310 State Street 53703   (608) 258-8084

Collection: Specialty used and new.
# of Vols: 30,000
Specialties: Science fiction; mystery; horror; fantasy.
Hours: Mon-Sat 10-7. Sun 12-5. Call for seasonal hours.
Services: Accepts want lists, mail order.
Travel: On pedestrian mall between Johnson and Gorham.
Credit Cards: Yes
Owner: Maureen V. Meehan & Ron Czerwien
Year Estab: 1993
Comments: Stock is approximately 80% used.

Avol's Bookstore   **Open Shop**
240 West Gilman Street 53703   (608) 255-4730

Collection: General stock of mostly hardcover.
# of Vols: 100,000+
Specialties: Scholarly; art; film; natural sciences; music; architecture.
Hours: Mon-Sat 10-9. Sun 12-5.
Services: Appraisals, accepts want lists, mail order.
Travel: Rte 151 exit (East Washington Ave) off I-90/94. Proceed south on Rte
                 151 to State Capitol. After going around square, park as close as pos-
                 sible to State St pedestrian mall. Alternate approach: Rte 12/18 exit off
                 I-90/94. Proceed west on Rte 12/18, then north on John Nolen and west
                 on Broom. Shop is just north of State Street pedestrian mall.
Credit Cards: Yes
Owner: Ron Czerwien & Maureen Meehan
Year Estab: 1980
Comments: A large, well organized shop with most subjects represented (The
                 owners' mystery, sci fi and horror books are located at their sister
                 store, Alternate Realties, a few blocks away.) The books we saw were
                 in generally good condition. No book savvy visitor to Madison should
                 miss a stop here.

Booked For Murder   **Open Shop**
2701 University Avenue 53705   (608) 238-2701
Web page: http://userpages.itis.com/booked   Fax: (608) 238-8701
                                                    E-mail: booked4m@aol.com
Collection: Specialty. Primarily new and some used.

# of Vols:	Few hundred (used)
Specialties:	Mystery
Hours:	Mon-Fri 9-8. Sat 9-5. Sun 12-5.
Travel:	Located in Lakepoint Commons Shopping Center.
Credit Cards:	Yes
Owner:	Mary Helen Becker
Year Estab:	1988
Comments:	Used stock consists of out of print titles.

Bookworks   **Open Shop**
109 State Street 53703   (608) 255-4848

Collection:	General stock of hardcover and paperback.
# of Vols:	50,000
Hours:	Mon-Sat 11-6. Sun 12-5.
Services:	Accepts want lists, book repair, drop spine box construction.
Travel:	At eastern end of pedestrian mall, close to the State Capitol.
Credit Cards:	Yes
Owner:	Peter Dast
Year Estab:	1991
Comments:	The best way to describe this shop is to refer to it as eclectic. Its books are in generally good condition and are of mixed vintage. There are plenty of paperbacks (primarily on a lower level) but more than enough hardcovers to satisfy the most ardent collector. As is often the case, what one sees when visiting is frequently the result of the owner's most recent buys and just prior to our visit the owner had acquired a very nice fantasy collection.

Frugal Muse Books, Music & Video   **Open Shop**
7475 Mineral Point Road 53717   (608) 833-8668

Collection:	General stock of hardcover, paperback, CDs and videos.
# of Vols:	75,000
Hours:	Mon-Sat 9-9. Sun 10-6.
Services:	Accepts want lists, mail order.
Travel:	Mineral Point Rd exit off Rte 12. Proceed east on Mineral Point Rd. Shop is in High Pointe Centre.
Credit Cards:	Yes
Owner:	David Danielson, William Sickels and Andy Gaylor
Year Estab:	1994
Comments:	A pleasant surprise. When we first entered the shop we thought we were going to find mostly new books, CDs, paperbacks and only a smattering of hardcover items, and those of only recent vintage. Of course, there were new books, videos and CDs, but the shop *also* offers quite a respectable selection of used hardcover books, most in quite good condition. Serious as well as more popular subjects were well represented. Quite reasonably priced. Certainly worth a visit. The owners have a second, smaller shop, on the other side of Madison. (See North Gate Books below.)

Glaeve Gallery   **Open Shop**
514 State Street 53703   (608) 255-3997
Web page: www.glaeve.com   Fax: (608) 255-3917
                                            E-mail: gfglaeve@aol.com

Collection:	Specialty new and used.
Specialties:	Art, including folk, Native American and ethnic.
Hours:	Mon-Sat 10-6. Sun 11-5.
Travel:	On pedestrian mall.
Credit Cards:	Yes
Owner:	Gerry Glaeve
Year Estab:	1989
Comments:	Approximately 80% of the stock is new. The shop is also an art gallery.

Half Price Books, Records, Magazines   **Open Shop**
4250 East Towne Boulevard 53704   (608) 244-1189
                                            Fax: (608) 244-3327

Collection:	General stock of used and new hardcover and paperback.
# of Vols:	175,000
Hours:	Mon-Thu 9-9. Fri & Sat 9-9. Sun 10-6.
Travel:	In Essex Square shopping center at intersection of Rte 151 and Eagan. Proceeding west on Rte 151, turn left on Eagan.

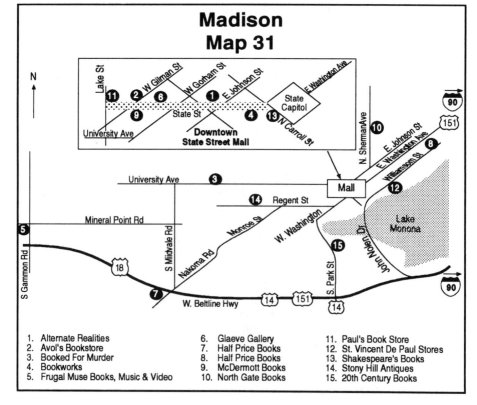

Madison
Map 31

1. Alternate Realities	6. Glaeve Gallery	11. Paul's Book Store
2. Avol's Bookstore	7. Half Price Books	12. St. Vincent De Paul Stores
3. Booked For Murder	8. Half Price Books	13. Shakespeare's Books
4. Bookworks	9. McDermott Books	14. Stony Hill Antiques
5. Frugal Muse Books, Music & Video	10. North Gate Books	15. 20th Century Books

Half Price Books, Records, Magazines
4543 West Beltline Highway 53711

Open Shop
(608) 273-1140
Fax: (608) 273-4324

Collection:	General stock of new and used hardcover and paperback.
# of Vols:	130,000
Hours:	Mon-Thu 9-9. Fri & Sat 9am-10pm. Sun 10-6.
Travel:	Just off Beltline Rd at Rte 18/151 (Verona Rd) in Nakoma Plaza.

McDermott Books
449D State Street 53703

Open Shop
Tel & Fax: (608) 284-0744
E-mail: mcdermottbooks@globaldialog.com

Collection:	General stock of hardcover and paperback.
# of Vols:	85,000
Specialties:	All academic areas, especially philosophy, history and literature.
Hours:	Mon, Thu, Fri 10-9. Tue, Wed, Sat 10-7. Sun 10-5.
Services:	Appraisals, search service, accepts want lists, mail order.
Travel:	Just off pedestrian mall between Gorham and Gilman.
Credit Cards:	Yes
Owner:	Pat McDermott & Lisa Bitney
Year Estab:	1995
Comments:	A bi-level shop with a solid collection of hardcover and paperback books with an emphasis on mostly quality titles. Easy to browse. Considering the shop's proximity to several other quality dealers in the area, you can't go wrong stopping here.

North Gate Books
1213 North Sherman Avenue 53704

Open Shop
(608) 242-0000

Collection:	General stock of used and new hardcover and paperback, CDs and videos.
# of Vols:	25,000
Hours:	Mon-Sat 10-8. Sun 12-5.
Travel:	Rte 151 off I-90/94. Proceed south on East Washington Ave, then right on Aberg Ave and left on Sherman. Shop is in North Gate Shopping Ctr.
Credit Cards:	Yes
Year Estab:	1997
Owner:	David Danielson, William Sickels and Andy Gaylor
Comments:	See Frugal Muse above.

Paul's Book Store
670 State Street 53703

Open Shop
(608) 257-2968

Collection:	General stock of hardcover and paperback.
# of Vols:	25,000-30,000
Hours:	Mon-Sat 9-7. Sun 1-5.
Travel:	At western end of pedestrian mall.
Credit Cards:	Yes
Owner:	Caryl Askins
Year Estab:	1950's

(Madison)

Comments:	Normally, this shop is open at the hours listed above. However, we arrived in Madison on Memorial Day and the sign outside the shop indicated that it would be open at 1pm that afternoon. Unfortunately, because of our tight schedule, we could not wait and our observations of the store had to be limited to our view from the front window. What we saw gives us the sense that we missed a good opportunity since there certainly seemed to be a healthy variety of hardcover volumes on hand, some scholarly, some more popular, as well as a fair selection of paperbacks. Despite our bad luck, we don't think you could go wrong here.

St. Vincent De Paul Stores   **Open Shop**
1309 Williamson Street 53703   (608) 257-0673

Collection:	General stock of hardcover and paperback.
Hours:	Mon-Fri 9-5:45. Sat 9-4:15.
Travel:	Rte 151 exit off I-90/94. Proceed south on East Washington Ave, then left on Baldwin. Shop is at corner of Baldwin and Williamson.
Comments:	A non profit store. All books are donated. A second store with a smaller stock is located at 4293 West Beltline Highway (608) 278-2924. Same hours.

Shakespeare's Books   **Open Shop**
18 North Carroll Street 53703   (608) 255-5521
                                                                   Fax: (608) 255-5511
                                                                   E-mail: shakebks@interloc.com

Collection:	General stock of hardcover and paperback.
# of Vols:	250,000
Specialties:	Americana; travel; modern first editions; magazines (from late 19th century).
Hours:	Daily 10-6.
Services:	Search service, accepts want lists, mail order.
Travel:	Shop is across from the State Capitol, around the corner from the State Street pedestrian mall.
Credit Cards:	Yes
Owner:	Harold Langhammer
Year Estab:	1933
Comments:	Unfortunately, the shop was closed on the day of our return trip to Madison. If things have changed from our earlier observations (see below), please let us know.
	Without question, one of the larger selections of used books in Wisconsin and the Midwest. Plan to spend lots of time in this bi-level shop as a true book lover can easily get lost in the many aisles that display books, in universally good condition, in every subject area and in depth. A separate room in the rear of the first floor contains attractive displays of rare, interesting and antiquarian books.

Stony Hill Antiques   **Open Shop**
2140 Regent Street 53705   (608) 231-1247

Collection:	General stock of mostly hardcover.
# of Vols:	5,000
Specialties:	Wisconsin; Americana.
Hours:	Tue-Sat 10-5.
Travel:	One half mile west of university football stadium.
Credit Cards:	Yes
Owner:	David Ward
Year Estab:	1976
Comments:	Also sells fine art, antiques, oriental and tribal rugs.

20th Century Books   **Open Shop**
1115 South Park Street 53715   (608) 251-6226

Collection:	Specialty. Mostly new and some used.
# of Vols:	30,000
Specialties:	Popular culture; science fiction; mystery; comics; television; film.
Hours:	Mon-Sat 10-5:30. Sun 12-5.
Services:	Accepts want lists, mail order.
Travel:	Park St exit off Rte 12/18. Proceed north on Park. From downtown, proceed south on Rte 151.
Credit Cards:	Yes
Owner:	Hank Luttrell
Year Estab:	1979
Comments:	You have to be either a comic book or sci fi aficionado to appreciate a shop like this which carries a healthy supply of new comics books and comic reprints as well as new sci fi, horror and fantasy titles. The shop does, however, also have an extensive collection of used paperbacks and hardcover books, including many vintage items. As the shop is not for everyone, let your taste be your guide.

Manitowoc
(Map 30, page 440)

The Book Nook   **Open Shop**
2516 Wollmer Street 54220   (920) 682-2665
                                                              E-mail: jeppler@lsol.net

Collection:	General stock of mostly used paperback and hardcover.
# of Vols:	70,000
Hours:	Mon-Fri 10-5. Sat 10-3. Sun by appointment.
Travel:	Exit 149 off I-43. Proceed east on Rte 42, then left on 26th St.
Credit Cards:	Yes
Owner:	Judith Eppler
Year Estab:	1985
Comments:	While the vast majority of the shop's stock consists of paperbacks, there are enough older fiction volumes (in the basement) and mystery titles to make the shop worth visiting if you're in the general area.

Markesan
(Map 30, page 440)

Lakeview's Happy Tales Bookshop   **Open Shop**
W1778 County Road K 53946   (920) 398-3375

Collection:	General stock of hardcover and paperback and ephemera.
# of Vols:	100,000
Hours:	May-Sept only: Sat 11-3 Other times by appointment or chance.
Services:	Search service, accepts want lists, mail order.
Travel:	Rte 73 to Road K. East on Road K, north on Road N, left on Lakeview.
Credit Cards:	No
Owner:	Leonore Dickman
Comments:	Almost every square inch of space in this former one room school-house, including a basement level, is devoted to the display of books. With some exceptions, the hardcover books are predominately older volumes ranging from attractive illustrated titles to more modern book club editions and library discards. We saw many items that were in questionable condition but also quite a few that a sharp eyed scout might turn around for a neat profit. Reasonably priced. Children's books galore, plus paperbacks, cookbooks, mystery, general fiction, and a little bit of everything. The owner also displays at the Portage Antique Mall in Portage. See below.

Marshfield
(Map 30, page 440)

Thimbleberry Used Books   **Open Shop**
132 South Central Avenue 54449   (715) 387-3049

Collection:	General stock of paperback and hardcover.
# of Vols:	9,000
Hours:	Tue-Fri 10-6. Sat 10-3.
Travel:	In downtown. Central Ave is Rte 13.
Year Estab:	1996
Comments:	Stock is approximately 70% paperback.

Middleton
(Map 30, page 440)

T.S. Vandoros Rare Books   **By Appointment**
5827 Highland Terrace 53562   (608) 836-8254
                                                     Fax: (608) 836-1788

Collection:	Specialty
Specialties:	Victorian novel (first editions), especially Charles Dickens; modern first editions (mainly English); signed; fine bindings; fine printing.
Services:	Appraisals, catalog, accepts want lists.
Credit Cards:	No
Owner:	Takis S. Vandoros
Year Estab:	1982

Milton
(Map 30, page 440)

Campus Antiques Mall   **Antique Mall**
609 Campus Street 53563   (608) 868-3324
Hours: Mon-Sat 10-5. Sun and holidays 12-5.
Travel: Between Fort Atkinson and Janesville at junction of Rtes 59 and 26.

Milwaukee
(Map 32, page 460 & Map 30, page 440)

John Angelos, Books   **By Appointment**
4803 West Washington Boulevard 53208   (414) 475-1487
Collection: Specialty
# of Vols: 1,000
Specialties: Photography; art; architecture; literature.
Services: Appraisals, lists, mail order.
Credit Cards: No
Year Estab: 1979

The Autograph Alcove   **By Appointment**
6939 Harvey Avenue 53213   (414) 771-7844
                                                           Fax: (414) 771-7880
Collection: Specialty
Specialties: Autographs; manuscripts; signed books; newspapers.
Services: Appraisals, search service, accepts want lists, auctions.
Credit Cards: No
Owner: William Luetge & James Twelmeyer
Year Estab: 1979

Bayview Books   **Open Shop**
2261 South Howell Avenue 53207   (414) 744-0742
Collection: General stock.
# of Vols: 100,000
Hours: Mon-Sat 12-6. Other times by appointment.
Services: Accepts want lists.
Travel: Holt Ave exit off I-94. Proceed east on Holt, then north on Howell.
                  Shop is near intersection of Kinnickinnic, Howell and Lincoln.
Credit Cards: No
Owner: George John
Year Estab: 1959
Comments: An old fashioned book shop with character. The owner, a laid back
                  gentleman, has been in the business for over 35 years and rightfully
                  takes pride in the quality of the books he displays. Most subjects are
                  represented, including a good selection of scholarly volumes. We found
                  the books to be very reasonably priced. If you're visiting only a few
                  shops in town, this is one that should not be missed.

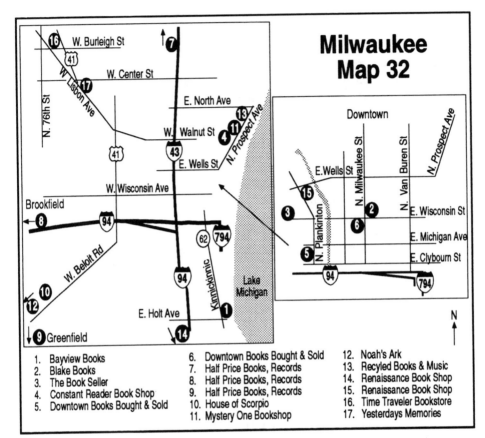

Milwaukee Map 32

Downtown

1. Bayview Books
2. Blake Books
3. The Book Seller
4. Constant Reader Book Shop
5. Downtown Books Bought & Sold
6. Downtown Books Bought & Sold
7. Half Price Books, Records
8. Half Price Books, Records
9. Half Price Books, Records
10. House of Scorpio
11. Mystery One Bookshop
12. Noah's Ark
13. Recyled Books & Music
14. Renaissance Book Shop
15. Renaissance Book Shop
16. Time Traveler Bookstore
17. Yesterdays Memories

Blake Books

714 Milwaukee Street 53202

Open Shop
(414) 272-1000
E-mail: ckbooks@mailbag.com

Collection:	General stock of mostly hardcover.
# of Vols:	25,000
Hours:	Mon-Sat 11-6. Best to call ahead.
Services:	Search service, accepts want lists, mail order.
Travel:	Eastbound on I-94: Follow signs to I-794, then Van Buren exit off I-794. Proceed north on Van Buren for three blocks, then left on Wisconsin and right on Milwaukee. Shop is just ahead on right. Westbound (north-bound) on I-94: Take first exit at far right (Downtown). Continue left (north) on Plankinton, then right on Wisconsin and left on Milwaukee.
Credit Cards:	No
Owner:	Roger Hunt & Christopher Key
Year Estab:	1994
Comments:	A large shop that just keeps on going from one room to the next. While there are some paperbacks on hand, the shop is overwhelmingly hard-cover. Every subject imaginable is covered, many in depth. In our view, definitely worth a visit.

The Book Seller
814 West Wisconsin Avenue 53233

Open Shop
(414) 286-2142

Collection: General stock of hardcover and paperback.
Hours: Mon-Fri 8:30-4:30. Sat 9-1.
Travel: Downtown, between 8 & 9th Streets.
Comments: A non profit shop run by the Friends of the Library.

Constant Reader Book Shop
1625-27 East Irving Place 53202

Open Shop
(414) 291-0452

Collection: General stock.
# of Vols: 22,000
Specialties: Modern first editions; maritime; hunting; fishing; mystery; science fiction; music; film; plays; military; Americana.
Hours: Mon-Sat 9-7. Sun 11-5.
Services: Appraisals, search service, accepts want lists, mail order.
Travel: Lincoln Memorial Dr exit off I-794. Proceed north on Lincoln Memorial, then left on Lafayette Hill Dr. Left at the top of the hill. Follow Lafayette to Oakland, then left on Oakland and proceed for one block to Irving Pl. Shop is at end of block.
Credit Cards: No
Owner: David W. Hurlbutt
Year Estab: 1979
Comments: A nice sized shop with a good selection of books in most areas. The generally good condition of the books suggests that the owner exercises care in the selection of the items he displays.

Downtown Books Bought & Sold
327 East Wisconsin Avenue 53202

Open Shop
(414) 276-5330

Collection: General stock of paperback and hardcover.
# of Vols: 250,000
Hours: Mon-Sat 10-6. Sun 12-5.
Travel: See Blake Books above.
Credit Cards: No
Owner: Keith Pajot
Year Estab: 1990
Comments: Another store that just goes and on and on in terms of bookcases, rooms, hallways and even a loft area for comic books and pulps. The store offers a good supply of hardcover titles (in some instances, we saw several duplicates on the shelves) as well as paperbacks in almost every subject. Quite reasonably priced and within a few hundred yards of a similar shop and two more shops just a few more streets away.

Downtown Books Bought & Sold
715 North Plankinton Avenue 53203

Open Shop
(414) 276-6477

Collection: General stock of hardcover and paperback.
# of Vols: 5,000-10,000 (hardcover)
Hours: Mon-Sat 10-6. Sun 12-5.

(Milwaukee)

Travel:	Eastbound on I-94: follow signs to I-794, then Plankinton Ave exit off I-794. Proceed north on Plankinton. Westbound (northbound) on I-94: Take first exit at far right (Downtown). Continue left (north) on Plankinton. Shop is between Wisconsin and Wells.
Credit Cards:	No
Owner:	Keith Pajot
Year Estab:	1990
Comments:	A tightly packed tri-level shop. The books, both hardcover and paperback, were, at the time of our visit, most reasonably priced. In trying to use every available inch of space for display, the browser is occasionally forced to squeeze between shelves; sometimes the squeeze is worth it. At the time of our visit, the owner was in the process of setting up a third, by appointment shop, where he planned to display some of his better books. See below.

Downtown Books Fine Arts Bookshop
324 East Michigan Avenue

By Appointment
(414) 272-4770

Collection:	Specialty
# of Vols:	10,000
Specialties:	Art; architecture; photography; antiques; illustrated.
Owner:	Keith Pajot
Year Estab:	1998

Half Price Books, Records, Magazines
6814 West Brown Deer Road 53223

Open Shop
(414) 354-1235
Fax: (414) 354-4848

Collection:	General stock of new and used hardcover and paperback.
Hours:	Mon-Sat 9am-10pm. Sun 10-6.
Travel:	Brown Deer Rd exit off I-43. Proceed west on Brown Deer to 68th St. Shop is located in strip shopping center.

House of Scorpio
5922 West Burnham Street 53219

Open Shop
(414) 545-7470

Collection:	Specialty. Primarily new with some used.
Specialties:	Metaphysics; self help; astrology.
Hours:	Tue-Fri 11-7:30. Sat 11-6.
Travel:	Hawley Rd exit off I-94. Proceed south on Hawley (60th St) for 1½ miles, then left on Burnham.
Credit Cards:	No
Owner:	Barbara & Dean O'Connor
Year Estab:	1972

Ingrid's Books and Antiques
PO Box 71036 53211

By Appointment
(414) 967-0370
E-mail: ingrid@globaldialog.com

Collection:	General stock and ephemera.

# of Vols:	1,500
Services:	Accepts want lists, search service, mail order.
Credit Cards:	Yes
Owner:	Katherine Servais
Year Estab:	1990

Mystery One Bookshop   **Open Shop**
2109 North Prospect Avenue 53202   (414) 347-4077
Web page: www.mysteryone.com   E-mail: mystery@execpc.com

Collection:	Specialty new and used.
# of Vols:	1,000 (used)
Specialties:	Mystery
Hours:	Mon-Sat 11-6, except Fri till 8.
Credit Cards:	Yes
Owner:	Richard Katz
Year Estab:	1992
Comments:	Used books are hardcover first editions.

Noah's Ark   **Open Shop**
4201 South 108th Street 53228   (414) 427-5760

Collection:	Specialty books, magazines and ephemera.
# of Vols:	300-500 (books), 10,000+ magazines.
Specialties:	Movies; television; sports; cartoons.
Hours:	Mon-Fri 11-6. Sat 11-4.
Travel:	Rte 45 exit off I-94. Proceed south on Rte 45, west on Beloit and south on Rte 100 (108th St).
Owner:	Art Rickun

Andrew Oren Military Books   **By Appointment**
3156 South Kinnickinnic Avenue 53207   Eve: (414) 744-3927
                                                     Day: (414) 747-7057

Collection:	Specialty
# of Vols:	1,500
Specialties:	Military; Civil War.
Services:	Appraisals, catalog, accepts want lists.
Credit Cards:	No
Year Estab:	1991

Recyled Books & Music   **Open Shop**
2239 North Prospect Avenue 53202   (414) 276-1321
                                                     E-mail: book@ticon.net

Collection:	General stock of hardcover and paperback, records and CDs.
# of Vols:	25,000+
Hours:	Mon-Sat 11-10. Sun 12-10.
Services:	Accepts want lists, mail order.
Travel:	Van Buren exit off I-794. Proceed north on Van Buren, then right on Wisconsin and proceed to end. Bear left onto Prospect. Shop is two miles head in the Prospect Mall (an indoor mall).

(Milwaukee)

Credit Cards:	Yes
Owner:	William F. Frickensmith
Year Estab:	1989
Comments:	The shop carries a mix of paperback and hardcover items as well as LPs and ephemera. The books we saw were in mixed condition. Most were of recent vintage although a few older volumes were on hand.

Renaissance Book Shop   **Open Shop**
834 North Plankinton Avenue 53202   (414) 271-6850

Collection:	General stock of hardcover and paperback.
# of Vols:	300,000
Hours:	Mon-Fri 12-7. Sat 12-5.
Services:	Accepts want lists, search service, mail order.
Travel:	Downtown, between Wells & Kilbourn. From 1-43 southbound: Wells St exit. From I-94 see Downtown Books above.
Credit Cards:	No
Owner:	Robert John
Year Estab:	1963
Comments:	The comments below are based on our earlier visit to Milwaukee. Unfortunately, on the day we arrived in the city for a return visit, the shop was closed making it impossible for us to determine if any changes had occurred during the intervening years. We were, however, happily able to visit the owner's second shop at the airport (see below) where we had a very positive experience.

The good news is that this shop has volume. Its claim to 300,000 books is not an exaggeration. In addition to the ground floor level, there's a basement as well as a second and third floor. Another plus is that the books are extremely well organized and labeled with almost every subject area well represented. We also saw quite a number of antiquarian items. The less favorable news is that on some of the shelves we found books that in others shops would have been discarded as worn, water damaged, etc.

Renaissance Book Shop   **Open Shop**
5300 South Howell Street 53207   (414) 747-4526

Collection:	General stock of hardcover and paperback and magazines.
# of Vols:	50,000
Hours:	Daily 8am-10pm.
Services:	Accepts want lists, search service, mail order.
Travel:	Located on second level of Milwaukee International Airport. (Airport exit off I-94.) Park in hourly parking lot and exit on Level 3. Ticket validated with a minimum purchase.
Credit Cards:	No
Owner:	Robert John
Year Estab:	1963

Comments: Twice before in our travels (with one of us kicking and screaming along the way) we drove out to an airport location where a used book dealer was displaying his wares. It's still difficult for us to comprehend the rational for such locations, but who are we to argue with success. This shop, in addition to carrying lots of paperbacks and hardcover items that might ordinarily be seen at an airport book shop, also has some very fine books on display, including several signed first editions, a number of antiquarian items and a good share of titles dealing with far more serious subjects. If you're traveling by air to Milwaukee, you should definitely drop by. (A sign indicates that the shop will ship your books.) If your travels are by car and you have some extra time while visiting the city, you may want to take a ride out to the airport; you won't be sorry. We clocked the trip in non rush hour at 15-20 minutes from downtown.

Time Traveler Bookstore
Open Shop
7143 West Burleigh Street 53210   (414) 442-0203

Collection:	General stock and ephemera.
# of Vols:	5,000
Specialties:	Wisconsin; paper Americana.
Hours:	Mon-Fri 11-3:30. Sat 11-4.
Services:	Accepts want lists, mail order.
Travel:	Burleigh exit off Rte 45. Proceed east on Burleigh to intersection with Lisbon.
Credit Cards:	No
Owner:	Robert E. Sampon
Year Estab:	1976
Comments:	A very small shop with books that are older and marginally collectible. The dealer also displays at Fox River Antique Mall in Appleton.

Yesterdays Memories
Open Shop
5631 West Center Street 53210   (414) 444-6210

Collection:	General stock, ephemera and records.
# of Vols:	10,000 (See Comments)
Specialties:	Wisconsin; Judaica; sports; children's; music.
Hours:	Daily 10-6 but a call ahead is advised.
Services:	Appraisals, mail order.
Travel:	Hawley Rd exit off I-94. Proceed north on Hawley, then left on Center.
Credit Cards:	No
Owner:	Michael Corenthal
Year Estab:	1969
Comments:	As the name implies, this shop has lots of books and ephemera that date back to what the owner would no doubt consider "the good old days." If you're into nostalgia and have a pretty good idea of what you're looking for, you could probably save some time (as we did) by calling ahead so that the owner could advise you of the likelihood of your finding materials in your particular area of interest. (The owner

may also need time to check his storage area as only a portion of the stock listed above is on display at the store.) While the shop offers older books in all categories, you'll need patience to find them as the shop is cluttered, crowded and not always organized. We wished more items had been priced.

Mineral Point
(Map 30, page 440)

The Foundry Books   **Open Shop**
105 Commerce 53565   (608) 987-4363
Web page: www.foundrybooks.com   Fax: (608) 987-3627
                                        E-mail: connors@foundrybooks.com

Collection:	General stock.
# of Vols:	15,000 (See Comments)
Specialties:	Wisconsin
Hours:	May-Oct: Daily 12-6. Nov-Apr: Fri-Sun 12-6. Other times by chance or appointment.
Services:	Search service, accepts want lists, catalog.
Travel:	At intersection of Rtes 151 and 23, turn south on Rte 23 which becomes Commerce St.
Credit Cards:	Yes
Owner:	Dean Connors
Year Estab:	1995
Comments:	A relatively small shop with a quality collection in local and regional topics, Wisconsin, hunting and fishing as well as books of a more general nature. The shop is not far from Sauk City, and to prove it, several shelves display the works of August Derleth, a local writer. Not inexpensive. We don't know if you'll have the pleasure of meeting the crusty gentleman who greeted us when we visited but we suspect his bark is worse than his bite. At the time of our visit, the number of books on display was less than that noted above.

Mineral Point Book Center   **Open Shop**
114 High Street   (608) 987-2320
Mailing address: PO Box 359 Mineral Point WI 53565   (608) 348-3139
                                             E-mail: ppmtn@mhtc.net

Collection:	General stock.
# of Vols:	3,000
Specialties:	Children's; books on books; cookbooks (ethnic and regional).
Hours:	Apr-Oct: Mon-Sat, except closed Wed, 10-5. Sun 10-4. Dec-Mar: Sat 10-5. Sun 10-4.
Services:	Search service, accepts want lists, mail order.
Travel:	From Rte 151, take Church St to High St. Shop is directly across from Library Park.
Credit Cards:	Yes
Owner:	James & Gayle Bull
Year Estab:	1997

Comments: A nice shop with enough room to display a modest selection of books offered by both the owners and several other dealers. The specialties listed above are well represented. As the owner is considering the possibility of moving to another site in town, you may wish to call ahead to be certain of the shop's current location.

Monona
(Map 30, page 440)

O.Z. Enterprises
4510 Shore Acres Road 53716

By Appointment
(608) 221-0584

Collection:	General stock.
# of Vols:	3,000-4,000
Owner:	John Baltes
Year Estab:	1992

Monroe
(Map 30, page 440)

Fireside Books
1517 11th Street 53566

Open Shop
(608) 329-7323

Collection:	General stock of hardcover and paperback.
# of Vols:	16,000
Hours:	Wed-Fri 11-6. Sat 10-5. (Closed Jan & Feb).
Services:	Accepts want lists.
Travel:	Rte 69 to downtown Monroe. Turn east on 11th St. Shop is one block before the square.
Credit Cards:	No
Owner:	Carrie Backe
Year Estab:	1993
Comments:	Stock is evenly divided between hardcover and paperback.

Mosinee
(Map 30, page 440)

Daltonbooks
302 Main Street 54455

Open Shop
(715) 693-2226

Collection:	General stock of mostly paperback.
# of Vols:	30,000
Hours:	Mon-Fri, except closed Wed, 10:45-5. Sat 10:45-1.

Oconomowoc
(Map 30, page 440)

Booksmith
418 East Wisconsin Avenue 53066
Web page: www.execpc.com/booksmith/

Open Shop
(414) 560-0001
Fax: (414) 560-0002
E-mail: mwiin@execpc.com

Collection:	General stock of paperback and hardcover.

# of Vols:	20,000
Specialties:	Children's series; Wisconsin; cookbooks; mystery; science fiction.
Hours:	Mon 10-4. Tue-Fri 10-8. Sat 10-6. Sun 11-4. Jun-Sept: Sun, Mon, Thu 11-4. Wed & Fri 11-8, Sat 10-6.
Services:	Search service, accepts want lists, mail order.
Travel:	Exit 282 (Rte 67) off I-94. Proceed north on Rte 67 for 2-3 miles, then veer right (near a traffic light) onto bypass and continue as it loops around to the traffic light at the end of the road. Turn right on Wisconsin Ave (Rte 16W/67N) and continue for about one mile. Shop is one right.
Credit Cards:	Yes
Owner:	Maria Smith Winter
Year Estab:	1997
Comments:	A very attractive bi-level shop located in a former private residence. The books are displayed in a charming fashion and run the gamut from hardcover vintage items and more recent titles to paperbacks. Several titles drew our interest. Prices were, we thought, a trifle higher than we have seen elsewhere for similar volumes.

Oregon
(Map 30, page 440)

Knollwood Books
110 North Main Street
Mailing address: PO Box 197 Oregon WI 53575

By Appointment
(608) 835-8861
Fax: (608) 835-8421
E-mail: books@tdsnet.com

Collection:	Specialty
# of Vols:	10,000
Specialties:	Astronomy; meteorology; space exploration.
Services:	Appraisals, search service, catalog, accepts want lists.
Credit Cards:	Yes
Owner:	Lee & Peggy Price
Year Estab:	1992

Oshkosh
(Map 30, page 440)

The Book Place
2211 Oregon Street, #A4 54901

Open Shop
(920) 426-3500

Collection:	General stock of mostly paperback.
# of Vols:	45,000
Hours:	Mon, Wed, Fri 10-6. Thu & Fri 10-5. Sat 10-3.

Originals Mall of Antiques
1475 South Washburn Street

Antique Mall
(920) 235-0495

Hours:	Daily 10-6.
Travel:	On Rte 41 (west frontage road) between 9th Ave and 20th Ave exits, two miles north of the EAA Museum.

Osseo
(Map 30, page 440)

Many Little Things Antique Mall   **Antique Mall**
13812 West 7th Street 54758   (715) 597-2879
                                                                    (888) 425-1297

Hours: Jan-Apr: Mon-Sat 10-5. Sun 11-4. May-Dec: Mon-Sat 9-5. Sun 10-4.
Travel: One half mile west of junction of I-94 and Rte 10.

Portage
(Map 30, page 440)

Portage Antique Mall   **Antique Mall**
114 West Cook Street 53901   (608) 742-1640

Hours: Daily 9:30-5.
Travel: Downtown, at intersection of Rtes 33 & 51.

Racine
(Map 30, page 440)

Ace & Bubba Treasure Hunters   **Open Shop**
218 Sixth Street 53403   (414) 633-3308

Collection: General stock.
# of Vols: 4,000+
Specialties: Children's; children's series; history.
Hours: Mon-Sat 10-5.
Services: Appraisals
Travel: Rte 20 exit off I-94. Proceed east on Rte 20, then left on Main and left
                 on Sixth St. Shop is 1/2 block ahead.
Credit Cards: Yes
Owner: Pam Pionke
Year Estab: 1989
Comments: A pleasant shop combining antiques, vintage clothing and used books.
                 The books, located on the first floor and in the basement, consist mostly
                 of older but not antiquarian titles and are very reasonably priced. What
                 the shop may lack in volume it makes up for in its helpful husband and
                 wife team, both of whom stand ready to please.

BotanaBooks & Art   **By Appointment**
PO Box 085756 53408   (800) 723-8502
Web page: www.botana.com   Fax: (414) 633-0830
                                                    E-mail: BobGoebel@Botana.com

Collection: Specialty books and ephemera.
Specialties: Botany; horticulture; orchids (books and art).
Services: Appraisals, search service, catalog, accepts want lists.
Credit Cards: Yes
Owner: Robert J. Goebel
Year Estab: 1973

Martha Merrell's Bookstore   **Open Shop**
312 Sixth Street 53403   (414) 632-0215

Collection: General stock of mostly used hardcover and paperback.
# of Vols: 25,000
Specialties: Maritime; western Americana; religion; literary criticism; history; na-
                 ture.
Hours: Mon-Fri 10-6. Sat 10-4. Sun (Jun-Aug only) 12-4.
Services: Appraisals
Travel: See Ace & Bubba Treasure Hunters above.
Credit Cards: Yes
Owner: Andrew M. McClean, Ph.D.
Year Estab: 1991
Comments: This shop sells new books, CDs and cassettes and a nice selection of
                 mixed vintage used books in generally very good condition. While we
                 were not able to spot any truly rare items during our visit, there were
                 some first editions and better books to select from. As is the case with
                 all used book shops, one never knows what volumes may be on display
                 during your visit. Note: The shop was previously known as the "Old
                 Book Corner."

Rib Mountain
(Map 30, page 440)

Rib Mountain Antique Mall   **Antique Mall**
3300 Eagle Avenue 54401   (715) 848-5564

Hours: Mon-Sat 10-5. Sun 12-5.
Travel: Exit 190 off Rte 51 north. East on N. Mountain Rd. Right on Eagle Ave.

Rice Lake
(Map 30, page 440)

Old Bookshop of Rice Lake   **Open Shop**
37 North Main Street 54868   (715) 234-4788
                                          E-mail: djohns11@chibardun.net

Collection: General stock of paperback and hardcover.
# of Vols: 18,000
Specialties: World War II; sciences; history; older romance fiction.
Hours: Tue-Fri 10-5, except Thu till 6. Sat 10-3.
Services: Search service.
Travel: From Rte 53, take Rte "O" exit to Rice Lake. Turn north at Rte SS.
                 Cross bridge. Shop is one block ahead after the light.
Credit Cards: No
Owner: Betty Johnson
Year Estab: 1994
Comments: While there were probably fewer hardcover books than paperbacks,
                 those that we did see were in generally good condition and quite reason-
                 ably priced. The shop offers a nice selection and we spotted several
                 titles worth going out of one's way for.

River Falls
(Map 30, page 440)

Books on the Rebound
128 A North Second Street 54022

Open Shop
(715) 426-9990

Collection:	General stock of hardcover and paperback and ephemera.
# of Vols:	2,000
Hours:	Tue-Fri 10-6. Sat 10-2.
Services:	Book repair.
Travel:	From I-94 at Hudson, proceed south on Rte 35 to River Falls exit. Turn right at stop sign and continue to 2nd light (Main and Maple). Right on Maple. Shop is one block ahead, on Maple, just east of Second St.
Credit Cards:	No
Owner:	Elizabeth Dressler
Year Estab:	1996
Comments:	Stock is approximately 70% hardcover. The shop is also an espresso coffee shop.

Seymour

Crabbe Reader
214 South Main Street 54165

Open Shop
(920) 833-9504

Collection:	General stock of mostly paperback.
# of Vols:	22,000
Hours:	Mon-Thu 10-5. Fri 10-7. Sat 10-4.

Sheboygan
(Map 30, page 440)

Book Boutique
1220 North 14th Street 53081

Open Shop
(920) 458-3177

Collection:	General stock of paperback and hardcover.
# of Vols:	20,000
Hours:	Mon-Fri 10-5. Sat 10-4.
Travel:	Erie Ave exit off Rte 23. Proceed east on Erie, then north on 14th St. Shop is 1½ blocks ahead on left.
Credit Cards:	No
Year Estab:	1983
Comments:	Stock is approximately 70% paperback.

Book Store
1032 Lincoln Avenue 53081

Open Shop
(920) 452-6640

Collection:	General stock of mostly used paperback.
# of Vols:	50,000
Hours:	Mon-Fri 9:30-5:30. Sat 10-4. Sun 11-4.

Spring Green
(Map 30, page 440)

The Spring Green General Store
137 South Albany Street 53588

General Store
(608) 588-7070

Hours:	Mon-Fri 9-6. Sat 8-6. Sun 8-4.
Travel:	One block west of Rte 23 and next to railroad tracks.

The Winsted Shop
140 South Winsted Street
Mailing address: PO Box 9 Spring Green WI 53588

Open Shop
(608) 588-7544

Collection:	General stock of new and used hardcover.
# of Vols:	500-1,000 (used)
Specialties:	Frank Lloyd Wright; Wisconsin.
Hours:	Mon-Sat 9-5:30. Sun 12:30-4:30.
Services:	Search service, accepts want lists.
Travel:	From Rte 14, proceed south on Rte 23. Shop is on Rte 23.
Credit Cards:	Yes
Owner:	Virgil & Helen Steele
Year Estab:	1967

Stevens Point
(Map 30, page 440)

Downtown Antiques Shop
1100 Main Street 54481

Antique Mall
(715) 342-1442

Hours:	Mon-Fri 10-6. Sat 10-5. Sun 12-4.
Travel:	Rte 10 exit off Rte 51/39. Proceed west on Rte 10 to downtown following signs for business district.

Mike Plonsker Books
101 Division North 54481

Open Shop
(715) 344-5805

Collection:	General stock of hardcover and paperback.
# of Vols:	10,000
Hours:	Spring: Mon-Fri 12-5. Winter: Tue-Fri 11-5:30. Sat 10-4.
Services:	Accepts want lists.
Travel:	Rte 51 to Bus Rte 51. Shop is one mile north of intersection of Rtes 51 & 10 at corner of Maria Dr and Bus Rte 51. Shop is located on lower level of a strip mall.
Credit Cards:	No
Year Estab:	1996
Comments:	Despite the advice we have repeatedly given to our readers concerning the importance of calling ahead, we arrived in Stevens Point (having just left Markesan and on our way to Wausau) without making that important phone call. As luck would have it, we found a sign on the door reading "Store Closed, 5/25-6/6. Will return 6/8." All we are able to tell our readers, therefore, is that we were able to view through the window a significant number of hardcover books along with a scatter-

ing of paperbacks; there is no way we could make a judgment regarding either the variety or quality of the books. Should you have an opportunity to visit this shop, please share your impressions with us.

Sturtevant
(Map 30, page 440)

School Days Antiques Mall
9500 Durand Avenue 53177

Antique Mall
(414) 866-1069

Hours:	Tue-Sat 10-5. Sun 12-5.
Travel:	Located on Rte 11, two miles east of I-94.

Superior
(Map 30, page 440)

E-Z Reading
1210 Tower Avenue 54880

Open Shop
(715) 394-4933

Collection:	General stock of mostly paperback.
# of Vols:	21,000
Hours:	Mon-Fri 10-6. Sat 10-4.

Walworth
(Map 30, page 440)

On The Square Antique Mall
Junction Rte 67 & 14
Mailing address: PO Box 921 Walworth WI 53184

Antique Mall
(414) 275-9858

Hours:	Daily 10-5.

Washburn
(Map 30, page 440)

Chequamegon Book & Coffee Co.
2 East Bayfield Street 54891

Open Shop
(715) 373-2899
Fax: (715) 373-0240

Collection:	General stock.
# of Vols:	50,000
Hours:	May-Dec: Mon-Sat 10-6. Sun 11-5. Call for winter hours.
Services:	Appraisals, search service, accepts want lists, mail order.
Travel:	On Rte 13, on route to Apostle Island National Park.
Credit Cards:	Yes
Owner:	Carol & Richard Avol
Year Estab:	1996
Comments:	If you've driven this far north, pat yourself on the back as you enter this shop and enjoy a nice array of both used books and attractive, bargain priced remainders. The books cover almost every category imaginable and are in quite good condition. Some paperbacks and a few oldies. Certainly worth a visit. The proprietors previously owned Avol's Bookstore in Madison, WI.

Waukesha
(Map 30, page 440)

The Book Place
233 West Newhall Avenue 53186

By Appointment
(414) 542-2355
E-mail: booksrch@execpc.com

Collection:	General stock.
# of Vols:	300+
Services:	Search service, accepts want lists, mail order.
Owner:	Carolyn I. & Richard E. Huttner
Year Estab:	1984

Waupaca
(Map 30, page 440)

Bookcellar
118 South Main Street 54981

Open Shop
(715) 258-2555

Collection:	General stock of mostly paperback.
Hours:	Mon-Fri 12-6. Sat 9-3.

Wausau
(Map 30, page 440)

Et Al's Read & Unread Books
419 1st Street
Mailing address: PO Box 583 Wausau WI 54402

Open Shop
(715) 675-3301

Collection:	General stock.
# of Vols:	5,000
Specialties:	Modern first editions.
Hours:	Tue-Fri 12-8:30. Sat 11-7. Other times by appointment.
Services:	Search service, accepts want lists, mail order.
Travel:	Exit 192 off Rte 51. Proceed east on Rte 52 (Stewart Ave) to downtown where traffic flows left onto 2nd St. Continue on 2nd St, then left on Scott and left on 1st.
Credit Cards:	No
Owner:	Allen J. Post
Year Estab:	1995
Comments:	While the collection is modest in size, we are pleased to report that, for a change, a shop reporting its specialty as "modern first editions" actually carries a reasonable number of such volumes—and in generally good condition. At the time of our visit, we also saw a small number of vintage paperbacks, some Modern Library volumes and other titles of a more general interest.

Gold Dog Books
2301 North 18th Street 54403

By Appointment
(715) 848-6157
Fax: (715) 842-7159
E-mail: waychar@dwave.net

Collection:	General stock.

# of Vols:	3,000-4,000
Services:	Accepts want lists, search service.
Credit Cards:	No
Owner:	Wayne & Charmaine Schultz
Year Estab:	1991
Comments:	Also displays at Rib Mountain Antique Mall in Rib Mountain. See above.

West Salem
(Map 30, page 440)

Historic Salem
99 Jefferson Street
Mailing address: PO Box 884 West Salem WI 54669

Open Shop
(608) 786-1675

Collection:	General stock of hardcover and paperback.
# of Vols:	15,000 (hardcover)
Specialties:	Hamlin Garland; Zona Gale.
Hours:	Apr 15-Dec 25: Mon-Fri 9-9. Sat & Sun 9-5. Dec 25-Apr 15: Daily 9-5.
Services:	Accepts want lists, mail order.
Travel:	West Salem exit off I-90. Turn north off exit and make first left after the interstate (following the sign for downtown). Turn left at the bottom of the ramp onto Jefferson St.
Credit Cards:	No
Owner:	Errol Kindschy
Year Estab:	1986

Wisconsin Dells
(Map 30, page 440)

Antique Mall of Wisconsin Dells I
720 Oak Street 53965

Antique Mall
(608) 254-2422

Hours:	June 15-Labor Day 9-9. Remainder of year: Daily 10-5.
Travel:	Exit 87 off I-90.

Antique Mall of Wisconsin Dells II
Highway 12

Antique Mall
(608) 356-7600

Hours:	Daily 10-8.
Travel:	At exit 92 off I-90.

Ravenswood Books
51 Bowman Road 53965

By Appointment
(608) 253-7861

Collection:	General stock.
# of Vols:	10,000
Specialties:	Americana in Wisconsin Dells; Frank Lloyd Wright in Spring Garden.
Services:	Accepts want lists, mail order.
Credit Cards:	No
Owner:	David & Sharon Lake
Year Estab:	1976
Comments:	Also displays in antique malls in Wisconsin Dells (see below) and in the Spring Green General Store in Spring Green (see above).

Wisconsin Rapids

Book Nook
130 2nd Avenue South 54495   (715) 421-0410
Collection: General stock of mostly paperback.
# of Vols: 20,000
Hours: Mon-Thu 9:30-5. Fri 9:30-6. Sat 9:30-4.

Woodruff
(Map 30, page 440)

A Good Book/The Mill Antiques
1405 Highway 47 South   (715) 356-5468
Mailing address: PO Box 1456 Woodruff WI 54568
Collection: General stock of hardcover and paperback and ephemera.
# of Vols: 100,000+
Hours: Labor Day-Memorial Day: Wed-Sat 10-5. Jun-Sep: Mon-Sat 10-5. Also
                     holiday Sundays. Best to call ahead.
Travel: From Rte 51, turn east on Rte 47 south.
Credit Cards: Yes
Owner: Dennis N. Howard
Year Estab: 1968
Comments: Located in a large bi-level metal prefab building, this shop carries
                     paperbacks, comics books as well as a mix of older and sometimes
                     interesting hardcover volumes. We spotted several sets, a few items
                     that could certainly be considered collectible and plenty of more com-
                     mon titles. Generally speaking, we would say that prices were some-
                     what higher than we have seen elsewhere for similar items. If you're
                     looking for old furniture, glassware and other non book collectibles,
                     you'll have lots to choose from here. At the time of our visit, the book
                     portion of the shop was in the process of being reorganized and books
                     were shelved in several different locations. Also, the number of vol-
                     umes on display was less than the number cited above.

Aardvark Book Depot
(414) 225-9881
PO Box 11394 Shorewood 53211
E-mail: aardvark@aero.net

Collection:	General stock.
# of Vols:	25,000
Specialties:	Native Americans; anthropology; travel.
Services:	Search service, accepts want lists.
Credit Cards:	Yes
Owner:	Gene Muehlbauer & Mary Hoberg
Year Estab:	1989
Comments:	Also displays at antique malls in Sturtevant and Oshkosh. See above.

B & B Crafts
Tel & Fax: (920) 235-4669
1235 North Westfield Street Oshkosh 54901

Collection:	Specialty new and used.
Specialties:	Mining; gold prospecting.
Services:	Search service, catalog, accepts want lists.
Credit Cards:	No
Owner:	Robert Fox
Year Estab:	1985
Comments:	Stock is approximately 85% new.

Badger Trading Co.
(920) 739-1339
PO Box 2402 Appleton 54913

Collection:	General stock, prints and ephemera.
# of Vols:	2,000
Specialties:	Antiques; decorative arts.
Services:	Catalog, accepts want lists.
Credit Cards:	No
Owner:	Tod Loberg
Year Estab:	1978

BNZ Enterprises
(715) 539-3637
W2928 County Highway G Merrill 54452

Collection:	Specialty
# of Vols:	1,500
Specialties:	Religion (Catholic pre-1962); history; children's.
Services:	Catalog, accepts want lists, search service.
Credit Cards:	No
Owner:	Bell & Nancy Zeitz
Year Estab:	1992

The Bookplate
(920) 459-7901
1303 South 10th Street Sheboygan 53081
E-mail: bookplte@execpc.com

Collection:	General stock of hardcover and paperback.
Specialties:	Children's
Services:	Search service, catalog, accepts want lists.
Credit Cards:	No

Owner: Amara Martin
Year Estab: 1996

Dusty Dreams Books   (715) 341-6113
324 Woodland Drive Stevens Point 54481

Collection: General stock.
Owner: Betty Coates
Year Estab: 1990
Comments: Also displays as Downtown Antiques Shop in Stevens Point. See above.

Raymond Dworczyk Rare Books   (414) 383-2659
2114 West Rogers Street Milwaukee 53204

Collection: General stock.
# of Vols: 50,000
Specialties: Illustrated; Americana; military.
Services: Appraisals, occasional catalog, accepts want lists.
Credit Cards: No
Year Estab: 1944

W. Bruce Fye Antiquarian Books   (715) 384-8128
1607 North Wood Avenue Marshfield 54449   Fax: (715) 389-2990
                                             E-mail: bfye@tznet.com

Collection: Specialty
Specialties: Medicine
Services: Catalog
Credit Cards: No
Owner: W. Bruce & Lois Fye
Year Estab: 1973

Heirloom Books and Collectibles   (920) 435-8223
PO Box 22162 Green Bay 54305   Fax: (920) 435-8646
                                             E-mail: heirloom@gbonline.com

Collection: General stock.
# of Vols: 2,000+
Services: Search service, accepts want lists.
Credit Cards: Yes
Owner: Kathy Roork
Year Estab: 1991
Comments: Also displays at Memories Antique Mall in Appleton. See above.

James Hyer, Bookseller   (920) 478-3644
N7609 Airport Road Waterloo 53594

Collection: General stock.
# of Vols: 20,000-25,000
Specialties: Wisconsin
Services: Search service, accepts want lists.
Credit Cards: No
Year Estab: 1950's

Lakeshore Books (920) 684-8770
1202 Marshall Street Manitowoc 54220

Collection:	General stock of hardcover and paperback and ephemera.
# of Vols:	12,000
Specialties:	Vintage paperbacks; older fiction.
Services:	Catalog, accepts want lists.
Credit Cards:	No
Owner:	Gary Kott
Year Estab:	1980

Louis & Clark Booksellers (608) 231-6850
PO Box 5093 Madison 53705   E-mail: Louis_and_Clark@compuserve.com

Collection:	Specialty
# of Vols:	5,000
Specialties:	Cookbooks; beverages; food industry; household management; etiquette; travel.
Services:	Search service, catalog, accepts want lists.
Credit Cards:	No
Owner:	Lillian A. Clark
Year Estab:	1990

Maple Lawn Antiques (414) 425-3854
S. 71 W. 13382 Woods Road Muskego 53150   Fax: (414) 427-8394
E-mail: sternw@earthlink.net

Collection:	General stock.
# of Vols:	6,000
Specialties:	Antique reference.
Credit Cards:	Yes
Owner:	Diane Stern
Year Estab:	1974
Comments:	Collection may be viewed by appointment.

Paper Mountain Books (608) 348-3139
150 Bavley Avenue Platteville 53818   E-mail: ppmtn@mhtc.net
Web page: www.papermountain.com

Collection:	General stock.
Specialties:	Children's; books on books; cookbooks.
Credit Cards:	Yes
Owner:	James & Gayle Bull
Year Estab:	1974

P.I.E.S. (Private Investigator Entertainment Service)
PO Box 341218 Milwaukee 53234

Collection:	Specialty
Specialties:	Detective
Services:	Catalog, accepts want lists.
Owner:	Gary Warren Niebuhr
Year Estab:	1990

J.L. Skaggs (608) 868-3861
600 College Street Milton 53563

Collection: General stock.
Services: Accepts want lists.

J. Tuttle Maritime Books (608) 238-SAIL
1806 Laurel Crest Madison 53705   Fax: (608) 238-7249
Web page: www.interloc.com/~tuttlemb/   E-mail: tuttlebk@aol.com

Collection: Specialty
# of Vols: 18,000
Specialties: Maritime (from 1600 to 1990's).
Services: Appraisals, search service, catalog, accepts want lists.
Credit Cards: Yes
Year Estab: 1980

Untamed Shrew Books (920) 478-3644
N7609 Airport Road Waterloo 53594

Collection: Specialty
# of Vols: 20,000
Specialties: Women's history and literature.
Services: Catalog, search service, accepts want lists.
Credit Cards: No
Owner: Joan Hyer
Year Estab: 1982

Wood Violet Books (608) 837-7207
3814 Sunhill Drive Madison 53718   Fax: (608) 825-3073
E-mail: wvbooks@aol.com

Collection: Specialty new and some used.
Specialties: Herbs; gardening; cookbooks.
Services: Search service, catalog.
Credit Cards: Yes
Owner: Debra Cravens
Year Estab: 1984

Specialty Index

Adventure
Fickes Crime Fiction 419
Africa
Marrow of Tradition Books 361
Old Main Book Shoppe 28
Gerald Rilling 64
Agriculture
The American Botanist 45
Just Books 329
Lancaster & Simpson 304
Midge's Dollhouse & Antiques 321
Pine Stock Books and Antiques 61
The Sporting Horse Gallery 168
Stroud Booksellers 433
Dennis Sutterer Books 143
Terrace Horticultural Books 285
Alaska
Artis Books & Antiques 195
Campfire Books 130
Freddie The Bookie 252
Almanacs
Bibliotective 234
American history
Bell's Books & Candles 346
Bibliodisia Books 32
Black Swan Books 165
The Book Gallery 165
Bookman's Alley 50
Bookzeller 68
D.R. Doerres Rendezvous Trader 150
Four Score Books and Ect. 257
Hooked On History 67
Jillson's Nauticals & Antiques 201
Leonard's Antiques and Books 115
Lien's Book Shop 283
Midway Bookstore 294
Ross & Haines Old Books Co. 449
Edwin Schaeffer 47
Twice Read Books 61
American literature
Bibliodisia Books 32
Richard Cady-Antiquarian Bookseller 34
The Fine Books Company 240
Anthony Garnett Fine Books 338
Glenn Books 325

John Wm. Martin-Bookseller 60
John Quinn, Bookseller 152
Paul Rohe Books 93
Americana
Alkahest Bookshop 48
Archer's Used And Rare Books 395
Bay Books 365
Beechwold Books 383
Bicentennial Book Shop 223
The Book Harbor 412
Books on High 383
Broad Ripple Bookshop 109
B. Caldwell - Bookseller 331
Gerald J. Cielec-Books 88
Circle City Antiquarian Books 110
Constant Reader Book Shop 461
James Cummings, Bookseller 450
Dann Collectibles 239
R. Dunaway, Bookseller 337
Raymond Dworczyk Rare Books 478
84 Charing Cross, EH? 231
Elegant Book & Map Co. 418
Enchanted Books, Antiques, Etc. 392
ETBooks 221
Exnowski Enterprises 250
Forest Park Books 105
Fourth Street Book Shop 242
Glenn Books 325
Glover's Bookery 167
Thatcher C. Goetz, Books 216
John M. Gram 239
Hamill & Barker Antiquarian Booksellers 51
Susan Heller - Pages for Sages 377
Hoffman's Bookshop 384
Thomas J. Joyce and Company 36
John K. King Books 207
Leaves of Grass Books 198
Left Bank Bookstall 91
Legacy Books 179
The Legacy Company 150
Little Journeys Bookshop 397
Mike Maddigan 139
Jerry Merkel 421
Michiana Antiques & Books 194
Mossback Books 208
Donald S. Mull - Books 172
Kenneth Nebenzahl, Inc. 56

Ralph Newman Bibliopole Ltd.   38
North Coast Americana   403
Ohio Book Store   372
Old Erie Street Bookstore   378
Paper Moone   333
Barbara Parks - Books   243
Peninsula Books   250
Ravenswood Books   475
ReReadables   399
Rowsburg Bookstore   404
Bob Rund-Books   54
L.J. Ryan, Scholarly Books   385
John Rybski, Bookseller   42
Shakespeare's Books   456
Shaw's Books   219
John Wallace Skinner Americana   379
Spivey's Books, Old Maps, Fine Art   327
Harry L. Stern, Ltd.   43
Stan Stites Books   93
Stonehill's Books   28
Stony Hill Antiques   457
Titles, Inc.   58
John Wade   425
Weekend Bookman   253
What Goes Round   442
Wilder Books   48
Robert Williams   94
Wise Owl Books   451
Pat & Bill Wisney-Books   262
Timothy B. Wuchter   262
Yesterday's Books   237

Ancient history
The Antiquarian, Ltd.   30
John B. Doukas   256
Dove Booksellers   227
Powell's Bookstore, South   40
Edwin Schaeffer   47

Animals
Paterson-Ford Booksellers   172
The Sporting Horse Gallery   168
WXICOF   348
(See also Cats, Dogs, Horses)

Anthropology
Aardvark Book Depot   477
Ancient Society Books   86
N. Fagin Books   35
Wm Caxton Ltd   447

Antiquarian
Archives Book Shop   210
John B. Doukas   256
Les Enluminures Ltd.   35
The Gentlemen Soldier   122
Graton & Graton   57
River Gallery   59

Antiques & collectibles
Acorn Books   315
Antiques at Hall House   396
Badger Trading Co.   477
Bookends and Fine Collectables   51
Byrd's Books & Collectibles   317
Cleveland Antiquarian Books   376
Dickens' Book Shop   396
Downtown Books Fine Arts   462
Galerie De Boicourt   251
The Library   151
Maple Lawn Antiques   479
Midtown Book Center   297
Shaw's Books   219
Shirley's Book Services   236

Appalachia
Trans Allegheny Books   427

Archaeology
Ancient Society Books   86
Deux Amasse Books   241
N. Fagin Books   35
John M. Gram   239
Richard A. Hand, Bookseller   420
Edwin Schaeffer   47
Flo Silver Books   132
Topaz-Mineral Exploration   261
Karen Wickliff Books   386

Archery
Evans Firearms and Archery   166
Fair Chase   451

Architecture
John Angelos, Books   459
Avol's Bookstore   452
Bay Books   365
Bookends and Fine Collectables   51
Booklegger's Used Books   32
Cleveland Antiquarian Books   376
John Dinsmore & Associates   166
Downtown Books Fine Arts   462
Hammond's Books   338
James & Mary Laurie, Booksellers   281
The Legacy Company   150
Marion The Antiquarian Librarian   200
Powell's Bookstore, South   40
Prairie Avenue Bookshop   41
Ed Ripp: Bookseller   41
St. Croix Antiquarian Booksellers   297
Helena Szépe, Books   44
Titles, Inc.   58
White Raven Books   254

Arctic
Artis Books & Antiques   195
Charles David Dyer - Books   398
Greenfield Books   320

Armor
Adams Walls of Books 315

Art
A Collector's Bookshop 334
A Place in History 392
Acorn Books 315
Alkahest Bookshop 48
John Angelos, Books 459
Avol's Bookstore 452
Bank Lane Books 86
Richard S. Barnes & Co. 86
Bay Books 365
Biermaier's B. H. Books 278
Book Beat 235
The Book House 336
The Book House 319
Book Stall Of Rockford 78
Bookends and Fine Collectables 51
Booklegger's Used Books 32
Bookman's Alley 50
Booksellers Row 33
Broad Ripple Bookshop 109
B. Caldwell - Bookseller 331
Gerald J. Cielec-Books 88
Classic Book Shop 242
Cleveland Antiquarian Books 376
Columbia Books 316
Cordell-Wilson Booksellers 314
Country Comfort Antiques & Books 299
Cross Street Book Shop 252
Stephen Daiter Gallery 34
Deux Amasse Books 241
John Dinsmore & Associates 166
Discount Books 376
Downtown Books Fine Arts 462
ETBooks 221
N. Fagin Books 35
Forest Park Books 105
Galerie De Boicourt 251
Gemini Fine Books & Arts 58
Glaeve Gallery 454
Hammond's Books 338
Susan Heller - Pages for Sages 377
Hooked On Books 343
Jane Addams Book Shop 27
Keramos 257
James & Mary Laurie, Booksellers 281
The Legacy Company 150
Marion The Antiquarian Librarian 200
Materiality 442
Midway Bookstore 294
Morrie's Books 213
My Bookhouse 409
O'Gara & Wilson Booksellers 39

Old Main Book Shoppe 28
Paragon Book Gallery 39
Powell's Bookstore, South 40
Powell's Bookstore, North 40
Prospero's Books 326
Rain Dog Books 41
Rhythm & Views 93
Ed Ripp: Bookseller 41
Robert Joseph Co. 373
Stephen Rose Fine Arts 112
Bernie Rost-Books 42
L.A. Rubin Rare Books 202
John Rybski, Bookseller 42
St. Croix Antiquarian Booksellers 297
Shaw's Books 219
Flo Silver Books 132
Snowy Egret Books 295
Helena Szépe, Books 44
Titles, Inc. 58
Toad Hall Books & Records 78
Trails' End Books 112
Turtle Island Books 44
Upstart Crow Books 143
White Raven Books 254
The World of Books 413

Art conservation
Materiality 442

Art, fine
Anthony Garnett Fine Books 338
Leonard's Antiques and Books 115
Loganberry Books 377
Metropolis Art Books 208
Old Erie Street Bookstore 378
Karen Wickliff Books 386

Art, folk
Galerie De Boicourt 251
Glaeve Gallery 454

Artist monographs
Ed Ripp: Bookseller 41

Arts & crafts
The Book Harbor 412
Ginkgo Leaf Press 89

Asia
The Cellar Book Shop 207
China Book Gallery 302
Deux Amasse Books 241
Gregory and Beverly Gamradt 303
Keramos 257
Paragon Book Gallery 39
Richard G. Peterson, Bookseller 304
Michael G. Price 259
Duane Robeck- Bookseller 305

Assasinations & Conspiracies
A-albionic Research 255

Association copies
Archives Book Shop 210
Jett W. Whitehead - Rare Books 201

Astrology
House of Scorpio 462
Insight Metaphysical Bookstore 27
Mayflower Bookshop 201
Occult Bookstore 39
Ramtek International 424
Sqecial Media 168
Turtle Island Books 44

Astronomy
Knollwood Books 468

Austen, Jane
Blenheim Books 175
Jane Austen Books 89

Autographs
Abraham Lincoln Book Shop 29
Americas Antiquarium 86
The Autograph Alcove 459
Richard Cady-Antiquarian Bookseller 34
Cleveland Antiquarian Books 376
Collector Book and Print Gallery 369
Historical Newspapers 80
History Makers Rare Find Gallery 111
Main Street Fine Books & Manuscripts 54
Monastery Hill Bindery 38
Shaw's Books 219
Wilder Books 48

Automotive
Casanova Books 443
Gerhart's Rare & Out-of-Print Books 89
GT Motors 226
John K. King Books 207
John King Books North 214
Magina Books 227
Russell S. Rein, Books & Records 253
Science Book Service 306
Shaw's Books 219
Art Spindler 260
Dennis Sutterer Books 143
T.E. Warth, Esq., Automotive Books 277

Aviation
ABT Books 403
Acorn Bookshop 382
Articles of War 79
Bookphil Out of Print & Signed 395
Books on High 383
The Bookseller 359
Casanova Books 443
Exnowski Enterprises 250

Grandview Book Gallery 319
Jefferson Street Book Sellers 127
The Reading Doctor 401
P.R. Schwan, Bookseller 121
Margaret Soderberg, Bookseller 447

Baja California
Bee Creek Books 302

Baseball
Archer's Used And Rare Books 395
The Christensen Gallery 235
Mary Ann's Books 258
Mostly Baseball 179
Philip Riggs, Books 373
Yannigan's 404
(See also Sports)

Baum, Frank
Armchair Adventures 160
Books on the Sun Porch 149
Excellence in Books 148
Mike Maddigan 139
Robert Williams Bound To Please Books 94

Beat generation
Country Comfort Antiques and Books 299
John Dinsmore & Associates, 166
Sqecial Media 168

Beverages
Louis & Clark Booksellers 479
The Wine And Food Library 199

Bibles
Richard Owen Roberts, Booksellers 83

Biblical studies
Dove Booksellers 227
Rowsburg Bookstore 404

Bibliography
Melvin McCosh, Bookseller 304
Midnight Bookman 129

Biography
A Place in History 392
A-albionic Research 255
ABC Collectables 301
Bloomsday Books 324
Candy Books 418
Caveat Emptor 102
Cordell-Wilson Booksellers 314
James Cummings, Bookseller 450
Deerlilly Farms 346
H & B Booksellers 202
Haunted Bookshop On The Creek 146
Lowry's Books 249
Jerry Merkel 421
Morrie's Books 213
The Mystery Nook 75

The Old Book Shop 321
ReReadables 399
Richard Owen Roberts, Booksellers 83
Robert Joseph Co. 373
Snowball Bookshop 364
Wabash River Books 128

Black studies
Beasley Books 30
Books of Choice 302
Booksellers Row 33
The Bookworm 369
Country Comfort Antiques and Books 299
Cross Street Book Shop 252
Freddie The Bookie 252
Ginkgo Leaf Press 89
Jay's African-American Books 207
Marrow of Tradition Books 361
Barbara Parks - Books 243
John Quinn, Bookseller 152
R.D. Book Search 423
Twice-Loved Books 415
Wilder Books 48
Wooden Spoon Books 199
Yesteryear Books 62

Bly, Robert
Ally Press 301

Books on books
Arch Books 301
Bags End 333
Matthew Bisiotti & Company 363
Richard Cady-AntiquarianBookseller 34
Circleback Books 369
Sam Gatteno Books 219
Ginkgo Leaf Press 89
Timothy Hawley Books 178
Susan Heller - Pages for Sages 377
Sheldon Jaffery: Books 377
Peter Keisogloff Rare Books 377
Leaves of Grass Books 198
John Wm. Martin-Bookseller 60
Martinton Book Co. 91
Midnight Bookman 129
Midway Bookstore 294
Mineral Point Book Center 466
Paper Mountain Books 479
Ed Ripp: Bookseller 41
Shaw's Books 219
J.E. Sheldon Fine Books 260
Titles, Inc. 58
West Side Book Shop 199
White Raven Books 254

Botany
Archer's Used & Rare Books 395

BotanaBooks & Art 469
N. Fagin Books 35
Natural History Books 151

British history (See English history)

Broadsides
Jett W. Whitehead - Rare Books 201

Bromfield, Louis
Little Journeys Bookshop 397

Brontes
Blenheim Books 175

Buffalo soliders
Afro Sol 222

Burroughs, Edgar Rice
Mike Parise, Books 422
Toad Hall Books & Records 78
Yorty's Half-Priced Books of Michigan 241

Business
Morgan Adams Books 164
Cordell-Wilson Booksellers 314
Elegant Book & Map Co. 418
Ramtek International 424
John Rybski, Bookseller 42

Canadian authors
The Looking Glass 414

Canoes and kayaks
The Wilderness Collection 262

Carribean
Marrow of Tradition Books 361

Cartoons
Noah's Ark 463

Cartography (See Maps & Atlases)

Cats
ABT Books 403
Seven Gables Books & Antiques 287
(See also Animals)

Caves
Glover's Bookery 167

Celtic
Unicorn, Ltd. 433

Charles Dickens
T.S. Vandoros Rare Books 458

Chemistry
Albert G. Clegg, Bookseller 212

Chess
Chessco 150
Lindsay Chess Supplies 253
Pella Books 151
Waukegan Bridge Center 82

Chicago
Aah! Rare Chicago   85
Bibliodisia Books   32
Robert S. Brooks, Bookseller   87
Chicago Historical Bookworks   51
Thomas J. Joyce and Company   36
Ed Ripp: Bookseller   41
Phyllis Tholin, Books   51
Titles, Inc.   58

Chicano & Latino
March, Inc.   37

Children's
A-Z Collectables   299
ABC Books   341
ABC Collectables   301
AC Books   103
Ace & Bubba Treasure Hunters   469
Morgan Adams Books   164
All Booked Up   169
Almond Tree Antiques   359
Amelia's Book House   448
Arch Books   301
Archer's Antiques & Books   331
As Time Goes By   286
E.J. Bankey   301
Richard S. Barnes & Co.   86
Bay Books   365
Frank G. Bezak - Bookseller   63
Bicentennial Book Shop   223
BNZ Enterprises   477
Book Beat   235
The Book House   336
The Book House   319
The Bookcase   287
Bookdales   289
The Bookery   145
Bookhaven of Springfield   406
Bookman Extraordinaire   46
Bookop Shop   256
The Bookplate   477
Books Bound   273
Books N' Things   416
Books Of The Ages   418
Books on High   383
Books on the Sun Porch   149
Books On Main   390
Byrd's Books & Collectibles   317
B. Caldwell - Bookseller   331
Caraway Book Company   166
Cattermole 20thC Children's Books   402
Children's Planet   170
Cindamar   402
Circleback Books   369
Cleveland Antiquarian Books   376

Collectors' Choice   403
Columbia Books   316
Country Comfort Antiques andn Books   299
Country Bookshelf   103
Crossroad Rare Books & Bindery   397
Curious Book Shop   210
A. Dalrymple, Bookseller   256
Dan's Books   288
Dann Collectibles   239
Ann Dumler Children's Books   59
84 Charing Cross, EH?   231
Enchanted Books, Antiques, Etc.   392
Estate Books   88
Fact and Fiction   296
The Fine Books Company   240
Cynthia K. Fowler Books   170
Sheila Frank, Bookseller   217
H.M. George Books   280
Betsy Gerboth   303
Susan Heller - Pages for Sages   377
Idlewood Rare Books   116
Jack's Corner Bookstore   238
Jane Addams Book Shop   27
Jim's Books   257
JW Books   131
Kaleidoscope Books & Collectibles   198
Gail Klemm-Books   90
Lantern Enterprises   226
Margaret Lee Antiques & Bookseller   236
Leipold's of Excelsior   275
Links To The Past   249
The Little Bookshop   412
E. Llewellyn, Bookseller   346
Loganberry Books   377
Looking Glass Books   227
Mad Hatter Collectible Books   258
Barb Mader - Books   293
Marvelous Books   347
Mary Twyce Books & Paper   300
McNeilly Books   92
Michiana Antiques & Books   194
Midtown Book Center   297
Midway Bookstore   294
Mineral Point Book Center   466
My Bookhouse   409
The Mystery Nook   75
The Old Book Shop   321
Old Delavan Book Co.   444
Old Main Book Shoppe   28
Old Town Books   274
Palos Books   73
Paper Peddlers   406
Paper Mountain Books   479
Barbara Parks - Books   243
Eleanor Pasotti   131

Peace of the Past 54
Peddler's Wagon 347
Puffabelly Station 65
The Rare Bookworm 424
The Reading Doctor 401
S & S Booksellers 305
St. Croix Antiquarian Booksellers 297
Dale St. Peter Books 82
Seven Gables Books & Antiques 287
Shirley's Book Services 236
Stillwater Children's Books 298
Stonehill's Books 28
Talponia Books Limited 193
Toad Hall Books & Records 78
Trails' End Books 112
Treasures From The Castle 261
Turnabout Books 295
Village Books 76
Volume I Books 220
John Wade 425
Weidler Book Source 94
Karen Wickliff Books 386
Wild Rumpus 286
Windy Hill Books 137
Wonderland Books 381
Wooten's Books 203
The World of Books 413
WXICOF 348
Yesterdays Memories 465
Yesterday's Books 237
Yesteryear Books 62
(See also Little Golden Books and Pop-ups)

Children's illustrated
Armchair Adventures 160
Bookop Shop 256
Circleback Books 369
Circle City Antiquarian Books 110
A. Dalrymple, Bookseller 256
Cynthia K. Fowler Books 170
Lost N' Found Books 131
Dorothy Meyer 38
Novelty Shop 405
Old Delavan Book Co. 444
Stillwater Children's Books 298
Mary Wehler, Books 20
Robert Williams Bound To Please Books 94
Wonderland Books 381

Children's series
Ace & Bubba Treasure Hunters 469
Acorn Books 247
Antiques at Hall House 396
Frank G. Bezak - Bookseller 63
Books on High 383
Booksmith 467

Robert S. Brooks, Bookseller 87
Circle City Antiquarian Books 110
Dan's Books 288
Mike DeBaptiste, Books 418
Good News Books 124
Granny's Trunk 101
Grandview Book Gallery 319
Gordon W. Huber 420
J O'Donoghue Books 270
Kaleidoscope Books & Collectibles 198
Leipold's of Excelsior 275
Mary Twyce Books & Paper 300
Dorothy Meyer 38
My Bookhouse 409
Gil O'Gara Antiquarian 151
Old Delavan Book Co. 444
Stillwater Children's Books 298
Victoria's Books 20
Robert Williams Bound To Please Books 94
Wise Owl Books 451

Christie, Agatha
Dale Weber Books 261

Christmas
Storey Book Antiques & Books 81

Churchill, Sir Winston
Blenheim Books 175
Dale Weber Books 261

Civil War
A Place in History 392
Abraham Lincoln Book Shop 29
AC Books 103
Adams Walls of Books 315
A. Amitin's Book Shop 334
Articles of War 79
Balcony Books 221
Bits & Pieces of History 70
Black Swan Books 165
The Book Harbor 412
The Book Shoppe 387
The Book Trader 279
Books Books Books 429
Books on the Square 81
Books On Main 390
The Bookstore 428
The Bookstack 104
Broad Ripple Bookshop 109
Camp Pope Bookshop 146
Chicago Historical Bookworks 51
Choice Books 26
Estate Books 88
Four Score Books and Ect. 257
Glover's Bookery 167
Half Price Books of the Ozarks 342
Harry's Books 176

Heartland Books 84
History Hardbacks 74
History Makers Rare Find Gallery 111
Michael A. Hogle Company 236
Hooked On History 67
Legacy Books 179
Main Street Fine Books & Manuscripts 54
The Mt. Sterling Rebel 174
Donald S. Mull - Books 172
Ralph Newman Bibliopole Ltd. 38
Old Main Book Shoppe 28
Andrew Oren Military Books 463
ReReadables 399
John Rybski, Bookseller 42
Swiss Village Book Store 340
T & S Books 160
C.E. Turley 430
Twice Told Books 172
Mary Wehler, Books 20
Weidler Book Source 94
Wise Owl Books 451
Yorty's Half-Priced Books of Michigan 241

Cleveland
Bay Books 365
John Wallace Skinner Americana 379

Coffee table books
Schenk Enterprises 163

Color plate books
Bookman Extraordinaire 46
Sam Gatteno Books 219
Natural History Books 151
Prints Ancient & Modern 211
George Ritzlin Maps & Books 57

Comics (collectible)
Bookery Fantasy 390
Capital City Comics & Books 226
Joe Sarno's Comic Kingdom 42
20th Century Books 457
Yesterday 44

Computers
Books & Bytes 68
Fostoria Trading Post 145

Confidence games
David Meyer Magic Books 92

Cookbooks
A Reader's Corner 169
ABC Books 341
Acorn Books 315
Morgan Adams Books 164
Almond Tree Antiques 359
Arnold's Of Michigan 228
Autonomy House Publications 130
The Book Gallery 165

The Bookcase 287
Bookdales 289
Bookhaven of Springfield 406
Booklegger's Used Books 32
Bookop Shop 256
Books on High 383
Books On Main 390
Booksmith 467
The Bookstack 104
Candy Books 418
Cindamar 402
The Cookbook Cottage 170
Corner Cupboard Cookbooks 130
Deerlilly Farms 346
Dickens' Book Shop 396
DreamWeaver Books 107
Enchanted Books, Antiques, Etc. 392
Felicitas Cookbooks 296
Freddie The Bookie 252
Heartland Books 84
Hooked On Books 343
Jane Addams Book Shop 27
Kay's Treasured Kookbooks 60
Joyce Klein (Little Treasures) 71
Margaret Lee Antiques and Bookseller 236
Leipold's of Excelsior 275
Louis & Clark Booksellers 479
Magina Books 227
Midtown Book Center 297
Mineral Point Book Center 466
James A. Monnig, Bookseller 258
Morrie's Books 213
Paper Mountain Books 479
Barbara Parks - Books 243
Pauper's Books 366
Plain Tales Books 92
Publix Books 423
P.R. Schwan, Bookseller 121
Shirley's Book Services 236
Snowball Bookshop 364
Toad Hall Books & Records 78
Trails' End Books 112
Turnabout Books 295
Twice Read Books 61
Volume I Books 220
What Goes Round 442
The Wine And Food Library 199
Wood Violet Books 480
Wooden Spoon Books 199
WXICOF 348

Counter culture
Black Bird Books 74
Country Comfort Antiques and Books 299
Prospero's Books 326

Country houses
Deerlilly Farms 346

Creation/evolution
Science Book Service 401

Cults
Science Book Service 401

Cultural studies
The Book House on Grand 292

Curwood, James Oliver
Jim's Books 257
David L. White - Books 261
Win's Books 262
Yorty's Half-Priced Books of Michigan 241

Darwin, Charles
Natural History Books 151

Decorative arts
Badger Trading Co. 477
Deerlilly Farms 346
Keramos 257
The Library 151
Metropolis Art Books 208
Ed Ripp: Bookseller 41
Barry Scott 42

Derleth, August
Wise Owl Books 451

Deserts
Bee Creek Books 302

Design
Stephen Daiter Gallery 34
Stephen Rose Fine Arts 112

Detroit
John King Books North 214

Diaries & Journals
James Cummings, Bookseller 450
Snowy Egret Books 295
John T. Zubal, Inc. 380

Dibdin, T.F
Sam Gatteno Books 219

Dictionaries & Other Reference
Rulon-Miller Books 305
ABC Collectables 301
Minnehaha Books 284

Diving
Margaret Lee Antiques and Bookseller 236

Dogs
Carol Butcher Books 418
Purple Shamrock 348
Seven Gables Books & Antiques 287
(See also Animals)

Early printing
Sam Gatteno Books 219
Hamill & Barker Antiquarian Booksellers 51
Sheldon Jaffery: Books 377
Barry Scott 42
Stroud Booksellers 433
Helena Szépe, Books 44
John Wade 425

Eckert, Allan
Taylor Search Service 260

Economics
Klimas Books 90

Eiseley, Loren
The Looking Glass 414

English history
The Book Harbor 412
Jane Austen Books 89
Paterson-Ford Booksellers 172
Richard G. Peterson, Bookseller 304

English literature
The Antiquarian, Ltd. 30
Richard Cady-Antiquarian Bookseller 34
The Fine Books Company 240
Anthony Garnett Fine Books 338
Glenn Books 325
Hartfield Fine and Rare Books 197
John Wm. Martin-Bookseller 60
Publix Books 423
John Quinn, Bookseller 152
Paul Rohe Books 93
T.S. Vandoros Rare Books 458

Entomology
Snowy Egret Books 295

Environment
N. Fagin Books 35
Pauper's Books 366

Erotica
Larry Laws 90

ESP/Paranormal
Shirley's Old Book Shop 344
Invisible Ink: Books on Ghosts 420

Espionage
Big Sleep Books 335
Bookphil Out of Print & Signed 395
The Mystery Nook 75

Ethnic studies
Exnowski Enterprises 250
N. Fagin Books 35
John Rybski, Bookseller 42

Etiquette
Louis & Clark Booksellers 479

Exploration
Americas Antiquarium 86
The Bookman Of Kent 417
Classic Arms Books 291
Theodore J. Holston Jr., Bookseller 303
Kenneth Nebenzahl, Inc. 56
Peninsula Books 250
Topaz-Mineral Exploration 261
West Side Book Shop 199

Fairs and expositions
Larry Laws 90
Michiana Antiques & Books 194

Fantasy
The Aleph Bookshop 48
Alternate Realities 452
Apparitions Comics & Books 224
Armchair Adventures 160
Karl M. Armens - Books 145
As Time Goes By 286
Book Jungle 342
The Book Trader II 450
Dark Star Books & Comics 387
Dawn Treader Book Shop 196
Deadly Passions Bookshop 224
Dragon's Lair 387
Dreamhaven 280
Else Fine Books 206
Flea Market Books 394
Foul Play 412
The Griffon 127
Ken Hebenstreit, Bookseller 243
Gordon W. Huber 420
Midway Bookstore 294
Remember When 449
S & S Books 305
The Stars Our Destination 43
Tabula Rasa 425
Timber City Books 152
Uncle Hugo's Science Fiction Bookstore 286
The Village Bookshelf 398
The Way Station 140

Farmer, Phillip Jose
Black Bird Books 74

Fashion
Deerlilly Farms 346
George Ritzlin Maps & Books 57

Film
A Place in History 392
Avol's Bookstore 452
The Book Harbor 412
Book World 23
Constant Reader Book Shop 461
Harold's Book Shop 293

Larry Laws 90
Metro-Golden Memories Shop 37
Noah's Ark 463
Gil O'Gara Antiquarian 151
Paper Peddlers 406
Tally Ho Studios 425
20th Century Books 457

Fine bindings
Archives Book Shop 210
Bibliodisia Books 32
Bookman Extraordinaire 46
Richard Cady-Antiquarian Bookseller 34
Cleveland Antiquarian Books 376
Country Comfort Antiques and Books 299
The Dust Jacket 370
Sam Gatteno Books 219
The Gentlemen Soldier 122
Susan Heller - Pages for Sages 377
Thomas J. Joyce and Company 36
Peter Keisogloff Rare Books 377
Monastery Hill Bindery 38
Old Erie Street Bookstore 378
L.A. Rubin Rare Books 202
Barry Scott 42
Shaw's Books 219
Titles, Inc. 58
T.S. Vandoros Rare Books 458
Patrick Vargo, Antiquarian Books 202
Karen Wickliff Books 386

Fine printing
Timothy Hawley Books 178
Old Erie Street Bookstore 378
T.S. Vandoros Rare Books 458

First editions
ABC Collectables 301
The Aleph Bookshop 48
Archives Book Shop 210
Bibliodisia Books 32
The Book House 336
Books & Beyond 87
Books Books Books 429
Books on High 383
Books on the Sun Porch 149
Robert S. Brooks, Bookseller 87
B. Caldwell - Bookseller 331
Chicago Historical Bookworks 51
Dawn Treader Book Shop 196
Duttenhofer's Books 370
Jackie Foote Used Books 256
The Gentlemen Soldier 122
Glenn Books 325
Grave Matters - Mysteries 371
H & B Booksellers 202
Hahn's House of Mystery 371

Thomas J. Joyce and Company 36
Peter Keisogloff Rare Books 377
James & Mary Laurie, Booksellers 281
Marion The Antiquarian Librarian 200
John Wm. Martin-Bookseller 60
The Mystery Nook 75
Palos Books 73
John Quinn, Bookseller 152
Rain Dog Books 41
The Rare Bookworm 424
Paul Rohe Books 93
Titles, Inc. 58
Toad Hall Books & Records 78
Upstart Crow Books 143
T.S. Vandoros Rare Books 458
Victoria's Books 20
Jett W. Whitehead - Rare Books 201
Wilder Books 48
Yesterday's Books 247

Fisher, Harrison
Frogtown Books 410

Fishing
Angling Book Hunter 229
Artis Books & Antiques 195
Bee Creek Books 302
Matthew Bisiotti & Company 363
The Bookstack 104
Campfire Books 130
Casanova Books 443
Classic Arms Books 291
Constant Reader Book Shop 461
The Fisherman's Bookshelf 88
Galaxy Of Books 85
Highwood Bookshop 248
Theodore J. Holston Jr., Bookseller 303
Leipold's of Excelsior 275
Gerald Pettinger 152
Pisces and Capricorn Books 193
Philip Riggs, Books 373
St. Croix Antiquarian Bookseller 297
Shaw's Books 219
Yesterday's Books 237

Folklore
George Barry, Books 255
Karen Wickliff Books 386

Fore-edge paintings
Bookman Extraordinaire 46
D. J. Flynn-Books 88
Hartfield Fine and Rare Books 197

Foreign language books
Dawn Treader Book Shop 196
Globe International Antiquarian Books 36
The Griffon 127
Kruklitis' Latvian Bookstore 258

Russian Language Specialties 246
Shirley's Old Book Shop 344
Helena Szépe, Books 44
(See also Germany)

Free masonry
Occult Bookstore 39

French Canadiana
John M. Gram 239

Fur trade
D.R. Doerres Rendezvous Trader 150

Gale, Zona
Historic Salem 475

Gambling
David Meyer Magic Books 92

Games & Cards
Bay Books 365
Bullfrog Books 110
Pella Books 151
Waukegan Bridge Center 82
(See also Chess)

Gardening
ABT Books 403
The American Botanist, Bookseller 45
BotanaBooks & Art 469
Columbia Books 316
Deerlilly Farms 346
Just Books 329
Lancaster & Simpson 304
Midtown Book Center 297
Stroud Booksellers 433
Raymond M. Sutton, Jr. Books 177
Terrace Horticultural Books 285
Robert D. Wagner 330
White Raven Books 254
Wood Violet Books 480

Garland, Hamlin
Historic Salem 475

Gay & Lesbian
Second Hand Stories 339
Six Steps Down Bookstore 379

Genealogy
The Book Shoppe 387
D. Gratz, Books 419
Legacy Books 179
Madigan's Books 91
Pennyroyal Books 163
C.E. Turley 430
Ye Olde Genealogie Shoppe 112

Geology
Albert G. Clegg, Bookseller 212
84 Charing Cross, EH? 231
N. Fagin Books 35

QuestAntiques-Books-Collectibles 259
Topaz-Mineral Exploration 261

Germany/German material
Anni's Antiques & Books 150
Exnowski Enterprises 250
Larry Laws 90

Golf
Frogtown Books 410
Shaw's Books 219
Dennis Sutterer Books 143
Taylor Search Service 260
(See also Sports)

Gone With The Wind
Frogtown Books 410

Grand Canyon
Bee Creek Books 302

Grant, Ulysses
Main Street Fine Books & Manuscripts 54

Great Lakes
Arnold's Of Michigan Antiquarian 228
Artis Books & Antiques 195
First Edition Too Bookstore 203
Thatcher C. Goetz, Books 216
Jillson's Nauticals & Antiques 201
North Wind Books 209
Peninsula Books 250
Shaw's Books 219
Talponia Books Limited 193

Grey, Zane
Jim's Books 257
Win's Books 262

Gruelle, J
J.E. Sheldon Fine Books 260

Guns
Campfire Books 130
Casanova Books 443
Evans Firearms and Archery 166
Fair Chase 451
Highwood Bookshop 248
Theodore J. Holston Jr., Bookseller 303
Neuman's Oak Point Books 62
Old House Bookstore 69
Gerald Pettinger 152
Philip Riggs, Books 373

Hearn, Lafcadio
Bags End 333

Hendry, James B.
David L. White - Books 261

Henry, Patrick
Bible Scholar Books 417

Herbs
Terrace Horticultural Books 285
Wood Violet Books 480

Herpetology
Natural History Books 151

Hill, Grace Livingstone
Yorty's Half-Priced Books of Michigan 241

Historical fiction
Owen D. Kubik Fine Books 388

History
A Collector's Bookshop 334
A Place in History 392
AC Books 103
Ace & Bubba Treasure Hunters 469
Acorn Books 315
Bags End 333
Balcony Books 221
Richard S. Barnes & Co. 86
Bay Books 365
Beverly Books 32
Bloomsday Books 324
BNZ Enterprises 477
The Book Gallery 165
The Book House 336
The Book House 319
Book Stall Of Rockford 78
The Book Stop 56
The Bookery 145
Bookhaven of Springfield 406
Books on the Sun Porch 149
The Bookstore 428
Browse Awhile Books 409
Richard Cady-Antiquarian Bookseller 34
B. Caldwell - Bookseller 331
Caveat Emptor 102
Choice Books 26
Cindamar 402
Cordell-Wilson Booksellers 314
Curious Book Shop 210
DreamWeaver Books 107
The Dust Jacket 370
Elegant Book & Map Co. 418
Fireside Book Company 383
Footnotes Bookshop 178
Four Score Books and Ect. 257
Ginkgo Leaf Press 89
The Griffon 127
H & B Booksellers 202
Half Price Books of the Ozarks 342
Hammond's Books 338
Heartland Books 84
Hooked On Books 343
Hyde Brothers Booksellers 106
Charles H. Kerr Co. 36

Left Bank Bookstall	91	Else Fine Books	206
Mackinaw Book Company	222	Foul Play	412
Martha Merrell's Bookstore	470	The Gallery Bookstore	35
Melvin McCosh, Bookseller	304	Green Lion Books	292
McDermott Books	455	Ken Hebenstreit, Bookseller	243
Midway Bookstore	294	Invisible Ink: Books on Ghosts	420
Miller's Antiques	240	Jack's Used Books	67
Minnehaha Books	284	Sheldon Jaffery: Books	377
My Bookhouse	409	Mythos Books	347
My Father's Books	326	Pac-Rats	157
Novel Ideas	45	PDW Books	304
O'Gara & Wilson Booksellers	39	S & S Books	305
Ohio Book Store	372	The Stars Our Destination	43
Old Bookshop of Rice Lake	470	Turtle Island Books	44
Out of Print Books	378	The Village Bookshelf	398
Palos Books	73	White Chapel Productions	53
Pella Books	151	White Rabbit Used Books	119
Pennyroyal Books	163	Yesterday's Books	247

Horses

Proud Mary's Booksellers	176	Matthew Bisiotti & Company	363
Rain Dog Books	41	Black Swan Books	165
Regarding Books	424	Carol Butcher Books	418
Richard Owen Roberts, Booksellers	83	Glover's Bookery	167
Ross & Haines Old Books Co.	449	The Sporting Horse Gallery	168
Royal Oak Books	244	Lila Trudel Books	425
Susie's	362	*(See also Animals)*	
Tabula Rasa	425		

Hotels/restaurants

Timber City Books	152	Louis & Clark Booksellers	479
Twice Read Books	61	The Wine And Food Library	199

Household management

Upstart Crow Books	143	Louis & Clark Booksellers	479
Volume I Books	220		

How-to books

Wabash River Books	128	Morgan Adams Books	164
Karen Wickliff Books	386		

Humanities

Wooten's Books	203	Armchair Books	70
(See also American history & English history)		Between The Lines	130
		Books In General	196

Holocaust

Freddie The Bookie	252	Thomas W. Burrows, Bookseller	87
		James Cummings, Bookseller	450

Homeschooling

		John Dinsmore & Associates	166
Cherie's Books	177	Notting Hill Books	294
Notting Hill Books	294	O'Gara & Wilson Booksellers	39
The Rare Bookworm	424	Powell's Bookstore, North	40
		Priceless Books	81

Homesteading

Just Books	329		

Hunting

		Angling Book Hunter	229

Horatio Alger

Milton F. Ehlert - Books	217	Artis Books & Antiques	195
		Matthew Bisiotti & Company	363

Horror

The Aleph Bookshop	48	The Bookstack	104
Alternate Realities	452	Carol Butcher Books	418
Books on the Sun Porch	149	Campfire Books	130
Box of Rocks	157	Casanova Books	443
Byrd's Books & Collectibles	317	Classic Arms Books	291
Dark Star Books & Comics	387		
Dragon's Lair	387		
Dreamhaven	280		

Constant Reader Book Shop 461
Evans Firearms and Archery 166
Fair Chase 451
Galaxy Of Books 85
Gunnerman Books 257
Highwood Bookshop 248
Theodore J. Holston Jr., Bookseller 303
Leipold's of Excelsior 275
Neuman's Oak Point Books 62
Old House Bookstore 69
Gerald Pettinger 152
Pisces and Capricorn Books 193
Philip Riggs, Books 373
St. Croix Antiquarian Booksellers 297
Shaw's Books 219
Yesterday's Books 237

Hypnotism
Sqecial Media 168

Illinois
Bibliodisia Books 32
Books on the Square 81
Choice Books 26
Thomas J. Joyce and Company 36
Prairie Archives, Booksellers 80
3R's HoneyBee Bookshoppe 55

Illuminated manuscripts
Bruce Ferrini Rare Books 361
Sam Gatteno Books 219
Graton & Graton 57
George Ritzlin Maps & Books 57

Illustrated
Arch Books 301
George Barry, Books 255
The Book Harbor 412
The Book House 336
The Book House 319
Bookdales 289
Bookends and Fine Collectables 51
The Bookman Of Kent 417
Books Of The Ages 418
Richard Cady-Antiquarian Bookseller 34
Collectors' Choice 403
Columbia Books 316
Dan's Books 288
Downtown Books Fine Arts 462
Ann Dumler Children's Books 59
Raymond Dworczyk Rare Books 478
Milton F. Ehlert - Books 217
The Fine Books Company 240
Forest Park Books 105
Frogtown Books 410
Sam Gatteno Books 219
The Gentlemen Soldier 122
Glenn Books 325

Klaus Grunewald - Bookdealer 325
Susan Heller - Pages for Sages 377
T.S. Hotter Antiquarian Maps 443
Idlewood Rare Books 116
Thomas J. Joyce and Company 36
Peter Keisogloff Rare Books 377
E. Llewellyn, Bookseller 346
Loganberry Books 377
Marion The Antiquarian Librarian 200
Marvelous Books 347
Midway Bookstore 294
Monastery Hill Bindery 38
Old Town Books 274
Ed Ripp: Bookseller 41
Bernie Rost-Books 42
L.A. Rubin Rare Books 202
S & S Booksellers 305
John Wallace Skinner Americana 379
Stonehill's Books 28
John Wade 425
Wilder Books 48
Wooten's Books 203

Immigration
Bohling Book Company 255

Incunabula
Sam Gatteno Books 219
Hamill & Barker AntiquarianBooksellers 51

Indiana
Antiquarian Book Company 106
Chuck's Books 114
Country Bookshelf 103
Gateway Collectibles 118
Good News Books 124
Hyde Brothers Booksellers 106
Idlewood Rare Books 116
Meridian Street Books 116
Trails' End Books 112

International relations
L.J. Ryan, Scholarly Books 385

Iowa
Bought Again Books 138
Excellence in Books 148

James, Jesse
The Bookcase 287

Johnson, Samuel
Hartfield Fine and Rare Books 197

Judaica
The Book House on Grand 292
Candy Books 418
Morrie's Books 213
Yesterdays Memories 465

Kansas
Klaus Grunewald - Bookdealer 325

Kentucky
All Booked Up 169
Black Swan Books 165
Glover's Bookery 167
Harry's Books 176
Legacy Books 179
Donald S. Mull - Books 172
Ohio Book Store 372
Poor Richard's Books 162
Proud Mary's Booksellers 176
J. Sampson Antiques & Books 163
Twice Told Books 172
Kipling, Rudyard
Richard G. Peterson, Bookseller 304
Labor
Six Steps Down Bookstore 379
Volume I Books 220
Wooden Spoon Books 199
Lakeside Classics
Americas Antiquarium 86
Robert S. Brooks, Bookseller 87
Chicago Historical Bookworks 51
D.R. Doerres Rendezvous Trader 150
Forest Park Books 105
Latin America
Dale Seppa 306
Flo Silver Books 132
Law
Greenfield Books 320
Thomas J. Joyce and Company 36
Klimas Books 90
Legibus 60
National Law Resource 92
Professional Book Service 423
Lewis, C.S.
Blenheim Books 175
Life saving
Jillson's Nauticals & Antiques 201
Lighthouses
Jillson's Nauticals & Antiques 201
Limited editions
Cleveland Antiquarian Books 376
Peter Keisogloff Rare Books 377
Peripatetic Bibliophile 218
Jett W. Whitehead - Rare Books 201
Limited Editions Club
Bookman Extraordinaire 46
Klaus Grunewald - Bookdealer 325
Susan Heller - Pages for Sages 377
Shaw's Books 219
Lincoln, Abraham
Abraham Lincoln Book Shop 29

Books on the Square 81
Historical Newspapers 80
History Hardbacks 74
Michael A. Hogle Company 236
Main Street Fine Books & Manuscripts 54
Ralph Newman Bibliopole Ltd. 38
Old Main Book Shoppe 28
Prairie Archives, Booksellers 80
Mary Wehler, Books 20
Yesteryear Books 62
Lincoln, Joseph
Yorty's Half-Priced Books of Michigan 241
Lindsay, Vachel
Prairie Archives, Booksellers 80
Linguistics
Bookcellar 101
Bullfrog Books 110
Rulon-Miller Books 305
Bernard Wheel 72
Literary criticism
A Collector's Bookshop 334
Babbitt's Books 26
James Cummings, Bookseller 450
R. Dunaway, Bookseller 337
Martha Merrell's Bookstore 470
John Wm. Martin-Bookseller 60
John Quinn, Bookseller 152
St. Croix Antiquarian Booksellers 297
Wm Caxton Ltd 447
Wooden Spoon Books 199
Literary first editions
Norma Adler 46
Karl M. Armens - Books 145
The Asphodel Book Shop 366
Richard Cady-Antiquarian Bookseller 34
Dinkytown Antiquarian Bookstore 280
Else Fine Books 206
The Fine Books Company 240
Anthony Garnett Fine Books 338
Idlewood Rare Books 116
The Legacy Company 150
The Little Bookshop 412
My Bookhouse 409
Paper Moone 333
Dennis Sutterer Books 143
West Side Book Shop 199
Timothy B. Wuchter 262
(See also Modern first editions)
Literature
A Place in History 392
Morgan Adams Books 164
John Angelos, Books 459
The Antiquarian, Ltd. 30

The Armadillo's Pillow 30
As Time Goes By 286
Beasley Books 30
Bicentennial Book Shop 223
Biermaier's B. H. Books 278
Black Swan Books 165
Blenheim Books 175
Bloomsday Books 324
The Book House in Dinkytown 278
The Book Stop 56
The Book Trader II 450
Booklegger's Used Books 32
Bookman's Alley 50
Bookphil Out of Print & Signed 395
Books of Choice 302
Books Revisited 291
Booksellers Row 33
The Booksmith 71
Bookzeller 68
Thomas W. Burrows, Bookseller 87
Casterbridge Books 87
Chapman Street Books 275
The Christensen Gallery 235
Discount Books 376
R. Dunaway, Bookseller 337
Exnowski Enterprises 250
Ginkgo Leaf Press 89
Roger Griffith Bookseller 23
The Griffon 127
Hamill & Barker Antiquarian Booksellers 51
Haunted Bookshop On The Creek 146
Heartland Books 84
Ken Hebenstreit, Bookseller 243
Susan Heller - Pages for Sages 377
Hooked On Books 343
Arthur Hudgins 293
Hyde Brothers Booksellers 106
Jay's African-American Books 207
John K. King Books 207
James & Mary Laurie, Booksellers 281
Leaves of Grass Books 198
Marrow of Tradition Books 361
Melvin McCosh, Bookseller 304
McDermott Books 455
Midtown Book Center 297
Midway Bookstore 294
Minnehaha Books 284
Notting Hill Books 294
Old Erie Street Bookstore 378
Pauper's Books 366
Pella Books 151
Prospero's Books 326
R.D. Book Search 423
L.J. Ryan, Scholarly Books 385
St. Croix Antiquarian Booksellers 297

Barry Scott 42
Selected Works 42
Stan Stites Books 93
Tabula Rasa 425
Phyllis Tholin, Books 51
Untamed Shrew Books 480
Upstart Crow Books 143
Karen Wickliff Books 386
Wilder Books 48
Wm Caxton Ltd 447
Wooden Spoon Books 199

Literature, avant garde
Gemini Fine Books & Arts 58
Twice-Loved Books 415

Literature, Irish
Bloomsday Books 324

Literature, modern
Books on High 383
Collector Book and Print Gallery 369
Fireside Book Company 383
Hahn's House of Mystery 371
Tony Lamy, Bookseller 420
The Little Bookshop 412
Nailler Books 429
Peripatetic Bibliophile 218
Frank S. Pollack 57
Wm. M. Ripley Rare Books 198
Mike Sarki, Rogue Books 179
P.C. Schmidt, Bookseller 211
Second Storey Bookshop 137
Spivey's Books, Old Maps, Fine Art 327
Wm Caxton Ltd 447
Yesterday's Books 247
(See also American literature & English literature)

Little Golden Books
Books on the Sun Porch 149
Old Delavan Book Co. 444
The Rare Bookworm 424
Wonderland Books 381

Livre d'artistes
Gemini Fine Books & Arts 58
Peter Keisogloff Rare Books 377

Local history
Booklady 50
Legacy Books 179
Little Journeys Bookshop 397
Madigan's Books 91
Michiana Antiques & Books 194
Mighty Fine Books 117
Old House Bookstore 69
Rowsburg Bookstore 404
Snowbound Books 229

T & S Books	160
Toad Hall Books & Records	78
White Chapel Productions	53
Ye Olde Genealogie Shoppe	112

Machen, J. Gresham

Bible Scholar Books	417

Magazines & Periodicals

A Williams Books	278
Afro Sol	222
B & D Collectibles	411
Big Book Store	206
Bookphil Out of Print & Signed	395
Casterbridge Books	87
Curious Book Shop	210
John Dinsmore & Associates	166
The Gallery Bookstore	35
Grave Matters - Mysteries	371
Orval J. Imel	112
Magazine Memories	67
Main Street Galleries	446
Paper Peddlers	406
Plunkett/Higgins Books	270
Shakespeare's Books	456
Don Smith's Nat'l Geographic Magazines	179
Tally Ho Studios	425
Timber City Books	152
Toad Hall Books & Records	78
Robert Williams Bound To Please Books	94
Yesterday	44
Yesterday's Books	237

Magic

Greenfield Books	320
Magic, Inc.	37
David Meyer Magic Books	92
Occult Bookstore	39
Sqecial Media	168
Turtle Island Books	44
Wooten's Books	203

Mammalogy

Natural History Books	151

Manuscripts & Documents

Archives Book Shop	210
The Autograph Alcove	459
Branchwater Books & Ephemera	256
Richard Cady-Antiquarian Bookseller	34
Cleveland Antiquarian Books	376
Les Enluminures Ltd.	35
Sam Gatteno Books	219
Historical Newspapers	80
History Makers Rare Find Gallery	111
The Legacy Company	150
Ralph Newman Bibliopole Ltd.	38
Barry Scott	42

Harry L. Stern, Ltd.	43
Wilder Books	48

Maps & atlases

Americas Antiquarium	86
Antiquarian Prints & Maps	236
Bay Books	365
Phyllis Y. Brown	337
Cleveland Antiquarian Books	376
Collector Book and Print Gallery	369
Elegant Book & Map Co.	418
Graton & Graton	57
Historical Newspapers	80
T.S. Hotter Antiquarian Maps	443
James & Mary Laurie, Booksellers	281
Margaret Lee Antiques and Bookseller	236
Kenneth Nebenzahl, Inc.	56
Prints Ancient & Modern	211
George Ritzlin Maps & Books	57
River Gallery	59
Sign Of The Unicorn	451
John Wallace Skinner Americana	379
Spivey's Books, Old Maps, Fine Art	327
Harry L. Stern, Ltd.	43
Stan Stites Books	93
Topaz-Mineral Exploration	261

Maritime (See Nautical)

Mark Twain

Admirable Books	394
Becky Thatcher Book Shop	320
Swiss Village Book Store	340

Marsh, George

David L. White - Books	261

Mathematics & Statistics

Bullfrog Books	110
David Netzorg	259
Science Book Service	306

Media

The Book Harbor	412
Bookery Fantasy	390
Sheila Frank, Bookseller	217
Metro-Golden Memories Shop	37
Noah's Ark	463
Tally Ho Studios	425
20th Century Books	457

Medicine

Avebury Books	365
The Bookworm	369
Discount Books	376
W. Bruce Fye Antiquarian Medical Books	478
Greenfield Books	320
Hamill & Barker Antiquarian Booksellers	51
Thomas J. Joyce and Company	36
James & Mary Laurie, Booksellers	281

Mayflower Bookshop 201
A.A. Miran Arts and Books 421
Mossback Books 208
Professional Book Service 423
Publix Books 423
The Science Bookshelf 260
Barry Scott 42
Shaw's Books 219
Source Book Store 141
The Sporting Horse Gallery 168
Yesteryear Books 62
Yorty's Half-Priced Books of Michigan 241

Medieval history
Beadsman Books 86
Karen Wickliff Books 386

Men's works
Ally Press 301

Metalworking
Evans Firearms and Archery 166

Metaphysics
Alice's Book Shelf 391
The Book Stop 56
Galaxy Of Books 85
House of Scorpio 462
Insight Metaphysical Bookstore 27
Magus Books 283
Mayflower Bookshop 201
Sqecial Media 168
Turtle Island Books 44
What Goes Round 442

Meteorology
Knollwood Books 468

Michigan
Argos Book Shop 216
Arnold's Of Michigan 228
Artis Books & Antiques 195
The Book Stop 238
Curious Book Shop 210
Milton F. Ehlert - Books 217
ETBooks 221
First Edition Too Bookstore 203
Sheila Frank, Bookseller 217
Thatcher C. Goetz, Books 216
John M. Gram 239
John K. King Books 207
John King Books North 214
Lantern Enterprises 226
Peninsula Books 250
Shaw's Books 219
J.E. Sheldon Fine Books 260
Shirley's Book Services 236
Snowbound Books 229
Topaz-Mineral Exploration 261

Richard Wertz, Bookseller 261
David L. White - Books 261
Pat & Bill Wisney-Books 262
Yesterday's Books 237
Yorty's Half-Priced Books of Michigan 241

Middle East
Deux Amasse Books 241
Gregory and Beverly Gamradt 303

Midwest
A. Amitin's Book Shop 334
Bohling Book Company 255
Books Bound 273
Books Revisited 291
Chicago Historical Bookworks 51
Collector Book and Print Gallery 369
Golden Raintree Books 120
Green Gryphon Books 212
Left Bank Bookstall 91
Lowry's Books 249
Mike Maddigan 139
North Woods Books 274
North Coast Paper Mill 422
North Wind Books 209
Old House Bookstore 69
Peninsula Books 250
Shirley's Old Book Shop 344
Twice Sold Tales 157

Midwest authors
Aah! Rare Chicago 85
Antiquarian Book Company 106
Books on the Sun Porch 149
Collector Book and Print Gallery 369
H.M. George Books 280
Good News Books 124
Green Gryphon Books 212
Idlewood Rare Books 116
Barb Mader - Books 293
David L. White - Books 261
(See also individual authors)

Military
A-Z Collectables 299
Abraham Lincoln Book Shop 29
Acorn Bookshop 382
Afro Sol 222
Antiques at Hall House 396
Articles of War 79
Balcony Books 221
Beulahland 222
Big League Company 272
Black Swan Books 165
The Book Harbor 412
The Book Trader 279
Book World 23
The Bookery 145

Bookphil Out of Print & Signed 395
Books on High 383
Books Revisited 291
The Bookseller 359
Bookzeller 68
B. Caldwell - Bookseller 331
Candy Books 418
Casanova Books 443
Classic Arms Books 291
Constant Reader Book Shop 461
Copperfield & Twist Bookstore 415
Crossroad Rare Books & Bindery 397
D.R. Doerres Rendezvous Trader 150
The Dust Jacket 370
Raymond Dworczyk Rare Books 478
Milton F. Ehlert - Books 217
Fourth Street Book Shop 242
Freddie The Bookie 252
Galaxy Of Books 85
John M. Gram 239
Grandview Book Gallery 319
H & B Booksellers 202
History Hardbacks 74
Hooked On History 67
Jillson's Nauticals & Antiques 201
John K. King Books 207
John King Books North 214
Kisselburg Military Books 303
Owen D. Kubik Fine Books 388
The Literate Veteran 421
The Little Bookshop 412
Lowry's Books 249
Magina Books 227
Anthony Maita 91
McNeilly Books 92
Meridian Street Books 116
Jerry Merkel 421
Midway Bookstore 294
Miller's Antiques 240
My Wife's Books 240
Old Army Books 167
Old Erie Street Bookstore 378
Andrew Oren Military Books 463
Overlord Military Collectibles 339
Palos Books 73
Philco Books 304
Proud Mary's Booksellers 176
The Reading Doctor 401
Ross & Haines Old Books Co. 449
John Rybski, Bookseller 42
Dale St. Peter Books 82
Edwin Schaeffer 47
Shaw's Books 219
Spivey's Books, Old Maps, Fine Art 327

Toad Hall Books & Records 78
Twice Read Books 61

Mining
B & B Crafts 477
84 Charing Cross, EH? 231
Quest Antiques-Books-Collectibles 259

Minnesota
As Time Goes By 286
The Bookcase 287
Bookdales 289
Country Comfort Antiques and Books 299
Harold's Book Shop 293
Leipold's of Excelsior 275
Mary Twyce Books & Paper 300
Once Read Reads 276

Missouri
ABC Books 341
Adams Walls of Books 315
Americana Antiques 344
Antiquarium Books & Collectibles 322
Blue Nile Books 329
B. Caldwell - Bookseller 331
Columbia Books 316
Klaus Grunewald - Bookdealer 325

Missouri Trail
The Old Book Shop 321

Modern first editions
Allison's Signed Books & Autographs 85
Amelia's Book House 448
Americana Books 104
Arbor Books 195
Autumn Leaves Books 58
Beasley Books 30
Bibliomania Book Store 417
Black Swan Books 165
Book Beat 235
The Book Gallery 165
The Bookcase 287
Bookdales 289
Books of Choice 302
Broad Ripple Bookshop 109
Buckeye Bookshop 360
Chuck's Books 114
Constant Reader Book Shop 461
Copperfield & Twist Bookstore 415
Country Comfort Antiques and Books 299
Cross Street Book Shop 252
John Dinsmore & Associates 166
DreamWeaver Books 107
The Dust Jacket 370
Milton F. Ehlert - Books 217
Et Al's Read & Unread Books 474
Fireproof Books 303

First Impressions | 88
Flea Market Books | 394
Sheila Frank, Bookseller | 217
Gemini Fine Books & Arts | 58
H.M. George Books | 280
Half Price Books of the Ozarks | 342
Ken Hebenstreit, Bookseller | 243
Susan Heller - Pages for Sages | 377
Hooked On Books | 343
Impact Books | 271
Jack's Used Books | 67
Barry A. Klaung | 90
McNeilly Books | 92
Old Erie Street Bookstore | 378
Plain Tales Books | 92
R.D. Book Search | 423
M. Sand Books | 93
Shakespeare's Books | 456
Talponia Books Limited | 193
3R's HoneyBee Bookshoppe | 55
Turnabout Books | 295
Twice Told Books | 172
T.S. Vandoros Rare Books | 458
Village Books | 76
John Wade | 425
J.F. Whyland Books | 113
Wallace M. Wojtkowski, Bookseller | 128

Modern Library
Books on High | 383

Mormons
John Hajicek | 346
The Old Book Shop | 321
Old House Bookstore | 69

Mountaineering
Charles David Dyer - Books | 398
Theodore J. Holston Jr., Bookseller | 303

Museums
Materiality | 442

Music
Archer's Used And Rare Books | 395
Armchair Books | 70
Avol's Bookstore | 452
Beasley Books | 30
Beechwold Books | 383
Candy Books | 418
Constant Reader Book Shop | 461
Cross Street Book Shop | 252
John Dinsmore & Associates | 166
Lantern Enterprises | 226
Montagnana Books | 92
David Netzorg | 259
Paper Peddlers | 406
Professional Book Service | 423
Rhythm & Views | 93

Toad Hall Books & Records | 78
Upstart Crow Books | 143
Yesterdays Memories | 465

Mystery
A Novel Idea | 408
Acorn Books | 247
Morgan Adams Books | 164
Alternate Realities | 452
Amelia's Book House | 448
Antiquarium Books & Collectibles | 322
Karl M. Armens - Books | 145
As Time Goes By | 286
Aunt Agatha's | 195
Beasley Books | 30
Bibliotective | 234
Big Bang Books | 255
Big Sleep Books | 335
The Book Harbor | 412
Bookdales | 289
Booked For Murder | 452
Bookhaven of Springfield | 406
Books and Things | 359
Books on High | 383
Booksmith | 467
Bookworm & Bugjuice | 418
Cindamar | 402
Clues! Mystery Bookseller | 324
Collector Book and Print Gallery | 369
Constant Reader Book Shop | 461
Copperfield & Twist Bookstore | 415
The Corner Shop | 123
Curious Book Shop | 210
Dark Star Books & Comics | 414
Dawn Treader Book Shop | 196
Deadly Passions Bookshop | 224
Dickens' Book Shop | 396
Dragon's Lair | 387
Fickes Crime Fiction | 419
Else Fine Books | 206
The Fine Books Company | 240
Foul Play | 412
Fountain Of Mystery Books | 111
The Gallery Bookstore | 35
Grave Matters - Mysteries | 371
Green Gryphon Books | 212
Green Lion Books | 292
The Griffon | 127
Grounds For Thought | 366
Hahn's House of Mystery | 371
Haunted Bookshop On The Creek | 146
Heartland Books | 84
Ken Hebenstreit, Bookseller | 243
Hooked On Books | 343
Gordon W. Huber | 420
Hyde Brothers Booksellers | 106

J O'Donoghue Books	270
Jack's Used Books	67
Sheldon Jaffery: Books	377
Jane Addams Book Shop	27
Kaldi's Coffeehouse & Bookstore	371
Kaleidoscope Books & Collectibles	198
Peter Keisogloff Rare Books	377
Tony Lamy, Bookseller	420
The Looking Glass	414
Mail Order Mysteries	258
Murder By The Book	421
Murder Is Served	388
My Bookhouse	409
Mystery One Bookshop	463
The Mystery Nook	75
Nailler Books	429
Novelty Shop	405
The Old Book Shop	321
Old Horizons Book Shoppe	204
Once Again Gently Used Books	172
Once Upon A Crime	284
Pella Books	151
Philco Books	304
P.I.E.S.	479
Frank S. Pollack	57
R.D. Book Search	423
Remember When	449
S & S Books	305
M. Sand Books	93
Schenk Enterprises	163
P.C. Schmidt, Bookseller	211
The Science Bookshelf	260
Scotland Yard Books	84
Snowball Bookshop	364
Something Wicked This Way Comes	225
Strange Birds Books	424
Taylor Search Service	260
Timber City Books	152
Turnabout Books	295
Turtle Island Books	44
20th Century Books	457
Uncle Buck's Mysteries	93
Uncle Edgar's Mystery Bookstore	286
The Village Bookshelf	398
Yesterday's Books	247
J.D. Zucatti, Bookseller	244

(See also Sherlock Holmes, Christie, Poe)

Mythology

George Barry, Books	255
Exnowski Enterprises	250

Napoleon

Balcony Books	221
Peter M. Holmes Fine Books	281

National Geographic (See Magazines)

Native Americans

Aardvark Book Depot	477
The Book Gallery	165
Country Comfort Antiques and Books	299
Exnowski Enterprises	250
Glaeve Gallery	454
North Coast Americana	403
Shenandoah Books, etc.	441
John Wallace Skinner Americana	379
Wm Caxton Ltd	447
Yesteryear Books	62

Natural history

ABC Collectables	301
Acorn Bookshop	382
Bay Books	365
Thomas C. Bayer	255
The Bookstack	104
Broad Ripple Bookshop	109
Circle City Antiquarian Books	110
The Dust Jacket	370
C.H. Fischer, Books	419
Galaxy Of Books	85
Theodore J. Holston Jr., Bookseller	303
Hyde Brothers Booksellers	106
Natural History Books	151
North Woods Books	274
Gerald Pettinger	152
Publix Books	423
Shaw's Books	219
Flo Silver Books	132
Snowy Egret Books	295
Raymond M. Sutton, Jr. Books	177
West Side Book Shop	199
Karen Wickliff Books	386
Wm Caxton Ltd	447
WXICOF	348

Nature

Acorn Books	315
Adams Walls of Books	315
Angling Book Hunter	229
The Book House	319
Chapman Street Books	275
Looking Glass Books	227
Martha Merrell's Bookstore	470
North Coast Americana	403
Snowy Egret Books	295
Susie's	362
What Goes Round	442

Nautical

Arnold's Of Michigan	228
Bookends and Fine Collectables	51
Bookphil Out of Print & Signed	395
Constant Reader Book Shop	461
Greenfield Books	320

Susan Heller - Pages for Sages 377
Hidden Room Book Shoppe 246
Jillson's Nauticals & Antiques 201
Just Books 329
Margaret Lee Antiques and Bookseller 236
Leyshon's Books Etc. 421
Mackinaw Book Company 222
Martha Merrell's Bookstore 470
The Reading Doctor 401
P.R. Schwan, Bookseller 121
Science Book Service 306
Shaw's Books 219
Art Spindler 260
Tall Ships Books 152
J. Tuttle Maritime Books 480

Needlecrafts
Elegant Book & Map Co. 418
Peddler's Wagon 347
Village Books 76

New age
A-albionic Research 255
Alice's Book Shelf 391
Bookzeller 68
White Rabbit Used Books 119

New York City
John Dinsmore & Associates 166

Newspapers
The Autograph Alcove 459
Historical Newspapers 80
Magazine Memories 67
Yesterday 44

Nostalgia
The Library 151

Notable Trials Series of British Trails
Pisces and Capricorn Books 193

Numismatics
Casanova Books 443
Cash Coin Connection 302
Larry Laws 90
Ramtek International 424
Dale Seppa 306
World Exonumia Press 94

Occult
A-albionic Research 255
The Bookworm 369
Grandview Book Gallery 319
Greenfield Books 320
Harold's Book Shop 293
Magus Books 283
Occult Bookstore 39
Ramtek International 424
S & S Books 305
J.E. Sheldon Fine Books 260

Turtle Island Books 44
White Rabbit Used Books 119

Ohio
After Five Booksellers 417
Archer's Used And Rare Books 395
Bay Books 365
The Book Harbor 412
The Book Shoppe 387
Books on High 383
Books On Main 390
The Bookseller 359
Bookworm's Buffet 382
Crossroad Rare Books & Bindery 397
C.H. Fischer, Books 419
Hoffman's Bookshop 384
Mountain Heritage Books 433
Ohio Book Store 372
ReReadables 399
Rowsburg Bookstore 404
Stagecoach Antiques 362

Older fiction
Autumn Leaves Books 58
The Book Shelf 74
Books Et Cetra 241
Good News Books 124
Lakeshore Books 479
Leipold's of Excelsior 275
Midge's Dollhouse & Antiques 321
Old Bookshop of Rice Lake 470

Orchids
BotanaBooks & Art 469

Oriental rugs
Cleveland Antiquarian Books 376

Orinthology
Natural History Books 151
Snowy Egret Books 295

Outdoor living
Artis Books & Antiques 195
Bookphil Out of Print & Signed 395
Casanova Books 443
Chapman Street Books 275

Pacific Rim
The Cellar Book Shop 207
Twice Sold Tales 157

Paleontology
Albert G. Clegg, Bookseller 212
Timber City Books 152

Palmistry
Ramtek International 424
J.E. Sheldon Fine Books 260

Performing arts
Armchair Books 70

Flea Market Books 394
Larry Laws 90
Loganberry Books 377
Priceless Books 81
Rhythm & Views 93
Shaw's Books 219
(See also Music, Theater)

Petroleum
Russell S. Rein, Books & Records 253

Philately
Casanova Books 443
Forgotten Lore 257
Philatelic Bibliopole 179
Ramtek International 424

Philosophy
A Reader's Corner 169
Acorn Books 315
The Armadillo's Pillow 30
Beverly Books 32
Bible Scholar Books 417
Bookcellar 101
The Bookery 145
Booklegger's Used Books 32
Books on High 383
Bookzeller 68
James Cummings, Bookseller 450
Dawn Treader Book Shop 196
Footnotes Bookshop 178
Good Question 150
The Griffon 127
Klaus Grunewald - Bookdealer 325
Klimas Books 90
Loome Theological Booksellers 296
McDermott Books 455
Midtown Book Center 297
Occult Bookstore 39
O'Gara & Wilson Booksellers 39
The Out-of-Print Book Shoppe 285
Powell's Bookstore, South 40
Prospero's Books 326
Rain Dog Books 41
Richard Owen Roberts, Booksellers 83
Rowsburg Bookstore 404
L.J. Ryan, Scholarly Books 385
St. Croix Antiquarian Booksellers 297
Schenk Enterprises 163
Selected Works 42
Sqecial Media 168
Turtle Island Books 44
Twice Read Books 61
Twice-Loved Books 415
Upstart Crow Books 143
Wm Caxton Ltd 447

Photography
John Angelos, Books 459
Bay Books 365
Book Beat 235
Booklegger's Used Books 32
Casanova Books 443
Gerald J. Cielec-Books 88
Stephen Daiter Gallery 34
Downtown Books Fine Arts 462
H.M. George Books 280
Hoffman's Bookshop 384
James & Mary Laurie, Booksellers 281
The Legacy Company 150
Metropolis Art Books 208
Midway Bookstore 294
Old Main Book Shoppe 28
Mike Parise, Books 422
Rhythm & Views 93
Ed Ripp: Bookseller 41
Stephen Rose Fine Arts 112
Bernie Rost-Books 42
Titles, Inc. 58
Trails' End Books 112
Wilder Books 48

Photoplay editions
My Bookhouse 409
Toad Hall Books & Records 78

Physics
Science Book Service 306

Poe, Edgar Allan
Dale Weber Books 261

Poetry
Acorn Books 315
Ally Press 301
Robert L. Barth, Bookseller 178
Bell's Books & Candles 346
The Book House on Grand 292
The Booksmith 71
Bookzeller 68
Casterbridge Books 87
Discount Books 376
Duttenhofer's Books 370
Ginkgo Leaf Press 89
Haunted Bookshop On The Creek 146
Kaldi's Coffeehouse & Bookstore 371
Leipold's of Excelsior 275
Notting Hill Books 294
Paper Moone 333
The Rare Bookworm 424
Mike Sarki, Rogue Books 179
Second Storey Bookshop 137
Upstart Crow Books 143
What Goes Round 442

Jett W. Whitehead - Rare Books   201
The World of Books   413

Political science
A Place in History   392
The Booksellers Shoppe   119
Caveat Emptor   102
Footnotes Bookshop   178
Edwin Schaeffer   47
Six Steps Down Bookstore   379

Pop-ups
A. Dalrymple, Bookseller   256
Stonehill's Books   28
Wonderland Books   381

Popular culture
20th Century Books   457

Porter, Gene Stratton
Americana Books   104
Antiquarian Book Company   106
Books on the Sun Porch   149
Jim's Books   257
Links To The Past   249
Win's Books   262
Yorty's Half-Priced Books of Michigan   241

Presidents
ABC Collectables   301
Historical Newspapers   80
History Makers Rare Find Gallery   111
Hooked On History   67
Swiss Village Book Store   340

Press books
Beechwold Books   383

Printing
Timothy Hawley Books   178
Midnight Bookman   129

Prisoners of war
Freddie The Bookie   252

Private press
Bags End   333
Bell's Books & Candles   346
Bibliodisia Books   32
Robert S. Brooks, Bookseller   87
John Dinsmore & Associates   166
Anthony Garnett Fine Books   338
The Gentlemen Soldier   122
Glenn Books   325
Timothy Hawley Books   178
Idlewood Rare Books   116
Thomas J. Joyce and Company   36
James & Mary Laurie, Booksellers   281
Midnight Bookman   129
Peripatetic Bibliophile   218

The Reading Doctor   401
Ed Ripp: Bookseller   41
Dale Weber Books   261

Proofs & ARCs
Hahn's House of Mystery   371

Psychology/psychiatry
Ally Press   301
Avebury Books   365
Beasley Books   30
The Book House on Grand   292
Richard Owen Roberts, Booksellers   83
Turtle Island Books   44

Pulps
Antiquarium Books & Collectibles   322
The Armadillo's Pillow   30
Bookery Fantasy   390
Curious Book Shop   210
DreamWeaver Books   107
The Gallery Bookstore   35
Grandview Book Gallery   319
Grave Matters - Mysteries   371
Kaleidoscope Books & Collectibles   198
Murder By The Book   421
Plunkett/Higgins Books   270

Puppetry
David Meyer Magic Books   92

Radical studies
A-albionic Research   255
Beasley Books   30
Books Galore   316
Charles H. Kerr Co.   36
Pauper's Books   366
Revolution Books   208
Volume I Books   220
Wooden Spoon Books   199

Railroads
ABT Books   403
Bohling Book Company   255
Bookends and Fine Collectables   51
Grandview Book Gallery   319
Leyshon's Books Etc.   421
The Old Book Shop   321
Stroud Booksellers   433

Religion
A Reader's Corner   169
ABC Books   341
As Time Goes By   286
Baker Book House   217
Beadsman Books   86
Bell's Books & Candles   346
Bible Scholar Books   417
BNZ Enterprises   477

The Bookcase 287
Bookcellar 101
Bookhaven of Springfield 406
Books on High 383
The Booksellers Shoppe 119
The Bookworm 369
Thomas W. Burrows, Bookseller 87
Carol Butcher Books 418
James Cummings, Bookseller 450
Ex Libris Theological Books 35
FBS 252
Footnotes Bookshop 178
Good Books 89
Good News Books 124
Granny's Trunk 101
The Griffon 127
Haunted Bookshop On The Creek 146
Heartland Books 84
HIS Used Christian Book Shop 120
Huizinga's Books 209
Hyde Brothers Booksellers 106
John Paul II Bookstore 219
Kregel Bookstore 218
Loome Theological Booksellers 296
Lowry's Books 249
Martha Merrell's Bookstore 470
Meridian Street Books 116
Midge's Dollhouse & Antiques 321
Minnehaha Books 284
Jeffrey Neumann 422
Notting Hill Books 294
O'Gara & Wilson Booksellers 39
The Old Book Shop 321
Old House Bookstore 69
The Out-of-Print Book Shoppe 285
Palos Books 73
Pella Books 151
R & R Books 423
Rare Christian Books 317
Reformation Heritage Books 259
Richard Owen Roberts, Booksellers 83
Rowsburg Bookstore 404
Royal Oak Books 244
L.J. Ryan, Scholarly Books 385
S & S Books 305
Rev. D.A. Schroeder 348
Science Book Service 401
Selected Works 42
Snowball Bookshop 364
Steel's Used Christian Books 328
Stroud Booksellers 433
Dennis Sutterer Books 143
Phyllis Tholin, Books 51
Turtle Island Books 44
Twice Read Books 61

Karen Wickliff Books 386

Renaissance
Harry L. Stern, Ltd. 43
Upstart Crow Books 143

Riley, James Whitcomb
Win's Books 262

Rivers, River Boats and Rivermen
Bee Creek Books 302
Leyshon's Books Etc. 421
Source Book Store 141
Swiss Village Book Store 340
T & S Books 160

Rivers of America Series (See Series Americana

Rogers, Bruce
Midnight Bookman 129

Romance
The Book Shelf 74
The Book Stop 56
Books Et Cetra 241
Flea Market Books 394
Good News Books 124
Snowball Bookshop 364
Turnabout Books 295

Royalty
Susie's 362

Ruling class
A-albionic Research 255

School books
AC Books 103
Books on the Sun Porch 149
The Country Tutor School Books 225
The Rare Bookworm 424
The Reading Doctor 401

Science
Acorn Books 247
Acorn Bookshop 382
After Five Booksellers 417
Avebury Books 365
Avol's Bookstore 452
Thomas C. Bayer 255
The Book House in Dinkytown 278
Books In General 196
Bullfrog Books 110
Albert G. Clegg, Bookseller 212
Cross Street Book Shop 252
Excellence in Books 148
Hamill & Barker Antiquarian Booksellers 51
Klimas Books 90
James & Mary Laurie, Booksellers 281
Leonard's Antiques and Books 115
Mayflower Bookshop 201

Martinton Book Co.	91
Old Bookshop of Rice Lake	470
Out of Print Books	378
Professional Book Service	423
QuestAntiques-Books-Collectibles	259
Rain Dog Books	41
Ramtek International	424
Science Book Service	306
Science Book Service	401
The Science Bookshelf	260
Barry Scott	42
Snowy Egret Books	295
Helena Szépe, Books	44
Karen Wickliff Books	386

Science fiction

A Collector's Bookshop	334
ABC Books	341
Acorn Books	247
Acorn Bookshop	382
Morgan Adams Books	164
The Aleph Bookshop	48
Alternate Realities	452
Amelia's Book House	448
Antiquarium Books & Collectibles	322
Apparitions Comics & Books	224
Armchair Adventures	160
Karl M. Armens - Books	145
As Time Goes By	286
Big Bang Books	255
Big League Company	272
The Book Harbor	412
Book Jungle	342
The Book Stop	56
The Book Trader II	450
Book World	23
Bookery Fantasy	390
The Booksellers Shoppe	119
Booksmith	467
Bookworm & Bugjuice	418
Box of Rocks	157
Byrd's Books & Collectibles	317
Cindamar	402
Constant Reader Book Shop	461
Curious Book Shop	210
Dark Star Books & Comics	414
Dark Star Books & Comics	387
Dawn Treader Book Shop	196
Deadly Passions Bookshop	224
Dragon's Lair	387
Dreamhaven	280
The Fine Books Company	240
Else Fine Books	206
Flea Market Books	394
Foul Play	412

Fountain Of Mystery Books	111
The Gallery Bookstore	35
Great Escape	171
Green Gryphon Books	212
Green Lion Books	292
The Griffon	127
Grounds For Thought	366
Hooked On Books	343
Gordon W. Huber	420
Hyde Brothers Booksellers	106
J O'Donoghue Books	270
Kaleidoscope Books & Collectibles	198
Midway Bookstore	294
More O'Books	27
Pac-Rats	157
Palos Books	73
Mike Parise, Books	422
Remember When	449
S & S Books	305
M. Sand Books	93
Joe Sarno's Comic Kingdom	42
P.C. Schmidt, Bookseller	211
Snowball Bookshop	364
The Stars Our Destination	43
Tabula Rasa	425
Tally Ho Studios	425
Timber City Books	152
Toad Hall Books & Records	78
Turtle Island Books	44
20th Century Books	457
Uncle Hugo's Science Fiction Bookstore	286
The Village Bookshelf	398
The Way Station	140
White Rabbit Used Books	119
Yesterday's Books	247
J.D. Zucatti, Bookseller	244

Scotland

Paterson-Ford Booksellers	172
Margaret Soderberg, Bookseller	447
Unicorn, Ltd.	433

Scouting

Dan's Books	288
Good Ol' Days Books	419

Seckatary Hawkins

Armchair Adventures	160

Self help

Morgan Adams Books	164
House of Scorpio	462
Lancaster & Simpson	304
Snowball Bookshop	364

Series Americana

Forest Park Books	105
Timothy B. Wuchter	262

Sets
Archives Book Shop 210
Cleveland Antiquarian Books 376
Sherlock Holmes
Bibliotective 234
Robert S. Brooks, Bookseller 87
Grave Matters - Mysteries 371
Thomas J. Joyce and Company 36
Murder By The Book 421
The Village Bookshelf 398
Shute, Nevil
The Looking Glass 414
Signed
Allison's Signed Books & Autographs 85
A. Amitin's Book Shop 334
Archives Book Shop 210
The Autograph Alcove 459
Beadsman Books 86
84 Charing Cross, EH? 231
H.M. George Books 280
Hahn's House of Mystery 371
Susan Heller - Pages for Sages 377
Peter Keisogloff Rare Books 377
Mighty Fine Books 117
The Mystery Nook 75
Paul Rohe Books 93
Toad Hall Books & Records 78
T.S. Vandoros Rare Books 458
Victoria's Books 20
White Raven Books 254
Jett W. Whitehead - Rare Books 201
Timothy B. Wuchter 262
Social sciences
The Book House in Dinkytown 278
Good Question 150
Grounds For Thought 366
Jane Addams Book Shop 27
L.J. Ryan, Scholarly Books 385
Southern Americana
Twice Told Books 172
Southwest Americana
B. Caldwell - Bookseller 331
Space exploration
Knollwood Books 468
Sports
ABC Collectables 301
Bicentennial Book Shop 223
Big League Company 272
Books Revisited 291
Curious Book Shop 210
Dan's Books 288
Susan Heller - Pages for Sages 377

Theodore J. Holston Jr., Bookseller 303
Mary Ann's Books 258
Miller's Antiques 240
Mostly Baseball 179
Noah's Ark 463
North Woods Books 274
Palos Books 73
Philco Books 304
Shaw's Books 219
Yesterdays Memories 465
Yesterday 44
(See also Baseball, Golf)
Steinbeck, John
Books on the Sun Porch 149
Collectors' Choice 403
Stuart, Jesse
Estate Books 88
Suspense
Fickes Crime Fiction 419
Ken Hebenstreit, Bookseller 243
Uncle Edgar's Mystery Bookstore 286
Taber, Gladys
Links To The Past 249
Win's Books 262
Yorty's Half-Priced Books of Michigan 241
Tarkington, Booth
Verl's Books 132
Technology
Acorn Books 247
Avebury Books 365
Thomas C. Bayer 255
Book Stall Of Rockford 78
Bookhaven of Springfield 406
Books In General 196
Branchwater Books & Ephemera 256
Cross Street Book Shop 252
Discount Books 376
Elegant Book & Map Co. 418
Granny's Trunk 101
Ashley Kennedy 90
Leonard's Antiques and Books 115
Martinton Book Co. 91
Materiality 442
Mossback Books 208
David Netzorg 259
Ramtek International 424
Rhythm & Views 93
Science Book Service 306
Dennis Sutterer Books 143
Karen Wickliff Books 386
Textiles
Galerie De Boicourt 251
Taylor Search Service 260

Theater
Acorn Books 315
Constant Reader Book Shop 461
Sheila Frank, Bookseller 217
Haunted Bookshop On The Creek 146
Larry Laws 90
Paper Peddlers 406
Second Stage Books 396
(See also Performing arts)

Thurber, James
Books on High 383
Hoffman's Bookshop 384

Trade catalogs
Autonomy House Publications 130
Bay Books 365
Broken Kettle Books 144
Elegant Book & Map Co. 418

Transportation
Avebury Books 365
Bay Books 365
Science Book Service 306
(See also Automotive, Railroads, Rivers)

Travel
Aardvark Book Depot 477
Americas Antiquarium 86
Bay Books 365
Bohling Book Company 255
Bookman Extraordinaire 46
The Bookman Of Kent 417
Robert S. Brooks, Bookseller 87
Deux Amasse Books 241
Gerhart's Rare & Out-of-Print Auto Books 89
Leonard's Antiques and Books 115
Louis & Clark Booksellers 479
Mighty Fine Books 117
Kenneth Nebenzahl, Inc. 56
Out-of-the-Way Books 205
Peninsula Books 250
Plain Tales Books 92
Russell S. Rein, Books & Records 253
Shakespeare's Books 456
Shaw's Books 219
Flo Silver Books 132
West Side Book Shop 199

Traver, Robert
Snowbound Books 229

True crime
Archer's Used And Rare Books 395
Aunt Agatha's 195
Big Sleep Books 335
Bookphil Out of Print & Signed 395
Cordell-Wilson Booksellers 314

Fountain Of Mystery Books 111
The Mystery Nook 75

Truman, Harry
The Old Book Shop 321

Tudor, Tasha
Books Of The Ages 418

U.S. government publications
Bee Creek Books 302
John T. Zubal, Inc. 380

UFOs
Insight Metaphysical Bookstore 27

University press
Between The Lines 130
Calhoun Book Store 302

Utopian societies
Golden Raintree Books 120

Veterinary
The Sporting Horse Gallery 168

Viewbooks
North Coast Americana 403

Vikings
Unicorn, Ltd. 433

Vintage paperbacks
Americana Books 104
Antiquarium Books & Collectibles 322
Antique Enterprises 206
Big Bang Books 255
Books Are Everything 178
Books on the Square 81
Buck Creek Books 114
Dreamhaven 280
DreamWeaver Books 107
Flea Market Books 394
The Gallery Bookstore 35
Grave Matters - Mysteries 371
Great Books 288
Green Lion Books 292
Hymie's Vintage Records Etc. 281
Kaleidoscope Books & Collectibles 198
Lakeshore Books 479
Munchkin Book Shop 408
My Bookhouse 409
The Open Book 343
Plunkett/Higgins Books 270
Second Stage Books 396
Toad Hall Books & Records 78
Turnabout Books 295
The Village Bookshelf 398

Virginia
Mountain Heritage Books 433

Vonnegut, Kurt
Verl's Books 132

West Virginia
Books Books Books 429
Mountain Heritage Books 433
Stroud Booksellers 433
C.E. Turley 430

Western Americana
Americas Antiquarium 86
Karl M. Armens - Books 145
Articles of War 79
Bits & Pieces of History 70
Bohling Book Company 255
Country Comfort Antiques and Books 299
D.R. Doerres Rendezvous Trader 150
Estate Books 88
Excellence in Books 148
Thatcher C. Goetz, Books 216
Grandview Book Gallery 319
H & B Booksellers 202
Heartland Books 84
Hooked On History 67
James & Mary Laurie, Booksellers 281
The Little Bookshop 412
Martha Merrell's Bookstore 470
The Old Book Shop 321
Old House Bookstore 69
Ross & Haines Old Books Co. 449
St. Croix Antiquarian Booksellers 297
Dennis Sutterer Books 143
Swiss Village Book Store 340
Weidler Book Source 94
Yesteryear Books 62

Western Reserve
Bay Books 365

Westerns
AC Books 103
Dinkytown Antiquarian Bookstore 280
Green Lion Books 292
Old Horizons Book Shoppe 204
Remember When 449
Second Storey Bookshop 137

White, Stewart Edward
David L. White - Books 261

Whitman 2300 Series
Dan's Books 288

Wisconsin
Booksmith 467
Country Comfort Antiques and Books 299
The Foundry Books 466
James Hyer, Bookseller 478
Mary Twyce Books & Paper 300
Stony Hill Antiques 457
Time Traveler Bookstore 465
The Winsted Shop 472

Wise Owl Books 451
Yesterdays Memories 465

Wizard of Oz (See Baum, Frank)

Wodehouse, P.G.
Taylor Search Service 260

Women's studies
Acorn Books 315
Dann Collectibles 239
Sheila Frank, Bookseller 217
Jane Addams Book Shop 27
Jane Austen Books 89
Loganberry Books 377
Barbara Parks - Books 243
Six Steps Down Bookstore 379
Sqecial Media 168
Phyllis Tholin, Books 51
Twice-Loved Books 415
Untamed Shrew Books 480
What Goes Round 442
Wm Caxton Ltd 447

Woodcut novels
Ed Ripp: Bookseller 41

Woodworking
Evans Firearms and Archery 166

Woolf, V.
Blenheim Books 175

World War I & II
Adams Walls of Books 315
Argonne Books 417
Books on High 383
Glover's Bookery 167
Hooked On History 67
Kisselburg Military Books 303
Mighty Fine Books 117
Old Bookshop of Rice Lake 470
The Reading Doctor 401

WPA guides
Forest Park Books 105
Timothy B. Wuchter 262

Wright, Frank Lloyd
Ravenswood Books 475
The Winsted Shop 472

Wright, Harold Bell
Archer's Antiques & Books 331
Links To The Past 249
Win's Books 262

Wyeth, N.C.
Dann Collectibles 239

Zoology
N. Fagin Books 35
Snowy Egret Books 295

The Used Book Lover's Guide Series
Your guide to over 6,000 used book dealers.

New England Guide (Rev Ed)
750 dealers • 383 pp • $16.95
ISBN 0-9634112-4-1

Mid-Atlantic Guide (Rev Ed)
1,100 dealers • 439 pp • $18.95
ISBN 0-9634112-7-6

South Atlantic Guide (Rev Ed)
950 dealers • 375 pages • $17.95
ISBN 0-9634112-8-4

Midwest Guide (Rev Ed)
1,300 dealers • 511 pp • $19.95
ISBN 0-9634112-9-2

Pacific Coast Guide
1,350 dealers • 474 pp • $18.95
ISBN 0-9634112-5-X

Central States Guide
1,250 dealers • 465 pp • $18.95
ISBN 0-9634112-6-8

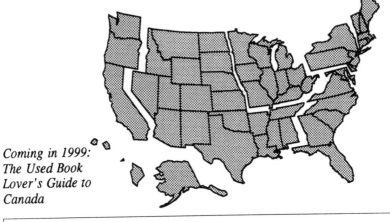

Coming in 1999:
The Used Book
Lover's Guide to
Canada

Keeping Current

As a service to our readers, we're happy to make available, at cost, Supplements for each of our guides.

The Supplements, published annually, provide our readers with additional listings as well as information concerning dealers who have either moved or gone out of business.

Much of the information in the Supplements comes to us from loyal readers who, in using our guides, have been kind enough to provide us with this valuable data based on their own book hunting experiences.

Should you wish to receive the next Supplement for the book(s) you currently own, complete the Order Form on the next page and enclose $2.50 for each Supplement, plus postage. Please note the date of any earlier Supplement/s you may have. **The new Supplements will be mailed as they become available.**

ORDER FORM

Book Hunter Press
PO Box 193 • Yorktown Heights, NY 10598
(914) 245-6608 • Fax: (914) 245-2630
E-mail: bookhuntpr@aol.com

GUIDES	Price	# of Copies	Disc.	Unit Cost	Total
New England (Rev)	16.95				
Mid-Atlantic (Rev)	18.95				
South Atlantic (Rev)	17.95				
Midwest (Rev)	19.95				
Pacific Coast	18.95				
Central States	18.95				

ANNUAL SUPPLEMENTS * (See Keeping Current on previous page)					
New England (Rev)	2.50				
Mid-Atlantic (Rev)	2.50				
South Atlantic (Rev)	2.50				
Midwest (Rev)	2.50				
Pacific Coast	2.50				
Central States	2.50				

The latest Supplement is automatically included with NEW orders.

SPECIAL DISCOUNTS
Any combination of books
2-5 copies: 20%
6 or more copies: 40%

Subtotal

Shipping

(NYS residents only) Sales Tax

TOTAL

SHIPPING Guides: For single copies: Book rate: $3.00. Priorty or foreign: $5.00.
Add $1.00 for each additional copy. Supplements: 50¢ each.

Name_____

Company_____

Address_____

City_____ State_____ Zip_____

Phone_____

MC Card _____ Visa _____ Exp Date _____

Card # _____

Signature_____